Contents

Page

Introduction

The introduction pages contain lots of valuable advice and information. They include tips on studying for and passing the exam, also the content of the syllabus and what has been examined.

Computer-based learning products from BPP

If you want to reinforce your studies by **interactive** learning, try BPP's **i-Learn** product, covering major syllabus areas in an interactive format. For **self-testing**, try **i-Pass,** which offers a large number of **objective test questions**, particularly useful where objective test questions form part of the exam.

Learn Online

Learn Online uses BPP's wealth of teaching experience to produce a fully **interactive** e-learning resource **delivered via the Internet**. The site offers comprehensive **tutor support** and features areas such as **study**, **practice**, **email service**, **revision** and **useful resources**.

Visit our website www.bpp.com/cima/learnonline to sample aspects of Learn Online free of charge.

Learning to Learn Accountancy

BPP's ground-breaking **Learning to Learn Accountancy** book is designed to be used both at the outset of your CIMA studies and throughout the process of learning accountancy. It challenges you to consider how you study and gives you helpful hints about how to approach the various types of paper which you will encounter. It can help you **focus your studies on the subject and exam**, enabling you to **acquire knowledge**, **practise and revise efficiently and effectively**.

CIMA

Managerial Paper P7

FINANCIAL ACCOUNTING AND TAX PRINCIPLES

For exams in November 2006 and May 2007

Study Text

In this May 2006 new edition

- A user-friendly format for easy navigation
- Exam-centred topic coverage, directly linked to CIMA's learning outcomes and syllabus content
- Regular **fast forward** summaries emphasising the points
- **Exam focus points** showing you what the examiner will want you to do
- **Questions** and **quick quizzes** to test your understanding
- **Exam question bank** containing exam standard questions with answers
- A full index
- Fully up to date for revised and new IFRS

BPP's **i-Learn** and **i-Pass** products also support this paper.

BPP PROFESSIONAL EDUCATION

First edition 2004
Third edition May 2006

ISBN 0 7517 2643 5 (previous ISBN 0 7517 2296 0)

British Library Cataloguing-in-Publication Data
A catalogue record for this book
is available from the British Library

Published by

BPP Professional Education
Aldine House, Aldine Place
London W12 8AW

www.bpp.com

Printed in Great Britain by
WM Print
45-47 Frederick Street
Walsall
WS2 9NE

We are grateful to the Chartered Institute of Management Accountants for permission to reproduce past examination questions and questions from the pilot paper. The suggested solutions in the exam answer bank have been prepared by BPP Professional Education.

The BPP Effective Study Package

Recommended period of use	The BPP Effective Study Package
From the outset and throughout	**Learning to Learn Accountancy** Read this invaluable book as you begin your studies and refer to it throughout your studies.
Three to twelve months before the exam	**Study Text and i-Learn** Use the Study Text to acquire knowledge, understanding, skills and the ability to apply techniques. Use BPP's **i-Learn** product to reinforce your learning.
Throughout	**Learn Online** Study, practise, revise and use other helpful resources with BPP's fully interactive e-learning site, including full tutor support.
Throughout	**i-Pass** **i-Pass**, our computer-based testing package, provides objective test questions in a variety of formats and is ideal for self-assessment.
One to six months before the exam	**Practice & Revision Kit** Try the numerous examination-format questions in our Kit, and compare your answers with the suggested solutions. Examiners emphasise that tackling exam-standard questions is essential preparation for your exams. Then attempt the two mock exams.
From three months before the exam until the last minute	**Passcards** Work through these short, memorable notes which are focused on the topics most likely to come up in your exam and which you can take anywhere.
One to six months before the exam	**Success CDs** The CDs cover the vital elements of your syllabus in less than 90 minutes per subject. They also contain exam hints to help you fine tune your strategy.

You can purchase these products by visiting www.bpp.com/mybpp

How the BPP Study Text can help you pass

It provides you with the knowledge and understanding, skills and application techniques that you need to be successful in your exams

This Study Text has been targeted at the **Financial Accounting and Tax Principles** syllabus.

- It is **comprehensive**. It covers the syllabus content. No more, no less.
- It is written at the **right level**. Each chapter is written with CIMA's precise learning outcomes in mind.
- It is aimed at the **exam**. We have taken account of recent exams, guidance the examiner has given and the assessment methodology.

It allows you to study in the way that best suits your learning style and the time you have available, by following your personal Study Plan (see page (viii))

You may be studying at home on your own, or you may be attending a full-time course. You may like to read every word, or you may prefer to skim-read and practise questions the rest of the time. However you study, you will find the BPP Study Text meets your needs in designing and following your personal Study Plan.

It ties in with the other components of the BPP Effective Study Package to ensure you have the best possible chance of passing the exam (see page (v))

Help yourself study for your CIMA exams

Exams for professional bodies such as CIMA are very different from those you have taken at college or university. You will be under **greater time pressure before** the exam – as you may be combining your study with work. Here are some hints and tips.

The right approach

1 **Develop the right attitude**

Believe in yourself	Yes, there is a lot to learn. But thousands have succeeded before and you can too.
Remember why you're doing it	You are studying for a good reason: to advance your career.

2 **Focus on the exam**

Read through the Syllabus and Learning outcomes	These tell you what you are expected to know and are supplemented by **Exam focus points** in the text.
Study the Exam paper section	Past papers are likely to be good guides to what you should expect in the exam.

3 **The right method**

See the whole picture	Keeping in mind how all the detail you need to know fits into the whole picture will help you understand it better. • The **Approaching and passing P7** section in the Introduction pages summarises what P7 is about, the skills you need to pass P7 and what you can do to improve your chances of passing. • The **Pilot paper** shows you how the exam fits together and gives examples of the types of question you may be asked. • The **Introduction** of each chapter puts the material in context. • The **Syllabus content, Learning outcomes** and **Exam focus points** show you what you need to **grasp**.
Use your own words	To absorb the information and to practise your written communication skills you need to **put it into your own words.** • **Take notes.** • Answer the **questions** in each chapter. • Draw **mindmaps**. • Try **'teaching' a subject** to a colleague or friend.
Give yourself cues to jog your memory	The BPP Study Text uses **bold** to **highlight key points**. • Try **colour coding** with a highlighter pen. • Write **key points** on cards.

4 **The right recap**

Review, review, review	Regularly reviewing a topic in summary form can **fix it in your memory**. The BPP Study Text helps you to review in many ways. • **Chapter roundups** summarise the 'fast forward' key points in each chapter. Use them to recap each study session. • The **Quick quiz** actively tests your grasp of the essentials. • Go through the **Examples** in each chapter a second or third time.

Developing your personal Study Plan

BPP's **Learning to Learn Accountancy** book emphasises the need to use a study plan. Planning and sticking to the plan are key elements of learning successfully.

There are five steps you should work through.

Step 1 **How do you learn?**

First you need to be aware of your style of learning. BPP's **Learning to Learn Accountancy** book commits a chapter to this **self-discovery**. What types of intelligence do you display when learning? You might be advised to brush up on certain study skills before launching into this Study Text.

BPP's **Learning to Learn Accountancy** book helps you to identify what intelligences you show more strongly and then details how you can tailor your study process to your preferences. It also includes handy hints on how to develop intelligences you exhibit less strongly, but which might be needed as you study accountancy.

Step 2 **What do you prefer to do first?**

If you prefer to get to grips with a theory before seeing how it's applied, we suggest you concentrate first on the explanations we give in each chapter before looking at the examples and case studies. If you prefer to see first how things work in practice, skim through the detail in each chapter, and concentrate on the examples and case studies, before supplementing your understanding by reading the detail.

Step 3 **How much time do you have?**

Work out the time you have available per week, given the following.

- The standard you have set yourself
- The time you need to set aside later for work on the Practice & Revision Kit and Passcards
- The other exam(s) you are sitting
- Practical matters such as work, travel, exercise, sleep and social life

		Hours
Note your time available in box A.	A	

Step 4 **Allocate your time**

- Take the time you have available per week for this Study Text shown in box A, multiply it by the number of weeks available and insert the result in box B. B [ ]
- Divide the figure in box B by the number of chapters in this text and insert the result in box C. C [ ]

Remember that this is only a rough guide. Some of the chapters in this book are longer and more complicated than others, and you will find some subjects easier to understand than others.

Step 5 **Implement**

Set about studying each chapter in the time shown in box C, following the key study steps in the order suggested by your particular learning style.

This is your personal **Study Plan**. You should try to combine it with the study sequence outlined below. You may want to modify the sequence to adapt it to your **personal style**.

BPP's **Learning to Learn Accountancy** gives further guidance on developing a study plan, and deciding where and when to study.

Tackling your studies

The best way to approach this Study Text is to tackle the chapters in order. Taking into account your individual learning style, you could follow this sequence for each chapter.

Key study steps	Activity
Step 1 **Topic list**	The topic list helps you navigate each chapter; each numbered topic is a numbered section in the chapter.
Step 2 **Introduction**	This sets your objectives for study by giving you the big picture in terms of the context of the chapter, the learning outcomes the chapter covers, and the content you will read. It tells you **why** the topics covered in the chapter need to be studied.
Step 3 **Knowledge brought forward boxes**	These highlight information and techniques that it is assumed you have 'brought forward' with you from your earlier studies. Remember that you may be tested on these areas in the exam. If you are unsure of these areas, you should consider revising your more detailed study material from earlier papers.
Step 4 **Fast forward**	Fast forward boxes give you a quick summary of the content of each of the main chapter sections. They are listed together in the roundup at the end of each chapter to help you review each chapter quickly.
Step 5 **Explanations**	Proceed methodically through each chapter, particularly focussing on areas highlighted as significant in the chapter introduction, or areas that are frequently examined.
Step 6 **Key terms and Exam focus points**	• Key terms can often earn you easy marks if you state them clearly and correctly in an exam answer. They are highlighted in the index at the back of this text. • Exam focus points state how the topic has been or may be examined, difficulties that can occur in questions about the topic, and examiner feedback on common weaknesses in answers.

Key study steps	Activity
Step 7 **Note taking**	Take brief notes, if you wish. Don't copy out too much. Remember that being able to record something yourself is a sign of being able to understand it. Your notes can be in whatever format you find most helpful; lists, diagrams, mindmaps.
Step 8 **Examples**	Work through the examples very carefully as they illustrate key knowledge and techniques.
Step 9 **Case studies**	Study each one, and try to add flesh to them from your own experience. They are designed to show how the topics you are studying come alive in the real world.
Step 10 **Questions**	Attempt each one, as they will illustrate how well you've understood what you've read.
Step 11 **Answers**	Check yours against ours, and make sure you understand any discrepancies.
Step 12 **Chapter roundup**	Review it carefully, to make sure you have grasped the significance of all the important points in the chapter.
Step 13 **Quick quiz**	Use the Quick quiz to check how much you have remembered of the topics covered and to practise questions in a variety of formats.
Step 14 **Question(s) in the Exam question bank**	Attempt the Question(s) suggested at the very end of the chapter. You can find these at the end of the Study Text, along with the Answers so you can see how you did.
Step 15 **Objective test questions**	Use the bank of OTs at the back of this Study Text to practise, and to determine how much of the Study Text you have absorbed. If you have bought i-Pass, use this too.

Short of time: Skim study technique?

You may find you simply do not have the time available to follow all the key study steps for each chapter, however you adapt them for your particular learning style. If this is the case, follow the **skim study** technique below.

Read the **topic list, chapter introduction** and **knowledge brought forward boxes**.

↓

Skim through the **explanations**, focusing on the points highlighted as important in the **fast forward boxes**.

↓

Read the **key terms** and **exam focus points** carefully.

↓

Go through the **examples**.

↓

Prepare outline **answers** to the **questions**.

↓

Revisit the fast forwards in the **chapter roundups**.

↓

Answer the **quick quiz** and look back at any areas where you got questions wrong.

↓

Do a plan for the **question(s) in the exam question bank** and review our answers carefully.

↓

Brief notes may help you skim study, although you may simply rely on the **passcards** for notes you can use for revision.

Moving on...

When you are ready to start revising, you should still refer back to this Study Text.

- As a source of **reference** (you should find the index particularly helpful for this)
- As a way to **review** (the Fast forwards, Exam focus points, Chapter roundups and Quick quizzes help you here)

Remember to keep careful hold of this Study Text – you will find it invaluable in your work.

More advice on Study Skills can be found in BPP's **Learning to Learn Accountancy** book.

Approaching and passing P7

What P7 is about

P7 consists of three fairly distinct areas covering:

- Tax
- Financial accounting standards and accounts preparation
- Financial management

Taxation

As P7 is designed to be an international paper you don't need specific knowledge of any individual country's tax regime. Instead the paper focuses on the elements that are common to most of the major tax regimes. P7 aims to give you knowledge of different kinds of taxation, how tax is administered, the role of the taxation authorities and what is regarded as tax avoidance and evasion. As this is an international paper, you also have to be aware of the international tax dimension and how foreign tax obligations can arise.

Financial accounting

The financial accounting part of the syllabus consists of two main areas. Firstly you are expected to know about the regulation of accounts; why regulation is necessary and the processes of establishing and enforcing the rules that accountants are expected to apply when they prepare company accounts. As accountants, you will have to deal with external auditors; this syllabus also therefore requires you to understand the role of external auditors and interpret external audit reports.

The second area is concerned with the preparation of accounts for a single company. It's assumed that you know the basic elements of accounts preparation from previous studies. P7 requires more detailed knowledge of the contents of the main financial statements (income statement, balance sheet and cash flow statement) and also how accounting standards impact upon the main statements and the notes to the accounts.

Financial management

The financial management element of the syllabus concentrates on what's required for the business's day-to-day operations and short-term financing requirements: its working capital of inventory, receivables, payables and cash. P7 covers how working capital is measured and managed, how an organisation determines its short-term financing requirements and where it can invest surplus cash.

What's required

Knowledge

As the majority of marks are available for questions worth 5 marks or less, the examiner has a lot of opportunity to test your knowledge of the detail of the syllabus, in particular key definitions, the features of tax regimes and the accounting regulatory process. You will also not only have to answer short questions on the requirements of accounting standards, but in addition use your knowledge of the standards to prepare extracts from accounts that comply with those standards.

Explanation

As well as stating your knowledge, you will also sometimes be asked to demonstrate the more advanced skill of explaining the requirements of accounting standards. Explaining means providing simple definitions and covering the reasons **why** regulations have been made and what the problems are that the standards are designed to counter. You'll gain higher marks if your explanations are clearly focussed on the question and you can supplement your explanations with examples.

Calculations

Calculation questions will be of two types:

- Short calculations for five marks or less, including taxation calculations, calculations that are required by accounting standards, and calculations that provide you with insights into working capital management and short-term financing
- Longer calculations for which you will have to prepare proformas. The majority of marks in Section C of P7 will be available for these. The proformas you will need to prepare are the main financial accounting statements, and cash budgets to assist financial management

Interpretation and recommendation

Particularly in financial management questions, you will have to interpret the results of the calculations you carry out. You must understand that interpretation isn't just saying figures have increased or decreased; it means explaining **why** figures have changed and also the consequences of the changes. You will also have to provide recommendations on how the business can improve its day-to-day working capital management and what sources of short-term finance it will need.

Passing P7

Cover the whole syllabus

80% of the marks available to you will be for compulsory questions. This gives the examiner plenty of opportunity to test all major areas of the syllabus on **every** paper, but sadly doesn't give you much opportunity to avoid questions you don't like. In particular you must spend some time on the rules and regulatory background issues as these may be covered in 5 mark, as well as shorter 2 mark, questions.

Practise

Our text gives you ample opportunity to practise by providing questions within chapters, quick quiz questions and questions in the exam question bank at the end. In addition the BPP Practice and Revision Kit provides lots more question practice. It's particularly important to practise:

- Banks of objective test questions so that you get used to doing a number together
- More complicated shorter calculations. We highlight within the Text calculations that can cause problems and it's worth doing as many of these as possible
- Longer calculations and proformas. You will need to do these to answer the Section C questions well.

Develop time management skills

The examiner has identified time management as being a problem, with some candidates not leaving themselves enough time to do the shorter calculations. Particularly therefore towards the end of your course, you need to practise all types of question, only allowing yourself the time you will be given in the exam.

Develop business awareness

Although this is not a higher level paper, candidates with good business awareness can score well in a number of areas.

- Reading articles in CIMA's *Financial Management* magazine and the business press will help you understand the practical rationale for accounting standards and make it easier for you to apply accounting requirements correctly
- Looking through the accounts of major companies will familiarise you with the contents of accounts and help you comment on key figures and changes from year-to-year
- Being aware of the work of different departments in your own organisation or others you know about will help you discuss the practical management issues involved in running a business; for P7 particularly managing cash, inventory and other working capital.

The good news

The pass rates for the first two sittings of P7 exceeded CIMA's expectations; most candidates seemed to have good knowledge of most of the syllabus and attempted the longer calculations questions well.

Learning outcomes and Syllabus

Paper P7 Financial Accounting and Tax Principles

The syllabus comprises:

Topic and Study Weighting

A	Principles of Business Taxation	20%
B	Principles of Regulation of Financial Reporting	10%
C	Single Company Financial Accounts	45%
D	Managing Short Term Finance	25%

Learning aims

Students should be able to:

- Describe the types of business taxation rules and requirements likely to affect a company (in respect of itself and its employees)
- Describe and discuss how financial reporting can be regulated and the system of International Accounting Standards
- Prepare statutory accounts in appropriate form for a single company
- Assess and control the short term financial requirements of a business entity

Learning Outcomes and Syllabus Content

A – Principles of Business Taxation – 20%

Learning Outcomes

On completion of their studies students should be able to:

(i) Identify the principal types of taxation likely to be of relevance to an incorporated business in a particular country, including direct tax on the company's trading profits and capital gains, indirect taxes collected by the company, employee taxation, withholding taxes on international payments.

(ii) Describe the features of the principal types of taxation likely to be of relevance to an incorporated business in a particular country (eg in terms of who ultimately bears the tax cost, withholding responsibilities, principles of calculating the tax base).

(iii) Describe the likely record-keeping, filing and tax payment requirements associated with the principal types of taxation likely to be of relevance to an incorporated business in a particular country.

(iv) Describe the possible enquiry and investigation powers of taxing authorities.

(v) Identify situations in which foreign tax obligations (reporting and liability) could arise and methods for relieving foreign tax.

(vi) Explain the difference in principle between tax avoidance and tax evasion.

(vii) Describe sources of tax rules and explain the importance of jurisdiction.

(viii) Explain and apply the accounting rules contained in IAS 12 for current and deferred taxation..

Syllabus Content

(1) Concepts of direct versus indirect taxes, taxable person and competent jurisdiction.

(2) Sources of tax rules (eg domestic primary legislation and court rulings, practice of the relevant taxing authority, supranational bodies, such as the EU in the case of value added/sales tax, and international tax treaties).

(3) Direct taxes on company profits and gains:

- The principle of non-deductibility of dividends and systems of taxation defined according to the treatment of dividends in the hands of the shareholder (eg classical, partial imputation and imputation).
- The distinction between accounting and taxable profits in absolute terms (eg disallowable expenditure on revenue account, such as entertaining, and on capital account, such as formation and acquisition costs) and in terms of timing (eg deduction on a paid basis, tax depreciation substituted for book depreciation).
- The nature of rules recharacterising interest payments as dividends.
- Potential for variation in rules for calculating the tax base dependent on the nature or source of the income (schedular systems).
- The need for rules dealing with the relief of losses.
- The concept of tax consolidation (eg for relief of losses and deferral of capital gains on asset transfers within a group).

(4) Indirect taxes collected by the company:

- In the context of indirect taxes, the distinction between unit taxes (eg excise duties based on physical measures) and ad valorem taxes (eg sales tax based on value).
- The mechanism of value added/sales taxes, in which businesses are liable for tax on their outputs less credits for tax paid on their inputs, including the concepts of exemption and variation in tax rates depending on the type of output and disallowance of input credits for exempt outputs.

(5) Employee taxation:

- The employee as a separate taxable person subject to a personal income tax regime.
- Use of employer reporting and withholding to ensure compliance and assist tax collection.

(6) The need for record-keeping and record retention that may be additional to that required for financial accounting purposes.

(7) The need for deadlines for reporting (filing returns) and tax payments.

(8) Types of powers of tax authorities to ensure compliance with tax rules:

- Power to review and query filed returns
- Power to request special reports or returns
- Power to examine records (generally extending back some years)
- Powers of entry and search
- Exchange of information with tax authorities in other jurisdictions

(9) International taxation:

- The concept of corporate residence and the variation in rules for its determination across jurisdictions (eg place of incorporation versus place of management).

- Types of payments on which withholding tax may be required (especially interest, dividends, royalties and capital gains accruing to non-residents).
- Means of establishing a taxable presence in another country (local company and branch).
- The effect of double tax treaties (based on the OECD Model Convention) on the above (eg reduction of withholding tax rates, provisions for defining a permanent establishment).
- Principles of relief for foreign taxes by exemption, deduction and credit.

(10) The distinction between tax avoidance and tax evasion, and how these vary among jurisdictions (including the difference between the use of statutory general anti-avoidance provisions and case law based regimes).

(11) Accounting treatment of taxation and disclosure requirements under IAS 12.

Note: Examples of general principles should be drawn from a 'benchmark' tax regime (eg the UK, USA, etc) or an appropriate local tax regime. Details of any specific tax regime will NOT be examined.

B – Principles of Regulation of Financial Reporting – 10%

Learning Outcomes

On completion of their studies students should be able to:

(i) Explain the need for regulation of published accounts and the concept that regulatory regimes vary from country to country.

(ii) Explain potential elements that might be expected in a regulatory framework for published accounts.

(iii) Describe the role and structure of the International Accounting Standards Board (IASB) and the International Organisation of Securities Commissions (IOSCO).

(iv) Explain the IASB's Framework for the Presentation and Preparation of Financial Statements.

(v) Describe the process leading to the promulgation of an international accounting standard (IAS).

(vi) Describe ways in which IASs can interact with local regulatory frameworks.

(vii) Explain in general terms, the role of the external auditor, the elements of the audit report and types of qualification of that report.

Syllabus Content

(1) The need for regulation of accounts.

(2) Elements in a regulatory framework for published accounts (eg company law, local GAAP, review of accounts by public bodies).

(3) GAAP based on prescriptive versus principles-based standards.

(4) The role and structure of the IASB and IOSCO.

(5) The IASB's Framework for the Presentation and Preparation of Financial Statements.

(6) The process leading to the promulgation of a standard practice.

(7) Ways in which IASs are used: adoption as local GAAP, model for local GAAP, persuasive influence in formulating local GAAP.

(8) The powers and duties of the external auditors, the audit report and its qualification for accounting statements not in accordance with best practice.

C – Single Company Financial Accounts – 45%

Learning outcomes

On completion of their studies students should be able to:

(i) Prepare financial statements in a form suitable for publication, with appropriate notes.

(ii) Prepare a cash flow statement in a form suitable for publication.

(iii) Explain and apply the accounting rules contained in IASs dealing with reporting performance, tangible fixed assets and inventories.

(iv) Explain the accounting rules contained in IASs governing share capital transactions.

(v) Explain the principles of the accounting rules contained in IASs dealing with disclosure of related parties to a business, construction contracts (and related financing costs), research and development expenditure, intangible fixed assets (other than goodwill on consolidation), impairment of assets, post-balance sheet events, contingencies, and leases (lessee only).

Syllabus Content

(1) Preparation of the financial statements of a single company, including the statement of changes in equity (IAS 1).

(2) Preparation of cash flow statements (IAS 7).

(3) Reporting performance: recognition of revenue, measurement of profit or loss, extraordinary items, prior period items, discontinued operations and segment reporting (IAS 1, 8, 14, 18 & IFRS 5).

(4) Property, Plant and Equipment (IAS 16): the calculation of depreciation and the effect of revaluations, changes to economic useful life, repairs, improvements and disposals.

(5) Inventories (IAS 2).

(6) Issue and redemption of shares, including treatment of share issue and redemption costs (IAS 32 and IAS 39), the share premium account, the accounting for maintenance of capital arising from the purchase by a company of its own shares.

(7) The disclosure of related parties to a business (IAS 24).

(8) Construction contracts and related financing costs (IAS 11 & 23): determination of cost, net realisable value, the inclusion of overheads and the measurement of profit on uncompleted contracts.

(9) Research and development costs (IAS 38): criteria for capitalisation.

(10) Intangible Assets (IAS 38) and goodwill (excluding that arising on consolidation): recognition, valuation and amortisation.

(11) Impairment of Assets (IAS 36) and its effect on the above.

(12) Post-balance sheet events (IAS 10).

(13) Provisions and contingencies (IAS 37).

(14) Leases (IAS 17) – Operating and finance leases in the books of the lessee.

D – Managing Short Term Finance – 25%

Learning Outcomes

On completion of their studies students should be able to:

(i) Calculate and interpret working capital ratios for business sectors.

(ii) Prepare and analyse cash-flow forecasts over a twelve-month period.

(iii) Identify measures to improve a cash forecast situation

(iv) Compare and contrast the use and limitations of cash management models and identify when each model is most appropriate.

(v) Analyse trade debtor information.

(vi) Evaluate debtor and creditor policies.

(vii) Evaluate appropriate methods of stock management.

(viii) Identify alternatives for investment of short-term cash surpluses.

(ix) Identify sources of short-term funding.

(x) Identify appropriate methods of finance for trading internationally.

Syllabus Content

(1) Working capital ratios (eg debtor days, stock days, creditor days, current ratio, quick ratio) and the working capital cycle.

(2) Working capital characteristics of different businesses (eg supermarkets being heavily funded by creditors) and the importance of industry comparisons.

(3) Cash-flow forecasts, use of spreadsheets to assist in this in terms of changing variables (eg interest rates, inflation) and in consolidating forecasts.

(4) Variables that are most easily changed, delayed or brought forward in a forecast.

(5) The link between cash, profit and the balance sheet.

(6) The Baumol and Miller–Orr cash management models.

(7) The credit cycle from receipt of customer order to cash receipt.

(8) Evaluation of payment terms and settlement discounts.

(9) Preparation and interpretation of age analyses of debtors and creditors.

(10) Establishing collection targets on an appropriate basis (eg motivational issues in managing credit control).

(11) The payment cycle from agreeing the order to make payments.

(12) Centralised versus decentralised purchasing.

(13) The relationship between purchasing and stock control.

(14) Principles of the economic order quantity (EOQ) model and criticisms thereof.

(15) Types and features of short-term finance: trade creditors, overdrafts, short-term loans and debt factoring.

(16) Use and abuse of trade creditors as a source of finance.

(17) The principles of investing short term (i.e. maturity, return, security, liquidity and diversification).

(18) Types of investments (eg interest-bearing bank accounts, negotiable instruments including certificates of deposit, short-term treasury bills, and securities).

(19) The difference between the coupon on debt and the yield to maturity.

(20) Export finance (eg documentary credits, bills of exchange, export factoring, forfaiting).

Syllabus changes

Section A of this new syllabus on Principles of Business Taxation was covered briefly in Paper 6 *Financial Accounting*, but is now more fully covered and given 20% of the syllabus weighting.

Section B was also covered in Paper 6. Much of the content of Section C was also examined in Paper 6. Topics examinable for Paper 6 but excluded from the P7 syllabus are Investment properties (IAS 40), Government grants (IAS 20) and operating and finance leases in the books of the lessor.

Section D on Managing short term finance covers topics that were previously examined in Paper 4 *Finance*.

P7 *Financial Accounting and Tax Principles* has a wide-ranging but very specific syllabus. As was the case with the previous syllabus, it may be that not all examinable standards have been specified.

The exam paper

Format of the paper

		Number of marks
Section A:	Around 20 multiple choice and other objective test questions, 2-4 marks each	50
Section B:	6 compulsory questions, 5 marks each	30
Section C:	1 out of 2 questions, 20 marks	20
		100

Time allowed: 3 hours

Section A will always contain some multiple choice questions but will not consist solely of multiple choice questions. Section A may contain types of objective test question that are different from those included in the pilot paper.

Further guidance on objective test questions and multiple choice questions is included on pages (xxi) and (xxii).

Section B questions will be mainly written discussion, although some calculations may be included. This section will require breadth of syllabus knowledge and also good time management skills.

Section C questions will be in various different styles including more complex calculations and analysis of data. Most questions will require calculation and written evaluation. Questions may include issues from a number of areas of the syllabus. Careful planning of answers will be essential.

November 2005 exam

			Marks
Section A			
1	20 objective test questions		50
Section B			
2	(a)	Discussion of tax avoidance and tax evasion	5
	(b)	Calculate EOQ and advise on discount	5
	(c)	Provisions and restructuring – calculate and explain	5
	(d)	Discuss qualitative characteristics from *Framework*	5
	(e)	Non-current assets and impairment	5
	(f)	Calculate yield to maturity	5
Section C			
Either			
3	Income statement, statement of changes in equity and balance sheet		
or			20
4	Cash budget and advice on funding		
			100

Examiner's comments

Question 1 was generally well done, but some candidates are still not providing workings on 3 or 4-mark questions. Question 2 was less well done. Candidates were not prepared for yield to maturity and some did not know what the qualitative characteristics of financial information were. Question 3 was expected and most candidates did well at it. Question 4 was generally well done, although few candidates were able to calculate the forecast trade receivables.

May 2005 exam

Section A

1		20 objective test questions	50

Section B

2	(a)	Calculation of deferred tax charge and account balance	5
	(b)	Calculate working capital cycle	5
	(c)	List and explain elements of financial statements as per *Framework*	5
	(d)	Income statement and balance sheet extracts relating to construction contract	5
	(e)	Cash budget	5
	(f)	Calculate finance costs and prepare balance sheet extracts for finance lease using sum of the digits method	5

Section C

Either

3	Income statement and balance sheet	
or		20
4	Cash flow statement – indirect method	
		100

> *Examiner's comments*
>
> Time allocation was a problem for some candidates and there was evidence of rushed answers to questions 1 and 2. There was a lack of workings for Question 1 sub-questions and some questions requiring workings were left out altogether. Question 1 is worth 50 marks and should get 50% of the time allowed. Question 2 showed that some candidates were not prepared for deferred tax, long-term contracts or finance leases and some did not know what the five elements of financial statements were. Candidates had prepared well for income statement/balance sheet and cash flow questions and questions 3 and 4 were well answered.

Pilot paper

Section A

1 21 objective test questions ranging from 2 to 4 marks each.

Section B – Six short answer questions – 5 marks each

2 Depreciation, change to estimated useful economic life

3 Treatment of decommissioning costs

4 Cash flow forecast

5 Income statement and balance sheet extracts to reflect entries in respect of tax on profits and deferred tax

6 Explain definition of provision as per IAS 37

7 Income statement and balance sheet extracts to show entries for leased asset

Section C – One question out of 2 – 20 marks

8 Income statement, balance sheet and statement of changes in equity

9 Cash flow statement in accordance with IAS 7.

What the examiner means

The table below has been prepared by CIMA to help you interpret exam questions.

Learning objective	Verbs used	Definition
1 Knowledge What you are expected to know	• List • State • Define	• Make a list of • Express, fully or clearly, the details of/facts of • Give the exact meaning of
2 Comprehension What you are expected to understand	• Describe • Distinguish • Explain • Identify • Illustrate	• Communicate the key features of • Highlight the differences between • Make clear or intelligible/state the meaning of • Recognise, establish or select after consideration • Use an example to describe or explain something
3 Application How you are expected to apply your knowledge	• Apply • Calculate/compute • Demonstrate • Prepare • Reconcile • Solve • Tabulate	• Put to practical use • Ascertain or reckon mathematically • Prove with certainty or to exhibit by practical means • Make or get ready for use • Make or prove consistent/compatible • Find an answer to • Arrange in a table
4 Analysis How you are expected to analyse the detail of what you have learned	• Analyse • Categorise • Compare and contrast • Construct • Discuss • Interpret • Produce	• Examine in detail the structure of • Place into a defined class or division • Show the similarities and/or differences between • Build up or compile • Examine in detail by argument • Translate into intelligible or familiar terms • Create or bring into existence
5 Evaluation How you are expected to use your learning to evaluate, make decisions or recommendations	• Advise • Evaluate • Recommend	• Counsel, inform or notify • Appraise or assess the value of • Advise on a course of action

Tackling multiple choice questions

The MCQs in your exam will contain four or five possible answers. You have to **choose the option that best answers the question**. The three or four incorrect options are called distracters. There is a skill in answering MCQs quickly and correctly. By practising MCQs you can develop this skill, giving yourself a better chance of passing the exam.

You may wish to follow the approach outlined below, or you may prefer to adapt it.

Step 1 Skim read all the MCQs and identify which appear to be the easier questions and which questions you will not need a calculator to answer.

Step 2 Remember that the examiner will not expect you to spend an equal amount of time on each MCQ; some can be answered instantly but others will take time to work out.

Step 3 Attempt each question **The questions** identified in Step 1 are questions which you should be able to answer during the 20 minutes reading time. Read the question thoroughly. You may prefer to work out the answer before looking at the options, or you may prefer to look at the options at the beginning. Adopt the method that works best for you.

You may find that you recognise a question when you sit the exam. Be aware that the detail and/or requirement may be different. If the question seems familiar, read the requirement and options carefully – do not assume that it is identical.

Step 4 Read the five options and see if one matches your own answer. Be careful with numerical questions, as the distracters are designed to match answers that incorporate **common errors**. Check that your calculation is correct. Have you followed the requirement exactly? Have you included every stage of the calculation?

Step 5 You may find that none of the options matches your answer.

- Re-read the question to ensure that you understand it and are answering the requirement
- Eliminate any obviously wrong answers
- Consider which of the remaining answers is the most likely to be correct and select that option

Step 6 If you are still unsure, make a note and continue to the next question. Likewise if you are nowhere near working out which option is correct, leave the question and come back to it later.

Step 7 Revisit unanswered questions. When you come back to a question after a break, you often find you can answer it correctly straightaway. If you are still unsure, have a guess. You are not penalised for incorrect answers, so **never leave a question unanswered!**

Step 8 **Rule off answers** to each MCQ in the answer booklet.

Tackling objective test questions

What is an objective test question?

An objective test (**OT**) question is made up of some form of **stimulus**, usually a question, and a **requirement** to do something.

- **MCQs.** Read through the information on page (xxiii) about MCQs and how to tackle them.
- **True or false**. You will be asked if a statement is true or false.
- **Data entry**. This type of OT requires you to provide figures such as the answer to a calculation, words to fill in a blank, single word answers to questions, or to identify numbers and words to complete a format.
- **Word-limited answers**. You may be asked to state, define or explain things in no more than a certain number of words or within a single line in the answer booklet.
- **Hot spots**. This question format may ask you to identify specific points on a graph or diagram.
- **Interpretation.** You may be asked to interpret or analyse graphical data.
- **Multiple response.** These questions provide you with a number of options and you have to identify those that fulfil certain criteria.
- **Listing**. You may be asked to list items in rank order.
- **Matching.** This OT question format could ask you to classify particular costs into one of a range of cost classifications provided, to match descriptions of variances with one of a number of variances listed, and so on.

OT questions in your exam

Section A of your exam will contain different types of OT questions. It is not certain how many questions in your exam will be MCQs and how many will be other types of OT, nor what types of OT you will encounter in your exam. Practising different types of OTs will prepare you well for whatever questions come up in your exam.

Dealing with OT questions

Again you may wish to follow the approach we suggest, or you may be prepared to adapt it.

Step 1 Work out **how long** you should allocate to each OT, taking into account the marks allocated to it. Remember that you will not be expected to spend an equal amount of time on each one; some can be answered instantly but others will take time to work out.

Step 2 **Jot down answers, workings or ideas** for as many OTs as possible on the question paper during the 20 minutes reading time.

Step 3 **Attempt each question**. Read the question thoroughly, and note in particular what the question says about the **format** of your answer and whether there are any **restrictions** placed on it (for example the number of words you can use).

You may find that you recognise a question when you sit the exam. Be aware that the detail and/or requirement may be different. If the question seems familiar read the requirement and options carefully – do not assume that it is identical.

Step 4 Read any options you are given and select which ones are appropriate. Check that your calculations are correct. Have you followed the requirement exactly? Have you included every stage of the calculation?

Step 5 You may find that you are unsure of the answer.

- Re-read the question to ensure that you understand it and are answering the requirement
- Eliminate any obviously wrong options if you are given a number of options from which to choose

Step 6 If you are still unsure, **continue to the next question**.

Step 7 Revisit questions you are uncertain about. When you come back to a question after a break you often find you are able to answer it correctly straightaway. If you are still unsure have a guess. You are not penalised for incorrect answers, so **never leave a question unanswered!**

Step 8 Make sure you show your **workings** clearly on calculation OTs, as you may gain some credit for workings even if your final answer is incorrect.

Step 9 Rule off answers to each OT in the answer booklet.

CIMA – Managerial Level

Paper P7

Financial Accounting and Tax Principles

Pilot paper

Instructions to candidates:

You are allowed three hours to answer this question paper.
In the real exam, you are allowed 20 minutes reading time before the examination begins during which you should read the question paper, and if you wish, make annotations on the question paper. However, you will **not** be allowed, **under any circumstances**, to open the answer book and start writing or use your calculator during this reading time.
You are strongly advised to carefully read the question requirement before attempting the question concerned.
Section A   Answer ALL sub-questions in this section
Section B   Answer ALL six short-answer question
Section C   Answer ONE question out of two

DO NOT OPEN THIS PAPER UNTIL YOU ARE READY TO START UNDER EXAMINATION CONDITIONS

SECTION A – 50 marks

Answer ALL sub-questions in this section

Question 1

1.1 Which ONE of the following transactions is most likely to affect the overall amount of working capital?

A Receipt of full amount of cash from a customer to settle their trade receivable account.
B Payment of a trade payable account in full.
C Sale of a non-current asset on credit at its net book value.
D Purchase of inventory on credit. **(2 marks)**

1.2 B entered into a three-year contract to build a leisure centre for an entity. The contract value was $6 million. B recognises profit on the basis of certified work completed.

At the end of the first year, the following figures were extracted from B's accounting records:

	$000
Certified value of work completed (progress payments billed)	2,000
Cost of work certified as complete	1,650
Cos of work-in-progress (not included in completed work)	550
Estimated cost of remaining work required to complete the contract	2,750
Progress payments received from entity	1,600
Cash paid to suppliers for work on the contract	1,300

What values should B record for this contract as 'gross amounts due from customers' and 'current liabilities – trade and other payables'?

	Gross amounts due from customers	*Current liabilities – trade and other payables*
A	$950,000	$350,000
B	$950,000	$900,000
C	$1,250,000	$600,000
D	$2,550,000	$900,000

(2 marks)

1.3 IAS 8 –*Accounting Policies, Changes in Accounting Estimates and Errors* specifies the definition and treatment of a number of different items. Which of the following is NOT specified by IAS 8?

A The effect of a change in an accounting estimate.
B Prior period adjustments.
C Provisions.
D Errors **(2 marks)**

1.4 In no more than 15 words, complete the following sentence:

'A direct tax is one that...' **(2 marks)**

1.5 A company uses the Baumol cash management model. Cash disbursements are constant at $20,000 each month. Money on deposit earns 5% a year, while money in the current account earns a zero return. Switching costs (that is, for each purchase or sale of securities) are $30 for each transaction.

What is the optimal amount (to the nearest $100) to be transferred in each transaction? **(2 marks)**

1.6 List (using no more than five words per item) the four main sources of tax rules in a country.

(4 marks)

1.7 WM's major supplier, INT, supplies electrical tools and is one of the largest companies in the industry, with international operations. Deliveries from INT are currently made monthly, and are constant throughout the year. Delivery and invoicing both occur in the last week of each month.

Details of the credit terms offered by INT are as follows:

Normal credit period	*Cash discount*	*Average monthly purchases*
40 days	2% for settlement in 10 days	$100,000

WM always takes advantage of the cash discount from INT.

Calculate the annual rate of interest (to two decimal places) implied in the cash discount offered by INT. Assume a 365-day year. **(3 marks)**

1.8 A company has a current ratio of 2 :1. Due to having significant surplus cash balances, it has decided to pay its trade payable accounts after 30 days in future, rather than after 50 days, as it has in the past.

What will be the effect of this change on the company's current ratio and its cash operating cycle?

	Current ratio	*Cash operating cycle*
A	Increase	Increase
B	Increase	Decrease
C	Decrease	Increase
D	Decrease	Decrease

(2 marks)

1.9 The following balances were extracted from the books of A:

	Year ended 31 March 20X3
	$000
Revenue	300
Cost of sales	200
Gross profit	100

	At 31 March 20X3
	$000
Closing inventory	15
Trade receivables	36
Trade payables	28

Assume all revenue is credit sales and costs of sales equates to inventory purchases. What is A's average working capital cycle for the year ended 31 March 20X3? **(3 marks)**

1.10 Double tax relief is used to

A ensure that you do not pay tax twice on any of your income.
B mitigate taxing overseas income twice.
C avoid taxing dividends received from subsidiaries in the same country twice.
D provide relief where a company pays tax at double the normal rate. **(2 marks)**

1.11 A withholding tax is:

A tax withheld from payment to the tax authorities.
B tax paid less an amount withheld from payment.
C tax deducted at source before payment of interest or dividends.
D tax paid on increases in value of investment holdings. **(2 marks)**

1.12 Tax on an entity's trading profits could be referred to as:

(i) Income tax
(ii) Profits tax
(iii) Indirect tax
(iv) Direct tax
(v) Earnings tax

Which TWO of the above would most accurately describe tax on an entity's trading profits:

A (i) and (iii)
B (i) and (iv)
C (ii) and (iii)
D (iv) and (v) **(2 marks)**

1.13 An entity commenced business on 1 April 20X2. Revenue in April 20X2 was $20,000, but this is expected to increase at 2% a month. Credit sales amount to 60% of total sales. The credit period allowed is one month. Bad debts are expected to be 3% of credit sales, but other customers are expected to pay on time. Cash sales represent the other 40% of revenue.

How much cash is expected to be received in May 20X2? **(3 marks)**

1.14 Which of the following types of taxes is regarded as an indirect tax?

A Taxes on income.
B Taxes on capital gains.
C Taxes on inherited wealth.
D Sales tax (Value added tax). **(2 marks)**

1.15 E has an accounting profit before tax of $95,000. The tax rate on trading profits applicable to E for the year is 25%. The accounting profit included non-taxable income from government grants of $15,000 and non-tax allowable expenditure of $10,000 on entertaining expenses.

How much tax is E due to pay for the year? **(2 marks)**

1.16 Which TWO of the following are underlying assumptions in the International Accounting Standards Board's Framework for the preparation and presentation of financial statements?

(i) Accruals
(ii) Relevance
(iii) Comparability
(iv) Going concern
(v) Reliability

A (i) and (v)
B (ii) and (v)
C (iii) and (iv)
D (i) and (iv) **(2 marks)**

1.17 The International Accounting Standards Board's Framework for the preparation and presentation of financial statements defines elements of financial statements. In no more than 30 words define an asset. **(2 marks)**

The following data is to be used to answer questions 1.18 and 1.19 below

X acquired the business and assets from the owners of an unincorporated business: the purchase price was satisfied by the issue of 10,000 equity shares with a nominal market value of $10 each and $20,000 cash. The market value of X shares at the date of acquisition was $20 each.

The assets acquired were:

- Net tangible non-current assets with a book value of $20,000 and current value of $25,000.
- Patents for a specialised process valued by a specialist valuer at $15,000.
- Brand name, valued by a specialist brand valuer on the basis of a multiple of earnings at $50,000.
- Publishing rights of the first text from an author that the management of X expects to become a best seller. The publishing rights were a gift from the author to the previous owners at no cost. The management of X has estimated the future value of the potential best seller at $100,000. However, there is no reliable evidence available to support the estimate of the management.

1.18 In no more than 30 words, explain the accounting treatment to be used for the publishing rights of the first text. **(2 marks)**

1.19 Calculate the value of goodwill to be included in the accounts of X for this purchase. **(4 marks)**

1.20 SK sells bathroom fittings throughout the country in which it operates. In order to obtain the best price, it has decided to purchase all its annual demand of 10,000 shower units from a single supplier. RR has offered to provide the required number of showers each year under an exclusive long-term contract.

Demand for shower units is at a constant rate all year. The cost to SK of holding one shower unit in Inventory for one year is $4 plus 3% of the purchase price.

RR is located only a few miles from the SK main showroom. It has offered to supply each shower unit at $400 with a transport charge of $200 per delivery. It has guaranteed such a regular and prompt delivery service that SK believes it will not be necessary to hold any safety Inventory (that is buffer Inventory) if it uses RR as its supplier.

Using the economic order quantity model (EOQ model), calculate the optimal order size, assuming that RR is chosen as the sole supplier of shower units for SK. **(3 marks)**

1.21 Which of the following would be LEAST LIKELY to arise from the introduction of a Just-in-Time inventory ordering system?

A Lower inventory holding costs.
B Less risk of inventory shortages.
C More frequent deliveries.
D Increased dependence on suppliers. **(2 marks)**

(Total marks = 50)

SECTION B – 30 marks

Answer ALL six short-answer questions

Question 2

A new type of delivery vehicle, when purchased on 1 April 20X0 for $20,000, was expected to have a useful life of four years. It now appears that the original estimate of the useful life was too short, and the vehicle is now expected to have a useful life of six years, from the date of purchase. All delivery vehicles are depreciated using the straight-line method and are assumed to have zero residual value.

Required

As the trainee management accountant, draft a memo to the transport manager explaining whether it is possible to change the useful life of the new delivery vehicle. Using appropriate International Accounting Standards, explain how the accounting transactions relating to the delivery vehicle should be recorded in the income statement for the year ended 31 March 20X3 and the balance sheet at that date **(5 marks)**

Question 3

NDL drilled a new oil well, which started production on 1 March 20X3. The licence granting permission to drill the new oil well included a clause that requires NDL to "return the land to the state it was in before drilling commenced".

NDL estimates that the oil well will have a 20-year production life. At the end of that time, the oil well will be de-commissioned and work carried out to reinstate the land. The cost of this de-commissioning work is estimated to be $20 million.

Required

As the trainee management accountant, draft a memo to the production manager explaining how NDL must treat the de-commissioning costs in its financial statements for the year to 31 March 20X3. Your memo should refer to appropriate International Accounting Standards. **(5 marks)**

Question 4

HRD owns a number of small hotels. The room occupancy rate varies significantly from month to month. There are also high fixed costs. As a result, the cash generated each month has been very difficult to estimate.

Christmas is normally a busy period and large cash surpluses are expected in December. There is, however, a possibility that a rival group of hotels will offer large discounts in December and this could damage December trade for HRD to a significant extent.

January is a poor period for the industry and therefore all the company's hotels will close for the month, resulting in a negative cash flow. The Finance Director has identified the following possible outcomes and their associated probabilities:

	$000	*Probability*
Expected cash balance at 30 November 20X3	+175	1.0
Net operating cash flow in December 20X3	+700	0.7
	–300	0.3
Net operating cash flow in January 20X4	–900	1.0

Assume cash flows arise at month ends.

After January 20X4, trade is expected to improve, but there is still a high degree of uncertainty in relation to the cash surpluses or deficits that will be generated in each month.

Required

Calculate the expected cash balance or overdraft of HRD at 31 January 20X4.

Explain why your answer may not be useful for short-term cash planning and outline alternative approaches that could be used. **(5 marks)**

Question 5

On 1 January 20X3, SPJ had an opening debit balance of $5,000 on its tax account, which represented the balance on the account after settling its tax liability for the previous year. SPJ had a credit balance on its deferred tax account of $1·6 million at the same date.

SPJ has been advised that it should expect to pay $1 million tax on its trading profits for the year ended 31 December 20X3 and increase its deferred tax account balance by $150,000.

Required

Prepare extracts from the income statement for the year ended 31 December 20X3, balance sheet at that date and notes to the accounts showing the tax entries required. **(5 marks)**

Question 6

IAS 37 defines the meaning of a provision and sets out when a provision should be recognised.

Required

Using the IAS 37 definition of a provision, explain how a provision meets the International Accounting Standards Board's Framework for the preparation and presentation of financial statements definition of a liability. **(5 marks)**

Question 7

A lessee leases a non-current asset on a non-cancellable lease contract of five years, the details of which are:

- The asset has a useful life of five years.
- The rental is $21,000 per annum payable at the end of each year.
- The lessee also has to pay all insurance and maintenance costs.
- The fair value of the asset was $88,300.

The lessee uses the sum of digits method to calculate finance charges on the lease.

Required

Prepare income statement and balance sheet extracts for years one and two of the lease. **(5 marks)**

SECTION C – 20 marks

Answer ONE question out of two

Question 8

AZ is a quoted manufacturing entity. Its finished products are stored in a nearby warehouse until ordered by customers. AZ has been re-organising the business to improve performance.

The trial balance for AZ at 31 March 20X3 was as follows:

	$000	$000
7% Loan Notes (redeemable 20X7)		18,250
Retained earnings at 31 March 20X2		14,677
Administrative expenses	16,020	
Bank and Cash	26,250	
Cost of goods manufactured in the year to 31 March 20X3 (excluding depreciation)	94,000	
Distribution costs	9,060	
Dividends paid	1,000	
Dividends received		1,200
Equity shares $1 each, fully paid		20,000
Interest paid	639	
Inventory as 30 March 20X2	4,852	
Plant and Equipment	30,315	
Allowance for depreciation at 31 March 20X2:		
Plant and Equipment		6,060
Vehicles		1,670
Allowance for doubtful trade receivables		600
Restructuring costs	121	
Sales revenue		124,900
Share issue expenses	70	
Share premium		500
Trade payables		8,120
Trade receivables	9,930	
Vehicles	3,720	
	195,977	195,977

Additional information provided

(i) Non-current assets are being depreciated as follows:

Plant & Equipment	20% per annum straight line
Vehicles	25% per annum reducing balance

Depreciation of plant and equipment is considered to be part of cost of sales, while depreciation of vehicles should be included under distribution costs.

(ii) Tax due for the year to 31 March 20X3 is estimated at $15,000.

(iii) The closing inventory at 31 March 20X3 was $5,180,000.

(iv) A dividend of 5 cents per ordinary share was paid in February 20X3.

(v) The 7% loan notes are 10-year loans due for repayment by 31 March 20X7. AZ incurred no other interest charges in the year to 31 March 20X3.

(vi) The restructuring costs in the trial balance represent the cost of the final phase of a major fundamental restructuring of the entity to improve competitiveness and future profitability.

(vii) At 31 March 20X3, AZ was engaged in defending a legal action against the entity. Legal advisers have indicated that it is reasonably certain that the outcome of the case will be against the entity. The amount of compensation is currently estimated at $25,000 and has not been included in the trial balance.

(viii) On 1 October 20X2, AZ issued 1,000,000 equity shares at $1·50 each. All money had been received and correctly accounted for by the year end.

Required

Prepare AZ's income statement for the year to 31 March 20X3, a balance sheet at that date, and a statement of changes in equity for the year. These should be in a form suitable for presentation to the shareholders, in accordance with the requirements of International Accounting Standards.

Notes to the financial statements are NOT required, but all workings must be clearly shown. DO NOT prepare a statement of accounting policies or a statement of recognised income and expenses.

(20 marks)

Question 9

The following information has been extracted from the draft financial statements of TEX, a manufacturing entity:

TEX – Income statement for the year ended 30 September 20X3

	$000
Revenue	15,000
Cost of sales	(9,000)
Gross profit	6,000
Other operating expenses	(2,300)
	3,700
Finance cost	(124)
Profit before tax	3,576
Income tax expense	(1,040)
Profit for the period	2,536

TEX – Balance sheets at 30 September

	20X3		20X2	
	$000	*$000*	*$000*	*$000*
Assets				
Non-current assets		18,160		14,500
Current assets:				
Inventories	1,600		1,100	
Trade receivables	1,500		800	
Bank	150		1,200	
		3,250		3,100
Total assets		21,410		17,600

	20X3		20X2	
	$000	$000	$000	$000
Equity and liabilities				
Equity:				
Issued capital		10,834		7,815
Retained earnings		5,836		4,400
		16,670		12,215
Non-current liabilities:				
Interest-bearing borrowings	1,700		2,900	
Deferred tax	600		400	
		2,300		3,300
Current liabilities:				
Trade payables	700		800	
Dividend payable	700		600	
Tax	1,040		685	
		2,440		2,085
		21,410		17,600

Non-current assets

	Property $000	*Plant* $000	*Total* $000
At 30 September 20X2			
Cost	8,400	10,800	19,200
Depreciation	1,300	3,400	4,700
Net book value	7,100	7,400	14,500
At 30 September 20X3			
Cost	11,200	13,400	24,600
Depreciation	1,540	4,900	6,440
Net book value	9,660	8,500	18,160

(i) Plant disposed of during the year had an original cost of $2,600,000 and accumulated depreciation of $900,000; cash received on disposal was $730,000.

(ii) All additions to non-current assets were purchased for cash.

(iii) Dividends totalling $1,100,000 were declared before the balance sheet date.

Required

Prepare TEX's cash flow statement and associated notes for the year ended 30 September 20X3, in accordance with IAS 7 – *Cash flow statements*. **(20 marks)**

CIMA professional development requirements

Soon, you will possess a professional qualification. You know its value by the effort you have put in. To uphold the prestige of the qualification, CIMA, with the other professional bodies that form the International Federation of Accountants (IFAC), requires its members to undertake continuous professional development (CPD). Happily, BPP Professional Education is here to support you in your professional development with materials, courses and qualifications.

For further information, please see CIMA's website: www.cimaglobal.com

Professional development with BPP

You do not have to do exams for professional development (PD) – but you need relevant technical updating and you may also benefit from other work-related training. BPP can provide you with both. Visit our professional development website, www.bpp.com/pd for details of our PD courses in accounting, law, general business skills and other important areas. Offering defined hours of structured CPD, and delivered by top professionals throughout the year and in many locations, our courses are designed to fit around your busy work schedule. Our unique PD passport will give you access to these PD services at an attractive discount.

For further information, please see BPP's website: www.bpp.com/pd

Oxford Institute of International Finance, (OXIIF) MBA

BPP supports the OXFII MBA. The MBA, accredited by AMBA (the Association of MBAs), lasts 30 months, and is taught by distance learning. Experts from Oxford Brookes University give online seminars to a global student base over the Internet. BPP provides the user-friendly materials. Flexibility, global reach and value for money underpin a high-quality learning experience.

The qualification features an introductory module (*Foundations of Management*). Other modules include *Global Business Strategy, Managing Self Development*, and *Organisational Change and Transformation.*

Research Methods are also taught, as they underpin the **research dissertation**.

For further information, please see the Oxford Institutes's website: www.oxfordinstitute.org and BPP's website: www.bpp.com/mba

Diploma in International Financial Reporting

The Diploma in International Financial Reporting is designed for those whose country-specific accounting knowledge needs to be supplemented by knowledge of international accounting standards. BPP offers books and courses in this useful qualification.

For further information, please see ACCA's website: www.accaglobal.com and BPP's website: www.bpp.com/dipifr

Tax and financial services

If you are interested in tax, BPP trains for CIMA's CPD module in Business Taxation. We also offer courses for the ATT (tax technician) and CTA (Chartered Tax Adviser, formerly ATII) qualifications. You can also buy our user-friendly CTA texts to keep up-to date with tax practice.

For further information, please see BPP's website: www.bpp.com/att and www.bpp.com/cta

If your role involves selling financial services products, such as pensions, or offering investment advice, BPP provides learning materials and training for relevant qualifications. BPP also offers training for specialist financial markets qualifications (eg CFA®) and insolvency.

For further information, please see BPP's website: www.bpp.com/financialadvisers

Other business qualifications

BPP supports many business disciplines, such as market research, marketing, human resources management and law. We are the official provider of distance learning programmes for the Market Research Society. We train for the Chartered Institute of Personnel and Development qualification, with a number of other supporting qualifications in training and personnel management. BPP's law school is an industry leader.

Visit www.bpp.com for further details of all that we can offer you. BPP's personalised online information service, My BPP, will help you keep track of the details you submit to BPP.

Part A

Principles of regulation of financial reporting

1

The regulatory framework

Introduction

Accounting is regulated by local statute (such as company law), by Stock Exchange requirements and by accounting standards.

We are looking here at the role of the International Accounting Standards Board and the development of International Accounting Standards and International Financial Reporting Standards. We will be dealing with some of these standards in detail later in the text.

Topic list	Learning outcomes	Syllabus references	Ability required
1 The International Accounting Standards Board (IASB)	B(iii)	B(4)	Comprehension
2 Setting of International Financial Reporting Standards	B(v), (vi)	B(6), (7)	Comprehension
3 Criticisms of the IASB	B(iii)	B(4)	Comprehension
4 Conceptual framework and GAAP	B(i), (ii)	B(1), (2), (3)	Comprehension
5 The IASB's framework	B(iv)	B(5)	Comprehension
6 IAS 18 *Revenue*	C(iv)	C(6)	Application

1 The International Accounting Standards Board (IASB)

FAST FORWARD

The IASB replaced the IASC in 2001. It is responsible for setting International Accounting Standards (IASs) and International Financial Reporting Standards (IFRSs). All new standards are now IFRSs.

1.1 Formation of the IASB

The International Accounting Standards Board is an independent, privately-funded accounting standard setter based in London.

In March 2001 the IASC Foundation was formed as a not-for-profit corporation incorporated in the USA. The IASC Foundation is the parent entity of the IASB.

From April 2001 the IASB assumed accounting standard setting responsibilities from its predecessor body, the International Accounting Standards Committee (IASC). This restructuring was based upon the recommendations made in the *Recommendations on Shaping IASC for the Future.*

1.2 How the IASB is made up

The 14 members of the IASB come from nine countries and have a variety of backgrounds with a mix of auditors, preparers of financial statements, users of financial statements and an academic. The Board consists of 12 full-time members and two part-time members.

1.3 Objectives of the IASB

The formal objectives of the IASB, formulated in its mission statement are:

(a) To develop, in the public interest, a single set of high quality, understandable and enforceable global accounting standards that require transparent and comparable information in general purpose financial statements, and to promote the use and application of these standards.

(b) To co-operate with national accounting standard setters to achieve convergence in accounting standards around the world.

1.4 Structure of the IASB

The structure of the IASB has the following main features.

(a) The IASC Foundation is an independent corporation having two main bodies – the Trustees and the IASB.

(b) The IASC Foundation trustees appoint the IASB members, exercise oversight and raise the funds needed.

(c) The IASB has sole responsibility for setting accounting standards.

(d) There are also two further bodies, the Standards Advisory Council and the International Financial Reporting Interpretations Committee (see below).

The structure can be illustrated as follows.

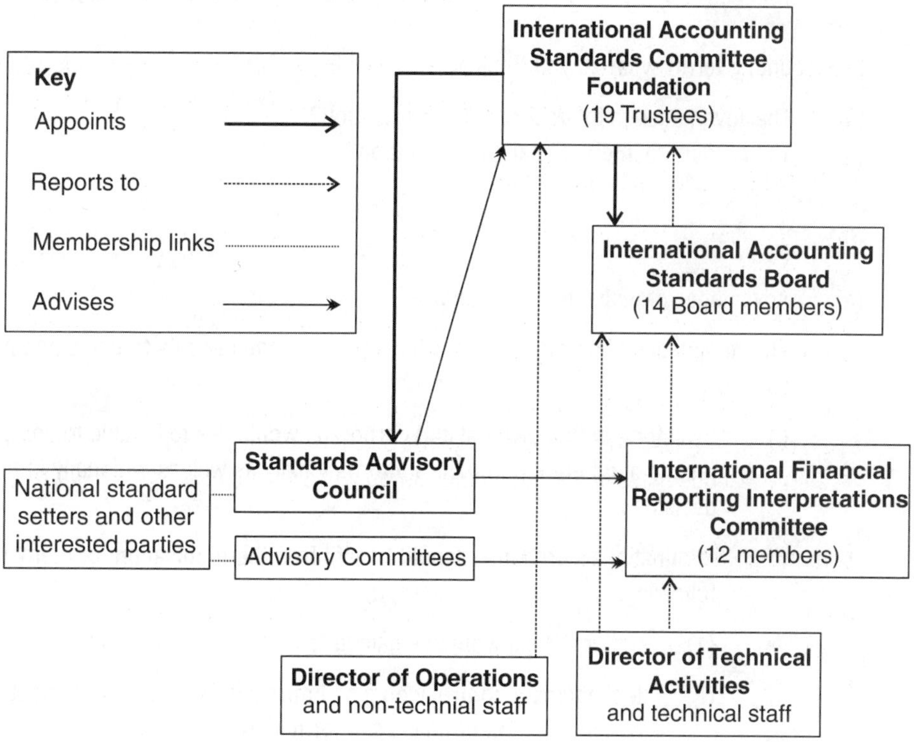

Trustees. The Trustees comprise a group of nineteen individuals, with diverse geographic and functional backgrounds. The Trustees appoint the Members of the Board, the International Financial Reporting Interpretations Committee and the Standards Advisory Council. In addition to monitoring IASC's effectiveness and raising its funds, the Trustees will approve IASC's budget and have responsibility for constitutional changes. Trustees were appointed so that initially there were six from North America, six from Europe, four from Asia Pacific, and three others from any area, as long as geographic balance is maintained.

(a) The International Federation of Accountants (IFAC) suggested candidates to fill five of the nineteen Trustee seats and international organisations of preparers, users and academics each suggested one candidate.

(b) The remaining eleven Trustees are 'at-large' in that they were not selected through the constituency nomination process.

Standards Advisory Council. The Standards Advisory Council provides a formal vehicle for further groups and individuals with diverse geographic and functional backgrounds to give advice to the Board and, at times, to advise the Trustees.

International Financial Reporting Interpretations Committee. The IFRIC provides timely guidance on the application and interpretation of International Financial Reporting Standards. It normally deals with complex accounting issues that could give rise to a diversity of accounting treatments. In this way it assists the IASB in setting and improving financial reporting standards.

Question

International harmonisation

In accounting terms what do you think are:

(a) The advantages to international harmonisation?
(b) The barriers to international harmonisation?

Answer

(a) Advantages of global harmonisation

The advantages of harmonisation will be based on the benefits to users and preparers of accounts, as follows.

(i) Investors, both individual and corporate, would like to be able to compare the financial results of different companies internationally as well as nationally in making investment decisions.

(ii) Multinational companies would benefit from harmonisation for many reasons including the following.

(1) Better access would be gained to foreign investor funds.

(2) Management control would be improved, because harmonisation would aid internal communication of financial information.

(3) Appraisal of foreign entities for take-overs and mergers would be more straightforward.

(4) It would be easier to comply with the reporting requirements of overseas stock exchanges.

(5) Preparation of group accounts would be easier.

(6) A reduction in audit costs might be achieved.

(7) Transfer of accounting staff across national borders would be easier.

(iii) Governments of developing countries would save time and money if they could adopt international standards and, if these were used internally, governments of developing countries could attempt to control the activities of foreign multinational companies in their own country. These companies could not 'hide' behind foreign accounting practices which are difficult to understand.

(iv) Tax authorities. It will be easier to calculate the tax liability of investors, including multinationals who receive income from overseas sources.

(v) Regional economic groups usually promote trade within a specific geographical region. This would be aided by common accounting practices within the region.

(vi) Large international accounting firms would benefit as accounting and auditing would be much easier if similar accounting practices existed throughout the world.

(b) Barriers to harmonisation

(i) Different purposes of financial reporting. In some countries the purpose is solely for tax assessment, while in others it is for investor decision-making.

(ii) Different legal systems. These prevent the development of certain accounting practices and restrict the options available.

(iii) Different user groups. Countries have different ideas about who the relevant user groups are and their respective importance. In the USA investor and creditor groups are given prominence, while in Europe employees enjoy a higher profile.

(iv) Needs of developing countries. Developing countries are obviously behind in the standard setting process and they need to develop the basic standards and principles already in place in most developed countries.

(v) Nationalism is demonstrated in an unwillingness to accept another country's standard.

(vi) Cultural differences result in objectives for accounting systems differing from country to country.

(vii) Unique circumstances. Some countries may be experiencing unusual circumstances which affect all aspects of everyday life and impinge on the ability of companies to produce proper reports, for example hyperinflation, civil war, currency restriction and so on.

(viii) The lack of strong accountancy bodies. Many countries do not have strong independent accountancy or business bodies which would press for better standards and greater harmonisation.

1.5 The IASB and current accounting standards

The IASB's predecessor body, the IASC, had issued 41 International Accounting Standards (IASs) and on 1 April 2001 the IASB adopted all of these standards and now issues its own International Financial Reporting Standards (IFRSs). So far seven new IFRSs have been issued.

1.6 The IASB and IOSCO

The International Organisation of Securities Commissions (IOSCO) is the representative of the world's securities markets regulators. High quality information is vital for the operation of an efficient capital market, and differences in the quality of the accounting policies and their enforcement between countries leads to inefficiencies between markets. IOSCO has been active in encouraging and promoting the improvement and quality of IASs over the last ten years. Most recently, this commitment was evidenced by the agreement between IASC and IOSCO to work on a programme of 'core standards' which could be used by publicly listed entities when offering securities in foreign jurisdictions.

The 'core standards' project resulted in fifteen new or revised IASs and was completed in 1999 with the issue of IAS 39 *Financial instruments: recognition and measurement.* IOSCO spent a year reviewing the results of the project and released a report in May 2000 which recommended to all its members that they allow multinational issuers to use IASs, as supplemented by reconciliation, disclosure and interpretation where necessary, to address outstanding substantive issues at a national or regional level.

IASB staff and IOSCO continue to work together to resolve outstanding issues and to identify areas where new IASB standards are needed.

1.7 European Commission and IASs/IFRSs

All listed entities in EU member states were required to report under IFRS in their consolidated financial statements from January 2005.

To this end the IASB undertook an **improvements project**, dealing with **revisions to IAS**, for example in the area of materiality, presentation, leases, related parties and earnings per share. This has been matched in, for example, the UK, by a **convergence project**, bringing UK GAAP into line with IASs where these are better.

2 Setting of International Financial Reporting Standards

FAST FORWARD

International Financial Reporting Standards (IFRSs) are set in a similar manner to the previous setting of IASs in accordance with the IASB's due process.

2.1 Due process

The overall agenda of the IASB is initially set by discussion with the Standards Advisory Council. The process for developing an individual standard involves the following steps.

Step 1 During the early stages of a project, IASB may establish an **Advisory Committee** to give advice on issues arising in the project. Consultation with the Advisory Committee and the Standards Advisory Council occurs throughout the project.

Step 2 IASB may develop and publish **Discussion Documents** for public comment.

Step 3 Following the receipt and review of comments, the IASB develops and publishes an **Exposure Draft** for public comment.

Step 4 Following the receipt and review of comments, the IASB issues a final **International Financial Reporting Standard**.

The period of exposure for public comment is normally 90 days. However, in exceptional circumstances, proposals may be issued with a comment period of 60 days.

2.2 Co-ordination with national standard setters

Close co-ordination between IASB due process and due process of national standard setters is important to the success of the IASB's mandate.

The IASB is exploring ways in which to integrate its due process more closely with national due process. Such integration may grow as the relationship between IASB and national standard setters evolves. In particular, the IASB is exploring the following procedure for projects that have international implications.

(a) IASB and national standard setters would co-ordinate their work plans so that when the IASB starts a project, national standard setters would also add it to their own work plans so that they can play a full part in developing international consensus. Similarly, where national standard setters start projects, the IASB would consider whether it needs to develop a new Standard or review its existing Standards. Over a reasonable period, the IASB and national standard setters should aim to review all standards where significant differences currently exist, giving priority to the areas where the differences are greatest.

(b) National standard setters would not be required to vote for IASB's preferred solution in their national standards, since each country remains free to adopt IASB standards with amendments or to adopt other standards. However, the existence of an international consensus is clearly one factor that members of national standard setters would consider when they decide how to vote on national standards.

(c) The IASB would continue to publish its own Exposure Drafts and other documents for public comment.

(d) National standard setters would publish their own exposure document at approximately the same time as IASB Exposure Drafts and would seek specific comments on any significant divergences between the two exposure documents. In some instances, national standard setters may include in their exposure documents specific comments on issues of particular relevance to their country or include more detailed guidance than is included in the corresponding IASB document.

(e) National standard setters would follow their own full due process, which they would ideally choose to integrate with the IASB's due process. This integration would avoid unnecessary delays in completing standards and would also minimise the likelihood of unnecessary differences between the standards that result.

2.3 IASB liaison members

Seven of the full-time members of the IASB have formal liaison responsibilities with national standard setters in order to promote the convergence of national accounting standards and International Accounting Standards. The IASB envisages a partnership between the IASB and these national standard setters as they work together to achieve convergence of accounting standards world-wide.

The countries with these liaison members are Australia and New Zealand, Canada, France, Germany, Japan, UK and USA.

In addition all IASB members have contact responsibility with national standards setter not having liaison members and many countries are also represented on the Standards Advisory Council.

2.4 Current IASs/IFRs

The current list is as follows.

International Accounting Standards		Date of issue
IAS 1 (revised)	Presentation of financial statements	Dec 2003
IAS 2 (revised)	Inventories	Dec 2003
IAS 7 (revised)	Cash flow statements	Dec 1992
IAS 8 (revised)	Accounting policies, changes in accounting estimates and errors	Dec 2003
IAS 10 (revised)	Events after the balance sheet date	Dec 2003
IAS 11 (revised)	Construction contracts	Dec 1993
IAS 12 (revised)	Income taxes	Nov 2000
IAS 14 (revised)	Segment reporting	Aug 1997
IAS 16 (revised)	Property, plant and equipment	Dec 2003
IAS 17 (revised)	Leases	Dec 2003
IAS 18 (revised)	Revenue	Dec 1993
IAS 19 (revised)	Employee benefits	Nov 2000
IAS 20	Accounting for government grants and disclosure of government assistance	Jan 1995
IAS 21 (revised)	The effects of changes in foreign exchange rates	Dec 2003
IAS 23 (revised)	Borrowing costs	Dec 1993
IAS 24 (revised)	Related party disclosures	Dec 2003
IAS 26	Accounting and reporting by retirement benefit plans	Jan 1995
IAS 27 (revised)	Consolidated and separate financial statements	Dec 2003
IAS 28 (revised)	Investments in associates	Dec 2003
IAS 29	Financial reporting in hyperinflationary economies	Jan 1995
IAS 30	Disclosures in the financial statements of banks and similar financial institutions (not examinable)	Jan 1995
IAS 31 (revised)	Interests in joint ventures	Dec 2003

International Accounting Standards		Date of issue
IAS 32 (revised)	Financial instruments: disclosures and presentation	Dec 2003
IAS 33 (revised)	Earnings per share	Dec 2003
IAS 34	Interim financial reporting	Feb 1998
IAS 36 (revised)	Impairment of assets	June 1998
IAS 37	Provisions, contingent liabilities and contingent assets	Sept 1998
IAS 38 (revised)	Intangible assets	Sept 1998
IAS 39 (revised)	Financial instruments: recognition and measurement	Dec 2003
IAS 40	Investment property	Dec 2003
IAS 41	Agriculture	Feb 2001
IFRS 1	First time adoption of International Financial Reporting Standards	June 2003
IFRS 2	Share-based payment	Feb 2004
IFRS 3	Business combinations	Mar 2004
IFRS 4	Insurance contracts	Mar 2004
IFRS 5	Non-current assets held for sale and discontinued operations	Mar 2004
IFRS 6	Exploration for and evaluation of mineral resources	Dec 2004
IFRS 7	Financial instruments – disclosures	Aug 2005

Various exposure drafts and discussion papers are currently at different stages within the IAS process, but these are not of concern to you at this stage. By the end of your financial accounting studies, however, you will know *all* the standards, exposure and discussion papers!

2.5 Benchmark and allowed alternative treatment

Many of the old IASs permitted two accounting treatments for like transactions or events. One treatment is designated as the **benchmark treatment** (effectively the **preferred treatment**) and the other is known as the **alternative treatment**. However, as the standards are revised, many alternatives are being eliminated.

2.6 Scope and application of IASs

2.6.1 Scope

Any limitation of the applicability of a specific IAS is made clear within that standard. IASs are **not intended to be applied to immaterial items, nor are they retrospective**. Each individual IAS lays out its scope at the beginning of the standard.

2.6.2 Application

Within each individual country **local regulations** govern, to a greater or lesser degree, the issue of financial statements. These local regulations include accounting standards issued by the national regulatory bodies and/or professional accountancy bodies in the country concerned.

The IASC **concentrated on essentials** when producing IASs. This means that the IASC tried not to make IASs too complex, because otherwise they would be impossible to apply on a worldwide basis.

2.7 World-wide effect of IASs and the IASB

The IASB, and before it the IASC, has now been in existence for around 25 years, and it is worth looking at the effect it has had in that time.

As far as **Europe** is concerned, the consolidated financial statements of many of Europe's top multinationals are prepared in conformity with national requirements, EC directives and IASs. Furthermore, IASs are having a growing influence on national accounting requirements and practices. Many of these developments have been given added impetus by the internationalisation of capital markets.

In **Japan**, the influence of the IASC had, until recently, been negligible. This was mainly because of links in Japan between tax rules and financial reporting. The Japanese Ministry of Finance set up a working committee to consider whether to bring national requirements into line with IASs. The Tokyo Stock Exchange has announced that it will accept financial statements from foreign issuers that conform with home country standards.

This was widely seen as an attempt to attract foreign issuers, in particular companies from Hong Kong and Singapore. As these countries base their accounting on international standards, this action is therefore implicit acknowledgement by the Japanese Ministry of Finance of IAS requirements.

America and Japan have been two of the developed countries which have been most reluctant to accept accounts prepared under IASs, but recent developments suggest that such financial statements may soon be acceptable on these important stock exchanges.

In **America**, the Securities and Exchange Commission (SEC) agreed in 1993 to allow foreign issuers (of shares, etc) to follow IAS treatments on certain issues, including cash flow statements under IAS 7. The overall effect is that, where an IAS treatment differs from US GAAP, these treatments will now be acceptable. The SEC is now supporting the IASB because it wants to attract foreign listings.

3 Criticisms of the IASB

FAST FORWARD

In its attempt to formulate standards which are accepted internationally, the IASB has met opposition over various issues from companies, interest groups and countries.

We will begin by looking at some of the general problems created by **accounting standards**, particularly where they offer a choice of treatment.

3.1 Accounting standards and choice

It is sometimes argued that companies should be given a choice in matters of financial reporting on the grounds that accounting standards are detrimental to the quality of such reporting. There are arguments on both sides.

In favour of accounting standards (both national and international), the following points can be made.

- They **reduce or eliminate confusing variations** in the methods used to prepare accounts.
- They provide a **focal point for debate** and discussions about accounting practice.
- They oblige companies to **disclose the accounting policies** used in the preparation of accounts.
- They are a less rigid alternative to enforcing conformity by means of **legislation**.
- They have obliged companies to **disclose more accounting information** than they would otherwise have done if accounting standards did not exist.

Many companies are reluctant to disclose information which is not required by national legislation. However, the following arguments may be put forward **against standardisation** and **in favour of choice**.

- A set of rules which give backing to one method of preparing accounts might be **inappropriate in some circumstances**. For example, IAS 16 on depreciation is inappropriate for investment properties (properties not occupied by the entity but held solely for investment), which are covered by IAS 40 on investment property.

- Standards may be subject to **lobbying or government pressure** (in the case of national standards). For example, in the USA, the accounting standard FAS 19 on the accounts of oil and gas companies led to a powerful lobby of oil companies, which persuaded the SEC (Securities and Exchange Commission) to step in. FAS 19 was then suspended.
- Unlike IFRSs, many national standards are not based on a **conceptual framework of accounting**.
- There may be a **trend towards rigidity**, and away from flexibility in applying the rules.

3.2 Political problems

Any international body, whatever its purpose or activity, faces enormous political difficulties in attempting to gain **international consensus** and the IASB is no exception to this. How can the IASB reconcile the financial reporting situation between economies as diverse as third-world developing countries and sophisticated first-world industrial powers?

Developing countries are suspicious of the IASB, believing it to be dominated by the **USA.** This arises because acceptance by the USA listing authority, the Securities and Exchange Commission (SEC), of IASs is seen as a major hurdle to be overcome. For all practical purposes it is the American market which must be persuaded to accept IASs and IFRSs.

Developing countries have been catered for to some extent by the development of IAS 41 on **agriculture**, which is generally of much more relevance to such countries.

There are also tensions between the **UK/US model** of financial reporting and the **European model**. The UK/US model is based around investor reporting, whereas the European model is mainly concerned with tax rules, so shareholder reporting has a much lower priority.

The break-up of the former USSR and the move in many **Eastern European countries** to free-market economies has also created difficulties. It is likely that these countries will have to 'catch up' to international standards as their economies stabilise.

4 Conceptual framework and GAAP

FAST FORWARD

A conceptual framework provides the basis for the formulation of accounting standards.

4.1 The search for a conceptual framework

Key term

A **conceptual framework**, in the field we are concerned with, is a statement of generally accepted theoretical principles which form the frame of reference for financial reporting.

These theoretical principles provide the basis for the development of new accounting standards and the evaluation of those already in existence. The financial reporting process is concerned with providing information that is useful in the business and economic decision-making process. Therefore a conceptual framework will form the **theoretical basis** for determining which events should be accounted for, how they should be measured and how they should be communicated to the user. Although it is theoretical in nature, a conceptual framework for financial reporting has highly practical final aims.

The **danger of not having a conceptual framework** is demonstrated in the way some countries' standards have developed over recent years; standards tend to be produced in a haphazard and fire-fighting approach. Where an agreed framework exists, the standard-setting body act as an architect or designer, rather than a fire-fighter, building accounting rules on the foundation of sound, agreed basic principles.

The lack of a conceptual framework also means that fundamental principles are tackled more than once in different standards, thereby producing **contradictions and inconsistencies** in basic concepts, such as those of prudence and matching. This leads to ambiguity and it affects the true and fair concept of financial reporting.

Another problem with the lack of a conceptual framework has become apparent in the USA. The large number of **highly detailed standards** produced by the Financial Accounting Standards Board (FASB) has created a financial reporting environment governed by specific rules rather than general principles. This would be avoided if a cohesive set of principles were in place.

A conceptual framework can also bolster standard setters **against political pressure** from various 'lobby groups' and interested parties. Such pressure would only prevail if it was acceptable under the conceptual framework.

4.2 Advantages and disadvantages of a conceptual framework

4.2.1 Advantages

(a) The situation is avoided whereby standards are developed on a patchwork basis, where a particular accounting problem is recognised as having emerged, and resources are then channelled into **standardising accounting practice** in that area, without regard to whether that particular issue was necessarily the most important issue remaining at that time without standardisation.

(b) As stated above, the development of certain standards (particularly national standards) have been subject to considerable **political interference** from interested parties. Where there is a conflict of interest between user groups on which policies to choose, policies deriving from a conceptual framework will be **less open to criticism** that the standard-setter buckled to external pressure.

(c) Some standards may concentrate on the **income statement** whereas some may concentrate on the **valuation of net assets** (balance sheet).

4.2.2 Disadvantages

(a) Financial statements are intended for a **variety of users**, and it is not certain that a single conceptual framework can be devised which will suit all users.

(b) Given the diversity of user requirements, there may be a need for a variety of accounting standards, each produced for a **different purpose** (and with different concepts as a basis).

(c) It is not clear that a conceptual framework makes the task of **preparing and then implementing** standards any easier than without a framework.

Before we look at the IASB's attempt to produce a conceptual framework, we need to consider another term of importance to this debate: generally accepted accounting practice; or GAAP.

4.3 Generally Accepted Accounting Practice (GAAP)

Key term

GAAP signifies all the rules, from whatever source, which govern accounting.

In individual countries this is seen primarily as a **combination** of:

- National company law
- National accounting standards
- Local stock exchange requirements

Although those sources are the basis for the GAAP of individual countries, the concept also includes the effects of **non-mandatory sources** such as:

- International accounting standards
- Statutory requirements in other countries

In many countries, like the UK, GAAP does not have any statutory or regulatory authority or definition, unlike other countries, such as the USA. The term is mentioned rarely in legislation, and only then in fairly limited terms.

There are different views of GAAP in different countries. The UK position can be explained in the following extracts from *UK GAAP* (Davies, Paterson & Wilson, Ernst & Young, 5th edition).

> 'Our view is that GAAP is a dynamic concept which requires constant review, adaptation and reaction to changing circumstances. We believe that use of the term "principle" gives GAAP an unjustified and inappropriate degree of permanence. GAAP changes in response to changing business and economic needs and developments. As circumstances alter, accounting practices are modified or developed accordingly..... We believe that GAAP goes far beyond mere rules and principles, and encompasses contemporary permissible accounting **practice**.
>
> It is often argued that the term "generally accepted" implies that there must exist a high degree of practical application of a particular accounting practice. However, this interpretation raises certain practical difficulties. For example, what about new areas of accounting which have not, as yet, been generally applied? What about different accounting treatments for similar items – are they all generally accepted?
>
> It is our view that "generally accepted" does **not** mean "generally adopted or used". We believe that, in the UK context, GAAP refers to accounting practices which are regarded as permissible by the accounting profession. The extent to which a particular practice has been adopted is, in our opinion, not the overriding consideration. Any accounting practice which is legitimate in the circumstances under which it has been applied should be regarded as GAAP. The decision as to whether or not a particular practice is permissible or legitimate would depend on one or more of the following factors:
>
> - Is the practice addressed either in the accounting standards, statute or other official pronouncements?
> - If the practice is not addressed in UK accounting standards, is it dealt with in International Accounting Standards, or the standards of other countries such as the US?
> - Is the practice consistent with the needs of users and the objectives of financial reporting?
> - Does the practice have authoritative support in the accounting literature?
> - Is the practice being applied by other companies in similar situations?
> - Is the practice consistent with the fundamental concept of "true and fair"?'

This view is not held in all countries, however. In the USA particularly, the equivalent of a 'true and fair view' is 'fair presentation in accordance with GAAP'. Generally accepted accounting principles are defined as those principles which have 'substantial authoritative support'. Therefore accounts prepared in accordance with accounting principles for which there is not substantial authoritative support are presumed to be misleading or inaccurate.

The effect here is that 'new' or 'different' accounting principles are not acceptable unless they have been adopted by the mainstream accounting profession, usually the standard-setting bodies and/or professional accountancy bodies. This is much more rigid than the UK view expressed above.

4.3.1 GAAP and a conceptual framework

A conceptual framework for financial reporting can be defined as an attempt to codify existing GAAP in order to reappraise current accounting standards and to produce new standards.

5 The IASB's framework

FAST FORWARD

The *Framework* was produced by the IASC and adopted by the IASB. It provides the conceptual framework within which IASs and IFRSs are formulated.

5.1 A conceptual framework

In July 1989 the old IASC produced a document, *Framework for the preparation and presentation of financial statements* (*'Framework'*). The *Framework* is, in effect, the **conceptual framework** upon which all IASs are based and hence which determines how financial statements are prepared and the information they contain.

The *Framework* consists of several sections or chapters, following on after a preface and introduction. These **chapters** are as follows.

- The objective of financial statements
- Underlying assumptions
- Qualitative characteristics of financial statements
- The elements of financial statements
- Recognition of the elements of financial statements
- Measurement of the elements of financial statements
- Concepts of capital and capital maintenance

5.2 Preface

The preface to the *Framework* points out the fundamental reason why financial statements are produced worldwide, ie to **satisfy the requirements of external users**, but that practice varies due to the individual pressures in each country.

These pressures may be social, political, economic or legal, but they result in variations in practice from country to country, including the form of statements, the definition of their component parts (assets, liabilities etc), the criteria for recognition of items and both the scope and disclosure of financial statements.

5.3 Introduction

The introduction to the *Framework* lays out the purpose, status and scope of the document. It then looks at different users of financial statements and their information needs. (Note that the framework refers to the IASC. In practice this now means the IASB.)

5.3.1 Purpose and status

The introduction gives a list of the purposes of the *Framework*.

(a) Assist the Board of the IASC in the **development of future IASs** and in its review of existing IASs.

(b) Assist the Board of the IASC in **promoting harmonisation** of regulations, accounting standards and procedures relating to the presentation of financial statements by providing a basis for reducing the number of alternative accounting treatments permitted by IASs.

(c) Assist **national standard-setting bodies** in developing national standards.

(d) Assist **preparers of financial statements** in applying IASs and in dealing with topics that have yet to form the subject of an IAS.

(e) Assist **auditors** in forming an opinion as to whether financial statements conform with IASs.

(f) Assist **users of financial statements** in interpreting the information contained in financial statements prepared in conformity with IASs.

(g) Provide those who are interested in the work of IASC with **information** about its approach to the formulation of IASs.

The *Framework* is not an IAS and so does not overrule any individual IAS. In the (rare) cases of conflict between an IAS and the *Framework*, the **IAS will prevail**. These cases will diminish over time as the *Framework* will be used as a guide in the production of future IASs. The *Framework* itself will be revised occasionally depending on the experience of the IASB in using it.

5.3.2 Scope

The *Framework* deals with:

(a) The **objective** of financial statements.

(b) The **qualitative characteristics** that determine the usefulness of information in financial statements.

(c) The **definition, recognition and measurement** of the elements from which financial statements are constructed.

(d) Concepts of **capital and capital maintenance**.

The *Framework* is concerned with **'general purpose' financial statements** (ie a normal set of annual statements), but it can be applied to other types of accounts. A complete set of financial statements includes:

(a) A balance sheet
(b) An income statement
(c) A statement of changes in financial position (eg a cash flow statement)
(d) Notes, other statements and explanatory material

Supplementary information may be included, but some items are not included, namely commentaries and reports by the directors, the chairman, management etc.

All types of financial reporting entities are included (commercial, industrial, business; public or private sector).

Key term

A **reporting entity** is an entity for which there are users who rely on the financial statements as their major source of financial information about the entity. *(Framework)*

5.3.3 Users and their information needs

We have already looked at the users of accounting information in earlier studies. They consist of investors, employees, lenders, suppliers and other trade creditors, customers, government and their agencies and the public. You should be able to remember enough to do the following question.

Question — **Information needs**

Consider the information needs of the users of financial information listed above.

Answer

(a) **Investors** are the providers of risk capital

- (i) Information is required to help make a decision about buying or selling shares, taking up a rights issue and voting.
- (ii) Investors must have information about the level of dividend, past, present and future and any changes in share price.
- (iii) Investors will also need to know whether the management has been running the company efficiently.
- (iv) Investors will want to know about the liquidity position of the company, the company's future prospects, and how the company's shares compare with those of its competitors.

(b) **Employees** need information about the security of employment and future prospects for jobs in the company, and to help with collective pay bargaining.

(c) **Lenders** need information to help them decide whether to lend to a company. They will also need to check that the value of any security remains adequate, that the interest repayments are secure.

(d) **Suppliers** need to know whether the company will be a good customer and pay its debts.

(e) **Customers** need to know whether the company can continue producing and supplying goods.

(f) **Government's** interest in a company may be one of creditor or customer, as well as being specifically concerned with compliance with tax and company law, ability to pay tax and the general contribution of the company to the economy.

(g) The **public** at large would wish to have information for all the reasons mentioned above, but it could be suggested that it would be impossible to provide general purpose accounting information which was specifically designed for the needs of the public.

Financial statements cannot meet all these users' needs, but financial statements which meet the **needs of investors** (providers of risk capital) will meet most of the needs of other users.

The *Framework* emphasises that the preparation and presentation of financial statements is primarily the **responsibility of an entity's management**. Management also has an interest in the information appearing in financial statements.

5.4 The objective of financial statements

'The objective of financial statements is to provide information about the financial position, performance and changes in financial position of an entity that is useful to a wide range of users in making economic decisions.' (*Framework*)

Such financial statements will meet the needs of most users. The information is, however, **restricted**.

(a) It is based on **past events** not expected future events.
(b) It does not necessarily contain **non-financial information**.

The statements also show the results of **management's stewardship**.

5.5 Underlying assumptions

5.5.1 Accruals basis

Key term

> **Accruals basis**. The effects of transactions and other events are recognised when they occur (and not as cash or its equivalent is received or paid) and they are recorded in the accounting records and reported in the financial statements of the periods to which they relate. *(Framework)*

Financial statements prepared under the accruals basis show users past transactions involving cash and also obligations to pay cash in the future and resources which represent cash to be received in the future.

5.5.2 Going concern

Key term

> **Going concern**. The entity is assumed to be a going concern, that is, as continuing in operation for the foreseeable future. It is assumed that the entity has neither the intention nor the need to liquidate or curtail materially the scale of its operations. *(Framework)*

It is assumed that the entity has no intention to liquidate or curtail major operations. If it did, then the financial statements would be prepared on a **different (disclosed) basis.**

5.6 Qualitative characteristics of financial statements

The *Framework* states that qualitative characteristics are the attributes that make the information provided in financial statements useful to users. The four principal qualitative characteristics are **understandability, relevance, reliability and comparability**.

5.6.1 Understandability

Users must be able to understand financial statements. They are assumed to have some business, economic and accounting knowledge and to be able to apply themselves to study the information properly. **Complex matters should not be left out** of financial statements simply due to its difficulty if it is relevant information.

5.6.2 Relevance

The **predictive and confirmatory roles** of information are interrelated.

Key term

> **Relevance**. Information has the quality of relevance when it influences the economic decisions of users by helping them evaluate past, present or future events or confirming, or correcting, their past evaluations. *(Framework)*

Information on financial position and performance is often used to predict future position and performance and other things of interest to the user, eg likely dividend, wage rises. The **manner of showing information** will enhance the ability to make predictions, eg by highlighting unusual items.

The relevance of information is affected by its **nature and materiality**.

Key term

Materiality. Information is material if its omission or misstatement could influence the economic decisions of users taken on the basis of the financial statements. *(Framework)*

Information may be judged relevant simply because of its nature (eg remuneration of management). In other cases, both the nature and materiality of the information are important. Materiality is not a primary qualitative characteristic itself (like reliability or relevance), because it is merely a threshold or cut-off point.

5.6.3 Reliability

Information must also be reliable to be useful. The user must be able to depend on it being a **faithful representation**.

Key term

Reliability. Information has the quality of reliability when it is free from material error and bias and can be depended upon by users to represent faithfully that which it either purports to represent or could reasonably be expected to represent. *(Framework)*

5.6.4 Comparability

Users must be able to compare an entity's financial statements:

(a) **Through time** to identify trends.

(b) **With the financial statements** of other entities to evaluate their relative financial position, performance and changes in financial position.

The consistency of treatment is therefore important across like items over time, within the entity and across all entities.

The **disclosure of accounting policies** is particularly important here. Users must be able to distinguish between different accounting policies in order to be able to make a valid comparison of similar items in the accounts of different entities.

Comparability is **not the same as uniformity**. Entities should change accounting policies if they become inappropriate.

Corresponding information for **preceding periods** should be shown to enable comparison over time.

Exam focus point

Make sure you know these qualitative characteristics. They were examined in both of the 2005 exams.

5.6.5 True and fair view/fair presentation

The *Framework* does not attempt to define these concepts directly. It does state, however, that the application of the **principal 'qualitative' characteristics** and of **appropriate accounting standards** will usually result in financial statements which show a true and fair view, or present fairly.

5.7 The elements of financial statements

Transactions and other events are grouped together in broad **classes** and in this way their financial effects are shown in the financial statements. These broad classes are the elements of financial statements. The *Framework* lays out these elements as follows.

Elements of financial statements

Measurement of financial position in the balance sheet

- **Assets**
- **Liabilities**
- **Equity**

Measurement of performance in the income statement

- **Income**
- **Expenses**

A process of **sub-classification** then takes place for presentation in the financial statements, eg assets are classified by their nature or function in the business to show information in the best way for users to take economic decisions.

5.7.1 Financial position

We need to define the three terms listed under this heading above.

Key terms

Asset. A resource controlled by an entity as a result of past events and from which future economic benefits are expected to flow to the entity.

Liability. A present obligation of the entity arising from past events, the settlement of which is expected to result in an outflow from the entity of resources embodying economic benefits.

Equity. The residual interest in the assets of the entity after deducting all its liabilities.

These definitions are important, but they do not cover the **criteria for recognition** of any of these items, which are discussed in the next section of this chapter. This means that the definitions may include items which would not actually be recognised in the balance sheet because they fail to satisfy recognition criteria particularly, as we will see below, the **probable flow of any economic benefit** to or from the business.

Whether an item satisfies any of the definitions above will depend on the **substance and economic reality** of the transaction, not merely its legal form.

Exam focus point

These definitions should be learnt. The pilot paper had a question asking for the definition of an asset.

Question

Assets and liabilities

Consider the following situations. In each case, do we have an asset or liability within the definitions given by the *Framework?* Give reasons for your answer.

(a) Pat Co has purchased a patent for $20,000. The patent gives the company sole use of a particular manufacturing process which will save $3,000 a year for the next five years.

(b) Baldwin Co paid Don Brennan $10,000 to set up a car repair shop, on condition that priority treatment is given to cars from the company's fleet.

(c) Deals on Wheels Co provides a warranty with every car sold.

Answer

(a) This is an asset, albeit an intangible one. There is a past event, control and future economic benefit (through cost savings).

78155

(b) This cannot be classified as an asset. Baldwin Co has no control over the car repair shop and it is difficult to argue that there are 'future economic benefits'.

(c) This is a liability; the business has taken on an obligation. It would be recognised when the warranty is issued rather than when a claim is made.

5.7.2 Equity

Equity is defined above as a **residual**, but it may be sub-classified in the balance sheet. This will indicate legal or other restrictions on the ability of the entity to distribute or otherwise apply its equity. Some reserves are required by statute or other law, eg for the future protection of creditors. The amount shown for equity depends on the **measurement of assets and liabilities.** It has nothing to do with the market value of the entity's shares.

5.7.3 Performance

Profit is used as a **measure of performance**, or as a basis for other measures (eg EPS). It depends directly on the measurement of income and expenses, which in turn depend (in part) on the concepts of capital and capital maintenance adopted.

The elements of income and expense are therefore defined.

Key terms

> **Income**. Increases in economic benefits during the accounting period in the form of inflows or enhancements of assets or decreases of liabilities that result in increases in equity, other than those relating to contributions from equity participants.
>
> **Expenses**. Decreases in economic benefits during the accounting period in the form of outflows or depletions of assets or incurrences of liabilities that result in decreases in equity, other than those relating to distributions to equity participants. *(Framework)*

5.7.4 Capital maintenance adjustments

A **revaluation** gives rise to an increase or decrease in equity.

Key term

> **Revaluation**. Restatement of assets and liabilities. *(Framework)*

These increases and decreases meet the definitions of income and expenses. They are **not included** in the income statement under certain concepts of capital maintenance, however, but rather in equity.

5.8 Recognition of the elements of financial statements

Items which meet the definition of assets or liabilities may still not be recognised in financial statements because they must also meet certain **recognition criteria**.

Key term

> **Recognition**. The process of incorporating in the balance sheet or income statement an item that meets the definition of an element and satisfies the following criteria for recognition:
>
> (a) It is probable that any future economic benefit associated with the item will flow to or from the entity.
>
> (b) The item has a cost or value that can be measured with reliability. *(Framework)*

Regard must be given to **materiality**.

5.8.1 Probability of future economic benefits

Probability here means the **degree of uncertainty** that the future economic benefits associated with an item will flow to or from the entity. This must be judged on the basis of the **characteristics of the entity's environment** and the **evidence available** when the financial statements are prepared.

5.8.2 Reliability of measurement

The cost or value of an item, in many cases, **must be estimated**. The *Framework* states, however, that the use of reasonable estimates is an essential part of the preparation of financial statements and does not undermine their reliability. Where no reasonable estimate can be made, the item should not be recognised, although its existence should be disclosed in the notes, or other explanatory material.

Items may still qualify for recognition **at a later date** due to changes in circumstances or subsequent events.

5.8.3 Recognition of items

We can summarise the recognition criteria for assets, liabilities, income and expenses, based on the definition of recognition given above.

Item	Recognised in	When
Asset	The balance sheet	It is probable that the future economic benefits will flow to the entity and the asset has a cost or value that can be measured reliably.
Liability	The balance sheet	It is probable that an outflow of resources embodying economic benefits will result from the settlement of a present obligation and the amount at which the settlement will take place can be measured reliably.
Income	The income statement	An increase in future economic benefits related to an increase in an asset or a decrease of a liability has arisen that can be measured reliably.
Expenses	The income statement	A decrease in future economic benefits related to a decrease in an asset or an increase of a liability has arisen that can be measured reliably.

5.9 Measurement of the elements of financial statements

Measurement is defined as follows.

Key term

Measurement. The process of determining the monetary amounts at which the elements of the financial statements are to be recognised and carried in the balance sheet and income statement. *(Framework)*

This involves the selection of a particular **basis of measurement**. A number of these are used to different degrees and in varying combinations in financial statements. They are:

- **Historical cost**. The amount that was originally paid to acquire an asset.
- **Current cost**. The amount which would be needed at current prices to obtain an equivalent asset.
- **Realisable value**. The net amount expected to be received from selling an asset, or paid to settle a liability.
- **Present value**. The discounted present value of future cash flows that are expected to be received or paid in respect of an asset or liability.

5.10 Concepts of capital and capital maintenance

Most entities use a **financial concept of capital** when preparing their financial statements (see below). The concept of capital selected should be appropriate to the needs of the users of an entity's financial statements.

5.10.1 Concepts of capital maintenance and the determination of profit

First of all, we need to define the different concepts of capital.

Key term

> **Capital**. Under a financial concept of capital, such as invested money or invested purchasing power, the net assets or equity of the entity. The financial concept of capital is adopted by most entities.
>
> Under a physical concept of capital, such as operating capability, the productive capacity of the entity based on, for example, units of output per day. *(Framework*

The definition of profit is also important.

Key term

> **Profit**. The residual amount that remains after expenses (including capital maintenance adjustments, where appropriate) have been deducted from income. Any amount over and above that required to maintain the capital at the beginning of the period is profit. *(Framework)*

The main difference between the two concepts of capital maintenance is the treatment of the **effects of changes in the prices of assets and liabilities** of the entity. In general terms, an entity has maintained its capital if it has as much capital at the end of the period as it had at the beginning of the period. Any amount over and above that required to maintain the capital at the beginning of the period is profit.

(a) **Financial capital maintenance**: profit is the increase in nominal money capital over the period.

(b) **Physical capital maintenance**: profit is the increase in the physical productive capacity over the period.

6 IAS 18 *Revenue*

FAST FORWARD

> **Revenue recognition** is straightforward in most business transactions, but some situations are more complicated. It is necessary to determine the **substance of each transaction**, rather than the legal form.

6.1 Introduction

Accruals accounting is based on the **matching of costs with the revenue they generate**. It is crucially important under this convention that we can establish the point at which revenue may be recognised so that the correct treatment can be applied to the related costs. For example, the costs of producing an item of finished goods should be carried as an asset in the balance sheet until such time as it is sold; they should then be written off as a charge to the trading account. Which of these two treatments should be applied cannot be decided until it is clear at what moment the sale of the item takes place.

The decision has a **direct impact on profit** since under the prudence concept it would be unacceptable to recognise the profit on sale until a sale had taken place in accordance with the criteria of revenue recognition.

Revenue is generally recognised as **earned at the point of sale**, because at that point four criteria will generally have been met.

- The product or service has been **provided to the buyer**.
- The buyer has **recognised his liability** to pay for the goods or services provided. The converse of this is that the seller has recognised that ownership of goods has passed from himself to the buyer.
- The buyer has indicated his **willingness to hand over cash** or other assets in settlement of his liability.
- The **monetary value** of the goods or services has been established.

At earlier points in the business cycle there will not in general be **firm evidence** that the above criteria will be met. Until work on a product is complete, there is a risk that some flaw in the manufacturing process will necessitate its writing off; even when the product is complete there is no guarantee that it will find a buyer.

At later points in the business cycle, for example when cash is received for the sale, the recognition of revenue may occur in a period later than that in which the related costs were charged. Revenue recognition would then depend on fortuitous circumstances, such as the cash flow of a company's receivables, and might fluctuate misleadingly from one period to another.

However, there are times when revenue is **recognised at other times than at the completion of a sale**. For example, in the recognition of profit on long-term construction contracts. Under IAS 11 *Construction contracts*, contract revenue and contract costs associated with the construction contract should be recognised as revenue and expenses respectively by reference to the stage of completion of the contract activity at the balance sheet date.

(a) Owing to the length of time taken to complete such contracts, to defer taking profit into account until completion may result in the income statement reflecting, not so much a fair view of the activity of the company during the year, but rather the results relating to contracts which have been completed by the year end.

(b) Revenue in this case is recognised when production on, say, a section of the total contract is complete, even though no sale can be made until the whole is complete.

6.2 IAS 18 Revenue

FAST FORWARD

IAS 18 *Revenue* is concerned with the **recognition of revenues** arising from fairly common transactions.

- The sale of goods
- The rendering of services
- The use by others of entity assets yielding interest, royalties and dividends

IAS 18 governs the recognition of revenue in specific (common) types of transaction. Generally, recognition should be when it is probable that **future economic benefits** will flow to the entity and when these benefits can be **measured reliably**.

Income, as defined by the IASB's *Framework* document, includes both revenues and gains. Revenue is income arising in the ordinary course of an entity's activities and it may be called different names, such as sales, fees, interest, dividends or royalties.

Exam focus point

The November 2005 exam had a 4-mark question on IAS 18.

6.3 Scope

IAS 18 covers the revenue from specific types of transaction or events.

- **Sale of goods** (manufactured products and items purchased for resale)

- **Rendering of services**
- Use by others of entity assets yielding **interest, royalties and dividends**

Interest, royalties and dividends are included as income because they arise from the use of an entity's assets by other parties.

Key terms

Interest is the charge for the use of cash or cash equivalents or amounts due to the entity.

Royalties are charges for the use of non-current assets of the entity, eg patents, computer software and trademarks.

Dividends are distributions of profit to holders of equity investments, in proportion with their holdings, of each relevant class of capital.

The standard specifically **excludes** various types of revenue arising from leases, insurance contracts, changes in value of financial instruments or other current assets natural increases in agricultural assets and mineral ore extraction.

6.4 Definitions

The following definitions are given in the standard.

Key term

Revenue is the gross inflow of economic benefits during the period arising in the course of the ordinary activities of an entity when those inflows result in increases in equity, other than increases relating to contributions from equity participants.

Fair value is the amount for which an asset could be exchanged, or a liability settled, between knowledgeable, willing parties in an arm's length transaction. *(IAS 18)*

Revenue **does not include** sales taxes, value added taxes or goods and service taxes which are only collected for third parties, because these do not represent an economic benefit flowing to the entity. The same is true for revenues collected by an agent on behalf of a principal. Revenue for the agent is only the commission received for acting as agent.

6.5 Measurement of revenue

When a transaction takes place, the amount of revenue is usually decided by the **agreement of the buyer and seller**. The revenue is actually measured, however, as the **fair value of the consideration received**, which will take account of any trade discounts and volume rebates.

6.6 Identification of the transaction

FAST FORWARD

Generally revenue is recognised when the entity has transferred to the buyer the **significant risks and rewards of ownership** and when the revenue can be **measured reliably**.

Normally, each transaction can be looked at **as a whole**. Sometimes, however, transactions are more complicated, and it is necessary to break a transaction down into its **component parts**. For example, a sale may include the transfer of goods and the provision of future servicing, the revenue for which should be deferred over the period the service is performed.

At the other end of the scale, **seemingly separate transactions must be considered together** if apart they lose their commercial meaning. An example would be to sell an asset with an agreement to buy it back at a later date. The second transaction cancels the first and so both must be considered together.

6.7 Sale of goods

Revenue from the sale of goods should only be recognised when *all* these conditions are satisfied.

(a) The entity has transferred to the buyer the **significant risks and rewards** of ownership of the goods

(b) The entity retains neither **continuing managerial involvement** to the degree usually associated with ownership, nor effective control over the goods sold

(c) The amount of revenue can be **measured reliably**

(d) It is probable that the **economic benefits** associated with the transaction will flow to the entity

(e) The **costs incurred** or to be incurred in respect of the transaction can be measured reliably

The transfer of risks and rewards can only be decided by examining each transaction. Mainly, the transfer occurs at the same time as either the **transfer of legal title**, or the **passing of possession** to the buyer – this is what happens when you buy something in a shop.

If **significant risks and rewards remain with the seller**, then the transaction is *not* a sale and revenue cannot be recognised, for example if the receipt of the revenue from a particular sale depends on the buyer receiving revenue from his own sale of the goods.

It is possible for the seller to retain only an **'insignificant' risk of ownership** and for the sale and revenue to be recognised. The main example here is where the seller retains title only to ensure collection of what is owed on the goods. This is a common commercial situation, and when it arises the revenue should be recognised on the date of sale.

The probability of the entity receiving the revenue arising from a transaction must be assessed. It may only become probable that the economic benefits will be received when an uncertainty is removed, for example government permission for funds to be received from another country. Only when the uncertainty is removed should the revenue be recognised. This is in contrast with the situation where revenue has already been recognised but where the **collectability of the cash** is brought into doubt. Where recovery has ceased to be probable, the amount should be recognised as an expense, *not* an adjustment of the revenue previously recognised. These points also refer to services and interest, royalties and dividends below.

Matching should take place, ie the revenue and expenses relating to the same transaction should be recognised at the same time. It is usually easy to estimate expenses at the date of sale (eg warranty costs, shipment costs, etc). Where they cannot be estimated reliably, then revenue cannot be recognised; any consideration which has already been received is treated as a liability.

6.8 Rendering of services

When the outcome of a transaction involving the rendering of services can be estimated reliably, the associated revenue should be recognised by reference to the **stage of completion of the transaction** at the balance sheet date. The outcome of a transaction can be estimated reliably when *all* these conditions are satisfied.

(a) The amount of revenue can be **measured reliably**

(b) It is probable that the **economic benefits** associated with the transaction will flow to the entity

(c) The **stage of completion** of the transaction at the balance sheet date can be measured reliably

(d) The **costs incurred** for the transaction and the costs to complete the transaction can be measured reliably

The parties to the transaction will normally have to agree the following before an entity can make reliable estimates.

(a) Each party's **enforceable rights** regarding the service to be provided and received by the parties

(b) The **consideration** to be exchanged

(c) The **manner and terms of settlement**

There are various methods of determining the stage of completion of a transaction, but for practical purposes, when services are performed by an indeterminate number of acts over a period of time, revenue should be recognised on a **straight line basis** over the period, unless there is evidence for the use of a more appropriate method. If one act is of more significance than the others, then the significant act should be carried out *before* revenue is recognised.

In uncertain situations, when the outcome of the transaction involving the rendering of services cannot be estimated reliably, the standard recommends a **no loss/no gain approach**. Revenue is recognised only to the extent of the expenses recognised that are recoverable.

This is particularly likely during the **early stages of a transaction**, but it is still probable that the entity will recover the costs incurred. So the revenue recognised in such a period will be equal to the expenses incurred, with no profit.

Obviously, if the costs are not likely to be reimbursed, then they must be recognised as an expense immediately. **When the uncertainties cease to exist**, revenue should be recognised.

6.9 Interest, royalties and dividends

When others use the entity's assets yielding interest, royalties and dividends, the revenue should be recognised on the bases set out below when:

(a) it is probable that the **economic benefits** associated with the transaction will flow to the entity; and

(b) the amount of the revenue can be **measured reliably**.

The revenue is recognised on the following bases.

(a) **Interest** is recognised using the effective interest method set out in IAS 39 (not in your syllabus)

(b) **Royalties** are recognised on an accruals basis in accordance with the substance of the relevant agreement

(c) **Dividends** are recognised when the shareholder's right to receive payment is established

6.10 Disclosure

The following items should be disclosed.

(a) The **accounting policies** adopted for the recognition of revenue, including the methods used to determine the stage of completion of transactions involving the rendering of services

(b) The amount of each **significant category of revenue** recognised during the period including revenue arising from:

(i) The sale of goods

(ii) The rendering of services
(iii) Interest
(iv) Royalties
(v) Dividends

(c) The amount of revenue arising from **exchanges of goods or services** included in each significant category of revenue

Question

Revenue recognition

Given that prudence is the main consideration, discuss under what circumstances, if any, revenue might be recognised at the following stages of a sale.

(a) Goods are acquired by the business which it confidently expects to resell very quickly.
(b) A customer places a firm order for goods.
(c) Goods are delivered to the customer.
(d) The customer is invoiced for goods.
(e) The customer pays for the goods.
(f) The customer's cheque in payment for the goods has been cleared by the bank.

Answer

(a) A sale must never be recognised before the goods have even been ordered by a customer. There is no certainty about the value of the sale, nor when it will take place, even if it is virtually certain that goods will be sold.

(b) A sale must never be recognised when the customer places an order. Even though the order will be for a specific quantity of goods at a specific price, it is not yet certain that the sale transaction will go through. The customer may cancel the order, the supplier might be unable to deliver the goods as ordered or it may be decided that the customer is not a good credit risk.

(c) A sale will be recognised when delivery of the goods is made only when:

(i) the sale is for cash, and so the cash is received at the same time; or
(ii) the sale is on credit and the customer accepts delivery (eg by signing a delivery note).

(d) The critical event for a credit sale is usually the despatch of an invoice to the customer. There is then a legally enforceable debt, payable on specified terms, for a completed sale transaction.

(e) The critical event for a cash sale is when delivery takes place and when cash is received; both take place at the same time.

It would be too cautious or 'prudent' to await cash payment for a credit sale transaction before recognising the sale, unless the customer is a high credit risk and there is a serious doubt about his ability or intention to pay.

(f) It would again be over-cautious to wait for clearance of the customer's cheques before recognising sales revenue. Such a precaution would only be justified in cases where there is a very high risk of the bank refusing to honour the cheque.

Chapter Roundup

- The IASB replaced the IASC in 2001. It is responsible for setting International Accounting Standards (IASs) and International Financial Reporting Standards (IFRSs). All new standards are now IFRSs.
- International Financial Reporting Standards (IFRSs) are set in a similar manner to the previous setting of IASs in accordance with the IASB's due process.
- In its attempt to formulate standards which are accepted internationally, the IASB has met opposition over various issues from companies, interest groups and countries.
- A conceptual framework provides the basis for the formulation of accounting standards.
- The *Framework* was produced by the IASC and adopted by the IASB. It provides the conceptual framework within which IASs and IFRSs are formulated.
- **Revenue recognition** is straightforward in most business transactions but some situations are more complicated. It is necessary to determine the **substance of each transaction** rather than the legal form.
- IAS 18 *Revenue* is concerned with the recognition of revenues arising from:
  - the sale of goods
  - the rendering of services
  - the use by others of equity assets yielding interest, royalties and dividends
- Generally revenue is recognised when the entity has transferred to the buyer the **significant risks and rewards of ownership** and when the revenue can be **measured reliably**.

Quick Quiz

1 What recent decisions will have a beneficial effect on global harmonisation of accounting practices?

2 One objective of the IASB is to promote the preparation of financial statements using the euro.

True ☐

False ☐

3 How many IASs and IFRSs have been published?

4 A conceptual framework is:

A A theoretical expression of accounting standards
B A list of key terms used by the IASB
C A statement of theoretical principles which form the frame of reference for financial reporting
D The proforma financial statements

5 Which of the following are chapters in the IASB *Framework?*

A Subsidiaries, associates and joint ventures
B Profit measurement in financial statements
C The objective of financial statements
D Accounting for interests in other entities
E Recognition of the elements of financial statements
F Presentation of financial information
G Substance of transactions in financial statements
H Qualitative characteristics of financial statements
I Quantitative characteristics of financial statements

J Measurement of the elements of financial statements
K Concepts of capital and capital maintenance
L The elements of financial statements.

6 Which of the following arguments is not in favour of accounting standards?

A They reduce variations in methods used to produce accounts
B They oblige companies to disclose their accounting policies
C They are a less rigid alternative to legislation
D They may tend towards rigidity in applying the rules

Answers to Quick Quiz

1 The IOSCO endorsement, and the EC requirement that listed companies should use IAS from 2005.

2 False

3 41 IASs and 7 IFRSs

4 C

5 C, E, H, J, K and L.

6 D The other arguments are all in favour of accounting standards.

Now try the questions below from the Exam Question Bank

Number	Level	Marks	Time
Q6	Examination	5	9 mins
Q7	Examination	5	9 mins
Q8	Examination	5	9 mins
Q9	Examination	5	9 mins

2

External audit

Introduction

Here we look at the **role of the external auditor**. If you work for an organisation which is audited (internally or externally), you should try to talk to the auditors about the audit and gather as much information as possible. Because it is the audit of an organisation you know well, you should gain some insight into the role of the auditor.

The external auditors are employed to check the good **stewardship** of the directors of the company and the truth and fairness of the financial statements. To enable them to do this they have certain **rights and duties**.

When the audit is completed and the auditors are satisfied with the information and explanations provided, an **audit report** is issued. The audit report is the instrument by which the auditors express an **opinion** on the truth and fairness of the financial statements. In section 3 we look at the standard audit report and its **qualification** when the auditors are not completely satisfied with the results of the audit.

Although we refer to ISAs, you are **not** required to learn them for the exam.

Topic list	Learning outcomes	Syllabus references	Ability required
1 External audit	B (vii)	B (8)	Comprehension
2 Duties and rights of auditors	B (vii)	B (8)	Comprehension
3 The audit report	B (vii)	B (8)	Comprehension

1 External audit

FAST FORWARD

An audit is essentially an independent review. External auditors are regulated by statute and by professional bodies.

1.1 Why is an audit needed?

In the modern commercial environment, businesses which are operated as companies with limited liability need to produce accounts to indicate how successfully they are performing. However the owners of a business require something more than accounts because the managers responsible for preparing them may, either unintentionally or by deliberate manipulation, produce accounts which are misleading. An independent examination of the accounts is needed so that the owners of the business can assess how well management have discharged their *stewardship*.

1.2 Definition of an audit

FAST FORWARD

The key stages of an audit are to:

- Carry out procedures to obtain **sufficient appropriate audit evidence**
- Evaluate the **presentation** of accounts
- Issue a report containing a clear expression of **opinion**.

The International Auditing and Assurance Standards Board *Glossary of Terms* defines the objective of an audit as follows.

Key term

'The objective of an **audit** of financial statements is to enable the auditor to express an opinion whether the financial statements are prepared, in all material respects, in accordance with an identified financial reporting framework. The phrases used to express the auditor's opinion are 'give a true and fair view' or 'present fairly, in all material respects', which are equivalent terms. A similar objective applies to the audit of financial or other information prepared in accordance with appropriate criteria.'

We will look at some of the terms used here later on.

First of all, though, we need to look at what an audit is really about. The International Federation of Accountants (IFAC's) International Standard on Auditing (ISA) 200 *Objective and general principles governing an audit of financial statements* summarises what audits are all about.

ISA 200

The auditor should conduct an audit in accordance with International Standards on Auditing.

(Paragraph 5)

The standard also comments on the auditor's general approach to audit work.

ISA 200

The auditor should plan and perform the audit with an attitude of professional scepticism, recognising that circumstances may exist which cause the financial statements to be materially misstated. *(Paragraph 6)*

So, for example, the auditor would not simply accept what managers say during the audit of an entity, but would look for supporting evidence.

1.3 Scope of an audit

We talk of the *scope* of an audit here in the sense of the range of audit procedures which are required to achieve the objective of the audit.

ISA 200

The procedures required to conduct an audit in accordance with ISAs should be determined by the auditor having regard to the requirements of ISAs, relevant professional bodies, legislation, regulations and, where appropriate, the terms of the audit engagement and reporting requirements. *(Paragraph 7)*

1.4 Limitations of an audit

FAST FORWARD

Audits at best give **reasonable assurance** that the accounts are free from **material misstatement**.

An audit performed under ISAs should provide **'reasonable assurance'** that the financial statements, taken as a whole, are free from material misstatement (we will look at the definition of 'material' later). Reasonable assurance is concerned with the way evidence is built up throughout the audit, which provides the basis of the auditor's opinion. It therefore reflects the whole audit process.

The definition of the audit given above is comprehensive about what an audit is. The standard also makes it clear that the audit is *not*:

(a) A **guarantee** of the **future viability** of the entity
(b) An **assurance** of **management's effectiveness** and efficiency

The standard points out that there are inherent (ie existing and permanent characteristic or attribute) limitations in an audit which affect the auditor's ability to discover material misstatements. These inherent limitations arise from the following factors.

(a) The use of testing

(b) The inherent limitations of any accounting and internal control system (eg through staff collusion)

(c) The fact that most audit evidence is persuasive rather than conclusive (indicates what is probable rather than what is definite)

The auditor's **judgement** is also an issue here. Throughout every stage of the audit, the auditor's judgement is brought to bear. In particular, the auditor's judgement has a great impact on:

(a) The **gathering of audit evidence**, eg in deciding the nature, timing and extent of audit procedures

(b) The **drawing of conclusions** based on the audit evidence gathered, eg assessing the reasonableness of accounting estimates calculated by management

1.5 Responsibility for the financial statements

ISA 200 ends by making a very important point, which many non-auditors and members of the public fail to appreciate.

> 'While the auditor is responsible for forming and expressing an opinion on the financial statements, the responsibility for preparing and presenting the financial statements is that of the management of the entity. The audit of the financial statements does not relieve management of its responsibilities.'

1.6 The expectations gap

FAST FORWARD

The **expectations gap** is the difference between the work auditors actually carry out and the work non-auditors think they carry out.

There are some common misconceptions in relation to the role of the auditors, even among 'financially aware' people, including the following examples.

(a) Many people think that the **auditors report** is to the **directors** of a company, rather than the members.

(b) Some think that a **qualified audit report** is **more favourable** than an unqualified audit report, whereas the converse is true.

(c) There is a perception that it is the auditors' duty to detect fraud, when in fact the detection of fraud is the **responsibility** of the **directors**.

These findings highlight the 'expectations gap' between what auditors do and what people in general think that they do. Add the fact that many 'financially aware' people do not look at the report and accounts of a company they are considering investing in, and you have some sobering facts for the auditors to contemplate!

Public concern at large company failures has highlighted problems with the expectations gap. This has formed part of a general debate on corporate governance (ie how companies are governed) in many countries. Corporate governance developments have aimed to make the role of the auditor clearer and to regulate the relationship between the auditors and the management of the entity being audited.

In most countries, audits are required under national statute in the case of a large number of undertakings, including limited liability companies. Other organisations and entities requiring a statutory audit may include charities, investment businesses, trade unions and so on.

Non-statutory audits are performed by independent auditors because the owners, proprietors, members, trustees, professional and governing bodies or other interested parties want them, rather than because the law requires them.

Auditors may also give an **audit opinion** on **statements** other **than annual accounts**, including:

- Summaries of sales in support of a statement of royalties
- Statements of expenditure in support of applications for government grants
- The circulation figures of a newspaper or magazine

In all such audits the auditors must take into account any regulations contained in the internal rules or constitution of the undertaking. Examples of the regulations which the auditors would need to refer to in such assignments would include:

- The rules of clubs, societies and charities
- Partnership agreements

1.7 Auditor independence

The most important characteristics of the external auditor, and one which must never be compromised, is that he is **independent** of the organisation and its directors. For this reason, audit firms will rotate partners so that the same partner is not continually signing off the audit report for a client. This is intended to prevent the development of a familiarity as a result of which the auditor's independence may be called into question.

2 Duties and rights of auditors

2.1 Duties

FAST FORWARD

Auditors' duties generally include the duties to report explicitly on the **reasonableness** of the accounts audited and their **compliance** with legislation. They should also report on whether proper accounting records have been kept.

The auditors should be required to report on every balance sheet and income statement laid before the company in general meeting.

The auditors may also be required to consider the following.

Compliance with legislation	Whether the accounts have been prepared in accordance with the relevant legislation.
Truth and fairness of accounts	Whether the balance sheet shows a true and fair view of the company's affairs at the end of the period and the income statement (and a cash flow statement) show a true and fair view of the results for the period.
Proper records and returns	Whether proper accounting records have been kept and proper returns adequate for the audit received from branches not visited by the auditor.
Agreement of accounts to records	Whether the accounts are in agreement with the accounting records.
Consistency of other information	Whether the other information with the accounts is consistent with the accounts.

2.2 Rights

FAST FORWARD

Auditor's rights should include the rights of **access to records** and to receive information and explanations, also rights relating to attendance and speaking at general meetings.

The auditors must have certain rights to enable them to carry out their duties effectively.

The principal rights auditors should have, excepting those dealing with resignation or removal, are set out in the table below, and the following are notes on more detailed points.

Access to records	A right of access at all times to the books, accounts and vouchers of the company.
Information and explanations	A right to require from the company's officers such information and explanations as they think necessary for the performance of their duties as auditors.
Attendance at/notices of general meetings	A right to attend any general meetings of the company and to receive all notices of and communications relating to such meetings which any member of the company is entitled to receive.
Right to speak at general meetings	A right to be heard at general meetings which they attend on any part of the business that concerns them as auditors.
Rights in relation to written resolutions	A right to receive a copy of any written resolution proposed.
Right to require laying of accounts	A right to give notice in writing requiring that a general meeting be held for the purpose of laying the accounts and reports before the company.

Rights to information

It should be an offence for a company's officer knowingly or recklessly to make a statement in any form to an auditor which:

(a) Purports to convey any information or explanation required by the auditor
(b) Is materially misleading, false or deceptive

If auditors have not received all the information and explanations they deem necessary, they should state this fact in their report.

3 The audit report

3.1 Preparing the report

FAST FORWARD

ISA 700 *The auditor's report on financial statements* gives guidance on unqualified and modified audit reports.

ISA 700 *The Auditor's Report on Financial Statements* establishes standards and provides guidance on the form and content of the auditor's report issued as a result of an audit performed by an independent auditor of the financial statements of an entity.

ISA 700

The auditor should review and assess the conclusions drawn from the audit evidence obtained as the basis for the expression of an opinion on the financial statements. *(Paragraph 2)*

This review and assessment involves considering whether the financial statements have been **prepared** in accordance with an **acceptable financial reporting framework** being either IASs or relevant national standards or practices. Auditors may also have to consider whether the financial statements comply with statutory requirements.

ISA 700

The auditor's report should contain a clear written expression of opinion on the financial statements taken as a whole. *(Paragraph 4)*

3.2 Basic elements of the auditor's report

AUDITOR'S REPORT

(APPROPRIATE ADDRESSEE)

We have audited the accompanying [reference can be by page numbers] balance sheet of the ABC Company as of December 31, 20X1, and the related statements of income, and cash flows for the year then ended. These financial statements are the responsibility of the Company's management. Our responsibility is to express an opinion on these financial statements based on our audit.

We conducted our audit in accordance with International Standards on Auditing [or refer to relevant national standards or practices]. Those Standards require that we plan and perform the audit to obtain reasonable assurance about whether the financial statements are free of material misstatement. An audit includes examining, on a test basis, evidence supporting the amounts and disclosures in the financial statements. An audit also includes assessing the accounting principles used and significant estimates made by management, as well as evaluating the overall financial statement presentation. We believe that our audit provides a reasonable basis for our opinion.

In our opinion, the financial statements give a true and fair view of (or present fairly, in all material respects) the financial position of the company as of December 31, 20X1, and of the results of its operations and its cash flows for the year then ended in accordance with [IASs or relevant national standards] and comply with [relevant statutes or law].

AUDITOR

Date

Address

3.2.1 Title

ISA 700

The auditor's report should have an appropriate title. *(Paragraph 6)*

The term 'independent auditor' may be used in the title to distinguish the auditor's report from reports that might be issued by others, such as by officers of the entity.

3.2.2 Addressee

ISA 700

The auditor's report should be appropriately addressed as required by the circumstances of the engagement and local regulations. *(Paragraph 7)*

The report is ordinarily addressed either to the **shareholders** or the **board of directors** of the entity whose financial statements are being audited.

3.2.3 Opening or introductory paragraph

ISA 700

The auditor's report should identify the financial statements of the entity that have been audited including the date of and period covered by the financial statements.

The report should include a statement that the financial statements are the responsibility of the entity's management [varies according to the legal situation in each country], and a statement that the responsibility of the auditor is to express an opinion on the financial statements based on the audit.

(Paragraphs 8 and 9)

The preparation of financial statements requires management to make **significant accounting estimates** and **judgements**, as well as to determine the appropriate accounting principles and methods used in preparation of the financial statements. In contrast, the auditor's responsibility is to audit these financial statements in order to express an opinion thereon.

3.2.4 Scope paragraph

ISA 700

The auditor's report should describe the scope of the audit by stating that the audit was conducted in accordance with ISAs or in accordance with relevant national standards or practices as appropriate.

(Paragraph 12)

'Scope' refers to the auditor's ability to perform audit procedures deemed necessary in the circumstances. The reader needs this as an assurance that the audit has been carried out in accordance with established standards or practices. Unless otherwise stated, the auditing standards or practices followed are presumed to be those of the country indicated by the auditor's address.

ISA 700

The report should include a statement that the audit was planned and performed to obtain reasonable assurance about whether the financial statements are free of material misstatement.

The auditor's report should describe the audit as including:

(a) examining, on a test basis, evidence to support the financial statement amounts and disclosures;

(b) assessing the accounting principles used in the preparation of the financial statements;

(c) assessing the significant estimates made by management in the preparation of the financial statements; and

(d) evaluating the overall financial statement presentation. *(Paragraphs 13 and 14)*

3.2.5 Opinion paragraph

ISA 700

The auditor's report should clearly state the auditor's opinion as to whether the financial statements give a true and fair view (or are presented fairly, in all material respects) in accordance with the financial reporting framework and, where appropriate, whether the financial statements comply with statutory requirements.

(Paragraph 17)

The terms used to express the auditor's opinion are 'give a true and fair view' or 'present fairly, in all material respects', and are **equivalent**. Both terms indicate, amongst other things, that the auditor considers only those matters that are **material** to the financial statements.

The **financial reporting framework** is determined by IASs, rules issued by professional bodies, and the development of general practice within a country, with an appropriate consideration of fairness and with due regard to local legislation. To advise the reader of the context in which 'fairness' is expressed, the auditor's opinion would indicate the framework upon which the financial statements are based by using words such as 'in accordance with [indicate IASs or relevant national standards]'.

In addition to an opinion of the true and fair view (or fair presentation, in all material respects), the auditor's report may need to include an opinion as to whether the financial statements comply with other requirements specified by **relevant statutes or law**.

ISA 700

In any situation where it is not evident which country's auditing principles have been used, the country should be stated. *(Paragraph 12)*

Suitable wording would be '...in accordance with auditing principles generally accepted in Country X...'.

3.2.6 Date of report

ISA 700

The auditor should date the report as of the completion date of the audit. *(Paragraph 23)*

This informs the reader that the auditor has considered the effect on the financial statements and on the report of events and transactions of which the auditor became aware and that occurred up to that date.

ISA 700

Since the auditor's responsibility is to report on the financial statements as prepared and presented by management, the auditor should not date the report earlier than the date on which the financial statements are signed or approved by management. *(Paragraph 24)*

3.2.7 Auditor's address

ISA 700

The report should name a specific location, which is ordinarily the city where the auditor maintains the office that has responsibility for the audit. *(Paragraph 25)*

3.2.8 Auditor's signature

ISA 700

The report should be signed in the name of the audit firm, the personal name of the auditor or both, as appropriate. *(Paragraph 26)*

The firm as a whole usually assumes responsibility for the audit, but in some countries an individual partner may be required to take responsibility and sign in his or her own name.

3.3 Unqualified audit report

ISA 700

An *unqualified opinion* should be expressed when the auditor concludes that the financial statements give a true and fair view (or are presented fairly, in all material respects) in accordance with the identified financial reporting framework. *(Paragraph 27)*

An unqualified opinion also indicates implicitly that any **changes in accounting principles** or in the method of their application, and the effects thereof, have been properly determined and disclosed in the financial statements.

This section has introduced you to the standard unqualified audit report. The next paragraphs look at how the audit report is affected when problems of varying severity arise in the audit.

Question — Unqualified audit report

The following is an unqualified audit report which has been signed by the auditors of Kiln, a limited liability company.

AUDITORS' REPORT

TO THE SHAREHOLDERS OF KILN COMPANY

We have audited the accompanying balance sheet of the Kiln Company as of December 31, 20X3, and the related statements of income, and cash flows for the year then ended. These financial statements are the responsibility of the Company's management. Our responsibility is to express an opinion on these financial statements based on our audit.

We conducted our audit in accordance with International Standards on Auditing. Those Standards require that we plan and perform the audit to obtain reasonable assurance about whether the financial statements are free of material misstatement. An audit includes examining, on a test basis, evidence supporting the amounts and disclosures in the financial statements. An audit also includes assessing the accounting principles used and significant estimates made by management, as well as evaluating the overall financial statement presentation. We believe that our audit provides a reasonable basis for our opinion.

In our opinion, the financial statements give a true and fair view of (or present fairly, in all material respects) the financial position of the company as at December 31, 20X3, and of the results of its operations and its cash flows for the year then ended in accordance with IASs/IFRSs and comply with company law.

AUDITOR

Date

Address

Required

Explain the purpose and meaning of the following phrases taken from the above extracts of an unqualified audit report.

(a) '... the accompanying balance sheet ... and the related statements of income and cash flows ....'
(b) '... in accordance with International Standards on Auditing.'
(c) 'In our opinion ...'

Answer

(a) '...the accompanying balance sheet ... and the related statements of income and cash flows ...'

Purpose

The purpose of this phrase is to make it clear to the reader of an audit report the part of a company's annual report upon which the auditors are reporting their opinion.

Meaning

An annual report may include documents such as a five year summary and other voluntary information. However, only the income statement, balance sheet and associated notes are required to be audited in true and fair terms. IAS 7 also requires a cash flow statement for the financial statements to show a true and fair view. Page references (for instance, 8 to 20) may be used instead to cover the income statement, balance sheet, notes to the accounts and cash flow statement. The directors' report, or any equivalent, although examined and reported on by exception if it contains inconsistencies, is not included in these references.

(b) '...in accordance with International Standards on Auditing ....'

Purpose

This phrase is included in order to confirm to the reader that best practice, as laid down in ISAs, has been adopted by the auditors in both carrying out their audit and in drafting their audit opinion. This means that the reader can be assured that the audit has been properly conducted, and that should he or she wish to discover what such standards are, or what certain key phrases mean, he or she can have recourse to ISAs to explain such matters.

Meaning

Auditing Standards are those auditing standards prepared by the International Auditing and Assurance Standards Board (although local/national standards may be mentioned instead).

These prescribe the principles and practices to be followed by auditors in planning, designing and carrying out various aspects of their audit work, the content of audit reports, both qualified and unqualified and so on. Members of professional accountancy bodies are expected to follow all of these standards.

(c) 'In our opinion ...'

Purpose

Auditors are required to report on every balance sheet, income statement and cash flow statement laid before shareholders. In reporting, they are required to state their *opinion* on those accounts. Thus, the purpose of this phrase is to comply with the requirement to report an opinion.

Meaning

An audit report is an expression of opinion by suitably qualified auditors as to whether the financial statements give a true and fair view, and have been properly prepared in accordance with any relevant local legislation. *It is not a certificate*; rather it is a statement of whether or not, in the professional judgement of the auditors, the financial statements give a true and fair view.

3.4 Modified reports

Modified audit reports arise when auditors do not believe that they can state without reservation that the accounts give a true and fair view.

An auditor's report is considered to be modified in the following situations.

(a) **Matters that do not affect the auditor's opinion:** emphasis of a matter

(b) **Matters that do affect the auditor's opinion**

  (i) Qualified opinion
  (ii) Disclaimer of opinion
  (iii) Adverse opinion

3.5 Matters that do not affect the auditor's opinion

Key term

In certain circumstances, an auditor's report may be modified by adding an **emphasis of matter** to highlight a matter affecting the financial statements which is included in a note to the financial statements that more extensively discusses the matter. The addition of such an emphasis of matter paragraph **does not affect** the auditor's opinion. The auditor may also modify the auditor's report by using an emphasis of matter paragraph(s) to report matters other than those affecting the financial statements.

The paragraph would preferably be included after the opinion paragraph and would ordinarily refer to the fact that the auditor's opinion is not qualified in this respect.

ISA 700 distinguishes between **going concern matters** and other matters.

ISA 700

The auditor should modify the auditor's report by adding a paragraph to highlight a material matter regarding a going concern problem.

The auditor should consider modifying the auditor's report by adding a paragraph if there is a significant uncertainty (other than a going concern problem), the resolution of which is dependent upon future events and which may affect the financial statements. *(Paragraphs 31 and 32)*

Key term

An **uncertainty** is a matter whose outcome depends on future actions or events not under the direct control of the entity but that may affect the financial statements.

FAST FORWARD

Auditors are concerned with the correct **treatment** and **disclosure** of **inherent** and **fundamental uncertainties** which relate to uncertain future events.

The following example of an emphasis of matter paragraph is given by the ISA, which would be added to the end of the standard unqualified wording given above.

> Without qualifying our opinion we draw attention to Note X to the financial statements. The Company is the defendant in a lawsuit alleging infringement of certain patent rights and claiming royalties and punitive damages. The Company has filed a counter action, and preliminary hearing and discovery proceedings on both actions are in progress. The ultimate outcome of the matter cannot presently be determined, and no provision for any liability that may result has been made in the financial statements.

An illustration of an emphasis of matter paragraph relating to going concern is set out in ISA 570 *Going concern*.

> Without qualifying our opinion we draw attention to Note X in the financial statements. The Company incurred a net loss of XXX during the year ended December 31, 20X1 and, as of that date, the Company's current liabilities exceeded its current assets by XXX and its total liabilities exceeded its total assets by XXX. These factors, along with other matters as set forth in Note X, raise substantial doubt that the Company will be able to continue as a going concern.

This type of paragraph will usually be sufficient to meet the auditor's reporting responsibilities. In extreme cases, however, involving multiple uncertainties that are significant to the financial statements, a **disclaimer of opinion** may be required instead (see below).

The auditor may also modify the report by using an emphasis of matter paragraph for matters which do *not* affect the financial statements. This might be the case if amendment is necessary to other information in a document containing audited financial statements and the entity refuses to make the amendment. An emphasis of matter paragraph could also be used for **additional statutory reporting responsibilities**.

3.6 Matters that do affect the auditor's opinion

FAST FORWARD

> Auditors may modify their audit opinion on the grounds of **disagreement** or **limitation of scope**; these may be **material** or **pervasive**.

An auditor may not be able to express an unqualified opinion when either of the following circumstances exist and, in the auditor's judgement, the effect of the matter is or may be **material** to the financial statements:

(a) There is a **limitation on the scope** of the auditor's work.

(b) There is a **disagreement** with management regarding the acceptability of the accounting policies selected, the method of their application or the adequacy of financial statement disclosures.

There are different types and degrees of modified opinion.

(a) A limitation on scope may lead to a **qualified opinion** or a **disclaimer of opinion**.
(b) A disagreement may lead to a **qualified opinion** or an **adverse opinion**.

The ISA describes these different modified opinions and the circumstances leading to them as follows.

ISA 700

A **qualified opinion** should be expressed when the auditor concludes that an unqualified opinion cannot be expressed but that the effect of any disagreement with management, or limitation on scope is not so material and pervasive as to require an adverse opinion or a disclaimer of opinion. A qualified opinion should be expressed as being 'except for the effects of the matter to which the qualification relates'.

A **disclaimer of opinion** should be expressed when the possible effect of a limitation on scope is so material and pervasive that the auditor has not been able to obtain sufficient appropriate audit evidence and accordingly is unable to express an opinion on the financial statements.

An **adverse opinion** should be expressed when the effect of a disagreement is so material and pervasive to the financial statements that the auditor concludes that a qualification of the report is not adequate to disclose the misleading or incomplete nature of the financial statements. *(Paragraphs 37-39)*

ISA 700 Cont'd

Whenever the auditor expresses an opinion that is other than unqualified, a clear description of all the substantive reasons should be included in the report and, unless impracticable, a quantification of the possible effect(s) on the financial statements. *(Paragraph 40)*

This description would usually be set out in a **separate paragraph** preceding the opinion or disclaimer of opinion and may include a reference to a more extensive discussion (if any) in a note to the financial statements.

Limitation of scope is not part of the syllabus, so we will concentrate here on disagreement.

The auditor may disagree with management about matters such as the acceptability of accounting policies selected, the method of their application, or the adequacy of disclosures in the financial statements.

If the auditor has a disagreement with management about an item in the accounts, he will first seek to resolve the disagreement. If management cannot be persuaded to amend their treatment of the item in question, he will then have to consider how this affects the audit report.

ISA 700

If such disagreements are material to the financial statements, the auditor should express a qualified or an adverse opinion. *(Paragraph 45)*

The following examples are given in the standard.

Disagreement on accounting policies – inappropriate accounting method – qualified opinion

We have audited ...[as for unqualified].

We conducted our audit in accordance with ... [as for unqualified].

As discussed in Note X to the financial statements, no depreciation has been provided in the financial statements which practice, in our opinion, is not in accordance with International Accounting Standards. The provision for the year ended December 31, 20X1, should be $xxx based on the straight-line method of depreciation using annual rates of 5% for the building and 20% for the equipment. Accordingly, the non-current assets should be reduced by accumulated depreciation of $xxx and the loss for the year and accumulated deficit should be increased by $xxx and $xxx respectively.

In our opinion, except for the effect on the financial statements of the matter referred to in the preceding paragraph, the financial statements give a true and ... [as for unqualified].

Disagreement on accounting policies – inadequate disclosure - qualified opinion

We have audited ... [as for unqualified].

We conducted our audit in accordance with ... [as for unqualified].

On January 15, 20X2, the Company issued debentures in the amount of $xxx for the purpose of financing plant expansion. The debenture agreement restricts the payment of future cash dividends to earnings after December 31, 20X1. In our opinion, disclosure of this information is required by .... .

In our opinion, except for the omission of the information included in the preceding paragraph, the financial statements give a true and ... [as for unqualified].

Disagreement on accounting polices – inadequate disclosure – adverse opinion

We have audited ... [as for unqualified].

We conducted our audit in accordance with ... [as for unqualified].

[Paragraph(s) discussing the disagreement].

In our opinion, because of the effects of the matters discussed in the preceding paragraph(s), the financial statements do not give a true and fair view of (or do not 'present fairly') the financial position of the Company as of December 31, 20X1, and of the results of its operations and its cash flows for the year then ended in accordance with ... and do not comply with....

Exam focus point

Exam questions on audit reports are often about possible qualifications in specific situations. In most cases, the 'except for' qualification will be appropriate. CIMA have stated that it is unlikely that in the exam you will be given a scenario requiring an adverse opinion.

Question

Audit problems

During the course of your audit of the non-current assets of Eastern Engineering, a listed company, at 31 March 20X4 the following problem has arisen.

The company incurred development expenditure of $25,000 spent on a viable new product which will go into production next year and which is expected to last for ten years. The expenditure has been debited in full to the income statement. The profit before tax is $100,000.

Required

(a) List the general forms of qualified report available to auditors in drafting their report and state the circumstances in which each is appropriate.

(b) State whether you feel that a qualified audit report would be necessary for the circumstances outlined above, giving reasons.

(c) On the assumption that you decide that a qualified audit report is necessary with respect to the treatment of the development expenditure, draft the section of the report describing the matter (the whole report is not required).

(d) Outline the auditors' general responsibility with regard to a statement in the directors' or management report concerning the valuation of land and buildings.

Answer

(a) ISA 700 *The auditor's report on financial statements* suggests that the auditors may need to qualify their audit opinion where there is disagreement with the treatment or disclosure of a matter in the financial statements.

There can be two 'levels' of qualified opinion:

(i) *material but not pervasive,* where the circumstances prompting the uncertainty or disagreement is material but confined to one particular aspect of the financial statements, so that it does not affect their overall value to any potential user;

(ii) the more serious qualified opinion where the extent of the uncertainty or disagreement is such that it will be *pervasive* to the overall view shown by the financial statements, ie the financial statements are or could be misleading.

The general form of qualified report appropriate to each potential situation may be seen by the following table.

Circumstance	*Material but not pervasive*	*Pervasive*
Disagreement	Except for ...	Adverse opinion

(b) Whether a modification of the audit opinion would be required in relation to the circumstances described in the question would depend on whether or not the auditors considered them to be material. An item is likely to be considered as material in the context of a company's financial statements if its omission, misstatement or non-disclosure would prevent a proper understanding of those statements on the part of a potential user. Whilst for some audit purposes materiality will be considered in absolute terms, more often than not it will be considered as a relative term.

Development costs debited to the income statement

The situation here is one of disagreement, since best accounting practice, as laid down by IAS 38, requires that development costs should be taken to the income statement over the useful life of the product to which they relate.

This departure from IAS 38 does not seem to be justifiable and would be material to the reported pre-tax profits for the year, representing as it does 22.5% of that figure.

Whilst this understatement of profit would be material to the financial statements, it is not likely to be seen as pervasive and therefore an 'except for' qualified opinion would be appropriate.

(c) *Qualified audit report extract*

'As explained in note ... development costs in respect of a potential new product have been deducted in full against profit instead of being spread over the life of the relevant product as required by IAS 38; the effect of so doing has been to decrease profits before and after tax for the year by $22,500.
Except for ...'

(d) The auditors' general responsibility with regard to the statement in the directors' report concerning the valuation of land and buildings is to satisfy themselves that this is consistent with the treatment and disclosure of this item in the audited financial statements. If the auditors are not satisfied on the question of consistency then they may have to consider qualifying the opinion in their audit report.

3.7 The audit report as a means of communication

Unqualified audit reports may not appear to give a great deal of information. The report says a lot, however, by implication.

The real problem here is that, unfortunately, most users do not know that this is what an unqualified audit report tells them. This issue is also confused by the fact that most users do not understand the responsibilities of either the auditors or the directors in relation to the financial statements.

Different countries have tackled this problem in different ways. The role of auditors has been included in the debate on corporate governance in many Western countries, leading to further rules which are nevertheless voluntary, not mandatory.

Exam focus point

This is a small section of the syllabus and is unlikely to give rise to complex questions. The May 2005 exam asked for a short discussion on the usefulness of the audit report and the November exam asked what the auditor would do first when finding an item about which he disagreed with management.

Chapter Roundup

- An audit is essentially an independent review.
- External auditors are regulated by statute and professional bodies.
- The key stages of an audit are to:
  - Carry out procedures to obtain **sufficient appropriate audit evidence**
  - **Evaluate** the **presentation** of accounts
  - Issue a report containing a **clear expression** of **opinion**
- Audits at best give **reasonable assurance** that the accounts are free from material misstatement.
- The **expectations gap** is the difference between the work auditors actually carry out and the work non-auditors think they carry out.
- Auditors' **duties** generally include the duties to report explicitly on the **reasonableness** of the accounts audited and their **compliance** with legislation.
- Auditors may have a duty to **report** on other matters, such as whether proper accounting records have been kept, by **exception.**
- Auditors' rights should include the rights of **access** to **records** and to receive **information** and **explanations**, also rights relating to **attendance** and **speaking** at **general meetings**.
- **ISA 700** *The auditor's report on financial statements* gives guidance on unqualified and qualified audit reports.
- Auditors may modify their audit opinion on the grounds of **disagreement or limitation of scope**; these may be **material** or **material and pervasive.**
- Auditors are also concerned with the correct **treatment** and **disclosure** of **inherent** and **fundamental uncertainties**, which relate to uncertain future events.

Quick Quiz

1. Define an audit of financial statements.
2. What work should auditors do when undertaking an audit?
3. What is the main reason why an audit is considered to be necessary?
4. What advantages is a partnership likely to gain from an audit?
5. What are the main statutory duties of the auditors?
6. What are the statutory rights of the auditors?
7. What are the basic elements of the auditors' report?
8. When will a qualified opinion be issued?

Answers to Quick Quiz

1 An audit is the work required to enable the auditor to express an opinion as to whether the financial statements are prepared, in all material respects, in accordance with an identified financial reporting framework.

2
- Carry out procedures designed to obtain sufficient appropriate evidence
- Evaluate the overall presentation of the financial statements
- Issue an audit report

3 The audit gives the financial statements credibility.

4
- It can settle accounts between partners
- The tax authorities are more likely to accept the accounts
- The negotiation of finance will be easier
- Sleeping partners will find the audit useful in giving them a confirmation of their profit share.

5 The auditor must report on every balance sheet and income statement laid before the company in general meeting. They must also report on compliance with relevant legislation, truth and fairness of accounts, proper records and returns, consistency and agreement.

6
- Access to records
- Attendance at general meetings
- Receipt of written resolutions
- Information and explanations
- Right to speak at general meetings
- Right to require the laying of the accounts

7
- The report should be addressed to its recipients
- It should identify the financial statements audited
- Separate sections should deal with the responsibilities of the directors and the responsibility of the auditors
- Scope paragraph
- Opinion paragraph
- Signature of the auditors
- Date of the audit report

8 When there is limitation of scope preventing the auditors from forming an opinion or where there is disagreement.

Now try the questions below from the Exam Question Bank

Number	Level	Marks	Time
Q10	Examination	5	9 mins
Q11	Examination	5	9 mins

Part B

Single company financial accounts

3

Presentation of published financial statements

Introduction

This chapter covers preparation of the accounts of non-group limited companies. It lays out the IAS 1 format for the balance sheet and income statement and the disclosures required in the notes to the accounts. The best way to gain familiarity with these formats and disclosures is by looking through the published accounts of limited companies and by doing practice questions.

Topic list	Learning outcomes	Syllabus references	Ability required
1 Purpose of financial statements	C (i)	C (1)	Comprehension
2 IAS 1 *Presentation of financial statements*	C (i)	C (1)	Application
3 Balance sheet	C (i)	C (1)	Comprehension
4 The current/non-current distinction	C (i)	C (1)	Application
5 Income statement	C (i)	C (1)	Application
6 Changes in equity	C (i)	C (1)	Comprehension
7 Notes to the financial statements	C (i)	C (1)	Comprehension

1 Purpose of financial statements

FAST FORWARD

Financial statements present the financial position and financial performance of an entity.

The purpose of financial statements is to provide users with information about the financial position, financial performance and cash flows of an entity. They show the results of managements' stewardship. Per IAS 1, financial statements provide information about an entity's:

(a) assets;
(b) liabilities;
(c) equity;
(d) income and expenses, including gains and losses;
(e) other changes in equity; and
(f) cash flows.

1.1 Fair presentation

Financial statements should **present fairly** the financial position, financial performance and cash flows of an entity. This requires:

- Representing transactions in accordance with the recognition criteria for assets, liabilities, income, expenses and equity set out in the *Framework.*
- Compliance with applicable IFRSs/IASs, and a statement of compliance.
- Selection, application and disclosure of accounting policies in accordance with IAS 8.

In the rare circumstances where management decides that compliance with a standard would not present a true and fair picture, they can depart from that requirements in order to achieve fair presentation. They should disclose:

- that the financial statements are a fair presentation of the entity's position, performance and cash flows
- that is has complied with all other relevant IFRSs
- details of the departure from an IFRS, why it was necessary and the financial impact of the departure

2 IAS 1 Presentation of financial statements

FAST FORWARD

IAS 1 covers the **form and content** of financial statements. The main components are:

- Balance sheet
- Income statement
- Statement of changes in equity
- Cash flow statement
- Notes to the financial statements

2.1 Overview

As well as covering accounting policies and other general considerations governing financial statements, IAS 1 *Presentation of financial statements* gives substantial guidance on the form and content of published financial statements. The standard looks at the balance sheet and income statement (the cash flow statement is covered by IAS 7). First of all, some general points are made about financial statements.

2.2 Profit or loss for the period

The income statement is the most significant indicator of a company's financial performance. So it is important to ensure that it is not misleading.

The income statement will be misleading if costs incurred in the current year are deducted not from the current year profits but from the balance of accumulated profits brought forward. This presents the current year's results more favourably.

IAS 1 stipulates that all items of income and expense recognised in a period shall be included in profit or loss unless a **Standard** or an **Interpretation** requires otherwise.

Circumstances where items may be excluded from profit or loss for the current year include the correction of errors and the effect of changes in accounting policies. These are covered in IAS 8.

2.3 How items are disclosed

IAS 1 specifies disclosures of certain items in certain ways.

- Some items must appear on the **face of the balance sheet or income statement**
- Other items can appear in a **note to the financial statements** instead
- **Recommended formats** are given which enterprises may or may not follow, depending on their circumstances

Obviously, disclosures specified by **other standards** must also be made, and we will mention the necessary disclosures when we cover each statement in turn. Disclosures in both IAS 1 and other standards must be made either on the face of the statement or in the notes unless otherwise stated, ie disclosures cannot be made in an accompanying commentary or report.

2.4 Identification of financial statements

As a result of the above point, it is most important that entities **distinguish the financial statements** very clearly from any other information published with them. This is because all IASs apply *only* to the financial statements (ie the main statements and related notes), so readers of the annual report must be able to differentiate between the parts of the report which are prepared under IASs, and other parts which are not.

The entity should **identify each component** of the financial statements very clearly. IAS 1 also requires disclosure of the following information in a prominent position. If necessary it should be repeated wherever it is felt to be of use to the reader in their understanding of the information presented.

- **Name** of the reporting entity (or other means of identification)
- Whether the accounts cover a **single entity** only or a group of entities
- The **balance sheet date** or the period covered by the financial statements (as appropriate)
- The **reporting currency**
- The **level of precision** used in presenting the figures in the financial statements

Judgement must be used to determine the best method of presenting this information. In particular, the standard suggests that the approach to this will be very different when the financial statements are communicated electronically.

The **level of precision** is important, as presenting figures in thousands or millions of units makes the figures more understandable. The level of precision must be disclosed, however, and it should not obscure necessary details or make the information less relevant.

2.5 Reporting period

It is normal for entities to present financial statements **annually** and IAS 1 states that they should be prepared at least as often as this. If (unusually) an entity's balance sheet date is changed, for whatever reason, the period for which the statements are presented will be less or more than one year. In such cases the entity should also disclose:

(a) the **reason(s) why** a period other than one year is used; and

(b) the fact that the comparative figures given **are not in fact comparable** (in particular for the income statement, changes in equity, cash flows and related notes).

For practical purposes, some entities prefer to use a period which **approximates to a year**, eg 52 weeks, and the IAS allows this approach as it will produce statements not materially different from those produced on an annual basis.

2.6 Timeliness

If the publication of financial statements is delayed too long after the balance sheet date, their usefulness will be severely diminished. The standard states that entities should be able to produce their financial statements **within six months of the balance sheet date.** An entity with consistently complex operations cannot use this as a reason for its failure to report on a timely basis. Local legislation and market regulation imposes specific deadlines on certain entities.

IAS 1 looks at the balance sheet and the income statement. We will not give all the detailed disclosures as some are outside the scope of your syllabus. Instead we will look at a **'proforma' set of accounts** based on the Standard.

3 Balance sheet

FAST FORWARD

IAS 1 discusses the distinction between current and non-current items in some detail, as we shall see in the next section. First of all we can look at the **suggested format** of the balance sheet (given in an appendix to the standard) and then look at further disclosures required.

3.1 Balance sheet example

The example given by the standard is as follows.

XYZ GROUP
BALANCE SHEET AS AT 31 DECEMBER 20X8

	20X8		20X7	
	$'000	$'000	$'000	$'000
Assets				
Non-current assets				
Property, plant and equipment	X		X	
Goodwill	X		X	
Other intangible assets	X		X	
Investments in associates	X		X	
Available-for-sale investments	X		X	
		X		X
Current assets				
Inventories	X		X	
Trade receivables	X		X	
Other current assets	X		X	
Cash and cash equivalents	X		X	
		X		X
Total assets		X		X
Equity and liabilities				
Equity attributable to equity holders of the parent				
Share capital	X		X	
Other reserves	X		X	
Retained earnings	X		X	
		X		X
Minority interest		X		X
Total equity		X		X
Non-current liabilities				
Long-term borrowings	X		X	
Deferred tax	X		X	
Long-term provisions	X		X	
Total non-current liabilities		X		X
Current liabilities				
Trade and other payables	X		X	
Short-term borrowings	X		X	
Current portion of long-term borrowings	X		X	
Current tax payable	X		X	
Short-term provisions	X		X	
Total current liabilities		X		X
Total equity and liabilities		X		X

IAS 1 specifies various items which must appear on the **face of the balance sheet** as a minimum disclosure.

(a) Property, plant and equipment
(b) Investment property
(c) Intangible assets
(d) Financial assets (excluding amounts shown under (e), (f) and (g))
(e) Investments accounted for using the equity method
(f) Biological assets

(g) Inventories
(h) Trade and other receivables
(i) Cash and cash equivalents
(j) Trade and other payables
(k) Provisions
(l) Financial liabilities (excluding items shown under (j) and (k))
(m) Current tax liabilities (as in IAS 12)
(n) Deferred tax liabilities and assets (as in IAS 12)
(o) Minority interest
(p) Issued capital and reserves

The face of the balance sheet shall also include line items that present:

(a) assets classified as held for sale in accordance with IFRS 5
(b) liabilities included in disposal groups classified as held for sale in accordance with IFRS 5.

Any **other line items**, headings or sub-totals should be shown on the face of the balance sheet when it is necessary for an understanding of the entity's financial position.

The example shown above is for illustration only (although we will follow the format in this Study Text). The IAS, however, does not prescribe the order or format in which the items listed should be presented. It simply states that they **must be presented separately** because they are so different in nature or function from each other.

Whether additional items are presented separately depends on judgements based on the assessment of the following factors.

(a) **Nature and liquidity of assets and their materiality**. Thus goodwill and assets arising from development expenditure will be presented separately, as will monetary/non-monetary assets and current/non-current assets.

(b) **Function within the entity.** Operating and financial assets, inventories, receivables and cash and cash equivalents are therefore shown separately.

(c) **Amounts, nature and timing of liabilities**. Interest-bearing and non-interest-bearing liabilities and provisions will be shown separately, classified as current or non-current as appropriate.

The standard also requires separate presentation where **different measurement bases** are used for assets and liabilities which differ in nature or function. According to IAS 16, for example, it is permitted to carry certain items of property, plant and equipment at cost or at a revalued amount.

3.2 Information presented either on the face of the balance sheet or by note

FAST FORWARD

IAS 1 specifies that certain items must be disclosed on the face of the financial statements.

Further **sub-classification** of the line items listed above should be disclosed either on the face of the balance sheet or in notes to the balance sheet. The classification will depend upon the nature of the entity's operations. As well as each item being sub-classified by its nature, any amounts payable to or receivable from any **group company or other related party** should also be disclosed separately.

The sub-classification details will in part depend on the requirements of IASs. The size, nature and function of the amounts involved will also be important and the factors listed in Section 3.1 should be considered. **Disclosures** will vary from item to item and IAS 1 gives the following examples.

(a) **Items of property, plant and equipment** are classified by class as described in IAS 16 *Property, plant and equipment*

(b) **Receivables** are analysed between amounts receivable from trade customers, other members of the group, receivables from related parties, prepayments and other amounts

(c) **Inventories** are sub-classified, in accordance with IAS 2 *Inventories,* into classifications such as merchandise, production supplies, materials, work in progress and finished goods

(d) **Provisions** are analysed showing separately provisions for employee benefit costs and any other items classified in a manner appropriate to the entity's operations

(e) **Equity capital and reserves** are analysed showing separately the various classes of paid in capital, share premium and reserves

The standard then lists some **specific disclosures** which must be made, either on the face of the balance sheet or the related notes.

(a) **Share capital disclosures (**for each class of share capital)

(i) Number of shares authorised

(ii) Number of shares issued and fully paid, and issued but not fully paid

(iii) Par value per share, or that the shares have no par value

(iv) Reconciliation of the number of shares outstanding at the beginning and at the end of the year

(v) Rights, preferences and restrictions attaching to that class including restrictions on the distribution of dividends and the repayment of capital

(vi) Shares in the entity held by the entity itself or by related group companies

(vii) Shares reserved for issuance under options and sales contracts, including the terms and amounts

(b) Description of the nature and purpose of **each reserve** within owners' equity

Some types of entity have no share capital, eg partnerships. Such entities should disclose information which is **equivalent** to that listed. This means disclosing the movement during the period in each category of equity interest and any rights, preferences or restrictions attached to each category of equity interest.

4 The current/non-current distinction

FAST FORWARD

You should appreciate the distinction between **current and non-current** assets and liabilities and the difference in treatment for operating cycle items and other non-operating items which are due after twelve months.

4.1 The current/non-current distinction

An entity must present **current** and **non-current** assets as separate classifications on the face of the balance sheet. A presentation based on liquidity should only be used where it provides more relevant and reliable information, in which case all assets and liabilities must be presented broadly **in order of liquidity**.

In either case, the entity should disclose any portion of an asset or liability which is expected to be recovered or settled **after more than twelve months**. For example, for an amount receivable which is due in instalments over 18 months, the portion due after more than twelve months must be disclosed.

The IAS emphasises how helpful information on the **operating cycle** is to users of financial statements. Where there is a clearly defined operating cycle within which the entity supplies goods or services, then information disclosing those net assets that are continuously circulating as **working capital** is useful.

This distinguishes them from those net assets used in the long-term operations of the entity. Assets that are expected to be realised and liabilities that are due for settlement within the operating cycle are therefore highlighted.

The liquidity and solvency of an entity is also indicated by information about the **maturity dates** of assets and liabilities. As we will see later, IAS 32 *Financial instruments: disclosure and presentation* requires disclosure of maturity dates of both financial assets and financial liabilities. (Financial assets include trade and other receivables; financial liabilities include trade and other payables.) In the case of non-monetary assets, eg inventories, such information is also useful.

4.2 Current assets

Key term

An asset should be classified as a **current asset** when it:

- is expected to be realised in, or is intended for sale or consumption in, the normal course of the entity's operating cycle; or
- is held primarily for trading purposes or is expected to be realised within twelve months of the balance sheet date; or
- is cash or a cash equivalent asset which is not restricted in its use.

All other assets shall be classified as non-current assets. *(IAS 1)*

Non-current assets include tangible, intangible, operating and financial assets of a long-term nature. Other terms with the same meaning can be used (eg 'fixed', 'long-term').

The term 'operating cycle' has been used several times above and the standard defines it as follows.

Key term

The **operating cycle** of an entity is the time between the acquisition of assets for processing and their realisation in cash or cash equivalents. *(IAS 1)*

Current assets therefore include inventories and trade receivables that are sold, consumed and realised as part of the normal operating cycle. **This is the case even where they are not expected to be realised within twelve months**.

Current assets will also include **marketable securities** if they are expected to be realised within twelve months of the balance sheet date. If expected to be realised later, they should be included in non-current assets.

4.3 Current liabilities

Key term

A liability should be classified as a **current liability** when:

- It is expected to be settled in the normal course of the entity's operating cycle; or
- It is held primarily for the purpose of being traded; or
- It is due to be settled within twelve months of the balance sheet date; or
- The entity does not have an unconditional right to defer settlement of the liability for at least twelve months after the balance sheet date.

All other liabilities should be classified as non-current liabilities. *(IAS 1)*

The categorisation of current liabilities is very similar to that of current assets. Thus, some current liabilities are part of the **working capital** used in the normal operating cycle of the business (ie trade payables and accruals for employee and other operating costs). Such items will be classed as current liabilities **even where they are due to be settled more than twelve months after the balance sheet date.**

There are also current liabilities which are not settled as part of the normal operating cycle, but which are due to be settled within twelve months of the balance sheet date. These include bank overdrafts, income taxes, other non-trade payables and the current portion of interest-bearing liabilities. Any interest-bearing liabilities that are used to finance working capital on a long-term basis, and that are not due for settlement within twelve months, should be classed as **non-current liabilities**.

A **long-term financial liability** due to be **settled within twelve months** of the balance sheet date should be classified as a **current liability**, even if an agreement to refinance, or to reschedule payments, on a long-term basis is completed after the balance sheet date and before the financial statements are authorised for issue.

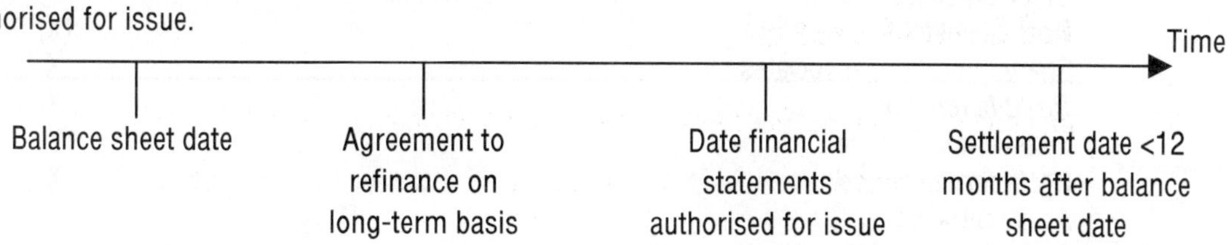

A **long-term financial liability** that is payable on **demand** because the entity **breached** a **condition** of its loan agreement should be classified as **current** at the balance sheet date even if the **lender** has agreed **after the balance sheet date**, and **before** the financial statements are **authorised for issue**, **not** to **demand payment** as a consequence of the breach.

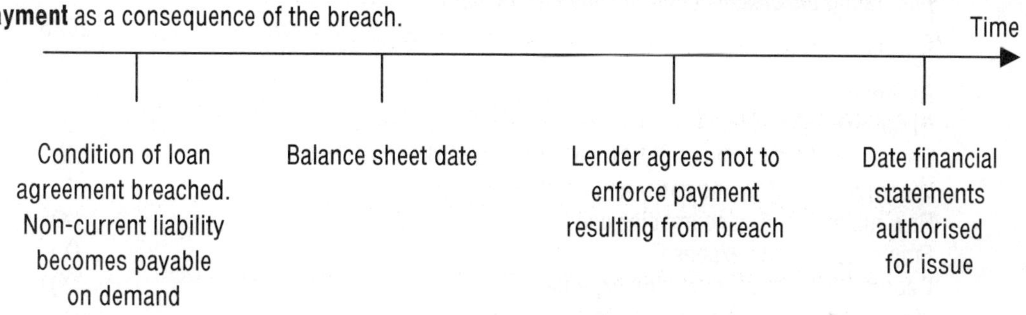

However, if the **lender** has **agreed** by the **balance sheet date** to provide a **period of grace** ending **at least twelve months after the balance sheet date** within which the entity can rectify the breach and during that time the lender cannot demand immediate repayment, the liability is classified as **non-current.**

5 Income statement

FAST FORWARD

The IAS 1 suggested formats for the balance sheet and income statement are not rigid, but items to be disclosed on the face of the income statement are specified, and this must be adhered to.

5.1 Formats

IAS 1 offers **two possible formats** for the income statement, the difference between the two being the classification of expenses: by function or by nature.

5.2 Examples of income statements

XYZ GROUP

INCOME STATEMENT FOR THE YEAR ENDED 31 DECEMBER 20X8

Illustrating the classification of expenses by function

	20X8	*20X7*
	$'000	$'000
Revenue	X	X
Cost of sales	(X)	(X)
Gross profit	X	X
Other income	X	X
Distribution costs	(X)	(X)
Administrative expenses	(X)	(X)
Other expenses	(X)	(X)
Finance costs	(X)	(X)
Share of profit of associates	X	X
Profit before tax	X	X
Income tax expense	(X)	(X)
Profit for the period	X	X
Attributable to:		
Equity holders of the parent	X	X
Minority interest	X	X
	X	X

Illustrating the classification of expenses by nature

	20X8	*20X7*
	$'000	$'000
Revenue	X	X
Other operating income	X	X
Changes in inventories of finished goods and work in progress	(X)	X
Work performed by the entity and capitalised	X	X
Raw material and consumables used	(X)	(X)
Employee benefits expense	(X)	(X)
Depreciation and amortisation expense	(X)	(X)
Impairment of property, plant and equipment	(X)	(X)
Other expenses	(X)	(X)
Finance cost	(X)	(X)
Share of profit of associates	X	X
Profit before tax	X	X
Income tax expense	(X)	(X)
Profit for the period	X	X
Attributable to:		
Equity holders of the parent	X	X
Minority interest	X	X
	X	X

5.3 Information presented on the face of the income statement

The standard lists the following as the **minimum** to be disclosed on the face of the income statement.

(a) Revenue

(b) Finance costs

(c) Share of profits and losses of associates and joint ventures accounted for using the equity method

(d) A single amount comprising the total of:

 (i) the post-tax profit or loss of discontinued operations

 (ii) the post-tax gain or loss recognised on the measurement to fair value less costs to sell or on the disposal of the assets constituting the discontinued operation

(e) Tax expense

(f) Profit or loss

The following items must be disclosed on the face of the income statement as allocations of profit or loss for the period.

(a) Profit or loss attributable to minority interest
(b) Profit or loss attributable to equity holders of the parent

The allocated amounts must not be presented as items of income or expense. There is a similar requirement for the statement of changes in equity or statement of recognised income and expense. (These relate to group accounts, not covered in this text.)

Income and expense items can only be **offset** when, and only when:

(a) It is permitted or required by an IFRS, or

(b) Gains, losses and related expenses arising from the same or similar transactions and events are immaterial, in which case they can be aggregated.

5.4 Information presented either on the face of the income statement or in the notes

The following items, where material, must be disclosed either on the face of the income statement or in the notes:

- write-downs of inventories or non-current assets and any write-down reversals
- disposals of property, plant and equipment or investments
- restructuring provisions and any reversals of provisions
- discontinued operations
- litigation settlements
- other reversals of provisions

An analysis of expenses must be shown either on the face of the income statement (as above, which is encouraged by the standard) or by note, using a classification based on *either* the nature of the expenses or their function. This **sub-classification of expenses** indicates a range of components of financial performance; these may differ in terms of stability, potential for gain or loss and predictability.

5.4.1 Nature of expense method

Expenses are not reallocated amongst various functions within the entity, but are aggregated in the income statement **according to their nature** (eg purchase of materials, depreciation, wages and salaries, transport costs). This is by far the easiest method, especially for smaller entities.

5.4.2 Function of expense/cost of sales method

You are likely to be more familiar with this method. Expenses are classified according to their function as part of cost of sales, distribution or administrative activities. This method often gives **more relevant information** for users, but the allocation of expenses by function requires the use of judgement and can be arbitrary. Consequently, perhaps, when this method is used, entities should disclose **additional information** on the nature of expenses, including staff costs, and depreciation and amortisation expense.

Which of the above methods is chosen by an entity will depend on **historical and industry factors**, and also the **nature of the organisation**. Under each method, there should be given an indication of costs which are likely to vary (directly or indirectly) with the level of sales or production. The choice of method should fairly reflect the main elements of the entity's performance.

5.5 Dividends

IAS 1 also requires disclosure of the amount of **dividends per share** (declared or proposed) for the period covered by the financial statements. This may be shown either on the face of the income statement or in the statement of changes in equity.

5.6 Further points

(a) All requirements previously set out in other Standards for the presentation of particular line items on the face of the balance sheet and income statement are now dealt with in IAS 1. These line items are: biological assets; liabilities and assets for current tax and deferred tax; and pre-tax gain or loss recognised on the disposal of assets or settlement of liabilities attributable to discontinuing operations.

(b) The section that set out the **presentation requirements** for the **net profit or loss** for the period in **IAS 8** has now been **transferred** to **IAS 1**.

(c) The following **disclosures** are **no longer required:**

  (i) The results of operating activities, as a line item on the face of the income statement. **'Operating activities'** are **not defined in IAS 1**

  (ii) **Extraordinary items**, as a line item on the face of the income statement (note that the disclosure of 'extraordinary items' is now **prohibited**)

  (iii) The **number** of an **entity's employees**

(d) An entity must disclose, in the summary of significant accounting policies and/or other notes, the **judgements** made by management in **applying** the **accounting policies** that have the **most significant effect** on the amounts of items recognised in the financial statements.

(e) An entity must disclose in the notes information regarding **key assumptions** about the **future**, and other sources of **measurement uncertainty**, that have a significant **risk of** causing a **material adjustment** to the carrying amounts of assets and liabilities within the **next financial year**.

(f) The following items must be disclosed on the **face of the income statement**.

  (i) Profit or loss attributable to **minority interest**
  (ii) Profit or loss attributable to **equity** holders of the parent

  The allocated amounts must not be presented as items of income or expense. There is a similar requirement for the statement of changes in equity or statement of recognised income and expense. (See the example formats above.)

6 Changes in equity

FAST FORWARD

The statement of **changes in equity** reconciles the movement in equity between periods, including both items passing through the income statement and movements on reserves. This reflects the increase or decrease in the net assets of the entity during the period.

6.1 Format

The revised IAS 1 requires a statement of changes in equity. This can be in the format illustrated below (showing all changes in equity) or in the form of a statement of recognised income and expense.

	Attributable to equity holders of the parent						
	Share capital	*Other reserves*	*Translation reserve*	*Retained earnings*	*Total*	*Minority interest*	*Total equity*
	$'000	$'000	$'000	$'000	$'000	$'000	$'000
Balance at 31 December 20X7 brought forward	X	X	(X)	X	X	X	X
Changes in equity for 20X8							
Loss on property revaluation		(X)			(X)	(X)	(X)
Available-for-sale investments:							
Valuation gains/(losses) taken to equity		(X)			(X)		(X)
Transferred to profit or loss on sale		X			X		X
Tax on items taken directly to or transferred from equity	–	X	X	–	X	X	X
Net income recognised directly in equity		(X)	(X)		(X)	(X)	(X)
Profit for the period		–	–	X	X	X	X
Total recognised income and expense for the period		(X)	(X)	X	X	X	X
Dividends				(X)	(X)	(X)	(X)
Issue of share capital	X				X		X
Balance at 31 December 20X8	X	X	(X)	X	X	X	X

6.2 Statement of recognised income and expense

This is an alternative method of presenting changes in equity. If this method is used, the notes to the financial statements must include a reconciliation of opening and closing balances of share capital, reserves and retained earnings, as illustrated in the statement of changes in equity. (The previous version of IAS 1 referred to the statement of recognised gains and losses.)

XYZ GROUP
STATEMENT OF RECOGNISED INCOME AND EXPENSE
FOR THE YEAR ENDED 31 DECEMBER 20X8

	20X8	20X7
	$'000	$'000
Gain/(loss) on revaluation of properties	(X)	X
Available-for-sale investments:		
Valuation gains/(losses) taken to equity	(X)	(X)
Transferred to profit or loss on sale	X	(X)
Tax on items taken directly to or transferred from equity	X	(X)
Net income recognised directly in equity	(X)	X
Net profit for the period	X	X
Total recognised income and expense for the period	X	X
Attributable to:		
Equity holders of the parent	X	X
Minority interest	X	X
	X	X
Effect of changes in accounting policy:		
Equity holders of the parent		(X)
Minority interest		(X)
		(X)

7 Notes to the financial statements

FAST FORWARD

The notes to the financial statements will **amplify** the information given in the balance sheet, income statement and statement of changes in equity. We have already noted above the information which the IAS allows to be shown by note rather than on the face of the statements. To some extent, then, the contents of the notes will be determined by the level of detail shown on the **face of the statements**.

7.1 Structure

The notes to the financial statements should perform the following functions.

(a) Provide information about the **basis on which the financial statements were prepared** and which **specific accounting policies** were chosen and applied to significant transactions/events

(b) Disclose any information, not shown elsewhere in the financial statements, which is **required by IFRSs**

(c) Show any additional information that is necessary for a **fair presentation** which is not shown on the face of the financial statements

The way the notes are presented is important. They should be given in a **systematic manner** and **cross referenced** back to the related figure(s) in the balance sheet, income statement or cash flow statement.

Notes to the financial statements will amplify the information shown therein by giving the following.

(a) More **detailed analysis** or breakdowns of figures in the statements
(b) **Narrative information** explaining figures in the statements
(c) **Additional information**, eg contingent liabilities and commitments

IAS 1 suggests a **certain order** for notes to the financial statements. This will assist users when comparing the statements of different entities.

(a) Statement of **compliance** with IFRSs

(b) Statement of the **measurement basis** (bases) and accounting policies applied

(c) **Supporting information** for items presented on the face of each financial statement in the same order as each line item and each financial statement is presented

(d) **Other disclosures**, eg:

  (i) Contingent liabilities, commitments and other financial disclosures
  (ii) Non-financial disclosures

The order of specific items may have to be varied occasionally, but a systematic structure is still required.

7.2 Presentation of accounting policies

The accounting policies section should describe the following.

- The **measurement basis** (or bases) used in preparing the financial statements
- The **other accounting policies** used, as required for a proper understanding of the financial statements

This information may be shown in the notes or sometimes as a **separate component** of the financial statements.

The information on measurement bases used is obviously fundamental to an understanding of the financial statements. Where **more than one basis is used**, it should be stated to which assets or liabilities each basis has been applied.

An entity must also disclose under accounting policies any judgements made by management in the application of accounting policies which have significantly affected amounts recognised in the financial statements. Management may make judgements determining:

(a) whether financial assets are held-to-maturity investments

(b) when substantially all the significant risks and rewards of ownership of a financial asset or lease have been transferred

(c) whether, in substance, particular sales of goods are financing arrangements and therefore do not give rise to revenue

7.3 Other disclosures

An entity shall disclose in the notes information about the key assumptions concerning the future, and other key sources of estimation uncertainty at the balance sheet date, that have a significant risk of causing a material adjustment to the carrying amounts of assets and liabilities within the next financial year. The notes shall include details of:

(a) the nature of those assets and liabilities
(b) their carrying amount as at the balance sheet date

Disclosure is not required for risk-bearing assets which are measured at fair value based on recently observed market prices.

An entity must disclose in the notes:

(a) The amount of **dividends proposed or declared before the financial statements** were **authorised** for issue but **not recognised as a distribution to equity holders** during the period, and the amount per share

(b) The amount of any **cumulative preference dividends** not recognised

IAS 1 ends by listing some **specific disclosures** which will always be required if they are not shown elsewhere in the financial statements.

(a) The **domicile and legal form** of the entity, its **country of incorporation** and the **address of the registered office** (or, if different, principal place of business)

(b) A description of the **nature of the entity's operations** and its **principal activities**

(c) The name of the **parent entity** and the **ultimate parent entity** of the group

Question — **Financial statements**

The accountant of Wislon Co has prepared the following list of account balances as at 31 December 20X7.

	$'000
50c ordinary shares (fully paid)	350
7% $1 preference shares (fully paid, non-cumulative, non-redeemable)	100
10% loan stock (secured)	200
Retained earnings 1.1.X7	242
General reserve 1.1.X7	171
Land and buildings 1.1.X7 (cost)	430
Plant and machinery 1.1.X7 (cost)	830

	$'000
Aggregate depreciation	
Buildings 1.1.X7	20
Plant and machinery 1.1.X7	222
Inventory 1.1.X7	190
Sales	2,695
Purchases	2,152
Preference dividend	7
Ordinary dividend (interim)	8
Loan interest	10
Wages and salaries	254
Light and heat	31
Sundry expenses	113
Suspense account	135
Trade accounts receivable	179
Trade accounts payable	195
Cash	126

Notes

(a) Sundry expenses include $9,000 paid in respect of insurance for the year ending 1 September 20X8. Light and heat does not include an invoice of $3,000 for electricity for the three months ending 2 January 20X8, which was paid in February 20X8. Light and heat also includes $20,000 relating to salesmen's commission.

(b) The suspense account is in respect of the following items.

	$'000
Proceeds from the issue of 100,000 ordinary shares	120
Proceeds from the sale of plant	300
	420
Less consideration for the acquisition of Mary & Co	285
	135

(c) The net assets of Mary & Co were purchased on 3 March 20X7. Assets were valued as follows

	$'000
Investments	231
Inventory	34
	265

All the inventory acquired was sold during 20X7. The investments were still held by Wislon at 31 December 20X7. Goodwill has not been impaired in value.

(d) The property was acquired some years ago. The buildings element of the cost was estimated at $100,000 and the estimated useful life of the asset was fifty years at the time of purchase. As at 31 December 20X7 the property is to be revalued at $800,000.

(e) The plant which was sold had cost $350,000 and had a net book value of $274,000 as on 1 January 20X7. $36,000 depreciation is to be charged on plant and machinery for 20X7.

(f) The loan notes have been in issue for some years.

(g) In December 20X7 the management decided to provide for:

(i) Loan interest due
(ii) A transfer to general reserve of $16,000
(iii) Audit fees of $4,000

(h) Inventory as at 31 December 20X7 was valued at $220,000 (cost).

(i) Taxation is to be ignored.

Required

Prepare the financial statements of Wislon Co as at 31 December 20X7. You do not need to produce notes to the statements.

Answer

WISLON CO
INCOME STATEMENT
FOR THE YEAR ENDED 31 DECEMBER 20X7

	$'000	$'000	$'000
Revenue			2,695
Less cost of sales			
Opening inventory		190	
Purchases (2,152 + 34) (W5)		2,186	
		2,376	
Less closing inventory		220	
			2,156
Gross profit			539
Profit on disposal of plant			26
			565
Expenses			
Wages, salaries and commission (254 + 20) (W2)		274	
Sundry expenses (113 – 6) (W1)		107	
Light and heat (31 – 20 + 3) (W2) (W1)		14	
Depreciation: buildings (W3)		2	
plant		36	
Audit fees		4	
Loan interest (W1)		20	
			457
Profit for the period			108

WISLON CO
BALANCE SHEET AS AT 31 DECEMBER 20X7

	$'000	$'000
Assets		
Non-current assets		
Property, plant and equipment		
Property at valuation		800
Plant: cost (W4)	480	
aggregate depreciation (W4)	182	
		298
Goodwill (W5)		20
Investments		231
Current assets		
Inventory	220	
Trade accounts receivable	179	
Prepayments (W1)	6	
Cash	126	
		531
Total assets		1,880

	$'000	$'000
Equity and liabilities		
Equity		
50c ordinary shares	400	
7% $1 preference shares	100	
Share premium	70	
Revaluation surplus (W3)	392	
General reserve	187	
Retained earnings	319	
		1,468
Non-current liabilities		
10% loan stock (secured)		200
Current liabilities		
Trade accounts payable	195	
Accrued expenses (W1)	17	
		212
Total equity and liabilities		1,880

WISLON CO
STATEMENT OF CHANGES IN EQUITY
FOR THE YEAR ENDED 31 DECEMBER 20X7

	Share capital $'000	*Share premium* $'000	*Revaluation reserve* $'000	*General reserve* $'000	*Retained earnings* $'000	*Total* $'000
At 1.1.X7	450	–	–	171	242	863
Surplus on revaluation of properties			392			392
Net profit for the period					108	108
Dividends					(15)	(15)
Transfer to reserve				16	(16)	–
Issue of share capital (W6)	50	70				120
Balance at 31.12.X7	500	70	392	187	319	1,468

Workings

(1) Normal adjustments are needed for accruals and prepayments (insurance, light and heat, loan interest and audit fees). The loan interest accrued is calculated as follows.

	$'000
Charge needed in income statement (10% × $200,000)	20
Amount paid so far, as shown in list of account balances	10
Accrual: presumably six months' interest now payable	10

The accrued expenses shown in the balance sheet comprise:	$'000
Loan interest	10
Light and heat	3
Audit fee	4
	17

Prepayment

Insurance (sundry expenses) $(\$9{,}000 \times \frac{8}{12}) = \$6{,}000$

(2) The misposting of $20,000 to light and heat is also adjusted, by reducing the light and heat expense, but charging $20,000 to salesmen's commission.

(3) Depreciation on the building is calculated as $\frac{\$100{,}000}{50} = \$2{,}000$.

The NBV of the property is then $430,000 – $20,000 – $2,000 = $408,000 at the end of the year. When the property is revalued a reserve of $800,000 – $408,000 = $392,000 is then created.

(4) The profit on disposal of plant is calculated as proceeds $300,000 (per suspense account) less NBV $274,000, ie $26,000. The cost of the remaining plant is calculated at $830,000 – $350,000 = $480,000. The depreciation provision at the year end is:

	$'000
Balance 1.1.X7	222
Charge for 20X7	36
Less depreciation on disposals (350 – 274)	(76)
	182

(5) Goodwill arising on the purchase of Mary & Co is:

	$'000
Consideration (per suspense account)	285
Assets at valuation	265
Goodwill	20

This is shown as an asset on the balance sheet. The investments, being owned by Wislon at the year end, are also shown on the balance sheet, whereas Mary's inventory, acquired and then sold, is added to the purchases figure for the year.

(6) The other item in the suspense account is dealt with as follows.

	$'000
Proceeds of issue of 100,000 ordinary shares	120
Less nominal value 100,000 × 50c	50
Excess of consideration over par value (= share premium)	70

(7) The transfer to general reserve increases it to $171,000 + $16,000 = $187,000.

Exam focus point

As only 20 marks are available for an accounts preparation question in Paper 7, you cannot be required to produce accounts plus a full set of notes. Questions are likely to require one or two specific notes or no notes.

But do prepare to do an accounts preparation question, including a statement of changes in equity. The examiner has stated that Section C will **not** always have a question requiring an income statement and balance sheet, but in this case, these topics are bound to be examined elsewhere in the paper.

Chapter Roundup

- Financial statements present the financial position and financial performance of an entity.
- IAS 1 covers the **form and content of** financial statements. The main components are:
  - Balance sheet
  - Income statement
  - Statement of changes in equity
  - Cash flow statement
  - Notes to the financial statements
- Each component must be **identified clearly**.
- The IAS 1 suggests **formats** for the balance sheet and income statement, but these are not rigid. Certain items are specified, however, for **disclosure on the face of the financial statements.**
- You should appreciate the distinction between **current and non-current** assets and liabilities and the difference in treatment for operating cycle items and other non-operating items which are due after twelve months.
- The statement of **changes in equity** reconciles the movement in equity between periods, including both items passing through the income statement and movements on reserves.
- The **notes** to the financial statements will amplify the information given in the financial statements. IAS 1 allows certain items to be shown by note rather than on the face of the statements. Where minimum disclosures are made on the face of the statements, more notes will be required.

Quick Quiz

1 Limited liability means that the shareholders of a company are not legally accountable.

True ☐

False ☐

2 IAS 1 states that entities should produce their financial statements within .... months of the balance sheet date.

3 Which of the following are examples of current assets?

(a) Property, plant and equipment
(b) Prepayments
(c) Cash equivalents
(d) Manufacturing licences
(e) Retained earnings

4 Provisions must be disclosed on the face of the balance sheet.

True ☐

False ☐

5 Which of the following must be disclosed on the face of the income statement?

(a) Tax expense
(b) Analysis of expenses
(c) Net profit or loss for the period.

6 What is the alternative to the statement of changes in equity?

7 Fill in the blanks.

The accounting policies section of the notes describes:

The .... used in preparing the financial statements and....................................... required for a proper understanding of the financial statements.

Answers to Quick Quiz

1 False. It means that if the company becomes insolvent, the maximum that an owner stands to lose is his share capital in the business.

2 Six

3 (b) and (c) only

4 True

5 (a) and (c) only. (b) may be shown in the notes.

6 The statement of recognised income and expense.

7 Measurement basis

Specific accounting policies

Now try the question below from the Exam Question Bank

Number	Level	Marks	Time
Q15	Examination	20	36 mins

Reporting financial performance

4

Introduction

This long chapter is mainly concerned with the **income statement**. **IAS 8** deals with accounting policies. It also looks at certain circumstances and transactions which require different treatment to normal profit or loss items.

IAS 14 on segment reporting requires publicly quoted entities to provide additional information on their results, breaking them down by different types of product and service and by geographical areas.

IFRS 5 on assets held for sale and discontinued operations is a new and important standard.

Topic list	Learning outcomes	Syllabus references	Ability required
1 IAS 8 *Accounting policies, changes in accounting estimates and errors*	C (iii)	C (3)	Evaluation
2 Accounting policies	C (iii)	C (3)	Evaluation
3 Changes in accounting policies	C (iii)	C (3)	Application
4 Changes in accounting estimates	C (iii)	C (3)	Application
5 Errors	C (iii)	C (3)	Application
6 IFRS 5 *Non-current assets held for sale and discontinued operations*	C (iii)	C (3)	Application
7 IAS 14 *Segment reporting*	C (iii)	C (3)	Application
8 Identifying reportable segments	C (iii)	C (3)	Application

1 IAS 8 Accounting policies, changes in accounting estimates and errors

FAST FORWARD

IAS 8 deals with the treatment of changes in accounting estimates, changes in accounting policies and errors.

The standard was extensively revised in December 2003. The new title reflects the fact that the material on determining net profit and loss for the period has been transferred to IAS 1.

1.1 Definitions

The following definitions are given in the standard. Apart from the definition of accounting policies, most of the definitions are either new or heavily amended.

Key terms

Accounting policies are the specific principles, bases, conventions, rules and practices adopted by an entity in preparing and presenting financial statements.

A **change in accounting estimate** is an adjustment of the carrying amount of an asset or a liability or the amount of the periodic consumption of an asset, that results from the assessment of the present status of, and expected future benefits and obligations associated with, assets and liabilities. Changes in accounting estimates result from new information or new developments and, accordingly, are not corrections of errors.

Material: as defined in IAS 1

Prior period errors are omissions from, and misstatements in, the entity's financial statements for one or more prior periods arising from a failure to use, or misuse of, reliable information that:

(a) Was available when financial statements for those periods were authorised for issue, and

(b) Could reasonably be expected to have been obtained and taken into account in the preparation and presentation of those financial statements.

Such errors include the effects of mathematical mistakes, mistakes in applying accounting policies, oversights or misinterpretations of facts, and fraud.

Retrospective application is applying a new accounting policy to transactions, other events and conditions as if that policy had always been applied.

Retrospective restatement is correcting the recognition, measurement and disclosure of amounts of elements of financial statements as if a prior period error had never occurred.

Prospective application of a change in accounting policy and of recognising the effect of a change in an accounting estimate, respectively, are:

(a) Applying the new accounting policy to transactions, other events and conditions occurring after the date as at which the policy is changed; and

(b) Recognising the effect of the change in the accounting estimate in the current and future periods affected by the change.

Impracticable Applying a requirement is impracticable when the entity cannot apply it after making every reasonable effort to do so. It is impracticable to apply a change in an accounting policy retrospectively or to make a retrospective restatement to correct an error if one of the following apply.

Key terms (continued)

(a) The effects of the retrospective application or retrospective restatement are not determinable.

(b) The retrospective application or retrospective restatement requires assumptions about what management's intent would have been in that period.

(c) The retrospective application or retrospective restatement requires significant estimates of amounts and it is impossible to distinguish objectively information about those estimates that: provides evidence of circumstances that existed on the date(s) at which those amounts are to be recognised, measured or disclosed; and would have been available when the financial statements for that prior period were authorised for issue, from other information. (*IAS 8*)

2 Accounting policies

FAST FORWARD

The material on accounting policies has been **transferred** into IAS 8 from IAS 1.

2.1 Developing accounting policies

Accounting policies are determined by **applying the relevant IFRS or IAS**.

Where there is no applicable IFRS or IAS management should use its **judgement** in developing and applying an accounting policy that results in information that is **relevant** and **reliable**. Management should refer to:

(a) The requirements and guidance in IFRSs and IASs dealing with **similar** and **related issues**

(b) The definitions, recognition criteria and measurement concepts for assets, liabilities and expenses in the ***Framework***

Management may also consider the most recent pronouncements of **other standard setting bodies** that use a similar conceptual framework to develop standards, other accounting literature and accepted industry practices if these do not conflict with the sources above.

An entity must select and apply its accounting policies for a period **consistently** for similar transactions, other events and conditions, unless an IFRS or an IAS specifically requires or permits categorisation of items for which different policies may be appropriate. If an IFRS or an IAS requires or permits categorisation of items, an appropriate accounting policy must be selected and applied consistently to each category.

3 Changes in accounting policies

3.1 Making changes

The same accounting policies are usually adopted from period to period, to allow users to analyse trends over time in profit, cash flows and financial position. **Changes in accounting policy will therefore be rare** and should be made only if required by one of three things.

(a) By **statute**

(b) By an **accounting standard setting body**

(c) If the change will result in a **more appropriate presentation** of events or transactions in the financial statements of the entity

The standard highlights two types of event **which do not constitute changes in accounting policy**.

(a) Adopting an accounting policy for a **new type of transaction** or event not dealt with previously by the entity.

(b) Adopting a **new accounting policy** for a transaction or event which has not occurred in the past or which was not material.

In the case of tangible non-current assets, if a policy of revaluation is adopted for the first time then this is treated, not as a change of accounting policy under IAS 8, but as a revaluation under IAS 16 *Property, plant and equipment*. The following paragraphs do not therefore apply to a change in policy to adopt revaluations.

A change in accounting policy **must be applied retrospectively**. **Retrospective application** means that the new accounting policy is applied to transactions and events as if it had always been in use. In other words, at the earliest date such transactions or events occurred, the policy is applied from that date.

Prospective application is **no longer allowed** under the revised IAS 8 unless it is **impracticable** (see Key Terms) to determine the cumulative amount of the adjustment.

3.2 Adoption of an IAS/IFRS

Where a new IAS or IFRS is adopted, IAS 8 requires any transitional provisions in the new IAS itself to be followed. If none are given in the IAS which is being adopted, then IAS 8 explains the required treatment.

3.3 Other changes in accounting policy

IAS 8 requires **retrospective application**, *unless* it is **impracticable** to determine the cumulative amount of the adjustment. Any resulting adjustment should be reported as an adjustment to the opening balance of retained earnings. Comparative information should be restated unless it is impracticable to do so.

This means that all comparative information must be restated **as if the new policy had always been in force**, with amounts relating to earlier periods reflected in an adjustment to opening reserves of the earliest period presented.

Prospective application is allowed only when it is impracticable to determine the cumulative effect of the change.

Certain **disclosures** are required when a change in accounting policy has a material effect on the current period or any prior period presented, or when it may have a material effect in subsequent periods.

(a) Reasons for the change

(b) Amount of the adjustment for the current period and for each period presented

(c) Amount of the adjustment relating to periods prior to those included in the comparative information

(d) The fact that comparative information has been restated or that it is impracticable to do so

An entity should also disclose information relevant to assessing the **impact of new IFRS** on the financial statements where these have **not yet come into force.**

Question — **Change of accounting policy**

Wick Co was established on 1 January 20X0. In the first three years' accounts development expenditure was carried forward as an asset in the balance sheet. During 20X3 the managers decided that for the current and future years, all development expenditure should be written off as it is incurred. This decision has not resulted from any change in the expected outcome of development projects on hand, but rather from a desire to favour the prudence concept. The following information is available.

(a) Movements on the development account.

Year	*Development expenditure incurred and capitalised during year*	*Transfer from capitalised development expenditure account to income statement*
	$'000	$'000
20X0	525	–
20X1	780	215
20X2	995	360

(b) The 20X2 accounts showed the following.

	$'000
Retained earnings b/f	2,955
Retained earnings for the year	1,825
Retained earnings c/f	4,780

(c) The retained profit for 20X3 after charging the actual development expenditure for the year was $2,030,000.

Required

Show how the change in accounting policy should be reflected in the reserves in the company's 20X3 accounts in accordance with IAS 8.

Ignore taxation.

Answer

If the new accounting policy had been adopted since the company was incorporated, the additional income statement charges for development expenditure would have been:

	$'000
20X0	525
20X1 (780 – 215)	565
	1,090
20X2 (995 – 360)	635
	1,725

This means that the reserves brought forward at 1 January 20X3 would have been $1,725,000 less than the reported figure of $4,780,000; while the reserves brought forward at 1 January 20X2 would have been $1,090,000 less than the reported figure of $2,955,000.

The statement of reserves in Wick Co's 20X3 accounts should, therefore, appear as follows.

	20X3	*Comparative (previous year) figures 20X2*	
	$'000	$'000	
Retained earnings at the beginning of year			
Previously reported	4,780	2,955	
Retrospective change in accounting policy (note 1)	1,725	1,090	
Restated	3,055	1,865	
Retained earnings for the year	2,030	1,190	(note 2)
Retained earnings at the end of the year	5,085	3,055	

Notes

1. The accounts should include a note explaining the reasons for and consequences of the change in accounting policy. (See above workings for 20X3 and 20X2.)
2. The retained profit shown for 20X2 is after charging the additional development expenditure of $635,000.

4 Changes in accounting estimates

FAST FORWARD

Changes in accounting estimates are **not** applied retrospectively.

4.1 What are estimates?

Estimates arise in relation to business activities because of the **uncertainties inherent within them**. Judgements are made based on the most up to date information and the use of such estimates is a necessary part of the preparation of financial statements. It does *not* undermine their reliability. Here are some examples of accounting estimates.

- A necessary **doubtful debt provision**
- **Useful lives** of depreciable assets
- Provision for **obsolescence of inventory**

The rule here is that the **effect of a change in an accounting estimate** should be included in the determination of net profit or loss in one of:

(a) The period of the change, if the change affects that period only
(b) The period of the change *and* future periods, if the change affects both

Changes may occur in the circumstances which were in force at the time the estimate was calculated, or perhaps additional information or subsequent developments have come to light.

An example of a change in accounting estimate which affects only the **current period** is the doubtful debt estimate. However, a revision in the life over which an asset is depreciated would affect both the **current and future periods**, in the amount of the depreciation expense.

Reasonably enough, the effect of a change in an accounting estimate should be included in the **same income statement classification** as was used previously for the estimate. This rule helps to ensure **consistency** between the financial statements of different periods.

The **materiality** of the change is also relevant. The nature and amount of a change in an accounting estimate that has a material effect in the current period (or which is expected to have a material effect in subsequent periods) should be disclosed. If it is not possible to quantify the amount, this impracticability should be disclosed.

5 Errors

FAST FORWARD

Prior period errors will require **retrospective correction** if they are **material**.

5.1 Prior period errors

Errors discovered during a current period which **relate to a prior period** may arise through:

(a) Mathematical mistakes

(b) Mistakes in the application of accounting policies
(c) Misinterpretation of facts
(d) Oversights
(e) Fraud

A more formal definition is given in the Key Terms at the beginning of this chapter.

Most of the time these errors can be **corrected through net profit or loss for the current period**. Where they fulfil the definition of **material errors**, however, this is not appropriate.

5.2 Accounting treatment

Prior period errors: correct retrospectively. There is no longer any allowed alternative treatment.

This involves:

(a) Either restating the comparative amounts for the prior period(s) in which the error occurred,

(b) Or, when the error occurred before the earliest prior period presented, restating the opening balances of assets, liabilities and equity for that period

so that the financial statements are presented **as if the error had never occurred**.

Only where it is **impracticable** to determine the cumulative effect of an error on prior periods can an entity correct an error **prospectively**.

Various **disclosures** are required.

(a) **Nature** of the prior period error

(b) For each prior period, to the extent practicable, the **amount** of the correction.

 (i) For each financial statement line item affected
 (ii) If IAS 33 applies, for basic and diluted earnings per share

(c) The amount of the correction at the **beginning of the earliest prior** period presented

(d) If **retrospective restatement is impracticable** for a particular prior period, the **circumstances** that led to the existence of that condition and a description of how and from when the error has been corrected. Subsequent periods need not repeat these disclosures

Question — Prior period error

During 20X7 Global discovered that certain items had been included in inventory at 31 December 20X6, valued at $4.2m, which had in fact been sold before the year end. The following figures for 20X6 (as reported) and 20X7 (draft) are available.

	20X6	*20X7 (draft)*
	$'000	$'000
Sales	47,400	67,200
Cost of goods sold	(34,570)	(55,800)
Profit before taxation	12,830	11,400
Income taxes	(3,880)	(3,400)
Net profit	8,950	8,000

Reserves at 1 January 20X6 were $13m. The cost of goods sold for 20X7 includes the $4.2m error in opening inventory. The income tax rate was 30% for 20X6 and 20X7.

Required

Show the income statement for 20X7, with the 20X6 comparative, and retained earnings.

Answer

INCOME STATEMENT

	20X6	20X7
	$'000	$'000
Sales	47,400	67,200
Cost of goods sold (W1)	(38,770)	(51,600)
Profit before tax	8,630	15,600
Income tax (W2)	(2,620)	(4,660)
Net profit	6,010	10,940

RETAINED EARNINGS

	20X6	20X7
	$'000	$'000
Opening retained earnings		
As previously reported	13,000	21,950
Correction of prior period error (4,200 – 1,260)	–	(2,940)
As restated	13,000	19,010
Net profit for year	6,010	10,940
Closing retained earnings	19,010	29,950

Workings

1 *Cost of goods sold*

	20X6	20X7
	$'000	$'000
As stated in question	34,570	55,800
Inventory adjustment	4,200	(4,200)
	38,770	51,600

2 *Income tax*

	20X6	20X7
	$'000	$'000
As stated in question	3,880	3,400
Inventory adjustment (4,200 × 30%)	(1,260)	1,260
	2,620	4,660

Exam focus point

IAS 8 was examined in a 5 mark question in May 2005 and in an MCQ in November 2005.

6 IFRS 5 Non-current assets held for sale and discontinued operations

FAST FORWARD

IFRS 5 *Non-current assets held for sale and discontinued operations* requires assets 'held for sale' to be presented separately on the face of the balance sheet.

6.1 Background

IFRS 5 is the result of a short-term convergence project with the US Financial Accounting Standards Board (FASB). It replaces IAS 35 *Discontinuing operations.*

IFRS 5 requires assets and groups of assets that are 'held for sale' to be **presented separately** on the face of the balance sheet and the results of discontinued operations to be presented separately in the income statement. This is required so that users of financial statements will be better able to make **projections** about the financial position, profits and cash flows of the entity.

Key term

> **Disposal group**: a group of assets to be disposed of, by sale or otherwise, together as a group in a single transaction, and liabilities directly associated with those assets that will be transferred in the transaction. (In practice a disposal group could be a subsidiary, a cash-generating unit or a single operation within an entity.) *(IFRS 5)*

IFRS 5 does not apply to certain assets covered by other accounting standards:

(a) Deferred tax assets (IAS 12)

(b) Assets arising from employee benefits (IAS 19)

(c) Financial assets (IAS 39)

(d) Investment properties accounted for in accordance with the fair value model (IAS 40)

(e) Agricultural and biological assets that are measured at fair value less estimated point of sale costs (IAS 41)

(f) Insurance contracts (IFRS 4)

6.2 Classification of assets held for sale

A non-current asset (or disposal group) should be classified as **held for sale** if its carrying amount will be recovered **principally through a sale transaction** rather than **through continuing use**. A number of detailed criteria must be met:

(a) The asset must be **available for immediate sale** in its present condition.
(b) Its sale must be **highly probable** (ie, significantly more likely than not).

For the sale to be highly probable, the following must apply.

(a) Management must be **committed** to a plan to sell the asset.

(b) There must be an active programme to **locate a buyer.**

(c) The asset must be marketed for sale at a **price that is reasonable** in relation to its current fair value.

(d) The sale should be expected to take place **within one year** from the date of classification.

(e) It is unlikely that significant changes to the plan will be made or that the plan will be withdrawn.

An asset (or disposal group) can still be classified as held for sale, even if the sale has not actually taken place within one year. However, the delay must have been **caused by events or circumstances beyond the entity's control** and there must be sufficient evidence that the entity is still committed to sell the asset or disposal group. Otherwise the entity must cease to classify the asset as held for sale.

If an entity acquires a disposal group (eg, a subsidiary) exclusively with a view to its subsequent disposal it can classify the asset as held for sale only if the sale is expected to take place within one year and it is highly probable that all the other criteria will be met within a short time (normally three months).

An asset that is to be **abandoned** should not be classified as held for sale. This is because its carrying amount will be recovered principally through continuing use. However, a disposal group to be abandoned may meet the definition of a discontinued operation and therefore separate disclosure may be required (see below).

Question

Assets held for sale

On 1 December 20X3, a company became committed to a plan to sell a manufacturing facility and has already found a potential buyer. The company does not intend to discontinue the operations currently carried out in the facility. At 31 December 20X3 there is a backlog of uncompleted customer orders. The subsidiary will not be able to transfer the facility to the buyer until after it ceases to operate the facility and has eliminated the backlog of uncompleted customer orders. This is not expected to occur until spring 20X4.

Required

Can the manufacturing facility be classified as 'held for sale' at 31 December 20X3?

Answer

The facility will not be transferred until the backlog of orders is completed; this demonstrates that the facility is not available for immediate sale in its present condition. The facility cannot be classified as 'held for sale' at 31 December 20X3. It must be treated in the same way as other items of property, plant and equipment: it should continue to be depreciated and should not be separately disclosed.

6.3 Measurement of assets held for sale

Key terms

Fair value: the amount for which an asset could be exchanged, or a liability settled, between knowledgeable, willing parties in an arm's length transaction.

Costs to sell: the incremental costs directly attributable to the disposal of an asset (or disposal group), excluding finance costs and income tax expense.

Recoverable amount: the higher of an asset's fair value less costs to sell and its value in use.

Value in use: the present value of estimated future cash flows expected to arise from the continuing use of an asset and from its disposal at the end of its useful life.

A non-current asset (or disposal group) that is held for sale should be measured at the **lower of** its **carrying amount** and **fair value less costs to sell**. Fair value less costs to sell is equivalent to net realisable value.

An impairment loss should be recognised where fair value less costs to sell is lower than carrying amount. Note that this is an exception to the normal rule. IAS 36 *Impairment of assets* requires an entity to recognise an impairment loss only where an asset's recoverable amount is lower than its carrying value. Recoverable amount is defined as the higher of net realisable value and value in use. IAS 36 does not apply to assets held for sale.

Non-current assets held for sale **should not be depreciated**, even if they are still being used by the entity.

A non-current asset (or disposal group) that is **no longer classified as held for sale** (for example, because the sale has not taken place within one year) is measured at the **lower of**:

(a) Its **carrying amount** before it was classified as held for sale, adjusted for any depreciation that would have been charged had the asset not been held for sale

(b) Its **recoverable amount** at the date of the decision not to sell

6.4 Presenting discontinued operations

FAST FORWARD

The results of discontinued operations should be presented separately in the income statement.

Key terms

Discontinued operation: a component of an entity that has either been disposed of, or is classified as held for sale, and:

(a) Represents a separate major line of business or geographical area of operations

(b) Is part of a single co-ordinated plan to dispose of a separate major line of business or geographical area of operations, or

(c) Is a subsidiary acquired exclusively with a view to resale.

Component of an entity: operations and cash flows that can be clearly distinguished, operationally and for financial reporting purposes, from the rest of the entity.

An entity should **present and disclose information** that enables users of the financial statements to evaluate the financial effects of **discontinued operations** and disposals of non-current assets or disposal groups.

An entity should disclose a **single amount** on the **face of the income statement** comprising the total of:

(a) The **post-tax profit or loss** of discontinued operations and

(b) The post-tax gain or loss recognised on the **measurement to fair value less costs to sell** or on the disposal of the assets or disposal group(s) constituting the discontinued operation.

An entity should also disclose an **analysis** of this single amount into:

(a) The revenue, expenses and pre-tax profit or loss of discontinued operations

(b) The related income tax expense

(c) The gain or loss recognised on the measurement to fair value less costs to sell or on the disposal of the assets or disposal group(s) constituting the discontinued operation

(d) The related income tax expense

This may be presented either on the face of the income statement or in the notes. If it is presented on the face of the income statement it should be presented in a section identified as relating to discontinued operations, ie separately from continuing operations. This analysis is not required where the discontinued operation is a newly acquired subsidiary that has been classified as held for sale.

An entity should disclose the **net cash flows** attributable to the operating, investing and financing activities of discontinued operations. These disclosures may be presented either on the face of the cash flow statement or in the notes.

Gains and losses on the remeasurement of a disposal group that is not a discontinued operation but is held for sale should be included in profit or loss from continuing operations.

6.5 Illustration

The following illustration is taken from the implementation guidance to IFRS 5. Profit for the period from discontinued operations would be analysed in the notes.

XYZ GROUP
INCOME STATEMENT
FOR THE YEAR ENDED 31 DECEMBER 20X2

	20X2	*20X1*
	$'000	$'000
Continuing operations		
Revenue	X	X
Cost of sales	(X)	(X)
Gross profit	X	X
Other income	X	X
Distribution costs	(X)	(X)
Administrative expenses	(X)	(X)
Other expenses	(X)	(X)
Finance costs	(X)	(X)
Share of profit of associates	X	X
Profit before tax	X	X
Income tax expense	(X)	(X)
Profit for the period from continuing operations	X	X
Discontinued operations		
Profit for the period from discontinued operations	X	X
Profit for the period	X	X
Attributable to:		
Equity holders of the parent	X	X
Minority interest	X	X
	X	X

An alternative to this presentation would be to analyse the profit from discontinued operations in a separate column on the face of the income statement.

Question

Discontinued operation

On 20 October 20X3 the directors of a parent company made a public announcement of plans to close a steel works. The closure means that the group will no longer carry out this type of operation, which until recently has represented about 10% of its total sales revenue. The works will be gradually shut down over a period of several months, with complete closure expected in July 20X4. At 31 December output had been significantly reduced and some redundancies had already taken place. The cash flows, revenues and expenses relating to the steel works can be clearly distinguished from those of the subsidiary's other operations.

Required

How should the closure be treated in the financial statements for the year ended 31 December 20X3?

Answer

Because the steel works is being closed, rather than sold, it cannot be classified as 'held for sale'. In addition, the steel works is not a discontinued operation. Although at 31 December 20X3 the group was firmly committed to the closure, this has not yet taken place and therefore the steel works must be included in continuing operations. Information about the planned closure could be disclosed in the notes to the financial statements.

6.6 Presentation of a non-current asset or disposal group classified as held for sale

Non-current assets and disposal groups classified as held for sale should be **presented separately** from other assets in the balance sheet. The liabilities of a disposal group should be presented separately from other liabilities in the balance sheet.

(a) Assets and liabilities held for sale **should not be offset**.

(b) The **major classes** of assets and liabilities held for sale should be **separately disclosed** either on the face of the balance sheet or in the notes.

6.7 Additional disclosures

In the period in which a non-current asset (or disposal group) has been either classified as held for sale or sold the following should be disclosed.

(a) A **description** of the non-current asset (or disposal group)

(b) A description of the **facts and circumstances** of the disposal

(c) Any **gain or loss** recognised when the item was classified as held for sale

(d) If applicable, the **segment** in which the non-current asset (or disposal group) is presented in accordance with IAS 14 *Segment reporting*

Where an asset previously classified as held for sale is **no longer held for sale**, the entity should disclose a description of the facts and circumstances leading to the decision and its effect on results.

Exam focus point

Discontinued operations were examined in a Section B question in November 2005.

7 IAS 14 Segment reporting

FAST FORWARD

IAS 14 distinguishes:

- Business segments
- Geographical segments

It is important to distinguish between these.

7.1 Why segment reporting?

Large entities produce a wide range of products and services, often in several different countries. Further information on how the overall results of entities are made up from each of these product or geographical areas will help the users of the financial statements. This is the reason for **segment reporting**.

(a) The entity's **past performance** will be better understood
(b) The entity's **risks and returns** may be better assessed
(c) More **informed judgements** may be made about the entity as a whole

Risks and returns of a **diversified, multi-national company** can only be assessed by looking at the individual risks and rewards attached to groups of products or services or in different groups of products or services or in different geographical areas. These are subject to differing rates of profitability, opportunities for growth, future prospects and risks.

7.2 Scope

Only entities whose **equity or debt securities are publicly traded** (ie on a stock exchange) need disclose segment information. This includes entities issuing securities. Other entities that produce financial statements which comply with IASs are encouraged to disclose segment information voluntarily (in such cases IAS 14 must be followed entirely, not simply in part).

7.3 Definitions

There are so many definitions in the standard that they are broken down by category.

7.3.1 Definitions from other standards

The definitions of **operating activities, accounting policies** and **revenue** as given by IAS 8 (see above) and IAS 18 are reproduced.

7.3.2 Definitions of business segment and geographical segment

These are the most important definitions in the standard, and it is vital that you learn the listed factors for business and geographical segments as these affect the rest of the standard.

Key terms

A **business segment** is a distinguishable component of an entity that is engaged in providing an individual product or service or a group of related products or services and that is subject to risks and returns that are different from those of other business segments. Factors that should be considered in determining whether products and services are related include:

(a) The nature of the products or services

(b) The nature of the production processes

(c) The type or class of customer for the products or services

(d) The methods used to distribute the products or provide the services

(e) If applicable, the nature of the regulatory environment, for example, banking, insurance, or public utilities

A **geographical segment** is a distinguishable component of an entity that is engaged in providing products or services within a particular economic environment and that is subject to risks and returns that are different from those of components operating in other economic environments. Factors that should be considered in identifying geographical segments include:

(a) Similarity of economic and political conditions
(b) Relationships between operations in different geographical areas
(c) Proximity of operations
(d) Special risks associated with operations in a particular area
(e) Exchange control regulations
(f) The underlying currency risks

A **reportable segment** is a business segment or a geographical segment identified based on the foregoing definitions for which segment information is required to be disclosed by IAS 14.

(IAS 14)

All the products or services produced by a segment will be similar with respect to a **majority of the factors** in the definition of a **business segment** (these factors are given in no particular order).

The case is similar for **geographical segments**. These may consist of one country, two or more countries or a region within a country, but they do not include operations in economic environments with significantly differing risks and returns.

IAS 14 argues that entities are organised and managed according to the predominant sources of risk. Their structure and financial reporting systems can therefore be used to identify segments. These should indicate whether the entity's risks and returns are influenced mainly by the geographical **location of its operations** or by the **location of its markets**. Either method can be used to identify geographical segments (ie either by origin or destination of sales).

There is obviously a significant level of judgement required to determine the composition of a segment. The qualitative characteristics of financial statements, as laid out in the IASB's *Framework* should be considered.

7.3.3 Definitions of segment revenue, expense, result, assets and liabilities

These definitions come into play **once segments have been identified**.

Key terms

Segment revenue is revenue reported in the entity's income statement that is directly attributable to a segment and the relevant portion of entity revenue that can be allocated on a reasonable basis to a segment, whether from sales to external customers or from transactions with other segments of the same entity. Segment revenue does *not* include:

(a) Interest or dividend income, including interest earned on advances or loans to other segments, unless the segment's operations are primarily of a financial nature

(b) Gains on sales of investments or gains on extinguishment of debt unless the segment's operations are primarily of a financial nature

Segment expense is expense resulting from the operating activities of a segment that is directly attributable to the segment and the relevant portion of an expense that can be allocated on a reasonable basis to the segment, including expenses relating to sales to external customers and expenses relating to transactions with other segments of the same entity. Segment expense does not include:

(a) Interest, including interest incurred on advances or loans from other segments, unless the segment's operations are primarily of a financial nature

(b) Losses on sales of investments or losses on extinguishment of debt unless the segment's operations are primarily of a financial nature

(c) Income tax expense

(d) General administrative expenses, head office expenses, and other expenses that arise at the entity level and relate to the entity as a whole. However, costs are sometimes incurred at the entity level on behalf of a segment. Such costs are segment expenses if they relate to the segment's operating activities and they can be directly attributed or allocated to the segment on a reasonable basis

Segment result is segment revenue less segment expense. Segment result is determined before any adjustments for minority interest.

Segment assets are those operating assets that are employed by a segment in its operating activities and that either are directly attributable to the segment or can be allocated to the segment on a reasonable basis.

- If a segment's segment result includes interest or dividend income, its segment assets include the related receivables, loans, investments, or other income-producing assets.
- Segment assets do not include income tax assets.

Segment liabilities are those operating liabilities that result from the operating activities of a segment and that either are directly attributable to the segment or can be allocated to the segment on a reasonable basis.

- If a segment's segment result includes interest expense, its segment liabilities include the related interest-bearing liabilities.
- Segment liabilities do not include income tax liabilities

Segment accounting policies are the accounting policies adopted for preparing and presenting the financial statements of the consolidated group or entity as well as those accounting policies that relate specifically to segment reporting. (*IAS 14*)

You can see from these definitions that only those amounts **directly attributable** to a segment should be included in the segment information.

Normally, internal financial reporting will be along these lines. Occasionally, however, amounts may be allocated to segments for management purposes which seem arbitrary or subjective. Alternatively, an entity may not allocate all items to segments which should be on a reasonable basis. In both these cases, the segment figures would **require adjustment**.

In relation to **segment assets**, if depreciation or amortisation is included as a segment expense, then the **respective asset** must be shown as a segment asset. Such assets may be shared between segments, but assets **held for the head office or for general purposes should be excluded.**

Segment liabilities do *not* include borrowings, liabilities resulting from finance leases, and other liabilities undertaken for **financing rather than operating purposes**. As with depreciation, if interest expense is included in the segment result, the related interest-bearing debt must be included in segment liabilities.

Exam focus point

The May 2005 exam had a very simple question on IAS 14. Just make sure you understand the basics here.

8 Identifying reportable segments

FAST FORWARD

IAS 14 adopts a **management approach** to determining reportable segments.

8.1 Primary and secondary segments

IAS 14 requires management to assess the dominant source and nature of an entity's risks and returns in order to assess whether the **primary segment reporting format** will be by business segment or geographical segment. The other format will then be given as a **secondary segment report**.

Dominant source and nature	Primary segment report	Secondary segment report
Business	Business	Geographical
Geographical	Geographical	Business

How is this decision made? IAS 14 states that it should be based on:

(a) An entity's internal organisational and management structure

(b) The system of internal financial reporting to the board of directors and chief executive officer

There are borderline or difficult cases which must be considered, although these will be very rare: in most cases the choice should be fairly obvious.

Dominant source and nature	Primary segment report	Secondary segment report
Both	Business	Geographical
Neither	Management choice, but show one as primary and one as secondary	

Where risks and rates of return are strongly affected by **both** products/services **and** by geography, this will usually be evidenced by a 'matrix approach' to managing the company and internal reporting. A '**matrix**'

presentation, where both business and geographical segments are reported as primary segment reporting formats, will often be useful in such situations. This is neither required nor prohibited by IAS 14.

An organisation may be based around neither products/services nor geographical areas, but, say, by legal entity. Management should be able to assess which of the product/service or geographical influences is dominant, thus allowing **comparability** with other similar entities by the disclosure of segment information.

8.2 Business and geographical segments

Both types of segment, for external reporting purposes, should be those **organisational units** for which information is reported to the board/CEO.

Where directors have had to make a **choice** of which should be the primary reporting format, in the circumstances laid out in Paragraph 8.1 above, then they should use the factors given in the **definitions of business, geographical and reportable segments** in Section 7 above, rather than on the basis of internal financial reporting. There are, however, various rules to be followed.

(a) Internally reported segments that meet the definitions (given in Section 7 above) **should not be further segmented**, even when other segments exist which do not meet the definitions.

(b) For those segments which do not meet the definitions, management should look at the **next lower level of segmentation** that reports information along product/service or geographical lines according to the definitions in Section 7.

(c) Where lower-level segments identified in (b) meet the relevant definitions, the criteria discussed below for identifying reportable segments should be applied to those segments.

If this procedure were not followed, an entity would be creating segments for external reporting purposes only. The approach adopted by the standard, of looking at the organisational and management structure and internal financial reporting system, is often called the **'management approach'**. The components for which information is reported internally are sometimes called **'operating segments'**.

8.3 Reportable segments

There are various rules on what comprises a reportable segment.

8.3.1 Combining segments

Internally reported business segments (two or more) can be **combined** to form a single business or geographical segment if they are **substantially similar**. This will only be the case if:

(a) They demonstrate similar **long-term financial performance** *and*
(b) They are similar in **all the factors** given in the definition of segments (see Section 7)

8.3.2 Material segments: 10% threshold rule

There is a **materiality rule**, which we could call the 10% rule. A business or geographical segment is a reportable segment if the majority of its revenue is earned from sales to external customers *and* any of the following applies.

(a) Segment internal and external **revenue** is 10% or more of total internal and external revenue of all segments.

(b) Segment **result** (profit *or* loss) is 10% or more of the combined result of all segments in profit *or* the combined result of all segments in loss (whichever is greater in absolute amount).

(c) Segment assets are 10% or more of the total assets of all segments.

8.3.3 Non-material segments

The question then arises as to what should be done with an internally reported segment which is below all the thresholds of significance given in Paragraph 8.3.2. The choice is as follows.

(a) The segment is designated as a reportable segment **despite its size**

(b) If not, **combine with other segments that are also below the thresholds** to form a separately reportable segment. These must be similar, according to the definition of business/geographical segments.

(c) If neither of the above, include the segment as an **unallocated reconciling item**.

8.3.4 75% rule

There is yet another rule! This, presumably, is to prevent entities from avoiding reporting some segmental information by bundling it up in 'unallocated reconciling items'. This rule states that the total revenue of identified reportable segments must represent **75% or more of the total revenue of the entity**. Where this is not the case, the management must identify further reportable segments, even where they do not meet the 10% threshold. This will carry on until the 75% of total has been achieved.

8.4 Segment accounting policies

An entity should adopt the **same accounting policies** for preparing segment information as it uses for preparing the financial statements of the entity. Additional segment information prepared on the basis of other policies (eg for internal purposes) may be disclosed, as long as it *is* reported internally *and* the basis of measurement used is reported.

Assets that are jointly used can be allocated to each relevant segment *only if* their related revenues and expenses are also allocated to those segments.

IAS 14 provides a **decision tree** (on the next page) which applies all of these rules, which you may find helpful.

Question — **Segment reporting**

The Multitrade Co has three divisions (all based in the home country, the UK), A. B and C. Details of their revenues, results and net assets are given below.

	$'000
Division A	
Sales to B	304,928
Other UK sales	57,223
Middle East export sales	406,082
Pacific fringe export sales	77,838
	846,071
Division B	
Sales to C	31,034
Export sales to Europe	195,915
	226,949
Division C	
Export sales to North America	127,003

	Head office	Division A	Division B	Division C
		$'000	$'000	$'000
Operational profit/(loss) before tax		162,367	18,754	(8,303)
Re-allocated costs from				
Head office		48,362	24,181	24,181
Interest costs		3,459	6,042	527
	$'000			
Non-current assets	49,071	200,921	41,612	113,076
Net current assets	47,800	121,832	39,044	92,338
Non-current liabilities	28,636	16,959	6,295	120,841

Required

Prepare a segment report in accordance with IAS 14 for publication in Multitrade's accounts, on the basis that the primary report will be based on business segments.

Answer

Ignoring comparative figures, Multitrade Co's segment report would look like this.

CLASSES OF BUSINESS

	Group	*Division A*	*Division B*	*Division C*
	$'000	$'000	$'000	$'000
Revenue *				
Total sales	1,200,023	846,071	226,949	127,003
Inter-segment sales	335,962	304,928	31,034	–
Sales to third parties	864,061	541,143	195,915	127,003
Profit before taxation				
Segment profit/(loss)	172,818	162,367	18,754	(8,303)
Common costs **	96,724			
Operating profit	76,094			
Net interest	10,028			
Group profit before tax	66,066			
Net assets				
Segment net assets	608,823	322,753	80,656	205,414
Unallocated assets	96,871			
Unallocated non-current liabilities	(172,731)			
Total net assets	532,963			

Tutor's hint. As the interest charge does not relate specifically to each segment, the non-current liabilities are also not allocated to each segment.

GEOGRAPHICAL SEGMENTS

	Group	*United Kingdom*	*Middle East*	*Pacific fringe*	*Europe*	*North America*
	$'000	$'000	$'000	$'000	$'000	$'000
Revenue						
Sales by segment ***						
Sales to third parties	864,061	57,223	406,082	77,838	195,915	127,003

* Revenue, profit, net interest and net assets should be the same as those shown in the accounts.

** Common costs and unallocated assets are those items in the accounts which cannot reasonably be allocated to any one segment. An example of a common cost is the cost of maintaining the holding company share register, and an example of an unallocated asset might be the head office building.

*** Sales by segment may be disclosed by origin or destination. Here all sales originate in the UK, so it is sensible to disclose sales by destination.

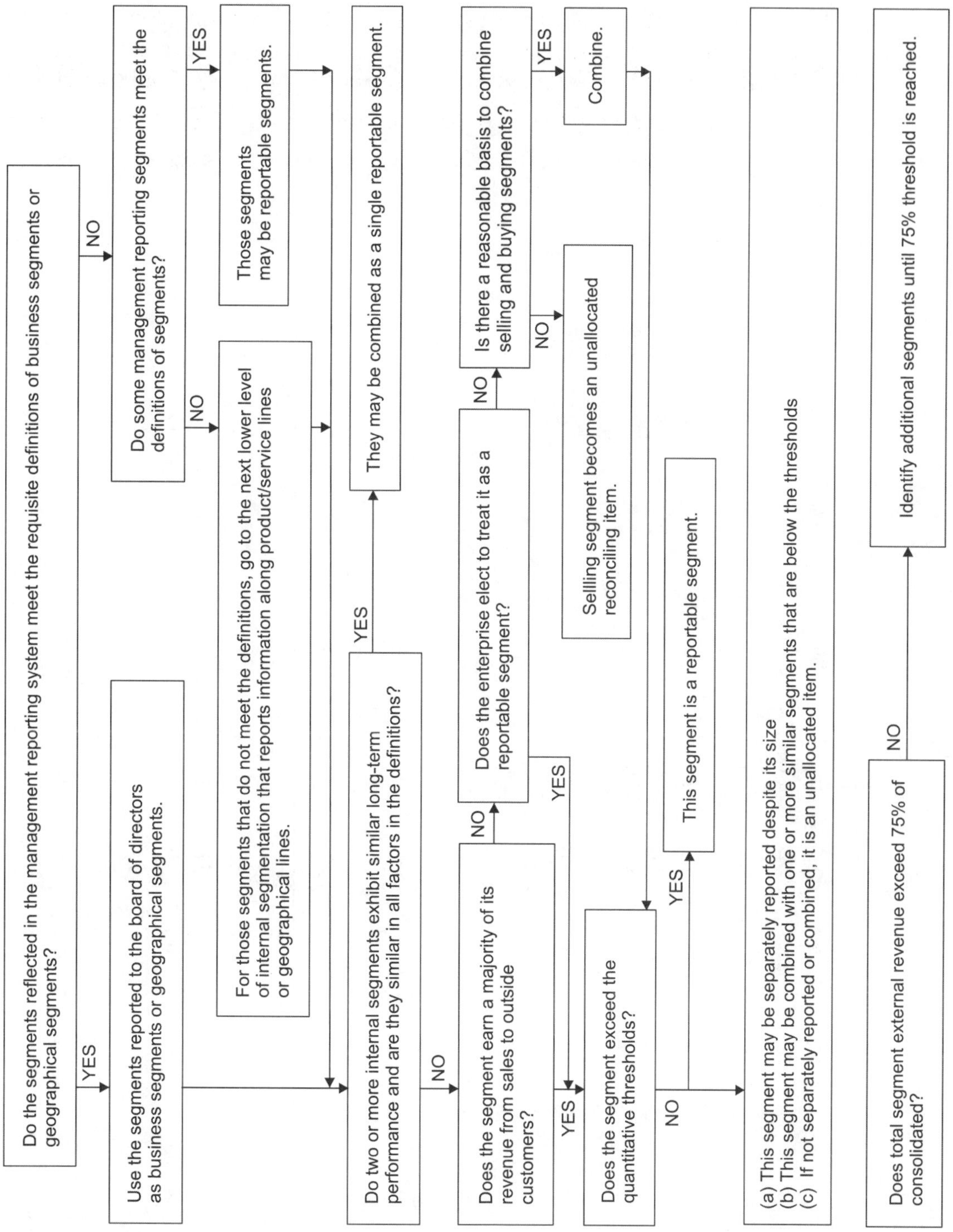

8.5 Example

IAS 14 gives the following illustrative example of a segmental report for a diversified multinational. You will not meet anything as complex as this in your exam, but it shows those items which are allocated between segments and those which are not.

	Paper products		*Office products*		*Publishing*		*Other operations*		*Eliminations*		*Consolidated*	
	20X2	*20X1*	*20X2*	*20X1*	*20X2*	*20X1*	*20X2*	*20X1*	*20X2*	*20X1*	*20X2*	*20X1*
	$m	$m	$m	$m	$m	$m	$m	$m	$m	$m	$m	$m
Revenue												
External sales	55	50	20	17	19	16	7	7				
Inter-segment sales	15	10	10	14	2	4	2	2	(29)	(30)		
Total revenue	70	60	30	31	21	20	9	9	(29)	(30)	101	90
Result												
Segment result	20	17	9	7	2	1	0	0	(1)	(1)	30	24
Unallocated corporate expenses											(7)	(9)
Operating profit											23	15
Interest expense											(4)	(4)
Interest income											2	3
Share of net profits of associates	6	5					2	2			8	7
Income taxes											(7)	(4)
Profit											22	17
Other information												
Segment assets	54	50	34	30	10	10	10	9			108	99
Investment in equity method associates	20	16					12	10			32	26
Unallocated corporate assets											35	30
Consolidated total assets											175	155
Segment liabilities	25	15	8	11	8	8	1	1			42	35
Unallocated corporate liabilities											40	55
Consolidated total liabilities											82	90
Capital expenditure	12	10	3	5	5		4	3				
Depreciation	9	7	9	7	5	3	3	4				
Non cash expenses other than depreciation	8	2	7	3	2	2	2	1				

Chapter Roundup

- The material on accounting policies has been transferred into IAS 8 from IAS 1.
- Changes in accounting estimates are **not** applied retrospectively.
- Prior period errors will require **retrospective** correction if they are **material**.
- **IFRS 5** *Non-current assets held for sale and discontinued operations* requires assets 'held for sale' to be presented separately on the face of the balance sheet.
- The results of discontinued operations should be presented separately in the income statement.
- Another important aspect of reporting financial performance is **segment reporting**.
- **IAS 14** adopts a **management approach** to determining reportable segments.
- The most important **definitions** are of:
  - Business segments
  - Geographical segments
- These definitions include **factors** which are used to determine whether products/services are related or whether a geographical segment exists. You must **learn these** as the rest of the standard is based on them.
- Other definitions are also important. You should be particularly careful about what is **included in and excluded from**:
  - Segment revenue
  - Segment expense
  - Segment assets
  - Segment liabilities
- Do not worry too much about the detailed **disclosure requirements**. These are unlikely to be of great importance in the exam.

Quick Quiz

1. How should a prior period error be corrected under IAS 8?
2. Give three circumstances when a change in accounting policy might be required.
3. When can a non-current asset be classified as held for sale?
4. How should an asset held for sale be measured?
5. How does IFRS 5 define a discontinued operation?
6. What approach should normally be taken when deciding whether business or geographical segments should be the primary reporting format?

Answers to Quick Quiz

1 By adjusting the opening balance of retained earnings.

2 (a) By statute
(b) By the IASB
(c) For a more appropriate presentation

3 See Para 6.2

4 At the lower of its carrying amount and fair value less costs to sell.

5 See Para 6.4

6 Assess the dominant source and nature of the entity's risks and returns.

Now try the question below from the Exam Question Bank

Number	Level	Marks	Time
Q13	Examination	5	9 mins

5

Accounting for non-current assets

Introduction

IAS 16 should be familiar to you from your earlier studies, as should the mechanics of accounting for depreciation, revaluations of long-term (non-current) assets and disposals of non-current assets. Some questions are given here for revision purposes.

IAS 36 on impairment is a recent, therefore topical, standard.

IAS 16 and **IAS 36** have recently been revised.

IAS 23 deals with the treatment of funds used in self-constructed assets.

Topic list	Learning outcomes	Syllabus references	Ability required
1 Depreciation accounting	C (iii)	C (4)	Application
2 IAS 16 *Property, plant and equipment*	C (iii)	C (4)	Application
3 IAS 36 *Impairment of assets*	C (iii)	C (11)	Application
4 IAS 23 *Borrowing costs*	C (iii)	C (8)	Application

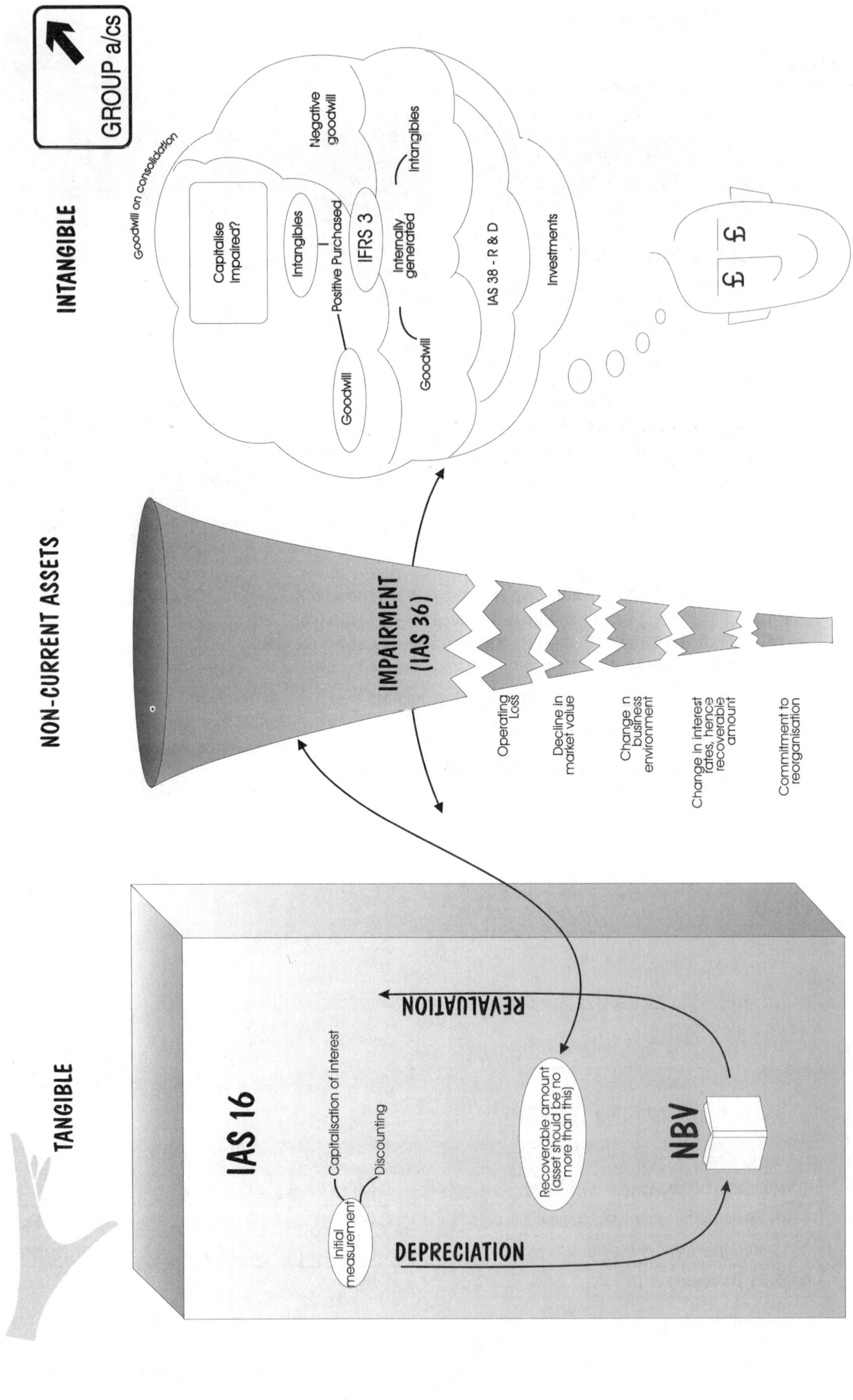
GROUP a/cs
INTANGIBLE
Goodwill on consolidation
Capitalise
Impaired?
Negative goodwill
Intangibles
Positive Purchased
IFRS 3
Goodwill
Internally generated
Intangibles
Goodwill
IAS 38 - R & D
Investments
£
£
NON-CURRENT ASSETS
IMPAIRMENT (IAS 36)
Operating Loss
Decline in market value
Change n business environment
Change in interest rates, hence recoverable amount
Commitment to reorganisation
TANGIBLE
IAS 16
Initial measurement
Capitalisation of interest
Discounting
REVALUATION
Recoverable amount (asset should be no more than this)
NBV
DEPRECIATION

1 Depreciation accounting

FAST FORWARD

The **cost of a non-current asset**, less its estimated residual value, is allocated fairly between accounting periods by means of depreciation. The provision for depreciation is both:

- Charged against profit
- Deducted from the value of the non-current asset in the balance sheet

1.1 Non-current assets

Where assets held by an entity have a **limited useful life** to that entity it is necessary to apportion the value of an asset used in a period against the revenue it has helped to create. If an asset's life extends over more than one accounting period, it earns profits over more than one period. It is a **non-current asset**.

With the exception of land held on freehold or very long leasehold, **every non-current asset eventually wears out over time**. Machines, cars and other vehicles, fixtures and fittings, and even buildings do not last for ever. When a business acquires a non-current asset, it will have some idea about how long its useful life will be, and it might decide what to do with it.

(a) Keep on using the non-current asset until it becomes **completely worn out**, useless, and worthless.

(b) **Sell off** the non-current asset at the end of its useful life, either by selling it as a second-hand item or as scrap.

Since a non-current asset has a cost, and a limited useful life, and its value eventually declines, it follows that a charge should be made in the income statement to reflect the use that is made of the asset by the business. This charge is called **depreciation**.

1.2 Scope

Depreciation accounting is governed by IAS 16 *Property, plant and equipment* which we will look at in Section 2 of this chapter. However, this section will deal with some of the IAS 16 definitions concerning depreciation.

Key terms

Depreciation is the result of systematic allocation of the depreciable amount of an asset over its useful life.

Property, plant and equipment are tangible items that:

- Are expected to be used during more than one accounting period; and
- Are held for use in the production or supply of goods and service, for rental to others, or for administrative purposes

Useful life is one of two things.

- The period over which an asset is expected to be available for use by an entity
- The number of production or similar units expected to be obtained from the asset by the entity.

Depreciable amount of a depreciable asset is the cost of an asset or other amount substituted for cost, less its residual value.

(IAS 16)

An 'amount substituted for cost' will normally be a **current market value** after a revaluation has taken place.

1.3 Depreciation

IAS 16 requires the depreciable amount of a depreciable asset to be allocated on a **systematic basis** to each accounting period during the useful life of the asset. **Every part of an item of property, plant and equipment with a cost that is significant in relation to the total cost of the item must be depreciated separately**.

One way of defining depreciation is to describe it as a means of **spreading the cost** of a non-current asset over its useful life, and so matching the cost against the full period during which it earns profits for the business. Depreciation charges are an example of the application of the accruals assumption.

There are situations where, over a period, an asset has **increased in value**, ie its current value is greater than the carrying value in the financial statements. You might think that in such situations it would not be necessary to depreciate the asset. The standard states, however, that this is irrelevant, and that depreciation should still be charged to each accounting period, based on the depreciable amount, irrespective of a rise in value.

An entity is required to begin depreciating an item of property, plant and equipment when it is available for use and to continue depreciating it until it is derecognised even if it is idle during the period.

1.4 Useful life

The following factors should be considered when **estimating the useful life** of a depreciable asset.

- Expected **physical wear and tear**
- **Obsolescence**
- Legal or other **limits** on the use of the assets

Once decided, the useful life should be **reviewed at least every financial year end** and depreciation rates adjusted for the current and future periods if expectations vary significantly from the original estimates. The effect of the change should be disclosed in the accounting period in which the change takes place.

The assessment of useful life requires **judgement** based on previous experience with similar assets or classes of asset. When a completely new type of asset is acquired (ie through technological advancement or through use in producing a brand new product or service) it is still necessary to estimate useful life, even though the exercise will be much more difficult.

The standard also points out that the physical life of the asset might be longer than its useful life to the entity in question. One of the main factors to be taken into consideration is the **physical wear and tear** the asset is likely to endure. This will depend on various circumstances, including the number of shifts for which the asset will be used, the entity's repair and maintenance programme and so on. Other factors to be considered include obsolescence (due to technological advances/improvements in production/reduction in demand for the product/service produced by the asset) and legal restrictions, eg length of a related lease.

1.5 Residual value

In most cases the residual value of an asset is **likely to be immaterial**. If it is likely to be of any significant value, that value must be estimated at the date of purchase or any subsequent revaluation. The amount of residual value should be estimated based on the current situation with other similar assets, used in the same way, which are now at the end of their useful lives. Any expected costs of disposal should be offset against the gross residual value.

1.6 Depreciation methods

Consistency is important. The depreciation method selected should be applied consistently from period to period unless altered circumstances justify a change. When the method *is* changed, the effect should be quantified and disclosed and the reason for the change should be stated.

Various methods of allocating depreciation to accounting periods are available, but whichever is chosen must be applied **consistently** (as required by IAS 1), to ensure comparability from period to period. Change of policy is not allowed simply because of the profitability situation of the entity.

You should be familiar with the various **accepted methods of allocating depreciation** and the relevant calculations and accounting treatments, which are revised in questions at the end of this section.

1.7 Disclosure

An accounting policy note should disclose the **valuation bases** used for determining the amounts at which depreciable assets are stated, along with the other accounting policies.

IAS 16 also requires the following to be disclosed for each major class of depreciable asset.

- **Depreciation methods** used
- **Useful lives** or the depreciation rates used
- **Gross amount** of depreciable assets and the related accumulated depreciation at the beginning and end of the period

1.8 What is depreciation?

The need to depreciate non-current assets arises from the **accruals assumption**. If money is expended in purchasing an asset then the amount expended must at some time be charged against profits. If the asset is one which contributes to an entity's revenue over a number of accounting periods it would be inappropriate to charge any single period (eg the period in which the asset was acquired) with the whole of the expenditure. Instead, some method must be found of spreading the cost of the asset over its useful economic life.

This view of depreciation as a process of allocation of the cost of an asset over several accounting periods is the view adopted by IAS 16. It is worth mentioning here two **common misconceptions** about the purpose and effects of depreciation.

(a) It is sometimes thought that the net book value (NBV) of an asset is equal to its net realisable value and that the object of charging depreciation is to **reflect the fall in value of an asset over its life**. This misconception is the basis of a common, but incorrect, argument which says that freehold properties (say) need not be depreciated in times when property values are rising. It is true that historical cost balance sheets often give a misleading impression when a property's NBV is much below its market value, but in such a case it is open to a business to incorporate a revaluation into its books, or even to prepare its accounts based on current costs. This is a separate problem from that of allocating the property's cost over successive accounting periods.

(b) Another misconception is that depreciation is provided **so that an asset can be replaced at the end of its useful life**. This is not the case.

  (i) If there is no intention of replacing the asset, it could then be argued that there is no need to provide for any depreciation at all.

  (ii) If prices are rising, the replacement cost of the asset will exceed the amount of depreciation provided.

Question — Depreciation

A lorry bought for a business cost $17,000. It is expected to last for five years and then be sold for scrap for $2,000. Usage over the five years is expected to be:

Year 1	200 days
Year 2	100 days
Year 3	100 days
Year 4	150 days
Year 5	40 days

Required

Work out the depreciation to be charged each year under:

(a) The straight line method
(b) The reducing balance method (using a rate of 35%)
(c) The machine hour method

Answer

(a) Under the straight line method, depreciation for each of the five years is:

$$\text{Annual depreciation} = \frac{\$(17{,}000 - 2{,}000)}{5} = \$3{,}000$$

(b) Under the reducing balance method, depreciation for each of the five years is:

Year	*Depreciation*		
1	35% × $17,000	=	$5,950
2	35% × ($17,000 – $5,950) = 35% × $11,050	=	$3,868
3	35% × ($11,050 – $3,868) = 35% × $7,182	=	$2,514
4	35% × ($7,182 – $2,514) = 35% × $4,668	=	$1,634
5	Balance to bring book value down to $2,000 = $4,668 – $1,634 – $2,000	=	$1,034

(c) Under the machine hour method, depreciation for each of the five years is calculated as follows.

Total usage (days) = 200 + 100 + 100 + 150 + 40 = 590 days

$$\text{Depreciation per day} = \frac{\$(17{,}000 - 2{,}000)}{590} = \$25.42$$

Year	*Usage (days)*	*Depreciation ($) (days × $25.42)*
1	200	5,084.00
2	100	2,542.00
3	100	2,542.00
4	150	3,813.00
5	40	1,016.80
		14,997.80

Note. The answer does not come to exactly $15,000 because of the rounding carried out at the 'depreciation per day' stage of the calculation.

Question — Depreciation

(a) What are the purposes of providing for depreciation?

(b) In what circumstances is the reducing balance method more appropriate than the straight-line method? Give reasons for your answer.

Answer

(a) The accounts of a business try to recognise that the cost of a non-current asset is gradually consumed as the asset wears out. This is done by gradually writing off the asset's cost in the income statement over several accounting periods. This process is known as depreciation, and is an example of the accruals assumption. IAS 16 *Property, plant and equipment* requires that depreciation should be allocated on a systematic basis to each accounting period during the useful life of the asset.

With regard to the accrual principle, it is fair that the profits should be reduced by the depreciation charge; this is not an arbitrary exercise. Depreciation is not, as is sometimes supposed, an attempt to set aside funds to purchase new non-current assets when required. Depreciation is not generally provided on freehold land because it does not 'wear out' (unless it is held for mining etc).

(b) The reducing balance method of depreciation is used instead of the straight line method when it is considered fair to allocate a greater proportion of the total depreciable amount to the earlier years and a lower proportion to the later years on the assumption that the benefits obtained by the business from using the asset decline over time.

In favour of this method it may be argued that it links the depreciation charge to the costs of maintaining and running the asset. In the early years these costs are low and the depreciation charge is high, while in later years this is reversed.

Question — Accounting entries

A business purchased two rivet-making machines on 1 January 20X5 at a cost of $15,000 each. Each had an estimated life of five years and a nil residual value. The straight line method of depreciation is used.

Owing to an unforeseen slump in market demand for rivets, the business decided to reduce its output of rivets, and switch to making other products instead. On 31 March 20X7, one rivet-making machine was sold (on credit) to a buyer for $8,000.

Later in the year, however, it was decided to abandon production of rivets altogether, and the second machine was sold on 1 December 20X7 for $2,500 cash.

Prepare the machinery account, provision for depreciation of machinery account and disposal of machinery account for the accounting year to 31 December 20X7.

Answer

MACHINERY ACCOUNT

		$			$
20X7			*20X7*		
1 Jan	Balance b/f	30,000	31 Mar	Disposal of machinery account	15,000
			1 Dec	Disposal of machinery account	15,000
		30,000			30,000

PROVISION FOR DEPRECIATION OF MACHINERY

		$			$
20X7			*20X7*		
31 Mar	Disposal of machinery account*	6,750	1 Jan	Balance b/f	12,000
1 Dec	Disposal of machinery account**	8,750	31 Dec	Income statement***	3,500
		15,500			15,500

* Depreciation at date of disposal = $6,000 + $750

** Depreciation at date of disposal = $6,000 + $2,750

*** Depreciation charge for the year = $750 + $2,750

DISPOSAL OF MACHINERY

		$			$
20X7			*20X7*		
31 Mar	Machinery account	15,000	31 Mar	Account receivable (sale price)	8,000
1 Dec	Machinery account	15,000	31 Mar	Provision for depreciation	6,750
			1 Dec	Cash (sale price)	2,500
			1 Dec	Provision for depreciation	8,750
			31 Dec	Income statement (loss on disposal)	4,000
		30,000			30,000

You should be able to calculate that there was a loss on the first disposal of $250, and on the second disposal of $3,750, giving a total loss of $4,000.

Workings

1 At 1 January 20X7, accumulated depreciation on the machines will be:

2 machines × 2 years × $\frac{\$15{,}000}{5}$ per machine pa = $12,000, or $6,000 per machine

2 Monthly depreciation is $\frac{\$3{,}000}{12}$ = $250 per machine per month

3 The machines are disposed of in 20X7.

(a) On 31 March – after 3 months of the year. Depreciation for the year on the machine = 3 months × $250 = $750.

(b) On 1 December – after 11 months of the year. Depreciation for the year on the machine = 11 months × $250 = $2,750

2 IAS 16 Property, plant and equipment

FAST FORWARD

IAS 16 *Property, plant and equipment* provides the basic rules on **depreciation**, including important definitions of depreciation, depreciable assets, useful life and depreciable amount.

2.1 Application of IAS 16

This standard covers all aspects of accounting for property, plant and equipment. This represents the bulk of items which are **'tangible' non-current assets**. The standard was revised in December 2003.

2.2 Scope

IAS 16 should be followed when accounting for property, plant and equipment *unless* another international accounting standard requires a **different treatment**.

IAS 16 **does not apply** to the following.

(a) Biological assets related to agricultural activity
(b) Mineral rights and mineral reserves, such as oil, gas and other non-regenerative resources

However, the standard applies to property, plant and equipment used to develop these assets.

2.3 Definitions

The standard gives a large number of definitions.

Key terms

Property, plant and equipment are tangible assets that:

- are held for use in the production or supply of goods or services, for rental to others, or for administrative purposes; and
- are expected to be used during more than one period.

Cost is the amount of cash or cash equivalents paid or the fair value of the other consideration given to acquire an asset at the time of its acquisition or construction.

Residual value is the net amount which the entity expects to obtain for an asset at the end of its useful life after deducting the expected costs of disposal.

Entity-specific value is the present value of the cash flows an entity expects to arise from the continuing use of an asset and from its disposal at the end of its useful life, or expects to incur when settling a liability.

Fair value is the amount for which an asset could be exchanged between knowledgeable, willing parties in an arm's length transaction.

Carrying amount is the amount at which an asset is recognised in the balance sheet after deducting any accumulated depreciation and accumulated impairment losses.

An **impairment loss** is the amount by which the carrying amount of an asset exceeds its recoverable amount. *(IAS 16)*

Exam focus point

These definitions are important. Make sure you know them all for the exam.

2.4 Recognition

In this context, recognition simply means incorporation of the item in the business's accounts, in this case as a non-current asset. The recognition of property, plant and equipment depends on two criteria.

(a) It is probable that **future economic benefits** associated with the asset will flow to the entity
(b) The cost of the asset to the entity can be **measured reliably**

These recognition criteria apply to **subsequent expenditure** as well as costs incurred initially. There are no longer any separate criteria for recognising subsequent expenditure.

Property, plant and equipment can amount to **substantial amounts** in financial statements, affecting the presentation of the company's financial position (in the balance sheet) and the profitability of the entity, through depreciation and also if an asset is wrongly classified as an expense and taken to the income statement.

2.4.1 First criterion: future economic benefits

The **degree of certainty** attached to the flow of future economic benefits must be assessed. This should be based on the evidence available at the date of initial recognition (usually the date of purchase). The entity should thus be assured that it will receive the rewards attached to the asset and it will incur the associated risks, which will only generally be the case when the rewards and risks have actually passed to the entity. Until then, the asset should not be recognised.

2.4.2 Second criterion: cost measured reliably

It is generally easy to measure the cost of an asset as the **transfer amount on purchase**, ie what was paid for it. **Self-constructed assets** can also be measured easily by adding together the purchase price of all the constituent parts (labour, material etc) paid to external parties.

2.5 Separate items

Most of the time assets will be identified individually, but this will not be the case for **smaller items**, such as tools, dies and moulds, which are sometimes classified as inventory and written off as an expense.

Major components or spare parts, however, should be recognised as property, plant and equipment.

For very **large and specialised items**, an apparently single asset should be broken down into its composite parts. This occurs where the different parts have different useful lives and different depreciation rates are applied to each part, eg an aircraft, where the body and engines are separated as they have different useful lives.

2.6 Safety and environmental equipment

When such assets as these are acquired they will qualify for recognition where they enable the entity to **obtain future economic benefits** from related assets in excess of those it would obtain otherwise. The recognition will only be to the extent that the carrying amount of the asset and related assets does not exceed the total recoverable amount of these assets.

2.7 Initial measurement

Once an item of property, plant and equipment qualifies for recognition as an asset, it will initially be **measured at cost**.

2.7.1 Components of cost

The standard lists the components of the cost of an item of property, plant and equipment.

- **Purchase price**, less any trade discount or rebate
- **Import duties** and non-refundable purchase taxes
- **Directly attributable costs** of bringing the asset to working condition for its intended use, eg:
  - The cost of site preparation
  - Initial delivery and handling costs
  - Installation costs
  - Testing
  - Professional fees (architects, engineers)
- Initial estimate of the cost of dismantling and removing the asset and restoring the site on which it is located

The revised IAS 16 provides **additional guidance on directly attributable** costs included in the cost of an item of property, plant and equipment.

(a) These costs bring the asset to the location and working conditions necessary for it to be capable of operating in the manner intended by management, including those costs to test whether the asset is functioning properly.

(b) These are determined after deducting the net proceeds from selling any items produced when bringing the asset to its location and condition.

The revised standard also states that income and related expenses of operations that are **incidental** to the construction or development of an item of property, plant and equipment should be **recognised** in the income statement.

The following costs **will not be part of the cost** of property, plant or equipment unless they can be attributed directly to the asset's acquisition, or bringing it into its working condition.

- Administration and other general overhead costs
- Start-up and similar pre-production costs
- Initial operating losses before the asset reaches planned performance

All of these will be recognised as an **expense** rather than an asset.

In the case of **self-constructed assets**, the same principles are applied as for acquired assets. If the entity makes similar assets during the normal course of business for sale externally, then the cost of the asset will be the cost of its production under IAS 2 *Inventories*. This also means that abnormal costs (wasted material, labour or other resources) are excluded from the cost of the asset. An example of a self-constructed asset is when a building company builds its own head office.

2.7.2 Exchanges of assets

The revised IAS 16 specifies that exchange of items of property, plant and equipment, regardless of whether the assets are similar, are measured at **fair value**, **unless the exchange transaction lacks commercial substance** or the fair value of neither of the assets exchanged can be **measured reliably**. If the acquired item is not measured at fair value, its cost is measured at the carrying amount of the asset given up.

2.7.3 Subsequent expenditure

Expenditure incurred in replacing or renewing a component of an item of property, plant and equipment must be **recognised in the carrying amount of the item**. The carrying amount of the replaced or renewed component must be derecognised. A similar approach is also applied when a separate component of an item of property, plant and equipment is identified in respect of a major inspection to enable the continued use of the item.

2.8 Measurement subsequent to initial recognition

FAST FORWARD

When a non-current asset is **revalued**, depreciation is charged on the revalued amount.

The standard offers two possible treatments here, essentially a choice between keeping an asset recorded at **cost** or revaluing it to **fair value**.

(a) **Cost model.** Carry the asset at its cost less depreciation and any accumulated impairment losses.

(b) **Revaluation model.** Carry the asset at a revalued amount, being its fair value at the date of the revaluation less any subsequent accumulated depreciation and subsequent accumulated impairment losses. The revised IAS 16 makes clear that the **revaluation model is available only if the fair value of the item can be measured reliably**.

2.8.1 Revaluations

The **market value** of land and buildings usually represents fair value, assuming existing use and line of business. Such valuations are usually carried out by professionally qualified valuers.

In the case of **plant and equipment**, fair value can also be taken as **market value**. Where a market value is not available, however, depreciated replacement cost should be used. There may be no market value where types of plant and equipment are sold only rarely or because of their specialised nature (ie they would normally only be sold as part of an ongoing business).

The frequency of valuation depends on the **volatility of the fair values** of individual items of property, plant and equipment. The more volatile the fair value, the more frequently revaluations should be carried out. Where the current fair value is very different from the carrying value then a revaluation should be carried out.

Most importantly, when an item of property, plant and equipment is revalued, **the whole class of assets to which it belongs should be revalued.**

All the items within a class should be **revalued at the same time**, to prevent selective revaluation of certain assets and to avoid disclosing a mixture of costs and values from different dates in the financial statements. A rolling basis of revaluation is allowed if the revaluations are kept up to date and the revaluation of the whole class is completed in a short period of time.

How should any **increase in value** be treated when a revaluation takes place? The debit will be the increase in value in the balance sheet, but what about the credit? IAS 16 requires the increase to be credited to a **revaluation surplus** (ie part of owners' equity), *unless* the increase is reversing a previous decrease which was recognised as an expense. To the extent that this offset is made, the increase is recognised as income; any excess is then taken to the revaluation reserve.

2.9 Example: revaluation reserve

Binkie Co has an item of land carried in its books at $13,000. Two years ago a slump in land values led the company to reduce the carrying value from $15,000. This was taken as an expense in the income statement. There has been a surge in land prices in the current year, however, and the land is now worth $20,000.

Account for the revaluation in the current year.

Solution

The double entry is:

DEBIT	Asset value (balance sheet)	$7,000	
CREDIT	Income statement		$2,000
	Revaluation surplus		$5,000

The case is similar for a **decrease in value** on revaluation. Any decrease should be recognised as an expense, except where it offsets a previous increase taken as a revaluation surplus in owners' equity. Any decrease greater than the previous upwards increase in value must be taken as an expense in the income statement.

2.10 Example: revaluation decrease

Let us simply swap round the example given above. The original cost was $15,000, revalued upwards to $20,000 two years ago. The value has now fallen to $13,000.

Account for the decrease in value.

Solution

The double entry is:

DEBIT	Revaluation surplus	$5,000	
DEBIT	Income statement	$2,000	
CREDIT	Asset value (balance sheet)		$7,000

There is a further complication when a **revalued asset is being depreciated**. As we have seen, an upward revaluation means that the depreciation charge will increase. Normally, a revaluation surplus is only realised when the asset is sold, but when it is being depreciated, part of that surplus is being realised as the asset is used. The amount of the surplus realised is the difference between depreciation charged on the revalued amount and the (lower) depreciation which would have been charged on the asset's original cost. **This amount can be transferred to retained (ie realised) earnings but *not* through the income statement.**

2.11 Example: revaluation and depreciation

Crinckle Co bought an asset for $10,000 at the beginning of 20X6. It had a useful life of five years. On 1 January 20X8 the asset was revalued to $12,000. The expected useful life has remained unchanged (ie three years remain).

Account for the revaluation and state the treatment for depreciation from 20X8 onwards.

Solution

On 1 January 20X8 the carrying value of the asset is $10,000 – (2 × $10,000 ÷ 5) = $6,000. For the revaluation:

DEBIT	Asset value (balance sheet)	$6,000	
CREDIT	Revaluation reserve		$6,000

The depreciation for the next three years will be $12,000 ÷ 3 = $4,000, compared to depreciation on cost of $10,000 ÷ 5 = $2,000. So each year, the extra $2,000 can be treated as part of the surplus which has become realised:

DEBIT	Revaluation surplus	$2,000	
CREDIT	Retained earnings		$2,000

This is a movement on owners' equity only, not an item in the income statement.

2.12 Depreciation

The standard states:

- The **depreciable amount** of an item of property, plant and equipment should be allocated on a systematic basis over its useful life.
- The **depreciation method** used should reflect the pattern in which the asset's economic benefits are consumed by the entity.
- The **depreciation charge** for each period should be recognised as an expense unless it is included in the carrying amount of another asset.

Land and buildings are dealt with separately even when they are acquired together because land normally has an unlimited life and is therefore not depreciated. In contrast buildings do have a limited life and must be depreciated. Any increase in the value of land on which a building is standing will have no impact on the determination of the building's useful life.

Depreciation is usually treated as an **expense**, but not where it is absorbed by the entity in the process of producing other assets. For example, depreciation of plant and machinery may be incurred in the production of goods for sale (inventory items). In such circumstances, the depreciation is included in the cost of the new assets produced.

2.12.1 Review of useful life

A review of the **useful life** of property, plant and equipment should be carried out at **least each financial year end** and the depreciation charge for the current and future periods should be adjusted if expectations have changed significantly from previous estimates. Changes are changes in accounting estimates and are accounted for prospectively as adjustments to future depreciation.

2.12.2 Review of depreciation method

The **depreciation method** should also be reviewed **at least each financial year end** and, if there has been a significant change in the expected pattern of economic benefits from those assets, the method should be changed to suit this changed pattern. When such a change in depreciation method takes place the change should be accounted for as a **change in accounting estimate** and the depreciation charge for the current and future periods should be adjusted.

2.12.3 Impairment of asset values

An **impairment loss** should be treated in the same way as a **revaluation decrease** ie the decrease should be **recognised as an expense**. However, a revaluation decrease (or impairment loss) should be charged directly against any related revaluation surplus to the extent that the decrease does not exceed the amount held in the revaluation surplus in respect of that same asset.

A **reversal of an impairment** loss should be treated in the same way as a **revaluation increase**, ie a revaluation increase should be recognised as income to the extent that it reverses a revaluation decrease or an impairment loss of the same asset previously recognised as an expense.

2.13 Retirements and disposals

FAST FORWARD

When a non-current asset is **sold**, there is likely to be a profit or loss on disposal. This is the difference between the net sale price of the asset and its net book value at the time of disposal.

When an asset is permanently **withdrawn from use, or sold or scrapped**, and no future economic benefits are expected from its disposal, it should be withdrawn from the balance sheet.

Gains or losses are the difference between the net disposal proceeds and the carrying amount of the asset. They should be recognised as income or expense in the income statement. This applies also to **revalued assets**. The gain or loss on disposal is the difference between the carrying value at the date of disposal and the proceeds.

2.14 Derecognition

An entity is required to **derecognise the carrying amount** of an item of property, plant or equipment that it disposes of on the date the **criteria for the sale of goods** in IAS 18 *Revenue* would be met. This also applies to parts of an asset.

An entity cannot classify as revenue a gain it realises on the disposal of an item of property, plant and equipment.

2.15 Disclosure

The standard has a long list of disclosure requirements, for each class of property, plant and equipment.

(a) **Measurement bases** for determining the gross carrying amount (if more than one, the gross carrying amount for that basis in each category)

(b) **Depreciation methods** used

(c) **Useful lives** or depreciation rates used

(d) **Gross carrying amount** and accumulated depreciation (aggregated with accumulated impairment losses) at the beginning and end of the period

(e) **Reconciliation** of the carrying amount at the beginning and end of the period showing:

  (i) Additions

  (ii) Disposals and assets classified as 'held for sale' in accordance with IFRS 5

  (iii) Acquisitions through business combinations

  (iv) Increases/decreases during the period from revaluations and from impairment losses

  (v) Impairment losses recognised in profit or loss

  (vi) Impairment losses reversed in profit or loss

  (vii) Depreciation

  (viii) Net exchange differences (from translation of statements of foreign entity)

  (ix) Other changes.

The financial statements should also disclose the following.

(a) Existence and amounts of **restrictions on title**, and items pledged as security for liabilities
(b) Accounting policy for **the estimated costs of restoring the site**
(c) Amount of expenditures on account of **items in the course of construction**
(d) Amount of commitments to **acquisitions**

Revalued assets require further disclosures.

(a) Basis used to revalue the assets

(b) Effective date of the revaluation

(c) Whether an independent valuer was involved

(d) Nature of any indices used to determine replacement cost

(e) Carrying amount of each class of property, plant and equipment that would have been included in the financial statements had the assets been carried at cost less accumulated depreciation and accumulated impairment losses.

(f) Revaluation surplus, indicating the movement for the period and any restrictions on the distribution of the balance to shareholders.

The standard also **encourages disclosure** of additional information, which the users of financial statements may find useful.

(a) The carrying amount of temporarily idle property, plant and equipment

(b) The gross carrying amount of any fully depreciated property, plant and equipment that is still in use

(c) The carrying amount of property, plant and equipment retired from active use and held for disposal

(d) The fair value of property, plant and equipment when this is materially different from the carrying amount

The following format (with notional figures) is commonly used to disclose non-current asset movements.

	Total $	Land and buildings $	Plant and equipment $
Cost or valuation			
At 1 January 20X4	50,000	40,000	10,000
Revaluation surplus	12,000	12,000	–
Additions in year	4,000	–	4,000
Disposals in year	(1,000)	–	(1,000)
At 31 December 20X4	65,000	52,000	13,000
Depreciation			
At 1 January 20X4	16,000	10,000	6,000
Charge for year	4,000	1,000	3,000
Eliminated on disposals	(500)	–	(500)
At 31 December 20X4	19,500	11,000	8,500
Net book value			
At 31 December 20X4	45,500	41,000	4,500
At 1 January 20X4	34,000	30,000	4,000

Question

IAS 16

(a) In a balance sheet prepared in accordance with IAS 16, what does the net book value (carrying value) represent?

(b) In a set of financial statements prepared in accordance with IAS 16, is it correct to say that the net book value (carrying value) figure in a balance sheet cannot be greater than the market (net realisable) value of the partially used asset as at the balance sheet date? Explain your reasons for your answer.

Answer

(a) In simple terms the net book value of an asset is the cost of an asset less the 'accumulated depreciation', that is all depreciation charged so far. It should be emphasised that the main purpose of charging depreciation is to ensure that profits are fairly reported. Thus depreciation is concerned with the income statement rather than the balance sheet. In consequence the net book value figure in the balance sheet can be quite arbitrary. In particular, it does not necessarily bear any relation to the market value of an asset and is of little use for planning and decision making.

An obvious example of the disparity between net book value and market value is found in the case of buildings, which may be worth more than ten times as much as their net book value.

(b) Net book value can in some circumstances be higher than market value (net realisable value). IAS 16 *Property, plant and equipment* states that the carrying value of an asset cannot be greater than its 'recoverable amount'. However 'recoverable amount' as defined in IAS 16 is the amount recoverable from further use. This may be higher than the market value.

This makes sense if you think of a specialised machine which could not fetch much on the secondhand market but which will produce goods which can be sold at a profit for many years.

3 IAS 36 Impairment of assets

FAST FORWARD

Impairment is determined by comparing the carrying amount of the asset with its **recoverable amount**.

3.1 Impairment

There is an established principle that assets should not be carried at above their recoverable amount. An entity should write down the carrying value of an asset to its recoverable amount if the carrying value of an asset is not recoverable in full. IAS 36 was published in June 1998 and has recently been revised. It puts in place a detailed methodology for carrying out impairment reviews and related accounting treatments and disclosures.

3.2 Scope

IAS 36 applies to all tangible, intangible and financial assets except inventories, assets arising from construction contracts, deferred tax assets, assets arising under IAS 19 *Employee benefits* and financial assets within the scope of IAS 32 *Financial instruments, disclosure and presentation*. This is because those IASs already have rules for recognising and measuring impairment. Note also that IAS 36 does not apply to non-current assets held for sale, which are dealt with under IFRS 5 *Non-current assets held for sale and discontinued operations*.

Key terms

Impairment: a fall in the value of an asset, so that its 'recoverable amount' is now less than its carrying value in the balance sheet.

Carrying amount: is the amount at which an asset is recognised after deducting any accumulated depreciation and accumulated impairment losses. *(IAS 36)*

The basic principle underlying IAS 36 is relatively straightforward. If an asset's value in the accounts is higher than its realistic value, measured as its 'recoverable amount', the asset is judged to have suffered an impairment loss. It should therefore be reduced in value, by the amount of the **impairment loss**. The amount of the impairment loss should be **written off against profit** immediately.

The main accounting issues to consider are therefore as follows.

(a) How is it possible to **identify when** an impairment loss may have occurred?
(b) How should the **recoverable amount** of the asset be measured?
(c) How should an 'impairment loss' be **reported in the accounts**?

3.3 Identifying a potentially impaired asset

An entity should carry out a **review of its assets at each balance sheet date**, to assess whether there are any indications of impairment to any assets. The concept of **materiality** applies, and only material impairment needs to be identified.

If there are indications of possible impairment, the entity is required to make a formal estimate of the **recoverable amount** of the assets concerned.

IAS 36 suggests how **indications of a possible impairment** of assets might be recognised. The suggestions are based largely on common sense.

(a) **External sources of information**

(i) A fall in the asset's market value that is significantly more than would normally be expected from passage of time or normal use.

(ii) Significant adverse changes in the technological, market, economic or legal environment in which the entity operates.

(iii) An increase in market interest rates or other market rates of return on investments likely to affect the discount rate used in calculating value in use.

(iv) The carrying amount of the entity's net assets being more than its market capitalisation.

(b) **Internal sources of information**: evidence of obsolescence or physical damage, adverse changes in the use to which the asset is put, or the asset's economic performance

Even if there are no indications of impairment, the following assets must **always** be tested for impairment annually.

(a) An intangible asset with an **indefinite useful life**
(b) **Goodwill** acquired in a business combination

3.4 Measuring the recoverable amount of the asset

What is an asset's recoverable amount?

Key term

> The **recoverable amount of an asset** should be measured as the *higher value* of:
>
> (a) the asset's fair value less costs to sell; and
> (b) its value in use. *(IAS 36)*

An asset's fair value less costs to sell is the amount net of selling costs that could be obtained from the sale of the asset. Selling costs include sales transaction costs, such as legal expenses.

(a) If there is **an active market** in the asset, the net selling price should be based on the **market value**, or on the price of recent transactions in similar assets.

(b) If there is **no active market** in the assets it might be possible to **estimate** a net selling price using best estimates of what 'knowledgeable, willing parties' might pay in an arm's length transaction.

Net selling price **cannot** be reduced, however, by including within selling costs any **restructuring or reorganisation expenses**, or any costs that have already been recognised in the accounts as liabilities.

The concept of 'value in use' is very important.

Key term

> The **value in use** of an asset is measured as the present value of future cash flows expected to be derived from an asset or cash-generating unit.

The cash flows used in the calculation should be **pre-tax cash flows** and a **pre-tax discount rate** should be applied to calculate the present value.

The calculation of **value in use** must reflect the following.

(a) An estimate of the **future cash flows** the entity expects to derive from the asset
(b) Expectations about **possible variations** in the amount and timing of future cash flows
(c) The **time value of money**
(d) The price for bearing the **uncertainty** inherent in the asset, and
(e) **Other factors** that would be reflected in pricing future cash flows from the asset

Calculating a value in use therefore calls for estimates of future cash flows, and the possibility exists that an entity might come up with **over-optimistic estimates** of cash flows. The IAS therefore states the following.

(a) Cash flow projections should be based on **'reasonable and supportable' assumptions**.

(b) Projections of cash flows, normally up to a maximum period of five years, should be based on the most **recent budgets or financial forecasts**.

(c) Cash flow projections beyond this period should be obtained by extrapolating short-term projections, using either a **steady or declining growth rate** for each subsequent year (unless a rising growth rate can be justified). The long term growth rate applied should not exceed the average long term growth rate for the product, market, industry or country, unless a higher growth rate can be justified.

3.4.1 Composition of estimates of future cash flows

These should include the following.

(a) Projections of **cash inflows** from **continuing use** of the asset

(b) Projections of **cash outflows** necessarily incurred to **generate the cash inflows** from continuing use of the asset

(c) **Net cash flows** received/paid on **disposal** of the asset at the end of its useful life

There is an underlying principle that future cash flows should be estimated for the asset in its current condition. Future cash flows relating to restructurings to which the entity is not yet committed, or to future costs to add to, replace part of, or service the asset are excluded.

Estimates of future cash flows should **exclude** the following.

(a) Cash inflows/ outflows from financing activities
(b) Income tax receipts/payments

The amount of net cash inflow/outflow on **disposal** of an asset should assume an arm's length transaction.

Foreign currency future cash flows should be forecast in the currency in which they will arise and will be discounted using a rule appropriate for that currency. The resulting figure should then be translated into the reporting currency at the spot rate at the balance sheet date.

The **discount rate** should be a current pre-tax rate (or rates) that reflects the current assessment of the time value of money and the risks specific to the asset. The discount should not include a risk weighting if the underlying cash flows have already been adjusted for risk.

3.5 Recognition and measurement of an impairment loss

The rule for assets at historical cost is:

Rule to learn

If the recoverable amount of an asset is lower than the carrying amount, the carrying amount should be reduced by the difference (ie the impairment loss) which should be charged as an expense in the income statement.

The rule for assets held at a revalued amount (such as property revalued under IAS 16) is:

Rule to learn

The impairment loss is to be treated as a revaluation decrease under the relevant IAS.

In practice this means:

- To the extent that there is a revaluation surplus held in respect of the asset, the impairment loss should be charged to revaluation surplus.
- Any excess should be charged to the income statement.

The IAS goes into quite a large amount of detail about the important concept of cash generating units. As a basic rule, the recoverable amount of an asset should be calculated for the **asset individually**. However, there will be occasions when it is not possible to estimate such a value for an individual asset, particularly in the calculation of value in use. This is because cash inflows and outflows cannot be attributed to the individual asset.

FAST FORWARD

If it is not possible to calculate the recoverable amount for an individual asset, the recoverable amount of the asset's cash generating unit should be measured instead.

Key term

A cash generating unit is the smallest identifiable group of assets for which independent cash flows can be identified and measured.

Question — Cash generating unit

Can you think of some examples of how a cash generating unit would be identified?

Answer

Here are two possibilities.

(a) A mining company owns a private railway that it uses to transport output from one of its mines. The railway now has no market value other than as scrap, and it is impossible to identify any separate cash inflows with the use of the railway itself. Consequently, if the mining company suspects an impairment in the value of the railway, it should treat the mine as a whole as a cash generating unit, and measure the recoverable amount of the mine as a whole.

(b) A bus company has an arrangement with a town's authorities to run a bus service on four routes in the town. Separately identifiable assets are allocated to each of the bus routes, and cash inflows and outflows can be attributed to each individual route. Three routes are running at a profit and one is running at a loss. The bus company suspects that there is an impairment of assets on the loss-making route. However, the company will be unable to close the loss-making route, because it is under an obligation to operate all four routes, as part of its contract with the local authority. Consequently, the company should treat all four bus routes together as a cash generating unit, and calculate the recoverable amount for the unit as a whole.

Question — Cash generating unit

Minimart belongs to a retail store chain Maximart. Minimart makes all its retail purchases through Maximart's purchasing centre. Pricing, marketing, advertising and human resources policies (except for hiring Minimart's cashiers and salesmen) are decided by Maximart. Maximart also owns 5 other stores in the same city as Minimart (although in different neighbourhoods) and 20 other stores in other cities. All stores are managed in the same way as Minimart. Minimart and 4 other stores were purchased 5 years ago and goodwill was recognised.

What is the cash-generating unit for Minimart?

Answer

In identifying Minimart's cash-generating unit, an entity considers whether, for example:

(a) Internal management reporting is organised to measure performance on a store-by-store basis.
(b) The business is run on a store-by-store profit basis or on a region/city basis.

All Maximart's stores are in different neighbourhoods and probably have different customer bases. So, although Minimart is managed at a corporate level, Minimart generates cash inflows that are largely independent from those of Maximart's other stores. Therefore, it is likely that Minimart is a cash-generating unit.

Question **Cash generating unit**

Mighty Mag Publishing Co owns 150 magazine titles of which 70 were purchased and 80 were self-created. The price paid for a purchased magazine title is recognised as an intangible asset. The costs of creating magazine titles and maintaining the existing titles are recognised as an expense when incurred. Cash inflows from direct sales and advertising are identifiable for each magazine title. Titles are managed by customer segments. The level of advertising income for a magazine title depends on the range of titles in the customer segment to which the magazine title relates. Management has a policy to abandon old titles before the end of their economic lives and replace them immediately with new titles for the same customer segment.

What is the cash-generating unit for an individual magazine title?

Answer

It is likely that the recoverable amount of an individual magazine title can be assessed. Even though the level of advertising income for a title is influenced, to a certain extent, by the other titles in the customer segment, cash inflows from direct sales and advertising are identifiable for each title. In addition, although titles are managed by customer segments, decisions to abandon titles are made on an individual title basis.

Therefore, it is likely that individual magazine titles generate cash inflows that are largely independent one from another and that each magazine title is a separate cash-generating unit.

If an active market exists for the output produced by the asset or a group of assets, this asset or group should be identified as a cash generating unit, even if some or all of the output is used internally.

Cash generating units should be identified consistently from period to period for the same type of asset unless a change is justified.

The group of assets less liabilities that are considered for impairment should be the same as those considered in the calculation of the recoverable amount. (For the treatment of goodwill and corporate assets see below.)

3.6 Example: recoverable amount and carrying amount

Fourways Co is made up of four cash generating units. All four units are being tested for impairment.

(a) Property, plant and equipment and separate intangibles would be allocated to the cash generating units as far as possible.

(b) Current assets such as inventories, receivables and prepayments would be allocated to the relevant cash generating units.

(c) Liabilities (eg payables) would be deducted from the net assets of the relevant cash generating units.

(d) The net figure for each cash generating unit resulting from this exercise would be compared to the relevant recoverable amount, computed on the same basis.

3.7 Goodwill and the impairment of assets

3.7.1 Allocating goodwill to cash-generating units

Goodwill acquired in a business combination does not generate cash flows independently of other assets. It must be **allocated** to each of the acquirer's **cash-generating units** (or groups of cash-generating units) that are expected to benefit from the synergies of the combination. Each unit to which the goodwill is so allocated should:

(a) Represent the **lowest level** within the entity at which the goodwill is monitored for internal management purposes

(b) Not be **larger than a reporting segment** determined in accordance with IAS 14 *Segment reporting*

It may be impractical to complete the allocation of goodwill before the first reporting date after a business combination, particularly if the acquirer is accounting for the combination for the first time using provisional values. The initial allocation of goodwill must be completed before the end of the first reporting period after the acquisition date.

3.7.2 Testing cash-generating units with goodwill for impairment

There are two situations to consider.

(a) Where goodwill has been allocated to a cash-generating unit

(b) Where it has not been possible to allocate goodwill to a specific cash-generating unit, but only to a group of units

A cash-generating unit to which goodwill has been allocated is tested for impairment annually. The **carrying amount** of the unit, including goodwill, is **compared with the recoverable amount**. If the carrying amount of the unit exceeds the recoverable amount, the entity must recognise an impairment loss.

Where goodwill relates to a cash-generating unit but has not been allocated to that unit, the unit is tested for impairment by **comparing its carrying amount** (excluding goodwill) **with its recoverable amount**. The entity must recognise an impairment loss if the carrying amount exceeds the recoverable amount.

The annual impairment test may be performed at any time during an accounting period, but must be performed at the **same time every year**.

3.8 Corporate assets

Corporate assets are group or divisional assets such as a head office building, computer equipment or a research centre. Essentially, corporate assets are assets that do not generate cash inflows independently from other assets, hence their carrying amount cannot be fully attributed to a cash-generating unit under review.

In testing a cash generating unit for impairment, an entity should identify all the corporate assets that relate to the cash-generating unit.

(a) If a portion of the carrying amount of a corporate asset **can be allocated** to the unit on a reasonable and consistent basis, the entity compares the carrying amount of the unit (including the portion of the asset) with its recoverable amount.

(b) If a portion of the carrying amount of a corporate asset **cannot be allocated** to the unit on a reasonable and consistent basis, the entity:

  (i) Compares the carrying amount of the unit (excluding the asset) with its recoverable amount and recognises any impairment loss

(ii) Identifies the smallest group of cash-generating units that includes the cash-generating unit to which the asset belongs and to which a portion of the carrying amount of the asset can be allocated on a reasonable and consistent basis

(iii) Compares the carrying amount of that group of cash-generating units (including the portion of the asset allocated to the group of units) with the recoverable amount of the group of units and recognises any impairment loss

3.9 Accounting treatment of an impairment loss

If, and only if, the recoverable amount of an asset is less than its carrying amount in the balance sheet, an impairment loss has occurred. This loss should be **recognised immediately**.

(a) The asset's **carrying amount** should be reduced to its recoverable amount in the balance sheet.

(b) The **impairment loss** should be recognised immediately in the income statement (unless the asset has been revalued in which case the loss is treated as a revaluation decrease).

After reducing an asset to its recoverable amount, the **depreciation charge** on the asset should then be based on its new carrying amount, its estimated residual value (if any) and its estimated remaining useful life.

An impairment loss should be recognised for a **cash generating unit** if (and only if) the recoverable amount for the cash generating unit is less than the carrying amount in the balance sheet for all the assets in the unit. When an impairment loss is recognised for a cash generating unit, the loss should be allocated between the assets in the unit in the following order.

(a) First, to the **goodwill** allocated to the cash generating unit
(b) Then to all other assets in the cash-generating unit, on a **pro rata basis**

In allocating an impairment loss, the carrying amount of an asset should not be reduced below the highest of:

(a) Its fair value less costs to sell
(b) Its value in use (if determinable)
(c) Zero

Any remaining amount of an impairment loss should be recognised as a liability if required by other IASs.

3.10 Example: impairment loss 1

A company that extracts natural gas and oil has a drilling platform in the Caspian Sea. It is required by legislation of the country concerned to remove and dismantle the platform at the end of its useful life. Accordingly, the company has included an amount in its accounts for removal and dismantling costs, and is depreciating this amount over the platform's expected life.

The company is carrying out an exercise to establish whether there has been an impairment of the platform.

(a) Its carrying amount in the balance sheet is \$3m.

(b) The company has received an offer of \$2.8m for the platform from another oil company. The bidder would take over the responsibility (and costs) for dismantling and removing the platform at the end of its life.

(c) The present value of the estimated cash flows from the platform's continued use is \$3.3m.

(d) The carrying amount in the balance sheet for the provision for dismantling and removal is currently \$0.6m.

What should be the value of the drilling platform in the balance sheet, and what, if anything, is the impairment loss?

Solution

Fair value less costs to sell	=	$2.8m
Value in use	=	PV of cash flows from use less the carrying amount of the provision/liability = $3.3m – $0.6m = $2.7m
Recoverable amount	=	Higher of these two amounts, ie $2.8m
Carrying value	=	$3m
Impairment loss	=	$0.2m

The carrying value should be reduced to $2.8m

3.11 Example: impairment loss 2

A company has acquired another business for $4.5m: tangible assets are valued at $4.0m and goodwill at $0.5m.

An asset with a carrying value of $1m is destroyed in a terrorist attack. The asset was not insured. The loss of the asset, without insurance, has prompted the company to estimate whether there has been an impairment of assets in the acquired business and what the amount of any such loss is. The recoverable amount of the business (a single cash generating unit) is measured as $3.1m.

Solution

There has been an impairment loss of $1.4m ($4.5m – $3.1m).

The impairment loss will be recognised in the income statement. The loss will be allocated between the assets in the cash generating unit as follows.

(a) A loss of $1m can be attributed directly to the uninsured asset that has been destroyed.

(b) The remaining loss of $0.4m should be allocated to goodwill.

The carrying value of the assets will now be $3m for tangible assets and $0.1m for goodwill.

3.12 Reversal of an impairment loss

The annual review of assets to determine whether there may have been some impairment should be **applied to all assets**, including assets that have already been impaired in the past.

In some cases, the recoverable amount of an asset that has previously been impaired might turn out to be **higher** than the asset's current carrying value. In other words, there might have been a reversal of some of the previous impairment loss.

(a) The reversal of the impairment loss should be **recognised immediately** as income in the income statement unless the asset has been revalued in accordance with IAS 16. In this case, it will be treated as a revaluation increase.

(b) The carrying amount of the asset should be increased to its **new recoverable amount**.

Rule to learn

> An impairment loss recognised in prior periods for an asset other than goodwill shall be reversed if, and only if, there has been a change in the estimates used to determine the asset's recoverable amount since the last impairment loss was recognised.

The asset cannot be revalued to a carrying amount that is higher than its value would have been if the asset had not been impaired originally, ie its **depreciated carrying value** had the impairment not taken place. Depreciation of the asset should now be based on its new revalued amount, its estimated residual value (if any) and its estimated remaining useful life.

Note: An impairment loss recognised for **goodwill** shall not be reversed in a subsequent period.

Question

Impairment loss

A cash generating unit comprising a factory, plant and equipment etc and associated purchased goodwill becomes impaired because the product it makes is overtaken by a technologically more advanced model produced by a competitor. The recoverable amount of the cash generating unit falls to $60m, resulting in an impairment loss of $80m, allocated as follows.

	Carrying amounts before impairment	*Carrying amounts after impairment*
	$m	$m
Goodwill	40	–
Patent (with no market value)	20	–
Property, plant and equipment	80	60
Total	140	60

After three years, the entity makes a technological breakthrough of its own, and the recoverable amount of the cash generating unit increases to $90m. The carrying amount of the property, plant and equipment had the impairment not occurred would have been $70m.

Required

Calculate the reversal of the impairment loss.

Answer

The reversal of the impairment loss is recognised to the extent that it increases the carrying amount of the property, plant and equipment to what it would have been had the impairment not taken place, ie a reversal of the impairment loss of $10m is recognised and the property, plant and equipment written back to $70m. Reversal of the impairment is not recognised in relation to the goodwill. IAS 36 does not allow the reversal of an impairment loss recognised for goodwill.

Exam focus point

The November 2005 exam had a 5-mark question on non-current assets and impairment.

3.13 Disclosure

IAS 36 calls for substantial disclosure about impairment of assets. The information to be disclosed includes the following.

(a) For each class of assets, the amount of **impairment losses recognised** and the amount of any **impairment losses recovered** (ie reversals of impairment losses)

(b) For each individual asset or cash generating unit that has suffered a **significant impairment loss**, details of the nature of the asset, the amount of the loss, the events that led to recognition of the loss, whether the recoverable amount is fair value price less costs to sell or value in use, and if the recoverable amount is value in use, the basis on which this value was estimated (eg the discount rate applied)

3.14 Section summary

The main aspects of IAS 36 to consider are:

- **Indications** of impairment of assets
- **Measuring recoverable amount**, as net selling price or value in use
- **Measuring value in use**
- **Cash generating units**

- **Accounting treatment** of an impairment loss, for individual assets and cash generating units
- **Reversal** of an impairment loss

4 IAS 23 Borrowing costs

FAST FORWARD

IAS 23 looks at the treatment of borrowing costs, particularly where the related borrowings are applied to the **construction of certain assets**. These are what are usually called 'self-constructed assets'.

4.1 Definitions

Only two definitions are given by the standard.

Key terms

Borrowing costs. Interest and other costs incurred by an entity in connection with the borrowing of funds.

Qualifying asset. An asset that necessarily takes a substantial period of time to get ready for its intended use or sale. *(IAS 23)*

The standard lists what may be **included in borrowing costs**.

- Interest on bank overdrafts and short-term and long-term borrowings
- Amortisation of discounts or premiums relating to borrowings
- Amortisation of ancillary costs incurred in connection with the arrangement of borrowings
- Finance charges in respect of finance leases recognised in accordance with IAS 17
- Exchange differences arising from foreign currency borrowings to the extent that they are regarded as an adjustment to interest costs

The standard also gives **examples of qualifying assets**.

- Inventories that require a substantial period of time to bring them to a saleable condition
- Manufacturing plants
- Power generation facilities
- Investment properties

Inventories produced in bulk over short periods and on a regular basis are **not qualifying assets**, nor are assets ready for sale or their intended use when purchased.

4.2 Benchmark treatment

The benchmark treatment for borrowing costs is the most straightforward and prudent. They should be **recognised as an expense** in the period in which they were incurred, regardless of how the borrowings were applied. The accounting policy adopted for borrowing costs should be disclosed.

4.3 Allowed alternative treatment: capitalisation

Under the alternative treatment, certain borrowing costs may be **capitalised**. Any other borrowing costs remaining must still be recognised as an expense as under the benchmark treatment.

Only borrowing costs that are **directly attributable** to the acquisition, construction or production of a qualifying asset can be capitalised as part of the cost of that asset. The standard lays out the criteria for determining which borrowing costs are eligible for capitalisation.

4.3.1 Borrowing costs eligible for capitalisation

Those borrowing costs directly attributable to the acquisition, construction or production of a qualifying asset must be identified. These are the borrowing costs that **would have been avoided** had the expenditure on the qualifying asset not been made. This is obviously straightforward where funds have been borrowed for the financing of one particular asset.

Difficulties arise, however, where the enterprise uses a **range of debt instruments** to finance a wide range of assets, so that there is no direct relationship between particular borrowings and a specific asset. For example, all borrowings may be made centrally and then lent to different parts of the group or enterprise. Judgement is therefore required, particularly where further complications can arise (eg foreign currency loans).

Once the relevant borrowings are identified, which relate to a specific asset, then the **amount of borrowing costs available for capitalisation** will be the actual borrowing costs incurred on those borrowings during the period, *less* any investment income on the temporary investment of those borrowings. It would not be unusual for some or all of the funds to be invested before they are actually used on the qualifying asset.

Question

Borrowing costs

On 1 January 20X6 Stremans Co borrowed $1.5m to finance the production of two assets, both of which were expected to take a year to build. Production started during 20X6. The loan facility was drawn down on 1 January 20X6, and was utilised as follows, with the remaining funds invested temporarily.

	Asset A	*Asset B*
	$'000	$'000
1 January 20X6	250	500
1 July 20X6	250	500

The loan rate was 9% and Stremans Co can invest surplus funds at 7%.

Required

Ignoring compound interest, calculate the borrowing costs which may be capitalised for each of the assets and consequently the cost of each asset as at 31 December 20X6.

Answer

		Asset A	*Asset B*
		$	$
Borrowing costs			
To 30 June 20X6	$500,000/$1,000,000 × 9% × 6/12	22,500	45,000
To 31 December 20X6	$500,000/$1,000,000 × 9% × 6/12	22,500	45,000
		45,000	90,000
Less investment income			
To 30 June 20X6	$250,000/$500,000 × 7% × 6/12	(8,750)	(17,500)
		36,250	72,500
		$	$
Cost of assets			
Expenditure incurred		500,000	1,000,000
Borrowing costs		36,250	72,500
		536,250	1,072,500

In a situation where **borrowings are obtained generally**, but are applied in part to obtaining a qualifying asset, then the amount of borrowing costs eligible for capitalisation is found by applying the 'capitalisation rate' to the expenditure on the asset.

The **capitalisation rate** is the weighted average of the borrowing costs applicable to the enterprise's borrowings that are outstanding during the period, *excluding* borrowings made specifically to obtain a qualifying asset. However, there is a cap on the amount of borrowing costs calculated in this way: it must not exceed actual borrowing costs incurred.

Sometimes one overall weighted average can be calculated for a group or enterprise, but in some situations it may be more appropriate to use a weighted average for borrowing costs for **individual parts of the group or enterprise**.

Question

Borrowing costs

Acruni Co had the following loans in place at the beginning and end of 20X6.

	1 January 20X6	*31 December* 20X6
	$m	$m
10% Bank loan repayable 20Y1	120	120
9.5% Bank loan repayable 20X9	80	80
8.9% loan stock repayable 20X6	–	150

The 8.9% loan stock was issued to fund the construction of a qualifying asset (a piece of mining equipment), construction of which began on 1 July 20X6.

On 1 January 20X6, Acruni Co began construction of a qualifying asset, a piece of machinery for a hydro-electric plant, using existing borrowings. Expenditure drawn down for the construction was: $30m on 1 January 20X6, $20m on 1 October 20X6.

Required

Calculate the borrowing costs to be capitalised for the hydro-electric plant machine.

Answer

$$\text{Capitalisation rate} = \text{weighted average rate} = \left(10\% \times \frac{120}{120+80}\right) + \left(9.5\% \times \frac{80}{120+80}\right) = 9.8\%$$

Borrowing costs = ($30m × 9.8%) + ($20m × 9.8% × 3/12)
= $3.43m

4.3.2 Carrying amount exceeds recoverable amount

A situation may arise whereby the carrying amount (or expected ultimate cost) of the qualifying asset exceeds its recoverable amount or net realisable value. In these cases, the carrying amount must be **written down or written off**, as required by other IASs. In certain circumstances (again as allowed by other IASs), these amounts may be written back in future periods.

4.3.3 Commencement of capitalisation

Three events or transactions must be taking place for capitalisation of borrowing costs to be started.

(a) Expenditure on the asset is being incurred
(b) Borrowing costs are being incurred

(c) Activities are in progress that are necessary to prepare the asset for its intended use or sale

Expenditure must result in the payment of cash, transfer of other assets or assumption of interest-bearing liabilities. **Deductions from expenditure** will be made for any progress payments or grants received in connection with the asset. IAS 23 allows the **average carrying amount** of the asset during a period (including borrowing costs previously capitalised) to be used as a reasonable approximation of the expenditure to which the capitalisation rate is applied in the period. Presumably more exact calculations can be used.

Activities necessary to prepare the asset for its intended sale or use extend further than physical construction work. They encompass technical and administrative work prior to construction, eg obtaining permits. They do *not* include holding an asset when no production or development that changes the asset's condition is taking place, eg where land is held without any associated development activity.

4.3.4 Suspension of capitalisation

If active development is **interrupted for any extended periods**, capitalisation of borrowing costs should be suspended for those periods.

Suspension of capitalisation of borrowing costs is not necessary for **temporary delays** or for periods when substantial technical or administrative work is taking place.

4.3.5 Cessation of capitalisation

Once substantially all the activities necessary to prepare the qualifying asset for its intended use or sale are complete, then capitalisation of borrowing costs should cease. This will normally be when **physical construction of the asset is completed**, although minor modifications may still be outstanding.

The asset may be completed in **parts or stages**, where each part can be used while construction is still taking place on the other parts. Capitalisation of borrowing costs should cease for each part as it is completed. The example given by the standard is a business park consisting of several buildings.

4.3.6 Disclosure

The following should be disclosed in the financial statements in relation to borrowing costs.

(a) **Accounting policy** adopted

(b) Amount of borrowing costs **capitalised during the period**

(c) **Capitalisation rate** used to determine the amount of borrowing costs eligible for capitalisation

4.4 Section summary

- There are two treatments allowed for borrowing costs.
  - **Benchmark treatment**: write off in the period incurred
  - **Allowed alternative**: capitalise those costs directly attributable to qualifying assets
- You may be asked to discuss the pros and cons of the capitalisation of borrowing costs.

  For capitalisation

  - Borrowing costs are part of the **total cost** of bringing an asset into use.
  - Capitalisation gives greater **comparability** between companies: a purchase price includes interest incurred by the seller, so a construction cost should also include interest.

Against capitalisation

– Finance costs are **not the most direct of costs** and may relate to the business as a whole.

– There will still be a lack of comparability due to **different financing policies**: businesses with loan financing will have higher values for assets than equity-backed businesses.

Chapter Roundup

- The **cost of a non-current asset**, less its estimated residual value, is allocated fairly between accounting periods by means of depreciation. The provision for depreciation is both:
  - Charged against profit
  - Deducted from the value of the non-current asset in the balance sheet
- IAS 16 *Property, plant and equipment* provides the basic rules on **depreciation**, including important definitions of depreciation, depreciable assets, useful life and depreciable amount.
- When a non-current asset is **revalued**, depreciation is charged on the revalued amount.
- When a non-current asset is **sold**, there is likely to be a profit or loss on disposal. This is the difference between the net sale price of the asset and its net book value at the time of disposal.
- Impairment is determined by comparing the carrying amount of the asset with its **recoverable amount**.
- The recoverable amount of an asset is the higher of the asset's **fair value less costs to sell** and **its value in use**.
- When it is not possible to calculate the recoverable amount of a single asset, then that of its **cash generating unit** should be measured instead.
- IAS 23 looks at the treatment of borrowing costs, particularly where the related borrowings are applied to the **construction of certain assets**. These are what are usually called self-constructed assets.

Quick Quiz

1 Define depreciation.

2 Which of the following elements can be included in the production cost of a non-current asset?

A Purchase price
B Architect's fees
C Import duties
D Installation costs

3 Market value can usually be taken as fair value.

True ☐

False ☐

4 Define impairment.

Answers to Quick Quiz

1 The result of the systematic allocation of the depreciable amount of an asset over its useful life.

2 All of them.

3 True

4 A fall in value of an asset, so that its 'recoverable amount' is less than its carrying value.

Now try the question below from the Exam Question Bank

Number	Level	Marks	Time
Q17	Examination	5	9 mins

Intangible non-current assets

6

Introduction

We begin our examination of intangible non-current assets with a discussion of a recently revised IAS on the subject (**IAS 38**).

Goodwill and its treatment is a controversial area, as is the accounting for items similar to goodwill, such as brands. In Section 3 we look in more detail at the IAS 38 provisions covering research and development.

Topic list	Learning outcomes	Syllabus references	Ability required
1 IAS 38 *Intangible assets*	C (v)	C (10)	Evaluation
2 Goodwill	C (v)	C (10)	Evaluation
3 Research and development costs	C (v)	C (9)	Application

1 IAS 38 Intangible assets

FAST FORWARD

Intangible assets are defined by **IAS 38** as non-monetary assets without physical substance. They must be:

- **Identifiable**
- **Controlled** as a result of a past event
- Able to provide **future economic benefits**

IAS 38 *Intangible assets* was originally published in September 1998. It has recently been revised to reflect changes introduced by IFRS 3 *Business combinations.*

1.1 The objectives of the standard

(a) To establish the criteria for when intangible assets may or should be **recognised**
(b) To specify how intangible assets should be **measured**
(c) To specify the **disclosure requirements** for intangible assets

It applies to all intangible assets with certain **exceptions**: deferred tax assets (IAS 12), leases that fall within the scope of IAS 17, financial assets, insurance contracts, assets arising from employee benefits (IAS 19), non-current assets held for sale and mineral rights and exploration and extraction costs for minerals etc (although intangible assets used to develop or maintain these rights are covered by the standard). It does *not* apply to goodwill acquired in a business combination, which is dealt with under IFRS 3 *Business combinations.*

1.2 Definition of an intangible asset

The definition of an intangible asset is a key aspect of the standard, because the rules for deciding whether or not an intangible asset may be **recognised** in the accounts of an entity are based on the definition of what an intangible asset is.

Key term

An **intangible asset** is an identifiable non-monetary asset without physical substance. The asset must be:

(a) controlled by the entity as a result of events in the past, and
(b) something from which the entity expects future economic benefits to flow.

Examples of items that might be considered as intangible assets include computer software, patents, copyrights, motion picture films, customer lists, franchises and fishing rights. An item should not be recognised as an intangible asset, however, unless it **fully meets the definition** in the standard. The guidelines go into great detail on this matter.

1.3 Intangible asset: must be identifiable

An intangible asset must be identifiable in order to distinguish it from goodwill. With non-physical items, there may be a problem with **'identifiability'**.

(a) If an intangible asset is **acquired separately through purchase**, there may be a transfer of a legal right that would help to make an asset identifiable.

(b) An intangible asset may be identifiable if it is **separable**, ie if it could be rented or sold separately. However, 'separability' is not an essential feature of an intangible asset.

1.4 Intangible asset: control by the entity

Another element of the definition of an intangible asset is that it must be under the control of the entity as a result of a past event. The entity must therefore be able to enjoy the future economic benefits from the asset, and prevent the access of others to those benefits. A **legally enforceable right** is evidence of such control, but is not always a *necessary* condition.

(a) Control over **technical knowledge or know-how** only exists if it is protected by a **legal right**.

(b) The skill of employees, arising out of the benefits of **training costs**, are most unlikely to be recognisable as an intangible asset, because an entity does not control the future actions of its staff.

(c) Similarly, **market share and customer loyalty** cannot normally be intangible assets, since an entity cannot control the actions of its customers.

1.5 Intangible asset: expected future economic benefits

An item can only be recognised as an intangible asset if economic benefits are expected to flow in the future from ownership of the asset. Economic benefits may come from the **sale** of products or services, or from a **reduction in expenditures** (cost savings).

An intangible asset, when recognised initially, must be measured at **cost**. It should be recognised if, and only if **both** the following occur.

(a) It is probable that the **future economic benefits** that are attributable to the asset will **flow to the entity.**

(b) The **cost can be measured reliably**.

Management has to exercise its judgement in assessing the degree of certainty attached to the flow of economic benefits to the entity. External evidence is best.

(a) If an intangible asset is **acquired separately**, its cost can usually be measured reliably as its purchase price (including incidental costs of purchase such as legal fees, and any costs incurred in getting the asset ready for use).

(b) When an intangible asset is acquired as **part of a business combination** (ie an acquisition or takeover), the cost of the intangible asset is its fair value at the date of the acquisition.

IFRS 3 explains that the fair value of intangible assets acquired in business combinations can normally be measured with sufficient reliability to be **recognised separately** from goodwill.

Quoted market prices in an active market provide the most reliable estimate of the fair value of an intangible asset. If no active market exists for an intangible asset, its fair value is the amount that the entity would have paid for the asset, at the acquisition date, in an arm's length transaction between knowledgeable and willing parties, on the basis of the best information available. In determining this amount, an entity should consider the outcome of recent transactions for similar assets. There are techniques for estimating the fair values of unique intangible assets (such as brand names) and these may be used to measure an intangible asset acquired in a business combination.

In accordance with IAS 20, intangible assets acquired by way of government grant and the grant itself may be recorded initially either at cost (which may be zero) or fair value.

1.6 Exchanges of assets

If one intangible asset is exchanged for another, the cost of the intangible asset is measured at fair value unless:

(a) The exchange transaction lacks commercial substance, or

(b) The fair value of neither the asset received nor the asset given up can be measured reliably.

Otherwise, its cost is measured at the carrying amount of the asset given up.

1.7 Internally generated goodwill

Rule to learn

Internally generated goodwill may **not** be recognised as an **asset**.

The standard deliberately precludes recognition of internally generated goodwill because it requires that, for initial recognition, the cost of the asset rather than its fair value should be capable of being measured reliably and that it should be identifiable and controlled. Thus you do not recognise an asset which is subjective and cannot be measured reliably.

1.8 Research and development costs

Research

Research activities by definition do not meet the criteria for recognition under IAS 38. This is because, at the research stage of a project, it cannot be certain that future economic benefits will probably flow to the entity from the project. There is too much uncertainty about the likely success or otherwise of the project. **Research costs should therefore be written off as an expense as they are incurred**. Development costs may be capitalised if they meet certain strict criteria. We will look at this in detail in Section 3.

1.9 Other internally generated intangible assets

The standard **prohibits** the recognition of **internally generated brands**, **mastheads**, **publishing titles and customer lists** and similar items as intangible assets. These all fail to meet one or more (in some cases all) of the definition and recognition criteria and in some cases are probably indistinguishable from internally generated goodwill.

1.10 Cost of an internally generated intangible asset

The costs allocated to an internally generated intangible asset should be only costs that can be **directly attributed** or allocated on a reasonable and consistent basis to creating, producing or preparing the asset for its intended use. The principles underlying the costs which may or may not be included are similar to those for other non-current assets and inventory.

The cost of an internally operated intangible asset is the sum of the **expenditure incurred from the date when** the intangible asset first **meets the recognition criteria**. If, as often happens, considerable costs have already been recognised as expenses before management could demonstrate that the criteria have been met, this earlier expenditure should not be retrospectively recognised at a later date as part of the cost of an intangible asset.

Question **Intangible asset**

Doug Co is developing a new production process. During 20X3, expenditure incurred was $100,000, of which $90,000 was incurred before 1 December 20X3 and $10,000 between 1 December 20X3 and 31 December 20X3. Doug Co can demonstrate that, at 1 December 20X3, the production process met the criteria for recognition as an intangible asset. The recoverable amount of the know-how embodied in the process is estimated to be $50,000.

How should the expenditure be treated?

Answer

At the end of 20X3, the production process is recognised as an intangible asset at a cost of $10,000. This is the expenditure incurred since the date when the recognition criteria were met, that is 1 December 20X3. The $90,000 expenditure incurred before 1 December 20X3 is expensed, because the recognition criteria were not met. It will never form part of the cost of the production process recognised in the balance sheet.

1.11 Recognition of an expense

All expenditure related to an intangible which does not meet the criteria for recognition either as an identifiable intangible asset or as goodwill arising on an acquisition should be **expensed as incurred**. The IAS gives examples of such expenditure.

- Start up costs
- Training costs
- Advertising costs
- Business relocation costs

Prepaid costs for services, for example advertising or marketing costs for campaigns that have been prepared but not launched, can still be recognised as a **prepayment**.

If tangible asset costs have been expensed in previous financial statements, they may not be recognised as part of the cost of the asset.

1.12 Measurement of intangible assets subsequent to initial recognition

FAST FORWARD

Intangible assets should initially be measured at cost, but subsequently they can be carried at **cost or at a fair value**.

The standard allows two methods of valuation for intangible assets after they have been first recognised.

Applying the **cost model**, an intangible asset should be **carried at its cost**, less any accumulated depreciation and less any accumulated impairment losses.

The **revaluation model** allows an intangible asset to be carried at a revalued amount, which is its **fair value** at the date of revaluation, less any subsequent accumulated amortisation and any subsequent accumulated impairment losses.

(a) The fair value must be able to be measured reliably with reference to an **active market** in that type of asset.

(b) The **entire class** of intangible assets of that type must be revalued at the same time (to prevent selective revaluations).

(c) If an intangible asset in a class of revalued intangible assets cannot be revalued because there is **no active market** for this asset, the asset should be carried at its **cost less any accumulated amortisation and impairment losses**.

(d) Revaluations should be made with such **regularity** that the carrying amount does not differ from that which would be determined using fair value at the balance sheet date.

Point to note

This treatment is **not** available for the **initial recognition** of intangible assets. This is because the cost of the asset must be reliably measured.

The guidelines state that there **will not usually be an active market** in an intangible asset; therefore the revaluation model will usually not be available. For example, although copyrights, publishing rights and film rights can be sold, each has a unique sale value. In such cases, revaluation to fair value would be inappropriate. A fair value might be obtainable however for assets such as fishing rights or quotas or taxi cab licences.

Where an intangible asset is revalued upwards to a fair value, the amount of the revaluation should be credited directly to equity under the heading of a **revaluation surplus**.

However, if a revaluation surplus is a **reversal of a revaluation decrease** that was previously charged against income, the increase can be recognised as income.

Where the carrying amount of an intangible asset is revalued downwards, the amount of the **downward revaluation** should be charged as an expense against income, unless the asset has previously been revalued upwards. A revaluation decrease should be first charged against any previous revaluation surplus in respect of that asset.

Question — Revaluation

An intangible asset is measured by a company at fair value. The asset was revalued by $400 in 20X3, and there is a revaluation surplus of $400 in the balance sheet. At the end of 20X4, the asset is valued again, and a downward valuation of $500 is required.

Required

State the accounting treatment for the downward revaluation.

Answer

In this example, the downward valuation of $500 can first be set against the revaluation surplus of $400. The revaluation surplus will be reduced to 0 and a charge of $100 made as an expense in 20X4.

When the revaluation model is used, and an intangible asset is revalued upwards, the cumulative revaluation **surplus may be transferred to retained earnings** when the surplus is eventually realised. The surplus would be realised when the asset is disposed of. However, the surplus may also be realised over time as the **asset is used** by the entity. The amount of the surplus realised each year is the difference between the amortisation charge for the asset based on the revalued amount of the asset, and the amortisation that would be charged on the basis of the asset's historical cost. The realised surplus in such case should be transferred from revaluation surplus directly to retained earnings, and should not be taken through the income statement.

1.13 Useful life

An entity should **assess** the useful life of an intangible asset, which may be **finite or indefinite**. An intangible asset has an indefinite useful life when there is **no foreseeable limit** to the period over which the asset is expected to generate net cash inflows for the entity.

Many factors are considered in determining the useful life of an intangible asset, including: expected usage; typical product life cycles; technical, technological, commercial or other types of obsolescence; the stability of the industry; expected actions by competitors; the level of maintenance expenditure required; and legal or similar limits on the use of the asset, such as the expiry dates of related leases. Computer software and many other intangible assets normally have short lives because they are susceptible to technological obsolescence. However, uncertainty does not justify choosing a life that is unrealistically short.

The useful life of an intangible asset that arises from **contractual or other legal rights** should not exceed the period of the rights, but may be shorter depending on the period over which the entity expects to use the asset.

1.14 Amortisation period and amortisation method

An intangible asset with a finite useful life should be amortised over its **expected useful life**.

(a) Amortisation should start when the asset is **available for use**.

(b) Amortisation should cease at the earlier of the date that the asset is classified **as held for sale** in accordance with IFRS 5 *Non-current assets held for sale and discontinued operations* and the date that the asset is **derecognised**.

(c) The amortisation method used should reflect the **pattern in which the asset's future economic benefits are consumed**. If such a pattern cannot be predicted reliably, the straight-line method should be used.

(d) The amortisation charge for each period should normally be recognised **in profit or loss**.

The **residual value** of an intangible asset with a finite useful life is **assumed to be zero** unless a third party is committed to buying the intangible asset at the end of its useful life or unless there is an active market for that type of asset (so that its expected residual value can be measured) and it is probable that there will be a market for the asset at the end of its useful life.

The amortisation period and the amortisation method used for an intangible asset with a finite useful life should be **reviewed at each financial year-end**.

1.15 Intangible assets with indefinite useful lives

An intangible asset with an indefinite useful life **should not be amortised**. (IAS 36 requires that such an asset is tested for impairment at least annually.)

The useful life of an intangible asset that is not being amortised should be **reviewed each year** to determine whether it is still appropriate to assess its useful life as indefinite. Reassessing the useful life of an intangible asset as finite rather than indefinite is an indicator that the asset may be impaired and therefore it should be tested for impairment.

Question — Useful life

It may be difficult to establish the useful life of an intangible asset, and judgement will be needed. Consider how to determine the useful life of a *purchased* brand name.

Answer

Factors to consider would include the following.

(a) Legal protection of the brand name and the control of the entity over the (illegal) use by others of the brand name (ie control over pirating)

(b) Age of the brand name

(c) Status or position of the brand in its particular market

(d) Ability of the management of the entity to manage the brand name and to measure activities that support the brand name (eg advertising and PR activities)

(e) Stability and geographical spread of the market in which the branded products are sold

(f) Pattern of benefits that the brand name is expected to generate over time

(g) Intention of the entity to use and promote the brand name over time (as evidenced perhaps by a business plan in which there will be substantial expenditure to promote the brand name)

1.16 Disposals/retirements of intangible assets

An intangible asset should be eliminated from the balance sheet when it is disposed of or when there is no further expected economic benefit from its future use. On disposal the gain or loss arising from the **difference between the net disposal proceeds and the carrying amount** of the asset should be taken to the income statement as a gain or loss on disposal (ie treated as income or expense).

1.17 Disclosure requirements

The standard has fairly extensive disclosure requirements for intangible assets. The financial statements should disclose the **accounting policies** for intangible assets that have been adopted.

For **each class of intangible assets**, disclosure is required of the following.

- The **method of amortisation** used
- The **useful life** of the assets or the amortisation rate used
- The **gross carrying amount**, the **accumulated amortisation** and the **accumulated impairment losses** as at the beginning and the end of the period
- A **reconciliation of the carrying amount** as at the beginning and at the end of the period (additions, retirements/disposals, revaluations, impairment losses, impairment losses reversed, amortisation charge for the period, net exchange differences, other movements)
- The carrying amount of **internally-generated intangible assets**

The financial statements should also disclose the following.

- In the case of intangible assets that are assessed as having an indefinite useful life, the carrying amounts and the reasons supporting that assessment
- For intangible assets acquired by way of a **government grant** and initially recognised at fair value, the **fair value initially recognised**, the **carrying amount**, and the accounting treatment for subsequent remeasurements
- The carrying amount, nature and remaining amortisation period of any intangible asset that is **material to the financial statements of the entity as a whole**
- The existence (if any) and amounts of intangible assets whose **title is restricted** and of intangible assets that have been **pledged as security** for liabilities
- The amount of any **commitments for the future acquisition of intangible assets**

Where intangible assets are accounted for at revalued amounts, disclosure is required of the following.

- The **effective date of the revaluation** (by class of intangible assets)
- The **carrying amount** of revalued intangible assets
- The carrying amount that would have been shown (by class of assets) **if the cost model had been used**, and the amount of amortisation that would have been charged

- The amount of any **revaluation surplus** on intangible assets, as at the beginning and end of the period, and movements in the surplus during the year (and any restrictions on the distribution of the balance to shareholders)

The financial statements should also disclose the amount of research and development expenditure that has been charged as an expense of the period.

1.18 Section summary

- An intangible asset should be recognised if, and only if, it is probable that future economic benefits will flow to the entity and the cost of the asset can be measured reliably.
- An asset is initially recognised at cost and subsequently carried either at cost or revalued amount.
- Costs that do not meet the recognition criteria should be expensed as incurred.
- An intangible asset with a finite useful life should be amortised over its useful life. An intangible asset with an indefinite useful life should not be amortised.

2 Goodwill

FAST FORWARD

If a business has **goodwill**, it means that the value of the business as a going concern is greater than the value of its separate tangible assets. The valuation of goodwill is extremely subjective and fluctuates constantly. For this reason, non-purchased goodwill is **not** shown as an asset in the balance sheet.

2.1 Internally generated goodwill

Goodwill is **created by good relationships** between a business and its customers.

(a) By building up a **reputation** (by word of mouth perhaps) for high quality products or high standards of service

(b) By **responding promptly and helpfully** to queries and complaints from customers

(c) Through the **personality of the staff** and their attitudes to customers

The value of goodwill to a business might be **extremely significant**. However, goodwill is not usually valued in the accounts of a business at all, and we should not normally expect to find an amount for goodwill in its balance sheet. For example, the welcoming smile of the bar staff may contribute more to a bar's profits than the fact that a new electronic cash register has recently been acquired. Even so, whereas the cash register will be recorded in the accounts as a non-current asset, the value of staff would be ignored for accounting purposes.

On reflection, we might agree with this omission of goodwill from the accounts of a business.

(a) The goodwill is **inherent** in the business but it has not been paid for, and it does not have an 'objective' value. We can guess at what such goodwill is worth, but such guesswork would be a matter of individual opinion, and not based on hard facts.

(b) Goodwill **changes** from day to day. One act of bad customer relations might damage goodwill and one act of good relations might improve it. Staff with a favourable personality might retire or leave to find another job, to be replaced by staff who need time to find their feet in the job, etc. Since goodwill is continually changing in value, it cannot realistically be recorded in the accounts of the business.

2.2 Purchased goodwill

FAST FORWARD

When someone **purchases a business** as a going concern the purchaser and vendor will fix an agreed price which includes an element in respect of goodwill. The amount at which goodwill is calculated is not an accounting problem, but a matter of agreement between the two parties.

There is one exception to the general rule that goodwill has no objective valuation. This is **when a business is sold**. People wishing to set up in business have a choice of how to do it – they can either buy their own long-term assets and inventory and set up their business from scratch, or they can buy up an existing business from a proprietor willing to sell it. When a buyer purchases an existing business, he will have to purchase not only its long-term assets and inventory (and perhaps take over its accounts payable and receivable too) but also the goodwill of the business.

Purchased goodwill is shown in the balance sheet because it has been paid for. It has no tangible substance, and so it is an **intangible non-current asset**.

Exam focus point

The Pilot Paper had a 4-mark question on calculating the goodwill arising on purchase of an unincorporated business.

2.3 How is the value of purchased goodwill decided?

When a business is sold, there is likely to be some purchased goodwill in the selling price. But **how is the amount of this purchased goodwill decided**?

This is not really a problem for accountants, who must simply record the goodwill in the accounts of the new business. The value of the goodwill is a **matter for the purchaser and seller to agree upon in fixing the purchase/sale price**. However, two methods of valuation are worth mentioning here.

(a) The seller and buyer agree on a price **without specifically quantifying the goodwill.** The purchased goodwill will then be the difference between the price agreed and the value of the tangible assets in the books of the new business.

(b) However, the calculation of goodwill often precedes the fixing of the purchase price and becomes a **central element of negotiation**. There are many ways of arriving at a value for goodwill and most of them are related to the profit record of the business in question.

No matter how goodwill is calculated within the total agreed purchase price, the goodwill shown by the purchaser in his accounts will be **the difference between the purchase consideration and his own valuation of the tangible net assets acquired**. If A values his tangible net assets at $40,000, goodwill is agreed at $21,000 and B agrees to pay $61,000 for the business but values the tangible net assets at only $38,000, then the goodwill in B's books will be $61,000 – $38,000 = $23,000.

2.4 IFRS 3 Business combinations

FAST FORWARD

Purchased goodwill arising on a business combination is retained in the balance sheet as an intangible asset under the requirements of **IFRS 3**. It must then be reviewed for impairment annually.

IFRS 3 covers the accounting treatment of goodwill acquired in a business combination.

It is possible to define goodwill in different ways. The IFRS 3 definition of goodwill is different from the more traditional definition and emphasises benefits, rather than the method of calculation.

Key terms

> **Goodwill**. Future economic benefits arising from assets that are not capable of being individually identified and separately recognised. *(IFRS 3)*
>
> **Goodwill**. Any excess of the cost of the business combination over the acquirer's interest in the net fair value of the identifiable assets, liabilities and contingent liabilities acquired. *(IFRS 3)*

Goodwill acquired in a business combination is **recognised as an asset** and is initially measured at **cost**. Cost is the excess of the cost of the combination over the acquirer's interest in the net fair value of the acquiree's identifiable assets, liabilities and contingent liabilities.

After initial recognition goodwill acquired in a business combination is measured **at cost less any accumulated impairment losses**. It is **not amortised**. Instead it is tested for impairment at least annually, in accordance with IAS 36 *Impairment of assets.*

Negative goodwill arises when the acquirer's interest in the net fair value of the acquiree's identifiable assets, liabilities and contingent liabilities exceeds the cost of the business combination. IFRS 3 refers to negative goodwill as the 'excess of acquirer's interest in the net fair value of acquiree's identifiable assets, liabilities and contingent liabilities over cost'.

Negative goodwill can arise as the result of **errors** in measuring the fair value of either the cost of the combination or the acquiree's identifiable net assets. It can also arise as the result of a **bargain purchase**. Where there is negative goodwill, an entity should first **reassess** the amounts at which it has measured both the cost of the combination and the acquiree's identifiable net assets. This exercise should identify any errors.

Any negative goodwill remaining should be **recognised immediately in profit or loss** (that is, in the income statement).

IFRS 3 requires extensive **disclosures**. These include a **reconciliation** of the carrying amount of goodwill at the beginning and end of the period, showing separately:

(a) The gross amount and accumulated impairment losses at the beginning of the period
(b) Additional goodwill recognised during the period
(c) Impairment losses recognised during the period
(d) Net exchange differences arising during the period, and
(e) The gross amount and accumulated impairment losses at the end of the period

Question

Goodwill

What are the main characteristics of goodwill which distinguish it from other intangible non-current assets? To what extent do you consider that these characteristics should affect the accounting treatment of goodwill? State your reasons.

Answer

Goodwill may be distinguished from other intangible non-current assets by reference to the following characteristics.

(a) It is incapable of realisation separately from the business as a whole.

(b) Its value has no reliable or predictable relationship to any costs which may have been incurred.

(c) Its value arises from various intangible factors such as skilled employees, effective advertising or a strategic location. These indirect factors cannot be valued.

(d) The value of goodwill may fluctuate widely according to internal and external circumstances over relatively short periods of time.

(e) The assessment of the value of goodwill is highly subjective.

It could be argued that, because goodwill is so different from other intangible non-current assets it does not make sense to account for it in the same way. Thus the capitalisation and amortisation treatment would not be acceptable. Furthermore, because goodwill is so difficult to value, any valuation may be misleading, and it is best eliminated from the balance sheet altogether. However, there are strong arguments for treating it like any other intangible non-current asset. This issue remains controversial.

3 Research and development costs

FAST FORWARD

If the criteria laid down by IAS 38 are satisfied, development costs may be capitalised. They are then amortised, beginning from the time when the development project is available for use.

3.1 Deferred development costs

Deferred development costs are the other type of intangible non-current asset you need to know about. Large companies may spend significant amounts of money on research and development (R & D) activities. Obviously, any amounts so expended must be credited to cash and debited to an account for research and development expenditure. The accounting problem is **how to treat the debit balance on R & D account** at the balance sheet date.

There are two possibilities.

(a) The debit balance may be classified as an **expense** and transferred to the income statement. This is referred to as 'writing off' the expenditure. The argument here is that it is an expense just like rent or wages and its accounting treatment should be the same.

(b) The debit balance may be classified as an **asset** and included in the balance sheet. This is referred to as 'capitalising' or 'carrying forward' or 'deferring' the expenditure. This argument is based on the accrual assumption. If R & D activity eventually leads to new or improved products which generate revenue, the costs should be carried forward to be matched against that revenue in future accounting periods.

So the main question surrounding research and development (R & D) costs is whether they should be treated as an expense or capitalised as an asset. This question is dealt with in IAS 38 *Intangible assets.*

IAS 38 was originally published in September 1998 and replaced IAS 9 *Research and development costs.*

3.2 Definitions

The following definitions are given by the standard.

Key terms

An **intangible asset** is an identifiable non-monetary asset without physical substance.

Research is original and planned investigation undertaken with the prospect of gaining new scientific or technical knowledge and understanding.

Development is the application of research findings or other knowledge to a plan or design for the production of new or substantially improved materials, devices, products, processes, systems or services prior to the commencement of commercial production or use.

Amortisation is the systematic allocation of the depreciable amount of an intangible asset over its useful life.

Depreciable amount is the cost of an asset, or other amount substituted for cost in the financial statements, less its residual value.

Key terms continued

Useful life is either:

- the period of time over which an asset is expected to be used by the enterprise; or
- the number of production or similar units expected to be obtained from the asset by the enterprise (*IAS 38*)

Exam focus point

These definitions are very important. You must learn them as they will form an integral part of any discussion of IAS 38.

Although these definitions are usually well-understood, **in practice** it may not be so easy to identify the activities encompassed by R & D and the dividing line between the categories may be indistinct. Identification often depends on the type of business involved, the projects it undertakes and how it is organised.

The standard gives examples of activities which might be included in either research or development, or which are neither but may be closely associated with both.

- **Research**
  - Activities aimed at obtaining new knowledge
  - The search for applications of research findings or other knowledge
  - The search for product or process alternatives
  - The formulation and design of possible new or improved product or process alternatives
- **Development**
  - The design, construction and testing of pre-production prototypes and models
  - The design of tools, jigs, moulds and dies involving new technology
  - The design, construction and operation of a pilot plant that is not of a scale economically feasible for commercial production
  - The design, construction and testing of a chosen alternative for new/improved materials

3.3 Components of research and development costs

Research and development costs will include all costs that are **directly attributable** to research and development activities, or that can be **allocated on a reasonable basis.**

The standard lists the costs which may be included in R & D, where applicable (note that **selling costs are excluded**).

- **Salaries, wages** and other employment related costs of personnel engaged in R & D activities
- Costs of **materials and services** consumed in R & D activities
- **Depreciation** of property, plant and equipment to the extent that these assets are used for R & D activities
- **Overhead costs**, other than general administrative costs, related to R & D activities; these costs are allocated on bases similar to those used in allocating overhead costs to inventories (see IAS 2 *Inventories*)
- **Other costs**, such as the amortisation of patents and licences, to the extent that these assets are used for R & D activities

3.4 Recognition of R & D costs

The relationship between the R & D costs and the **economic benefit** expected to derive from them will determine the allocation of those costs to different periods. Recognition of the costs as an asset will only occur where it is probable that the cost will produce future economic benefits for the enterprise and where the costs can be measured reliably.

(a) In the case of **research costs**, this will not be the case due to uncertainty about the resulting benefit from them; and so they should be expensed in the period in which they arose.

(b) **Development activities** tend to be much further advanced than the research stage and so it may be possible to determine the likelihood of future economic benefit. Where it is possible to do so, the development costs should be carried forward as an asset.

3.4.1 Research costs

Research costs should be recognised as an **expense in the period in which they are incurred**. They should not be recognised as an asset in a later period.

3.4.2 Development costs

Alternative treatments are given for development costs, the use of which depends on the situation. Most of the time, development costs will be recognised as an **expense in the period in which they are incurred** unless the criteria for asset recognition identified below are met. Development costs initially recognised as an expense should not be recognised as an asset in a later period.

Development expenditure should be recognised as an asset only when the business can demonstrate **all** of the following.

- The technical feasibility of **completing** the intangible asset so that it will be available for use or sale
- Its intention to complete the intangible asset and **use or sell** it
- Its **ability** to use or sell the intangible asset
- How the intangible asset will generate probable **future economic benefits**. Among other things, the enterprise should demonstrate the existence of a market for the output of the intangible asset itself or, if it is to be used internally, the usefulness of the intangible asset
- The availability of adequate technical, financial and other **resources** to complete the development and to use or sell the intangible asset
- Its ability to **measure reliably** the expenditure attributable to the intangible asset during its development

There is also an important point about the carrying amount of the asset and recoverability. The development costs of a project recognised as an asset should not exceed the amount that it is probable will be **recovered from related future economic benefits**, after deducting further development costs, related production costs, and selling and administrative costs directly incurred in marketing the product.

3.5 Amortisation of development costs

Once capitalised as an asset, development costs must be **amortised** and recognised as an expense to match the costs with the related revenue or cost savings. This must be done on a systematic basis, so as to reflect the pattern in which the related economic benefits are recognised.

It is unlikely to be possible to **match exactly** the economic benefits obtained with the costs which are held as an asset simply because of the nature of development activities. The enterprise should consider either:

(a) the revenue or other benefits from the sale/use of the product/process; *or*
(b) the period of time over which the product/process is expected to be sold/used.

Point to note

If the pattern cannot be determined reliably, the straight-line method should be used.

The amortisation will begin when the **asset is available for use**.

3.6 Impairment of development costs

FAST FORWARD

Impairment rules follow **IAS 36**. There are substantial disclosure requirements.

As with all assets, impairment (fall in value of an asset) is a possibility, but perhaps even more so in cases such as this. The development costs should be **written down** to the extent that the unamortised balance (taken together with further development costs, related production costs, and selling and administrative costs directly incurred in marketing the product) is no longer probable of being recovered from the expected future economic benefit.

3.7 Disclosure

For **each class of intangible assets** (including development costs), IAS 38 requires the following disclosures.

- The **method of amortisation** used
- The **useful life** of the assets or the amortisation rate used
- The **gross carrying amount**, the **accumulated amortisation** and the **accumulated impairment losses** as at the beginning and the end of the period
- A **reconciliation of the carrying amount** as at the beginning and at the end of the period (additions, retirements/disposals, revaluations, impairment losses, impairment losses reversed, amortisation charge for the period, net exchange differences, other movements)
- The carrying amount of **internally-generated intangible assets**

Question — **Research and development**

Y Co is a research company which specialises in developing new materials and manufacturing processes for the furniture industry. The company receives payments from a variety of manufacturers, which pay for the right to use the company's patented fabrics and processes.

Research and development costs for the year ended 30 September 20X5 can be analysed as follows.

	$
Expenditure on continuing research projects	1,420,000
Amortisation of development expenditure capitalised in earlier years	240,000
New projects started during the year:	
Project A	280,000
New flame-proof padding. Expected to cost a total of $800,000 to develop. Expected total revenue $2,000,000 once work completed - probably late 20X6	
Project B	150,000
New colour-fast dye. Expected to cost a total of $3,000,000 to complete. Future revenues are likely to exceed $5,000,000. The completion date is uncertain because external funding will have to be obtained before research work can be completed.	
Project C	110,000
Investigation of new adhesive recently developed in aerospace industry. If this proves effective then Y Co may well generate significant income because it will be used in place of existing adhesives.	
	2,200,000

The company has a policy of capitalising all development expenditure where permitted by IAS 38.

Explain how the three research projects A, B and C will be dealt with in Y Co's income statement and balance sheet.

In each case, explain your proposed treatment in terms of IAS 38 *Intangible assets* and, where relevant, in terms of the fundamental accounting assumptions of going concern and accruals, and the prudence concept.

Answer

Project A

This project meets the criteria in IAS 38 for development expenditure to be recognised as an asset. These are as follows.

(a) The product or process is clearly defined and the costs attributable to the product or process can be separately identified and measured reliably.

(b) The technical feasibility of the product or process can be demonstrated.

(c) The enterprise intends to produce and market, or use, the product or process and has the ability to do so.

(d) The existence of a market for the product or process or, if it is to be used internally rather than sold, its usefulness to the enterprise, can be demonstrated.

(e) Adequate resources exist, or their availability can be demonstrated, to complete the project and market or use the product or process.

The capitalisation of development costs in a company which is a going concern means that these are accrued in order that they can be matched against the income they are expected to generate.

Hence the costs of $280,000 incurred to date should be transferred from research and development costs to capitalised development expenditure and carried forward until revenues are generated; they should then be matched with those revenues.

Project B

Whilst this project meets most of the criteria discussed above which would enable the costs to be carried forward it fails on the requirement that 'adequate resources exist, or their availability can be demonstrated, to complete the project'.

Hence it would be prudent to write off these costs. Once funding is obtained the situation can then be reassessed and these and future costs may be capitalised. In this case the prudence concept overrides the accruals assumption.

Project C

This is a research project according to IAS 38, ie original and planned investigation undertaken with the prospect of gaining new scientific or technical knowledge or understanding.

There is no certainty as to its ultimate success or commercial viability and therefore it cannot be considered to be a development project. IAS 38 therefore requires that costs be written off as incurred. Once again, prudence overrides the accruals assumption.

Question

Disclosure

Show how the research and development costs in the question above will be disclosed in the accounts of Y Co. Assume the cost of capitalised development expenditure brought forward is $1,480,000, and that accumulated amortisation of $240,000 has been charged at the beginning of the year.

Show extracts from:

(a) Income statement
(b) Balance sheet
(c) Notes to the accounts

Answer

(a) INCOME STATEMENT (EXTRACT)

	$
Research expenditure (Project C + 1,420,000)	1,530,000
Development costs (Project B)	150,000
Amortisation of capitalised development costs	240,000

(b) BALANCE SHEET (EXTRACT)

	$
Non current assets	
Intangible assets	
Deferred development costs	1,280,000

(c) NOTE TO ACCOUNTS

Deferred development costs

	$
Cost	
Balance b/f	1,480,000
Additions during year (Project A)	280,000
Balance c/f	1,760,000
Amortisation	
Balance b/f	240,000
Charge during year	240,000
Balance c/f	480,000
Net book value at 30 September 20X5	1,280,000
Net book value at 30 September 20X4	1,240,000

Chapter Roundup

- **Intangible assets** are defined by **IAS 38** as non-monetary assets without physical substance. They must be:
  - Identifiable
  - Controlled as a result of a past event
  - Able to provide future economic benefits
- Intangible assets should initially be measured at cost, but subsequently they can be carried at **cost or at a fair value**.
- If a business has **goodwill**, it means that the value of the business as a going concern is greater than the value of its separate tangible assets. The valuation of goodwill is extremely subjective and fluctuates constantly. For this reason, non-purchased goodwill is **not** shown as an asset in the balance sheet.
- When someone **purchases a business** as a going concern the purchaser and vendor will fix an agreed price which includes an element in respect of goodwill. The amount at which goodwill is calculated is not an accounting problem, but a matter of agreement between the two parties.
- **Purchased goodwill** arising on a business combination is retained in the balance sheet as an intangible asset under the requirements of **IFRS 3**. It must then be reviewed for impairment annually.
- If the criteria laid down by IAS 38 are satisfied, development costs may be capitalised. They are then amortised, beginning from the time when the development project is available for use.
- **Impairment** rules follow **IAS 36**. There are substantial disclosure requirements.

Quick Quiz

1 Intangible assets can only be recognised in a company's accounts if:

- It is probable that .... will flow to the entity
- The cost can be ....

2 What are the criteria which must be met before development expenditure can be deferred?

3 Start up costs must be expensed.

True ☐

False ☐

4 Peggy buys Phil's business for $30,000. The business assets are a bar valued at $20,000, inventories at $3,000 and receivables of $3,000. How much is goodwill valued at?

5 How is goodwill measured under IFRS 3?

6 How should negative goodwill be accounted for under IFRS 3?

Answers to Quick Quiz

1 Future economic benefits. Measured reliably.

2 See Para 3.4.2. Learn these six requirements.

3 True

4 $30,000 – $20,000 – $3,000 – $3,000 = $4,000

5 Cost less accumulated impairment losses

6 Recognised in profit or loss immediately

Now try the question below from the Exam Question Bank

Number	Level	Marks	Time
Q18	Examination	5	9 mins

7

IAS 17: Leases

Introduction

Leasing transactions are extremely common so this is an important practical subject. **Lease accounting is regulated by IAS 17**, which was introduced because of abuses in the use of lease accounting by companies. IAS 17 was revised in December 2003.

These companies effectively 'owned' an asset and 'owed' a debt for its purchase, but showed neither the asset nor the liability on the balance sheet because they were not required to do so. This is called '**off balance sheet finance**'.

Topic list	Learning outcomes	Syllabus references	Ability required
1 Types of lease	C (v)	C (14)	Evaluation
2 Lessees	C (v)	C (14)	Application

1 Types of lease

FAST FORWARD

Under **finance leases**:

- Assets acquired should be capitalised
- The interest element of instalments should be charged against profit.

Operating leases are **rental agreements** and all instalments are charged against profit.

1.1 IAS 17

Where goods are acquired other than on immediate cash terms, arrangements have to be made in respect of the future payments on those goods. In the simplest case of **credit sales**, the purchaser is allowed a period of time (say one month) to settle the outstanding amount and the normal accounting procedure in respect of receivables/payables will be adopted. However, in recent years there has been considerable growth in leasing agreements (some types of lease are called **hire purchase agreements** in some countries).

IAS 17 *Leases* standardises the accounting treatment and disclosure of assets held under lease.

In a leasing transaction there is a **contract** between the lessor and the lessee for the hire of an asset. The lessor retains legal ownership but conveys to the lessee the right to use the asset for an agreed period of time in return for specified rentals. IAS 17 defines a lease and recognises two types.

Key terms

Lease. An agreement whereby the lessor conveys to the lessee in return for a payment or a series of payments the right to use an asset for an agreed period of time.

Finance lease. A lease that transfers substantially all the risks and rewards incident to ownership of an asset. Title may or may not eventually be transferred.

Operating lease. A lease other than a finance lease. *(IAS 17)*

A **finance lease** may be a **hire purchase agreement**. (The difference is that under a hire purchase agreement the customer eventually, after paying an agreed number of instalments, becomes entitled to exercise an option to purchase the asset. Under other leasing agreements, ownership remains forever with the lessor.)

In this chapter the **user** of an asset will often be referred to simply as the **lessee**, and the **supplier** as the **lessor**. You should bear in mind that identical requirements apply in the case of hirers and vendors respectively under hire purchase agreements.

To expand on the definition above, a finance lease should be presumed if at the inception of a lease the **present value of the minimum lease payments** is approximately equal to the **fair value of the leased asset**.

The present value should be calculated by using the **interest rate implicit in the lease**.

Key terms

Minimum lease payments. The payments over the lease term that the lessee is or can be required to make, excluding contingent rent, costs for services and taxes to be paid by and be reimbursable to the lessor, together with:

(a) For a lessee, any amounts guaranteed by the lessee or by a party related to the lessee

(b) For a lessor, any residual value guaranteed to the lessor by one of the following.

  (i) The lessee
  (ii) A party related to the lessee
  (iii) An independent third party financially capable of meeting this guarantee

However, if the lessee has the option to purchase the asset at a price which is expected to be sufficiently lower than fair value at the date the option becomes exercisable for it to be reasonably certain, at the inception of the lease, that the option will be exercised, the minimum lease payments comprise the minimum payments payable over the lease term to the expected date of exercise of this purchase option and the payment required to exercise it.

Interest rate implicit in the lease

The discount rate that, at the inception of the lease, causes the aggregate present value of

(a) the minimum lease payments, and
(b) the unguaranteed residual value

to be equal to the sum of

(a) the fair value of the leased asset, and
(b) any initial direct costs of the lessor

Initial direct costs are **incremental costs** that are directly attributable to **negotiating** and **arranging** a lease, except for such costs incurred by manufacturer or dealer lessors. Examples of initial direct costs include amounts such as **commissions, legal fees** and relevant internal costs.

Lease term. The non-cancellable period for which the lessee has contracted to lease the asset together with any further terms for which the lessee has the option to continue to lease the asset, with or without further payment, when at the inception of the lease it is reasonably certain that the lessee will exercise the option.

A non-cancellable lease is a lease that is cancellable only in one of the following situations.

(a) Upon the occurrence of some remote contingency

(b) With the permission of the lessor

(c) If the lessee enters into a new lease for the same or an equivalent asset with the same lessor

(d) Upon payment by the lessee of an additional amount such that, at inception, continuation of the lease is reasonably certain

The **inception of the lease** is the earlier of the date of the lease agreement and the date of commitment by the parties to the principal provisions of the lease. As at this date:

(a) a lease is classified as either an operating lease or a finance lease; and

(b) in the case of a finance lease, the amounts to be recognised at the commencement of the lease term are determined.

Economic life is either:

(a) the period over which an asset is expected to be economically usable by one or more users, or

(b) the number of production or similar units expected to be obtained from the asset by one or more users.

Useful life is the estimated remaining period, from the beginning of the lease term, without limitation by the lease term, over which the economic benefits embodied in the asset are expected to be consumed by the entity.

Guaranteed residual value is:

(a) for a lessee, that part of the residual value which is guaranteed by the lessee or by a party related to the lessee (the amount of the guarantee being the maximum amount that could, in any event, become payable).

(b) for a lessor, that part of the residual value which is guaranteed by the lessee or by a third party unrelated to the lessor who is financially capable of discharging the obligations under the guarantee.

Unguaranteed residual value is that portion of the residual value of the leased asset, the realisation of which by the lessor is not assured or is guaranteed solely by a party related to the lessor.

Gross investment in the lease is the aggregate of:

(a) the minimum lease payments receivable by the lessor under a finance lease, and
(b) any unguaranteed residual value accruing to the lessor.

Net investment in the lease is the gross investment in the lease discounted at the interest rate implicit in the lease.

Unearned finance income is the difference between:

(a) the gross investment in the lease, and
(b) the net investment in the lease.

The **lessee's incremental borrowing rate of interest** is the rate of interest the lessee would have to pay on a similar lease or, if that is not determinable, the rate that, at the inception of the lease, the lessee would incur to borrow over a similar term, and with a similar security, the funds necessary to purchase the asset.

Contingent rent is that portion of the lease payments that is not fixed in amount but is based on a factor other than just the passage of time (eg percentage of sales, amount of usage, price indices, market rates of interest). *(IAS 17)*

There are further definitions in IAS 17, but (fortunately!) these go beyond the scope of your syllabus.

1.2 Accounting for operating leases

Operating leases do not really pose an accounting problem. The lessee pays amounts periodically to the lessor and these are **charged to the income statement**. The lessor treats the leased asset as a non-current asset and depreciates it in the normal way. Rentals received from the lessee are credited to the income statement in the lessor's books.

Where the lessee is offered an incentive such as a **rent-free period** or **cashback incentive**, this is effectively a **discount**, which will be spread over the period of the operating lease in accordance with the accruals principle. For instance, if a company entered into a 4-year operating lease but was not required to make any payments until year 2, the total payments to be made over years 2-4 should be charged evenly over years 1-4.

Where a cashback incentive is received, the total amount payable over the lease term, less the cashback, should be charged evenly over the term of the lease. This can be done by crediting the cashback received to deferred income and releasing it to the income statement over the lease term.

1.3 Accounting for finance leases

For assets held under **finance leases or hire purchase** this accounting treatment would not disclose the reality of the situation. If a **lessor** leases out an asset on a finance lease, the asset will probably never be seen on his premises or used in his business again. It would be inappropriate for a lessor to record such an asset as a non-current asset. In reality, what he owns is a **stream of cash flows receivable** from the lessee. **The asset is an amount receivable rather than a non-current asset.**

Similarly, a **lessee** may use a finance lease to fund the 'acquisition' of a major asset which he will then use in his business perhaps for many years. **The substance of the transaction is that he has acquired a non-**

current asset, and this is reflected in the accounting treatment prescribed by IAS 17, even though in law the lessee never becomes the owner of the asset.

The following summary diagram should help you when deciding whether a lease is an operating lease or a finance lease.

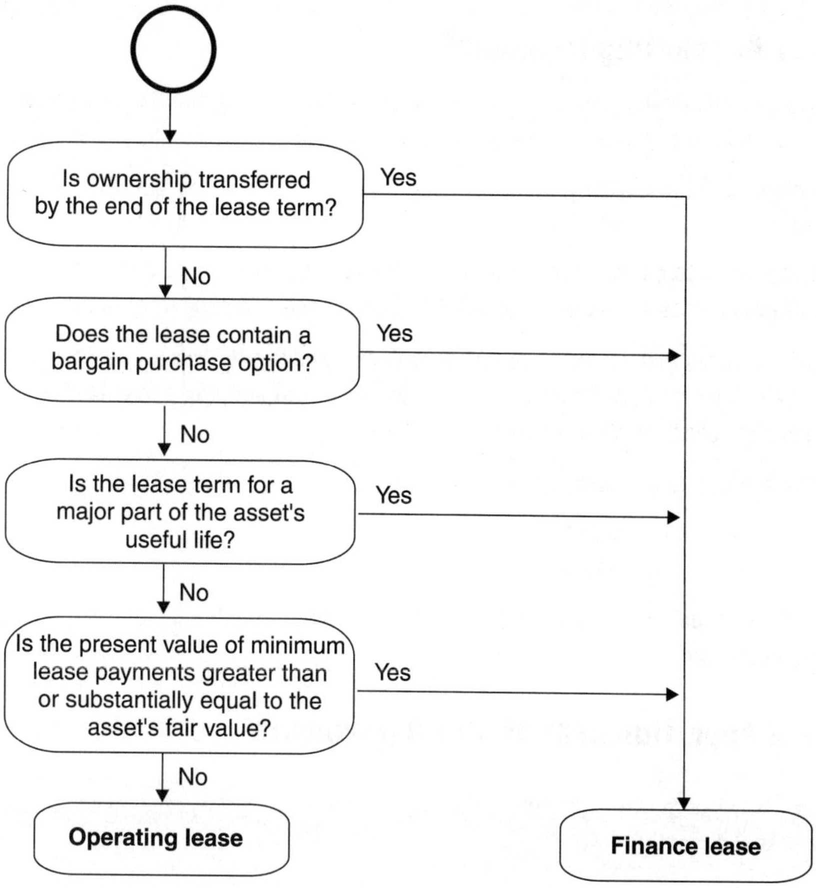

The standard also gives additional indicators of a lease that should be classified as a finance lease.

- the leased assets are of such a specialised nature that only the lessee can use them without major modifications
- if the lessee can cancel the lease, he must bear any losses suffered by the lessor associated with the cancellation
- the lessee has the ability to continue the lease for a secondary period at a rent that is substantially lower than market rent
- gains or losses due to fluctuation in the fair value of the residual value of the asset accrue to the lessee

The revised IAS 17 states that when classifying a lease of **land and buildings** the **land** element is normally classified as an **operating lease unless title passes to the lessee** at the end of the contract.

Exam focus point

You may be required to decide whether a lease is an operating lease or a finance lease. Make sure you understand the criteria.

2 Lessees

Exam focus point

> You are not required to know the accounting treatment of a finance lease in the books of the lessor.

2.1 Accounting treatment

IAS 17 requires that, when an asset changes hands under a **finance lease**, **lessor and lessee should account for the transaction as though it were a credit sale.** In the lessee's books therefore:

DEBIT Asset account
CREDIT Lessor (liability) account

The amount to be recorded in this way is the **lower of** the **fair value** and the **present value** of the **minimum lease payments**. This will generally be the purchase price of the asset.

IAS 17 states that it is not appropriate to show liabilities for leased assets as deductions from the leased assets. A distinction should be made between **current and non-current** lease liabilities, if the entity makes this distinction for other liabilities.

The asset should be **depreciated** (on the bases set out in IASs 16 and 38) over the shorter of:

- The lease term
- The asset's useful life

If there is reasonable certainty of eventual ownership of the asset, then it should be depreciated over its useful life.

2.2 Apportionment of rental payments

FAST FORWARD

> You must learn (through repeated practice) how to apply the actuarial and sum-of-the-digits methods of **interest allocation**.

When the lessee makes a rental payment it will comprise two elements.

(a) An **interest charge** on the finance provided by the lessor. This proportion of each payment is interest payable and interest receivable in the income statements of the lessee and lessor respectively.

(b) A repayment of part of the **capital cost** of the asset. In the lessee's books this proportion of each rental payment must be debited to the lessor's account to reduce the outstanding liability. In the lessor's books, it must be credited to the lessee's account to reduce the amount owing (the debit of course is to cash).

The accounting problem is to decide what proportion of each instalment paid by the lessee represents interest, and what proportion represents a repayment of the capital advanced by the lessor. There are three apportionment methods you may encounter:

- The straight line method
- The actuarial method
- The sum-of-the-digits method

Exam focus point

> An examination question will always make it clear which method should be used. In theory, the aim is that the income statement finance charge should reduce over the lease term in line with the outstanding liability. If you are given an interest rate, you will be expected to use the actuarial method. If not, use the sum-of-the-digits method. In both May and November 2005 there was a question specifying the use of the sum-of-the-digits method.

The **straight-line method** is simple but does not provide a constant rate of interest. The interest amount is simply allocated equally over the lease periods. You are not likely to be asked to use this method in the exam, but you should know about it.

The **actuarial method** is the best and most scientific method. It derives from the common-sense assumption that the interest charged by a lessor company will equal the rate of return desired by the company, multiplied by the amount of capital it has invested.

(a) At the beginning of the lease the capital invested is equal to the fair value of the asset (less any initial deposit paid by the lessee).

(b) This amount reduces as each instalment is paid. It follows that the interest accruing is greatest in the early part of the lease term, and gradually reduces as capital is repaid. In this section, we will look at a simple example of the actuarial method.

The **sum-of-the-digits** method approximates to the actuarial method, splitting the total interest (without reference to a rate of interest) in such a way that the greater proportion falls in the earlier years. The procedure is as follows.

(a) Assign a digit to each instalment. The digit 1 should be assigned to the final instalment, 2 to the penultimate instalment and so on.

(b) Add the digits. A quick method of adding the digits is to use the formula $\frac{n(n+1)}{2}$ where n is the number of instalments. If there are twelve instalments, then the sum of the digits will be 78. For this reason, the sum of the digits method is sometimes called the **rule of 78**.

(c) Calculate the interest charge included in each instalment. Do this by multiplying the total interest accruing over the lease term by the fraction:

$$\frac{\text{Digit applicable to the instalment}}{\text{Sum of the digits}}$$

2.3 Example: apportionment methods

On 1 January 20X0 Bacchus Co, wine merchants, buys a small bottling and labelling machine from Silenus Co under a finance lease. The cash price of the machine was $7,710 while the amount to be paid was $10,000. The agreement required the immediate payment of a $2,000 deposit with the balance being settled in four equal annual instalments commencing on 31 December 20X0. The charge of $2,290 represents interest of 15% per annum, calculated on the remaining balance of the liability during each accounting period. Depreciation on the plant is to be provided for at the rate of 20% per annum on a straight line basis assuming a residual value of nil.

You are required to show the breakdown of each instalment between interest and capital, using in turn each of the apportionment methods described above.

Solution

In this example, enough detail is given to use either of the apportionment methods. In an examination question, you would normally be directed to use one method specifically.

(a) **Sum-of-the-digits method**

Each instalment is allocated a digit as follows.

Instalment	*Digit*
1st (20X0)	4
2nd (20X1)	3
3rd (20X2)	2
4th (20X3)	1
	10

Or using the formula, $\frac{4 \times 5}{2} = 10$.

The $2,290 interest charges can then be apportioned.

		$
1st instalment	$2,290 × 4/10	916
2nd instalment	$2,290 × 3/10	687
3rd instalment	$2,290 × 2/10	458
4th instalment	$2,290 × 1/10	229
		2,290

The breakdown is then as follows.

	1st instalment	*2nd instalment*	*3rd instalment*	*4th instalment*
	$	$	$	$
Interest	916	687	458	229
Capital repayment (balance)	1,084	1,313	1,542	1,771
	2,000	2,000	2,000	2,000

(b) **Actuarial method**

Interest is calculated as 15% of the outstanding *capital* balance at the beginning of each year. The outstanding capital balance reduces each year by the capital element comprised in each instalment. The outstanding capital balance at 1 January 20X0 is $5,710 ($7,710 fair value less $2,000 deposit).

	Total	*Capital*	*Interest*
	$	$	$
Capital balance at 1 Jan 20X0		5,710	
1st instalment (interest = $5,710 × 15%)	2,000	1,144	856
Capital balance at 1 Jan 20X1		4,566	
2nd instalment (interest = $4,566 × 15%)	2,000	1,315	685
Capital balance at 1 Jan 20X2		3,251	
3rd instalment (interest = $3,251 × 15%)	2,000	1,512	488
Capital balance at 1 Jan 20X3		1,739	
4th instalment (interest = $1,739 × 15%)	2,000	1,739	261
	8,000		2,290
Capital balance at 1 Jan 20X4		–	

2.4 Journal entries

The entries at 1 January 20X0 will be:

(a)	DEBIT	Asset account	$7,710	
	CREDIT	Lessor payable: Silenus		$7,710
(b)	DEBIT	Lessor payable: Silenus	$2,000	
	CREDIT	Bank		$2,000

Entries at 31 December 20X0 will be:

(c)	DEBIT	Lessor payable: Silenus	$2,000	
	CREDIT	Bank		$2,000
(d)	DEBIT	Interest payable/finance charges (income statement)	$856	
	CREDIT	Lessor payable: Silenus		$856

Entry (b) is the deposit. Entry (c) is the first instalment.

Entry (d) ensures that the interest element is recorded and is an annual adjustment. It is, of course, possible to make the full correct entry as each instalment is paid:

DEBIT	Interest payable/finance charges (income statement)	$856	
	Lessor payable: Silenus	$1,144	
CREDIT	Bank		$2,000

However, in practice in many companies the interest/finance charge calculation is only made annually when preparing published accounts.

Thus, at the year end, whatever system is used during the year, the balance on the lessor payable will represent the outstanding capital liability. Future interest/finance charges are not a true liability as the capital could be paid off at any time, thus avoiding these charges.

Exam focus point

> In the exam, if you are required to use the actuarial method you will be given the interest rate. If you are given the interest rate, assume the actuarial method is required.

Question

Sum-of-the-digits method

Dundas Co purchased a machine under a finance lease on 1 January 20X6. The agreement provided for an immediate payment of $2,000, following by five equal instalments of $3,056, each instalment to be paid on 30 June and 31 December respectively. The cash price of the machine was $10,000. Dundas estimated that it would have a useful economic life of five years, and its residual value would then be $1,000. At the end of the lease, ownership will pass to Dundas Co.

In apportioning interest to respective accounting periods, the company uses the 'sum of digits' method.

Required

(a) Write up the following ledger accounts for each of the three years to 31 December 20X6, 20X7 and 20X8 respectively.

(i) Machine lease loan account

(ii) Machine lease interest suspense account

(b) Show the following balance sheet extracts relating to the machine as at 31 December 20X6, 20X7 and 20X8 respectively.

(i) Non-current assets: machine at net book value

(ii) Current liabilities: obligation under finance lease

(iii) Non-current liabilities: obligation under finance lease

Answer

(a) (i)

MACHINE LEASE LOAN ACCOUNT

20X6		$	*20X6*		$
1.1	Bank	2,000	1.1	Machine	10,000
30.6	Bank	3,056	1.1	Machine interest	7,280
31.12	Bank	3,056			
31.12	Balance c/d	9,168			
		17,280			17,280
20X7			*20X7*		
30.6	Bank	3,056	1.1	Balance b/d	9,168
31.12	Bank	3,056			
31.12	Balance c/d	3,056			
		9,168			9,168
20X8			*20X8*		
30.6	Bank	3,056	1.1	Balance b/d	3,056

(ii) MACHINE LEASE INTEREST SUSPENSE ACCOUNT

		$			$
20X6			20X6		
1.1	Machine lease		31.12	Income statement	4,368
	Loan a/c	7,280	31.12	Balance c/d	2,912
		7,280			7,280
20X7			20X7		
1.1	Balance b/d	2,912	31.12	Income statement	2,427
			31.12	Balance c/d	485
		2,912			2,912
20X8			20X8		
1.1	Balance b/d	485	31.12	Income statement	485

Note: In this example the total interest has been credited to the loan account and debited to an interest suspense account at the inception of the lease. It would be equally correct to just credit the loan account with $10,000 and split each instalment between capital and interest, the interest going straight to an interest expense account.

Working

	$
Sum of the digits = 5 + 4 + 3 + 2 + 1 = 15 (5 half year periods)	
Interest charge 20X6 = $\$7,280 \times \frac{5+4}{15}$	4,368
Interest charge 20X7 = $\$7,280 \times \frac{3+2}{15}$	2,427
Interest charge 20X8 = $\$7,280 \times \frac{1}{15}$	485
	7,280

(b) (i) Non-current assets: machines at net book value

		$
At 31.12.X6	Machines at cost	10,000
	Accumulated depreciation	1,800
	Net book value	8,200
At 31.12.X7	Machines at cost	10,000
	Accumulated depreciation	3,600
	Net book value	6,400
At 31.12.X8	Machines at cost	10,000
	Accumulated depreciation	5,400
	Net book value	4,600

Working

	$
Depreciation: cost	10,000
residual value	1,000
	9,000

Economic life* = 5 years

Annual depreciation charge on a straight-line basis $= \frac{\$9,000}{5}$

$= \$1,800$ per year

* *Note.* Eventual ownership is certain – see para 2.1.

(ii) *Current payables: obligation under finance lease*

	$
At 31.12.X6	3,685
At 31.12.X7	2,571
At 31.12.X8	–

Workings

		$
31.12.X6	Balance per loan account	9,168
	Less due in 20X8	(3,056)
	Less interest element	(2,427)
		3,685
31.12.X7	Balance per loan account	3,056
	Less interest element	(485)
		2,571

(iii) *Non-current payables: obligation under finance lease*

	$
At 31.12.X6	2,571
At 31.12.X7	–
At 31.12.X8	–

For working see (b)(ii) above.

Exam focus point

When doing lease calculations, you must highlight the **answer**. Question 1.5 in November 2005 asked for the finance charge for the second year of a lease. Many candidates worked out all five years finance charge and either did not specify the correct answer or gave the wrong figure.

2.5 Disclosure requirements for lessees

FAST FORWARD

You must also learn the disclosure requirements of IAS 17 (revised).

IAS 17 (revised) requires the following disclosures by lessees in respect of **operating leases**.

- The total of future minimum lease payments under non-cancellable operating leases for each of the following periods:
  - not later than one year;
  - later than one year and not later than five years
  - Later than five years

  This disclosure note is required because, although operating leases do not give rise to a balance sheet creditor, they are non-cancellable and so they do entail a future financial commitment, which should be disclosed.

IAS 17 (revised) requires the following disclosures by lessees, in respect of **finance leases**.

- The **net carrying amount** at the balance sheet date for each class of asset
- A **reconciliation** between the total of minimum lease payments at the balance sheet date, and their present value. In addition, an entity should disclose the total of minimum lease payments at the balance sheet date, and their present value, for each of the following periods:
  - Not later than one year
  - Later than one year and not later than five years
  - Later than five years

- **Contingent rents** recognised in income for the period
- Total of **future minimum sublease payments** expected to be received under non-cancellable subleases at the balance sheet date
- A **general description** of the lessee's significant leasing arrangements including, but not limited to, the following:
  - The basis on which contingent rent payments are determined
  - The existence and terms of renewal or purchase options and escalation clauses
  - Restrictions imposed by lease arrangements, such as those concerning dividends, additional debt, and further leasing

IAS 17 encourages (but does not require) further disclosures, as appropriate.

2.6 Example: lessee disclosures

These disclosure requirements will be illustrated for Bacchus Co (above example). We will assume that Bacchus Co makes up its accounts to 31 December and uses the actuarial method to apportion finance charges.

Solution

The company's accounts for the first year of the lease, the year ended 31 December 20X0, would include the information given below.

BALANCE SHEET AS AT 31 DECEMBER 20X0 (EXTRACTS)

	$	$
Non-current assets		
Assets held under finance leases		
Plant and machinery at cost	7,710	
Less accumulated depreciation (20% × $7,710)	1,542	
		6,168
Current liabilities		
Obligations under finance leases		1,315
Non-current liabilities		
Obligations under finance leases		
$(1,512 + 1,739)		3,251

(Notice that only the outstanding **capital** element is disclosed under liabilities, ie the total of the minimum lease payments with future finance charges separately deducted.)

INCOME STATEMENT
FOR THE YEAR ENDED 31 DECEMBER 20X0

	$
Interest payable and similar charges	
Interest on finance leases	856

For **operating leases** the disclosures are as follows.

(a) The total of future minimum lease payments under non-cancellable operating leases for each of the following periods:

(i) Not later than one year
(ii) Later than one year and not later than five years
(iii) Later than five years

(b) The total of future minimum sublease payments expected to be received under non-cancellable subleases at the balance sheet date;

(c) Lease and sublease payments recognised in income for the period, with separate amounts for minimum lease payments, contingent rents, and sublease payments;

(d) A general description of the lessee's significant leasing arrangements including, but not limited to, the following

(i) The basis on which contingent rent payments are determined

(ii) The existence and terms of renewal or purchase options and escalation clauses

(iii) Restrictions imposed by lease arrangements, such as those concerning dividends, additional debt, and further leasing

The following diagram gives a useful summary of the **accounting treatment for a finance lease by a lessee.**

Accounting for a finance lease by a lessee

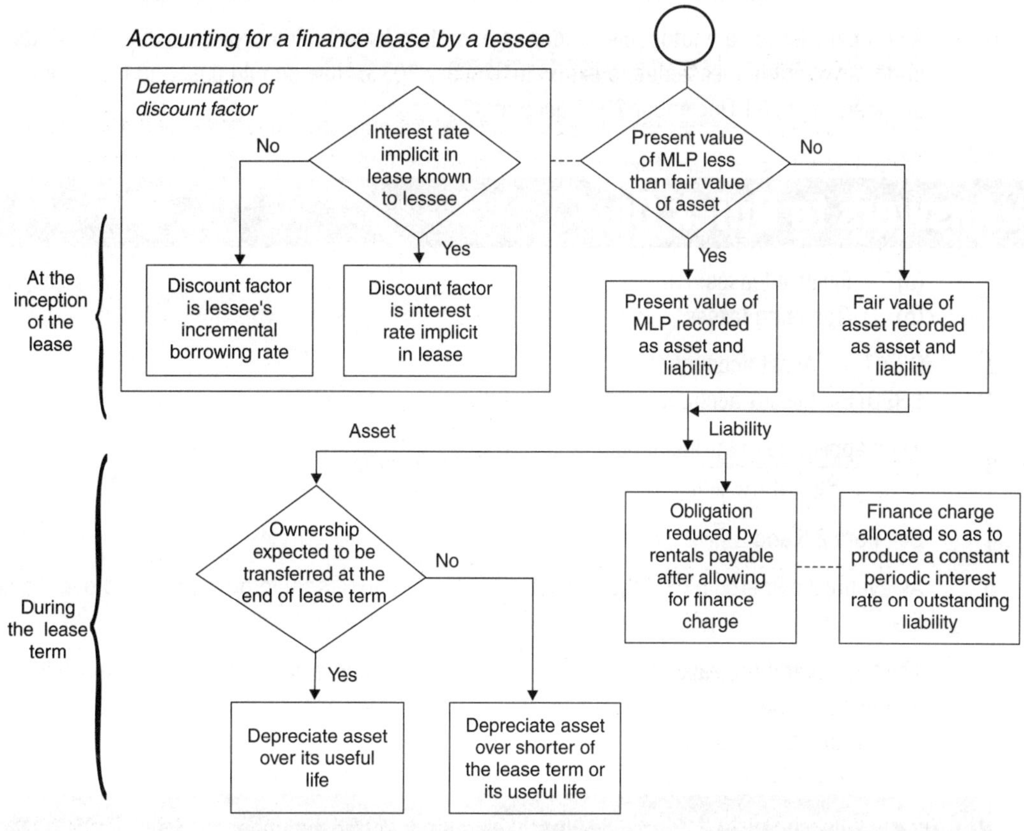

MLP = Minimum lease payments

Chapter Roundup

- Under finance leases:
  - Assets acquired should be capitalised
  - Interest element of instalments should be charged against profit.
- Operating leases are rental agreements and all instalments are charged against profit.
- You must learn (through repeated practice) how to apply the actuarial and sum-of-the-digits methods of interest allocation.
- You must also learn the disclosure requirements of IAS 17 (revised).

Quick Quiz

1 (a) .... leases transfer substantially all the risks and rewards of ownership.

(b) .... leases are usually short-term rental agreements with the lessor being responsible for the repairs and maintenance of the asset.

2 A business acquires an asset under a finance lease. What is the double entry?

3 What is the formula to calculate each period's interest using sum of the digits?

4 List the disclosures required under IAS 17 for lessees.

5 A lorry has an expected useful life of six years. It is acquired under a four year finance lease and will probably be kept for its entire six year life. Over which period should it be depreciated?

6 A company leases a photocopier under an operating lease which expires in June 20X2. Its office is leased under an operating lease due to expire in January 20X3. How should past and future operating leases be disclosed in its 31 December 20X1 accounts?

Answers to Quick Quiz

1 (a) Finance leases
(b) Operating leases

2 DEBIT Asset account
CREDIT Lessor account

3 $$\frac{\text{Digit applicable to the instalment}}{\text{Sum of the digits}} \times \text{Total interest charge}$$

4 See Para 2.5 and 2.6.

5 As eventual ownership of the lorry is reasonably certain, it should be depreciated over its six year useful life.

6 The total operating lease rentals charged though the income statement should be disclosed. The payments committed to should be disclosed analysing them between those falling due in the next year and the second to fifth years.

Now try the question below from the Exam Question Bank

Number	Level	Marks	Time
Q14	Examination	5	9 mins

IAS 7: Cash flow statements

8

Introduction

The importance of the distinction between cash and profit and the scant attention paid to this by the income statement has resulted in the development of cash flow statements.

This chapter adopts a systematic approach to the preparation of cash flow statements in examinations; you should learn this method and you will then be equipped for any problems in the exam itself.

The third section of the chapter looks at the information which is provided by the cash flow statement and how it should be analysed.

Topic list	Learning outcomes	Syllabus references	Ability required
1 IAS 7 *Cash flow statements*	C (ii)	C (2)	Application
2 Preparing a cash flow statement	C (i)	C (2)	Application
3 Interpretation of cash flow statements	C (ii)	C (2)	Application

1 IAS 7 Cash flow statements

FAST FORWARD

Cash flow statements are a useful addition to the financial statements of companies because it is recognised that accounting profit is not the only indicator of a company's performance.

1.1 Cash flow and profit

It has been argued that 'profit' does not always give a useful or meaningful picture of a company's operations. Readers of a company's financial statements might even be **misled by a reported profit figure**.

(a) Shareholders might believe that if a company makes a profit after tax, of say, $100,000 then this is the amount which it could afford to **pay as a dividend**. Unless the company has **sufficient cash** available to stay in business and also to pay a dividend, the shareholders' expectations would be wrong.

(b) Employees might believe that if a company makes profits, it can afford to **pay higher wages** next year. This opinion may not be correct: the ability to pay wages depends on the **availability of cash**.

(c) Survival of a business entity depends not so much on profits as on its **ability to pay its debts when they fall due**. Such payments might include 'profit and loss' items such as material purchases, wages, interest and taxation etc, but also capital payments for new non-current assets and the repayment of loan capital when this falls due (for example on the redemption of debentures).

From these examples, it may be apparent that a company's performance and prospects depend not so much on the 'profits' earned in a period, but more realistically on liquidity or **cash flows**.

1.2 Funds flow and cash flow

Some countries, either currently or in the past, have required the disclosure of additional statements based on **funds flow** rather than cash flow. However, the definition of 'funds' can be very vague and such statements often simply require a rearrangement of figures already provided in the balance sheet and income statement. By contrast, a statement of cash flows is unambiguous and provides information which is additional to that provided in the rest of the accounts. It also lends itself to organisation by activity and not by balance sheet classification.

Cash flow statements are frequently given as an **additional statement**, supplementing the balance sheet, income statement and related notes. The group aspects of cash flow statements (and certain complex matters) have been excluded as they are beyond the scope of your syllabus.

1.3 Objective of IAS 7

The aim of IAS 7 is to provide information to users of financial statements about an entity's **ability to generate cash and cash equivalents**, as well as indicating the cash needs of the entity. The cash flow statement provides *historical* information about cash and cash equivalents, classifying cash flows between operating, investing and financing activities.

1.4 Scope

A cash flow statement should be presented as an **integral part** of an entity's financial statements. All types of entity can provide useful information about cash flows as the need for cash is universal, whatever the nature of their revenue-producing activities. Therefore **all entities are required by the standard to produce a cash flow statement.**

1.5 Benefits of cash flow information

FAST FORWARD

Cash flow statements concentrate on the sources and uses of cash and are a useful indicator of a company's **liquidity** and **solvency**.

The use of cash flow statements is very much **in conjunction** with the rest of the financial statements. Users can gain further appreciation of the change in net assets, of the entity's financial position (liquidity and solvency) and the entity's ability to adapt to changing circumstances by affecting the amount and timing of cash flows. Cash flow statements **enhance comparability** as they are not affected by differing accounting policies used for the same type of transactions or events.

Cash flow information of a historical nature can be used as an indicator of the amount, timing and certainty of future cash flows. Past forecast cash flow information can be **checked for accuracy** as actual figures emerge. The relationship between profit and cash flows can be analysed as can changes in prices over time.

1.6 Definitions

The standard gives the following definitions, the most important of which are **cash** and **cash equivalents**.

Key terms

Cash comprises cash on hand and demand deposits.

Cash equivalents are short-term, highly liquid investments that are readily convertible to known amounts of cash and which are subject to an insignificant risk of changes in value.

Cash flows are inflows and outflows of cash and cash equivalents.

Operating activities are the principal revenue-producing activities of the entity and other activities that are not investing or financing activities.

Investing activities are the acquisition and disposal of non-current assets and other investments not included in cash equivalents.

Financing activities are activities that result in changes in the size and composition of the contributed equity capital and borrowings of the entity. *(IAS 7)*

1.7 Cash and cash equivalents

The standard expands on the definition of cash equivalents: they are not held for investment or other long-term purposes, but rather to meet short-term cash commitments. To fulfil the above definition, an investment's **maturity date should normally be three months from its acquisition date**. It would usually be the case then that equity investments (ie shares in other companies) are *not* cash equivalents. An exception would be where preferred shares were acquired with a very close maturity date.

Loans and other borrowings from banks are classified as investing activities. In some countries, however, **bank overdrafts** are repayable on demand and are treated as part of an entity's total cash management system. In these circumstances an overdrawn balance will be included in cash and cash equivalents. Such banking arrangements are characterised by a balance which fluctuates between overdrawn and credit.

Movements between different types of cash and cash equivalent are not included in cash flows. The investment of surplus cash in cash equivalents is part of cash management, not part of operating, investing or financing activities.

1.8 Presentation of a cash flow statement

IAS 7 requires cash flow statements to report cash flows during the period classified by **operating, investing and financing activities.**

1.9 Example: simple cash flow statement

Flail Co commenced trading on 1 January 20X1 with a medium-term loan of $21,000 and a share issue which raised $35,000. The company purchased non-current assets for $21,000 cash, and during the year to 31 December 20X1 entered into the following transactions.

(a) Purchases from suppliers were $19,500, of which $2,550 was unpaid at the year end.
(b) Wages and salaries amounted to $10,500, of which $750 was unpaid at the year end.
(c) Interest on the loan of $2,100 was fully paid in the year and a repayment of $5,250 was made.
(d) Sales revenue was $29,400, including $900 receivables at the year end.
(e) Interest on cash deposits at the bank amounted to $75.
(f) A dividend of $4,000 was proposed as at 31 December 20X1.

You are required to prepare a historical cash flow statement for the year ended 31 December 20X1.

Solution

FLAIL CO
CASH FLOW STATEMENT FOR
THE YEAR ENDED 31 DECEMBER 20X1

	$	$
Cash flows from operating activities		
Cash received from customers ($29,400 – $900)	28,500	
Cash paid to suppliers ($19,500 – $2,550)	(16,950)	
Cash paid to and on behalf of employees ($10,500 – $750)	(9,750)	
Interest paid	(2,100)	
Interest received	75	
Net cash flow from operating activities		(225)
Investing activities		
Purchase of non-current assets		(21,000)
Financing activities		
Issue of shares	35,000	
Proceeds from medium-term loan	21,000	
Repayment of medium-term loan	(5,250)	
Net cash flow from financing activities		50,750
Net increase in cash and cash equivalents		29,525
Cash and cash equivalents at 1 January 20X1		–
Cash and cash equivalents at 31 December 20X1		29,525

Note that the dividend is only proposed and so there is no related cash flow in 20X1.

Exam focus point

Both the pilot paper and the May 2005 paper had a 20-mark cash flow statement question. Make sure you learn this well

1.11 Example: finance lease rental

The notes to the financial statements of Hayley Co show the following in respect of obligations under finance leases.

Year ended 30 June	20X5	20X4
	$'000	$'000
Amounts payable within one year	12	8
Within two to five years	110	66
	122	74
Less finance charges allocated to future periods	(14)	(8)
	108	66

Interest paid on finance leases in the year to 30 June 20X5 amounted to $6,000. Additions to property, plant and equipment acquired under finance leases were shown in the non-current asset note at $56,000.

Required

Calculate the capital repayment to be shown in the cash flow statement of Hayley Co for the year to 30 June 20X5.

Solution

OBLIGATIONS UNDER FINANCE LEASES

	$'000		$'000
Capital repayment (bal fig)	14	Bal 1.7.X4	66
Bal 30.6.X5	108	Additions	56
	122		122

1.12 Reporting cash flows from operating activities

The standard offers a choice of method for this part of the cash flow statement.

(a) **Direct method:** disclose major classes of gross cash receipts and gross cash payments

(b) **Indirect method**: net profit or loss is adjusted for the effects of transactions of a non-cash nature, any deferrals or accruals of past or future operating cash receipts or payments, and items of income or expense associated with investing or financing cash flows

The **direct method is the preferred method** because it discloses information, not available elsewhere in the financial statements, which could be of use in estimating future cash flows. The example below shows both methods.

1.12.1 Using the direct method

There are different ways in which the **information about gross cash receipts and payments** can be obtained. The most obvious way is simply to extract the information from the accounting records. This may be a laborious task, however, and the indirect method below may be easier. The example and question above used the direct method.

1.12.2 Using the indirect method

This method is undoubtedly **easier** from the point of view of the preparer of the cash flow statement. The net profit or loss for the period is adjusted for the following.

(a) Changes during the period in inventories, operating receivables and payables

(b) Non-cash items, eg depreciation, provisions, profits/losses on the sales of assets

(c) Other items, the cash flows from which should be classified under investing or financing activities.

A **proforma** of such a calculation, taken from the IAS, is as follows and this method may be more common in the exam. (The proforma has been amended to reflect changes to IFRS.)

	$
Cash flows from operating activities	
Net profit before taxation	X
Adjustments for:	
Depreciation	X
Profit (loss) on disposal of a non-current asset	X
Investment income	(X)
Interest expense	X
Operating profit before working capital changes	X
Increase in trade and other receivables	(X)
Decrease in inventories	X
Decrease in trade payables	(X)
Cash generated from operations	X
Interest paid	(X)
Income taxes paid	(X)
Net cash from operating activities	X

It is important to understand why **certain items are added and others subtracted**. Note the following points.

(a) Depreciation is not a cash expense, but is deducted in arriving at the profit figure in the income statement. It makes sense, therefore, to eliminate it by adding it back.

(b) By the same logic, a loss on a disposal of a non-current asset (arising through underprovision of depreciation) needs to be added back and a profit deducted.

(c) An increase in inventories means less cash – you have spent cash on buying inventory.

(d) An increase in receivables means the company's debtors have not paid as much, and therefore there is less cash.

(e) If we pay off payables, causing the figure to decrease, again we have less cash.

1.12.3 Indirect versus direct

The direct method is encouraged where the necessary information is not too costly to obtain, but IAS 7 does not require it. In practice, therefore, the direct method is rarely used. It is not obvious that businesses in practice are right in favouring the indirect method. It could be argued that companies ought to monitor their cash flows carefully enough on an ongoing basis to be able to use the direct method at minimal extra cost.

1.13 Interest and dividends

Cash flows from interest and dividends received and paid should each be **disclosed separately**. Each should be classified in a consistent manner from period to period as either operating, investing or financing activities.

Dividends paid by the entity can be classified in **one of two ways**.

(a) As a **financing cash flow**, showing the cost of obtaining financial resources.

(b) As a component of **cash flows from operating activities** so that users can assess the entity's ability to pay dividends out of operating cash flows.

1.14 Taxes on income

Cash flows arising from taxes on income should be **separately disclosed** and should be classified as cash flows from operating activities *unless* they can be specifically identified with financing and investing activities.

Taxation cash flows are often **difficult to match** to the originating underlying transaction, so most of the time all tax cash flows are classified as arising from operating activities.

1.15 Components of cash and cash equivalents

The components of cash and cash equivalents should be disclosed and a **reconciliation** should be presented, showing the amounts in the cash flow statement reconciled with the equivalent items reported in the balance sheet.

It is also necessary to disclose the **accounting policy** used in deciding the items included in cash and cash equivalents, in accordance with IAS 1 *Presentation of Financial Statements*, but also because of the wide range of cash management practices worldwide.

1.16 Other disclosures

All entities should disclose, together with a **commentary by management**, any other information likely to be of importance, for example:

(a) Restrictions on the use of or access to any part of cash equivalents

(b) The amount of undrawn borrowing facilities which are available

(c) Cash flows which increased operating capacity compared to cash flows which merely maintained operating capacity

(d) Cash flows arising from each reported industry and geographical segment

1.17 Example of a cash flow statement

In the next section we will look at the procedures for preparing a cash flow statement. First, look at this **example**, adapted from the example given in the standard (which is based on a group and therefore beyond the scope of your syllabus).

Direct method

CASH FLOW STATEMENT (DIRECT METHOD)
YEAR ENDED 31 DECEMBER 20X7

	$m	$m
Cash flows from operating activities		
Cash receipts from customers	30,330	
Cash paid to suppliers and employees	(27,600)	
Cash generated from operations	2,730	
Interest paid	(270)	
Income taxes paid	(900)	
Net cash from operating activities		1,560
Cash flows from investing activities		
Purchase of property, plant and equipment	(900)	
Proceeds from sale of equipment	20	
Interest received	200	
Dividends received	200	
Net cash used in investing activities		(480)
Cash flows from financing activities		
Proceeds from issuance of share capital	250	
Proceeds from long-term borrowings	250	
Dividends paid*	(1,290)	
Net cash used in financing activities		(790)
Net increase in cash and cash equivalents		290
Cash and cash equivalents at beginning of period (Note)		120
Cash and cash equivalents at end of period (Note)		410

* This could also be shown as an operating cash flow

Indirect method

CASH FLOW STATEMENT (INDIRECT METHOD)
YEAR ENDED 31 DECEMBER 20X7

	$m	$m
Cash flows from operating activities		
Net profit before taxation	3,570	
Adjustments for:		
Depreciation	450	
Investment income	(500)	
Interest expense	400	
Operating profit before working capital changes	3,920	
Increase in trade and other receivables	(500)	
Decrease in inventories	1,050	
Decrease in trade payables	(1,740)	
Cash generated from operations	2,730	
Interest paid	(270)	
Income taxes paid	(900)	
Net cash from operating activities		1,560
Cash flows from investing activities		
Purchase of property, plant and equipment	(900)	
Proceeds from sale of equipment **	20	
Interest received	200	
Dividends received	200	
Net cash used in investing activities		(480)
Cash flows from financing activities		
Proceeds from issuance of share capital	250	
Proceeds from long-term borrowings	250	
Dividends paid*	(1,290)	
Net cash used in financing activities		(790)
Net increase in cash and cash equivalents		290
Cash and cash equivalents at beginning of period (Note)		120
Cash and cash equivalents at end of period (Note)		410

* This could also be shown as an operating cash flow

** The equipment was disposed of at its NBV, so no profit or loss arose.

The following note is required to both versions of the statement.

Note: Cash and cash equivalents

Cash and cash equivalents consist of cash on hand and balances with banks, and investments in money market instruments. Cash and cash equivalents included in the cash flow statement comprise the following balance sheet amounts.

	20X7	*20X6*
	$m	$m
Cash on hand and balances with banks	40	25
Short-term investments	370	95
Cash and cash equivalents	410	120

The company has undrawn borrowing facilities of $2,000m of which only $700m may be used for future expansion.

2 Preparing a cash flow statement

FAST FORWARD

You need to be aware of the **format** of the statement as laid out in IAS 7. Setting out the format is an essential first stage in preparing the statement, so this format must be learnt.

2.1 Working capital adjustments

In essence, preparing a cash flow statement is very straightforward. You should therefore simply learn the format and apply the steps noted in the example below. Note that the following items are treated in a way that might seem confusing, but the treatment is logical if you **think in terms of cash**.

(a) **Increase in inventory** is treated as **negative** (in brackets). This is because it represents a cash **outflow**; cash is being spent on inventory.

(b) An **increase in receivables** would be treated as **negative** for the same reasons; more receivables means less cash.

(c) By contrast an **increase in payables is positive** because cash is being retained and not used to settle accounts payable. There is therefore more of it.

Exam focus point

The pilot paper and the May 2005 paper both had a 20-mark question on preparation of a cash flow statement.

2.2 Example: preparation of a cash flow statement

Kane Co's income statement for the year ended 31 December 20X2 and balance sheets at 31 December 20X1 and 31 December 20X2 were as follows.

KANE CO
INCOME STATEMENT FOR THE YEAR ENDED 31 DECEMBER 20X2

	$'000	$'000
Sales		720
Raw materials consumed	70	
Staff costs	94	
Depreciation	118	
Loss on disposal of property, plant and equipment	18	
		300
Operating profit		420
Interest payable		28
Profit before tax		392
Taxation		124
Profit for the period		268

Note: Total dividends paid during the year were $66,000.

BPP PROFESSIONAL EDUCATION

KANE CO
BALANCE SHEETS AS AT 31 DECEMBER

	20X2		*20X1*	
	$'000	$'000	$'000	$'000
Assets				
Property, plant and equipment				
Cost	1,596		1,560	
Depreciation	318		224	
		1,278		1,336
Current assets				
Inventory	24		20	
Trade receivables	76		58	
Bank	48		56	
		148		134
Total assets		1,426		1,470
Equity and liabilities				
Capital and reserves				
Share capital	360		340	
Share premium	36		24	
Retained earnings	716		514	
		1,112		878
Non-current liabilities				
Long-term loans		200		500
Current liabilities				
Trade payables	12		6	
Taxation	102		86	
		114		92
		1,426		1,470

During the year, the company paid $90,000 for a new piece of machinery.

Required

Prepare a cash flow statement for Kane Co for the year ended 31 December 20X2 in accordance with the requirements of IAS 7, using the indirect method.

Solution

Step 1 **Set out the proforma cash flow statement** with the headings required by IAS 7. You should leave plenty of space. Ideally, use three or more sheets of paper, one for the main statement, one for the notes and one for your workings. It is obviously essential to know the formats very well.

Step 2 Begin with the **reconciliation of profit before tax to net cash from operating activities** as far as possible. When preparing the statement from balance sheets, you will usually have to calculate such items as depreciation, loss on sale of non-current assets, profit for the year and tax paid (see Step 4). Note that you may not be given the tax charge in the income statement. You will then have to assume that the tax paid in the year is last year's year-end provision and calculate the charge as the balancing figure.

Step 3 Calculate the cash flow figures for dividends paid, purchase or sale of non-current assets, issue of shares and repayment of loans if these are not already given to you (as they may be).

Step 4 If you are not given the profit figure, open up a working for the income statement. Using the opening and closing balances of retained earnings, the taxation charge and dividends paid and proposed, you will be able to calculate profit for the year as the balancing figure to put in the net profit to net cash flow from operating activities section.

Step 5 You will now be able to complete the statement by slotting in the figures given or calculated.

KANE CO
CASH FLOW STATEMENT FOR THE YEAR ENDED 31 DECEMBER 20X2

	$'000	$'000
Net cash flow from operating activities		
Profit before tax	392	
Depreciation charges	118	
Interest expense	28	
Loss on sale of property, plant and equipment	18	
Increase in inventories	(4)	
Increase in receivables	(18)	
Increase in payables	6	
Cash generated from operations	540	
Interest paid	(28)	
Dividends paid	(66)	
Tax paid (86 + 124 – 102)	(108)	
Net cash flow from operating activities		338
Cash flows from investing activities		
Payments to acquire property, plant and equipment	(90)	
Receipts from sales of property, plant and equipment (W)	12	
Net cash flows from investing activities		(78)
Cash outflow from financing activities		
Issues of share capital (360 + 36 – 340 – 24)	32	
Long-term loans repaid (500 – 200)	(300)	
Net cash outflow from financing activities		(268)
Decrease in cash and cash equivalents		(8)
Cash and cash equivalents at 1.1.X2		56
Cash and cash equivalents at 31.12.X2		48

Working: property, plant and equipment

COST

	$'000		$'000
At 1.1.X2	1,560	At 31.12.X2	1,596
Purchases	90	Disposals (balance)	54
	1,650		1,650

ACCUMULATED DEPRECIATION

	$'000		$'000
At 31.1.X2	318	At 1.1.X2	224
Depreciation on disposals (balance)	24	Charge for year	118
	342		342

	$'000
NBV of disposals	30
Net loss reported	(18)
Proceeds of disposals	12

Question

Cash flow statement

Set out below are the financial statements of Emma Co. You are the financial controller, faced with the task of implementing IAS 7 *Cash flow statements*.

EMMA CO
INCOME STATEMENT FOR THE YEAR ENDED 31 DECEMBER 20X2

	$'000
Sales revenue	2,553
Cost of sales	1,814
Gross profit	739
Distribution costs	125
Administrative expenses	264
Operating profit	350
Interest received	25
Interest paid	75
Profit before taxation	300
Taxation	140
Profit for the period	160

EMMA CO
BALANCE SHEETS AS AT 31 DECEMBER

	20X2	*20X1*
Assets	$'000	$'000
Non-current assets		
Property, plant and equipment	380	305
Intangible assets	250	200
Investments	–	25
Current assets		
Inventories	150	102
Receivables	390	315
Short-term investments (highly liquid)	50	–
Cash in hand	2	1
Total assets	1,222	948
Equity and liabilities		
Equity		
Share capital ($1 ordinary shares)	200	150
Share premium account	160	150
Revaluation reserve	100	91
Retained earnings	260	180
Non-current liabilities		
Long-term loan	170	50
Current liabilities		
Trade payables	127	119
Bank overdraft	85	98
Taxation	120	110
Total equity and liabilities	1,222	948

The following information is available.

(a) The proceeds of the sale of non-current asset investments amounted to $30,000.

(b) Fixtures and fittings, with an original cost of $85,000 and a net book value of $45,000, were sold for $32,000 during the year.

(c) The following information relates to property, plant and equipment.

	31 December 20X2	20X1
	$'000	$'000
Cost	720	595
Accumulated depreciation	340	290
Net book value	380	305

(d) 50,000 $1 ordinary shares were issued during the year at a premium of 20c per share.

(e) Dividends totalling $80,000 were paid in 20X2.

Required

Prepare a cash flow statement for the year to 31 December 20X2 using the format laid out in IAS 7.

Answer

EMMA CO
CASH FLOW STATEMENT FOR THE YEAR ENDED 31 DECEMBER 20X2

	$'000	$'000
Net cash flows from operating activities		
Profit before tax	300	
Depreciation charge (W1)	90	
Net interest charge	50	
Loss on sale of property, plant and equipment (45 – 32)	13	
Profit on sale of non-current asset investments (30 – 25)	(5)	
(Increase)/decrease in inventories	(48)	
(Increase)/decrease in receivables	(75)	
Increase/(decrease) in payables	8	
Cash generated from operating activities	333	
Interest received	25	
Interest paid	(75)	
Dividends paid	(80)	
Tax paid (110 + 140 – 120)	(130)	
Net cash flows from operating activities		73
Cash flows from investing activities		
Payments to acquire property, plant and equipment (W2)	(201)	
Payments to acquire intangible non-current assets	(50)	
Receipts from sales of property, plant and equipment	32	
Receipts from sale of non-current asset investments	30	
Net cash outflow from investing activities		(189)
Cash flows from financing activities		
Issue of share capital	60	
Long-term loan	120	
Net cash flows from financing		180
Increase in cash and cash equivalents		64
Net cash and cash equivalents at 1.1 X2 (Note)		(97)
Cash and cash equivalents at 31.12.X2 (Note)		(33)

NOTES TO THE CASH FLOW STATEMENT

Note: analysis of the balances of cash and cash equivalents as shown in the balance sheet

	20X2	*20X1*	*Change in year*
	$'000	$'000	$'000
Cash in hand	2	1	1
Short term investments	50	–	50
Bank overdraft	(85)	(98)	13
	(33)	(97)	64

Workings

1 Depreciation charge

	$'000	$'000
Depreciation at 31 December 20X2		340
Depreciation 31 December 20X1	290	
Depreciation on assets sold (85 – 45)	40	
		250
Charge for the year		90

2 Purchase of property, plant and equipment

PROPERTY, PLANT AND EQUIPMENT

	$'000		$'000
1.1.X2 Balance b/d	595	Disposals	85
Revaluation (100 – 91)	9		
Purchases (bal fig)	201	31.12.X2 Balance c/d	720
	805		805

Exam focus point

The pilot paper and the May 2005 exam both had 20-mark cash flow statement questions. In November 2005, this was replaced by a 20-mark cash budget question and there were short questions totalling 6 marks on cash flow statements. It may come back as a 20-mark question. This is an important exam topic. Make sure you know the format.

3 Interpretation of cash flow statements

FAST FORWARD

Note that you may be expected to **analyse** or **interpret** a cash flow statement.

3.1 Uses of the cash flow statement

IAS 7 *Cash flow statements* was introduced on the basis that it would provide better, more comprehensive and more useful information than what was already shown in the financial statements. So what kind of information does the cash flow statement, along with its notes, provide?

Some of the main areas where IAS 7 should provide information not found elsewhere in the financial statements are as follows.

(a) The **relationships between profit and cash** can be seen clearly and analysed accordingly.

(b) **Cash equivalents** are highlighted, giving a better picture of the liquidity of the company.

(c) **Financing inflows and outflows must be shown, rather than simply passed through reserves.**

One of the most important things to realise at this point is that it is wrong to try to assess the health or predict the death of a reporting entity solely on the basis of a single indicator. When analysing cash flow data, the **comparison should not just be between cash flows and profit, but also between cash flows over a period of time** (say three to five years).

Cash is not synonymous with profit on an annual basis, but you should also remember that the 'behaviour' of profit and cash flows will be very different. **Profit is smoothed out** through accruals, prepayments, provisions and other accounting conventions. This does not apply to cash, so the **cash flow figures** are likely to be **'lumpy'** in comparison. You must distinguish between this 'lumpiness' and the trends which will appear over time.

The **relationship between profit and cash flows will vary constantly**. Note that healthy companies do not always have reported profits exceeding operating cash flows. Similarly, unhealthy companies can have operating cash flows well in excess of reported profit. The value of comparing them is in determining the extent to which earned profits are being converted into the necessary cash flows.

Profit is not as important as the extent to which a company can **convert its profits into cash on a continuing basis.** This process should be judged over a period longer than one year. The cash flows should be compared with profits over the same periods to decide how successfully the reporting entity has converted earnings into cash.

Cash flow figures should also be considered in terms of their specific relationships with each other over time. A form of **'cash flow gearing'** can be determined by comparing operating cash flows and financing flows, particularly borrowing, to establish the extent of dependence of the reporting entity on external funding.

Other relationships can be examined.

(a) Operating cash flows and investment flows can be related to match cash recovery from investment to investment.

(b) Investment can be compared to distribution to indicate the proportion of total cash outflow designated specifically to investor return and reinvestment.

(c) A comparison of tax outflow to operating cash flow minus investment flow will establish a 'cash basis tax rate'.

The 'ratios' mentioned above can be monitored **inter- and intra-firm** and the analyses can be undertaken in monetary, general price-level adjusted, or percentage terms.

3.2 The advantages of cash flow accounting

The advantages of cash flow accounting are as follows.

(a) Survival in business depends on the **ability to generate** cash. Cash flow accounting directs attention towards this critical issue.

(b) Cash flow is **more comprehensive** than 'profit' which is dependent on accounting conventions and concepts.

(c) **Creditors** (long and short-term) are more interested in an entity's ability to repay them than in its profitability. Whereas 'profits' might indicate that cash is likely to be available, cash flow accounting is more direct with its message.

(d) Cash flow reporting provides a better means of **comparing the results** of different companies than traditional profit reporting.

(e) Cash flow reporting **satisfies the needs of all users** better.

(i) For **management**, it provides the sort of information on which decisions should be taken: (in management accounting, 'relevant costs' to a decision are future cash flows); traditional profit accounting does not help with decision-making.

(ii) For **shareholders and auditors**, cash flow accounting can provide a satisfactory basis for stewardship accounting.

(iii) As described previously, the information needs of **creditors and employees** will be better served by cash flow accounting.

(f) Cash flow forecasts are **easier to prepare**, as well as more useful, than profit forecasts.

(g) They can in some respects be **audited more easily** than accounts based on the accruals concept.

(h) The accruals concept is confusing, and cash flows are **more easily understood**.

(i) Cash flow accounting should be both retrospective, and also include a forecast for the future. This is of **great information value** to all users of accounting information.

(j) **Forecasts** can subsequently be **monitored** by the publication of variance statements which compare actual cash flows against the forecast.

Question

Disadvantages

Can you think of some possible disadvantages of cash flow accounting?

Answer

The main disadvantages of cash accounting are essentially the advantages of accruals accounting (proper matching of related items). There is also the practical problem that few businesses keep historical cash flow information in the form needed to prepare a historical cash flow statement and so extra record keeping is likely to be necessary.

3.3 Criticisms of IAS 7

The inclusion of **cash equivalents** has been criticised because it does not reflect the way in which businesses are managed: in particular, the requirement that to be a cash equivalent an investment has to be within three months of maturity is considered **unrealistic**.

The management of assets similar to cash (ie 'cash equivalents') is not distinguished from other investment decisions.

Chapter Roundup

- **Cash flow statements** are a useful addition to the financial statements of companies because it is recognised that accounting profit is not the only indicator of a company's performance.
- Cash flow statements concentrate on the sources and uses of cash and are a useful indicator of a company's **liquidity and solvency**.
- You need to be aware of the **format** of the statement as laid out in **IAS 7**; setting out the format is an essential first stage in preparing the statement, so this format must be learnt.
- Remember the **step-by-step preparation procedure** and use it for all the questions you practise.
- Note that you may be expected to **analyse** or **interpret** a cash flow statement.

Quick Quiz

1 What is the aim of a cash flow statement?

2 The standard headings in an IAS 7 cash flow statement are:

- O..................... a.......................
- I..................... a.......................
- F..................... a.......................
- Net...................... in C......................... and ....

3 Cash equivalents are current asset investments which will mature or can be redeemed within three months of the year end.

True ☐

False ☐

4 Why are you more likely to encounter the indirect method as opposed to the direct method?

5 List five advantages of cash flow accounting.

Answers to Quick Quiz

1 To indicate an entity's ability to generate cash and cash equivalents.

2
- Operating activities
- Investing activities
- Financing activities
- Net increase (decrease) in cash and cash equivalents

3 False. See the definition in paragraph 1.6 if you are not sure about this.

4 The indirect method utilises figures which appear in the financial statements. The figures required for the direct method may not be readily available.

5 See paragraph 3.2.

Now try the questions below from the Exam Question Bank

Number	Level	Marks	Time
Q20	Examination	20	36 mins
Q21	Examination	20	36 mins

9

Miscellaneous standards

Introduction

IAS 10 and IAS 37 are very important as they can affect many items in the accounts. Students sometimes get them confused with each other, so make sure you learn all the relevant definitions and understand the standard accounting treatment.

Related party disclosures are important to users of accounts. Make sure you understand why. You must also know what constitutes a related party.

1 IAS 10 (revised) Events after the balance sheet date

FAST FORWARD

IAS 10 deals with **events occurring after the balance sheet date.** It distinguishes between adjusting and non-adjusting events and gives examples. You should be able to define and discuss all these terms and apply them to practical examples.

1.1 Purpose of IAS 10

The financial statements are significant indicators of a company's success or failure. It is important, therefore, that they include all the information necessary for an understanding of the company's position.

IAS 10 (Revised) *Events after the balance sheet date* requires the provision of additional information in order to facilitate such an understanding. IAS 10 deals with events **after** the balance sheet date which may affect the position at the balance sheet date.

1.2 Definitions

The standard gives the following definition.

Key term

Events occurring after the balance sheet date are those events, both favourable and unfavourable, that occur between the balance sheet date and the date on which the financial statements are authorised for issue. Two types of events can be identified.

- Those that provide evidence of conditions that existed at the balance sheet date – *adjusting*
- Those that are indicative of conditions that arose after the balance sheet date – *non-adjusting*

(IAS 10)

1.3 Events occurring after the balance sheet date

Between the balance sheet date and the date the financial statements are authorised (ie for issue outside the organisation), events may occur which show that assets and liabilities at the balance sheet date should be adjusted, or that disclosure of such events should be given.

1.4 Events requiring adjustment

The standard requires adjustment of assets and liabilities in certain circumstances.

An entity shall adjust the amounts recognised in its financial statements to reflect adjusting events after the balance sheet date. An entity shall not adjust the amounts recognised in its financial statements to reflect non-adjusting events after the balance sheet date. *(IAS 10)*

An **example** of additional evidence which becomes available after the balance sheet date is where a **customer goes bankrupt, thus confirming that the trade account receivable balance at the year end is uncollectable.**

In relation to **going concern**, the standard states that, where operating results and the financial position have deteriorated after the balance sheet date, it may be necessary to reconsider whether the going concern assumption is appropriate in the preparation of the financial statements.

Examples of **adjusting events** would be:

- evidence of a permanent diminution in property value prior to the year end
- sale of inventory after the balance sheet date for less than its carrying value at the year end
- insolvency of a customer with a balance owing at the year end

- amounts received or paid in respect of legal or insurance claims which were in negotiation at the year end
- determination after the year end of the sale or purchase price of assets sold or purchased before the year end
- evidence of a permanent diminution in the value of a long-term investment prior to the year end
- discovery of error or fraud which shows that the financial statements were incorrect

1.5 Events not requiring adjustment

The standard then looks at events which do **not** require adjustment.

The standard gives the following examples of events which do **not** require adjustments:

- acquisition of, or disposal of, a subsidiary after the year end
- announcement of a plan to discontinue an operation
- major purchases and disposals of assets
- destruction of a production plant by fire after the balance sheet date
- announcement or commencing implementation of a major restructuring
- share transactions after the balance sheet date
- litigation commenced after the balance sheet date

But note that, while they may be non-adjusting, some events after the balance sheet date will require disclosure.

If non-adjusting events after the balance sheet date are material, non-disclosure could influence the economic decisions of users taken on the basis of the financial statements. Accordingly, an entity shall disclose the following for each material category of non-adjusting event after the balance sheet date:

(a) the nature of the event; and
(b) an estimate of its financial effect, or a statement that such an estimate cannot be made.

(IAS 10)

The **example** given by the standard of such an event is where the **value of an investment falls between the balance sheet date and the date the financial statements are authorised** for issue. The fall in value represents circumstances during the current period, not conditions existing at the previous balance sheet date, so it is not appropriate to adjust the value of the investment in the financial statements. Disclosure is an aid to users, however, indicating 'unusual changes' in the state of assets and liabilities after the balance sheet date.

The rule for **disclosure** of events occurring after the balance sheet date which relate to conditions that arose after that date, is that disclosure should be made if non-disclosure would hinder the user's ability to make **proper evaluations** and decisions based on the financial statements. An example might be the acquisition of another business.

1.6 Dividends

Dividends on equity shares declared by the entity after the balance sheet date should not be recognised as a liability at the balance sheet date, but should be disclosed, either on the face of the balance sheet as a separate component of equity or in the notes to the financial statements.

Exam focus point

It is of course quite unusual for a company to declare a dividend before the balance sheet date, but CIMA have stated that the examiner may take advantage of this loophole in questions, so that a proposed dividend will appear as a liability.

1.7 Disclosures

The following **disclosure requirements** are given **for events** which occur after the balance sheet date which do not require adjustment. If disclosure of events occurring after the balance sheet date is required, the following information should be provided.

(a) The nature of the event
(b) An estimate of the financial effect, or a statement that such an estimate cannot be made

Question — Adjusting or not?

State whether the following events occurring after the balance sheet date require an adjustment to the assets and liabilities of the financial statements.

(a) Purchase of an investment
(b) A change in the rate of corporate tax, applicable to the previous year
(c) An increase in pension benefits
(d) Losses due to fire
(e) A bad debt suddenly being paid
(f) The receipt of proceeds of sales or other evidence concerning the net realisable value of inventory
(g) A sudden decline in the value of property held as a long-term asset

Answer

(b), (e) and (f) require adjustment.

Exam focus point

Both the May 2005 and November 2005 exams had a question on IAS 10. This is a relatively easy topic, so make sure you understand what constitutes an adjusting event.

2 IAS 37 Provisions, contingent liabilities and contingent assets

FAST FORWARD

Under IAS 37 a **provision** should be recognised when

- An entity has a **present obligation**, legal or constructive
- It is probable that a **transfer of economic benefits** will be required to settle it
- A **reliable estimate** can be made of its amount

2.1 Dealing with uncertainty

As we have seen with regard to post balance sheet events, financial statements must include **all the information necessary for an understanding of the company's financial position**. Provisions, contingent liabilities and contingent assets are 'uncertainties' that must be accounted for consistently if we are to achieve this understanding.

2.2 Objective

IAS 37 *Provisions, contingent liabilities and contingent assets* aims to ensure that appropriate **recognition criteria** and **measurement bases** are applied to provisions, contingent liabilities and contingent assets and that **sufficient information** is disclosed in the **notes** to the financial statements to enable users to understand their nature, timing and amount.

2.3 Provisions

You will be familiar with provisions (allowances) for depreciation and doubtful debts from your earlier studies. The provisions addressed by IAS 37 are, however, rather different.

Before IAS 37, there was no accounting standard dealing with provisions. Companies wanting to show their results in the most favourable light used to make large 'one off' provisions in years where a high level of underlying profit was generated. These provisions, often known as 'big bath' provisions, were then available to shield expenditure in future years when perhaps the underlying profits were not as good.

In other words, provisions were used for profit smoothing. Profit smoothing is misleading.

Important!

> The key aim of IAS 37 is to ensure that provisions are made only where there are valid grounds for them.
>
> IAS 37 views a provision as a liability.

Key terms

> A **provision** is a **liability** of uncertain timing or amount.
>
> A **liability** is an obligation of an entity to transfer economic benefits as a result of past transactions or events. *(IAS 37)*

The IAS distinguishes provisions from other liabilities such as trade payables and accruals. This is on the basis that for a provision there is **uncertainty** about the timing or amount of the future expenditure. Whilst uncertainty is clearly present in the case of certain accruals the uncertainty is generally much less than for provisions.

2.4 Recognition

IAS 37 states that a provision should be **recognised** as a liability in the financial statements when:

- An entity has a **present obligation** (legal or constructive) as a result of a past event
- It is probable that a **transfer of economic benefits** will be required to settle the obligation
- A **reliable estimate** can be made of the obligation

2.5 Meaning of obligation

It is fairly clear what a legal obligation is. However, you may not know what a **constructive obligation** is.

Key term

> IAS 37 defines a **constructive obligation** as
>
> 'An obligation that derives from an entity's actions where:
>
> - by an established pattern of past practice, published policies or a sufficiently specific current statement the entity has indicated to other parties that it will accept certain responsibilities; and
> - as a result, the entity has created a valid expectation on the part of those other parties that it will discharge those responsibilities.

Question — Recognising a provision

In which of the following circumstances might a provision be recognised?

(a) On 13 December 20X9 the board of an entity decided to close down a division. The accounting date of the company is 31 December. Before 31 December 20X9 the decision was not communicated to any of those affected and no other steps were taken to implement the decision.

(b) The board agreed a detailed closure plan on 20 December 20X9 and details were given to customers and employees.

(c) A company is obliged to incur clean up costs for environmental damage (that has already been caused).

(d) A company intends to carry out future expenditure to operate in a particular way in the future.

Answer

(a) No provision would be recognised as the decision has not been implemented.

(b) A provision would be made in the 20X9 financial statements.

(c) A provision for such costs is appropriate.

(d) No present obligation exists and under IAS 37 no provision would be appropriate. This is because the entity could avoid the future expenditure by its future actions, maybe by changing its method of operation.

2.5.1 Probable transfer of economic benefits

For the purpose of the IAS, a transfer of economic benefits is regarded as **'probable'** if the event is **more likely than not** to occur. This appears to indicate a probability of more than 50%. However, the standard makes it clear that where there is a number of similar obligations the probability should be based on considering the population as a whole, rather than one single item.

2.6 Example: transfer of economic benefits

If a company has entered into a warranty obligation then the probability of transfer of economic benefits may well be extremely small in respect of one specific item. However, when considering the population as a whole the probability of some transfer of economic benefits is quite likely to be much higher. If there is a **greater than 50% probability** of some transfer of economic benefits then a **provision** should be made for the **expected amount**.

2.7 Measurement of provisions

Important!

> The amount recognised as a provision should be the best estimate of the expenditure required to settle the present obligation at the balance sheet date.

The estimates will be determined by the **judgement** of the entity's management supplemented by the experience of similar transactions.

Allowance is made for **uncertainty**. Where the provision being measured involves a large population of items, the obligation is estimated by weighting all possible outcomes by their discounted probabilities, ie **expected value**.

purchasing the field in the first place is not only the cost of the field itself but also the costs of putting it right again. Thus all the costs of abandonment may be capitalised.

(f) **Restructuring**. This is considered in detail below.

2.10 Provisions for restructuring

One of the main purposes of IAS 37 was to target abuses of provisions for restructuring. Accordingly, IAS 37 lays down **strict criteria** to determine when such a provision can be made.

Key term

IAS 37 defines a **restructuring** as:

A programme that is planned and is controlled by management and materially changes either:

- the scope of a business undertaken by an entity; or
- the manner in which that business is conducted.

The IAS gives the following **examples** of events that may fall under the definition of restructuring.

- The **sale or termination** of a line of business
- The **closure of business locations** in a country or region or the **relocation** of business activities from one country region to another
- **Changes in management structure**, for example, the elimination of a layer of management
- **Fundamental reorganisations** that have a material effect on the **nature and focus** of the entity's operations

The question is whether or not an entity has an obligation - legal or constructive - at the balance sheet date.

- An entity must have a **detailed formal plan** for the restructuring.
- It must have **raised a valid expectation** in those affected that it will carry out the restructuring by starting to implement that plan or announcing its main features to those affected by it

Important!

A mere management decision is not normally sufficient. Management decisions may sometimes trigger off recognition, but only if earlier events such as negotiations with employee representatives and other interested parties have been concluded subject only to management approval.

Where the restructuring involves the **sale of an operation** then IAS 37 states that no obligation arises until the entity has entered into a **binding sale agreement**. This is because until this has occurred the entity will be able to change its mind and withdraw from the sale even if its intentions have been announced publicly.

2.10.1 Costs to be included within a restructuring provision

The IAS states that a restructuring provision should include only the **direct expenditures** arising from the restructuring, which are those that are both:

- **Necessarily entailed** by the restructuring; and
- Not associated with the **ongoing activities** of the entity.

The following costs should specifically **not** be included within a restructuring provision.

- **Retraining** or relocating continuing staff
- **Marketing**
- **Investment in new systems** and distribution networks

2.10.2 Disclosure

Disclosures for provisions fall into two parts.

- Disclosure of details of the **change in carrying value** of a provision from the beginning to the end of the year
- Disclosure of the **background** to the making of the provision and the uncertainties affecting its outcome

Exam focus point

The November 2005 exam had question which gave a number of scenarios and asked which one would require a provision to be set up.

2.11 Contingent liabilities

FAST FORWARD

An entity should not **recognise** a contingent asset or liability but they should be **disclosed.**

Now that you understand provisions it will be easier to understand contingent assets and liabilities.

Key term

IAS 37 defines a **contingent liability** as:

- A possible obligation that arises from past events and whose existence will be confirmed only by the occurrence or non-occurrence of one or more uncertain future events not wholly within the entity's control; or
- A present obligation that arises from past events but is not recognised because:
  - It is not probable that a transfer of economic benefits will be required to settle the obligation; or
  - The amount of the obligation cannot be measured with sufficient reliability.

As a rule of thumb, probable means **more than 50%** likely. **If an obligation is probable, it is not a contingent liability** - instead, a **provision is needed**.

2.11.1 Treatment of contingent liabilities

Contingent liabilities **should not be recognised in financial statements** but they **should be disclosed**. The required disclosures are:

- A brief description of the nature of the contingent liability
- An estimate of its financial effect
- An indication of the uncertainties that exist
- The possibility of any reimbursement

2.12 Contingent assets

Key term

IAS 37 defines a **contingent asset** as:

A possible asset that arises from past events and whose existence will be confirmed by the occurrence of one or more uncertain future events not wholly within the entity's control.

A contingent asset must not be recognised. Only when the realisation of the related economic benefits is **virtually certain** should recognition take place. At that point, **the asset is no longer a contingent asset**!

2.12.1 Disclosure: contingent liabilities

A **brief description** must be provided of all material contingent liabilities unless they are likely to be remote. In addition, provide

- An estimate of their **financial effect**
- Details of **any uncertainties**
- Details of any possible reimbursement

2.12.2 Disclosure: contingent assets

Contingent assets must only be disclosed in the notes if they are **probable**. In that case a brief description of the contingent asset should be provided along with an estimate of its likely financial effect.

2.12.3 'Let out'

IAS 37 permits reporting entities to avoid disclosure requirements relating to provisions, contingent liabilities and contingent assets if they would be expected to **seriously prejudice** the position of the entity in dispute with other parties. However, this should only be employed in **extremely rare** cases. Details of the general nature of the provision/contingencies must still be provided, together with an explanation of why it has not been disclosed.

You must practise the questions below to get the hang of IAS 37. But first, study the flow chart, taken from IAS 37, which is a good summary of its requirements.

Exam focus point

> If you learn this flow chart you should be able to deal with most questions you are likely to meet in an exam.

Question — Provide or not? (1)

During 20X0 Smack Co gives a guarantee of certain borrowings of Pony Co, whose financial condition at that time is sound. During 20X1, the financial condition of Pony Co deteriorates and at 30 June 20X1 Pony Co files for protection from its creditors.

What accounting treatment is required:

(a) At 31 December 20X0?
(b) At 31 December 20X1?

Answer

(a) At 31 December 20X0

There is a present obligation as a result of a past obligating event. The obligating event is the giving of the guarantee, which gives rise to a legal obligation. However, at 31 December 20X0 no transfer of economic benefits is probable in settlement of the obligation.

No provision is recognised. The guarantee is disclosed as a contingent liability unless the probability of any transfer is regarded as remote.

(b) At 31 December 20X1

As above, there is a present obligation as a result of a past obligating event, namely the giving of the guarantee.

At 31 December 20X1 it is probable that a transfer of economic events will be required to settle the obligation. A provision is therefore recognised for the best estimate of the obligation.

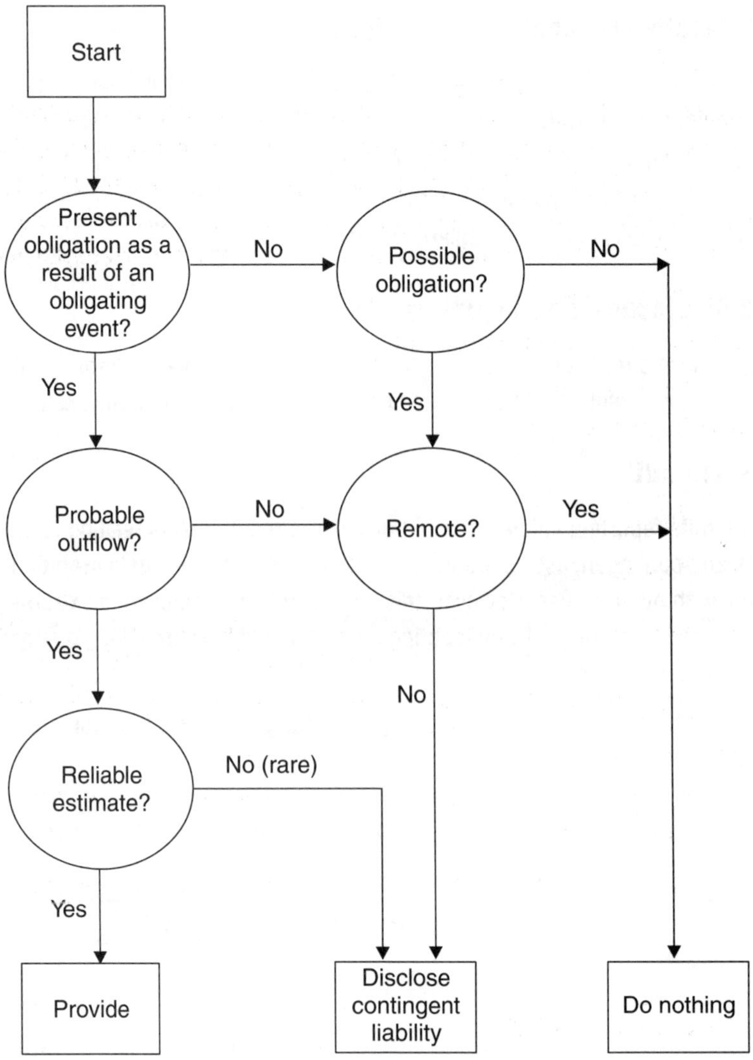

Question

Provide or not? (2)

Warren Co gives warranties at the time of sale to purchasers of its products. Under the terms of the warranty the manufacturer undertakes to make good, by repair or replacement, manufacturing defects that become apparent within a period of three years from the date of the sale. Should a provision be recognised?

Answer

Warren Co **cannot avoid** the cost of repairing or replacing all items of product that manifest manufacturing defects in respect of which warranties are given before the balance sheet date, and a provision for the cost of this should therefore be made.

Warren Co is obliged to repair or replace items that fail within the entire warranty period. Therefore, in respect of **this year's sales**, the obligation provided for at the balance sheet date should be the cost of making good items for which defects have been notified but not yet processed, **plus** an estimate of costs in respect of the other items sold for which there is sufficient evidence that manufacturing defects **will** manifest themselves during their remaining periods of warranty cover.

Question — **Provide or not? (3)**

After a wedding in 20X0 ten people died, possibly as a result of food poisoning from products sold by Callow Co. Legal proceedings are started seeking damages from Callow but it disputes liability. Up to the date of approval of the financial statements for the year to 31 December 20X0, Callow's lawyers advise that it is probable that it will not be found liable. However, when Callow prepares the financial statements for the year to 31 December 20X1 its lawyers advise that, owing to developments in the case, it is probable that it will be found liable.

What is the required accounting treatment:

(a) At 31 December 20X0?
(b) At 31 December 20X1?

Answer

(a) At 31 December 20X0

On the basis of the evidence available when the financial statements were approved, there is no obligation as a result of past events. No provision is recognised. The matter is disclosed as a contingent liability unless the probability of any transfer is regarded as remote.

(b) At 31 December 20X1

On the basis of the evidence available, there is a present obligation. A transfer of economic benefits in settlement is probable.

A provision is recognised for the best estimate of the amount needed to settle the present obligation.

2.13 Section summary

- The objective of IAS 37 is to ensure that appropriate recognition criteria and measurement bases are applied to provisions and contingencies and that sufficient information is disclosed.
- The IAS seeks to ensure that provisions are **only recognised** when a **measurable obligation** exists. It includes detailed rules that can be used to ascertain when an obligation exists and how to measure the obligation.
- The standard attempts to **eliminate 'profit smoothing'**.

3 IAS 24 Related party disclosures

FAST FORWARD

IAS 24 is primarily a **disclosure statement.** It is concerned with improving the quality of information provided by published accounts.

3.1 Why was a standard needed?

In the absence of information to the contrary, it is assumed that a reporting entity has **independent discretionary power** over its resources and transactions and pursues its activities independently of the interests of its individual owners, managers and others. Transactions are presumed to have been undertaken on an **arm's length basis**, ie on terms such as could have obtained in a transaction with an external party, in which each side bargained knowledgeably and freely, unaffected by any relationship between them.

These assumptions may not be justified when **related party relationships** exist, because the requisite conditions for competitive, free market dealings may not be present. Whilst the parties may endeavour to achieve arm's length bargaining the very nature of the relationship may preclude this occurring.

3.2 Objective

The objective of IAS 24 is to ensure that an entity's financial statements contain the disclosures necessary to draw attention to the possibility that its financial position and profit or loss may have been affected by the existence of related parties and by transactions and outstanding balances with such parties.

3.3 Scope

The standard applies in:

- identifying related parties and related party transactions
- identifying outstanding balances between related parties
- identifying circumstances in which disclosure is required
- determining the disclosures to be made

Note that the standard does not apply to the *measurement* of related party transactions. It is only concerned with disclosure.

Under the standard a party is a **related party** if:

(a) directly or indirectly the party

  (i) controls, is controlled by, or is under common control with, the entity (this includes parents, subsidiaries, fellow subsidiaries)

  (i) has an interest in the entity that gives it significant influence over the entity; or

  (iii) has joint control over the entity

(b) the party is an associate of the entity

(c) the party is a joint venture in which the entity is a venturer

(d) the party is a member if the key management personnel of the entity or its parent

(e) the party is a close member of the family of any individual referred to in (a) or (d)

(f) the party is an entity that is controlled, jointly controlled or significantly influenced by, or a significant proportion of whose voting rights are held by, any individual referred to in (d) or (e)

(g) the party is a post-employment benefit plan for the benefit of employees of the entity, or of any entity that is a related party of the entity

The following are not necessarily related parties:

(a) two entities simply because they have a director or other member of key management personnel in common

(b) two venturers simply because they share control over a joint venture

(c) (i) providers of finance
  (ii) trade unions
  (iii) public utilities; and
  (iv) government departments and agencies

(d) a customer, supplier, franchisor, distributor or general agent with whom the entity transacts a significant volume of business, merely by virtue of the resulting economic dependence. (In other words, this is not designated as *significant influence*.)

Exam focus point

> You will not be examined on related party transactions involving parent companies, subsidiaries, associates, joint ventures or post-retirement benefit plans.

3.4 Definitions

The following important definitions are given in the standard:

> **Related party transaction**. A transfer of resources, services or obligations between related parties, regardless of whether a price is charged.
>
> **Control**. The power to govern the financial and operating policies of an entity so as to obtain benefits from its activities.
>
> **Joint control**. The contractually agreed sharing of control over an economic activity.
>
> **Significant influence**. The power to participate in the financial and operating policy decisions of an entity, but not control over those policies. Significant influence may be gained by share ownership, statute or agreement.
>
> **Key management personnel**. Those persons having authority and responsibility for planning, directing and controlling the activities of the entity, directly or indirectly, including any director of that entity.
>
> **Compensation**. All employee benefits. This includes:
>
> (a) short-term employee benefits such as wages, salaries and social security contributions, paid annual leave and paid sick leave, profit-sharing and bonuses
>
> (b) post-employment benefits such as pensions, other retirement benefits, post-employment life insurance and post-employment medical care
>
> (c) other long-term benefits, including long-service leave or sabbatical leave
>
> (d) termination benefits; and
>
> (e) share-based payment (IAS 24)

3.5 Disclosures

(a) **Relationships between parents and subsidiaries** are to be disclosed irrespective of whether any transactions have taken place.

(b) **Key management personnel compensation** is to be disclosed in total and for each of the categories (a) to (e) above.

(c) **Transactions between related parties** require disclosure of the relationship as well as details concerning the transaction, including the amount of the transaction(s), the amount of any outstanding balance(s) and any provisions or expenses in respect of doubtful debts due from related parties.

3.6 Transactions

The standard gives the following examples of transactions that are disclosed if they are with a related party:

(a) purchases or sales of goods
(b) purchases or sales of property and other assets
(c) rendering or receiving of services
(d) leases
(e) transfers of research and development
(f) transfers under licence agreement

(g) transfers under finance arrangements (such as loans)
(h) provisions of guarantees or collateral; and
(i) settlement of liabilities on behalf of the entity, or by the entity on behalf of another party

Exam focus point

In both of the exams so far, questions on IAS 24 have simply been on what constitutes a related party. Make sure you know this.

Chapter Roundup

- IAS 10 deals with **events occurring after the balance sheet date.** IAS 10 distinguishes between adjusting and non-adjusting events and gives examples.
- Under IAS 37 *a* **provision** should be recognised
  - When an entity has a **present obligation**, legal or constructive; and
  - It is probable that a **transfer of economic benefits** will be required to settle it; and
  - A **reliable estimate** can be made of its amount
- An entity **should not recognise a contingent asset or liability** but they **should be disclosed.**
- **IAS 24** is primarily a **disclosure statement.** It is concerned with improving the quality of information provided by published accounts.

Quick Quiz

1 Define events occurring after the balance sheet date.

2 A customer goes bankrupt after the balance sheet date and his debt must be written off.

Adjusting event ☐

Non-adjusting event ☐

3 Inventory is lost in a fire after the balance sheet date.

Adjusting event ☐

Non-adjusting event ☐

4 A provision is a ……………..………… of ………………….…… timing or amount.

5 A programme is undertaken by management which converts the previously wholly owned chain of restaurants they ran into franchises. Is this restructuring?

6 Define contingent asset and contingent liability.

7 Banks lending money to a company are deemed related parties by IAS 24.

True ☐

False ☐

Answers to Quick Quiz

1 Those events unfavourable and favourable, which occur between the balance sheet date and the date on which the financial statements are authorised for issue.

2 Adjusting

3 Non-adjusting

4 Liability of uncertain timing or amount

5 Yes. The manner in which the business is conducted has changed.

6 Refer to paragraphs 2.11 and 2.12

7 False (see Para 3.3).

Now try the questions below from the Exam Question Bank

Number	Level	Marks	Time
Q19	Examination	20	36 mins
Q22	Examination	5	9 mins

10

Inventories and construction contracts

Introduction

You have encountered inventory and its valuation in your earlier studies. Inventory and short-term work-in-progress valuation has a direct impact on a company's gross profit and it is usually a material item in any company's accounts. This is therefore an important subject area. If you have any doubts about accounting for inventories and methods of inventory valuation you would be advised to go back to your earlier study material and revise this topic.

Section 1 of this chapter goes over some of this ground again, concentrating on the effect of IAS 2. Section 2 goes on to discuss a new area, construction contracts, which are effectively long-term work in progress. You should find this topic fairly logical as long as you work through the examples and question carefully.

Topic list	Learning outcomes	Syllabus references	Ability required
1 Inventories and short-term WIP (IAS 2)	C (iii)	C (5)	Application
2 IAS 11 *Construction contracts*	C (iii)	C (8)	Application

1 Inventories and short-term WIP (IAS 2)

FAST FORWARD

IAS 2 *Inventories* requires that the balance sheet should show **inventories** classified in a manner appropriate to the entity. Common **classifications** are:

- Merchandise
- Production supplies
- Materials
- Work-in-progress
- Finished goods

1.1 Valuing inventory

In most businesses the value put on inventory is an important factor in the determination of profit. Inventory valuation is, however, a highly subjective exercise and consequently there is a wide variety of different methods used in practice.

1.2 IAS 2 (revised) Inventories

IAS 2 was revised in December 2003. It lays out the required accounting treatment for inventories (sometimes called stocks) under the historical cost system. The major area of contention is the cost **value of inventory** to be recorded. This is recognised as an asset of the entity until the related revenues are recognised (ie the item is sold) at which point the inventory is recognised as an expense (ie cost of sales). Part or all of the cost of inventories may also be expensed if a write-down to **net realisable value** is necessary. The revised IAS also provides guidance on the cost formulas that are used to assign costs to inventories.

In other words, the fundamental accounting assumption of **accruals** requires costs to be matched with associated revenues. In order to achieve this, costs incurred for goods which remain unsold at the year end must be carried forward in the balance sheet and matched against future revenues.

1.3 Scope

The following items are **excluded** from the scope of the standard.

- Work in progress under **construction contracts** (covered by IAS 11 *Construction contracts,* see Section 2)
- **Financial instruments** (ie shares, bonds)
- **Biological assets**

Certain inventories are exempt from the standard's **measurement rules**, ie those held by:

- Producers of **agricultural and forest products**
- **Commodity broker-traders**

1.4 Definitions

The standard gives the following important definitions.

Key terms

Inventories are assets:

- held for sale in the ordinary course of business;
- in the process of production for such sale; or
- in the form of materials or supplies to be consumed in the production process or in the rendering of services.

Net realisable value is the estimated selling price in the ordinary course of business less the estimated costs of completion and the estimated costs necessary to make the sale.

Fair value is the amount for which an asset could be exchanged or a liability settled between knowledgeable, willing parties in an arm's length transaction. (*IAS 2*)

Inventories can **include** any of the following.

- **Goods purchased and held for resale**, eg goods held for sale by a retailer, or land and buildings held for resale
- **Finished goods** produced
- **Work in progress** being produced
- Materials and supplies awaiting use in the production process (**raw materials**)

1.5 Measurement of inventories

The standard states that **'Inventories should be measured at the lower of cost and net realisable value.'**

Exam focus point

This is a very important rule and you will be expected to apply it in the exam.

1.6 Cost of inventories

The cost of inventories will consist of all costs of:

(a) **Purchase**
(b) **Costs of conversion**
(c) **Other costs** incurred in bringing the inventories to their **present location and condition**

1.6.1 Costs of purchase

The standard lists the following as comprising the costs of purchase of inventories:

(a) **Purchase price** *plus*

(b) **Import duties** and other taxes *plus*

(c) Transport, handling and any other costs **directly attributable** to the acquisition of finished goods, services and materials *less*

(d) **Trade discounts**, rebates and other similar amounts

1.6.2 Costs of conversion

Costs of conversion of inventories consist of two main parts.

(a) Costs **directly related** to the units of production, eg direct materials, direct labour

(b) Fixed and variable **production overheads** that are incurred in converting materials into finished goods, allocated on a systematic basis.

You may have come across the terms 'fixed production overheads' or 'variable production overheads' elsewhere in your studies. The standard defines them as follows.

Key terms

Fixed production overheads are those indirect costs of production that remain relatively constant regardless of the volume of production, eg the cost of factory management and administration.

Variable production overheads are those indirect costs of production that vary directly, or nearly directly, with the volume of production, eg indirect materials and labour. *(IAS 2)*

The standard emphasises that fixed production overheads must be allocated to items of inventory on the basis of the **normal capacity of the production facilities**. This is an important point.

(a) **Normal capacity** is the expected achievable production based on the average over several periods/seasons, under normal circumstances.

(b) The above figure should take account of the capacity lost through **planned maintenance**.

(c) If it approximates to the normal level of activity then the **actual level of production** can be used.

(d) **Low production** or **idle plant** will *not* result in a higher fixed overhead allocation to each unit.

(e) **Unallocated overheads** must be recognised as an expense in the period in which they were incurred.

(f) When production is **abnormally high**, the fixed production overhead allocated to each unit will be reduced, so avoiding inventories being stated at more than cost.

(g) The allocation of variable production overheads to each unit is based on the **actual use** of production facilities.

1.6.3 Other costs

Any other costs should only be recognised if they are incurred in bringing the inventories to their **present location and condition**.

The standard lists types of cost which **would not be included** in cost of inventories. Instead, they should be recognised as an **expense** in the period they are incurred.

- **Abnormal amounts** of wasted materials, labour or other production costs
- **Storage costs** (except costs which are necessary in the production process before a further production stage)
- **Administrative overheads** not incurred to bring inventories to their present location and condition
- **Selling costs**

1.6.4 Techniques for the measurement of cost

Two techniques are mentioned by the standard, both of which produce results which **approximate to cost**, and so both of which may be used for convenience.

(a) **Standard costs** are set up to take account of normal production values: amount of raw materials used, labour time etc. They are reviewed and revised on a regular basis.

(b) **Retail method**: this is often used in the retail industry where there is a large turnover of inventory items, which nevertheless have similar profit margins. The only practical method of inventory valuation may be to take the total selling price of inventories and deduct an overall average profit margin, thus reducing the value to an approximation of cost. The percentage will take account of reduced price lines. Sometimes different percentages are applied on a department basis.

1.7 Cost formulae

FAST FORWARD

The use of **LIFO** is **prohibited** under the revised IAS 2.

Cost of inventories should be assigned by **specific identification** of their individual costs for:

(a) Items that are **not ordinarily interchangeable**
(b) Goods or services produced and segregated for **specific projects**

Specific costs should be attributed to individual items of inventory when they are segregated for a specific project, but not where inventories consist of a large number of interchangeable (ie identical or very similar) items. In the latter case the rule is as specified below.

1.7.1 Accounting treatment

Rule to learn

The cost of inventories should be assigned by using the **first-in, first-out (FIFO)** or **weighted average** cost formula. (The LIFO formula (last in, first out) is **not permitted** by the revised IAS 2.)

Under the weighted average cost method, a recalculation can be made after each purchase, **or alternatively only at the period end**.

1.8 Net realisable value (NRV)

As a general rule assets should not be carried at amounts greater than those expected to be realised from their sale or use. In the case of inventories this amount could fall below cost when items are **damaged or become obsolete**, or where the **costs to completion have increased** in order to make the sale.

In fact we can identify the principal situations in which **NRV is likely to be less than cost**, ie where there has been:

(a) An **increase in costs** or a **fall in selling price**

(b) A **physical deterioration** in the condition of inventory

(c) **Obsolescence** of products

(d) A decision as part of the company's marketing strategy to manufacture and sell products at a **loss**

(e) **Errors in production or purchasing**

A write down of inventories would normally take place on an item by item basis, but similar or related items may be **grouped together**. This grouping together is acceptable for, say, items in the same product line, but it is not acceptable to write down inventories based on a whole classification (eg finished goods) or a whole business.

The assessment of NRV should take place **at the same time** as estimates are made of selling price, using the most reliable information available. Fluctuations of price or cost should be taken into account if they relate directly to **events after the balance sheet date,** which confirm conditions existing at the end of the period.

The reasons why inventory is held must also be taken into account. Some inventory, for example, may be held to satisfy a firm contract and its NRV will therefore be the **contract price**. Any additional inventory of the same type held at the period end will, in contrast, be assessed according to general sales prices when NRV is estimated.

Net realisable value must be reassessed at the end of each period and compared again with cost. If the NRV has risen for inventories held over the end of more than one period, then the previous write down must be **reversed** to the extent that the inventory is then valued at the lower of cost and the new NRV. This may be possible when selling prices have fallen in the past and then risen again.

On occasion a write down to NRV may be of such size, incidence or nature that it must be **disclosed separately**.

1.9 Recognition as an expense

The following treatment is required **when inventories are sold**.

(a) The **carrying amount** is recognised as an expense in the period in which the related revenue is recognised

(b) The amount of any **write-down of inventories** to NRV and all losses of inventories are recognised as an expense in the period the write-down or loss occurs

(c) The amount of any **reversal of any write-down of inventories**, arising from an increase in NRV, is recognised as a reduction in the amount of inventories recognised as an expense in the period in which the reversal occurs

1.10 Disclosure

FAST FORWARD

Full details are required of inventory carried at **NRV** as well as the reversal of any previous write down.

The financial statements should disclose the following.

(a) **Accounting policies** adopted in measuring inventories, including the cost formula used

(b) **Total carrying amount of inventories** and the carrying amount in classifications appropriate to the entity

(c) **Carrying amount** of inventories carried at fair value less costs to sell

(d) The amount of inventories **recognised as an expense** in the period

(e) The amount of any **write-down** of inventories **recognised as an expense** in the period

(f) The amount of any **reversal of any write-down** that is recognised as a reduction in the amount of inventories recognised as an expense in the period

(g) **Circumstances or events** that led to the reversal of a write-down of inventories

(h) Carrying amount of inventories **pledged as security for liabilities**

This information is of great relevance to users of financial statements, particularly the change in assets from period to period. The standard lists common **classifications for inventories**.

- Merchandise
- Production supplies
- Materials
- Work in progress
- Finished goods

The financial statements must also disclose one of two things.

(a) The **amount of inventories** recognised as an expense during the period; or
(b) The **costs** recognised as an expense during the period, classified by their nature

The choice reflects differences in **the way the income statement can be presented**.

Where the entity discloses the amount of **costs** recognised, classified by their nature, then the costs recognised as an expense will be disclosed for:

(a) Raw materials and consumables
(b) Labour costs
(c) Other operating costs
(d) The net change in inventories for the period

Question — Inventory valuation

You are the accountant at Water Pumps Co, and you have been asked to calculate the valuation of the company's inventory at cost at its year end of 30 April 20X5.

Water Pumps manufactures a range of pumps. The pumps are assembled from components bought by Water Pumps (the company does not manufacture any parts).

The company does not use a standard costing system, and work in progress and finished goods are valued as follows.

(a) Material costs are determined from the product specification, which lists the components required to make a pump.

(b) The company produces a range of pumps. Employees record the hours spent on assembling each type of pump, this information is input into the payroll system which prints the total hours spent each week assembling each type of pump. All employees assembling pumps are paid at the same rate and there is no overtime.

(c) Overheads are added to the inventory value in accordance with IAS 2 *Inventories.* The financial accounting records are used to determine the overhead cost, and this is applied as a percentage based on the direct labour cost.

For direct labour costs, you have agreed that the labour expended for a unit in work in progress is half that of a completed unit.

The draft accounts show the following materials and direct labour costs in inventory.

	Raw materials	*Work in progress*	*Finished goods*
Materials ($)	74,786	85,692	152,693
Direct labour ($)		13,072	46,584

The costs incurred in April, as recorded in the financial accounting records, were as follows.

	$
Direct labour	61,320
Selling costs	43,550
Depreciation and finance costs of production machines	4,490
Distribution costs	6,570
Factory manager's wage	2,560
Other production overheads	24,820
Purchasing and accounting costs relating to production	5,450
Other accounting costs	7,130
Other administration overheads	24,770

For your calculations assume that all work in progress and finished goods were produced in April 20X5 and that the company was operating at a normal level of activity.

Required

Calculate the value of overheads which should be added to work in progress and finished goods in accordance with IAS 2 *Inventories.*

Note. You should include details and a description of your workings and all figures should be calculated to the nearest $.

Answer

Calculation of overheads for inventory

Production overheads are as follows.

	$
Depreciation/finance costs	4,490
Factory manager's wage	2,560
Other production overheads	24,820
Accounting/purchase costs	5,450
	37,320

Direct labour = $61,320

$$\therefore \text{ Production overhead rate} = \frac{37{,}320}{61{,}320} = 60.86\%$$

Inventory valuation

	Raw materials	*WIP*	*Finished goods*	*Total*
	$	$	$	$
Materials	74,786	85,692	152,693	313,171
Direct labour	–	13,072	46,584	59,656
Production overhead (at 60.86% of labour)	–	7,956	28,351	36,307
	74,786	106,720	227,628	409,134

Variable overheads will be included in the cost of inventory.

2 IAS 11 Construction contracts

FAST FORWARD

The rules for calculating accounting entries on **construction contracts** can be summarised as follows.

- When the outcome of a construction contract can be estimated reliably, contract revenue and contract costs ... shall be recognised as revenue and expenses respectively by reference to the stage of completion of the contract.
- When it is probable that total contract costs will exceed total contract revenue, the expected loss shall be recognised as an expense immediately.

2.1 Income and expenditure

Imagine that you are the accountant at a construction company. Your company is building a large tower block that will house offices, under a contract with an investment company. It will take three years to build the block and over that time you will obviously have to pay for building materials, wages of workers on the building, architects' fees and so on. You will receive periodic payments from the investment company at various predetermined stages of the construction. How do you decide, in each of the three years, **what to include as income and expenditure** for the contract in the income statement?

This is the problem tackled by IAS 11 *Construction contracts*.

2.2 Example: construction contract

A numerical example might help to illustrate the problem. Suppose that a contract is started on 1 January 20X5, with an estimated completion date of 31 December 20X6. The final contract price is $1,500,000. In the first year, to 31 December 20X5:

(a) Costs incurred amounted to $600,000.

(b) Half the work on the contract was completed.

(c) Certificates of work completed have been issued, to the value of $750,000. (*Note.* It is usual, in a construction contract, for a qualified person such as an architect or engineer to inspect the work completed, and if it is satisfactory, to issue certificates. This will then be the notification to the customer that progress payments are now due to the contractor. Progress payments are commonly the amount of valuation on the work certificates issued, minus a precautionary retention of 10%).

(d) It is estimated with reasonable certainty that further costs to completion in 20X6 will be $600,000.

What is the contract profit in 20X5, and what entries would be made for the contract at 31 December 20X5 if:

(a) Profits are deferred until the completion of the contract?
(b) A proportion of the estimated revenue and profit is credited to the income statement in 20X5?

Solution

(a) If profits were deferred until the completion of the contract in 20X6, the revenue and profit recognised on the contract in 20X5 would be nil, and the value of work in progress on 31 December 20X5 would be $600,000. IAS 11 takes the view that this policy is unreasonable, because in 20X6, the total profit of $300,000 would be recorded. Since the contract revenues are earned throughout 20X5 and 20X6, a profit of nil in 20X5 and $300,000 in 20X6 would be contrary to the accruals concept of accounting.

(b) **It is fairer to recognise revenue and profit throughout the duration of the contract.**

As at 31 December 20X5 revenue of $750,000 should be matched with cost of sales of $600,000 in the income statement, leaving an attributable profit for 20X5 of $150,000.

The only balance sheet entry as at 31 December 20X5 is a receivable of $750,000 recognising that the company is owed this amount for work done to date. No balance remains for work in progress, the whole $600,000 having been recognised in cost of sales.

2.3 What is a construction contract?

A contract which needs IAS 11 treatment does not have to last for a period of more than one year. The main point is that the contract activity **starts in one financial period and ends in another**, thus creating the problem: to which of two or more periods should contract income and costs be allocated? In fact the definition given in the IAS of a construction contract is very straightforward.

Key term

Construction contract. A contract specifically negotiated for the construction of an asset or a combination of assets that are closely interrelated or interdependent in terms of their design, technology and function or their ultimate purpose or use. *(IAS 11)*

The standard differentiates between fixed price contracts and cost plus contracts.

Key terms

Fixed price contract. A contract in which the contractor agrees to a fixed contract price, or a fixed rate per unit of output, which in some cases is subject to cost escalation clauses.

Cost plus contract. A construction contract in which the contractor is reimbursed for allowable or otherwise defined costs, plus a percentage of these costs or a fixed fee.

Construction contracts may involve the building of one asset, eg a bridge, or a series of interrelated assets eg an oil refinery. They may also include **rendering of services** (eg architects) or restoring or demolishing an asset.

2.4 Combining and segmenting construction contracts

The standard lays out the factors which determine whether the construction of a **series of assets** under one contract should be treated as several contracts.

- **Separate proposals** are submitted for each asset
- **Separate negotiations** are undertaken for each asset; the customer can accept/reject each individually
- **Identifiable costs and revenues** can be separated for each asset

There are also circumstances where a **group of contracts** should be treated as **one single construction contract**.

- The group of contracts are negotiated as a **single package**
- Contracts are **closely interrelated**, with an overall profit margin
- The contracts are performed **concurrently** or **in a continuous sequence**

2.5 Contract revenue

Contract revenue will be the **amount specified in the contract**, subject to variations in the contract work, incentive payments and claims *if* these will probably give rise to revenue and *if* they can be reliably measured. The result is that contract revenue is measured at the **fair value** of received or receivable revenue.

The standard elaborates on the types of uncertainty, which depend on the outcome of future events, that affect the **measurement of contract revenue**.

- An **agreed variation** (increase/decrease)
- **Cost escalation clauses** in a fixed price contract (increase)
- **Penalties** imposed due to delays by the contractor (decrease)
- **Number of units** varies in a contract for fixed prices per unit (increase/decrease)

In the case of any variation, claim or incentive payment, two factors should be assessed to determine whether contract revenue should be recognised.

(a) Whether it is **probable** that the customer will accept the variation/claim, or that the contract is sufficiently advanced that the performance criteria will be met

(b) Whether the amount of the revenue can be **measured reliably**

2.6 Contract costs

Contract costs consist of:

- Costs relating **directly** to the contract

- Costs attributable to general contract activity which can be **allocated** to the contract, such as insurance, cost of design and technical assistance not directly related to a specific contract and construction overheads
- Any other costs which can be **charged to the customer** under the contract, which may include general administration costs and development costs

Costs that **relate directly** to a specific contract include the following.

- **Site labour costs**, including site supervision
- Costs of **materials** used in construction
- **Depreciation** of plant and equipment used on the contract
- Costs of **moving** plant, equipment and materials to and from the contract site
- Costs of **hiring** plant and equipment
- Costs of **design and technical assistance** that are directly related to the contract
- Estimated costs of **rectification and guarantee work**, including expected warranty costs
- **Claims from third parties**

General contract activity costs should be **allocated systematically and rationally**, and all costs with similar characteristics should be treated **consistently**. The allocation should be based on the **normal level** of construction activity. Borrowing costs may be attributed in this way (see IAS 23: Section 3).

Some costs **cannot be attributed** to contract activity and so the following should be **excluded** from construction contract costs.

- **General administration costs** (unless reimbursement is specified in contract)
- **Selling costs**
- **R&D** (unless reimbursement is specified in contract)
- **Depreciation** of idle plant and equipment not used on any particular contract

2.7 Recognition of contract revenue and expenses

Revenue and costs associated with a contract should be recognised according to the stage of completion of the contract at the balance sheet date, but *only when* the **outcome of the activity can be estimated reliably**. If a loss is predicted on a contract, then it should be recognised immediately. This is often known as the **percentage of completion method**.

A reliable estimate of the outcome of a construction contract can only be made when **certain conditions** have been met, and these conditions will be different for fixed price and cost plus contracts.

- **Fixed price contracts**
  - Probable that economic benefits of the contract will flow to the entity
  - Total contract revenue can be reliably measured
  - Stage of completion at the period end and costs to complete the contract can be reliably measured
  - Costs attributable to the contract can be identified clearly and be reliably measured (actual costs can be compared to previous estimates)
- **Cost plus contracts**
  - Probable that economic benefits of the contract will flow to the entity
  - Costs attributable to the contract (whether or not reimbursable) can be identified clearly and be reliably measured

The **percentage of completion method** is an application of the accruals assumption. Contract revenue is matched to the contract costs incurred in reaching the stage of completion, so revenue, costs and profit are attributed to the proportion of work completed.

We can **summarise** the treatment as follows.

- Recognise **contract revenue** as revenue in the accounting periods in which the work is performed
- Recognise **contract costs** as an expense in the accounting period in which the work to which they relate is performed
- Any **expected excess** of total contract costs over total contract revenue should be recognised as an expense immediately
- Any costs incurred which relate to **future activity** should be recognised as an asset if it is probable that they will be recovered (often called contract work in progress, ie amounts due from the customer)
- Where amounts have been recognised as contract revenue, but their **collectability** from the customer becomes doubtful, such amounts should be recognised as an expense, not a deduction from revenue

2.8 When can reliable estimates be made?

IAS 11 only allows contract revenue and costs to be recognised when the outcome of the contract can be predicted, ie when it is probable that the economic benefits attached to the contract will flow to the entity. IAS 11 states that this can only be when a contract has been agreed which establishes the following.

- The **enforceable rights** of each party in respect of the asset to be constructed
- The **consideration** that is to be exchanged
- **Terms and manner of settlement**

In addition, the entity should have an **effective internal financial budgeting and reporting system**, in order to review and revise the estimates of contract revenue and costs as the contract progresses.

2.9 Determining the stage of completion

How should you decide on the stage of completion of any contract? The standard lists several methods.

- Proportion of contract costs incurred for work carried out to date
- Surveys of work carried out
- Physical proportion of the contract work completed

2.10 Example: stage of completion

Centrepoint Co have a fixed price contract to build a tower block. The initial amount of revenue agreed is $220m. At the beginning of the contract on 1 January 20X6 our initial estimate of the contract costs is $200m. At the end of 20X6 our estimate of the total costs has risen to $202m.

During 20X7 the customer agrees to a variation which increases expected revenue from the contract by $5m and causes additional costs of $3m. At the end of 20X7 there are materials stored on site for use during the following period which cost $2.5m.

We have decided to determine the stage of completion of the contract by calculating the proportion that contract costs incurred for work to date bear to the latest estimated total contract costs. The contract costs incurred at the end of each year were 20X6: $52.52m, 20X7: $154.2m (including materials in store), 20X8 $205m.

Required

Calculate the stage of completion for each year of the contract and show how revenues, costs and profits will be recognised in each year.

Solution

We can summarise the financial data for each year end during the construction period as follows.

	20X6	*20X7*	*20X8*
	$'000	$'000	$'000
Initial amount of revenue agreed in the contract	220,000	220,000	220,000
Variation	–	5,000	5,000
Total contract revenue	220,000	225,000	225,000
Contract costs incurred to date	52,520	154,200	205,000
Contract costs to complete	149,480	50,800	–
Total estimated contract costs	202,000	205,000	205,000
Estimated profit	18,000	20,000	20,000
Stage of completion	26.0%	74.0%	100.0%

The stage of completion has been calculated using the formula:

$$\frac{\text{Contract costs incurred to date}}{\text{Total estimated contract costs}}$$

The stage of completion in 20X7 is calculated by deducting the $2.5m of materials held for the following period from the costs incurred up to that year end, ie $154.2m – $2.5m = $151.7m. $151.7m/$205m = 74%.

Revenue, expenses and profit will be recognised in the income statements as follows.

		To date	*Recognised in prior years*	*Recognised in current year*
		$'000	$'000	$'000
20X6	Revenue ($220m × 26%)	57,200		
	Costs ($202m × 26%)	52,520		
		4,680		
20X7	Revenue ($225m × 74%)	166,500	57,200	109,300
	Costs ($205m × 74%)	151,700	52,520	99,180
		14,800	4,680	10,120
20X8	Revenue ($225m × 100%)	225,000	166,500	58,500
	Costs ($205m × 100%)	205,000	151,700	53,300
		20,000	14,800	5,200

You can see from the above example that, when the stage of completion is determined using the contract costs incurred to date, only contract costs reflecting the work to date should be included in costs incurred to date.

- Exclude costs relating to **future activity**, eg cost of materials delivered but not yet used
- Exclude payments made to subcontractors **in advance** of work performed

2.11 Outcome of the contract cannot be predicted reliably

When the contract's outcome cannot be predicted reliably the following treatment should be followed.

- Only recognise revenue to the extent of contract costs incurred which are expected to be **recoverable**
- Recognise contract costs as an **expense** in the period they are incurred

This **no profit/no loss approach** reflects the situation near the beginning of a contract, ie the outcome cannot be reliably estimated, but it is likely that costs will be recovered.

Contract costs which **cannot be recovered** should be recognised as an expense straight away. IAS 11 lists the following situations where this might occur.

- The contract is **not fully enforceable**, ie its validity is seriously questioned
- The completion of the contract is subject to the outcome of **pending litigation or legislation**
- The contract relates to properties which will probably be **expropriated or condemned**
- The customer is **unable to meet its obligations** under the contract
- The contractor **cannot complete** the contract or in any other way meet its obligations under the contract

Where these **uncertainties cease to exist,** contract revenue and costs should be recognised as normal, ie by reference to the stage of completion.

2.12 Recognition of expected losses

Any loss on a contract should be **recognised as soon as it is foreseen**. The loss will be the amount by which total expected contract revenue is exceeded by total expected contract costs. The loss amount is not affected by whether work has started on the contract, the stage of completion of the work or profits on other contracts (unless they are related contracts treated as a single contract).

2.13 Changes in estimates

The effect of any change in the estimate of contract revenue or costs or the outcome of a contract should be accounted for as a **change in accounting estimate** under IAS 8 *Accounting policies, changes in accounting estimates and errors.*

2.14 Example: changes in estimates

The example below shows the effect of a change in estimate of costs on the figures that appear in the income statement and balance sheet.

Battersby Co enters into a three-year contract.

Estimated revenue = $20,000
Estimated total cost = $16,000.

However, during Year 2, management revises its estimate of total costs incurred and thus the outcome of the contract. As a result, during Year 2, a loss is recognised on the contract for the year, even though the contract will still be profitable overall.

	Year 1	*Year 2*	*Year 3*
	$	$	$
Estimated revenue	20,000	20,000	20,000
Estimated total cost	16,000	18,000	18,000
Estimated total profit	4,000	2,000	2,000
Cost incurred to date	$8,000	$13,500	$18,000
Percentage of completion	50%	75%	100%
Recognised profit/(loss) to date	$2,000	($500)	$500
Cumulative recognised profit	$2,000	$1,500	$2,000

Progress billings of $8,000, $8,000 and $4,000 are made on the last day of each year and are received in the first month of the following year. The balance sheet asset at the end of each year is:

Gross amounts due to/from customers	*Year 1*	*Year 2*	*Year 3*
	$	$	$
Costs incurred	8,000	13,500	18,000
Recognised profits	2,000	2,000	2,500
(Recognised losses)	–	(500)	(500)
(Progress billings)	(8,000)	(16,000)	(20,000)
Amount recognised as an asset/(liability) (unbilled contract revenue)	2,000	(1,000)	0

In addition, at each year end, the entity recognises a trade receivable for the amount outstanding at the end of the year of $8,000, $8,000 and $4,000.

2.15 Disclosures

The following should be disclosed under IAS 11

- Contract revenue recognised as **revenue in the period**
- **Methods used** to determine the **contract revenue**
- **Methods used** to determine **stage of completion** of contracts which are in progress

For **contracts in progress** at the balance sheet date, show the following.

- **Total costs incurred** and recognised profits (less recognised losses) to date
- **Advances** received
- **Retentions** (progress billings not paid until the satisfaction of certain conditions)

Amounts owed by customers and to sub-contractors for contract work must be **shown gross as an asset and a liability respectively**. These are determined by comparing the total costs incurred plus recognised profits to the sum of recognised losses and progress billings, as you will see in the question below.

Any **contingent gains or losses**, eg due to warranty costs, claims, penalties or possible losses, should be disclosed in accordance with IAS 37 *Provisions, contingent liabilities and contingent assets.*

2.16 Example: disclosure

Suppose that Tract Ore Co finishes its first year of operations in which all contract costs were paid in cash and all progress billings and advances were received in cash. For contracts W, X and Z only:

(a) contract costs include costs of materials purchased for use in the contract which have not been used at the period end; and

(b) customers have advanced sums to the contractor for work not yet performed.

The relevant figures for all contracts at the end of Tract Ore's first year of trading are as follows.

	V	*W*	*X*	*Y*	*Z*	*Total*
	$m	$m	$m	$m	$m	$m
Contract revenue recognised	37.7	135.2	98.8	52.0	14.3	338.0
Contract expenses recognised	28.6	117.0	91.0	65.0	14.3	315.9
Expected losses recognised	–	–	–	10.4	7.8	18.2
Recognised profits less recognised losses	9.1	18.2	7.8	(23.4)	(7.8)	3.9
Contract costs incurred in the period	28.6	132.6	117.0	65.0	26.0	369.2
Contract expenses recognised	28.6	117.0	91.0	65.0	14.3	315.9
Contract expenses that relate to future activity recognised as an asset	–	15.6	26.0	–	11.7	53.3

	V	*W*	*X*	*Y*	*Z*	*Total*
	$m	$m	$m	$m	$m	$m
Contract revenue	37.7	135.2	98.8	52.0	14.3	338.0
Progress billings	26.0	135.2	98.8	46.8	14.3	321.1
Unbilled contract revenue	11.7	–	–	5.2	–	16.9
Advances	–	20.8	5.2	–	6.5	32.5

Required

Show the figures that should be disclosed under IAS 11.

Solution

Following IAS 11, the required disclosures would be as follows.

	$m
Contract revenue recognised in the period	338.0
Contract costs incurred and recognised profits (less recognised losses) to date (W)	373.1
Advances received	32.5
Gross amount due from customers for contract work: asset (W)	57.2
Gross amount due to customers for contract work: liability (W)	(5.2)

Workings

These amounts are calculated as follows.

	V	*W*	*X*	*Y*	*Z*	*Total*
	$m	$m	$m	$m	$m	$m
Contract costs incurred	28.6	132.6	117.0	65.0	26.0	369.2
Recognised profits less recognised losses	9.1	18.2	7.8	(23.4)	(7.8)	3.9
	37.7	150.8	124.8	41.6	18.2	373.1
Progress billings	26.0	135.2	98.8	46.8	14.3	321.1
Due from customers	11.7	15.6	26.0		3.9	57.2
Due to customers				(5.2)		(5.2)

2.17 Summary of accounting treatment

The following summarises the accounting treatment for long-term contracts – **make sure that you understand it.**

2.17.1 Income statement

(a) **Revenue and costs**

(i) Sales revenue and associated costs should be recorded in the income statement as the contract activity progresses.

(ii) Include an appropriate proportion of total contract value as sales revenue in the income statement.

(iii) The costs incurred in reaching that stage of completion are matched with this sales revenue, resulting in the reporting of results which can be attributed to the proportion of work completed.

(iv) Sales revenue is the value of work carried out to date.

(b) **Profit recognised in the contract**

(i) It must reflect the proportion of work carried out.

(ii) It should take into account any known inequalities in profitability in the various stages of a contract.

2.17.2 Balance sheet

(a) **Asset**

	$
Costs incurred plus recognised profits	X
Progress billings plus recognised losses	(X)
Gross amount due from customers	X

(b) **Liability**

	$
Costs incurred plus recognised profits	X
Progress billings plus recognised losses	(X)
Gross amount due to customers	(X)

(c) Separate disclosure must also be made of:

(i) costs incurred and recognised profits (less recognised losses) to date
(ii) the amount of advances received
(iii) the amount of retentions

Question — Construction contracts

The main business of Santolina Co is construction contracts. At the end of September 20X3 there is an uncompleted contract on the books, details of which are as follows.

Date commenced	1.4.X1
Expected completed date	23.12.X3
	$
Final contract price	290,000
Costs to 30.9.X3	210,450
Value of work certified to 30.9.X3	230,000
Progress billings to 30.9.X3	210,000
Cash received to 30.9.X3	194,000
Estimated costs to completion at 30.9.X3	20,600

Required

Prepare calculations showing the amounts to be included in the balance sheet at 30 September 20X3 in respect of the above contract.

Answer

The estimated final profit is:

	$
Final contract price	290,000
Less costs to date	(210,450)
estimated future costs	(20,600)
Estimated final profit	58,950

The attributable profit is found as follows.

$$\text{Estimated final profit} \times \frac{\text{Work certified}}{\text{Total contract work}}$$

$$\$58,950 \times \frac{230,000}{290,000}$$

Attributable profit = $46,753

	$
Costs incurred plus recognised profits (210,450 + 46,753)	257,203
Progress billings	(210,000)
Gross amount due from customers (asset)	47,203

Exam focus point

The May and November 2005 papers both had a question on construction contracts. The November question gave details of a contract and asked how much revenue could be recognised. Make sure you understand this. The question in May carried 5 marks and asked for income statement and balance sheet extracts. You must know how to present 'Gross amount due to/from customers'.

2.18 IAS 11 example

This example is given in the appendix to IAS 11. Work through it and make sure you understand it.

A construction contractor has a fixed price contract for 9,000 (presumably $'000) to build a bridge. The initial amount of revenue agreed in the contract is 9,000. The contractor's initial estimate of contract costs is 8,000. It will take three years to build the bridge. By the end of year 1, the contractor's estimate of contract costs has increased to 8,050.

In year 2, the customer approves a variation resulting in an increase in contract revenue of 200 and estimated additional contract costs of 150. At the end of year 2, costs incurred include 100 for standard materials stored on site to be used in year 3 to complete the project.

The contractor determines the stage of completion of the contract by calculating the proportion that contract costs incurred for work performed to date bear to the latest estimated total contract costs. A summary of the financial data during the construction period is as follows:

	Year 1	*Year 2*	*Year 3*
Initial amount of revenue agreed in contract	9,000	9,000	9,000
Variation	–	200	200
Total contract revenue	9,000	9,200	9,200
Contract costs incurred to date	2,093	6,168	8,200
Contract costs to complete	5,957	2,023	–
Total estimated contract costs	8,050	8,200	8,200
Estimated profit	950	1,000	1,000
Stage of completion	26%	74%	100%

The stage of completion for year 2 (74%) is determined by excluding from contract costs incurred for work performed to date the 100 of standard materials stored at the site for use in year 3.

The amounts of revenue, expenses and profit recognised in the income statement in the three years are as follows:

	To date	Recognised in prior years	Recognised in current year
Year 1			
Revenue (9,000 × 26%)	2,340	–	2,340
Expenses (8,050 × 26%)	2,093	–	2,093
Profit	247	–	247
Year 2			
Revenue (9,200 × 74%)	6,808	2,340	4,468
Expenses (8,200 × 74%)	6,068	2,093	3,975
Profit	740	247	493
Year 3			
Revenue (9,200 × 100%)	9,200	6,808	2,392
Expenses	8,200	6,068	2,132
Profit	1,000	740	260

Here is another example illustrating the disclosures required under IAS 11.

A contractor has five contracts in progress at the end of year 1 as follows:

	A	B	C	D	E	Total
Contract revenue recognised	145	520	380	200	55	1,300
Contract expenses recognised	110	450	350	250	55	1,215
Expected losses recognised	–	–	–	40	30	70
Recognised profits less recognised losses	35	70	30	(90)	(30)	15
Contract costs incurred in the period	110	510	450	250	100	1,420
Contract costs incurred recognised as expenses	110	450	350	250	55	1,215
Contract costs relating to future activity (WIP)	–	60	100	–	45	205
Contract revenue (as above)	145	520	380	200	55	1,300
Progress billings	100	520	380	180	55	1,235
Unbilled contract revenue	45	–	–	20	–	65
Advances	–	80	20	–	25	125

The amounts to be disclosed in accordance with IAS 11 are as follows:

Contract revenue recognised as revenue in the period	1,300
Contract costs incurred and recognised profits less recognised losses to date	1,435
Advances received	125
Gross amount due from customers for contract work (asset)	220
Gross amounts due to customers for contract work (liability)	(20)

These amounts are calculated as follows:

	A	B	C	D	E	Total
Contract costs incurred	110	510	450	250	100	1,420
Recognised profits less recognised losses	35	70	30	(90)	(30)	15
	145	580	480	160	70	1,435
Progress billings	100	520	380	180	55	1,235
Due from customers	45	60	100	–	15	220
Due to customers	–	–	–	(20)	–	(20)

Note that, where you are dealing with a single construction contract, there will be *either* a gross amount due to customers *or* a gross amount due from customers. Here we are dealing with more than one contract and, instead of showing a net balance of 200 due from customers, the standard requires the asset and the liability to be shown separately.

Exam focus point

In the exam, **gross amounts due to customers** should be shown as a current liability.

Chapter Roundup

- IAS 2 *Inventories* requires that the balance sheet should show **inventories** classified in a manner appropriate to the entity. Common **classifications** are:

  Merchandise
  Production supplies
  Materials
  Work-in-progress
  Finished goods

- The use of **LIFO** is **prohibited** under the revised IAS 2.
- Full details are required of inventory carried at **NRV** as well as the reversal of any previous write down.
- The rules for calculating accounting entries on **construction contracts** can be summarised as follows.
  - Sales revenue taken on construction contracts should be debited to receivables (and credited to the income statement).
  - The amount due from customers is costs to date plus recognised profits less progress billings plus recognised losses.
  - Any amount due to customers will be the excess of progress payments plus recognised losses over costs to date plus recognised profits.

Quick Quiz

1 Net realisable value = Selling price **less** .... **less** ....

2 Which inventory costing method is allowed under IAS 2?

(a) FIFO (b) LIFO

3 Any expected loss on a construction contract must be recognised, in full, in the year it was identified.

True ☐ False ☐

4 How is the value of a construction contract disclosed in the balance sheet?

5 Which items in the income statement and balance sheet are potentially affected by construction contracts?

Answers to Quick Quiz

1 Net realisable value = selling price costs to completion **less** costs necessary to make the sale.

2 (a) FIFO. LIFO is not allowed.

3 True

4 See Paragraph 2.17

5 Income statement: revenue and cost of sales.
Balance sheet: inventories, receivables, liabilities.

Now try the questions below from the Exam Question Bank

Number	Level	Marks	Time
Q12	Examination	20	36 mins
Q16	Examination	20	36 mins

11

Distributable profits and capital transactions

Introduction

The topics in this chapter are relevant to all types of accounting transactions, providing a theoretical framework for the topics already covered and for accounting in general.

A great deal of national legislation governing distributions and capital transactions is concerned with protection of creditors (eg suppliers); the aim is to prevent companies favouring shareholders over creditors.

Topic list	Learning outcomes	Syllabus references	Ability required
1 The issue and forfeiture of shares	C (iv)	C (6)	Evaluation
2 Distributable profits	C (iv)	C (6)	Evaluation
3 Purchase of own shares	C (iv)	C (6)	Application
4 Financial Instruments	C (iv)	C (6)	Evaluation

1 The issue and forfeiture of shares

1.1 Share issues

A company can increase its share capital by means of a **share issue**. Here we will look at the specific accounting entries necessary for such an issue, including where a share premium account is required (when the price of the share is greater than its nominal value).

Exam focus point

Local rules and procedures may vary – below the UK rules are given.

1.2 General rules and procedures

Key term

As a general rule, if a company issues ordinary shares for **cash** it must first offer them to its existing ordinary shareholders in proportion to their shareholdings. This is called a **rights issue** because members may obtain new shares in right of their existing holdings.

If they do not accept the shares within 21 days, the company may then offer the shares to non-members. A private company may, by the terms of its memorandum or articles, permanently exclude the members' right of pre-emption (as just described). A public company may authorise its directors (by special resolution) to allot ordinary shares for cash without first offering the shares to members.

When a company issues shares it must obtain consideration at least equal in value to the nominal value of the shares (to issue shares **at par value** means to obtain equal value): shares cannot be issued at a discount. The entire consideration does not have to be received at the time of allotment, and the holder of such **partly-paid shares** is liable to pay the balance. Usually the company may make a 'call' for the balance or any part of it under a procedure laid down in the articles whenever the directors decide to do so. When a call has been made the capital is 'called-up' to that extent, and when the shareholders pay the call it is 'paid-up' to that extent (including in each case previous amounts due or paid). If the company goes into liquidation the liquidator is entitled to call up any balance outstanding.

Key term

Although a company may not allot shares for a consideration of less value than the nominal value of the shares, it is free to obtain a consideration of greater value. The excess of the consideration over the nominal value of the shares is **share premium** which must be credited to a statutory **share premium account** as part of the fixed capital.

Except when a **rights issue** is made to existing members, it is generally considered to be the duty of directors to obtain the highest possible price for the shares, and so to maximise the premium (if any). A rights issue is an issue of shares to existing shareholders. The shares are offered for cash but at a discount to the current market price, and are offered to shareholders in proportion to their existing holdings. For instance a '1 for 4' issue means that a shareholder can buy one new share for each four that he currently holds.

The **share premium account** may be repaid to members (or otherwise eliminated) under a reduction of share capital authorised by the court, but it may not be distributed as dividend because it is a **non-distributable reserve**. It may, however, be applied in the following ways:

(a) Issuing fully paid bonus shares to the members (explained below).

(b) Writing off:

- Preliminary expenses of company formation
- Share or loan stock issue expenses (including commissions and discounts)

(c) In certain circumstances, paying any premium payable when the company redeems redeemable shares or debentures.

Key term

In issuing shares a company, instead of requiring its members to provide new consideration, may capitalise available reserves in paying up the shares wholly or in part. This procedure, called making a **bonus issue** of shares, is only permitted to the extent that the articles provide for it (and the correct procedure must be observed).

Since reserves (which in some cases might be distributed as dividends) are part of the shareholders' funds, the effect is to convert them into permanent capital. The members pay for their additional shares by forgoing whatever rights they had to the reserves. Any reserve may be reclassified in this way, including a share premium account or other statutory reserve.

Examples of the treatment for both **bonus issues** and **rights issues** are given towards the end of this section.

1.3 Accounting for an issue of shares for cash

If subscription monies are payable in instalments, entries are made initially to **application and allotment accounts** and **call accounts**. Balances on these accounts are eventually transferred to share capital and share premium accounts. Issue costs will normally be debited to the share premium account.

Occasionally (though rarely nowadays) a shareholder may fail to pay amounts due on allotment or on a call. If the articles of association so allow, the company may (after due warning) confiscate the shares without refund of any amounts paid to date. The shares are not cancelled but their called up value is transferred from share capital account to a **forfeited shares account** (the share premium account, if any, is not affected) until they are reissued. Forfeited shares may be reissued at any price provided that the total amount received (from both applicants) is not less than the par value of the shares.

1.4 Example: accounting for an issue of shares for cash

Ibex wished to issue 500,000 $1 ordinary shares, 60c (including 10c premium) per share payable on application, 20c on allotment and the final 30c on call, four months later. The prospectus was published and applications for 600,000 shares were received. The directors rejected 'small' applicants for a total of 100,000 shares and allotted the remainder. Show the journal entries involved in respect of the issue, assuming that all cheques were banked on receipt.

Solution

JOURNAL

(a)	DEBIT	Bank	$360,000	
	CREDIT	Application and allotment account		$360,000
	Being amounts received on application			
(b)	DEBIT	Application and allotment account	$60,000	
	CREDIT	Bank		$60,000
	Being return of application money to unsuccessful subscribers			
(c)	DEBIT	Application and allotment account	$400,000	
	CREDIT	Share capital account		$350,000
	CREDIT	Share premium account		$50,000
	Being allotment of shares			

(At this stage the total of the balances on the share capital account and share premium account shows the total amount receivable on application and allotment, while the debit balance on the application and allotment account records how much of that amount is still outstanding.)

(d)	DEBIT	Bank	$100,000	
	CREDIT	Application and allotment account		$100,000
	Being receipt of amounts due on allotment			

(This entry closes the application and allotment account.)

(e)	DEBIT	Call account	$150,000	
	CREDIT	Share capital account		$150,000
	Being the amount of the call on shares to make them fully paid			

(The share capital account is credited with the full amount due on the call, and the call account records the actual receipt of the money.)

(f)	DEBIT	Bank	$150,000	
	CREDIT	Call account		$150,000
	Being receipt of call money due			

If, in the example, shares had been allotted on a proportional basis, each subscriber would have received five-sixths of the number of shares applied for. There would therefore be no need for entry (b) above, and each subscriber's surplus application money would be applied to the amount due from him on allotment. Entry (c) above would remain the same, but entry (d) would be:

DEBIT	Bank	$40,000	
CREDIT	Application and allotment account		$40,000
Being receipt of amounts due on allotment			

1.5 Example (continued)

After the call was made the money due on 10,000 of the shares was not received. The directors of Ibex (after due notice) forfeited the shares and subsequently reissued them at a price of 75c each. The journal entries (a) to (e) above would remain the same, but the subsequent entries would be:

(f)	DEBIT	Bank	$147,000	
	CREDIT	Call account		$147,000
	Being receipt of call money			

(If a balance sheet were drawn up at this stage, the debit balance on call account, being the $3,000 still receivable, would be shown as called up share capital not paid.)

(g)	DEBIT	Investments: own shares *	$3,000	
	CREDIT	Call account		$3,000
	Being the forfeiture of the shares (The shares are now held by the company ready for re-issue.)			

When the shares are reissued the journal entries made are as follows.

(h)	DEBIT	Bank	$7,500	
	CREDIT	Investments: own shares *		$7,500
	Being proceeds of reissue of shares			
(i)	DEBIT	Investments: own shares	$4,500	
	CREDIT	Share premium account		$4,500
	Being transfer of the premium on the reissued shares to share premium account.			

(This is an additional premium obtained on the reissue of shares and is the excess of reissue price over the unpaid calls: 10,000 @ 45c.)

* OR a forfeiture account

The combined example may be worked in ledger account form.

BANK ACCOUNT

	$		$
Application & allotment a/c	360,000	Application & allotment a/c	60,000
Application & allotment a/c	100,000	Balance c/d	554,500
Call a/c	147,000		
Investments: own shares	7,500		
	614,500		614,500

APPLICATION AND ALLOTMENT ACCOUNT

	$		$
Bank (100,000 @ 60c)	60,000	Bank (600,000 @ 60c)	360,000
Ordinary share capital a/c:		Bank (500,000 @ 20c)	100,000
(500,000 @ 70c)	350,000		
Share premium a/c:			
(500,000 @ 10c)	50,000		
	460,000		460,000

SHARE CAPITAL ACCOUNT: $1 ORDINARY SHARES

	$		$
Balance c/d	500,000	Application & allotment a/c	350,000
		Call a/c	150,000
	500,000		500,000

SHARE PREMIUM ACCOUNT

	$		$
Balance	54,500	Application & allotment a/c	50,000
		Investments: own shares	4,500
	54,500		54,500

CALL ACCOUNT

	$		$
Ordinary share capital a/c		Bank (490,000 @ 30c)	147,000
(500,000 @ 30c)	150,000	Investments : own shares	3,000
	150,000		150,000

INVESTMENTS: OWN SHARES

	$		$
Call a/c	3,000	Bank (10,000 @ 75c)	7,500
Share premium account	4,500		
	7,500		7,500

Ibex balance sheets would be as follows.

(a) After the call (but before forfeiture)

	$
Current assets	
Receivables: called up share capital not paid	3,000
Cash at bank	547,000
	550,000
Capital and reserves	
Called up share capital: 500,000 $1 ordinary shares	500,000
Share premium account	50,000
	550,000

(b) After the forfeiture (but before reissue)

	$
Current assets	
Investments: own shares	3,000
Cash at bank	547,000
	550,000
Capital and reserves	
Called up share capital: 500,000 $1 ord shares	500,000
Share premium account	50,000
	550,000

(c) After the reissue

	$
Current assets	
Cash at bank	554,500
Capital and reserves	
Called up share capital: 500,000 $1 ord shares fully paid	500,000
Share premium account	54,500
	554,500

Exam focus point

The May 2005 exam had a question on reissue of forfeited shares.

1.6 Example: bonus issues

BUBBLES CO
BALANCE SHEET (EXTRACT)

	$'000	$'000
Capital and reserves		
Share capital		
$1 ordinary shares (fully paid)		1,000
Reserves		
Share premium	500	
Retained earnings	2,000	
		2,500
		3,500

Bubbles decided to make a '3 for 2' bonus issue (ie 3 new shares for every 2 already held). The double entry is as follows.

		$'000	$'000
DEBIT	Share premium	500	
	Retained earnings	1,000	
CREDIT	Ordinary share capital		1,500

After the issue the balance sheet is as follows.

	$'000
Capital and reserves	
Share capital	
$1 ordinary shares (fully paid)	2,500
Reserves	
Retained earnings	1,000
	3,500

1,500,000 new ('bonus') shares are issued to existing shareholders, so that if Mr X previously held 20,000 shares he will now hold 50,000. The total value of his holding should theoretically remain the same however, since the net assets of the company remain unchanged and his share of those net assets remains at 2% (50,000/2,500,000; previously 20,000/1,000,000).

1.7 Example: rights issues

Bubbles (above) decides to make a rights issue, shortly after the bonus issue. The terms are '1 for 5 @ $1.20' (one new share for every five already held, at a price of $1.20). Assuming that all shareholders take up their rights (which they are not obliged to) the double entry is as follows.

		$'000	$'000
DEBIT	Cash	600	
CREDIT	Ordinary share capital		500
CREDIT	Share premium		100

Mr X who previously held 50,000 shares will now hold 60,000, and the value of his holding should increase (theoretically at least) because the net assets of the company will increase. The new balance sheet will show:

	$'000	$'000
Capital and reserves		
Share capital		
$1 ordinary shares		3,000
Reserves		
Share premium	100	
Retained earnings	1,000	
		1,100
		4,100

The increase in funds of $600,000 represents the cash raised from the issue of 500,000 new shares at a price of $1.20 each.

1.8 Summary of procedure and accounting entries

The following procedure is followed for the issue and forfeiture of shares.

(a) **Application**: where potential shareholders apply for shares in the company and send cash to cover the amount applied for.

(b) **Allotment**: the company allocates shares to the successful applicants and returns cash to unsuccessful applicants.

(c) **Call**: where the purchase price is payable in instalments, the company will call for instalments on their due dates of payment.

(d) **Forfeiture**: if a shareholder fails to pay a call, his shares may be forfeited without the need to return the money he has paid. These forfeited shares may then be reissued to other shareholders.

The following summarises the relevant accounting entries.

(a) DEBIT Bank
CREDIT Application and allotment a/c
Application proceeds

(b) DEBIT Application and allotment a/c
CREDIT Bank
Money returned to over-subscribers

(c) DEBIT Bank
CREDIT Application and allotment a/c
Cash on allotment

(d) DEBIT Application and allotment a/c
CREDIT Share capital
CREDIT Share premium
Allotment of shares

(e) DEBIT Call a/c
CREDIT Share capital
Call of final instalment owed

(f) DEBIT Bank
CREDIT Call a/c
Cash receipts banked

(g) DEBIT Investment: own shares (or forfeit a/c)
CREDIT Call a/c
Forfeited shares

(h) DEBIT Bank
CREDIT Investment: own shares
Reissue forfeited shares

(i) DEBIT Investment: own shares
CREDIT Share premium a/c
Additional premium on reissue

Question — Issue of shares

Haggot Co issued 50,000 $1 shares at $1.20 per share. Monies due were as follows.

On application	50c including premium
On allotment	30c
Call	40c

Applications were received amounting to $30,000 (ie for 60,000 shares).

At the call, 1,000 shares were forfeited. These were subsequently reissued for $1.10 cash.

Required

Write up the relevant ledger accounts for the above issue.

Answer

APPLICATION AND ALLOTMENT A/C

	$		$
Bank	5,000	Bank	30,000
Share capital	30,000	Bank	15,000
Share premium	10,000		
	45,000		45,000

BANK

	$		$
App & allot a/c	30,000	App & allot a/c	5,000
App & allot a/c	15,000		
Call	19,600		
Forfeit	1,100	C/d	60,700
	65,700		65,700

SHARE CAPITAL

	$		$
		App & allot	30,000
C/d	50,000	Call	20,000
	50,000		50,000

SHARE PREMIUM

	$		$
		App & allot a/c	10,000
C/d	10,700	Investments : own shares	700
	10,700		10,700

CALL A/C

	$		$
Share capital	20,000	Bank	19,600
		Forfeit	400
	20,000		20,000

INVESTMENT IN OWN SHARES

	$		$
Call a/c	400	Bank	1,100
Share premium	700		
	1,100		1,100

2 Distributable profits

FAST FORWARD

You should be able to calculate **maximum distributions available** to private and public companies and to discuss the meaning of distributable and realised profits.

2.1 Distributions

A **distribution** may be defined by national legislation, but we can state here that it is generally every description of distribution of a company's assets to members (shareholders) of the company, whether in cash or otherwise, with the **exception** of the following.

(a) An issue of **bonus shares**

(b) The **redemption or purchase of the company's own shares** out of capital (including the proceeds of a new issue) or out of unrealised profits

(c) The **reduction of share capital** by:

  (i) reducing the liability on shares in respect of share capital not fully paid up, or
  (ii) paying off paid-up share capital

(d) A distribution of assets to shareholders in a **winding up** of the company

In general, **companies must not make a distribution except out of profits available for the purpose.** These available profits are:

(a) Its **accumulated realised profits**, insofar as these have not already been used for an earlier distribution or for 'capitalisation'

(b) **Minus its accumulated realised losses**, insofar as these have not already been written off in a reduction or reconstruction scheme

Capital profits and revenue profits (if realised) are taken together and capital losses and revenue losses (if realised) are similarly grouped together. **Unrealised profits** cannot be distributed (for example profit on the revaluation of non-current assets); nor must a company apply unrealised profits to pay up debentures or any unpaid amounts on issued shares.

Capitalisation of realised profits is the use of profits for one of two purposes.

(a) To issue bonus shares
(b) As a transfer to any reserve for the redemption of capital (a **capital redemption reserve**)

Some countries may impose **further restrictions on the distributions of all companies**, or perhaps listed companies or other public interest companies.

For example, such a company may not be able to make a distribution if at the time either of these apply.

(a) The amount of its net assets is less than the combined total of its called-up share capital plus its undistributable reserves.

(b) The distribution will reduce the amount of its net assets to below the combined total of its called-up share capital plus its undistributable reserves.

'Undistributable reserves' are likely to include the following, although national legislation may dictate otherwise.

- The **share premium account** (capital paid in excess of par)
- Any reserve for the **redemption of capital**
- Any **accumulated surplus** of unrealised profits over unrealised losses
- Any **other reserve** which cannot be distributed, whether by statute, or the company's memorandum or articles of association (ie constitution)

Where such a restriction applies, all **accumulated distributable profits, both realised and unrealised, must exceed the accumulated realised and unrealised losses of the company** before any distribution can be made. The difference between the profits and losses is the maximum possible distribution.

In contrast with the basic definition of distributable profits, this restriction includes consideration of **unrealised** profits and losses, so that if unrealised losses exceed unrealised profits, the amount of distributions which can be made will be reduced by the amount of the 'deficit'.

2.2 Example: basic distributable profits vs special restrictions

Huddle Co is a private company and Publimco is a listed company. Both companies have a financial year ending on 31 December. On 31 December 20X5, the balance sheets of the companies, by a remarkable coincidence, were identical, as follows.

	Huddle Co		*Publimco*	
	$'000	$'000	$'000	$'000
Net assets		365		365
Share capital		300		300
Share premium account		60		60
Unrealised losses on asset revaluations		(25)		(25)
Realised profits	50		50	
Realised losses	(20)		(20)	
		30		30
		365		365

What is the maximum distribution that each company can make, if Huddle Co's distributable profits follow the basic definition, but Publimco has special restrictions over its distributable profits as noted above?

Solution

(a) The distributable profits of Huddle Co are $30,000.

(b) The distributable profits of Publimco are further restricted to $30,000 – $25,000 = $5,000 (or alternatively, $365,000 – $300,000 – $60,000 = $5,000. This is the surplus of net assets over share capital plus undistributable reserves (which in this example are represented by the share premium account).

2.3 Realised and distributable profits

National legislation may define **realised profits** but in other countries the definition may not be clear. As a general 'rule of thumb' we can state that profits in the **income statement** are realised, while **unrealised profits** are **credited directly to reserves.**

IAS 1 *Presentation of financial statements* provides a framework for recognising realised profits. If IAS 1, particularly the **prudence concept** is followed, income statement profits will be realised.

2.3.1 Exceptions

In the case of **sale of revalued non-current assets**, the **unrealised profit on revaluation** previously credited to the revaluation reserve may not pass through the income statement. It may nevertheless be regarded as **distributable**, unless local legislation states otherwise.

Where an asset has been revalued, the **increase in depreciation charge** can be treated as a realised profit.

Development expenditure is a realised loss in the year in which it is incurred, except when the costs are capitalised within IAS 38 guidelines, in which case the costs are amortised as realised losses over a number of years.

Provisions are generally treated as realised losses.

2.4 The relevant accounts

Which accounts should be used to determine the distributable profits? These are the **most recent audited annual accounts** of the company, prepared in compliance with national standards and legislation, or IASs. If the accounts are qualified by the auditors, the auditors must state in their report whether they consider that the proposed distribution would contravene any relevant legislation.

Companies may also be permitted to base a distribution on **interim accounts**, which need not be audited. However, in general, such interim accounts must be properly prepared and comply with IASs and show a true and fair view.

Question — **Distributable profits**

Explain the implications of the following items to profits available for distribution in a company, based on the provisions of relevant IASs.

(a) Development expenditure

(b) Net deficit on a revaluation reserve arising from an overall deficit on the revaluation of non-current assets

(c) Excess depreciation

(d) Goodwill

Answer

(a) For the purposes of calculating realised profits, development expenditure carried forward in the balance sheet should be treated as a realised loss. This means that development expenditure may not be regarded as part of net assets.

If, however, there are special circumstances which, in the opinion of the directors, justify the treatment of development expenditure as an asset and not as a loss, then this requirement need not apply. It is generally considered that, if the development expenditure qualifies for treatment as an asset under the provisions of IAS 38, then it may be treated as an asset and not a loss for the purposes of calculating distributable profits.

(b) A revaluation reserve is a non-distributable reserve because it reflects unrealised profits and losses. A permanent fall in value causing an overall deficit on the revaluation reserve should be taken to the income statement, ie it is a realised loss and therefore reduces distributable profits.

(c) Excess depreciation is the depreciation on revalued assets in excess of cost. Since excess depreciation is regarded as the realisation (through use) of part of the corresponding revaluation reserve, it is added back to profits available for distribution.

(d) Goodwill is kept on the balance sheet subject to an annual impairment review. Any impairment loss recognised will reduce distributable profits.

3 Purchase of own shares

FAST FORWARD

You must be able to carry out **simple calculations** showing the amounts to be transferred to the **capital redemption reserve** on purchase of own shares and how the amount of any **premium** on redemption would be treated.

3.1 Reduction of capital

Limited liability companies may be permitted to cancel unissued shares and in that way reduce their **authorised** share capital. That change does not alter the financial position of any company.

If a limited liability company wishes to **reduce its issued share capital** (and incidentally its authorised capital of which the issued capital is part) it may do so provided that certain conditions are met (set by national legislation). For example:

(a) It must have the power to do so in its **articles** of association
(b) It must pass a **special resolution**
(c) It must obtain **confirmation** of the reduction **from the court**

Requirement (a) is usually a matter of procedure. Articles usually contain the necessary power. If not, the company in general meeting would first pass a special resolution to alter the articles appropriately and then proceed to pass a special resolution to reduce the capital.

There are various basic methods of reducing share capital, and three of the most common are discussed here.

(a) **Extinguish or reduce liability on partly paid shares**. A company may have issued $1 (par) shares 75c paid up. The outstanding liability of 25c per share may be eliminated altogether by reducing each share to 75c (par) fully paid or some intermediate figure, eg 80c (par) 75c paid. Nothing is returned to the shareholders but the company gives up a claim against them for money which it could call up whenever needed.

(b) **Cancel paid up share capital which has been lost or which is no longer represented by available assets.** Suppose that the issued shares are $1 (par) fully paid but the net assets now represent a value of only 50c per share. The difference is probably matched by a debit balance on the retained reserves. The company could reduce the par value of its $1 shares to 50c (or some intermediate figure) and apply the amount to write off the debit balance wholly or in part. It would then be able to resume payment of dividends out of future profits without being obliged to make good past losses. The resources of the company are not reduced by this procedure of part cancellation of nominal value of shares but it avoids having to rebuild lost capital by retaining profits.

(c) **Pay off part of the paid up share capital out of surplus assets.** The company might repay to shareholders, say, 30c in cash per $1 share by reducing the par value of the share to 70c. This reduces the assets of the company by 30c per share.

3.2 Role of court in reduction of capital

In many countries the sanction of the court (or equivalent) may be required for a redemption of shares or reduction in capital. The purpose here is **creditor protection**. The reduction in capital must not put at risk a company's ability to pay its debts. If it did so, then shareholders would be favoured over creditors for distributions from the company. Creditors may be allowed to petition the court against the proposed transaction, but the company may be able to override this by paying off its creditors. The details will vary from country to country.

3.3 Share premium account

Whenever a company obtains for its shares a consideration in excess of their par value, it must usually transfer the excess to a share premium account (capital in excess of par account). The general rule is that the **share premium account is subject to the same restrictions as share capital**. However, it may be possible to make a bonus issue using the share premium account (reducing share premium in order to increase issued share capital).

There may be an **exemption** from the general rules on setting up a share premium account, in certain circumstances where new shares are issued as consideration for the acquisition of shares in another company.

Examples of the **other likely permitted uses of share premium** are to pay:

(a) Capital expenses such as preliminary expenses of forming the company
(b) A discount on the issue of shares or debentures
(c) A premium (if any) paid on redemption of debentures

Some companies may also be able to use a share premium account in purchasing or redeeming their own shares out of capital. It must be emphasised that these rules will vary from country to country according to national legislation.

3.4 Purchase by a company of its own shares

In some countries, there is a **general prohibition** against any voluntary acquisition by a company of its own shares. In other countries, it is possible for a company to voluntarily acquire and keep its own shares, although there may be a limit on the time for which they can be held. For the rest of the chapter, however, we will assume that any of its own shares purchased by a company cannot be held and must be **cancelled immediately**.

One way to preserve reserves for creditor protection is to prevent companies from repurchasing shares except by transferring a sum equal to the par value of shares purchased from distributable profit reserves to a non-distributable reserve, which here we will call the '**capital redemption reserve**'. This reduction in distributable reserves is an example of the **capitalisation of profits**, where previously distributable profits become undistributable.

Such regulations prevent companies from reducing their share capital investment so as to put creditors of the company at risk. This excess of non-distributable over distributable reserves is often referred to as the "creditor's buffer."

3.5 Example: capitalisation of profits

Suppose, for example, that Muffin Co decided to repurchase and cancel $100,000 of its ordinary share capital. A balance sheet of the company is currently as follows.

	$	$
Assets		
Cash		100,000
Other assets		300,000
		400,000
Equity and liabilities		
Equity		
Ordinary shares	130,000	
Retained earnings	150,000	
		280,000
Liabilities		
Trade accounts payable		120,000
		400,000

Now if Muffin were able to repurchase the shares without making any transfer from retained earnings to a capital redemption reserve, the effect of the share redemption on the balance sheet would be as follows.

		$
Assets		
Non-cash assets		300,000
Equity and liabilities		
Equity		
Ordinary shares	30,000	
Retained earnings	150,000	
		180,000
Trade accounts payable		120,000
		300,000

In this example, the company would still be able to pay dividends out of profits of up to $150,000. If it did, the creditors of the company would be highly vulnerable, financing $120,000 out of a total of $150,000 assets of the company.

The regulations prevent such extreme situations arising. On repurchase of the shares, Muffin would have been required to transfer $100,000 from its retained earnings to a non-distributable reserve, called here a capital redemption reserve. The effect of the repurchase of shares on the balance sheet would have been:

	$	$
Assets		
Non-cash assets		300,000
Equity and liabilities		
Equity		
Ordinary shares	30,000	
Reserves		
Distributable (retained earnings)	50,000	
Non-distributable (capital redemption reserve)	100,000	
		180,000
Trade accounts payable		120,000
		300,000

The maximum distributable profits are now $50,000. If Muffin paid all these as a dividend, there would still be $250,000 of assets left in the company, just over half of which would be financed by non-distributable equity capital.

3.6 Treasury shares

Since 2003, entities have been allowed to repurchase their own shares and retain them in treasury, rather than cancelling them. These 'treasury shares' can then be re-issued in the future or issued as part of an employee share scheme.

An entity is allowed to hold up to 10% of its issued share capital as 'treasury shares'. They are shown in the balance sheet as a deduction from equity.

For instance, a company has 500,000 $1 shares in issue and $200,000 in share premium. It reacquires 100,000 shares for $1.40.

The shares re-acquired are classified as treasury shares and presented as follows:

	$'000
Share capital: $1 shares fully paid	500
Share premium	200
	700
Treasury shares	(140)
	560

Exam focus point

The November 2005 exam had a question on treasury shares.

When a company repurchases its own shares, this should normally be financed:

(a) **Out of distributable profits,** OR
(b) **Out of the proceeds** of a new issue of shares.

In addition, if there is any premium on repurchase, it may be the rule that **the premium must be paid out of distributable profits**, except that if the shares were issued at a premium, then any premium payable on their repurchase may be paid out of the proceeds of a new share issue made for the purpose, up to an amount equal to the lesser of:

(a) the aggregate premiums received on issue of the shares; and
(b) the balance on the share premium account (including premium on issue of the new shares).

This may seem complicated, but it makes logical sense. A numerical example might help.

3.7 Example: repurchase of shares

Suppose that Jingle Co intends to repurchase 10,000 shares of $1 each at a premium of 5 cents per share. The repurchase must be financed in one of the following ways.

(a) Out of distributable profits (10,000 × $1.05 = $10,500).

(b) Out of the proceeds of a new share issue (say, by issuing 10,000 new $1 shares at par). The premium of $500 must be paid out of distributable profits.

(c) Out of a combination of a new share issue and distributable profits.

(d) Out of the proceeds of a new share issue where the shares to be repurchased were issued at a premium. For example, if the shares had been issued at a premium of 3c per share, then (assuming that the balance on the share premium account after the new share issue was at least $300) $300 of the premium on repurchase could be debited to the share premium account and only $200 need be debited to distributable profits.

The following rules may also assist.

(a) Where a company purchases its own shares wholly out of distributable profits, it must transfer to the capital redemption reserve an amount equal to the par value of the shares repurchased.

In example (a) above the accounting entries would be:

		$	$
DEBIT	Share capital account	10,000	
	Retained earnings (premium on repurchase)	500	
CREDIT	Cash		10,500
DEBIT	Retained earnings	10,000	
CREDIT	Capital redemption reserve		10,000

(b) Where a company purchases its shares wholly or partly out of the proceeds of a new share issue, it must transfer to the capital redemption reserve an amount by which the par value of the shares repurchased exceeds the *aggregate* proceeds from the new issue (ie par value of new shares issued plus share premium).

In example (b) the accounting entries would be:

		$	$
DEBIT	Share capital account (repurchased shares)	10,000	
	Retained earnings (premium)	500	
CREDIT	Cash (repurchase of shares)		10,500
DEBIT	Cash (from new issue)	10,000	
CREDIT	Share capital account		10,000

No credit to the capital redemption reserve is necessary because there is no decrease in the creditors' buffer.

(c) If the repurchase in the same example as in (b) were made by issuing 5,000 new $1 shares at par, and paying $5,500 out of distributable profits:

		$	$
DEBIT	Share capital account (repurchased shares)	10,000	
	Retained earnings (premium)	500	
CREDIT	Cash (repurchase of shares)		10,500
DEBIT	Cash (from new issue)	5,000	
CREDIT	Share capital account		5,000
DEBIT	Retained earnings	5,000	
CREDIT	Capital redemption reserve		5,000

(d) In the example (d) above (assuming a new issue of 10,000 $1 shares at a premium of 8c per share) the accounting entries would be:

		$	$
DEBIT	Cash (from new issue)	10,800	
CREDIT	Share capital account		10,000
	Share premium account		800
DEBIT	Share capital account (repurchased shares)	10,000	
	Share premium account	300	
	Retained earnings	200	
CREDIT	Cash (repurchase of shares)		10,500

No capital redemption reserve is required, as in (b) above. The repurchase is financed entirely by a new issue of shares.

3.8 Commercial reasons for altering capital structure

These include the following.

- Greater **security of finance**
- Better **image** for third parties
- A **'neater' balance sheet**
- **Borrowing repaid** sooner
- **Cost of borrowing** reduced

Question

Purchase of own shares

Set out below is the summarised balance sheet of A Co at 30 June 20X5.

	A
	$'000
Capital and reserves	
Called up share capital $1 ordinary shares	300
Share premium account	60
Retained earnings	160
	520
Net assets	520

On 1 July 20X5 A Co purchased and cancelled 50,000 of its own ordinary shares as follows.

A Co purchased its own shares at 150c each. The shares were originally issued at a premium of 20c. The repurchase was partly financed by the issue at par of 5,000 new shares of $1 each.

Required

Prepare the summarised balance sheet of A Co at 1 July 20X5 immediately after the above transactions have been effected.

Answer

Workings

	$	$
Cost of redemption (repurchase) (50,000 × $1.50)		75,000
Premium on redemption (50,000 × 50c)		25,000
No premium arises on the new issue.		
Distributable profits		
Retained earnings before redemption		160,000
Premium on redemption (must come out of distributable profits, no premium on new issue)		(25,000)
		135,000
Remainder of redemption costs	50,000	
Proceeds of new issue 5,000 × $1	(5,000)	
Remainder out of distributable profits		(45,000)
Balance on retained earnings		90,000
Transfer to capital redemption reserve		
Par value of shares redeemed		50,000
Proceeds of new issue		(5,000)
Balance to CRR		45,000

BALANCE SHEET AS AT 1 JULY 20X5

	$'000
Total assets	450
Equity and liabilities	
Ordinary shares	255
Share premium	60
Capital redemption reserve	45
	360
Retained earnings	90
	450

3.9 Redeemable preferred (preference) shares

We have been dealing up to now with the repurchase or redemption of **ordinary** shares. The rules and the necessary accounting for redemption of **redeemable preference shares** are quite different. IAS 32 classifies a redeemable preference share as a **liability**, not an equity instrument. This is explained in the next section on **financial instruments**.

4 Financial instruments

FAST FORWARD

IAS 32 and IAS 39 deal with financial instruments. IAS 32 deals with presentation and disclosure. IAS 39 sets out principles for recognising and measuring financial assets and liabilities.

4.1 IAS 32 and IAS 39

(a) IAS 32 *Financial instruments: Disclosure and presentation* deals with:

(i) The classification of financial instruments between liabilities and equity
(ii) Presentation of certain compound instruments
(iii) The disclosure of information about financial instruments

(b) IAS 39 *Financial instruments: Recognition and measurement* deals with:

(i) Recognition and derecognition
(ii) The measurement of financial instruments
(iii) Hedge accounting

We will not be dealing here with hedge accounting or derivatives. We will be considering the rules on financial instruments as they relate to the issue and redemption of shares.

4.2 Definitions

The most important definitions are common to both standards.

Key terms

Financial instrument. Any contract that gives rise to both a financial asset of one entity and a financial liability or equity instrument of another entity.

Financial asset. Any asset that is:

(a) cash

(b) an equity instrument of another entity

Key terms

(c) a contractual right to receive cash or another financial asset from another entity; or to exchange financial instruments with another entity under conditions that are potentially favourable to the entity, or

(d) a contract that will or may be settled in the entity's own equity instruments and is:

 (i) a non-derivative for which the entity is or may be obliged to receive a variable number of the entity's own equity instruments; or

 (ii) a derivative that will or may be settled other than by the exchange of a fixed amount of cash or another financial asset for a fixed number of the entity's own equity instruments.

Financial liability. Any liability that is:

(a) a contractual obligation:

 (i) to deliver cash or another financial asset to another entity, or

 (ii) to exchange financial instruments with another entity under conditions that are potentially unfavourable; or

(b) a contract that will or may be settled in the entity's own equity instruments and is:

 (i) a non-derivative for which the entity is or may be obliged to deliver a variable number of the entity's own equity instruments; or

 (ii) a derivative that will or may be settled other than by the exchange of a fixed amount of cash or another financial asset for a fixed number of the entity's own equity instruments.

Equity instrument. Any contract that evidences a residual interest in the assets of an entity after deducting all of its liabilities.

Fair value is the amount for which an asset could be exchanged, or a liability settled, between knowledgeable, willing parties in an arm's length transaction.

(IAS 32 and IAS 39)

4.3 Assets and liabilities

Examples of **financial assets** include:

(a) Trade receivables
(b) Options
(c) Shares (when used as an investment)

Examples of **financial liabilities** include:

(a) Trade payables
(b) Debenture loans payable
(c) Redeemable preference (non-equity) shares
(d) Forward contracts standing at a loss

As we have already noted, financial instruments include both of the following.

(a) **Primary instruments**: eg receivables, payables and equity securities

(b) **Derivative instruments**: eg financial options, futures and forwards, interest rate swaps and currency swaps, **whether recognised or unrecognised**

IAS 32 makes it clear that the following items are *not* financial instruments.

- **Physical assets**, eg inventories, property, plant and equipment, leased assets and intangible assets (patents, trademarks etc)

- **Prepaid expenses**, deferred revenue and most warranty obligations
- Liabilities or assets that are **not contractual** in nature
- Contractual rights/obligations that **do not involve transfer of a financial asset**, eg commodity futures contracts, operating leases

Question — Financial instruments

Can you give the reasons why the first two items listed above do not qualify as financial instruments?

Answer

Refer to the definitions of financial assets and liabilities given above.

(a) **Physical assets**: control of these creates an opportunity to generate an inflow of cash or other assets, but it does not give rise to a present right to receive cash or other financial assets.

(b) **Prepaid expenses, etc**: the future economic benefit is the receipt of goods/services rather than the right to receive cash or other financial assets.

(c) **Deferred revenue, warranty obligations**: the probable outflow of economic benefits is the delivery of goods/services rather than cash or another financial asset.

Contingent rights and obligations meet the definition of financial assets and financial liabilities respectively, even though many do not qualify for recognition in financial statements. This is because the contractual rights or obligations exist because of a past transaction or event (eg assumption of a guarantee).

4.4 Liabilities and equity

The main thrust of IAS 32 is that financial instruments should be presented according to their **substance, not merely their legal form**. In particular, entities which issue financial instruments should classify them (or their component parts) as **either financial liabilities, or equity**.

The classification of a financial instrument as a liability or as equity depends on the following.

- The **substance of the contractual arrangement** on initial recognition
- The definitions of a **financial liability** and an **equity instrument**

How should a **financial liability be distinguished from an equity instrument**? The critical feature of a **liability** is an **obligation** to transfer economic benefit. Therefore a financial instrument is a financial liability if there is a **contractual obligation** on the issuer either to deliver cash or another financial asset to the holder or to exchange another financial instrument with the holder under potentially unfavourable conditions to the issuer.

The financial liability exists **regardless of the way in which the contractual obligation will be settled**. The issuer's ability to satisfy an obligation may be restricted, eg by lack of access to foreign currency, but this is irrelevant as it does not remove the issuer's obligation or the holder's right under the instrument.

Where the above critical feature is *not* met, then the financial instrument is an **equity instrument**. IAS 32 explains that although the holder of an equity instrument may be entitled to a *pro rata* share of any distributions out of equity, the issuer does *not* have a contractual obligation to make such a distribution.

Although substance and legal form are often **consistent with each other**, this is not always the case. In particular, a financial instrument may have the legal form of equity, but in substance it is in fact a liability.

4.5 IAS 32 and redeemable (or cumulative) preference shares

Many entities issue **preference shares** which must be **redeemed** by the issuer for a fixed (or determinable) amount at a fixed (or determinable) future date. Alternatively, the holder may have the right to require the issuer to redeem the shares at or after a certain date for a fixed amount. In such cases, the issuer has an **obligation**. Therefore the instrument is a **financial liability** and should be classified as such. The issuer will also have an obligation to the holder of a preference share if the share is **cumulative**. In this case the issuer is obliged to pay the dividend each year, and the preference share will be classified as a liability. Preference shares which are non-cumulative and non-redeemable will be classified as equity.

The classification of the financial instrument is made when it is **first recognised** and this classification will continue until the financial instrument is removed from the entity's balance sheet.

4.6 Interest, dividends, losses and gains

As well as looking at balance sheet presentation, IAS 32 considers how financial instruments affect the income statement (and movements in equity). The treatment varies according to whether interest, dividends, losses or gains relate to a financial liability or an equity instrument.

(a) Interest, dividends, losses and gains relating to a financial instrument (or component part) classified as a **financial liability** should be recognised as **income or expense** in profit or loss.

(b) Distributions to holders of a financial instrument classified as an **equity instrument** should be **debited directly to equity** by the issuer.

(c) **Transaction costs** of an equity transaction shall be accounted for as a **deduction from equity**.

4.7 Section summary

- Financial instruments must be classified as **liabilities** or **equity**
- The **substance** of the financial instrument is more important than its **legal form**
- The **critical feature of a financial liability** is the contractual obligation to deliver cash or another financial instrument
- **Redeemable preference shares** are classified as a **financial liability**.
- **Interest, dividends, losses and gains** are treated according to whether they relate to a financial liability or an equity instrument

Exam focus point

The May 2005 exam had a question on the IAS 32 distinction between equity and liability.

4.8 Measurement of financial instruments: IAS 39

Financial instruments are initially measured at the **fair value** of the consideration given or received (ie, **cost**) **plus** (in most cases) **transaction costs** that are **directly attributable** to the acquisition or issue of the financial instrument.

The **exception** to this rule is where a financial instrument is designated as **at fair value through profit or loss**. In this case, **transaction costs** are **not** added to fair value at initial recognition.

The fair value of the consideration is normally the transaction price or market price. If market prices are not reliable, the fair value may be **estimated** using a valuation technique (for example, by discounting cash flows).

4.9 Definitions of Financial Instruments

IAS 39 defines four categories of financial instrument.

(a) **A financial asset or liability at fair value through profit or loss**

This Is prlmarily a financial instrument held for trading. It must have a quoted market price or its fair value must be capable of reliable measurement.

(b) **Held-to-maturity investments**

These have fixed or determinable payments and fixed maturity. The entity has the positive intention and ability to hold them to maturity.

(c) **Loans and receivables**

These are financial assets with fixed or determinable payments that are not quoted in an active market. They are not classified as held for trading and have not been designated as 'at fair value through profit or loss'.

(d) **Available-for-sale financial assets**

These are designated as available for sale but are not classified as 'financial assets or fair value through profit or loss'. They are therefore measured at fair value plus directly attributable transaction costs.

4.10 IAS 39 and redeemable preference shares

FAST FORWARD

Redeemable preference shares are classified as financial liabilities. The finance charge will be the dividends payable plus the redemption cost, less the amount received on issue. This is allocated over the term of the shares.

An entity which issues redeemable preference shares must account for the transaction according to IAS 39. Redeemable preference shares are classified as a **financial liability**. Payment of **dividends** on redeemable preference shares is treated as if it were payment of the **finance charge on a redeemable loan**.

4.11 Accounting for finance charges

How is the finance charge on a financial instrument calculated? It can be measured as the difference between the amount paid or received for the instrument, including any transaction costs, and all amounts received or paid subsequent to that – interest or dividends, amount payable or receivable on maturity. This amount must then be allocated over the life of the instrument.

IAS 39 prescribes the **effective interest method** of allocating the finance charge (or the interest receivable, in the case of the purchaser) over the life of the liability.

Key term

The **effective interest rate** is the rate that exactly discounts estimated future cash payments or receipts through the expected life of the financial instrument. (IAS 39)

4.12 Example: allocation of interest receivable

On 1 January 20X1 Abacus Co purchases a debt instrument for its fair value of $1,000. The debt instrument is due to mature on 31 December 20X5. The instrument has a principal amount of $1,250 and carries fixed interest of 4.72% paid annually.

How should Abacus Co account for the debt instrument over its five year term?

Solution

The interest receivable will be calculated as follows.

	$
Interest:	
5 years × $59 (1,250 × 4.72%)	295
Amount at maturity	1,250
Purchase cost	(1,000)
Interest receivable	545

This interest receivable must be allocated over the five year term. In this case the effective interest rate is 10%.

So the allocation would be as follows.

Year	*Financial asset at beginning of year*	*Interest income for year*	*Interest received during year*	*Financial asset at end of year*
	$	$	$	$
20X1	1,000	100	(59)	1,041
20X2	1,041	104	(59)	1,086
20X3	1,086	109	(59)	1,136
20X4	1,136	113	(59)	1,190
20X5	1,190	119	(59)	1,250

Each year the carrying amount of the financial asset is increased by the interest income for the year (DR Asset/CR Interest receivable in income statement) and reduced by the interest actually received during the year (DR Cash/CR Asset).

As Abacus was the **purchaser** of the financial instrument, we were dealing with **interest receivable**, rather than finance charge.

Now we will take the example of a finance charge.

4.13 Example: allocation of finance charge

On 1 January 20X1 Abacus Co also issues 20 million $1 5% preferred shares redeemable at par after 4 years. Issue costs are $2 million.

The finance charge is calculated as follows.

	$m
Receipt from issue (20m – 2m)	18
Dividend payable over 4 years (20 × 5% ×4)	(4)
Payable on redemption	(20)
Finance charge	(6)

The effective interest rate is approximately 8% and the allocation is as follows.

Year	*Balance sheet liability*	*Finance charge for year 8%*	*Dividends paid*	*Balance sheet liability*
	$m	$m	$m	$m
20X1	18	1.44	(1)	18.44
20X2	18.44	1.48	(1)	18.92
20X3	18.92	1.52	(1)	19.44
20X4	19.44	1.55	(1)	19.99

So by the redemption date the carrying value of the liability has been increased from the amount originally received ($18m) to the amount needed to redeem the shares ($20m).

Exam focus point

> If you were required to calculate finance charges or interest receivable on a financial instrument in the exam, you would be told the effective interest rate.

4.14 IFRS 7

IFRS 7 *Financial Instruments: Disclosures* adds to, and replaces, the disclosure requirements of IAS 32. The two main categories of disclosure required by IFRS 7 are:

(a) Information about the significance of financial instruments

(b) Information about the nature and extent of risks arising from financial instruments.

IFRS 7 comes into force in January 2007.

Chapter Roundup

- You should be able to calculate **maximum distributions available to companies** and to discuss the meaning of distributable and realised profits.
- You must be able to carry out **simple calculations** showing the amounts to be transferred to the **capital redemption reserve** on purchase of own shares, and how the amount of any **premium** on redemption would be treated.
- IAS 32 and IAS 39 deal with financial instruments. IAS 32 deals with presentation and disclosure. IAS 39 sets out principles for recognising and measuring financial assets and liabilities.
- Redeemable preference shares are classified as financial liabilities. The finance charge will be the dividends payable plus the redemption cost, less the amount received on issue. This is allocated over the term of the shares.

Quick Quiz

1 To which purposes can a share premium account be applied?

(i) Writing off share/debenture issue expenses
(ii) Paying a premium on redemption
(iii) Issuing fully paid bonus shares to members

Which is correct?

A (i) and (ii)
B (i) and (iii)
C (ii) and (iii)
D All the above

2 What are the profits generally available for distribution?

3 A public company cannot make a distribution if this will reduce its net assets to below the value of its called up share capital plus undistributable reserves.

True ☐

False ☐

4 If a company has not got the power to reduce its issued share capital, per the original articles of association, then it can never do so.

True ☐

False ☐

5 A company can redeem shares out of which sources of funds?

(i) Distributable profits
(ii) Proceeds of new shares
(iii) The share premium account

A All three
B (i) and (ii)
C (ii) and (iii)
D (i) and (iii)

Answers to Quick Quiz

1 D

2 Accumulated realised profits less accumulated realised losses.

3 True

4 False, it can pass a special resolution to change the articles.

5 B

Now try the question below from the Exam Question Bank

Number	Level	Marks	Time
Q23	Examination	5	9 mins

Part C
Principles of business taxation

12

General principles of taxation

Introduction

All businesses have to pay tax in some form. This chapter forms a general introduction to the subject.

In Section 1, we look at the general principles of taxation.

As taxation is so important to the business, Section 2 looks at how it is administered. Finally, in Section 3, we look at the collection of tax and powers of enforcement.

Topic list	Learning outcomes	Syllabus references
1 Principles of taxation	A(i), A(ii), A(vii)	A(1), A(2), A(3)
2 Administration of tax	A(ii), A(iii), A(iv)	A(6), A(7), A(8)
3 Collection and enforcement	A(i), A(ii), A(vi),	A(10)

1 Principles of taxation

1.1 General introduction

FAST FORWARD

Taxation can be one of two forms.

- Direct taxation
- Indirect taxation

Direct taxation is charged directly on the person, or enterprise, who is intended to pay the tax. Examples include personal income taxes, company income tax, tax on capital gains.

Indirect taxation is charged indirectly on the final consumer of the goods or services. An example of a sales tax (eg VAT in the UK; TVA in France).

The person liable to pay tax is called a **taxable person**. This includes an individual, an estate of a deceased person, a trust fund, a partnership, a limited company and any other body set up to carry out a trade for profit (eg the bar at a golf club).

A taxable person normally only pays tax in the country where he or she is resident. We will look at this in detail in Chapter 4. The tax authority able to charge tax is called the **competent jurisdiction**.

Question — Indirect tax

Which of the following is an indirect tax?

A Tax on capital gains
B Personal income tax
C Sales tax
D Company income tax

Answer

The answer is C, a sales tax. The others are all direct taxes.

1.2 Sources of tax rules

FAST FORWARD

Tax rules arise from a number of sources. There are four main ones.

- Domestic tax legislation and court rulings
- Domestic tax authority practice
- Supranational bodies
- International tax treaties

1.2.1 Domestic tax legislation and court rulings

The main source of tax rules arises from the domestic tax legislation of the country, eg in the UK, the annual Finance Act. Although the legislators try to think of all possible situations, business is always changing and so the law may have to be interpreted by the courts. This gives rise to court rulings that have the force of law.

1.2.2 Domestic tax authority practice

Every tax authority develops its own practice on how the law is applied. For example, UK tax law states that employees should be taxed on all 'benefits' supplied by the employer. However, in practice, certain benefits are exempted from the rules because it would be too time consuming to account for them and they yield little in the way of tax.

1.2.3 Supranational bodies

Supranational bodies, such as the European Union (EU), can affect tax rules. The EU has a number of rules on value added or sales tax, which have to be applied by all members of the EU. In addition, the EU has stated that all listed entities must use International Accounting Standards in their consolidated financial statements from 2005.

1.2.4 International tax treaties

Some businesses trade in many different countries of the world, so called 'multi-national' companies. This means that their profits will be subject to tax in the local countries they trade in, as well as the country where the company has its headquarters. This could mean that the company pays tax on certain profits twice. In order to avoid this 'double tax', countries enter into tax treaties which set out which country gets to tax the profits and to allow relief for local taxes paid, for example withholding taxes. We will look at this in more detail in Chapter 4.

1.3 Direct taxes

We will look at direct taxes on company profits in detail in Chapter 3, when we consider IAS 12 *Income taxes*. However it is worth looking at the general rules.

1.3.1 Taxable profit

FAST FORWARD

The financial statements show the **accounting profit** for the accounting period. However the local tax rules will normally require certain adjustments in order to arrive at the **taxable profit**.

Key term

Taxable profit is the accounting profit adjusted according to the tax rules and is the amount on which tax is actually paid.

1.3.2 Adjustments to accounting profit

The following statement shows the kind of adjustments needed to arrive at taxable profit.

		$'000	$'000
Accounting profit			5,000
Add: disallowable expenditure:	entertaining	50	
	formation and acquisition costs	100	
	book depreciation	250	
			400
			5,400
Less:	non-taxable income	10	
	tax allowable depreciation	140	
			(150)
Taxable profit			5,250

Here the accounting profit is $5m, but the tax will be paid on the taxable profit of $5.25m. If the tax rate is 30%, the tax due is $1,575,000 (30% × $5,250,000). Lay people usually expect the tax to be 30% of accounting profit ($1,500,000).

Note: 'Book depreciation' will have been deducted in the income statement but is not allowable for tax. 'Tax allowable depreciation' is based upon the rules laid down by the tax authority. In the UK this allowable deduction is referred to as 'capital allowance'.

Capital allowances are sometimes used to encourage businesses to invest. For instance, on some assets there may be 100% first year allowance. Over the life of an asset, capital allowances must account for the purchase price of the asset less any amount realised on disposal. When disposal takes place, there is often a 'balancing charge'; or 'balancing allowance'. For instance:

	$
Purchase price of asset	50,000
Capital allowances received	(40,000)
Remaining value for tax purposes	10,000
Realised on disposal	(15,000)
Balancing charge – tax due on	(5,000)

If the asset had realised $7,000 on disposal, the company would have received a balancing allowance of $3,000 – this is deducted from the taxable profit.

Items which are allowed or disallowed for tax purposes vary according to the tax regime. For instance, business entertaining is generally disallowed in the UK. In an exam question you will be told which expenses are allowed or disallowed.

Question

Taxable profit

Pax had an accounting profit for the year of $500,000. This includes non-taxable income of $15,000 and disallowable expenses of $25,000. What is the taxable profit for the period?

Answer

	$'000
Accounting profit	500
Add: disallowable expenses	25
	525
Less: non-taxable income	(15)
Taxable profit	510

1.3.3 Types of adjustment

The adjustments are of two types:

- absolute
- timing

Absolute adjustments are **permanently disallowed** for tax purposes, such as entertaining expenses and formation and acquisition costs in the example above. These types of expenses are never allowable. Some income may not be taxable at all, eg government grants.

Timing adjustments mean that the expenditure will eventually be **allowed in full**, but there are **timing differences** between the accounting 'book depreciation' and 'tax allowable depreciation'. In our example

1.3.2. the book depreciation is $250,000 but the tax allowable depreciation is only $140,000. There is a timing difference of $110,000. We will look at this again in Chapter 3, when we deal with deferred tax.

1.3.4 Recharacterisation rules

An otherwise profitable company may have high interest payments, leading to a low taxable income. This has an adverse effect on government tax revenue. In some countries, such as the US, interest payments above a certain level can be **recharacterised** as dividend payments, which are not an allowable expense. This is likely to be applied where the loans in question are between group companies. This has consequences because **advanced taxes** or **withholding taxes** may be payable.

Advanced taxes may be charged on dividends. This is a proportion of the dividend which is paid to the tax authorities as an advanced payment on account of the final tax liability. If the advanced tax rate is 20%, then the dividend is considered to be 80% and the advanced tax due is 20/80 or 1/4 of the dividend.

Withholding taxes arise when dividends are paid by a company in one tax jurisdiction to a company in a different tax jurisdiction. They are similar to advanced taxes, but can be reduced as a result of a double taxation treaty (see Chapter 13).

1.3.5 Schedular system and loss relief

Some countries, such as the UK, tax different types of income according to different rules. This is known as a **schedular system**. A business may receive income from a number of different sources, such as:

- trading profit
- capital gains
- loan interest
- royalties
- rent received.

Some governments want to tax income from different source at different rates.

For instance, in the UK, rental income may be taxed according to Schedule A rules but company profits are taxed according to a different set of rules under Schedule D1.

When losses arise, tax relief will be given according to the schedule rules. So losses on Schedule A rents are usually carried forward to be relieved against future profits on the same property. Company losses under Schedule D1 may also be carried forward to be relieved against future profits from the same trade. However, the company may also use losses in other ways, eg set against capital gains or carried back and set against profit of a previous year.

The position regarding **relief for trading losses** can best be summarised as follows. When an enterprise sustains a trading loss in its financial year, it cannot claim a refund of tax for that year. However, there are a number of other possible ways of relieving the loss.

- Carry it forward against future trading profits
- Offset it against other income or capital gains of the same period
- Carry it back against profits of previous periods
- Offset it against the profits of another group company (see section 1.3.6)

Some countries do not allow **capital gains/losses** to be offset against **trading gains/losses** and vice versa.

Some countries do not allow losses to be carried back and some restrict the number of years for which they can be carried forward. When a business ceases trading, there may be provision for **terminal losses**. In the UK, a business calculates the losses for the last twelve months ending on the day trade ceases. If necessary, **time apportionment** is used. These terminal losses can then be carried back and offset against the final year of assessment and the three previous tax years.

1.3.6 Group relief

Tax rules are also necessary to deal with tax losses in groups. In the UK, losses of one group subsidiary may be set against the profits of another group subsidiary. When assets are transferred between group companies, capital gains tax is deferred until the asset is sold outside the group. In effect, UK group relief rules treat the group as one entity for tax purposes.

This UK treatment is an example of **tax consolidation.** In general, if a group of enterprises are recognised as a **tax group**, it is possible for them to gain relief for trading losses by offsetting the losses of one group member against the profits of another group member. The rules for group relief will vary from country to country, as will the rules for recognition of a tax group (which may differ from the rules under which groups are recognised for financial reporting purposes).

Some countries also have their own regulations for recognising **tax groups for capital gains purposes**. It is not usually possible to offset capital losses and gains between the group members. However, there are usually provisions that allow the transfer of assets between group members without recognising a capital gain or loss. The calculation of the gain and the payment of the tax are usually **deferred** until the asset is sold outside the tax group. Good tax planning is needed to ensure that all asset sales to third parties take place through just one group member. These provisions can then be used to accumulate all the group's capital gains and losses in that member, thereby effectively obtaining offset.

Exam focus point

In any exam question you will be told what rules apply.

1.3.7 Basis of assessment

The rules for calculating a tax liability are known as the **basis of assessment**. This basis depends on the type of income and the taxable person. In the UK, the bases of assessment for the different types of income are embodied in the schedular system, discussed above. The basis of assessment also governs how the tax liability of a particular person or organisation is computed. The examples below are from the UK tax system.

- An employee is taxed on the income actually earned during the tax year.
- A self-employed person is taxed on the profits of his financial year.
- A limited liability company is taxed on the profits of its financial year.

In the UK, a tax year runs from 6 April in one year to 5 April in the following year. So the 2005/06 tax year runs from 6 April 2005 to 5 April 2006. An employee will be taxed on his or her earnings for the tax year.

However a self-employed person will prepare financial statements for his or her financial year and it is highly unlikely that this will be the same as the tax year. For example, the financial statements may cover the year from 1 January to 31 December 2005. Under the rules for Schedule D1, the whole of the profit will be taxed in the tax year 2005/06 ie the tax year in which the financial year ends.

In contrast, the profit for a limited liability company is taxed according to tax financial years. A tax financial year ends on 31 March. In calculating the tax due, the profit is split between tax financial years and taxed according. So if a company makes a taxable profit of $12,000 for the year ended 31 December 2005, $3,000 will be taxed on the rates for the year ended 31 March 2005 and $9,000 will be taxed on the rates for the year ended 31 March 2006.

If the tax rate on companies is 30% in the year ended 31 March 2005 and 25% in the year ended 31 March 2006. What is the total tax due on the profits for the year ended 31 December 2005?

The answer is $3,150 ($3,000 @ 30% + $9,000 @ 25%).

Exam focus point

> The above examples from the UK tax regime are **for illustration purposes only**. You do not need to learn these. If you are set a question on this in the exam, you will be given full details of the basis of assessment to be used.

1.4 Classification and characteristics of taxation – the tax base

Although the details of taxes differ between countries, there are certain classes and characteristics of taxation that are common to most tax regimes.

Taxes can be classified according to their **tax base** (what is being taxed). They can be based on any or all of the following items.

- Income or profits (personal income tax and company income tax)
- Assets (tax on capital gains, wealth and inheritance taxes)
- Consumption (taxes on alcohol, cigarettes or fuel and sales taxes)

We have considered tax on income or profits in section 1.3 above. In the rest of this section we will consider tax on assets and consumption.

1.4.1 Capital gains

When an asset is disposed of for more than its original cost, a 'capital gain' arises. Governments are naturally very anxious to tax this. Different tax jurisdictions have different rules concerning the taxation of capital gains.

In the UK, the largest capital gains are probably made on the sales of residential property, but these are exempt from taxation as long as the property constitutes a 'main residence'. Other items are also excluded, such as cars, boats and caravans, and the UK government probably makes most of its capital gains tax revenue from gains made on transfers of shares in companies listed on the Stock Exchange.

Some countries allow the original cost of the asset to be adjusted up to current prices by the use of an index, such as the Retail Price Index, before calculating the capital gain. This prevents the taxpayer from having to pay tax on a paper gain, which is simply the result of inflation. In addition, there may be an annual exemption from capital gains tax. In this case, each individual is allowed to make capital gains up to an annual limit each year. Any gains in excess of this amount are charged to tax.

An enterprise may sell an asset and realise a chargeable gain. However, it may then need to replace the asset. If the enterprise pays tax on the capital gain, this will reduce the proceeds available for reinvestment. Therefore, some countries allow the tax charge on the disposal of a business asset to be **deferred** until the replacement asset is disposed of. If this is a type of asset that will have to be continuously replaced (such as manufacturing machinery), then this deferral could go on indefinitely. In some tax jurisdictions, this is known as **rollover relief**.

1.4.2 Capital losses

Capital losses are generally accounted for in the same way as capital gains. Most countries allow capital losses to be offset against current or future capital gains. Note that where annual exemptions are available, these may be given after losses have been offset (as in the UK). In this case, the loss relief may effectively be lost.

1.4.3 Example: Capital gains and losses

Assume that an individual makes capital gains of $15,000 and capital losses of $4,000 in the same year. The tax regime requires losses to be offset against gains, before using the annual exemption of $7,500. How much is chargeable to tax?

Chargeable gain = \$15,000 – \$4,000 – \$7,500
= \$3,500

However if the losses were \$10,000, the chargeable gain would be calculated as follows.

Chargeable gain = \$15,000 – \$10,000 – \$5,000
= \$NIL

The taxpayer has effectively lost tax relief of \$2,500, unless he makes other gains during the year to use up the balance of the annual exemption (\$7,500 – \$5,000).

1.4.4 Wealth taxes

A number of countries levy wealth taxes, either on individuals or on enterprises or on both. This will involve measurement and valuation of assets each year. The tax is usually a straight percentage, for example 2%, of total net worth (total assets less total liabilities).

1.4.5 Inheritance tax

Inheritance taxes are usually levied on a deceased person's estate. As most people do not like the idea of inherited wealth, governments usually find that inheritance taxes are a popular option. Therefore, a number of countries do have inheritance taxes. However, the threat of this tax may make people give away their wealth before they die. Therefore some tax regimes also tax lifetime gifts.

The level where the tax starts to operate must not be set too low or too many people will find that they are liable to the tax. Therefore, there is likely to be an exemption of a considerable amount before the tax comes into force. There may also be exemptions for legacies to the surviving spouse, to charities and for certain lifetime gifts.

In the UK, there are a number of exemptions on lifetime gifts, these include:

- Gifts out of normal income
- Marriage gifts to close relatives
- Gifts to spouse
- Gifts to charities
- Potentially exempt transfers (no tax if the donor survives seven years after making the gift)

There are usually exemptions for business assets as well. This allows a family business to be passed on to the next generation without being taxed out of existence.

Tax authorities usually find that inheritance taxes are expensive to administer and that the tax yield is quite low. However, governments persist in using these taxes as they are popularly seen as being a redistribution of wealth from the 'privileged'.

1.4.6 Property taxes

Some countries operate systems under which people are taxed on their property – usually land and buildings, but sometimes including other assets. The UK has a system whereby individuals and businesses are taxed at a local level on the basis of the value of their property.

1.4.7 Consumption taxes

Consumption taxes are added to the purchase price of goods. They include excise duties and sales tax. They are often levied most heavily on those items not considered necessary to maintain life.

The UK has a long and proud tradition of taxing alcohol and cigarettes. The government is also very enthusiastic about taxing the motorist. It is hampered in its efforts only by the fact that increased duty on motor fuel increases distribution costs, which increases the cost of the foodstuffs trundled daily up and down the motorways. Foodstuffs are unfortunately necessary to life.

The other major consumption tax in the EU is currently tax on added value (TVA or VAT). This is levied on all goods and services except those specifically excluded (such as food and education). It is very cheap to collect and yields enormous revenues.

A consumption tax is an example of an indirect tax and we will be looking at indirect taxes in detail in Chapter 13.

1.4.8 Characteristics of taxation

The economist, Adam Smith, wrote about the **canons of taxation.** His original characteristics of a 'good tax' were **equity, certainty, convenience and efficiency.** In the US, these characteristics are included among the 10 principles that form the CPA Institute's 'Guiding Principles of Good Tax Policy'.

The three **major** principles recognised today are:

(a) **Equity**: the tax burden should be fairly distributed

(b) **Efficiency**: tax should be easy and cheap to collect.

(c) **Economic effects**: the government must consider the effect of taxation policy on various sectors of the economy.

Efficiency is best achieved by the use of 'unpaid tax collectors', such as businesses which have to charge and account for sales tax; and employers who have to collect and account for payroll taxes.

Economic effects are sometimes overlooked, with disastrous consequences. For instance, the increase in employers' tax in the UK had a serious effect on many government departments that carry huge payrolls. The government had neglected to take into account that it was, in fact, taxing itself.

1.5 Tax framework

When considering the tax framework, there are a number of general principles that you need to understand.

1.5.1 Tax rate structure

A government will structure its tax rates according to where it wishes the burden of taxation to fall. There is a general agreement that people on higher incomes should pay more tax, but governments have learned that punitive rates at the top lead to higher levels of avoidance and evasion.

In the UK, Harold Wilson's Labour government in the 1960s sought to 'soak the rich' with a top rate of 98%. This led to an exodus from the country of film stars and pop singers, who thereafter paid no UK tax at all.

There are four possible structures.

- A **proportional** tax rate structure taxes all income at the same rate, so the same proportion of all income is taken in tax.
- A **progressive** tax rate structure takes a higher proportion in tax as income rises.
- A **regressive** structure would take a decreasing proportion as income rises.
- A **stepped** tax rate structure increases the tax burden in stages.

Most Western countries use a progressive tax rate structure.

Exam focus point

Tax rate structures were tested in the November 2005 exam.

1.5.2 Tax gap

This is the gap between the tax theoretically collectable and the amount actually collected. The tax authorities work unceasingly to minimise this gap.

1.5.3 Hypothecation

The government can choose to ring-fence certain types of tax revenue as being for the purposes of certain types of expenditure. This prevents the money being spent on anything else and is known as **hypothecation**.

A recent example, in the UK, is the revenue from the 'congestion charge' levied on London motorists. This can only be spent on transport in the capital.

2 Administration of tax

FAST FORWARD

> Records may need to be kept for different periods and retained for longer intervals than normal accounting records.

2.1 Record keeping and retention

Obviously a business needs to keep records of the tax it pays. It makes no difference if the tax is a cost to the business (eg tax on business profits) or whether the business acts merely as a tax collector (eg employee tax).

However, tax records usually need to be kept in more detail than is strictly necessary for pure accounting purposes. For example, records of employee taxation will need to be kept in great dealt for every employee. This is so that the business can satisfy the tax authority that is has complied with the law.

Most tax authorities have the power to inspect business records to ensure compliance. If mistakes are made, the tax authority may be able to re-open earlier years and collect back taxes owed. In the UK, the Inland Revenue have the power to go back six tax years if errors are found. Therefore tax records may need to be kept longer than normal, eg payroll records are usually kept for at least six years in the UK.

Notice also that tax years may not be the same as accounting years. In the UK, the tax year runs from 6 April in one year to 5 April in the following year. Very few companies have a 5 April accounting year end.

Question — **Retention periods**

Blam is incorporated in the UK. Its company year end is 31 December. How long should it keep the records of employee taxation of the year ended 31 December 2000?

Answer

The year ended 31 December 2000 is part of the tax year ended 5 April 2001. Therefore the records need to be kept until at least 5 April 2007.

2.2 Returns

Businesses need to make **returns** of the different taxes that they have deducted on behalf of the government. They also make returns of their taxable profits, so that they pay the correct income tax and/or capital gains tax.

2.3 Deadlines

There are deadlines for reporting to the tax authorities. These deadlines apply both to the reporting of the taxable profit of the business and also for returns of taxes collected on behalf of the tax authorities.

For instance, in the UK, company income tax for small and medium enterprises has to be paid within 9 months of the end of the accounting period. The company tax return has to be submitted within 12 months of the end of the period. At this point, any adjustment will be made to the amount originally paid. This allows the government to collect tax before the company's tax liability is finalised.

In the UK, a business has to file a return on employee taxes deducted within 6 weeks of the end of the tax year. For the tax year ended 5 April 2006, returns of employee taxes must be made by 19 May 2006.

Similarly, there are deadlines for the submission of records of VAT (sales tax) and other excise duties. The business may be fined for submitting returns late.

Tax due to, or collected on behalf of, the tax authorities must also be paid within a time limit. In the UK, employee taxes must be paid to the Inland Revenue on a monthly basis. The tax deducted for the tax month ended 5 January 2006 needs to be paid by 19 January 2006. Interest is charged for late payment and there may also be penalties charged for persistent late payment.

Deadlines allow the tax authority to forecast their cash receipts and give them a framework within which interest or penalties for late payment can be imposed.

3 Collection and enforcement

3.1 Collection

The tax authorities in the UK have a specialised branch for collecting taxes due to the Government. The tax authorities review the returns received from taxpayers (whether individuals or businesses) and calculate the tax due. This figure is notified to the collector who then issues a demand to the taxpayer. If the tax is not paid on time, it is the collector who charges interest.

3.2 Enforcement

Tax authorities have the power to enforce compliance with the tax rules. These powers include the following.

(a) Power to review and query filed returns.
(b) Power to request special reports or returns.
(c) Power to examine records (generally extending back some years).
(d) Powers of entry and search.
(e) Exchange of information with tax authorities in other jurisdictions.

We have looked at (a) in Section 3.1 above. With regard to (b), the special report may take the form of asking for details of pay and tax deducted from an individual employee, where there are indications that the tax rules have been broken. There have been instances of casual employees having a number of jobs but using a number of false names, so that the tax authority has been defrauded.

(c) is generally carried out by appointment. However, where the tax authority believes fraud has occurred, it can obtain warrants to enter a business's premises and seize the records (d).

Point (e) has become very important as a counter-terrorism measure in recent years. One tax authority may become aware of funds being moved to another country in suspicious circumstances. It will then warn the tax authority in that other jurisdiction. Exchange of information is also useful in dealing with drug smuggling and money laundering. Tax authorities will only exchange information where a tax treaty exists with the other country.

3.3 Tax avoidance and tax evasion

FAST FORWARD

Tax avoidance is a way of arranging your affairs to take advantage of the tax rules to pay as little tax as possible. It is perfectly legal.

Tax evasion is a way of paying no tax by **illegal methods**, eg not declaring the income, money laundering.

Avoidance and evasion tend to be most common where the following situations apply:

- High tax rates, making it more worthwhile to avoid tax and to spend money on tax advice
- Imprecise wording of the tax laws, leaving loopholes to be exploited
- Insufficient penalties for tax evasion
- Perceived inequity in the tax laws, which makes evasion/avoidance seem more justified

When a tax authority becomes aware that so many businesses are avoiding tax by using a perceived loophole in the law, it may bring in **anti-avoidance legislation** to close the loophole. However this takes time and so modern laws usually include general anti-avoidance clauses in new tax bills to cover any loopholes. In other tax regimes, the tax authority may have to take the case to court to obtain a legal ruling as to whether a scheme is against the spirit of the law.

In countries such as the UK, case law is important in dealing with avoidance and evasion. The revenue authorities regularly bring cases against avoidance schemes and, where the court decides that transactions have been undertaken solely for the purpose of avoiding tax, it will rule that these transactions should be disregarded. This creates a precedent for future cases and in this way loopholes are closed.

However, in the long term, if it wishes to minimise avoidance and evasion, a tax authority has to concentrate on the following:

(a) reducing opportunity by deducting tax at source whenever possible and keeping the tax system as simple as possible

(b) increasing the risk of detection by having an efficient system of checking tax returns and good communications with other tax authorities

(c) maximising penalties for evasion and making sure that this is well publicised

(d) making sure that the tax system is perceived as equitable and that the tax administration deals fairly and courteously with taxpayers

Chapter Roundup

- Taxation can be one of two forms: **direct** or **indirect**.
- There are four main sources of tax rules.
  - Domestic tax legislation and court rulings
  - Domestic tax authority practice
  - Supranational bodies
  - International tax treaties
- The financial statements show the **accounting profit** for the accounting period. However the local tax rules will normally require certain adjustments in order to arrive at the **taxable profit**.
- Records may need to be kept for **different periods** and retained for **longer intervals** than normal accounting records.
- **Tax avoidance** is a way of arranging your affairs to take advantage of the tax rules to pay as little tax as possible. It is perfectly legal.
- **Tax evasion** is a way of paying no tax by illegal methods.

Quick Quiz

1 Taxable profit is the .... adjusted according to the tax rules and is the amount on which .... is actually paid. Complete the gaps.

2 Value added tax is an example of which kind of tax?

A Indirect tax
B Capital gains tax
C Direct tax
D Income tax

3 A withholding tax is:

A tax withheld from the tax authorities ☐

A tax deducted at source before payment of a dividend ☐

4 Tax evasion is illegal. True or false?

Answers to Quick Quiz

1 Accounting profit; tax

2 A

3 A tax deducted at source before payment of a dividend ☑

4 True

13

Types of taxation

Introduction

In this chapter we look at three types of taxation – indirect taxes, employee taxes and international taxation.

Topic list	Learning outcomes	Syllabus references
1 Indirect taxes	A(i), A(ii)	A(4)
2 Value added tax	A(i), A(ii)	A(4)
3 Employee tax	A(i), A(ii)	A(5)
4 International taxation	A(i), A(ii)	A(9)
5 Double taxation treaties	A(v), A(vii)	A(9)

1 Indirect taxes

1.1 Types of indirect taxes

FAST FORWARD

Indirect taxes are not actually paid by the company. Instead the company acts as a **tax collector** on behalf of the government. There are two types of indirect taxes.

- Unit taxes
- Ad valorem taxes

1.1.1 Unit taxes

Unit taxes are based on the number or weight of items, eg excise duties on cigarettes or tobacco.

1.1.2 Ad valorem taxes

Ad valorem taxes are based on the value, eg a sales tax or value added tax.

1.1.3 Import duty

Another form of indirect tax is the import duty. Import duties are often levied less to raise revenue than to protect domestic producers.

The US has traditionally had high import tariffs to protect its industries, but is now changing its position. For instance, a decade ago foreign cars were rarely seen in the US, now they are becoming very popular. The EU has of course removed most import tariffs between member states.

1.2 Excise duties

Excise duties are a 'unit' tax – they are levied on the **amount** of the commodity.

Governments apply excise duty to goods that have large sales volumes and are easy to **control**, ie there are a few large producers and products covered by the duty are easily defined.

Excise duty tends to be levied on four major commodities – alcohol, tobacco, oil products and motor vehicles. The tax is collected earlier in the supply chain than sales taxes. By the time the product reaches the final consumer the price will already include excise duty. For instance, each brewery will have an excise officer assigned to it, who will know exactly what quantities are being produced. Because they are collected early in the supply chain from a limited number of products, excise duties yield large amounts of revenue for low collection cost and are therefore popular with governments. They may seek to justify excise duty on the basis that increasing the cost of drinking, smoking and motoring is a means of curbing the consumer's enthusiasm for damaging his own health and that of the environment.

1.3 Wealth and property taxes

Some countries tax individuals and companies on the value of land and buildings or other valuable property or on 'total wealth' – for a company this would be its asset value.

2 Value Added Tax

A sales tax can be single-stage (such as the retail sales tax applied in the US) or multi-stage (chargeable and deductible at different points in the supply chain) such as VAT. As value is added the tax increases cumulatively. However the business deducts the VAT it pays and pays over the balance to the government. The incidence of the tax is therefore on the final consumer of the goods or services.

2.1 Example of VAT

		Price net of VAT	*VAT @ 17.5%*	*Total price*
		$	$	$
(a)	Manufacturer buys raw materials	40	7	47
	Manufacturer makes and sells television to wholesaler	200	35	235
	Manufacturer pays VAT		28	
(b)	Wholesaler buys television	200	35	235
	Wholesaler sells television to retailer	320	56	376
	Wholesaler pays VAT		21	
(c)	Retailer buys television	320	56	376
	Retailer sells television	480	84	564
	Retailer pays VAT		28	
(d)	Customer buys television	480	84	564

The total tax of $84 is paid by the customer (the end user). The tax amounts paid by the manufacturer, the wholesaler and the retailer will all have been reclaimed.

	$
Supplier of raw materials	7
Manufacturer	28
Wholesaler	21
Retailer	28
Total VAT paid	84

Question

Sales tax

In the example above, the amount of value added tax paid in total is:

A $7
B $21
C $28
D $84

Answer

D

2.2 Business liability

VAT on sales is called **output tax**, while VAT on purchases is called **input tax**. Basically the business owes the tax authority the output tax it collects but deducts from this liability the input tax it pays.

Output tax – Input tax = Amount paid to tax authority

Some activities may be **exempt from VAT**, eg banking services. Traders who carry on exempt activities cannot reclaim VAT on inputs relating to those activities. Organisations who carry out only exempt activities (such as banks) are not allowed to register for VAT.

In our example, we used a tax rate of 17.5%. However different outputs may be taxed at different rates. In the UK, there are three rates of VAT.

(a) Standard rate of 17.5%
(b) Reduced rate of 5%
(c) Zero rate (0%)

2.3 VAT registration

The example in Section 2.1 above assumes that the supplier, manufacturer, wholesaler and retailer are all VAT-registered traders.

A VAT-registered trader must carry out the following tasks.

(a) Charge VAT on the goods and services sold at the rate prescribed by the government.

(b) Pay VAT on goods and services purchased from other businesses.

(c) Pay to Customs and Excise the difference between the VAT collected on sales and the VAT paid to suppliers for purchases. Payments are made at quarterly intervals.

However, if the input VAT paid exceeds the output tax, then the trader can claim a refund from Customs and Excise.

2.4 Irrecoverable VAT

There are some circumstances in which traders are not allowed to reclaim VAT paid on their inputs. In these cases the trader must bear the cost of VAT and account for it accordingly. Three such cases need to be considered.

- Non-registered persons
- Registered persons carrying on exempt activities
- Non-deductible inputs

Non-registered persons are traders whose sales (outputs) are below a certain minimum level and so need not register for VAT. Non-registered persons will pay VAT on their inputs and, because they are not registered, they cannot reclaim it. The VAT paid will effectively increase their costs. Non-registered persons do not charge VAT on their outputs.

Registered persons may be carrying on exempt activities. All outputs of registered traders are either taxable or exempt. Taxable outputs are charged to VAT at zero per cent (zero-rated items) or at 17.5% (standard-rated items). Some items are charged at the lower rate of 5% (eg domestic fuel), but this has limited application in business accounts.

Traders carrying on only exempt activities (such as banks) cannot be registered for VAT. Some traders and companies carry on a mixture of taxable and exempt activities. Such traders need to apportion the VAT paid on inputs. Only VAT relating to taxable outputs may be reclaimed (see Section 2.5 below).

There are a few special cases where the input tax is not deductible even for a taxable person with taxable outputs. These are as follows.

- VAT on cars is never reclaimable unless a car is acquired new for resale, ie by a car dealer.
- VAT on business entertaining is not deductible other than VAT on entertaining staff.
- VAT on expenses incurred on domestic accommodation for directors.
- VAT on non-business items passed through the business accounts with limited relief where the goods are used partly in the business.
- VAT unrelated to the making of supplies in the course of a business.

Exam focus point

The November 2005 exam had a 2-mark question on calculating VAT payable.

2.5 Partial exemption

Where a trader has wholly exempt outputs (such as a bank or financial institution), he cannot reclaim any input tax and is not allowed to register for VAT. (Contrast this with traders who have totally zero-rated outputs, such as farmers, who are allowed to register and obtain a refund of all of their input tax).

However, where a registered trader makes both taxable and exempt supplies, partial exemption applies. A number of schemes exist under which the input tax can be apportioned.

The simplest method is that any input tax wholly attributable to exempt outputs is not deductible, any input tax wholly attributable to taxable supplies is deductible in full and any remaining input tax is apportioned according to the percentage of exempt outputs.

For instance, if 30% of outputs were exempt, the trader would be able to deduct 70% (100% - 30%) of unallocated input tax.

Example: A has total sales of $700,000 before VAT. Purchases total $450,000 excluding VAT. The sales tax rate is 15% and 10% of the sales are exempt. How much VAT does A have to pay?

	$
Output tax (700,000 × 15%) × 90%	94,500
Input tax (450,000 × 15 %) × 90%	(60,750)
Amount payable	33,750

Example: B has total sales of $700,000 before VAT. Purchases total $450,000 excluding VAT. The VAT rate is 15%, 10% of the sales are exempt and 20% of inputs are directly related to these exempt supplies. How much VAT does B have to pay?

	$
Output tax (700,000 × 15%) × 90%	94,500
Input tax (450,000 × 15%) × 80% × 90%*	(48,600)
Amount payable	45,900

*The proportion related to exempt supplies (20%) is deducted and the remaining input tax is apportioned between taxable and exempt supplies.

Note There are many examples of sales tax calculations in the Practice and Revision Kit. For those dealing with partial exemption in particular, see Q3: parts 1, 6 and 10; and Q6 part (e).

2.6 Single-stage sales tax

TVA or VAT is a multi-level sales tax ie it is applied at each stage of the sales process, from manufacturer to wholesaler to retailer to customer.

It is also possible to have a single-stage sales tax. In the US there is a state sales tax levied at the point of sale. This tax is not payable until the goods are actually purchased, so it does not appear on any price tags. Tourists are understandably unimpressed when they get to the till and find that they have to pay the amount on the price tag plus x%.

2.7 Incidence/effective incidence

It is important to distinguish between formal and effective incidence. The **incidence** of a tax is on the person or organisation that pays it.

However, while the **formal incidence** of a sales tax is on the registered trader who has to pay it to the government, the **effective incidence** is on the customer who eventually bears the tax burden.

Exam focus point

The November 2005 exam had a question on the definition of effective incidence.

3 Employee taxation

FAST FORWARD

Employee taxation is personal tax; the company acts as a tax collector.

3.1 Introduction

Employees are liable to personal taxation and are responsible for dealing with their own tax liabilities. In the UK employees are taxed under the personal tax regime.

However, many tax regimes require the employer to operate a withholding tax (PAYE in the UK). This means that tax is deducted from the employee's pay and paid over to the government. The employer then reports total pay and tax deducted to the tax authority at the end of the tax year. This system ensures that all employees comply with the tax rules.

If the employee feels that he or she has paid too much tax, it is up to the individual to deal with the tax authority and obtain a refund. The employer merely acts as a tax collector.

3.2 Taxable income

In the UK, an employee is taxed on all income earned from the employment. This includes 'non cash' items (called benefits in kind). A list of examples follows.

- Basic pay
- Overtime
- Bonus and allowances
- Commission
- Statutory pay (eg statutory sick pay, statutory maternity pay, statutory paternity pay, statutory adoption pay)
- Redundancy pay
- Holiday pay
- Benefits in kind
- Occupational pensions

The following are examples of benefits in kind under the UK legislation.

- Assets transferred to the employee
- Payments made on behalf of the employee
- Living accommodation provided by the employer
- Company car and fuel
- Company van
- Private medical insurance
- Relocation expenses
- Expenses reimbursed by employer

Employers, therefore, need to keep careful records of all payments made to, or on behalf of, their employees. In the UK, employers have to make a return of all benefits provided to each employee at the end of the tax year.

3.3 Deductible expenses

Sometimes an employee can claim that expenses were incurred **wholly, exclusively and necessarily**, in the course of his or her employment. These expenses are then deductible for tax purposes, eg professional subscriptions, business travel, charitable donations and contributions to pension plans.

3.4 Tax codes

In order to make sure that benefits are taxed or expenses are claimed correctly, in the UK the tax authorities issue a tax code. This shows the amount of tax-free pay an employee can earn before paying tax. The employer is given the code and deducts tax accordingly. The employee is sent a detailed notice of how the tax code is calculated. If the employee feels that the code is wrong, it is up to the employee to contact the tax authorities and sort it out. The employer is purely a tax collector.

While placing a burden on employers, this system has major advantages for the government:

- It allows the tax to be collected earlier than would be the case if it were assessed on the employee's earnings at the end of the year.
- The costs of administering the system are borne by employers, rather than by the government.
- It greatly reduces the risks of default or late payment, helping government to minimise the tax gap.

It also makes tax payment easier for individuals, who do not have to deal with a large bill once or twice a year.

3.5 Social security contributions

Some taxes are called **social security** contributions because, in theory, they are used to pay for social security items such as pensions. In fact, the money raised is used as part of the general tax revenue. However, it is politically more acceptable to raise social security contributions than to raise taxes. For example, the UK government added a 1% social security levy to pay for hospitals and their needs. In the UK the social security contribution is National Insurance. It is paid by both the employee and the employer.

4 International taxation

4.1 Corporate residence

FAST FORWARD

A company is resident in one country, even though it may trade in many countries. Usually a company is resident in the **place of incorporation**. However some tax authorities go on the basis of the **place of management**.

As an example, consider the case of a company incorporated in Jersey in the British Channel Islands. Jersey has its independent tax authority and is a 'tax haven' because of its low tax rates. Usually the UK authorities will accept that the company is resident in Jersey, provided its **place of management** is also in Jersey. However if the company is run from offices in London, all board meetings take place in London and, in general, its place of management is in London, then the UK tax authorities will consider the company resident in the UK, not Jersey.

4.2 Taxable presence

A company does not need to be resident in a country in order to establish a **taxable presence** there. It may set up an **overseas subsidiary** or it may trade through a **branch**. However because the subsidiary or branch are resident in the foreign country, their profits will be taxable in that country.

A business trading abroad will have to decide whether it should do so through a subsidiary or a foreign branch. This decision will not be made principally on the basis of tax considerations, but the following tax issues apply:

- the holding company is liable to tax on foreign dividends received, while money transferred from a branch will not be treated as a dividend
- losses made by a non-resident subsidiary are not available for group relief
- the enterprise will be subject to capital gains tax on any capital gains made by a branch. This will not normally apply to capital gains made by a subsidiary
- the tax authorities will look carefully at transfer pricing arrangements between parent and foreign subsidiary, as this could be used to transfer profits abroad

4.3 Withholding taxes

4.3.1 Payments affected

If a company makes payments to an individual or another company resident in a different tax jurisdiction, it may have to pay **withholding tax** to the tax authority of its own jurisdiction.

The reason for this is to stop companies paying all their earnings abroad and then stopping trading without paying any tax to the tax authorities of the country where they are resident. Therefore the local tax authority will take a payment on account of the final tax liability by deducing at source a withholding tax from all payments sent abroad. The withholding tax can be as low as 5% or as high as 40%.

Payments affected are usually the following.

- Interest payments
- Dividends
- Royalties
- Capital gains accruing to non-residents

4.3.2 Underlying tax

When an enterprise receives a dividend from a foreign enterprise, the dividend has been paid out of taxed profits. Under some tax systems, the enterprise can obtain relief for the tax levied in the foreign country on the amount out of which their dividend was paid. This is referred to as the **underlying tax**.

5 Double taxation treaties

5.1 Introduction

In order to establish more clearly which tax authority has jurisdiction, countries enter into **double taxation treaties**. These treaties seek to avoid a business having to pay tax twice on its income simply because it deals with two tax authorities.

A double taxation treaty (eg that between the UK and the USA) sets out which tax authority has jurisdiction. So a company incorporated in the UK which trades with the USA will be taxed primarily in the

UK. The treaty defines a **permanent establishment** and directs that the business will be taxed in the country where it has its permanent establishment.

Where a double taxation treaty exists, provisions are usually made to reduce withholding taxes, or even to avoid paying withholding tax at all.

Another feature of a double taxation treaty is that where a company pays tax in Country A, but is resident in Country B, the tax authorities of Country B will give relief for the tax paid in Country A.

5.2 Example of double taxation relief

Manifold pays tax of $5,000 on profits of $50,000 in Country A. Manifold is resident in Country B and will normally have to pay tax of $10,000 on the same profits. Countries A and B have a double taxation treaty whereby Country B will allow full credit for taxes paid in Country A. Therefore Manifold's tax bill in Country B is reduced by the $5,000 paid in Country A. The result is that Manifold still pays $10,000 tax in total, however it is divided between two different countries.

		$	$
Country A	– tax paid	5,000	5,000
Country B	– tax due	10,000	
	– double taxation relief	(5,000)	
	– tax paid	5,000	5,000
			10,000

5.3 Methods of giving relief

The above example shows the method of giving full **deduction** for foreign taxes. This is not the only way of giving double taxation relief.

Relief may be given by **exemption**. In this case, if income is taxed in Country A, then it will not be taxed in Country B.

Another way of giving relief is by **credit**. This usually occurs where the tax rate in Country A is higher than that in Country B. Instead of deducting the full amount of tax paid in Country A, Country B credits the amount it would have paid in Country B, as follows.

	$
Income taxable	10,000
Tax paid in Country A (20%)	2,000
Tax due in Country B (15%)	1,500
Double taxation relief (restricted to 15%)	(1,500)
Tax payable in Country B	NIL

5.4 Branch

An enterprise may choose to trade in another country by setting up a subsidiary or by trading through a branch. Unlike a subsidiary, a branch is considered to be an overseas operation of the enterprise.

Therefore, the enterprise will be taxed on the profits of the branch in the country where the enterprise is resident. There may also be foreign tax levied on the profits of the branch (in the country where the branch is resident) and these will usually attract double taxation relief.

5.5 OECD Model treaty

The Organisation for Economic Co-operation and Development has published a model tax convention. This can be used as a basis for double taxation treaties between countries.

Under the OECD model, an enterprise is considered to have residence in the country in which it has a **permanent establishment**.

A permanent establishment includes:

- A place of management (Section 1.1)
- A branch (Section 3.4)
- An office
- A factory
- A workshop
- A mine, well or quarry

Note that this means that residence is determined on the basis of the country where the business is carried on, rather than the country of incorporation, which could be different.

Exam focus point

> Students do not need to know the OECD model tax convention in detail. However, it does make good background reading and students may like to access the document by using the following link: http://www.oecd.org/dataoecd/52/34/1914467.pdf

5.6 Double residence

An enterprise will be liable for corporate income tax in the country in which it is resident. It can deemed to be resident either by having its place of management and control in the country or by having been incorporated in the country.

An enterprise incorporated in one country and managed and controlled in another, can thus face the problem of double residence. It is taxable in two countries. This is resolved under the provisions of double tax treaties, based on the OECD model.

Chapter Roundup

- Indirect taxes are not actually paid by the company. Instead the company acts as a **tax collector** on behalf of the government.
- There are two types of indirect taxes: **unit taxes** and **ad valorem taxes**.
- Employee taxation is personal tax; the company acts as the tax collector.
- A company is resident in one country, even though it may trade in many countries. Usually a company is resident in the **place of incorporation**. However some tax authorities go on the basis of **place of management**.

Quick Quiz

1 Value added tax is an example of which kind of tax?

A Unit tax
B Ad valorem tax
C Direct tax
D Income tax

2 Peter is a VAT registered trader. In the quarter to 31 March 20X5 Peter sold goods for £40,000 (excluding VAT) and bought stock to sell for £17,900 (including VAT). Show the VAT figures for his VAT return for this quarter.

3 A withholding tax is:

A tax withheld from the tax authorities ☐

A tax deducted at source before payment of a dividend ☐

Answers to Quick Quiz

1 B

2

	£
Output tax (£40,000 × 17.5%)	7,000
Input tax (£17,900 × 7/47)*	(2,666)
Net VAT payable	4,334

*17.5/117.5 = 7/47

3 A tax deducted at source before payment of a dividend.

Now try the question below from the Exam Question Bank

Number	Level	Marks	Time
Q1	Examination	5	9 mins
Q4	Examination	5	9 mins

14

IAS 12: Income taxes

Introduction

In almost all countries enterprises are taxed on the basis of their trading income. In some countries this may be called corporation or corporate tax, but we will follow the terminology of IAS 12 *Income taxes* and call it income tax.

In Section 1 we will look briefly at the two main systems for taxing corporate income: the **classical system** and the **imputation system**. Of course, each country will be different in its tax legislation and its method of accounting for taxation may reflect this.

There are two aspects of income tax which must be accounted for: **current tax** and **deferred tax**. These will be discussed in Sections 2 and 3 respectively.

Sections 4 to 7 cover the details of the standard, IAS 12.

Note. Throughout this chapter we will assume a current corporate income tax rate of 30% and a current personal income tax rate of 20%.

Topic list	Learning outcomes	Syllabus references
1 Systems of taxing corporate income	A(i)	A(3)
2 Current tax	A(i), A(viii)	A(3); A(11)
3 Deferred tax	A(i), A(viii)	A(3); A(11)
4 Taxable temporary differences	A(viii)	A(3); A(11)
5 Deductible temporary differences	A(viii)	A(3); A(11)
6 Measurement and recognition of deferred tax	A(viii)	A(3); A(11)
7 Presentation and disclosure of taxation	A(viii)	A(3); A(11)

1 Systems of taxing corporate income

1.1 Overview

In the rest of this chapter we will be looking at the question of how income tax is allocated between accounting periods. First of all, we will look at two different taxing methods, which are more to do with the **timing of payment** of tax, rather than with what the tax liability will be in the accounts.

The **taxable profits** of an enterprise essentially comprise its net profit before dividends, adjusted for certain items where the tax treatment differs from the accounting treatment.

The amount of tax to which a company is assessed on its profit for an accounting period is called its **tax liability** for that period. In general, an enterprise must pay its tax liability a certain amount of time after the period end (although in some countries, enterprises may have to make monthly or quarterly 'payments on account').

FAST FORWARD

There are two main systems of taxing corporate income: the classical system and the imputation system.

1.2 Classical system

Under the classical system of taxation, company income tax is charged on all of the profits of the enterprise, distributed or not. Dividends are paid out of taxed profits and are then chargeable to personal income tax in the hands of the shareholder. This system is simple to administer but gives rise to double taxation of dividends. Where the shareholder is a **company**, the dividend is not liable to UK corporation tax. If this were not the case, the dividend could end up being taxed three times, as it will be included in income by the receiving company and may then be distributed to its own individual shareholders, who will now pay tax on it.

1.3 Imputation system

Under the imputation system, the company income tax that has already been paid is **imputed** to the shareholder as a tax credit. He pays income tax on the dividend but deducts the tax credit. This avoids the problem of double taxation.

The shareholder receives the net dividend. He is taxed on the gross dividend (amount received plus tax credit) and the tax credit is then deducted from his liability. The company may have to pay the tax on the dividend in advance, as soon as the dividend is paid. This is referred to as '**advance tax**'.

1.3.1 Partial imputation system

It is also possible to have a system of **partial imputation**, where the taxpayer receives a tax credit of only part of the underlying company income tax.

Some tax jurisdictions operate a **split rate system** in which distributed profits are taxable at a lower rate than retained profits. This can function under the classical, imputation or partial imputation system.

1.4 Example: classical vs imputation system

Cadis Co supplies the following information.

	$
Year to 30 June 20X8	
Taxable profits	100,000
Dividend paid for the year (net)	24,500

The corporate income tax rate is 30% and shareholders pay income tax at 40% on dividends received.

Required

Calculate the total tax payable by Cadis Co and its shareholders as at 30 June 20X8 under:

(a) the classical system,
(b) the imputation system; and
(c) a partial imputation system where a tax credit of 25% is allowed.

Solution

(a) **Classical system**

		$
Corporate income tax paid by Cadis Co (100,000 × 30%)		30,000
Tax on dividends paid by shareholders (24,500 × 40%)		9,800
Total tax paid		39,800

(b) **Imputation system**

	$	$
Corporate income tax paid by Cadis Co		30,000
Shareholder:		
Net dividend received	24,500	
Tax credit (24,500 × 30/70)	10,500	
Gross dividend	35,000	
Tax at 40%	14,000	
Less tax credit	(10,500)	
		3,500
Total tax paid		33,500

(c) **Partial imputation system**

	$	$
Corporate income tax paid by Cadis Co		30,000
Shareholder:		
Net dividend received	24,500	
Tax credit (25%) (24,500 × 25/75)	8,167	
	32,667	
Tax at 40%	13,067	
Less tax credit	(8,167)	
		4,900
Total tax paid		34,900

Note that under the full imputation system (b), if company tax and income tax on individuals had been at the same rate, the shareholder's tax liability would have been nil. The payment due from shareholders in (b) is 10% of the gross dividend. This represents the difference between the company rate (30%) and the rate payable by individual shareholders (40%).

You can see that the classical system does not encourage the payment of dividends.

1.5 Section summary

- There are two main systems under which companies pay income tax: **classical** and **imputation**.
- The classical system is much **simpler** but most countries do not use it.
- Obviously, rates of tax and tax rules **vary from country to country**.
- In the **exam**, the examiner will lay out in detail what type of tax system is in operation.

Question — **Tax system**

What type of system is in place in your country?

How are taxes *paid* and how are they *accounted for*?

2 Current tax

FAST FORWARD

Taxation consists of two components: current tax and deferred tax.

2.1 Accounting entries

You may have assumed until now that accounting for income tax was a very simple matter for companies. You would calculate the amount of tax due to be paid on the company's taxable profits and you would:

DEBIT	Tax charge (income statement)
CREDIT	Tax liability (balance sheet)

with this amount.

However, it may take some time to finalise the company's accounts and therefore its tax liability.

Example: The company's tax charge for 20X5 is estimated at $55,000. The following entry is made in the financial statements:

DEBIT	Income statement (tax expense)	$55,000
CREDIT	Balance sheet (tax payable)	$55,000

When the final tax liability is agreed with the tax authority, the amount payable is $58,000, and this amount is paid and posted as:

DEBIT	Balance sheet (tax payable)	$58,000
CREDIT	Cash	$58,000

The balance sheet account now has a DR balance of $3,000. This represents an **underprovision** of tax for 20X5. This tax has been paid but not charged to the income statement.

In the accounts for 20X6, this underprovision will be accounted for. If the estimated liability for 20X6 is $60,000, the following entries will be made:

DEBIT	Income statement	$60,000	Being current tax
		$3,000	Being prior year underprovision
CREDIT	Balance sheet	$63,000	

The balance sheet will now have a balance of $60,000, being the amount payable for the current year.

Complexities also arise when we consider the future tax consequences of what is going on in the accounts now. This is an aspect of tax called **deferred tax**, which we will look at in the next section.

2.2 IAS 12 Income taxes

FAST FORWARD

IAS 12 covers both current and deferred tax.

The parts relating to current tax are fairly brief, because this is the simple and uncontroversial area of tax.

2.2.1 Definitions

These are some of the definitions given in IAS 12. We will look at the rest later.

Key terms

> **Accounting profit**. Net profit or loss for a period before deducting tax expense.
>
> **Taxable profit (tax loss)**. The profit (loss) for a period, determined in accordance with the rules established by the taxation authorities, upon which income taxes are payable (recoverable).
>
> **Tax expense (tax income)**. The aggregate amount included in the determination of net profit or loss for the period in respect of current tax and deferred tax.
>
> **Current tax**. The amount of income taxes payable (recoverable) in respect of the taxable profit (tax loss) for a period.
>
> *(IAS 12)*

Before we go any further, let us be clear about the difference between current and deferred tax.

(a) **Current tax** is the amount *actually payable* to the tax authorities in relation to the trading activities of the enterprise during the period.

(b) **Deferred tax** is an *accounting measure*, used to match the tax effects of transactions with their accounting impact and thereby produce less distorted results.

You should understand this a little better after working through Section 3.

2.2.2 Recognition of current tax liabilities and assets

IAS 12 requires any **unpaid tax** in respect of the current or prior periods to be recognised as a **liability**.

Conversely, any **excess tax** paid in respect of current or prior periods over what is due should be recognised as an asset.

Question

Tax charge and tax payable

In 20X8 Darton Co had taxable profits of $120,000. In the previous year (20X7) income tax on 20X7 profits had been estimated as $30,000. Tax is payable at 30%.

Required

Calculate tax payable and the charge for 20X8 if the tax due on 20X7 profits was subsequently agreed with the tax authorities as:

(a) $35,000; or
(b) $25,000.

Any under or over payments are not settled until the following year's tax payment is due.

Answer

(a)

	$
Tax due on 20X8 profits ($120,000 × 30%)	36,000
Underpayment for 20X7	5,000
Tax charge and liability	41,000

(b)

	$
Tax due on 20X8 profits (as above)	36,000
Overpayment for 20X7	(5,000)
Tax charge and liability	31,000

Alternatively, the rebate due could be shown separately as income in the income statement and as an asset in the balance sheet. An offset approach like this is, however, most likely.

Taking this a stage further, IAS 12 also requires recognition as an asset of the benefit relating to any tax loss that can be **carried back** to recover current tax of a previous period. This is acceptable because it is probable that the benefit will flow to the enterprise *and* it can be reliably measured.

2.2.3 Example: tax losses carried back

In 20X7 Eramu Co paid $50,000 in tax on its profits. In 20X8 the company made tax losses of $24,000. The local tax authority rules allow losses to be carried back to offset against current tax of prior years.

Required

Show the tax charge and tax liability for 20X8.

Solution

Tax repayment due on tax losses = 30% × $24,000 = $7,200.

The double entry will be:

DEBIT	Tax receivable (balance sheet)	$7,200
CREDIT	Tax repayment (income statement)	$7,200

The tax receivable will be shown as an asset until the repayment is received from the tax authorities.

Exam focus point

The November 2005 exam had a 3-mark question on calculating corporate income tax liability including losses brought forward.

2.2.4 Measurement

Measurement of current tax liabilities (assets) for the current and prior periods is very simple. They are measured at the **amount expected to be paid to (recovered from) the tax authorities**. The tax rates (and tax laws) used should be those enacted (or substantively enacted) by the balance sheet date.

2.2.5 Recognition of current tax

Normally, current tax is recognised as income or expense and included in the net profit or loss for the period, except in two cases.

(a) Tax arising from a **business combination** which is an acquisition is treated differently (not relevant for this syllabus).

(b) Tax arising from a transaction or event which is recognised **directly in equity** (in the same or a different period).

The rule in (b) is logical. If a transaction or event is charged or credited directly to equity, rather than to the income statement, then the related tax should be also. An example of such a situation is where, under IAS 8, an adjustment is made to the **opening balance of retained earnings** due to either a change in accounting policy that is applied retrospectively, or to the correction of a material error.

2.2.6 Presentation

In the balance sheet, **tax assets and liabilities** should be shown separately from other assets and liabilities.

Current tax assets and liabilities can be **offset**, but this should happen only when certain conditions apply.

(a) The enterprise has a **legally enforceable right** to set off the recognised amounts.

(b) The enterprise intends to settle the amounts on a **net basis**, or to realise the asset and settle the liability at the same time.

The **tax expense (income)** related to the profit or loss from ordinary activities should be shown on the face of the income statement.

The **disclosure requirements** of IAS 12 are extensive and we will look at these later in the chapter.

3 Deferred tax

FAST FORWARD

Deferred tax is an accounting measure used to match the tax effects of transactions with their accounting impact. It is quite complex.

Exam focus point

Students invariably find deferred tax very confusing. You are unlikely to be asked any very complicated questions on deferred tax in Paper 7, so concentrate on understanding and being able to explain the purpose of deferred tax and to carry out basic calculations.

3.1 What is deferred tax?

When a company recognises an asset or liability, it expects to **recover or settle the carrying amount** of that asset or liability. In other words, it expects to sell or use up assets, and to pay off liabilities. What happens if that recovery or settlement is likely to make future tax payments larger (or smaller) than they would otherwise have been if the recovery or settlement had no tax consequences? In these circumstances, IAS 12 requires companies to recognise a **deferred tax liability** (or **deferred tax asset**).

3.2 Definitions

Don't worry too much if you don't understand the concept of deferred tax yet; things should become clearer as you work through this section. First of all, here are the definitions relating to deferred tax given in IAS 12.

Key terms

Deferred tax liabilities are the amounts of income taxes payable in future periods in respect of taxable temporary differences.

Deferred tax assets are the amounts of income taxes recoverable in future periods in respect of:

- Deductible temporary differences
- The carry forward of unused tax losses
- The carry forward of unused tax credits

Temporary differences are differences between the carrying amount of an asset or liability in the balance sheet and its tax base. Temporary differences may be either:

- **Taxable temporary differences**, which are temporary differences that will result in taxable amounts in determining taxable profit (tax loss) of future periods when the carrying amount of the asset or liability is recovered or settled
- **Deductible temporary differences**, which are temporary differences that will result in amounts that are deductible in determining taxable profit (tax loss) of future periods when the carrying amount of the asset or liability is recovered or settled

The **tax base** of an asset or liability is the amount attributed to that asset or liability for tax purposes.

(IAS 12)

We need to look at some of these definitions in more detail.

3.3 Tax base

We can expand on the definition given above by stating that the **tax base of an asset** is the amount that will be deductible for tax purposes against any taxable economic benefits that will flow to the enterprise when it recovers the carrying value of the asset. Where those economic benefits are not taxable, the tax base of the asset is the same as its carrying amount.

Question — Tax base (1)

State the tax base of each of the following assets.

(a) A machine cost $10,000. For tax purposes, depreciation of $3,000 has already been deducted in the current and prior periods and the remaining cost will be deductible in future periods, either as depreciation or through a deduction on disposal. Revenue generated by using the machine is taxable, any gain on disposal of the machine will be taxable and any loss on disposal will be deductible for tax purposes.

(b) Interest receivable has a carrying amount of $1,000. The related interest revenue will be taxed on a cash basis.

(c) Trade receivables have a carrying amount of $10,000. The related revenue has already been included in taxable profit (tax loss).

(d) A loan receivable has a carrying amount of $1m. The repayment of the loan will have no tax consequences.

Answer

(a) The tax base of the machine is $7,000.
(b) The tax base of the interest receivable is nil.
(c) The tax base of the trade receivables is $10,000.
(d) The tax base of the loan is $1m.

In the case of a **liability**, the tax base will be its carrying amount, less any amount that will be deducted for tax purposes in relation to the liability in future periods. For revenue received in advance, the tax base of the resulting liability is its carrying amount, less any amount of the revenue that will *not* be taxable in future periods.

Question — Tax base (2)

State the tax base of each of the following liabilities.

(a) Current liabilities include accrued expenses with a carrying amount of $1,000. The related expense will be deducted for tax purposes on a cash basis.

(b) Current liabilities include interest revenue received in advance, with a carrying amount of $10,000. The related interest revenue was taxed on a cash basis.

(c) Current liabilities include accrued expenses with a carrying amount of $2,000. The related expense has already been deducted for tax purposes.

(d) Current liabilities include accrued fines and penalties with a carrying amount of $100. Fines and penalties are not deductible for tax purposes.

(e) A loan payable has a carrying amount of $1m. The repayment of the loan will have no tax consequences.

Answer

(a) The tax base of the accrued expenses is nil.
(b) The tax base of the interest received in advance is nil.
(c) The tax base of the accrued expenses is $2,000.
(d) The tax base of the accrued fines and penalties is $100.
(e) The tax base of the loan is $1m.

IAS 12 gives the following examples of circumstances in which the carrying amount of an asset or liability will be **equal to its tax base**.

- **Accrued expenses** which have already been deducted in determining an enterprise's current tax liability for the current or earlier periods.
- A **loan payable** is measured at the amount originally received and this amount is the same as the amount repayable on final maturity of the loan.
- **Accrued expenses** which will never be deductible for tax purposes.
- **Accrued income** will never be taxable.

3.4 Temporary differences

You may have found the definition of temporary differences somewhat confusing. Remember that accounting profits form the basis for computing **taxable profits**, on which the tax liability for the year is calculated; however, accounting profits and taxable profits are different. There are two reasons for the differences.

(a) **Permanent differences.** These occur when certain items of revenue or expense are excluded from the computation of taxable profits (for example, entertainment expenses may not be allowable for tax purposes).

(b) **Temporary differences.** These occur when items of revenue or expense are included in both accounting profits and taxable profits, but not for the same accounting period. For example, an expense which is allowable as a deduction in arriving at taxable profits for 20X7 might not be included in the financial accounts until 20X8 or later. In the long run, the total taxable profits and total accounting profits will be the same (except for permanent differences) so that timing differences originate in one period and are capable of reversal in one or more subsequent periods. Deferred tax is the tax attributable to **temporary differences.**

The distinction made in the definition between **taxable temporary differences** and **deductible temporary differences** can be made clearer by looking at the explanations and examples given in the standard and its appendices.

3.5 Section summary

- Deferred tax is an **accounting device**. It does *not* represent tax payable to the tax authorities.
- The **tax base** of an asset or liability is the value of that asset or liability for tax purposes.

- You should understand the difference between **permanent and temporary differences**.
- Deferred tax is the tax attributable to **temporary differences**.

4 Taxable temporary differences

FAST FORWARD

Deferred tax assets and liabilities arise from taxable and deductible temporary differences.

Exam focus point

The rule to remember here is that:

'All taxable temporary differences give rise to a deferred tax liability.'

4.1 Examples

The following are examples of circumstances that give rise to taxable temporary differences.

4.1.1 Transactions that affect the income statement

(a) **Interest revenue** received in arrears and included in accounting profit on the basis of time apportionment. It is included in taxable profit, however, on a cash basis.

(b) **Sale of goods revenue** is included in accounting profit when the goods are delivered, but only included in taxable profit when cash is received.

(c) **Depreciation** of an asset is accelerated for tax purposes. When new assets are purchased, allowances may be available against taxable profits which exceed the amount of depreciation chargeable on the assets in the financial accounts for the year of purchase.

(d) **Development costs** which have been capitalised will be amortised in the income statement, but they were deducted in full from taxable profit in the period in which they were incurred.

(e) **Prepaid expenses** have already been deducted on a cash basis in determining the taxable profit of the current or previous periods.

4.1.2 Transactions that affect the balance sheet

(a) **Depreciation of an asset** is not deductible for tax purposes. No deduction will be available for tax purposes when the asset is sold/scrapped.

(b) A borrower records a **loan** at proceeds received (amount due at maturity) less transaction costs. The carrying amount of the loan is subsequently increased by amortisation of the transaction costs against accounting profit. The transaction costs were, however, deducted for tax purposes in the period when the loan was first recognised.

4.1.3 Fair value adjustments and revaluations

(a) **Current investments** or financial instruments are carried at fair value. This exceeds cost, but no equivalent adjustment is made for tax purposes.

(b) Property, plant and equipment is **revalued** by an enterprise (under IAS 16), but no equivalent adjustment is made for tax purposes. This also applies to long-term investments (under IAS 25). As the tax base remains at the original value, there will be a difference between the carrying value and the tax base, leading to an increase in the deferred tax provision.

4.1.4 Differences that do not give rise to a deferred tax liability

Remember the rule we gave you above, that all taxable temporary differences give rise to a deferred tax liability? There are **two circumstances** given in the standard where this does *not* apply.

(a) The deferred tax liability arises from **goodwill** for which amortisation is not deductible for tax purposes.

(b) The deferred tax liability arises from the **initial recognition** of an asset or liability in a transaction which:

(i) Is *not* a business combination, *and*
(ii) At the time of the transaction affects neither accounting profit nor taxable profit

Try to **understand the reasoning** behind the recognition of deferred tax liabilities on taxable temporary differences.

(a) When an **asset is recognised**, it is expected that its carrying amount will be recovered in the form of economic benefits that flow to the enterprise in future periods.

(b) If the carrying amount of the asset is **greater than** its tax base, then taxable economic benefits will also be greater than the amount that will be allowed as a deduction for tax purposes.

(c) The difference is therefore a **taxable temporary difference** and the obligation to pay the resulting income taxes in future periods is a **deferred tax liability**.

(d) As the enterprise recovers the carrying amount of the asset, the taxable temporary difference will **reverse** and the enterprise will have taxable profit.

(e) It is then probable that economic benefits will flow from the enterprise in the form of **tax payments**, and so the recognition of all deferred tax liabilities (except those excluded above) is required by IAS 12.

4.2 Example: taxable temporary differences

A company purchased an asset costing $1,500. At the end of 20X8 the carrying amount is $1,000. The cumulative depreciation for tax purposes is $900 and the current tax rate is 25%.

Required

Calculate the deferred tax liability for the asset.

Solution

Firstly, what is the tax base of the asset? It is $1,500 – $900 = $600.

In order to recover the carrying value of $1,000, the enterprise must earn taxable income of $1,000, but it will only be able to deduct $600 as a taxable expense. The enterprise must therefore pay income tax of $400 × 25% = $100 when the carrying value of the asset is recovered.

The enterprise must therefore recognise a deferred tax liability of $400 × 25% = $100, recognising the difference between the carrying amount of $1,000 and the tax base of $600 as a taxable temporary difference.

4.3 Timing differences

Some temporary differences are often called **timing differences**, when income or expense is included in accounting profit in one period, but is included in taxable profit in a different period. The main types of taxable temporary differences which are timing differences and which result in deferred tax liabilities are included in the examples given above.

- **Interest received** which is accounted for on an accruals basis, but which for tax purposes is included on a cash basis.
- **Accelerated depreciation** for tax purposes.
- Capitalised and amortised **development costs**.

We will look briefly at other circumstances where temporary differences arise.

4.4 Revalued assets

Under IAS 16 assets may be revalued. If this affects the taxable profit for the current period, the tax base of the asset changes and **no temporary difference** arises.

If, however (as in some countries), the revaluation does *not* affect current taxable profits, the tax base of the asset is not adjusted. Consequently, the taxable flow of economic benefits to the enterprise as the carrying value of the asset is recovered will differ from the amount that will be deductible for tax purposes.

The difference between the carrying amount of a revalued asset and its tax base is a temporary difference and gives rise to a **deferred tax liability or asset**..

4.5 Initial recognition of an asset or liability

A temporary difference can arise on initial recognition of an asset or liability, eg if part or all of the cost of an asset will not be deductible for tax purposes. The **nature of the transaction** which led to the initial recognition of the asset is important in determining the method of accounting for such temporary differences.

If the transaction affects *either* accounting profit or taxable profit, an enterprise will **recognise any deferred tax liability** or asset. The resulting deferred tax expense or income will be recognised in the income statement.

Where a transaction affects **neither accounting profit nor taxable profit** it would be normal for an enterprise to recognise a deferred tax liability or asset and adjust the carrying amount of the asset or liability by the same amount (unless exempted by IAS 12 as under Paragraph 4.1.4 above). However, IAS 12 does *not* permit this recognition of a deferred tax asset or liability as it would make the financial statements less transparent. This will be the case both on initial recognition and subsequently, nor should any subsequent changes in the unrecognised deferred tax liability or asset as the asset is depreciated be made.

4.6 Example: initial recognition

As an example of the last paragraph, suppose Petros Co intends to use an asset which cost $10,000 in 20X1 through its useful life of five years. Its residual value will then be nil. The tax rate is 40%. Any capital gain on disposal would not be taxable (and any capital loss not deductible). Depreciation of the asset is not deductible for tax purposes.

Required

State the deferred tax consequences in each of years 20X1 and 20X2.

Solution

As at 20X1, as it recovers the carrying amount of the asset, Petros Co will earn taxable income of $10,000 and pay tax of $4,000. The resulting deferred tax liability of $4,000 would not be recognised because it results from the initial recognition of the asset.

As at 20X2, the carrying value of the asset is now $8,000. In earning taxable income of $8,000, the enterprise will pay tax of $3,200. Again, the resulting deferred tax liability of $3,200 is not recognised, because it results from the initial recognition of the asset.

The following question on accelerated depreciation should clarify some of the issues and introduce you to the calculations which may be necessary in the exam.

Question — Current and deferred tax

Jonquil Co buys equipment for $50,000 and depreciates it on a straight line basis over its expected useful life of five years. For tax purposes, the equipment is depreciated at 25% per annum on a straight line basis. Tax losses may be carried back against taxable profit of the previous five years. In year 20X0, the enterprise's taxable profit was $25,000. The tax rate is 40%.

Required

Assuming nil profits/losses after depreciation in years 20X1 to 20X5 show the current and deferred tax impact in years 20X1 to 20X5 of the acquisition of the equipment.

Answer

Jonquil Co will recover the carrying amount of the equipment by using it to manufacture goods for resale. Therefore, the enterprise's current tax computation is as follows.

			Year		
	20X1	*20X2*	*20X3*	*20X4*	*20X5*
	$	$	$	$	$
Taxable income*	10,000	10,000	10,000	10,000	10,000
Depreciation for tax purposes	12,500	12,500	12,500	12,500	0
Taxable profit (tax loss)	(2,500)	(2,500)	(2,500)	(2,500)	10,000
Current tax expense (income) at 40%	(1,000)	(1,000)	(1,000)	(1,000)	4,000

* ie nil profit plus $50,000 ÷ 5 depreciation add-back.

The enterprise recognises a current tax asset at the end of years 20X1 to 20X4 because it recovers the benefit of the tax loss against the taxable profit of year 20X0.

The temporary differences associated with the equipment and the resulting deferred tax asset and liability and deferred tax expense and income are as follows.

			Year		
	20X1	*20X2*	*20X3*	*20X4*	*20X5*
	$	$	$	$	$
Carrying amount	40,000	30,000	20,000	10,000	0
Tax base	37,500	25,000	12,500	0	0
Taxable temporary difference	2,500	5,000	7,500	10,000	0
Opening deferred tax liability	0	1,000	2,000	3,000	4,000
Deferred tax expense (income): bal fig	1,000	1,000	1,000	1,000	(4,000)
Closing deferred tax liability @ 40%	1,000	2,000	3,000	4,000	0

The enterprise recognises the deferred tax liability in years 20X1 to 20X4 because the reversal of the taxable temporary difference will create taxable income in subsequent years. The enterprise's income statement is as follows.

	Year				
	20X1	20X2	20X3	20X4	20X5
	$	$	$	$	$
Income	10,000	10,000	10,000	10,000	10,000
Depreciation	10,000	10,000	10,000	10,000	10,000
Profit before tax	0	0	0	0	0
Current tax expense (income)	(1,000)	(1,000)	(1,000)	(1,000)	4,000
Deferred tax expense (income)	1,000	1,000	1,000	1,000	(4,000)
Total tax expense (income)	0	0	0	0	0
Net profit for the period	0	0	0	0	0

4.7 Section summary

- With one or two exceptions, all taxable temporary differences give rise to a **deferred tax liability**.
- Many taxable temporary differences are **timing differences**.
- Timing differences arise when income or an expense is included in accounting profit in one period, but in taxable profit in a **different period**.

5 Deductible temporary differences

5.1 Definition

Refer again to the definition given in Section 3 above.

Exam focus point

> The rule to remember here is that:
>
> 'All deductible temporary differences give rise to a deferred tax asset.'

There is a proviso, however. The deferred tax asset must also satisfy the **recognition criteria** given in IAS 12. This is that a deferred tax asset should be recognised for all deductible temporary differences to the extent that it is **probable that taxable profit will be available** against which it can be utilised. This is an application of prudence. Before we look at this issue in more detail, let us consider the examples of deductible temporary differences given in the standard.

5.2 Transactions that affect the income statement

(a) **Retirement benefit costs** (pension costs) are deducted from accounting profit as service is provided by the employee. They are not deducted in determining taxable profit until the enterprise pays either retirement benefits or contributions to a fund. (This may also apply to similar expenses.)

(b) **Accumulated depreciation** of an asset in the financial statements is greater than the accumulated depreciation allowed for tax purposes up to the balance sheet date.

(c) The **cost of inventories** sold before the balance sheet date is deducted from accounting profit when goods/services are delivered, but is deducted from taxable profit when the cash is received. (*Note.* There is also a taxable temporary difference associated with the related trade receivable, as noted in Section 4 above.)

(d) The **NRV** of inventory, or the **recoverable amount** of an item of property, plant and equipment falls and the carrying value is therefore **reduced**, but that reduction is ignored for tax purposes until the asset is sold.

(e) **Research costs** (or organisation/other start-up costs) are recognised as an expense for accounting purposes but are not deductible against taxable profits until a later period.

(f) Income is **deferred** in the balance sheet, but has already been included in taxable profit in current/prior periods.

(g) A **government grant** is included in the balance sheet as deferred income, but it will not be taxable in future periods. (*Note.* A deferred tax asset may *not* be recognised here according to the standard.)

5.3 Fair value adjustments and revaluations

Current investments or **financial instruments** may be carried at fair value which is less than cost, but no equivalent adjustment is made for tax purposes.

Other situations discussed by the standard relate to **business combinations** and consolidation. (These are not relevant for this syllabus.)

5.4 Recognition of deductible temporary differences

We looked at the important recognition criteria in Section 5.1 above. As with temporary taxable differences, there are also circumstances where the overall rule for recognition of deferred tax asset is *not* allowed.

(a) Where the deferred tax asset arises from **negative goodwill** which is treated as deferred income in accordance with IAS 22.

(b) Where the deferred tax asset arises from **initial recognition** of an asset or liability in a transaction which:

(i) Is not a business combination, *and*
(ii) At the time of the transaction, affects neither accounting nor taxable profit/ tax loss.

Let us lay out the reasoning behind the recognition of deferred tax assets arising from deductible temporary differences.

(a) When a **liability is recognised**, it is assumed that its carrying amount will be settled in the form of outflows of economic benefits from the enterprise in future periods.

(b) When these resources flow from the enterprise, part or all may be deductible in determining taxable profits of a **period later** than that in which the liability is recognised.

(c) A **temporary tax difference** then exists between the carrying amount of the liability and its tax base.

(d) A **deferred tax asset** therefore arises, representing the income taxes that will be recoverable in future periods when that part of the liability is allowed as a deduction from taxable profit.

(e) Similarly, when the carrying amount of an asset is **less than its tax base**, the difference gives rise to a deferred tax asset in respect of the income taxes that will be recoverable in future periods.

5.5 Example: deductible temporary differences

Pargatha Co recognises a liability of $10,000 for accrued product warranty costs on 31 December 20X7. These product warranty costs will not be deductible for tax purposes until the enterprise pays claims. The tax rate is 25%.

Required

State the deferred tax implications of this situation.

Solution

What is the tax base of the liability? It is nil (carrying amount of $10,000 less the amount that will be deductible for tax purposes in respect of the liability in future periods).

When the liability is settled for its carrying amount, the enterprise's future taxable profit will be reduced by $10,000 and so its future tax payments by $10,000 × 25% = $2,500.

The difference of $10,000 between the carrying amount ($10,000) and the tax base (nil) is a deductible temporary difference. The enterprise should therefore recognise a deferred tax asset of $10,000 × 25% = $2,500 **provided that** it is probable that the enterprise will earn sufficient taxable profits in future periods to benefit from a reduction in tax payments.

5.6 Taxable profits in future periods

When can we be sure that sufficient taxable profit will be available against which a deductible temporary difference can be utilised? IAS 12 states that this will be assumed when sufficient **taxable temporary differences** exist which relate to the same taxation authority and the same taxable entity. These should be expected to reverse:

(a) In the same period as the expected reversal of the deductible temporary difference, *or*

(b) In periods into which a tax loss arising from the deferred tax asset can be carried back or forward.

Only in these circumstances is the deferred tax asset **recognised**, in the period in which the deductible temporary differences arise.

5.7 Unused tax losses and unused tax credits

An enterprise may have unused tax losses or credits (ie which it can offset against taxable profits) at the end of a period. Should a deferred tax asset be recognised in relation to such amounts? IAS 12 states that a deferred tax asset may be recognised in such circumstances **to the extent that it is probable future taxable profit will be available against which the unused tax losses/credits can be utilised**.

5.8 Reassessment of unrecognised deferred tax assets

For *all* unrecognised deferred tax assets, at each balance sheet date an enterprise should **reassess the availability of future taxable profits** and whether part or all of any unrecognised deferred tax assets should now be recognised. This may be due to an improvement in trading conditions which is expected to continue.

5.9 Section summary

- Deductible temporary differences give rise to a **deferred tax asset**.
- **Prudence** dictates that deferred tax assets can only be recognised when **sufficient future taxable profits** exist against which they can be utilised.

6 Measurement and recognition of deferred tax

We need to look at several issues in this section, the first of which is the most controversial internationally.

6.1 Basis of provision of deferred tax

There are various methods of accounting for deferred tax, only one of which is adopted by IAS 12.

- **Flow-through method**
- **Full provision method** (as under IAS 12)
- **Partial provision method** (as adopted in some countries, eg the UK until recently)

You must understand the differences between these methods and the conceptual reasons why **IAS 12 adopts the full provision method**.

6.2 Different methods compared

Under the **flow-through method**, the tax liability recognised is the expected legal tax liability for the period (ie no provision is made for deferred tax). The main **advantages** of the method are that it is straightforward to apply and the tax liability recognised is closer to many people's idea of a 'real' liability than that recognised under either full or partial provision. The main **disadvantages** of flow-through are that it can lead to large fluctuations in the tax charge and that it does not allow tax relief for non-current liabilities to be recognised until those liabilities are settled. In addition, profits may be overstated because there is no deferred tax charge leading to excessive dividend payments, distortion of earnings per share and of results in the eyes of shareholders.

The **full provision method** has the **advantage** that it recognises that each timing difference at the balance sheet date has an effect on future tax payments. If a company claims an accelerated tax allowance on an item of plant, future tax assessments will be bigger than they would have been otherwise. Future transactions may well affect those assessments still further, but that is not relevant in assessing the position at the balance sheet date. The **disadvantage** of full provision is that, under certain types of tax system, it gives rise to large liabilities that may fall due only far in the future, if at all. Furthermore, it may be said to be less realistic than the partial provision method, if more objective.

The **partial provision method** addresses this disadvantage by providing for deferred tax only to the extent that it is expected to be paid in the foreseeable future. This has an obvious intuitive appeal, but its effect is that deferred tax recognised at the balance sheet date includes the tax effects of future transactions that have not been recognised in the financial statements, and which the reporting company has neither undertaken nor even committed to undertake at that date. It is difficult to reconcile this with the IASC's *Framework* document, which defines assets and liabilities as arising from past events. Where partial provision is required, the difference between the amount provided and the maximum (ie under the full provision method) should usually be disclosed.

6.3 Example: the three methods compared

Suppose that Girdo Co begins trading on 1 January 20X7. In its first year it makes profits of \$5m, the depreciation charge is \$1m and the tax allowances on those assets is \$1.5m. The rate of corporation tax is 30%.

Solution: flow through method

The tax liability for the year is 30% × \$(5.0 + 1.0 – 1.5)m = \$1.35m. The potential deferred tax liability of 30% × (\$1.5m – \$1m) is completely ignored and no judgement is required on the part of the preparer.

Solution: full provision

The tax liability is $1.35m again, but the debit in the income statement is increased by the deferred tax liability of 30% × $0.5m = $150,000. The total charge to the income statement is therefore $1.5m which is an effective tax rate of 30% on accounting profits (ie 30% × $5.0m). Again, no judgement is involved in using this method.

Solution: partial provision

Is a deferred tax provision necessary under partial provision? We need to look ahead at future capital expenditure plans. Will tax allowances exceed depreciation over the next few years? If *yes*, no provision for deferred tax is required. If *no*, then a reversal is expected, ie there will be a year in which depreciation is greater than tax allowances. The deferred tax provision is made on the maximum reversal which will be created, and any not provided is disclosed by note.

If we assume that the review of expected future capital expenditure under the partial method required a deferred tax charge of $75,000 (30% × $250,000), we can then summarise the position.

6.4 Summary

The methods can be compared as follows.

Method	*Provision*	*Disclosure*
	$	$
Flow-through	–	–
Full provision	150,000	–
Partial provision	75,000	75,000

6.5 Changes in tax rates

Where the corporate rate of income tax **fluctuates from one year to another**, a problem arises in respect of the amount of deferred tax to be credited (debited) to the income statement in later years. The amount could be calculated using either of two methods.

(a) The **deferral method** assumes that the deferred tax account is an item of 'deferred tax relief' which is credited to profits in the years in which the timing differences are reversed. Therefore the tax effects of timing differences are calculated using tax rates current when the differences **arise**.

(b) The **liability method** assumes that the tax effects of timing differences should be regarded as amounts of tax ultimately due by or to the company. Therefore deferred tax provisions are calculated at the rate at which it is estimated that tax will be paid (or recovered) when the timing differences **reverse**.

IAS 12 requires deferred tax assets and liabilities to be measured at the tax rates expected to apply in the period **when the asset is realised or liability settled**, based on tax rates and laws enacted (or substantively enacted) at the balance sheet date. In other words, IAS 12 requires the **liability method** to be used.

6.6 Different rates of tax

In addition, in some countries different tax rates apply to different levels of taxable income. In such cases, deferred tax assets and liabilities should be measured using the **average rates** that are expected to apply to the taxable profit (loss) of the periods in which the temporary differences are expected to reverse.

6.7 Manner of recovery or settlement

In some countries, the way in which an enterprise **recovers or settles** the carrying amount of an asset or liability may affect:

(a) The tax rate applying when the enterprise recovers/settles the carrying amount of the asset/liability, *and/or*

(b) The tax base of the asset/liability

In such cases, the enterprise must consider the expected manner of recovery or settlement. Deferred tax liabilities and assets must be measured accordingly, using an **appropriate tax rate and tax base**.

6.8 Example: manner of recovery/settlement

Richcard Co has an asset with a carrying amount of \$10,000 and a tax base of \$6,000. If the asset were sold, a tax rate of 20% would apply. A tax rate of 30% would apply to other income.

Required

State the deferred tax consequences if the enterprise:

(a) Sells the asset without further use, or
(b) Expects to return the asset and recover its carrying amount through use.

Solution

(a) A deferred tax liability is recognised of $\$(10,000 - 6,000) \times 20\% = \$800$.
(b) A deferred tax liability is recognised of $\$(10,000 - 6,000) \times 30\% = \$1,200$.

6.9 Discounting

IAS 12 states that deferred tax assets and liabilities **should not be discounted** because of the complexities and difficulties involved.

6.10 Carrying amount of deferred tax assets

The carrying amount of deferred tax assets should be **reviewed at each balance sheet date** and reduced where appropriate (insufficient future taxable profits). Such a reduction may be reversed in future years.

6.11 Recognition

As with current tax, deferred tax should normally be recognised as income or an expense and included in the net profit or loss for the period in the **income statement**. The exception is where the tax arises from a transaction or event which is recognised (in the same or a different period) **directly in equity**.

The figures shown for deferred tax in the income statement will consist of **two components**.

(a) Deferred tax relating to **timing differences**.

(b) Adjustments relating to **changes in the carrying amount of deferred tax assets/ liabilities** (where there is no change in timing differences), eg changes in tax rates/ laws, reassessment of the recoverability of deferred tax assets, or a change in the expected recovery of an asset.

Items in (b) will be recognised in the income statement, *unless* they relate to items previously charged/credited to equity.

Deferred tax (and current tax) should be **charged/credited directly to equity** if the tax relates to items also charged/credited directly to equity (in the same or a different period).

Examples of IASs which allow certain items to be credited/charged directly to equity include:

(a) **Revaluations** of property, plant and equipment (IAS 16), and

(b) The effect of a **change in accounting policy** (applied retrospectively) or correction of a **material error**

6.12 Why do we recognise deferred tax?

(a) Adjustments for deferred tax are made in accordance with the **accruals concept** and in accordance with the definition of a **liability** in the Framework, ie a past event has given rise to an obligation in the form of increased taxation which will be payable in the future. The amount can be reliably estimated. A deferred tax asset similarly meets the definition of an **asset**.

(b) If the future tax consequences of transactions are not recognised, profit can be overstated, leading to overpayment of dividends and distortion of share price and EPS.

6.13 Section summary

- You should understand and be able to explain the different **bases for provision** of deferred tax.
  - Flow-through method (no tax provided)
  - Full provision method (tax provided in full, as per IAS 12)
  - Partial provision method (tax provided to the extent it is expected to be paid)
- You should be able to apply the **full provision method**.
- There are two methods of calculating deferred tax when **tax rates change**.
  - **Deferral method** (use tax rates current when differences **arise**)
  - **Liability method** (use tax rate expected when differences **reverse**: per IAS 12)
- You should be able to apply the **liability method**.
- Where different rates of tax apply to different types of income, the **manner of recovery/settlement** of assets/liabilities is important.

Exam focus point

The November 2005 exam had a 4-mark question on calculating deferred tax.

7 Presentation and disclosure of taxation

FAST FORWARD

IAS 12 contains rules for comprehensive presentation and disclosure of taxation items, which are summarised here.

7.1 Presentation of tax assets and liabilities

These should be **presented separately** from other assets and liabilities in the balance sheet. Deferred tax assets and liabilities should be distinguished from current tax assets and liabilities.

In addition, deferred tax assets/liabilities should *not* be classified as current assets/ liabilities, where an enterprise makes such as distinction.

There are only limited circumstances where **current tax** assets and liabilities may be **offset**. This should only occur if the enterprise:

(a) Has a legally enforceable right to set off the recognised amounts, *and*

(b) Intends either to settle on a net basis, or to realise the asset and settle the liability simultaneously

Similar criteria apply to the **offset of deferred tax assets and liabilities**.

7.2 Presentation of tax expense

The tax expense or income related to the profit or loss from ordinary activities should be presented on the **face of the income statement**.

7.3 Disclosure

As you would expect, the major components of tax expense or income should be disclosed separately. These will generally include the following.

(a) **Current tax expense** (income)

(b) Any adjustments recognised in the period for **current tax of prior periods** (ie for over/under statement in prior years)

(c) Amount of **deferred tax expense (income)** relating to the origination and reversal of **temporary differences**

(d) Amount of the benefit arising from a previously unrecognised tax loss, tax credit or temporary difference of a prior period that is used to **reduce current tax expense**

(e) Amount of the benefit from a previously unrecognised tax loss, tax credit or temporary difference of a prior period that is used to **reduce deferred tax expense**

(f) Deferred tax expense arising from the **write-down**, or reversal of a previous write-down, of a deferred tax asset

(g) Amount of tax expense (income) relating to those **changes in accounting policies** and **material errors** which are included in the determination of net profit or loss for the period in accordance with the allowed alternative treatment in IAS 8

There are substantial additional disclosures required by the standard. All these items should be shown separately.

(a) Aggregate current and deferred tax relating to items that are charged or credited to **equity**

(b) An explanation of the relationship between **tax expense (income)** and **accounting profit** in either or both of the following forms

(i) A numerical reconciliation between tax expense (income) and the product of accounting profit multiplied by the applicable tax rate(s), disclosing also the basis on which the applicable tax rate(s) is (are) computed, *or*

(ii) A numerical reconciliation between the average effective tax rate and the applicable tax rate, disclosing also the basis on which the applicable tax rate is computed

(c) An explanation of **changes in the applicable tax rate(s)** compared to the previous accounting period

(d) The amount (and expiry date, if any) of **deductible temporary differences**, unused tax losses, and unused tax credits for which no deferred tax is recognised in the balance sheet

(e) In respect of each type of **temporary difference**, and in respect of each type of **unused tax loss** and **unused tax credit**:

 (i) The amount of the deferred tax assets and liabilities recognised in the balance sheet for each period presented

 (ii) The amount of the deferred tax income or expense recognised in the income statement, if this is not apparent from the changes in the amounts recognised in the balance sheet

(f) In respect of **discontinued operations**, the tax expense relating to

 (i) The gain or loss on discontinuance, *and*

 (ii) The profit or loss from the ordinary activities of the discontinued operation for the period, together with the corresponding amounts for each prior period presented

In addition, an enterprise should disclose the amount of a deferred tax asset and the nature of the evidence supporting its recognition, when:

(a) The utilisation of the deferred tax asset is dependent on future taxable profits in excess of the profits arising from the reversal of existing taxable temporary differences, and

(b) The enterprise has suffered a loss in either the current or preceding period in the tax jurisdiction to which the deferred tax asset relates.

7.4 Example of tax presentation

Alpha has a balance brought forward on current tax of $5,000,000. Tax paid during the period was $4,900,000 and the provision for the period is $3,000,000.

Alpha also has a balance brought forward on deferred tax of $2,600,000. The charge to the income statement (profit and loss account) for the period is $400,000.

Draw up the current and deferred tax accounts for the accounting period and show the disclosure in the income statement and balance sheet.

Solution

CURRENT TAX

	$		$
Bank account	4,900,000	Bal b/f	5,000,000
Bal c/f	3,000,000	Income statement	2,900,000
	7,900,000		7,900,000
		Bal c/f	3,000,000

DEFERRED TAX

	$		$
Bal c/f	3,000,000	Bal b/f	2,600,000
		Income statement	400,000
	3,000,000		3,000,000
		Bal c/f	3,000,000

INCOME STATEMENT (EXTRACT)

Tax (Note 1)	3,300,000

BALANCE SHEET (EXTRACT)

Current liabilities	
Tax payable	3,000,000
Non current liabilities	
Deferred tax (Note 2)	3,000,000

Notes to the accounts

1 *Tax expense*

	$
Bal b/f	(5,000,000)
Tax paid	4,900,000
Tax for current period	3,000,000
Increase in deferred tax	400,000
Income statement	3,300,000

2 *Deferred tax*

	$
Bal b/f	2,600,000
Increase in period	400,000
	3,000,000

Chapter Roundup

- There are two main systems under which companies are taxed.
  - The **classical system**
  - The **imputation system**
- Taxation consists of **two components.**
  - Current tax
  - Deferred tax
- **IAS 12 *Income taxes*** covers both current and deferred tax.
- **Deferred tax** is an accounting measure, used to match the tax effects of transactions with their accounting impact. It is quite complex.
- **Deferred tax assets and liabilities** arise from taxable and deductible temporary differences.
- IAS 12 contains rules for comprehensive presentation and disclosure of taxation items.

Quick Quiz

1 What is the difference between the classical and imputation system of income tax?

2 The tax expense related to the profit from ordinary activities should be shown on the face of the income statement.

True ☐

False ☐

3 Deferred tax liabilities are the amounts of income taxes payable in future periods in respect of ....

4 Give three examples of taxable temporary differences.

5 Which of the following methods of accounting for deferred tax is adopted by IAS 12?

A Flow-through method
B Differential method
C Full provision method
D Partial provision method

Answers to Quick Quiz

1 See Sections 1.2 and 1.3

2 True

3 Taxable temporary differences

4 Any three of:

- Interest revenue
- Depreciation
- Development costs
- Prepayments
- Sale of goods revenue

5 C

Now try the questions below from the Exam Question Bank

Number	Level	Marks	Time
Q2	Examination	20	36 mins
Q3	Examination	5	9 mins
Q5	Examination	5	9 mins
Q24	Examination	5	9 mins

Part D

Managing short term finance

15

Working capital and the operating cycle

Introduction

In this chapter we consider functions of the financial manager relating to the **management of working capital** in general terms, including how much working capital the business requires and the impact on working capital of changes in the business.

Topic list	Learning outcomes	Syllabus references	Ability required
1 Working capital	D (i)	D (2)	Application
2 Working capital (liquidity) ratios	D (i)	D (1)	Analysis
3 Working capital requirements	D (i)	D (2)	Analysis

1 Working capital

1.1 What is working capital?

FAST FORWARD

The amount tied up in **working capital** is equal to the value of all inventory and receivables less payables. This amount directly affects the liquidity of the organisation.

Key term

Working capital is the capital available for conducting the day-to-day operations of an organisation; normally the excess of current assets over current liabilities. *(OT 2000)*

Every business needs adequate **liquid resources** to maintain day-to-day cash flow. It needs enough to pay wages and salaries as they fall due and enough to pay suppliers if it is to keep its workforce and ensure its supplies. Maintaining adequate working capital is not just important in the short term. Sufficient liquidity must be maintained in order to ensure the survival of the business in the long term as well. Even a profitable company may fail if it does not have adequate cash flow to meet its liabilities as they fall due.

1.2 Working capital characteristics of different businesses

Different businesses will have different working capital characteristics. There are three main aspects to these differences.

(a) Holding inventories (from their purchase from external suppliers, through the production and warehousing of finished goods, up to the time of sale)

(b) Taking time to pay suppliers and other payables

(c) Allowing customers (receivables) time to pay

The current assets of a business can be subdivided into **permanent current assets** (the core levels of inventory and receivables) and **fluctuating current assets**, which vary from period to period.

1.3 Examples

(a) Supermarkets and other retailers receive much of their sales in cash or by credit card or debit card. However, they typically buy from suppliers on credit. They may therefore have the advantage of significant cash holdings, which they may choose to invest.

(b) A company which supplies to other companies, such as a wholesaler, is likely to be selling and buying mainly on **credit**. Co-ordinating the flow of cash may be quite a problem. Such a company may make use of short-term borrowings (such as an overdraft) to manage its cash.

(c) Smaller companies with a limited trading record may face particularly severe problems. Lacking a long track record, such companies may find it difficult to obtain credit from suppliers. At the same time, customers will expect to receive the length of credit period that is normal for the particular business concerned. The firm may find itself squeezed in its management of cash.

1.4 What is working capital management?

Ensuring that sufficient liquid resources are maintained is a matter of working capital management. This involves achieving a balance between the requirement to minimise the risk of insolvency and the requirement to maximise the return on assets. Efficient working capital management is vital if the organisation is to stay in business. Profitable businesses can go under very quickly if liquidity is not maintained. The business must decide what level of cash and inventories are to be maintained and how they are to be funded.

A business pursuing an **aggressive** working capital policy will hold minimal cash and inventories and use short-term financing to fund both permanent and fluctuating current assets. This policy carries the highest risk of insolvency and the highest level of financial return.

A business pursuing a **conservative** policy will hold large levels of ready cash and safety inventory and use long-term funding for both non-current and most current assets. This is the least risky option but results in the lowest expected return.

An excessively conservative approach to working capital management resulting in high levels of cash holdings will harm profits because the opportunity to make a return on the assets tied up as cash will have been missed.

A **moderate** policy will match short-term finance to fluctuating current assets and non-fluctuating current assets will be matched by long-term funding.

1.5 The working capital cycle

FAST FORWARD

Working capital cycle is the period of time which elapses between the point at which cash begins to be expended on the production of a product and the collection of cash from a purchaser. *(OT 2000)*

The connection between investment in working capital and cash flow may be illustrated by means of the **working capital cycle** (also called the **cash cycle, operating cycle** or **trading cycle**).

The working capital cycle in a manufacturing business equals:

The average time that raw materials remain in inventory
Less the period of credit taken from suppliers
Plus the time taken to produce the goods
Plus the time finished goods remain in inventory after production is completed
Plus the time taken by customers to pay for the goods

If the turnover periods for inventories and receivables lengthen, or the payment period to payables shortens, then the operating cycle will lengthen and the investment in working capital will increase.

1.6 Example: working capital cycle

Wines Co buys raw materials from suppliers that allow Wines 2.5 months credit. The raw materials remain in inventory for one month, and it takes Wines 2 months to produce the goods. The goods are sold within a couple of days of production being completed and customers take on average 1.5 months to pay.

Required

Calculate Wines's working capital cycle.

Solution

We can ignore the time finished goods are in inventory as it is no more than a couple of days.

	Months
The average time that raw materials remain in inventory	1.0
Less: The time taken to pay suppliers	(2.5)
The time taken to produce the goods	2.0
The time taken by customers to pay for the goods	1.5
	2.0

The company's working capital cycle is 2 months. This can be illustrated diagrammatically as follows.

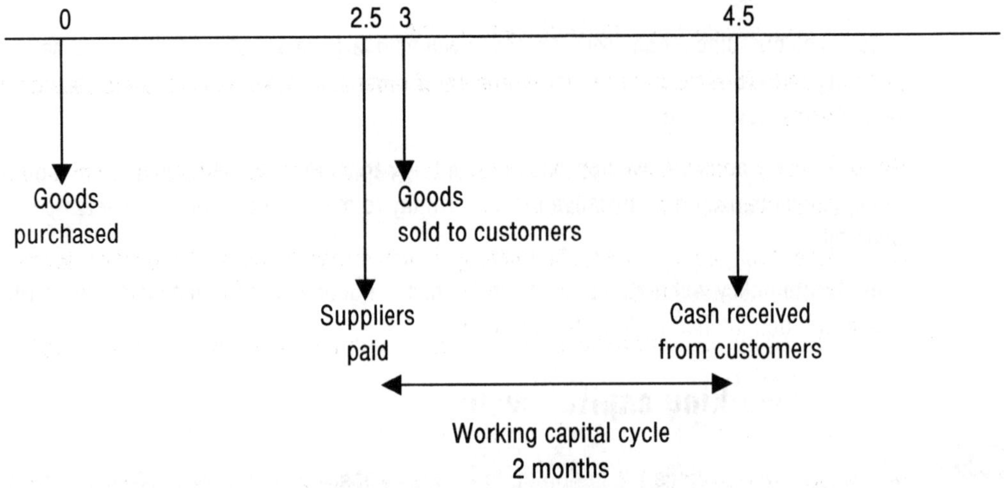

The working capital cycle is the period between the suppliers being paid and the cash being received from the customers.

1.7 Managing the cycle

A longer working capital cycle requires more financial resource, so management will seek whenever possible to reduce the length of the cycle. Their possible options are as follows.

(a) Reduce levels of raw materials inventory. This may be done by the introduction of some type of JIT system, which will necessitate more efficient links with suppliers. Production delays due to running out of inventory must be avoided.

(b) Reduce work in progress by reducing production volume or improving techniques and efficiency.

(c) Reduce finished goods inventory, perhaps by improving distribution. This may lead to delays in fulfilling customer orders.

(d) Delay payments to suppliers. This can lead to loss of discounts and of supplier goodwill.

(e) Reduce period of credit given to customers. This may mean offering discounts and more aggressive credit control may lead to loss of customers.

1.8 Cash flow planning

Since a company must have adequate cash inflows to survive, management should plan and control cash flows as well as profitability. **Cash budgeting** is an important element in short-term cash flow planning.

The purpose of cash budgets is to make sure that the organisation will have **enough cash inflows** to meet its cash outflows. If a budget reveals that a short-term cash shortage can be expected, steps will be taken to meet the problem and avoid the cash crisis (perhaps by arranging a bigger bank overdraft facility).

Cash budgets and cash flow forecasts on their own do not give full protection against a cash shortage and enforced liquidation of the business by creditors. There may be unexpected changes in cash flow patterns. When unforeseen events have an adverse effect on cash inflows, a company will only survive if it can maintain adequate cash inflows despite the setbacks.

Question — Cash flow patterns

Give examples of unforeseen changes which may affect cash flow patterns.

Answer

Your list probably included some of the following.

(a) A **change** in the **general economic environment**. An economic recession will cause a slump in trade.

(b) A **new product**, launched by a competitor, which takes business away from a company's traditional and established product lines.

(c) **New cost-saving product technology**, which forces the company to invest in the new technology to remain competitive.

(d) **Moves by competitors** which have to be countered (for example a price reduction or a sales promotion).

(e) **Changes in consumer preferences**, resulting in a fall in demand.

(f) **Government action** against certain trade practices or against trade with a country that a company has dealings with.

(g) **Strikes** or other industrial action.

(h) **Natural disasters**, such as floods or fire damage, which curtail an organisation's activities.

2 Working capital (liquidity) ratios

FAST FORWARD

Liquidity ratios may help to indicate whether a company has too much working capital (over-capitalised) or too little (overtrading).

2.1 The current ratio and the quick ratio

The standard test of liquidity is the **current ratio**. It can be obtained from the balance sheet.

Key term

$$\textbf{Current ratio} = \frac{\text{Current assets}}{\text{Current liabilities}}$$

A company should have enough current assets that give a promise of 'cash to come' to meet its commitments to pay its current liabilities. Obviously, a ratio in excess of 1 should be expected; an ideal is probably about 2. Otherwise, there would be the prospect that the company might be unable to pay its debts on time. In practice, a ratio comfortably in excess of 1 should be expected, but what is 'comfortable' varies between different types of businesses.

Some manufacturing companies might hold large quantities of raw material inventories, which must be used in production to create finished goods. Finished goods might be warehoused for a long time, or sold on lengthy credit. In such businesses, where inventory turnover is slow, most inventories are not very liquid assets, because the cash cycle is so long. For these reasons, we calculate an additional liquidity ratio, known as the quick ratio or acid test ratio.

Key term

Quick ratio, or **acid test ratio** = $\frac{\text{Current assets less inventories}}{\text{Current liabilities}}$

This ratio should ideally be at least 1 for companies with a slow inventory turnover. For companies with a fast inventory turnover, a quick ratio can be less than 1 without suggesting that the company is in cash flow difficulties.

2.2 The receivables collection period

FAST FORWARD

A rough measure of the average length of time it takes for a company's customers to pay what they owe is the '**receivable days**' ratio.

Key term

Receivable days ratio = $\frac{\text{Average trade receivables}}{\text{Average daily sales on credit terms}}$ *(OT 2000)*

An equivalent measure is the receivables turnover period.

Key term

Receivables turnover period = $\frac{\text{Average trade receivables}}{\text{Credit sales for the year}} \times 365$ days

The trade receivables are not the **total** figure for receivables in the balance sheet, which includes prepayments and non-trade receivables. The trade receivables figure will be itemised in an analysis of the total receivables, in a note to the accounts.

The estimate of receivables days is only approximate.

(a) The balance sheet value might be used instead of the average. However, don't forget that the balance sheet value of receivables might be abnormally high or low compared with the 'normal' level the company usually has.

(b) Sales revenue in the income statement excludes sales tax, but the receivables figure in the balance sheet includes sales tax. We are not strictly comparing like with like. If the figures are too distorted by sales tax, adjustment will be needed.

(c) Average receivables may not be representative of year-end sales if sales are growing rapidly.

2.3 The payables payment period

Similar measures can be used for payables.

FAST FORWARD

This indicates the average time taken, in calendar days, to pay for supplies received on credit.

Key terms

Payables days ratio = $\frac{\text{Average trade payables}}{\text{Average daily purchases on credit terms}}$ *(OT 2000)*

Payables payment period, or **payables turnover period** = $\frac{\text{Average trade payables}}{\text{Purchases on credit terms for year}} \times 365$ days

If the credit purchases information is not readily available, cost of sales can be used instead. Don't forget however that some elements of cost of sales (for example, labour costs) are not relevant to trade payables. Note also that credit purchases in the income statement do not include sales tax.

2.4 The inventory turnover period

FAST FORWARD

The inventory turnover period shows how long goods are being kept in inventory.

Another ratio worth calculating is the inventory turnover period. This is another estimated figure, obtainable from published accounts, which indicates the average number of days that items of inventory are held for. As with the average receivable collection period, it is only an approximate figure; there may be distortions caused by seasonal variations in inventory levels. However it should be reliable enough for finding changes over time.

Key terms

Inventory turnover = $\frac{\text{Inventory value}}{\text{Average daily cost of sales in period}}$

The inventory turnover period can also be calculated:

Inventory turnover period = $\frac{\text{Inventory value}}{\text{Cost of sales}} \times 365$ days

The ratio $\frac{\text{Average inventory}}{\text{Cost of sales}}$ is called the inventory turnover, and is another measure of how vigorously a business is trading. A lengthening inventory turnover period indicates:

(a) A slowdown in trading, or

(b) A build-up in inventory levels, perhaps suggesting that the investment in inventories is becoming excessive

Where a business is manufacturing goods for resale, inventory turnover will have three components:

Raw materials: $\frac{\text{average materials inventory}}{\text{purchases of raw materials}} \times 365$

WIP: $\frac{\text{average work in progress}}{\text{cost of sales}} \times 365$

Finished goods: $\frac{\text{average finished goods}}{\text{cost of sales}} \times 365$

Where average values are not available, closing values can be used.

Where no breakdown of inventories is supplied, just use the overall ratio: $\frac{\text{average inventory}}{\text{cost of sales}}$

If we add together the inventory days and the receivable days, this should give us an indication of how soon inventory is convertible into cash, thereby giving a further indication of the company's liquidity.

All the ratios calculated above will **vary industry by industry**; hence **comparisons** of ratios calculated with other similar companies in the same industry are important. There are organisations which specialise in **inter-firm comparison**. A company submits its figures to one of these organisations and receives an analysis of the average ratios for its industry. It can then compare its own performance to that of the industry as a whole.

3 Working capital requirements

3.1 The need for funds for investment in current assets

Current assets may be financed either by long-term funds or by current liabilities.

Liquidity ratios are a guide to the risk of cash flow problems and insolvency. If a company suddenly finds that it is unable to renew its short-term liabilities (for example, if the bank suspends its overdraft facilities, or suppliers start to demand earlier payment), there will be a danger of insolvency unless the company is able to turn enough of its current assets into cash quickly.

Current liabilities are often a cheap method of finance (trade payables do not usually carry an interest cost) and companies may therefore consider that, in the interest of higher profits, it is worth accepting some risk of insolvency by increasing current liabilities, taking the maximum credit possible from suppliers.

3.2 The volume of current assets required

The volume of current assets required will depend on the nature of the company's business. For example, a manufacturing company may require more inventories than a company in a service industry. As the volume of output by a company increases, the volume of current assets required will also increase.

Even assuming efficient inventory holding, receivable collection procedures and cash management, there is still a certain degree of choice in the total volume of current assets required to meet output requirements. Policies of low inventory-holding levels, tight credit and minimum cash holdings may be contrasted with policies of high inventories (to allow for safety or buffer inventories) easier credit and sizeable cash holdings (for precautionary reasons).

3.3 Over-capitalisation and working capital

FAST FORWARD

Over-capitalisation means that the organisation has an excess of working capital.

If there are excessive inventories, receivables and cash, and very few payables, there will be an over-investment by the company in current assets. Working capital will be excessive and the company will be in this respect over-capitalised. The return on investment will be lower than it should be, and long-term funds will be unnecessarily tied up when they could be invested elsewhere to earn profits.

Over-capitalisation with respect to working capital should not exist if there is good management, but the warning signs of excessive working capital would be unfavourable accounting ratios, including the following.

(a) **Sales/working capital**

The volume of sales as a multiple of the working capital investment should indicate whether, in comparison with previous years or with similar companies, the total volume of working capital is too high.

(b) **Liquidity ratios**

A current ratio greatly in excess of 2:1 or a quick ratio much in excess of 1:1 may indicate over-investment in working capital.

(c) **Turnover periods**

Excessive turnover periods for inventories and receivables, or a short period of credit taken from suppliers, might indicate that the volume of inventories or receivables is unnecessarily high, or the volume of payables too low.

3.4 Example: working capital ratios

Calculate liquidity and working capital ratios from the following accounts of a manufacturer of products for the construction industry, and comment on the ratios.

	20X8	*20X7*
	$m	$m
Sales revenue	2,065.0	1,788.7
Cost of sales	1,478.6	1,304.0
Gross profit	586.4	484.7

	20X8	20X7
	$m	$m
Current assets		
Inventories	119.0	109.0
Receivables (note 1)	400.9	347.4
Short-term investments	4.2	18.8
Cash at bank and in hand	48.2	48.0
	572.3	523.2

	20X8	20X7
	$m	$m
Payables: amounts falling due within one year		
Loans and overdrafts	49.1	35.3
Income taxes	62.0	46.7
Dividend	19.2	14.3
Payables (note 2)	370.7	324.0
	501.0	420.3
Net current assets	71.3	102.9

Notes

		20X8	*20X7*
		$m	$m
1	Trade receivables	329.8	285.4
2	Trade payables	236.2	210.8

3 We are not given a breakdown of inventories

Solution

	20X8	*20X7*
Current ratio	$\frac{572.3}{501.0} = 1.14$	$\frac{523.2}{420.3} = 1.24$
Quick ratio	$\frac{453.3}{501.0} = 0.90$	$\frac{414.2}{420.3} = 0.99$
Receivables' turnover period	$\frac{329.8}{2,065.0} \times 365 = 58$ days	$\frac{285.4}{1,788.7} \times 365 = 58$ days
Inventory turnover period	$\frac{119.0}{1,478.6} \times 365 = 29$ days	$\frac{109.0}{1,304.0} \times 365 = 31$ days

	20X8	20X7
Payables turnover period	$\frac{236.2}{1,478.6} \times 365 = 58$ days	$\frac{210.8}{1,304.0} \times 365 = 59$ days

The company is a manufacturing group serving the construction industry, and so would be expected to have a comparatively lengthy receivables turnover period, because of the relatively poor cash flow in the construction industry. It is clear that the company compensates for this by ensuring that they do not pay for raw materials and other costs before they have sold their inventories of finished goods (hence the similarity of receivables and payables turnover periods).

The company's current ratio is a little lower than average but its quick ratio is better than average and very little less than the current ratio. This suggests that inventory levels are strictly controlled, which is reinforced by the low inventory turnover period. It would seem that working capital is tightly managed, to avoid the poor liquidity which could be caused by a high receivables turnover period and comparatively high payables.

3.5 Overtrading

FAST FORWARD

Overtrading means that the organisation has too little working capital.

Key term

> **Overtrading** is the condition of a business which enters into commitments in excess of its available short-term resources. This can arise even if the company is trading profitably, and is typically caused by financing strains imposed by a lengthy operating cycle or production cycle. *(OT 2000)*

In contrast with over-capitalisation, overtrading happens when a business tries to do too much too quickly with too little long-term capital, so that it is trying to support too large a volume of trade with the capital resources at its disposal.

Even if an overtrading business operates at a profit, it could easily run into serious trouble because it is short of money. Such liquidity troubles stem from the fact that it does not have enough capital to provide the cash to pay its debts as they fall due.

3.6 Example: overtrading

Great Ambition appoints a new managing director who has great plans to expand the company. He wants to increase revenue by 100% within two years, and to do this he employs extra sales staff. He recognises that customers do not want to have to wait for deliveries, and so he decides that the company must build up its inventory levels. There is a substantial increase in the company's inventories. These are held in additional warehouse space which is now rented. The company also buys new cars for its extra sales representatives.

The managing director's policies are immediately successful in boosting sales, which double in just over one year. Inventory levels are now much higher, but the company takes longer credit from its suppliers, even though some suppliers have expressed their annoyance at the length of time they must wait for payment. Credit terms for receivables are unchanged, and so the volume of receivables, like the volume of sales, rises by 100%.

In spite of taking longer credit, the company still needs to increase its overdraft facilities with the bank, which are raised from a limit of $40,000 to one of $80,000. The company is profitable, and retains some profits in the business, but profit margins have fallen. **Gross profit margins** are lower because some prices have been reduced to obtain extra sales. **Net profit margins** are lower because overhead costs are higher. These include sales representatives' wages, car expenses and depreciation on cars, warehouse rent and additional losses from having to write off out-of-date and slow-moving inventory items.

The balance sheet of the company might change over time from (A) to (B).

	Balance sheet (A)		*Balance sheet (B)*	
	$	$	$	$
Non-current assets		160,000		210,000
Current assets				
Inventory	60,000		150,000	
Receivables	64,000		135,000	
Cash	1,000		–	
		125,000		285,000
Total assets		285,000		495,000
Current liabilities				
Bank	25,000		80,000	
Payables	50,000		200,000	
		75,000		280,000
Share capital	10,000		10,000	
Retained earnings	200,000		205,000	
		210,000		215,000
Total equity/liabilities		285,000		495,000
Sales revenue	$1,000,000			$2,000,000
Gross profit	$200,000			$300,000
Net profit	$50,000			$20,000

In situation (B), the company has reached its overdraft limit and has four times as many payables as in situation (A) but with only twice the sales revenue. Inventory levels are much higher, and inventory turnover is lower.

The company is overtrading. If it had to pay its next trade payable, or salaries and wages, before it received any income, it could not do so without the bank allowing it to exceed its overdraft limit. The company is profitable, although profit margins have fallen, and it ought to expect a prosperous future. But if it does not sort out its cash flow and liquidity, it will not survive to enjoy future profits.

Solutions to the problem

Suitable solutions to the problem would be measures to reduce the degree of overtrading. **New capital** from the shareholders could be injected. Short-term finance could be converted to longer-term finance. **Better control** could be applied to inventories and receivables. The company could **abandon ambitious plans** for increased sales and more non-current asset purchases until the business has had time to consolidate its position, and build up its capital base with retained profits. It partly requires the business to take a long-term view of future prospects, and **avoid short-termism**.

Key term

Short-termism is a bias towards paying particular attention to short-term performance, with a corresponding relative disregard to the long term. *(OT 2000)*

3.7 Symptoms of overtrading

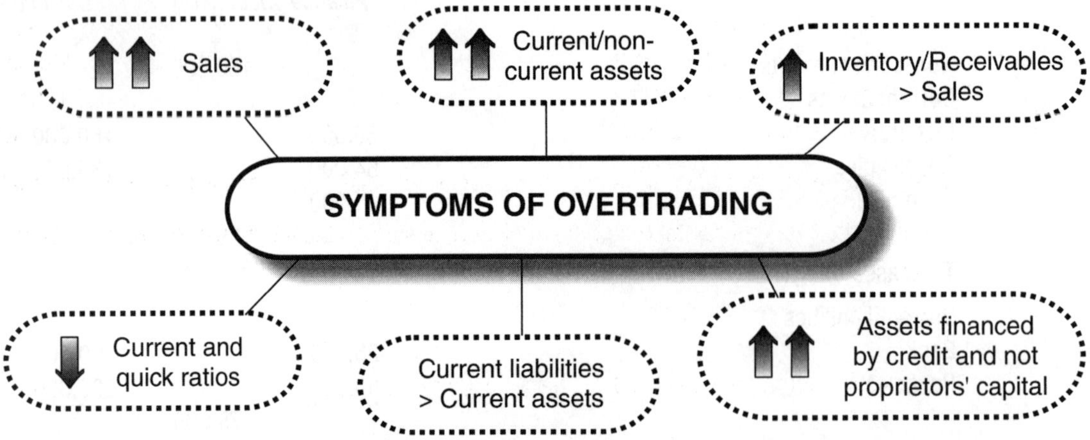

Apart from the danger of overtrading when a business seeks to increase its sales too rapidly without an adequate capital base, **other causes** are as follows.

(a) When a business repays a loan, it often replaces the old loan with a new one. However a business might **repay a loan** without **replacing it**, with the consequence that it has **less long-term capital** to finance its current level of operations.

(b) A business might be profitable, but in a period of inflation, its **retained profits** might be **insufficient** to pay for replacement non-current assets and inventories, which now cost more because of inflation. The business would then rely increasingly on credit, and find itself eventually unable to support its current volume of trading with a capital base that has fallen in real terms.

3.8 The working capital requirement

Computing the working capital requirement is a matter of calculating the value of current assets less current liabilities, perhaps by taking averages over a one year period.

3.9 Example: working capital requirements

The following data relate to Corn Co, a manufacturing company.

Sales for the year	$1,500,000
Costs as percentages of sales	
	%
Direct materials	30
Direct labour	25
Variable overheads	10
Fixed overheads	15
Selling and distribution	5

On average:

(a) Receivables take 2.5 months before payment.

(b) Raw materials are in inventory for three months.

(c) Work-in-progress represents two months worth of half produced goods.

(d) Finished goods represents one month's production.

(e) Credit is taken as follows.

(i)	Direct materials	2 months
(ii)	Direct labour	1 week
(iii)	Variable overheads	1 month
(iv)	Fixed overheads	1 month
(v)	Selling and distribution	0.5 months

Work-in-progress and finished goods are valued at material, labour and variable expense cost.

Compute the working capital requirement of Corn assuming the labour force is paid for 50 working weeks a year.

Solution

(a) The annual costs incurred will be as follows.

		$
Direct materials	30% of $1,500,000	450,000
Direct labour	25% of $1,500,000	375,000
Variable overheads	10% of $1,500,000	150,000
Fixed overheads	15% of $1,500,000	225,000
Selling and distribution	5% of $1,500,000	75,000

(b) The average value of current assets will be as follows.

		$	$
Raw materials	3/12 × $450,000		112,500
Work-in-progress			
Materials (50% complete)	1/12 × $450,000	37,500	
Labour (50% complete)	1/12 × $375,000	31,250	
Variable overheads (50% complete)	1/12 × $150,000	12,500	
			81,250
Finished goods			
Materials	1/12 × $450,000	37,500	
Labour	1/12 × $375,000	31,250	
Variable overheads	1/12 × $150,000	12,500	
			81,250
Receivables	2.5/12 × $1,500,000		312,500
			587,500

(c) Average value of current liabilities will be as follows.

		$	$
Materials	2/12 × $450,000	75,000	
Labour	1/50 × $375,000	7,500	
Variable overheads	1/12 × $150,000	12,500	
Fixed overheads	1/12 × $225,000	18,750	
Selling and distribution	0.5/12 × $75,000	3,125	
			116,875

(d) Working capital required is ($(587,500 – 116,875)) = 470,625

It has been assumed that all the direct materials are allocated to work-in-progress when production starts.

Exam focus point

This topic lends itself to short questions. The May 2005 exam had three questions on working capital issues.

Question — Overtrading

Define what is meant by the term 'overtrading' and describe some of the typical symptoms.

Answer

'**Overtrading**' refers to the situation where a company is **over-reliant** on **short-term finance** to support its operations. This is risky because short-term finance may be withdrawn relatively quickly if suppliers lose confidence in the business, or if there is a general tightening of credit in the economy, and this may result in a liquidity crisis and even bankruptcy, even though the firm is profitable. The fundamental solution to overtrading is to replace short term finance with longer term finance such as term loans or equity funds.

The term overtrading is used because the condition commonly arises when a company is **expanding rapidly**. In this situation, because of increasing volumes, more cash is frequently needed to pay input costs such as wages or purchases than is currently being collected from customers. The result is that the company runs up its overdraft to the limit and sometimes there is insufficient time to arrange an increase in facilities to pay other payables on the due dates.

These problems are often compounded by a general lack of attention to cost control and working capital management, such as receivables collection, because most management time is spent organising selling or production. The result is an unnecessary drop in profit margins.

When the overdraft limit is reached the company frequently raises funds from other expensive short term sources, such as receivables factoring or receivables prompt payment discounts, and delays payment to suppliers, instead of underpinning its financial position with equity funds or a longer term loan. The consequent under-capitalisation delays investment in non-current assets and staff and can further harm the quality of the firm's operations.

Question — Quick ratio

The figures below have been extracted from the accounts of Premier Co.

	$
Sales revenue	750,000
Cost of sales	500,000
Gross profit	250,000
Current assets	
Inventories	75,000
Trade receivables	100,000
Other receivables	10,000
Cash at bank and in hand	5,000
	190,000
Current liabilities	
Overdraft	30,000
Dividend	40,000
Trade payables	80,000
Other payables	10,000
	160,000
Net current assets	30,000

What is the quick ratio?

A 0.69
B 0.72
C 0.82
D 1.19

Answer

B The quick ratio is the ratio of current assets excluding inventories to current liabilities.

In this case: $\frac{190{,}000 - 75{,}000}{160{,}000} = 0.72$

Chapter Roundup

- The amount tied up in **working capital** is equal to the value of raw materials, work-in-progress, finished inventories and receivables less payables. The size of this net figure has a direct effect on the **liquidity** of an organisation.
- **Working capital cycle** is the period of time which elapses between the point at which cash begins to be expended on the production of a product and the collection of cash from a purchaser.
- **Liquidity ratios** may help to indicate whether a company is **over-capitalised**, with excessive working capital, or if a business is likely to fail. A business which is trying to do too much too quickly with too little long-term capital is **overtrading**.
- A rough measure of the average length of time it takes customers to pay is the **'receivable days'** ratio.
- The **payables payment period** indicates the average time taken to pay suppliers.
- The **inventory turnover period** shows how long goods are being kept in inventory.
- **Over-capitalisation** means that the organisation has an excess of working capital.
- **Overtrading** means that the organisation has too little working capital.

Quick Quiz

1 Which of the following is the most likely to be a symptom of overtrading?

A Static levels of inventory turnover
B Rapid increase in profits
C Increase in the level of the current ratio
D Rapid increase in sales

2 The operating cycle is:

	A The time	
Less	B The time	
Plus	C The time	
Plus	D The time	

Fill in the blanks.

3 Fill in the blanks with the following:

Current liabilities; current assets; inventories; 1.

Quick ratio = $\frac{\text{\_\_\_\_\_\_ less \_\_\_\_\_\_}}{\text{\_\_\_\_\_\_}}$ (This should be at least ....)

4 Which of the following describes *overcapitalisation* and which describes *overtrading*?

A A company with excessive investment in working capital
B A company trying to support too large a volume of trade with the capital resources at its disposal

5 Which of the following statements best defines the current ratio?

A The ratio of current assets to current liabilities.
For the majority of businesses it should be at least 2.

B The ratio of current assets to current liabilities.
For the majority of businesses it should be at least 1.

C The ratio of current assets excluding inventory to current liabilities.
For the majority of businesses it should be at least 1.

D The ratio of current assets excluding inventory to current liabilities.
For the majority of businesses it should be at least 2.

6 The receivables payment period is a calculation of the time taken to pay by all receivables.

True ☐

False ☐

7 A company has a current ratio of 2:1. It decides to use surplus cash balances to settle 40% of its total current liabilities. The current ratio will:

A Increase by more than 40%
B Decrease by more than 40%
C Increase by less than 40%
D Decrease by less than 40%

8 What is the working capital requirement of a company with the following average figures over a year?

	$
Inventory	3,750
Trade receivables	1,500
Cash and bank balances	500
Trade payables	1,800

Answers to Quick Quiz

1 D Rapid increase in sales

2 A The time raw materials remain in inventory
B The time period of credit taken from suppliers
C The time taken to produce goods
D The time taken by customers to pay for goods

3 Quick ratio = $\frac{\text{Current assets less inventories}}{\text{Current liabilities}}$ (This should be at least 1)

4 A Overcapitalisation
  B Overtrading

5 A The ratio of current assets to current liabilities: 2

6 False; the calculation normally only includes trade receivables.

7 C Current ratio = 2
  Settlement = 0.4
  New current ratio = 1.6/0.6 = 2.67

  Increase = (2.67/2) – 1 = 33.3%

8 Working capital requirement = current assets less current liabilities = 3,750 + 1,500 + 500 – 1,800
  = $3,950

Now try the question below from the Exam Question Bank

Number	Level	Marks	Time
Q27	Examination	20	36 mins

16

Cash flow forecasts

Introduction

Survival in business depends on the ability to generate cash. **Cash flow information** directs attention towards this critical issue. Cash flow is a more comprehensive concept than 'profit' which is dependent on accounting conventions and concepts.

The **cash budget** is an extremely important mechanism for monitoring cash flows, and cash budgets will appear frequently in this paper. Various complications about timing of cash flows or lack of particular figures will be included in cash budget questions.

At the heart of this chapter is the method for systematically preparing a cash budget. You must be able to set out a budget clearly, supported by appropriate workings.

1 Cash flows and profit

1.1 Types of cash transaction

There are many types of cash transaction. They can be distinguished by their purpose (ie what they are for), their form (how they are implemented), and their frequency. Sometimes the following distinctions are made.

(a) **Capital** and **revenue** items

 (i) Capital items relate to the long-term functioning of the business, such as raising money from shareholders, or acquiring non-current assets.

 (ii) Revenue items relate to day-to-day operations, as in the operating cycle, including other matters such as overdraft interest.

(b) **Exceptional** and **unexceptional** items

 (i) Exceptional items are unusual. An example would be the costs of closing down part of a business.

 (ii) Unexceptional items include everything else. You have to be careful using this distinction, as the phrase 'exceptional item' has a precise meaning in the preparation of a company's financial statements.

(c) **Regular** and **irregular** items

 (i) Regular items occur at predictable intervals. Such intervals might be frequent such as the payment of wages every week or month, or relatively infrequent, such as the disbursement of interim and final dividends twice a year. A capital item might be the regular repayment of principal and interest on leased property. Annual disbursements are sums of money paid at yearly intervals.

 (ii) Irregular items do not occur at regular intervals.

1.2 Cash flows and profit

FAST FORWARD

Trading profits and **cash flows** are different. A company can make losses but still have a net cash income from trading. A **company** can also make profits but have a net cash deficit on its trading operations.

(a) Cash may be obtained from a transaction which has **nothing** to do with **profit or loss**. For example, an issue of shares or loan stock for cash has no immediate effect on profit but is obviously a source of cash. Similarly, an increase in bank overdraft provides a source of cash for payments, but it is not reported in the income statement.

(b) Cash may be paid for the **purchase of non-current assets**, but the charge in the income statement is depreciation, which is only a part of an asset's cost.

(c) When a non-current asset is sold there is a profit or loss on sale **equal to the difference** between the **sale proceeds** and the **'net book value'** of the asset in the balance sheet at the time it is sold.

(d) One reason is changes in the amount of the company's inventories, receivables and payables.

 (i) **Profit** is sales minus the cost of sales.

 (ii) **Operational cash flow** is the difference between cash received and cash paid from trading.

(iii) Cash received differs from sales because of changes in the amount of receivables.

	$
Customers owing money at the start of the year	X
Sales during the year	X
Total money due from customers	X
Less customers owing money at the end of the year	(X)
Cash receipts from customers during the year	X

(iv) Cash paid differs from the cost of sales because of changes in the amount of inventories and payables.

	$
Closing inventories at the end of the year	X
Add cost of sales during the year	X
	X
Less opening inventories at the start of the year	(X)
Equals purchases	Y
	$
Payments owing to suppliers at the start of the year	X
Add purchases	Y
	X
Less payments still owing to suppliers at the end of the year	(X)
Equals **cash payments** to suppliers during the year	X

(v) Operational cash flow therefore differs from profit because of changes in the amount of receivables, inventories and payables between the start and end of a period.

Question

Profits and cash flow

Assume that Beta achieved sales revenue in a particular year of $200,000 and the cost of sales was $170,000. Inventories were $12,000, payables $11,000 and receivables $15,000 at the start of the year. At the end of the year, inventories were $21,000, payables were $14,000 and receivables $24,000.

Required

Find out the profits and the operational cash flow resulting from the year's trading.

Answer

	Profit $	*Operational cash flow* $
Sales	200,000	200,000
Opening receivables (∴ received in year)		15,000
Closing receivables (outstanding at year end)		(24,000)
Cash in		191,000
Cost of sales	170,000	170,000
Closing inventory (bought, but not used, in year)		21,000
Opening inventory (used, but not bought, in year)		(12,000)
Purchases in year		179,000
Opening payables (∴ paid in year)		11,000
Closing payables (outstanding at year end)		(14,000)
Cash out		176,000
Profit/operational cash flow	30,000	15,000

The difference between profit and cash flow has important implications.

(a) If a company is profitable but short of cash, one reason could be an increase in the other elements of working capital. If a company were to seek credit from a bank to finance the growth in working capital, the bank might ask the management whether **operational cash flows could be improved** by squeezing working capital, and:

- Reducing receivables
- Reducing inventories, or
- Taking more trade credit from suppliers

Better control over working capital could remove the need to borrow.

(b) If a company is making losses, it could try to maintain a positive operational cash flow by **taking more credit** (ie by increasing its payables and so reducing working capital). The credit managers of supplier companies should then consider whether to give the extra credit required, or whether to refuse because the risk would be too great.

Question — Profits compared with cash flow

Write brief notes on why the reported profit figure of a business for a period does not normally represent the amount of cash generated in that period.

Answer

The principal reasons why profit will not equal cash flow are as follows.

(a) The '**matching concept**' means that costs and revenues do not equal payments and receipts. Revenue is recognised in the income statement when goods are sold, and any revenue not received is recorded as a receivable. Similarly, costs are incurred when a resource is acquired or subsequently used, not when it happens to be paid for.

(b) **Some items appearing** in the income statement do not **affect cash flow**. For example, depreciation is a 'non-cash' deduction in arriving at profit.

(c) Similarly, items may **affect cash flow** but not profit. Capital expenditure decisions (apart from depreciation) and inventory level adjustments are prime examples.

Exam focus point

Exam questions in this area could ask you to calculate cash forecasts from profit and balance sheet forecasts or vice versa.

2 The purpose of cash forecasts

FAST FORWARD

Cash flow forecasts provide an early warning of liquidity problems and funding needs. Banks often expect business customers to provide a cash forecast as a condition of lending.

Cash forecasting ensures that sufficient funds will be available when they are needed to sustain the activities of an enterprise. Efficient financial planning also has to minimise interest payments and maximise the return from any spare cash. Interest rates will differ according to whether money is being lent to, or borrowed from, the bank. The **time value of money** is another important factor. The bank will charge a higher rate of interest on a long-term loan than on a short term loan and will pay a higher rate of interest on an account subject to a longer notice of withdrawal than on an account that requires only 24 hours notice.

All of these factors must be considered when forecasting cash requirements.

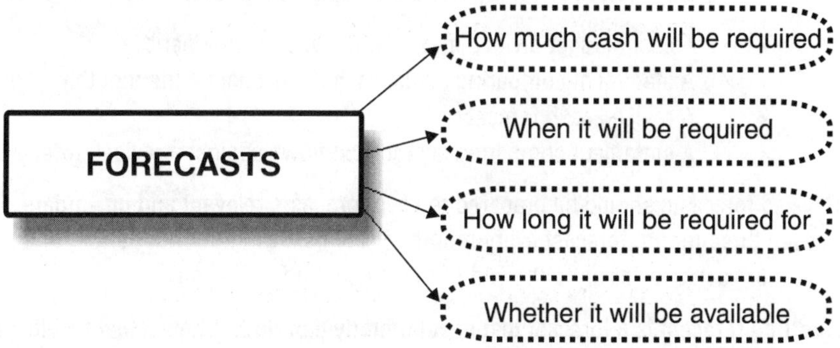

Banks have increasingly insisted that customers provide cash forecasts (or a business plan that includes a cash forecast) as a precondition of lending. A newly established company wishing to open a bank account will also normally be asked to supply a **business plan**. The cash and sales forecasts will also allow the bank to **monitor** the **progress** of the new company, and control its lending more effectively.

2.1 Deficiencies

Any forecast **deficiency** of cash will have to be funded.

(a) **Borrowing**. If borrowing arrangements are not already secured, a source of funds will have to be found. If a company cannot fund its cash deficits it could be wound up.

(b) The firm can make arrangements to **sell any short-term financial investments** to raise cash.

(c) The firm can delay payments to suppliers, or pull in payments from customers. This is sometimes known as **leading and lagging**.

Because cash forecasts cannot be entirely accurate, companies should have **contingency funding**, available from a surplus cash balance and liquid investments, or from a bank facility.

Forecasting gives management time to arrange its funding. If planned in advance, instead of a panic measure to avert a cash crisis, a company can more easily choose **when to borrow**, and will probably obtain a **lower interest rate**.

2.2 Forecasting a cash surplus

Many cash-generative businesses are less reliant on high quality cash forecasts. If a cash surplus is forecast, having an idea of both its size and how long it will exist could help decide how best to invest it.

In some cases, the amount of interest earned from surplus cash could be significant for the company's earnings. The company might then need a forecast of its interest earnings in order to indicate its prospective earnings per share to stock market analysts and institutional investors.

2.3 Types of forecast

FAST FORWARD

There are two broad types of cash forecast.

- Cash flow based forecasts (or cash budgets) in **receipts and payments format**
- **Balance sheet and financial statement based** forecasts

Key term

> A **cash budget** is a detailed budget of estimated cash inflows and outflows, incorporating both revenue and capital items. *(OT 2000)*

In companies that use cash flow reporting for control purposes, there will probably be:

- A cash budget divided into monthly or quarterly periods
- A statement comparing actual cash flows against the monthly or quarterly budget
- A revised cash forecast
- A statement comparing actual cash flows against a revised forecast

Revised forecasts should be prepared to keep forecasts relevant and up-to-date. Examples would be a revised three-month forecast every month for the next three-month period, or a revised forecast each month or each quarter up to the end of the annual budget period.

A **rolling forecast** is a forecast that is **continually updated**. When actual results are reported for a given time period (say for one month's results within an annual forecast period) a further forecast period is added and forecasts for intermediate time periods are updated. A rolling forecast can therefore be a 12-month forecast which is updated at the end of every month, with a further month added to the end of the forecast period and with figures for the intervening 11 months revised if necessary.

Cash flow control with budgets and revised forecasts

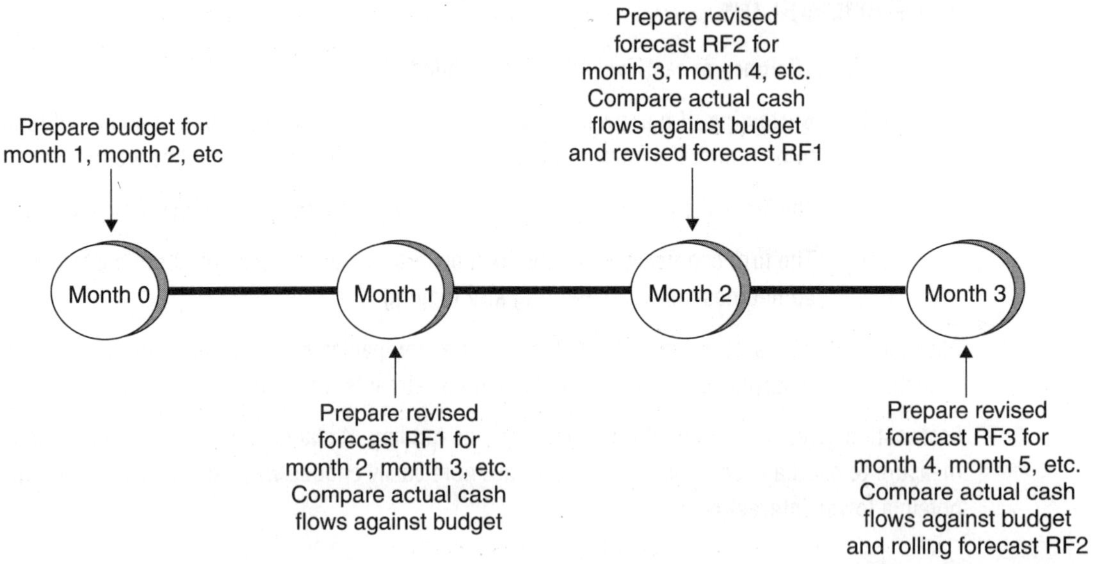

2.4 Strategic forecasts

FAST FORWARD

> Cash budgets and forecasts can be used for control reporting. Balance sheet based forecasts are used for long-term strategic analysis.

In **strategic forecasts**, a 'cash surplus' or 'funds deficit' is the **balancing item** after a forecast has been made for *all* the *other* items in the **balance sheet**.

For example, if a firm increases its credit period offered, leading to an increase in receivables, and intends to purchase non-current assets, what will be its requirements for cash? Such plans express the company's or group's likely future balance sheet as a consequence of adopting certain strategies.

Strategic forecasts should consider:

- The amount of funds required to pursue the chosen strategies
- The sources of those funds, including internally generated cash flows
- The strategy's potential consequences for liquidity and financial gearing

2.5 Assumptions of a forecast

Even fairly predictable items of income and spending (eg salary payments, and tax or social security deductions) cannot usually be forecast with total accuracy. Any forecast should therefore include a clear statement of the **assumptions** on which the figures are based. With clearly stated assumptions, a forecast can be tested for **reasonableness**.

For example, cash receipts from sales and receivables might be forecast on the assumption that sales will be a certain level, and customers will take a certain time to pay.

3 Cash budgets in receipts and payments format

FAST FORWARD

A cash budget is a detailed forecast of cash receipts, payments and balances over a planning period. It is formally adopted as part of the business plan or master budget for the period.

3.1 Assumptions

For each item of cash inflows or outflows, assumptions must be made about the **quantity** and timing of the flows. The total amount of receipts and payments will be derived from other budgets, such as the company's operating budgets and capital expenditure budget. Assumptions will already have been made for these to prepare the profit or loss budget. Assumptions about the **time to pay** must be introduced for cash forecasting.

The forecasting method can be either one or a combination of the following.

- Identifying a particular cash flow, and scheduling when it will be received or paid
- Projecting future trends and seasonal cycles in business activity and cash flows
- Analysing historical payment patterns of regular repeat payments

3.2 Preparing the cash budget

FAST FORWARD

Cash budgets are prepared by taking **operational budgets** and converting them into forecasts as to when receipts and payments occur. The forecast should indicate the highest and lowest cash balance in a period as well as the balance at the end.

The steps in preparing the cash budget are as follows:

Preparation

1 Set up a proforma cash budget

	Month 1	*Month 2*	*Month 3*
	$	$	$
Cash receipts			
Receipts from customers	X	X	X
Loan etc	X	X	X
	X	X	X
Cash payments			
Payments to suppliers	X	X	X
Wages etc	X	X	X
	X	X	X
Opening balance	X	X	X
Net cash flow (receipts - payments)	X	X	X
Closing balance	X	X	X

Sort out cash receipts

2 Establish budgeted sales month by month

3 Establish the length of credit period taken by customers

$$\text{Receivables collection period (no. of days credit)} = \frac{\text{average (or year - end) receivables during period}}{\text{total credit sales in period}} \times \text{no. of days in period}$$

4 Hence determine when budgeted sales revenue will be received as cash (by considering cash receipts from total receivables, ignoring any allowance for doubtful debts)

5 Establish when opening receivables will pay

6 Establish when any other cash income will be received

Sort out cash payments

7 Establish production quantities and material usage quantities each month

8 Establish material inventory changes and hence the quantity and cost of materials purchases each month

9 Establish the length of credit period taken from suppliers and hence calculate when cash payments to suppliers will be made

$$\text{Payables payment period (no. of days credit)} = \frac{\text{average (or year-end) payables during period}}{\text{total purchases on credit in period}} \times \text{no. of days in period}$$

10 Establish when amount due to opening payables will be paid

11 Establish when any other cash payments (excluding non-cash items such as depreciation) will be made

12 Show clearly on the bottom of the budget opening position, net cash flow and closing position

If an overdraft is shown, suggest delaying payments to suppliers, speeding up payments from customers, reducing production volumes or arranging further overdraft facilities

3.3 Cash payments

Assumptions about payments are easier to make than assumptions about income. Assumptions about payments to suppliers can take account of:

(a) The **credit terms** given by suppliers (or groups of suppliers), company policy on purchase orders and the administration of cheque payments, etc

(b) Any **specific supply arrangements**, (such as a delivery once every two months, with payment for each delivery at the end of the following month)

(c) **Past practice** (eg the proportion of invoices (by value) paid in the month of supply and invoice, the proportion paid in the month following, and so on)

(d) **Predictable dates** for certain payments, such as payments for rent, business rates, telephones, electricity and company tax

As a guideline, assumptions about payments should lean towards caution, ie if in doubt, budget for earlier payments.

3.4 Fixed cost expenditures

Some items of expenditure will be regarded as **fixed costs** in the operating budget. Salaries, office expenses and marketing expenditure are three such items. With some fixed costs, it could be assumed that there will be an **equal monthly expenditure** on each item, with cash payment in the month of expenditure perhaps, or in the month following. Other costs may not be monthly. If annual building rental is payable quarterly in advance, the budget should plan for payments on the specific dates.

3.5 Receipts

Assumptions about receipts might be more difficult to formulate than assumptions about payments.

(a) For a company that depends almost entirely on consumer sales by cash, credit card and debit card, the major uncertainty in the cash flow forecast will be the **volume of sales**. The timing of receipts from a large proportion of those sales will be predictable (payment with sale).

(b) Companies that have a **mixture of cash and credit sales** must attempt to **estimate** the **proportion** of **each** in the total sales figure, and then formulate assumptions for the timing pattern of receipts from credit sales.

(c) There are several ways of estimating when receipts will occur.

   (i) If the company has **specific credit terms**, such as a requirement to pay within 15 days of the invoice date, it could assume that:

      (1) Invoices will be sent out at the time of sale

      (2) A proportion, say 25%, will be paid within 15 days (1/2 month)

      (3) A proportion, say 65%, will be paid between 16 days and 30 days (one month after invoice)

      (4) A proportion (say 9%) will pay in the month following

      (5) There will be some bad debts (say 1%, a proportion that should be consistent with the company's budgeted expectations)

   (ii) If there is a policy of cash discounts for early payment, the **discounts allowed** should be provided for in the forecasts of receipts.

   (iii) The time **customers take to pay** can be estimated from past experience. Care should be taken to allow for seasonal variations and the possibility that payments can be slower at some times of the year than at others (for example, delays during holiday periods).

   (iv) **Payment patterns** can also vary from one country to another. Companies in France and Italy for example will often take several months after the invoice date to pay amounts due.

3.6 Calendar variations

Assumptions could be required to take account of calendar variations.

(a) **Days-in-the-month effect**. It could be assumed that receipts will be the same on every day of the 20th/21st/22nd/23rd etc working day each month. Alternatively, it could be assumed that receipts will be twice as high in the first five days of each month. Assumptions should generally be based on past experience.

(b) **Days-in-the-week effect**. Where appropriate, assumptions should be made about the cash inflows on each particular day of the week, with some days regularly producing higher cash inflows than other days. Such forecasts should be based on historical analysis.

Receipts for some companies, particularly retailers, follow a regular weekly pattern (with some variations for holidays and seasons of the year). Companies should be able to estimate total weekly takings in cash (notes and coins), cheques and credit card vouchers, the number of cheques and credit card vouchers handled and the deposit spread (for each day, the percentage of the total takings for the week, eg 10% on Monday, 15% on Tuesday).

3.7 Time periods and overdraft size

Dividing the forecast period into time periods should coincide as closely as possible with significant cash flow events, to provide management with information about the **high or low points for cash balances**. In other words, as well as predicting the **month end surplus or overdraft**, the **maximum overdraft *during* the month** should be predicted.

3.8 Example: timing of cash flows

Oak Tree Villa operates a retail business. Purchases are sold at cost plus 33$^1/_3$%. Or put another way, purchases are 75% of sales.

(a)

	Budgeted sales	*Labour cost*	*Expenses incurred*
	$	$	$
January	40,000	3,000	4,000
February	60,000	3,000	6,000
March	160,000	5,000	7,000
April	120,000	4,000	7,000

(b) It is management policy to have sufficient inventory in hand at the end of each month to meet sales demand in the next half month.

(c) Payables for materials and expenses are paid in the month after the purchases are made or the expenses incurred. Labour is paid in full by the end of each month.

(d) Expenses include a monthly depreciation charge of $2,000.

(e) (i) 75% of sales are for cash.
(ii) 25% of sales are on one month's interest-free credit.

(f) The company will buy equipment for cash costing $18,000 in February and will pay a dividend of $20,000 in March. The opening cash balance at 1 February is $1,000.

Required

(a) An income statement for February and March
(b) A cash budget for February and March

Solution

(a) INCOME STATEMENT

	February		March		Total	
	$	$	$	$	$	$
Sales		60,000		160,000		220,000
Cost of purchases (75%)		45,000		120,000		165,000
Gross profit		15,000		40,000		55,000
Less: labour	3,000		5,000		8,000	
expenses	6,000		7,000		13,000	
		9,000		12,000		21,000
		6,000		28,000		34,000

(b) *Workings*

(i) *Receipts:*

		$
in February	75% of Feb sales (75% × $60,000)	45,000
	+ 25% of Jan sales (25% × $40,000)	10,000
		55,000

		$
in March	75% of Mar sales (75% × $160,000)	120,000
	+25% of Feb sales (25% × $60,000)	15,000
		135,000

(ii)

	Purchases in January		*Purchases in February*
	$		$
Purchases:			
For Jan sales (50% of $30,000)	15,000		
For Feb sales (50% of $45,000)	22,500	(50% of $45,000)	22,500
For Mar sales	–	(50% of $120,000)	60,000
	37,500		82,500

These purchases are paid for in February and March.

(iii) *Expenses*. Cash expenses in January ($4,000 – $2,000) and February ($6,000 – $2,000) are paid for in February and March respectively. Depreciation is not a cash item.

CASH BUDGET

	February	*March*	*Total*
	$	$	$
Receipts from sales	55,000	135,000	190,000
Payments			
Trade payables	37,500	82,500	120,000
Expenses payables	2,000	4,000	6,000
Labour	3,000	5,000	8,000
Equipment purchase	18,000	–	18,000
Dividend	–	20,000	20,000
Total payments	60,500	111,500	172,000
Receipts less payments	(5,500)	23,500	18,000
Opening cash balance b/f	1,000	(4,500)*	1,000
Closing cash balance c/f	(4,500)*	19,000	19,000

Notes

* The cash balance at the end of February is carried forward as the opening cash balance for March.

1. The profit in February and March means that there is sufficient cash to operate the business as planned.
2. Steps should be taken either to ensure that an overdraft facility is available for the cash shortage at the end of February, or to defer certain payments so that the overdraft is avoided.

3.9 Cash budgets and opening receivables and payables

One situation which can be problematic is if you are required to analyse an **opening balance sheet** to decide how many outstanding receivables will pay what they owe in the first few months of the cash budget period, and how many outstanding payables must be paid.

3.10 Example: receivables and payables

For example, suppose that a balance sheet as at 31 December 20X4 shows that a company has the following receivables and payables.

Receivables	$150,000
Trade payables	$ 60,000

You are informed of the following.

(a) Customers are allowed two months to pay.
(b) 1½ months' credit is taken from trade suppliers.
(c) Sales and materials purchases were both made at an even monthly rate throughout 20X4.

Required

Determine in which months of 20X5 the customers will eventually pay and the suppliers will be paid.

Solution

(a) Since customers take two months to pay, the $150,000 of receivables in the balance sheet represent credit sales in November and December 20X4, who will pay in January and February 20X5 respectively. Since sales in 20X4 were at an equal monthly rate, the cash budget should plan for receipts of $75,000 each month in January and February from the receivables in the opening balance sheet.

(b) Similarly, since suppliers are paid after 1½ months, the balance sheet payables will be paid in January and the first half of February 20X5, which means that budgeted payments will be as follows.

	$
In January (purchases in second half of November and first half of December 20X4)	40,000
In February (purchases in second half of December 20X4)	20,000
Total payables in the balance sheet	60,000

(The balance sheet payables of $60,000 represent 1½ months' purchases, so that purchases in 20X4 must be $40,000 per month, which is $20,000 per half month.)

3.11 Example: a month-by-month cash budget in detail

Now you have some idea as to the underlying principles, let us put these to work. From the following information which relates to George and Zola, you are required to prepare a month by month cash budget for the second half of 20X5 and to append such brief comments as you consider might be helpful to management.

(a) The company's only product, a leather bag, sells at $40 and has a variable cost of $26 made up as follows.

Material $20
Labour $4
Variable overhead $2

(b) Fixed costs of $6,000 per month are paid on the 28th of each month.

(c) *Quantities sold/to be sold on credit*

May	*June*	*July*	*Aug*	*Sept*	*Oct*	*Nov*	*Dec*
1,000	1,200	1,400	1,600	1,800	2,000	2,200	2,600

(d) *Production quantities*

May	*June*	*July*	*Aug*	*Sept*	*Oct*	*Nov*	*Dec*
1,200	1,400	1,600	2,000	2,400	2,600	2,400	2,200

(e) Cash sales at a discount of 5% are expected to average 100 units a month.

(f) Customers are expected to settle their accounts by the end of the second month following sale.

(g) Suppliers of material are paid two months after the material is used in production.

(h) Wages are paid in the same month as they are incurred.

(i) 70% of the variable overhead is paid in the month of production, the remainder in the following month.

(j) Company tax of $18,000 is to be paid in October.

(k) A new delivery vehicle was bought in June, the cost of which, $8,000 is to be paid in August. The old vehicle was sold for $600, the buyer undertaking to pay in July.

(l) The company is expected to be $3,000 overdrawn at the bank at 30 June 20X5.

(m) The opening and closing inventories of raw materials, work in progress and finished goods are budgeted to be the same.

Solution

CASH BUDGET FOR 1 JULY TO 31 DECEMBER 20X5

	July	*Aug*	*Sept*	*Oct*	*Nov*	*Dec*	*Total*
	$	$	$	$	$	$	$
Receipts							
Credit sales	40,000	48,000	56,000	64,000	72,000	80,000	360,000
Cash sales	3,800	3,800	3,800	3,800	3,800	3,800	22,800
Sale of vehicles	600						600
	44,400	51,800	59,800	67,800	75,800	83,800	383,400
Payments							
Materials	24,000	28,000	32,000	40,000	48,000	52,000	224,000
Labour	6,400	8,000	9,600	10,400	9,600	8,800	52,800
Variable overhead (W1)	3,080	3,760	4,560	5,080	4,920	4,520	25,920
Fixed costs	6,000	6,000	6,000	6,000	6,000	6,000	36,000
Company tax				18,000			18,000
Purchase of vehicle		8,000					8,000
	39,480	53,760	52,160	79,480	68,520	71,320	364,720
Excess of receipts over payments	4,920	(1,960)	7,640	(11,680)	7,280	12,480	18,680
Balance b/f	(3,000)	1,920	(40)	7,600	(4,080)	3,200	(3,000)
Balance c/f	1,920	(40)	7,600	(4,080)	3,200	15,680	15,680

Working

Variable overhead

	June	*July*	*Aug*	*Sept*	*Oct*	*Nov*	*Dec*
	$	$	$	$	$	$	$
Variable overhead production cost	2,800	3,200	4,000	4,800	5,200	4,800	4,400
70% paid in month		2,240	2,800	3,360	3,640	3,360	3,080
30% in following month		840	960	1,200	1,440	1,560	1,440
		3,080	3,760	4,560	5,080	4,920	4,520

Comments

(a) There will be a small overdraft at the end of August but a much larger one at the end of October. It may be possible to delay payments to suppliers for longer than two months or to reduce purchases of materials or reduce the volume of production by running down existing inventory levels.

(b) If neither of these courses is possible, the company may need to negotiate overdraft facilities with its bank.

(c) The cash deficit is only temporary and by the end of December there will be a comfortable surplus. The use to which this cash will be put should ideally be planned in advance.

Exam focus point

The November 2005 exam had a 20-mark cash budget question in Section C. The pilot paper and the May 2005 paper both had a 5-mark question. This is an important topic. Make sure you can do a basic cash budget.

Question — Cash forecast

Tom Ward has worked for some years as a sales representative, but has recently been made redundant. He intends to start up in business on his own account, using $15,000 which he currently has invested. Tom maintains a bank account showing a small credit balance, and he plans to approach his bank for the necessary additional finance. Tom asks you for advice and provides the following additional information.

(a) Arrangements have been made to purchase non-current assets costing $8,000. These will be paid for at the end of September and are expected to have a five-year life, at the end of which they will possess a nil residual value.

(b) Inventories costing $5,000 will be acquired on 28 September and subsequent monthly purchases will be at a level sufficient to replace forecast sales for the month.

(c) Forecast monthly sales are $3,000 for October, $6,000 for November and December, and $10,500 from January 20X7 onwards.

(d) Selling price is fixed at the cost of inventory plus 50%.

(e) Two months' credit will be allowed to customers but only 1 month's credit will be received from suppliers of goods.

(f) Running expenses, including rent, are estimated at $1,600 per month, all paid in cash.

(g) Tom intends to make monthly cash drawings of $1,000.

Required

Prepare a forecast cash budget for the 6 months October 20X6 to March 20X7.

Answer

The opening cash balance at 1 October will consist of Tom's initial $15,000 less the $8,000 expended on non-current assets purchased in September, ie the opening balance is $7,000. Cash receipts from credit customers arise two months after the relevant sales.

Payments to suppliers are a little more tricky. We are told that cost of sales is 100/150 × sales. Thus for October cost of sales is 100/150 × $3,000 = $2,000. These goods will be purchased in October but not paid for until November. Similar calculations can be made for later months. The initial inventory of $5,000 is purchased in September and consequently paid for in October.

The forecast budget can now be constructed.

CASH FORECAST FOR THE SIX MONTHS ENDING 31 MARCH 20X7

	October	*November*	*December*	*January*	*February*	*March*
	$	$	$	$	$	$
Payments						
Suppliers	5,000	2,000	4,000	4,000	7,000	7,000
Running expenses	1,600	1,600	1,600	1,600	1,600	1,600
Drawings	1,000	1,000	1,000	1,000	1,000	1,000
	7,600	4,600	6,600	6,600	9,600	9,600
Receipts						
Customers	–	–	3,000	6,000	6,000	10,500
Surplus/(shortfall)	(7,600)	(4,600)	(3,600)	(600)	(3,600)	900
Opening balance	7,000	(600)	(5,200)	(8,800)	(9,400)	(13,000)
Closing balance	(600)	(5,200)	(8,800)	(9,400)	(13,000)	(12,100)

Question

Cash budget

You are presented with the following budgeted data for your organisation for the period November 20X1 to June 20X2. It has been extracted from functional budgets that have already been prepared.

	Nov X1	*Dec X1*	*Jan X2*	*Feb X2*	*Mar X2*	*Apr X2*	*May X2*	*June X2*
	$	$	$	$	$	$	$	$
Sales	80,000	100,000	110,000	130,000	140,000	150,000	160,000	180,000
Purchases	40,000	60,000	80,000	90,000	110,000	130,000	140,000	150,000
Wages	10,000	12,000	16,000	20,000	24,000	28,000	32,000	36,000
Overheads	10,000	10,000	15,000	15,000	15,000	20,000	20,000	20,000
Dividends		20,000						40,000
Capital expenditure			30,000			40,000		

You are also told the following.

(a) Sales are 40% cash, 60% credit. Credit sales are paid two months after the month of sales.
(b) Purchases are paid the month following purchase.
(c) 75% of wages are paid in the current month and 25% the following month.
(d) Overheads are paid the month after they are incurred.
(e) Dividends are paid three months after they are declared.
(f) Capital expenditure is paid two months after it is incurred.
(g) The opening cash balance on 1 January 20X2 is $15,000.

The managing director is pleased with the above figures as they show sales will have increased by more than 100% in the period under review. In order to achieve this he has arranged a bank overdraft with a ceiling of $50,000 to accommodate the increased inventory levels and wage bill for overtime worked.

Required

(a) Prepare a cash budget for the six month period January to June 20X2.

(b) Comment upon your results in the light of your managing director's comments and offer advice.

(c) If you have access to a computer spreadsheet package and you know how to use it, try setting up the cash budget on it. Then make a copy of the budget and try making changes to the estimates to see their effect on cash flow.

Answer

(a)

	January	*February*	*March*	*April*	*May*	*June*
	$'000	$'000	$'000	$'000	$'000	$'000
Sales revenue						
Cash (40%)	44	52	56	60	64	72
Credit (60%, 2 months)	48	60	66	78	84	90
	92	112	122	138	148	162
Purchases	60	80	90	110	130	140
Wages 75%	12	15	18	21	24	27
25%	3	4	5	6	7	8
Overheads	10	15	15	15	20	20
Dividends			20			
Capital expenditure			30			40
	85	114	178	152	181	235
b/f	15	22	20	(36)	(50)	(83)
Net cash flow	7	(2)	(56)	(14)	(33)	(73)
c/f	22	20	(36)	(50)	(83)	(156)

(b) The overdraft arrangements are quite inadequate to service the cash needs of the business over the six-month period. If the figures are realistic then action should be taken now to avoid difficulties in the near future. The following are possible courses of action.

(i) **Activities** could be **curtailed**.

(ii) Other **sources of cash** could be **explored**, for example a long-term loan to finance the capital expenditure and a factoring arrangement to provide cash due from receivables more quickly.

(iii) Efforts to **increase the speed of debt collection** could be made.

(iv) **Payments to suppliers** could be **delayed**.

(v) The **dividend payments** could be **postponed** (the figures indicate that this is a small company, possibly owner-managed).

(vi) Staff might be **persuaded to work at a lower rate** in return for, say, an annual bonus or a profit-sharing agreement.

(vii) **Extra staff** might be taken on to reduce the amount of overtime paid.

(viii) The **inventory holding policy** should be **reviewed**; it may be possible to meet demand from current production and minimise cash tied up in inventories.

4 Cleared funds cash forecasts

4.1 Cleared funds

FAST FORWARD

Cleared funds are used for short-term planning. They take clearance delays into account.

Float refers to the amount of money tied up between the time a payment is initiated and **cleared funds** become available in the recipient's bank account for immediate spending.

Knowing what **cleared funds** are likely to be has a direct and immediate relevance to cash management in the **short-term**. If a company expects to have insufficient cleared funds in the next few days to meet a payment obligation, it must either borrow funds to meet the obligation or (if possible) defer the payment until there are cash receipts to cover it.

A **cleared funds cash forecast** is a short-term cash forecast of the cleared funds available to a company in its bank accounts, or of the funding deficit that must be met by **immediate borrowing**. Cleared funds forecasts should be reviewed and updated regularly, *daily* for companies with large and uncertain cash flows. Uncertainty might be caused by the internal organisation of the recipient.

(a) The recipient might delay the banking of cheques.
(b) Cheques do sometimes get held up by bureaucracy.

4.2 Preparing a cleared funds forecast

There should be relatively few items in a cleared funds forecast, and each forecast should generally relate to a **particular bank account** unless balances can be netted against each other.

A cleared funds forecast can be prepared by a combination of three methods.

(a) **Obtaining information** from the **company's banks**.

(b) **Forecasting for other receipts and payments** that have occurred but have not yet been lodged with a bank. You should be already familiar with bank reconciliations.

(c) **Adapting the cash budget**.

  (i) Analyse the cash budget into suitable time periods.
  (ii) Identify cash book payments and receipts.
  (iii) Adjust these for float times.

Question — Types of forecast

Kim O'Hara runs an import/export retail business, largely on a cash basis. He likes to negotiate the best possible deals from his suppliers and this generally means a strict adherence to any payment terms so as to benefit from any settlement discounts: he also orders his supplies at the last possible moment, as he is a firm believer in 'just-in-time' philosophy. On the other hand Creighton, a listed company, is a large software house, dealing with major clients. Which type of forecast would be most appropriate to each business?

Answer

Kim O'Hara would be best served by a **cleared funds forecast**, Creighton by a **cash book based forecast**.

5 Cash forecasts based on financial statements

FAST FORWARD

A cash flow forecast can be prepared by projecting the movement in the balance sheet or income statement.

5.1 Balance sheet

The balance sheet is produced for **financial accounting purposes. It is not an estimate of cash inflows and outflows**. However a number of sequential forecasts can be produced, for example a forecast of the balance sheet at the end of each year for the next five years.

A balance sheet based forecast is an estimate of the company's balance sheet at a future date. It is used to identify either the cash surplus or the funding shortfall in the company's balance sheet at the **forecast date**.

5.2 Estimating a future balance sheet

A balance sheet estimate calls for some prediction of the amount/value of each item in the company's balance sheet, **excluding cash and short-term investments**, as these are what we are trying to predict. A forecast is prepared by taking each item in the balance sheet, and estimating what its value might be at the future date. The assumptions used are critical, and the following guidelines are suggested.

(a) Intangible **non-current assets** (gross book value) and long term investments, if there are any, should be taken at their current value unless there is good reason for another treatment.

(b) Some estimate of **non-current asset purchases** (and disposals) will be required. Revaluations can be ignored as they are not cash flows.

(c) **Current assets**. Balance sheet estimates of inventories and receivables can be based on fairly simple assumptions. The estimated value for inventories and receivables can be made in any of the following ways.

   (i) **Same as current amounts**. This is unlikely if business has boomed.

   (ii) **Increase by a certain percentage**, to allow for growth in business volume. For example, the volume of receivables might be expected to increase by a similar amount.

   (iii) **Decrease by a certain percentage**, to allow for tighter management control over working capital.

   (iv) **Assume to be a certain percentage** of the company's estimated **annual sales revenue** for the year.

   (v) The firm can assume that the operating cycle will more or less **remain the same**. In other words, if a firm's customers take two months to pay, this relationship can be expected to continue.

(d) **Current liabilities**. Some itemising of current liabilities will be necessary, because no single set of assumptions can accurately estimate them collectively.

   (i) **Trade payables and accruals** can be estimated in a similar way to current assets, as indicated above.

   (ii) Current liabilities include **bank loans** due for repayment within 12 months. These can be identified individually.

(iii) **Bank overdraft facilities** might be in place. It could be appropriate to assume that there will be no overdraft in the forecast balance sheet. Any available overdraft facility can be considered later when the company's overall cash requirements are identified.

(iv) **Taxation**. Any company tax payable should be estimated from anticipated profits and based on an estimated percentage of those profits.

(v) **Dividends payable**. Any ordinary dividend payable should be estimated from anticipated profits, and any preferred dividend payable can be predicted from the coupon rate of dividend for the company's preferred shares.

(vi) **Other payables** can be included if required and are of significant value.

(e) **Long-term payables**. Long-term payables are likely to consist of long-term loans, and any other long-term finance debt. Unless the company has already arranged further long-term borrowing, this item should include just existing long-term debts, minus debts that will be repaid before the balance sheet date.

(f) **Share capital and reserves**. With the exception of the retained earnings, the estimated balance sheet figures for share capital and other reserves should be the same as their current amount unless it is expected or known that a new issue of shares will take place before the balance sheet date.

(g) An estimate is required of the change in the company's **accumulated profits** in the period up to the balance sheet date. This reserve should be calculated as:

(i) The existing value of accumulated profits

(ii) Plus further retained profits anticipated in the period to the balance sheet date (ie post tax profits minus estimated dividends)

The various estimates should now be brought together into a balance sheet. The figures on each side of the balance sheet will not be equal, and there will be one of the following.

(a) A surplus of share capital and reserves over net assets (total assets minus total liabilities). If this occurs, the company will be forecasting a **cash surplus**.

(b) A surplus of net assets over share capital and reserves. If this occurs, the company will be forecasting a **funding deficit**.

5.3 Example

Alpha has an existing balance sheet and an estimated balance sheet in one year's time before the necessary extra funding is taken into account, as follows. (Note that for the purpose of this exercise liabilities have been deducted from assets.)

	Existing		*Forecast after one year*	
	$	$	$	$
Non-current assets		100,000		180,000
Current assets	90,000		100,000	
Short-term payables	(60,000)		(90,000)	
Net current assets		30,000		10,000
		130,000		190,000
Long-term payables		(20,000)		(20,000)
Deferred taxation		(10,000)		(10,000)
Total net assets		100,000		160,000

	Existing		Forecast after one year	
	$	$	$	$
Share capital and reserves				
Ordinary share capital		50,000		50,000
Other reserves		20,000		20,000
Retained earnings		30,000		50,000
		100,000		120,000

The company is expecting to increase its net assets in the next year by $60,000 ($160,000 – $100,000) but expects retained profits for the year to be only $20,000 ($50,000 – $30,000). There is an excess of net assets over share capital and reserves amounting to $40,000 ($160,000 – $120,000), which is a funding deficit. The company must consider ways of obtaining extra cash (eg by borrowing) to cover the deficit. If it cannot, it will need to keep its assets below the forecast amount, or to have higher short-term payables.

A revised projected balance sheet can then be prepared by introducing these new sources of funds. This should be checked for realism (eg by ratio analysis) to ensure that the proportion of the balance sheet made up by non-current assets and working capital, etc is sensible.

Main uses of balance sheet-based forecasts

(a) As longer-term (strategic) estimates, to assess the scale of funding requirements or cash surpluses the company expects over time

(b) To act as a check on the realism of cash flow-based forecasts (The estimated balance sheet should be **roughly** consistent with the net cash change in the cash budget, after allowing for approximations in the balance sheet forecast assumptions)

5.4 Deriving cash flow from income statement and balance sheet information

The previous paragraphs concentrated on preparing a forecast balance sheet, with estimated figures for receivables, payables and inventory. Cash requirements might therefore be presented as the **'balancing figure'**. However, it is possible to derive a forecast figure for cash flows using both the balance sheet and income statement.

This is examined in the example below, which is based on the first question (Profits and cash flow) in this chapter. For the time being, assume that there is no depreciation to worry about. The task is to get from profit to operational cash flow, by taking into account movements in working capital.

	Profit	*Operational cash flow*
	$	$
Sales	200,000	200,000
Opening receivables (∴ received in year)		15,000
Closing receivables (outstanding at year end)		(24,000)
Cash in		191,000
Cost of sales	170,000	170,000
Closing inventory (purchased, but not used, in year)		21,000
Opening inventory (used, but not purchased, in year)		(12,000)
Purchases in year		179,000
Opening payables (∴ paid in year)		11,000
Closing payables (outstanding at year end)		(14,000)
Cash out		176,000
Profit/operational cash flow	30,000	15,000

		Profit $	*Operational cash flow* $
Profit			30,000
(Increase)/Decrease in inventories	Opening	12,000	
	Closing	(21,000)	
			(9,000)
(Increase)/Decrease in receivables	Opening	15,000	
	Closing	(24,000)	
			(9,000)
Increase/(Decrease) in payables	Closing	14,000	
	Opening	(11,000)	
			3,000
Operational cash flow			15,000

In practice, a business will make many other adjustments. The profit figure includes items which do not involve the movement of cash, such as the annual depreciation charge, which will have to be added back to arrive at a figure for cash.

Both 'receipts and payments' forecasts and forecasts based on financial statements could be used alongside each other. The cash management section and the financial controller's section should reconcile differences between forecasts on a continuing basis, so that the forecast can be made more accurate as time goes on.

6 Inflation and cash budgeting

6.1 Index numbers

FAST FORWARD

When results of a business are being compared over a period of time for internal management purposes, it is up to managers of the business to agree and use an appropriate method of allowing for changing price levels. The usual method is to use a series of index numbers.

Key term

An **index** is a measure, over a period of time, of the average **changes** in the values (prices or quantities) of a group of items.

6.2 The use of index numbers in cash forecasting and budgeting

What is the use of index numbers in **cash budgeting and forecasting**? The person preparing the cash budget is not particularly interested in prices in 'real terms': instead, it is the exact monetary amount that he or she is interested in. After all, bank overdrafts, for example, are expressed in fixed monetary amounts which do not allow for inflation.

Index numbers are still useful, however.

(a) Index numbers might be used to **predict future cash inflows**. For example, if it is assumed that 500,000 units will be sold in three or four months time, an estimate of future monetary prices gives some idea of the amount **in cash terms** that can be expected if a forecast index of prices is applied to estimated sales volumes.

(b) Similarly, with cash outflows, an **estimated future price index** can suggest the **likely size of cash payments**.

(c) Their use in forecasting can also suggest a need for **increased borrowing limits**, which might be fixed in monetary terms.

Different items, such as capital items, costs of various kinds, and revenues, are likely to be subject to differing rates of inflation, and different indices may therefore be appropriate for different items.

Question

Budget estimates

You are assisting with the work on a maintenance department's budget for the next quarter of 20X4. The maintenance department's budget for the current quarter (just ending) is $200,000.

	Quantity used in current quarter	*Average price payable per unit*	
		Current quarter	*Next quarter*
	Units	$	$
Material A	9	10	10.20
Material B	13	12	12.50
Material C	8	9	9.00
Material D	20	25	26.00

A base weighted index for the next quarter stands at 103.5, compared to 100 for this quarter, for the price of input quantities.

Required

(a) Estimate the budget for the next quarter, assuming that the quantities of each material to be used:

(i) Remain the same
(ii) Increase by 10%

(b) Give reasons why your budget estimate could be in error.

Answer

(a) (i) The index suggests prices will increase by 3.5% and so produces a budget of $200,000 × 1.035 = $207,000.

(ii) The budget in (i) assumes that quantities consumed remain the same. If quantities increase by 10% the budget will be $207,000 × 110% = $227,700.

(b) The budget estimates could be in error for a number of reasons.

(i) The **estimates** of quantities and prices for next quarter could be inaccurate.

(ii) The **current budget** (of $200,000) may not be a **suitable basis** on which to base the next quarter's budget. It may have been incorrectly set or next period's workload may not reflect that of the current period.

(iii) The maintenance department may have a **budget limit** imposed on it and may not be allowed to increase its budget.

(iv) The **weightings** on which the index is made may **go out of date**.

7 Computer models and sensitivity analysis

7.1 Sensitivity analysis

Key term

> **Sensitivity analysis** is a modelling and risk assessment procedure in which changes are made to significant variables in order to determine the effect of these changes on the planned outcome. Particular attention is thereafter paid to variables identified as being of special importance. *(OT 2000)*

FAST FORWARD

> **Sensitivity analysis** tests the results of a forecast to see how sensitive the results are to changes in inputs (eg lower or higher interest rates). **Spreadsheet modelling** is used for this purpose.

Sensitivity analysis is a method commonly used in planning, especially by companies using a **spreadsheet model** or other **financial modelling package**. Changes are made to estimates of key variables to establish how they could critically affect the outcome of the plan.

Sensitivity analysis tests the 'responsiveness' of profitability or cash flow to changes in one of the budget variables. For example, it would be possible to test the income statement budget and cash budget for:

- An unforeseen 10% rise in material costs
- An unforeseen 5% drop in productivity
- A shortfall in sales volumes of, say, 10%
- A labour strike of, say, one month
- A delay of six months in opening a new plant or operation

Computer cash forecast models allow the user to test different assumptions and ask questions about the consequences of different future events or outcomes. Alternative methods of uncertainty analysis include:

(a) **Preparing** a **series** of **different forecasts**, each assuming a different scenario

(b) **Preparing cash forecasts** as a **range of possible outcomes**, from most pessimistic through most likely, to most optimistic

(c) **Carrying out sensitivity analysis** on key items of cash flow (in terms of quantity and timing) to identify the consequences for borrowing/investing

(d) **Using probability analysis** by assigning probabilities to a range of values for key uncertain cash flow items

7.2 Example: sensitivity analysis

A company setting up a subsidiary prepared a cash budget. As with many start-ups, initial expenditures were expected to be high in comparison with first year revenues. The company's budget year ended on 31 March and the operation was planned to commence on 1 June of the previous year. Selling to customers would not begin until 1 August. Revenue was forecast at $2 million for the period to 31 March.

The initial cash budget, illustrated below along with the revised budget, indicated a maximum deficit of about $750,000–$800,000 in September and October. The main areas of uncertainty were sales revenue, one major item of production cost and marketing costs.

Lower than anticipated revenues, and excessive production costs, would possibly create a bigger cash deficit than the company could afford. Management believed, however, that controls over marketing expenditure would ensure that such costs should not exceed budget.

The cash flow model was used for sensitivity analysis. Assumptions were changed. Estimated sales revenue was reduced by 25% and production costs increased by 50%. The output from the revised model indicated a resulting cash deficit of about $1.2 million, **just** within the funding limit the company would allow for the new operation. Management concluded that the budget was acceptable, but that revenue, production costs and marketing costs should be continually reviewed.

Original cash budget	*June* $'000	*July* $'000	*Aug* $'000	*Sept* $'000	*Oct* $'000	*Nov* $'000	*Dec* $'000	*Total* $'000
Sales	0	0	160	210	280	360	490	1,500
Total inflows	0	0	160	210	280	360	490	1,500
Set-up costs	120	20	0	0	0	0	0	140
Production	100	100	100	100	100	100	100	700
Distribution	0	0	20	20	20	20	20	100
Marketing and advertising	0	150	150	75	75	75	75	600
Staff costs	10	20	24	24	24	24	24	150
General overheads	6	14	16	16	16	16	16	100
Accommodation	0	25	0	0	25	0	0	50
Capital equipment	30	0	0	10	0	0	0	40
Total outflows	266	329	310	245	260	235	235	1,880
Net inflow/(outflow)	(266)	(329)	(150)	(35)	20	125	255	(380)
Cumulative cash flow	(266)	(595)	(745)	(780)	(760)	(635)	(380)	(380)

Revised cash budget	*June* $'000	*July* $'000	*Aug* $'000	*Sept* $'000	*Oct* $'000	*Nov* $'000	*Dec* $'000	*Total* $'000
Sales	0	0	120	158	210	270	367	1,125
Total inflows	0	0	120	158	210	270	367	1,125
Set-up costs	120	20	0	0	0	0	0	140
Production	150	150	150	150	150	150	150	1,050
Distribution	0	0	20	20	20	20	20	100
Marketing and advertising	0	150	150	75	75	75	75	600
Staff costs	10	20	24	24	24	24	24	150
General overheads	6	14	16	16	16	16	16	100
Accommodation	0	25	0	0	25	0	0	50
Capital equipment	30	0	0	10	0	0	0	40
Total outflows	316	379	360	295	310	285	285	2,230
Net inflow/(outflow)	(316)	(379)	(240)	(137)	(100)	(15)	82	(1,105)
Cumulative cash flow	(316)	(695)	(935)	(1,072)	(1,172)	(1,187)	(1,105)	(1,105)

7.3 Spreadsheets

FAST FORWARD

Spreadsheets make it possible to easily adjust forecasts for changes in variables such as interest or inflation rates.

Exam focus point

You should be familiar with spreadsheets already. We provide below an example of how a spreadsheet can be used in cash budgeting and forecasting.

7.4 Example: preparing a cash flow projection

A loan officer of a bank advising a small company wishes to assess the company's cash flow using a spreadsheet model. The cash flow projection is to provide a monthly cash flow analysis over a 5 year period. The following data is relevant.

(a) On 1 January 20X4 the company expects to have $15,000 in the bank. Sales in January are expected to be $25,000, and a growth rate of 1.25% per month in sales is predicted throughout the forecast period.

(b) The company buys inventory one month in advance and pays in cash. All sales are on credit. There are no bad debts.

(c) On average, payment is received from customers as follows.

  (i) 60% one month in arrears
  (ii) 40% two months in arrears

(d) The cost of sales is 65% of sales value. Overhead costs (cash expenses) are expected to be $6,500 per month, rising by 5% at the start of each new calendar year.

(e) Purchases of capital equipment and payments of tax, interest charges and dividends must also be provided for within the model. The loans officer has advised the company that the interest rate on bank overdrafts is expected to be 1.695% per month.

The loans officer might decide to label the spreadsheet rows and columns as follows.

	A	B	C	D	E	F
1:		*20X4*				
2:		*Jan*	*Feb*	*March*	*April*	*May*
3:		$	$	$	$	$
4:	Sales					
5:	Cash receipts:					
6:	One months in arrears					
7:	Two months in arrears					
8:	Three months in arrears					
9:	Total receipts					
10:						
11:	Cash payments:					
12:	Inventory					
13:	Overheads					
14:	Interest					
15:	Tax					
16:	Dividends					
17:	Capital purchases					
18:	Total payments					
19:						
20:	Cash receipts less payments					
21:	Balance b/f					
22:	Balance c/f					

Your task is to construct the necessary formulae.

Solution

The formulae required can be constructed in a variety of ways. One way would be to insert some 'constant' values into cells of the spreadsheet and then cross-refer each formula to these constants, or absolutes.

Row	Column A	B
23:	Sales growth factor per month	1.0125
24:	Interest rate per month	0.01695
25:	Debts paid within 1 month	0.6
26:	Debts paid within 2 months	0.4
27:	Debts paid within 3 months	0
28:	Bad debts	0
29:	Cost of sales as proportion of sales	0.65

Alternatively, these values could be specified in the formulae in the spreadsheet. The advantage of setting up key data like this separately is that in the event of a change in say, interest rates, only one figure needs to be changed and there is no need for a search through the spreadsheet for relevant formulae.

Examples of constructing formulae for the spreadsheet are as follows.

(a) The formulae for sales in February 20X4, in this example, would be (+B4 * B23), in March 20X1 (+C4 * B23), in April 20X4 (+D4 * B23) etc. Replication of the formula could be used to save input time.

(b) The formula for cash receipts in April 20X4 would be:

E6 = +D4 * B25
E7 = +C4 * B26
E8 = +B4 * B27
E9 = + E6 + E7 + E8

(c) Cash payments for inventory would be expressed as the cost of sales in the previous month; for February 20X4, the formula in cell C12 would be:

+ B4 * B29

(d) Total cash payments in May 20X4 would be the sum of cells F12 to F17, ie the formula in cell F18 would be:

@ SUM (F12..F17)

and so on.

Input data would include the opening cash balance on 1 January 20X4, dividend and tax payments, capital purchases, sales in January 20X4, the constant values (in our example in column B, rows 23 to 29) and the other data needed to establish cash receipts and payments in the first month or so of the forecast period (eg receipts in January 20X4 will depend on sales in November and December 20X3, which the simplified model shown here has not provided for).

With this input data, and the spreadsheet formulae, a full cash flow projection for the five year period can be produced and, if required, printed out.

Question — **Sensitivity analysis**

Whenever a forecast or budget is made, management should consider asking 'what if' questions, and so carry out a form of sensitivity analysis. Using the example above, how would you take account of the following changed assumptions? Describe what amendments would need to be made to the contents of individual cells.

(a) What if the payment pattern from customers is:

1 month in arrears	40%
2 months in arrears	50%
3 months in arrears	10%?

(b) What if sales growth is only ½% per month?

Answer

Using the spreadsheet model, the answers to these questions can be obtained simply and quickly, using the editing facility in the program.

(a) To test the consequences of slower payments by customers, it would merely be necessary to alter the contents of cells B25, B26 and B27 in our example from 0.6, 0.4 and 0 to 0.4, 0.5 and 0.1 respectively, and then to run the model again.

(b) Similarly, the consequences for cash flow of slower sales growth of only ½% per month can be tested by altering the value of Cell B23 in our example from 1.0125 to 1.005.

7.5 Quality control of forecasts

When actual results differ from budget, it can be tempting to conclude that plans never work out in practice. However, planning is a vital management activity, and if actual results differ from the plan, it is important to find out whether the *planning* processes can be improved.

Accuracy of cash flow forecasts can be enhanced by:

(a) **Reviewing actual cash flows** against the **forecasts**, learning from past mistakes, and

(b) **Updating rolling forecasts** or **revised forecasts**, where useful, to replace earlier, less reliable forecasts

A constant monthly amount for receipts and payments will often indicate either sloppy cash forecasting practice, or a high degree of uncertainty in the forecast, since it is rare for specific receivables and payables to remain unchanged except where there is a formal arrangement.

As a financial year progresses, the actual cash flows for the past months could show large variances from budget, but a rolling forecast indicates that the original budget for the end-of-year cash balance will still be achieved. This could occur if the rolling forecast has been prepared by adjusting the forecast for the unexpired months of the year, in order to keep the annual budget (on paper at least) for the end-of-year cash position. Where this occurs, suspicion must arise that the rolling forecast has been prepared with little thought.

Unchanged figures over a number of months of revised forecast submissions are also an indication of a **weak forecasting system**. It could be that business expectations have not changed; however there are few businesses that do not fluctuate with market conditions. A more likely explanation is that the rolling cash forecast has been prepared by copying the figures from the previous forecast or that a new revised forecast has not been prepared at all.

Question

Operating cash flow

Frosty Ice Cream had sales in the last year of $150,000, and purchases of $115,000. At the start of the year inventories were $15,000, receivables were $5,000 and payables were $10,000. At the end of the year inventories were $10,000, receivables were $8,000 and payables were $12,000.

What was the operating cash flow for the period?

A $30,000
B $32,000

C $34,000
D $40,000

Answer

C

	$
Sales	150,000
Add opening receivables	5,000
Less closing receivables	(8,000)
	147,000
Less purchases	(115,000)
Less opening payables	(10,000)
Add closing payables	12,000
Operating cash flow	34,000

Chapter Roundup

- **Trading profits** need to be distinguished from cash flows. A company can make losses but still have a net cash income from trading. A company can also make profits but have a net cash deficit on its trading operations.
- **Cash flow forecasts** provide an early warning of liquidity problems and funding needs. **Banks** often expect business customers to provide a cash forecast as a condition of lending.
- There are **two main ways** of preparing a cash forecast.
  - A forecast can be prepared of cash receipts and payments, and net cash flows (cash flow based forecasts).
  - Alternatively, a cash surplus or funding requirement can be prepared by constructing a forecast balance sheet (balance sheet-based forecast), or adjusting other financial statements.
- Cash budgets and forecasts can be used for **control reporting**. Balance sheet based forecasts are used for long-term strategic analysis.
- A **cash budget** is a detailed forecast of cash receipts, payments and balances over a planning period. It is formally adopted as part of the business plan or master budget for the period.
- Cash budgets are prepared by taking **operational budgets** and converting them into forecasts as to when receipts and payments occur. The forecast should indicate the highest and lowest cash balance in a period as well as the balance at the end.
- **Cleared funds** are used for short-term planning. They take clearance delays into account.
- A cash flow forecast can be prepared by projecting the movement in the balance sheet or income statement.
- A number of **statistical and modelling techniques** can be used to reduce uncertainty in cash flow forecasting. An example is the use of inflation indices.
- **Sensitivity analysis** tests the results of a forecast to see how sensitive the results are to changes in inputs (eg lower or higher interest rates). **Spreadsheet modelling** is used for this purpose.
- Spreadsheets make it possible to easily adjust forecasts for changes in variables such as interest or inflation rates.

Quick Quiz

1 Operational cash flows of a business could be improved directly by:

- *Reducing/Increasing* receivables
- *Reducing/Increasing* inventories
- *Reducing/Increasing* the credit period for the company's trade payables

Delete the word in italics that does not apply.

2 Explain what a rolling forecast is in not more than 20 words.

3 The 'float' is the time between (A) .... and (B) .... (Fill in the blanks)

4 List the twelve main steps involved in preparing a cash budget.

5 'Changes are made to estimates of key variables to establish how they could critically affect the outcome of the plan.' What technique does this describe?

6 Explain what an index is in not more than 30 words.

7 Heavy Metal is preparing its cash flow forecast for the next quarter. Which of the following items should be excluded from the calculations?

A The receipt of a bank loan that has been raised for the purpose of investment in a new rolling mill

B Depreciation of the new rolling mill

C A tax payment that is due to be made, but which relates to profits earned in a previous accounting period

D Disposal proceeds from the sale of the old rolling mill

Answers to Quick Quiz

1 The following words are those which you should *not* have deleted.

- *Reducing* receivables
- *Reducing* inventories
- *Increasing* the credit period for the company's trade payables

2 A forecast that is continually updated

3 (A) Initiation of a payment

(B) When cleared funds become available in the recipient's bank account

4 *Step*

1	Set up a proforma cash budget
2	Establish budgeted sales month by month
3	Establish the length of credit period taken by customers
4	Determine when budgeted sales revenue will be received as cash
5	Establish when opening receivables will pay
6	Establish when any other cash income will be received
7	Establish production quantities and material usage quantities each month

8	Establish material inventory changes and quantity and cost of month-by-month materials purchases
9	Establish length of credit period taken from suppliers and hence calculate when cash payments to suppliers will be made
10	Establish when amount due to opening payables will be pald
11	Establish when any other cash payments will be made
12	Show clearly on the bottom of the budget opening position, net cash flow and closing position

5 Sensitivity analysis

6 A measure over a period of time of the average changes in the values (prices or quantities) of a group of items

7 B This is a non-cash item and should therefore be excluded.

Now try the question below from the Exam Question Bank

Number	Level	Marks	Time
Q28	Examination	20	36 mins

17

Cash management

Introduction

How much cash should a company keep on hand or on 'short call' at a bank? The financial manager must balance **liquidity** with **profitability**. He must also be aware of the means to ease cash shortages. The Baumol and Miller-Orr models can be used to assist in cash management. You must understand these and be able to apply them.

Topic list	Learning outcomes	Syllabus references	Ability required
1 The need for cash management	D (iv)	D (6)	Comprehension
2 Cash management services	D (iv)	D (6)	Comprehension
3 Inventory approach to cash management	D (iv)	D (6)	Application
4 Applying probabilities in cash management	D (iv)	D (6)	Application

1 The need for cash management

FAST FORWARD

Optimal **cash** holding levels can be calculated from formal models.

Key term

Cash management models are sophisticated cash flow forecasting models which assist management in determining how to balance the cash needs of an organisation. Cash management models might help in areas such as optimising cash balances, in the management of customer, supplier, investor and company investor needs, in the decision to buy or invest shares or in the decision as to the optimum method of financing working capital. *(OT 2000)*

1.1 Cash flow problems

We have already used the concept of the **operating cycle**, which connects investment in working capital with cash flows. Cash flow problems can arise in several ways.

CASH FLOW PROBLEMS	
Making losses	Continual losses will eventually mean problems, whose timing depends on the size of losses and whether depreciation is significant; if it is, problems arise on replacement of assets
Inflation	Ever-increasing cash flows required just to replace used-up and worn out assets
Growth	Growth means business needs to support more receivables and inventory
Seasonal business	Cash flow difficulties may occur at certain times when cash inflows are low and outflows high, as inventories are being built up
One-off items of expenditure	Large items such as a loan repayment or the purchase of expensive non-current asset such as freehold land

1.2 Methods of easing cash shortages

FAST FORWARD

Cash shortages can be eased by postponing capital expenditure, selling assets, taking longer to pay creditors and pressing debtors for earlier payment (leading and lagging).

1.2.1 Improving the business

Cash deficits can arise out of **basic trading factors** underlying the business such as falling sales or increasing costs. Clearly, the way to deal with these items is to take normal business measures, rectifying the fall in sales by marketing activities or, if this cannot be achieved, by cutting costs.

1.2.2 Controlling the operating cycle: short-term deficiencies

Cash deficits can also arise out of the business's management of the operating cycle and from timing differences. The following are possibilities.

(a) **Borrowing** from the bank. This is only a short-term measure. It is possible that a bank will convert an overdraft into a long-term loan, or perhaps new overdraft limits can be set up.

(b) **Raising capital.** This is likely to be expensive and should be generally used for long-term investment, not short term cash management.

(c) **Different sources of finance** (such as leasing) might be used.

When a company cannot obtain resources from any other source such as a loan or an increased overdraft, it can take the following steps.

(a) **Postponing capital expenditure**

(i) It might be imprudent to postpone expenditure on non-current assets which are needed for the **development** and **growth** of the business.

(ii) On the other hand, some **capital expenditures** might be **postponable** without serious consequences. The routine replacement of motor vehicles is an example. If a company's policy is to replace company cars every two years, it may decide, if cash is short, to replace cars every three years.

(b) **Accelerating cash inflows which would otherwise be expected in a later period**

The most obvious way of bringing forward cash inflows would be to press receivables for earlier payment (leading and lagging receivables).

(c) **Reversing past investment decisions by selling assets previously acquired**

Some assets are less crucial to a business than others and so if cash flow problems are severe, the option of selling short-term investments or even property might have to be considered.

(d) **Negotiating a reduction in cash outflows, so as to postpone or even reduce payments**

There are several ways in which this could be done.

(i) **Longer credit** might be taken from suppliers (leading and lagging payables).

(ii) **Loan repayments** could be rescheduled by agreement with a bank.

(iii) A **deferral of the payment of tax** could be agreed with the taxation authorities.

(iv) **Dividend payments** could be **reduced**. Dividend payments are discretionary cash outflows, although a company's directors might be constrained by shareholders' expectations.

(v) **Inventory levels** could decrease to reduce the amount of money tied up in their production cost.

1.3 Example: leading and lagging

Assume that Gilbert Gosayne sells Nullas. Each Nulla costs $50 to make and is sold for $100. The bank has refused an overdraft to Gilbert Gosayne. Suppliers are normally paid at the end of Month 1; the Nullas are sold on the 15th of Month 2. Payment is received on the first day of Month 3.

(a) Under this system we have the following forecast.

	Inflows	*Outflows*	*Balance*
	$	$	$
Month 1 (end)	–	50	(50)
Month 2	–	–	(50)
Month 3 (beginning)	100	–	50

In other words the cash cycle means that the firm is in deficit for all of Month 2. As the bank has refused an overdraft, the suppliers will not be paid.

(b) If, however, Gilbert Gosayne persuades its suppliers to wait for two weeks until the 15th of Month 2 and offers a settlement discount of $5 to customers to induce them to pay on the 15th of Month 2, the situation is transformed.

	Inflows	*Outflows*	*Balance*
	$	$	$
Month 1	–	–	–
Month 2	95	50	45
Month 3	–	–	45

In practice, it is not that simple.

(a) Suppliers can object to their customers taking extra credit and it can also harm their businesses, thus jeopardising their ability to make future supplies. The customer also loses the possibility of taking advantage of trade discounts.

(b) Customers might refuse to pay early, despite the inducement of a discount.

In fact, a firm's customers and suppliers might be 'leading and lagging' themselves.

A firm might be in a position to choose which of its suppliers should be paid now rather than later. Certain suppliers have to be paid early, if they are powerful. The bank is a powerful supplier: it is worth keeping the bank happy even if the firm loses out on a few trade discounts in the process.

Shortening the operating cycle is helpful in dealing with **short-term deficiencies** and saving interest costs, but it is not necessarily a long term solution to the business's funding problems. This is because a shorter operating cycle time will **reduce the amount of cash** that a company needs to invest in its operating activities.

2 Cash management services

2.1 Computerised cash management

A relatively recent development in banking services is that of cash management services for corporate customers. A company with many different bank accounts can obtain information about the cash balance in each account through a computer terminal in the company's treasury department linked to the bank's computer. The company can then arrange to move cash from one account to another and so manage its cash position more efficiently.

2.2 Float

As already mentioned, the term 'float' is sometimes used to describe the amount of time between:

(a) The time when a **payment** is **initiated** (for example when a debtor sends a cheque in payment, probably by post), and

(b) The time when the **funds** become **available** for use in the recipient's bank account.

REASONS FOR LENGTHY FLOAT	
Transmission delay	Postal delays of a day, maybe longer
Lodgement delay	Delay in banking payments received, payee delaying presentation to bank of cash/cheques received
Clearance delay	Time for bank to clear cheque, payment not available for use by recipient until clearance (2-3 days in UK)

There are several measures that could be taken to reduce the float.

(a) The payee should ensure that the **lodgement delay** is kept to a minimum. **Cheques** received should be presented to the bank on the day of receipt.

(b) The payee might, in some cases, arrange to **collect cheques** from the payer's premises. This would only be practicable, however, if the payer is local. The payment would have to be large to make the extra effort worthwhile.

(c) The payer might be asked to pay through his own branch of a bank. The payer can give his bank detailed payment instructions, and use the credit clearing system of the bank giro. The **bank giro** is a means of making credit transfers for customers of other banks and other branches. The payee may include a bank giro credit slip on the bottom of his invoice, to help with this method of payment.

(d) **BACS** (Bankers' Automated Clearing Services), a system which provides for the computerised transfer of funds between banks, could be used. BACS is available to corporate customers of banks for making payments. The customer must supply a magnetic tape or disk to BACS, which contains details of payments, and payment will be made in two days.

(e) For regular payments **standing orders** or **direct debits** might be used.

(f) **CHAPS** (Clearing House Automated Payments System) is a computerised system for banks to make same-day clearances (that is, immediate payment) between each other. Each member bank of CHAPS can allow its own corporate customers to make immediate transfers of funds through CHAPS. However, there is a large minimum size for payments using CHAPS.

2.3 Example: cash management

Ryan Coates owns a chain of seven clothes shops. Takings at each shop are remitted once a week on Thursday evening to the head office, and are then banked at the start of business on Friday morning. As business is expanding, Ryan Coates has hired an accountant to help him. The accountant gave him the following advice.

'Sales revenue at the seven shops totalled $1,950,000 last year, at a constant daily rate, but you were paying bank overdraft charges at a rate of 11%. You could have reduced your overdraft costs by banking the shop takings each day, except for Saturday's takings. Saturday takings could have been banked on Mondays.'

Comment on the significance of this statement, stating your assumptions. The shops are closed on Sundays.

Solution

(a) A bank overdraft rate of 11% a year is approximately 11/365 = 0.03% a day.

(b) Annual takings of $1,950,000 would be an average of $1,950,000/312 = $6,250 a day for the seven shops in total, on the assumption that they opened for a 52 week year of six days a week (312 days).

(c) Using the approximate overdraft cost of 0.03% a day, the cost of holding $6,250 for one day instead of banking it is 0.03% × $6,250 = $1.875.

(d) Banking all takings up to Thursday evening of each week on Friday morning involves an unnecessary delay in paying cash into the bank. The cost of this delay would be either:

  (i) The opportunity cost of investment capital for the business, or
  (ii) The cost of avoidable bank overdraft charges

  It is assumed here that the overdraft cost is higher and is therefore more appropriate to use. It is also assumed that, for interest purposes, funds are credited when banked.

Takings on	*Could be banked on*	*Number of days delay incurred by Friday banking*
Monday	Tuesday	3
Tuesday	Wednesday	2
Wednesday	Thursday	1
Thursday	Friday	0
Friday	Saturday	6
Saturday	Monday	4
		16

In one week, the total number of days delay incurred by Friday banking is 16. At a cost of \$1.875 a day, the weekly cost of Friday banking was \$1.875 × 16 = \$30.00, and the annual cost of Friday banking was \$30.00 × 52 = \$1,560.

(e) *Conclusion*. The company could have saved about \$1,560 a year in bank overdraft charges last year. If the overdraft rate remains at 11% and sales continue to increase, the saving from daily banking would be even higher next year.

3 Inventory approach to cash management

FAST FORWARD

The **inventory approach** (Baumol's model) aims to minimise the costs of **holding cash** and **obtaining new funds**.

3.1 Baumol's model

There are a number of different formal cash management models designed to indicate the optimum amount of cash that a company should hold. One such model, **Baumol's model**, is based on the idea that deciding on optimum cash balances is a similar question to deciding on optimum inventory levels.

We can distinguish two types of cost which are involved in obtaining cash:

(a) The **fixed cost** represented, for example, by the issue cost of equity finance or the cost of negotiating an overdraft

(b) The **variable cost** (opportunity cost) of keeping the money in the form of cash

The total cost incurred for a period in holding a certain average level of cash is:

$$\frac{Qi}{2} + \frac{FS}{Q}$$

Where S = the amount of cash to be used in each time period
F = the fixed cost of obtaining new funds (cost per sale/purchase of securities)
i = the interest cost of holding cash or near cash equivalents
Q = the total amount to be raised to provide for S

We can then establish that the optimum amount of cash to obtain each time that new funds are needed is given by the following formula, whose derivation you do not need to know. Whenever cash holdings fall to a low 'safety' level, the 'optimum sale' quantity of securities such as shares or gilts would be sold in order to replenish holdings of cash.

Exam formula

$$\text{Optimal sale} = \sqrt{\frac{2 \times \text{annual cash disbursements} \times \text{cost per sale of securities}}{\text{interest rate}}}, \text{ ie } Q = \sqrt{\frac{2SF}{i}}$$

3.2 Example: inventory approach to cash management

F Co faces a fixed cost of $4,000 to obtain new funds. There is a requirement for $24,000 of cash over each period of one year for the foreseeable future. The interest cost of new funds is 12% per annum; the interest rate earned on short-term securities is 9% per annum. How much finance should F Co raise at a time?

Solution

The cost of holding cash is 12% – 9% = 3%

The optimum level of Q (the 're-order quantity') is:

$$\sqrt{\frac{2 \times 4{,}000 \times 24{,}000}{0.03}} = \$80{,}000$$

The optimum amount of new funds to raise is $80,000.

This amount is raised every 80,000 ÷ 24,000 = $3^1/_3$ years.

3.3 Drawbacks of the inventory approach

The inventory approach has the following drawbacks.

(a) In reality, **amounts required** over **future periods** will be **difficult to predict** with much certainty.

(b) There may be **costs** associated with running out of cash.

(c) There may be **other normal costs of holding cash** which increase with the average amount held.

(d) The model works satisfactorily for a firm which uses up its cash at a **steady rate**, but not if there are larger inflows and outflows of cash from time to time.

3.4 The Miller-Orr model

FAST FORWARD

The **Miller-Orr model** assumes cash flows are unpredictable. It is based on calculating upper and lower limits for cash balances, and selling or buying securities when these points are reached in order to return the business to the normal level of cash holdings.

In an attempt to produce a more realistic approach to cash management, various models more complicated than the inventory approach have been developed. One of these, the **Miller-Orr model**, manages to achieve a reasonable degree of realism while not being too elaborate.

We can begin looking at the Miller-Orr model by asking what will happen if there is no attempt to manage cash balances. Clearly, the cash balance is likely to 'meander' upwards or downwards. The Miller-Orr model imposes limits to this meandering. If the cash balance reaches an upper limit (point A in Figure 1) the firm buys sufficient securities to return the cash balance to a normal level (called the 'return point'). When the cash balance reaches a lower limit (point B in Figure 1), the firm sells securities to bring the balance back to the return point.

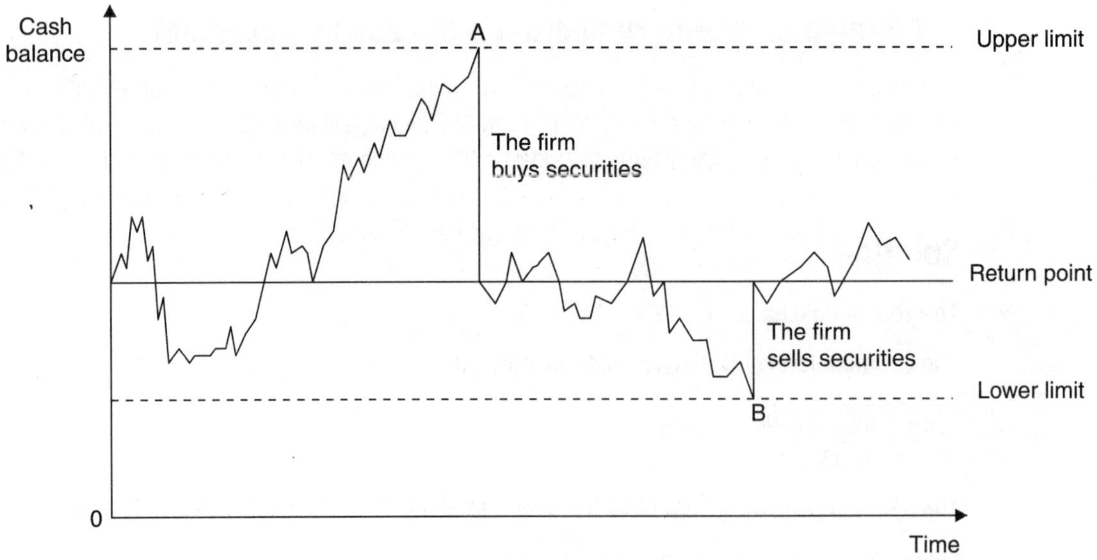

Figure 1 Applying the Miller-Orr model

How are the upper and lower limits and the return point set? Miller and Orr showed that the answer to this question depends on three factors:

- The variance of cash flows
- Transaction costs
- Interest rates

If the day-to-day variability of cash flows is high or the transaction cost in buying or selling securities is high, then wider limits should be set. If interest rates are high, the limits should be closer together.

To keep the interest costs of holding cash down, the return point is set at one-third of the distance (or 'spread') between the lower and the upper limit.

Return point = Lower limit + $^1/_3$ × spread

Exam formula

Spread between upper and lower cash balance limits, Miller-Orr model:

$$\text{Spread} = 3\left(\frac{\frac{3}{4} \times \text{transaction cost} \times \text{variance of cash flows}}{\text{interest rate}}\right)^{\frac{1}{3}}$$

3.5 Applying the Miller-Orr model

To use the Miller-Orr model, it is necessary to follow the steps below.

(a) **Set** the **lower limit** for the **cash balance**. This may be zero, or it may be set at some minimum safety margin above zero.

(b) **Estimate** the **variance of cash flows**, for example from sample observations over a 100-day period.

(c) **Note the interest rate** and the **transaction cost** for each sale or purchase of securities (the latter is assumed to be fixed).

(d) **Compute** the **upper limit** and the return point from the model and instruct an employee to implement the limits strategy.

Now try applying the Miller-Orr equations yourself in the following exercise.

Question

Miller-Orr model

The following data applies to a company.

(a) The minimum cash balance is $8,000.
(b) The variance of daily cash flows is 4,000,000, equivalent to a standard deviation of $2,000 per day.
(c) The transaction cost for buying or selling securities is $50.
(d) The interest rate is 0.025 per cent per day.

Required

Formulate a decision rule using the Miller-Orr model.

Answer

The spread between the upper and the lower cash balance limits is calculated as follows.

$$\text{Spread} = 3\left(\frac{3}{4} \times \frac{\text{transaction cost} \times \text{variance of cash flows}}{\text{interest rate}}\right)^{\frac{1}{3}}$$

$$= 3\left(\frac{3}{4} \times \frac{50 \times 4{,}000{,}000}{0.00025}\right)^{\frac{1}{3}} = \$25{,}303\text{, say } \$25{,}300$$

The upper limit and return point are now calculated.

Upper limit = Lower limit + $25,300 = $8,000 + $25,300 = $33,300

Return point = lower limit + $^1/_3$ × spread
= $8,000 + $^1/_3$ × $25,300 = $16,433, say $16,400

The decision rule is as follows. If the cash balance reaches $33,300, buy $16,900 (= 33,300 – 16,400) in marketable securities. If the cash balance falls to $8,000, sell $8,400 of marketable securities for cash.

3.6 Advantages and disadvantages of the Miller-Orr model

The usefulness of the Miller-Orr model is limited by the **assumptions** on which it is based.

(a) In practice, cash inflows and outflows are **unlikely** to be **entirely unpredictable** as the model assumes: for example, for a retailer, seasonal factors are likely to affect cash inflows; for any company, dividend and tax payments will be known well in advance.

(b) Excessively good or bad trading conditions may mean the company **never reaches** the lower or upper **limits** calculated.

However, the Miller-Orr model may save management time which might otherwise be spent in responding to those cash inflows and outflows which cannot be predicted.

3.7 Use of cash management models in practice

Some banks, especially in the USA, make cash management models available to their customers. These models vary from relatively simple spreadsheet-based models to more sophisticated systems such as those provided for multinational companies by the Chemical Bank.

Sophisticated models, such as that used by the Chemical Bank, can take account of a user's risk preferences by allowing limits to be set on the amount of funds allocated to any single investment. Users can manipulate variables to trace the effect on the short-term plan, which can help them to increase their awareness of the factors affecting day-to-day management decisions and the liquidity/profitability trade-off.

Exam focus point

The pilot paper had a question on the Baumol model and the May 2005 paper had a question on the Miller-Orr model. You are given both of the formulae in the exam, so make sure you can use them.

4 Applying probabilities in cash management

FAST FORWARD

Probabilities can be used to calculate the likelihood of different financial outcomes.

We can see how **probabilities** can be applied to cash management problems by looking at an example.

4.1 Example: probabilities in cash management

Sinkos Wim has an overdraft facility of $100,000, and currently has an overdraft balance at the bank of $34,000. The company maintains a cash float of $10,000 for transactions and precautionary purposes. It is unclear whether a long awaited economic recovery will take place, and the company has prepared cash budgets as set out below for the next three months using two different assumptions about economic events. The cash flows in months 2 and 3 depend on the cash flows in the previous month.

Estimated net cash flows

Month 1		*Month 2*		*Month 3*	
Probability	*Cash flow* $'000	*Probability*	*Cash flow* $'000	*Probability*	*Cash flow* $'000
		0.8	25	0.5	30
0.7	(40)			0.5	20
		0.2	10	0.5	10
				0.5	0
		0.8	0	0.5	(10)
0.3	(60)			0.5	(20)
		0.2	(10)	0.5	(40)
				0.5	(50)

Required

If the company intends to maintain a cash float of $10,000 at the end of each month, what is the probability that this will be possible at the end of each of months 1, 2 and 3 given the current overdraft limit?

Solution

The opening balance at the beginning of month 1 is $10,000.

Month 1				*Month 2*				*Month 3*			
Prob.	*Cash flow*	*Close bal.*	*Over-draft*	*Prob.*	*Cash flow*	*Close bal.*	*Over-draft*	*Prob.*	*Cash flow*	*Close bal.*	*Over-draft*
	$'000	$'000	$'000		$'000	$'000	$'000		$'000	$'000	$'000
								0.28	30	10	19
				0.56	25	10	49	0.28	20	10	29
0.7	(40)	10	74								
								0.07	10	10	54
				0.14	10	10	64	0.07	0	10	64
								0.12	(10)	6	100
				0.24	0	10	94	0.12	(20)	(4)	100
0.3	(60)	10	94								
								0.03	(40)	(34)	100
				0.06	(10)	6	100	0.03	(50)	(44)	100

The probabilities that the cash float of $10,000 can be maintained at the end of each month are as follows.

Month 1: 0.7 + 0.3 = 1.0
Month 2: 0.56 + 0.14 + 0.24 = 0.94
Month 3: 0.28 + 0.28 + 0.07 + 0.07 = 0.7

Question

Cash shortage

Using the figures in the above example, state the probabilities that the company completely runs out of cash at the end of each month.

Answer

Under none of the projected outcomes for months 1 and 2 does the company run out of cash.

For month 3, the probability of the company running out of cash is:

0.12 + 0.03 + 0.03 = 0.18

Probabilities can also be used to calculate the expected value of cash flows. If for example a business has a 0.6 chance of a cash inflow of $400,000 and a 0.4 chance of a cash outflow of $600,000 over the next month, the expected value of the cash flow is (0.6 × $400,000) – (0.4 × $600,000) = $0.

However expected values are only of use if the event could be repeated a number of times. As a one-off event to say the expected value of the cash flow over the next month is $0 is worthless; there will either be a large inflow or outflow. Managers will be concerned with making plans to invest surplus cash and dealing with the risks of a large cash outflow, possibly seeking extra finance.

Chapter Roundup

- Optimal **cash** holding levels can be calculated from formal models.
- The **inventory approach** (Baumol's model) aims to minimise the costs of **holding cash** and **obtaining new funds**.
- The **Miller-Orr model** assumes cash flows are unpredictable. It is based on calculating upper and lower limits for cash balances, and selling or buying securities when these points are reached in order to return the business to the normal level of cash holdings.
- **Cash shortages** can be eased by postponing capital expenditure, selling assets, taking longer to pay creditors and pressing debtors for earlier payment (leading and lagging).
- Businesses should also try to reduce **float,** the period between the time a payment is initiated and the time when funds become available.
- **Probabilities** can be used to calculate the likelihood of different financial outcomes.

Quick Quiz

1 The cash flow forecast prepared by Heavy Metal suggests that the overdraft limit will be exceeded during the second month of the forecast period due to the timing of the asset purchase. However, by the end of the quarter the overdraft should be back to a level similar to that at the start of the period. Which of the following courses of action would you recommend to overcome this problem?

A Acquire the asset using a finance lease rather than by outright purchase
B Seek help from a venture capital company
C Make a rights issue to raise the additional funds
D Negotiate with the bank for a short-term loan to cover the deficit

2 Possible reasons for a lengthy float are:

(A) .... delay
(B) .... delay
(C) .... delay

3 Hallas is a small manufacturing business that uses a large number of suppliers, many of which are located outside the UK. The accountant has suggested that Hallas could improve its cash position by sending payments out using surface mail rather than airmail as at present. If Hallas did this, which of the following would it be taking advantage of?

A Lodgement delay
B Clearance delay
C Transmission delay
D Collection delay

4 In the Miller-Orr cash management model:

Return point = Lower limit + [ ] × Spread

(Fill in the box)

5 The formula for Baumol's model is $Q = \sqrt{\frac{2SF}{i}}$. What do these terms stand for?

Answers to Quick Quiz

1 D Since the cash flow problems appear to be temporary in nature, it is appropriate to use a short-term solution. Additional long-term capital should not be required.

2 (A) Transmission delay
(B) Lodgement delay
(C) Clearance delay

3 C Transmission delay

4 One-third

5 S = amount of cash to be used in each time period
F = fixed costs of obtaining new funds
i = Interest cost of holding cash or near cash equivalents
Q = total amount to be raised to provide for S

Now try the question below from the Exam Question Bank

Number	Level	Marks	Time
Q29	Examination	20	36 mins

18

Borrowing and investing

Introduction

In this chapter, we discuss short- and medium-term finance. This involves looking at the use of bank loans and overdrafts. The choice between taking out a loan or overdraft is often very important. You should concentrate on understanding when different forms of borrowing might be most appropriate for a business.

We also look at different methods of **financing foreign trade**.

In the second part of this chapter, we look at the ways in which cash can be invested in the short-term, and identify the purpose and main features of various types of short-term investment. The characteristics of different types of instrument may be tested in an MCQ. Alternatively in a longer question you might be asked to explain which types of investment an investor might choose.

1 Budgeting for borrowings

FAST FORWARD

Maintenance of **liquidity** is an important corporate objective. Organisations may have problems due to **timing differences**, **risk** and **contingencies**.

1.1 Maintaining liquidity

As far as borrowing is concerned, there are three aspects to the **maintenance of liquidity**.

(a) The firm needs enough money to function operationally, pay salaries, suppliers and so on. Of course, eventually it will receive funds from customers, but the length of the cash cycle can mean reliance on **overdraft finance** at times.

(b) The firm needs to minimise the **risk** that some of its sources of finance will be removed from it.

(c) The firm also needs to provide against the **contingency** of any sudden movements in cash. Contingency measures can take the form of special arrangements with the bank, insurance policies and so on.

Some of these needs are more pressing than others.

(a) **Working capital**

Working capital is often financed by an overdraft – this is a result of lagged payments and receipts as discussed earlier and the willingness of businesses to offer credit.

(b) **Long-term finance**

This is used for major investments. Capital expenditure is easier to put off than, say, wages in a crisis, but a long-term failure to invest can damage the business and reduce its capacity.

(c) **Overseas finance**

The borrowing might be required to finance **assets overseas**, in which case the **currency** of the borrowing might be important.

Key terms

Bank borrowing can be obtained in the following ways.

(a) Overdraft facility. A company, through its current account, can borrow money on a short-term basis up to a certain amount. Overdrafts are repayable on demand.

(b) Term loan. The customer borrows a fixed amount and pays it back with interest over a period or at the end of it.

(c) Committed facility. The bank undertakes to make a stipulated amount available to a borrower, on demand.

(d) A revolving facility is a facility that is renewed after a set period. Once the customer has repaid the amount, the customer can borrow again.

(e) Uncommitted facility. The bank, if it feels like it, can lend the borrower a specified sum. The only purpose of this is that all the paperwork has been done up front. The bank has no obligation to lend.

2 Overdrafts

FAST FORWARD

Overdrafts are a form of short-term lending, technically repayable on demand. Businesses may not need to use the overdraft facilities that they have been granted.

OVERDRAFTS	
Amount	Should not exceed limit, usually based on known income
Margin	Interest charged at base rate plus margin on daily amount overdrawn and charged quarterly. Fee may be charged for large facility
Purpose	Generally to cover short-term deficits
Repayment	Technically repayable on demand
Security	Depends on size of facility
Benefits	Customer has flexible means of short-term borrowing; bank has to accept fluctuation

2.1 Overdraft as short-term borrowing

Where payments from a current account exceed the balance on the account for a temporary period, the bank finances the deficit by means of an **overdraft**. It is very much a form of **short-term lending**, available to both personal and business customers.

By providing an overdraft facility to a customer, the bank is committing itself to provide an overdraft to the customer whenever the customer wants it, up to the agreed limit. The bank will earn interest on the lending, but only to the extent that the customer uses the facility and goes into overdraft. If the customer does not go into overdraft, the bank cannot charge interest.

The bank will generally charge a **commitment fee** when a customer is granted an overdraft facility or an increase in his overdraft facility. This is a fee for granting an overdraft facility and agreeing to provide the customer with funds if and whenever he needs them.

2.2 Overdrafts and the operating cycle

Many businesses require their bank to provide financial assistance for normal trading over the **operating cycle**.

For example, suppose that a business has the following operating cycle.

	$	$
Inventories and receivables		10,000
Bank overdraft	1,000	
Payables	3,000	
		4,000
Working capital		6,000

The business now buys inventories costing $2,500 for cash, using its overdraft. Working capital remains the same, $6,000, although the bank's financial stake has risen from $1,000 to $3,500.

	$	$
Inventories and receivables		12,500
Bank overdraft	3,500	
Payables	3,000	
		6,500
Working capital		6,000

A bank overdraft provides support for normal trading finance. In this example, finance for normal trading rises from $(10,000 – 3,000) = $7,000 to $(12,500 – 3,000) = $9,500 and the bank's contribution rises from $1,000 out of $7,000 to $3,500 out of $9,500.

A feature of bank lending to support normal trading finance is that the amount of the overdraft required at any time will depend on the **cash flows of the business**: the timing of receipts and payments, seasonal variations in trade patterns and so on. An overdraft will increase in size if the customer writes more cheques, but will reduce in size when money is paid into the account.

There should be times when there will be no overdraft at all, and the account is in credit for a while. In other words, the customer's account may well **swing** from overdraft into credit, back again into overdraft and again into credit, and so on. The account would then be a **swinging account**. The purpose of the overdraft is to bridge the gap between cash payments and cash receipts.

When a business customer has an overdraft facility, and the account is always in overdraft, then it has a **solid core** (or **hard core**) instead of swing. For example, suppose that the account of Blunderbuss has the following record for the previous year:

	Average balance		*Range*		*Debit turnover*
Quarter to	$	$		$	$
31 March 20X5	40,000 debit	70,000 debit	–	20,000 debit	600,000
30 June 20X5	50,000 debit	80,000 debit	–	25,000 debit	500,000
30 September 20X5	75,000 debit	105,000 debit	–	50,000 debit	700,000
31 December 20X5	80,000 debit	110,000 debit	–	60,000 debit	550,000

These figures show that the account has been permanently in overdraft, and the hard core of the overdraft has been rising steeply over the course of the year (from a minimum overdraft of $20,000 in the first quarter to one of $60,000 in the fourth quarter).

If the hard core element of the overdraft appears to be becoming a long-term feature of the business, the bank might wish, after discussions with the customer, to convert the hard core of the overdraft into a medium-term loan, thus giving formal recognition to its more permanent nature. Otherwise annual reductions in the hard core of an overdraft would typically be a requirement of the bank.

2.3 The purpose of an advance for day-to-day trading

The purpose of a bank overdraft for normal day-to-day trading is to help with the financing of current assets. However, there are a number of different reasons why a business might need an overdraft facility. Only **some** of these reasons will be sound and acceptable to a bank.

Borrowing by a business will either:

- Increase the assets of the business, or
- Decrease its liabilities

2.4 Increasing business assets

If borrowing is to increase the business assets, a bank will first check whether the purpose is to acquire more **non-current assets** or more **current assets**. A customer might ask for an overdraft facility to help with day to day trading finance, when the *real* cause of his shortage of liquidity is really a decision to purchase a new non-current asset. There is nothing wrong with asking a bank for financial assistance with the purchase of non-current assets. But borrowing to purchase a non-current asset reduces the liquidity of the business, and might even make it illiquid.

Exam focus point

Factoring (Chapter 19) is of course another means of raising finance. An exam question could ask whether it is more beneficial to an entity to factor its debts or to raise finance by another means, such as an overdraft.

Question

Bank overdraft

The directors of Wrong Wreason have asked their bank for a $50,000 overdraft which they say will be used for normal trading operations. They present two balance sheets, one indicating the firm's position before the loan and one after. What do you think the bank's response will be?

WRONG WREASON – BALANCE SHEET (BEFORE)

	$	$
Non-current assets		200,000
Current assets	120,000	
Current liabilities: trade payables	60,000	
Working capital		60,000
		260,000
Share capital and reserves		260,000

WRONG WREASON – BALANCE SHEET (AFTER)

		$	$	$
Non-current assets (200,000 + 50,000)				250,000
Current assets			120,000	
Current liabilities:	bank overdraft	50,000		
	trade payables	60,000		
			110,000	
Working capital				10,000
				260,000
Share capital and reserves				260,000

Answer

Although the directors might believe that they are asking the bank to help with financing their current assets, they are really asking for assistance with the purchase of a non-current asset, because the bank lending would leave the total current assets of the company unchanged, but will increase the current liabilities. Consequently, bank borrowing on overdraft to buy a non-current asset would reduce the working capital of Wrong Wreason from $60,000 to $10,000. In contrast, borrowing $50,000 to finance extra current assets would have increased current assets from $120,000 to $170,000, and with current liabilities going from $60,000 to $110,000, total working capital would have remained unchanged at $60,000 and liquidity would arguably still be adequate.

An overdraft facility for **day-to-day trading** should therefore be either to **increase total current assets**, or to **reduce other current liabilities.**

2.5 Increasing total current assets

A request for an overdraft facility to increase total current assets can be pinpointed more exactly, to a wish by the company:

- To increase its inventory levels
- To increase its overall receivables
- To increase its overall sales turnover

The underlying guide to a bank's attitude to lending (in addition to avoiding risk) is whether the finance will be temporary (and 'swinging') or longer term. There might be a number of reasons for a business **increasing its inventory levels** without increasing its total sales.

REASONS FOR INCREASING INVENTORY LEVELS	
Large order	Overdraft suitable, temporary finance to enable business to fulfil order
Inventory build up anticipating seasonal peak	Overdraft suitable, temporary finance to support cost of inventory
Speculative purchase, eg buying raw materials	Overdraft suitable, provided finance temporary and not unacceptably risky
Permanent increase without increase in sales	Overdraft probably not suitable; need for review of finance facilities; inventory may be unsaleable

Reasons for a business wanting to **increase its total receivables** without increasing its sales turnover might be:

(a) A loss of efficiency in the credit control, invoicing and debt collection procedures of the business, or

(b) The inability of existing customers to pay without being allowed more credit

In both cases, the bank will be cautious about agreeing to an increased overdraft facility. Delays in invoicing should be eliminated by the business; however, if more credit must be allowed to maintain sales, a bank might agree to an overdraft facility for this purpose.

When a business **increases its sales turnover**, it will almost certainly have to increase its investment in inventories and receivables. It will probably be able to obtain more credit from trade payables, but the balance of the extra finance required will have to be provided out of extra proprietors' capital or other lending. A danger with business expansion is **overtrading**, and a bank will be wary of requests to support ambitious expansion schemes.

2.6 Using an overdraft to reduce other current liabilities

A bank might be asked to provide an overdraft facility to enable a business to pay its tax bills, or to reduce its volume of trade payables. The payment of tax might be sales tax (generally every quarter) or year end corporation tax. An overdraft facility to help a business to pay tax when it falls due is a 'legitimate' and acceptable purpose for an overdraft, although the bank might wish to know why the business had not set funds aside to pay the tax. A bank should be able to expect that the overdraft would soon be paid off out of profits from future trading.

An **extension** to an overdraft in order to pay trade suppliers must be for the purpose of **reducing the overall average volume of trade payables**, which in turn implies a significant change in the trade payables position of the business, all other things being equal. Why might such a reduction in total trade payables be required?

(a) **To take advantage of attractive purchase discounts offered by suppliers for early settlement of debts**. This should be an acceptable purpose for an extra overdraft to a bank, because taking the discount would reduce the costs and so increase the profits of the business.

(b) **To pay suppliers who are pressing for payment**. A bank will deal cautiously with such a request. It might be because the supplier is desperate for money. If the business *customer* is getting into difficulties, and is falling behind with paying his debts, a banker would take the view that agreeing to an increased overdraft would simply mean taking over debts that might one day never be paid, and so may not agree to such a proposition.

3 Loans

FAST FORWARD

Bank loans tend to be a **source** of **medium-term finance**, linked with the purchase of specific assets. Interest and repayments will be set in advance.

3.1 When a loan is appropriate

A customer might ask the bank for an overdraft facility when the bank would wish to suggest a loan instead; alternatively, a customer might ask for a loan when an overdraft would be more appropriate.

(a) In most cases, when a customer wants finance to help with 'day to day' trading and cash flow needs, an **overdraft** would be the **appropriate method** of financing. The customer should not be short of cash all the time, and should expect to be in credit in some days, but in need of an overdraft on others.

(b) When a customer wants to borrow from a bank for only a **short period of time**, even for the purchase of a major non-current asset such as an item of plant or machinery, an overdraft facility might be more suitable than a loan, because the customer will stop paying interest as soon as his account goes into credit.

(c) When a customer wants to borrow from a bank, but cannot see his way to repaying the bank except over the course of a few years, the **medium– or long-term nature** of the financing is best catered for by the provision of a loan rather than an overdraft facility.

3.2 Advantages of an overdraft over a loan

(a) The customer only pays interest when he is overdrawn.

(b) The bank has the flexibility to review the customer's overdraft facility periodically, and perhaps agree to additional facilities, or insist on a reduction in the facility.

(c) An overdraft can do the same job as a loan: a facility can simply be renewed every time it comes up for review.

(d) Being short-term debt, an overdraft will not affect the calculation of a company's gearing.

Bear in mind, however, that overdrafts are normally **repayable on demand**.

3.3 Advantages of a loan

(a) Both the customer and the bank **know exactly** what the repayments of the loan will be and how much interest is payable, and when. This makes planning (budgeting) simpler.

(b) The customer does not have to worry about the bank deciding to reduce or **withdraw** an overdraft facility before he is in a position to repay what is owed. There is an element of 'security' or 'peace of mind' in being able to arrange a loan for an agreed term.

(c) Loans normally carry a **facility letter** setting out the precise terms of the agreement.

For purchases of a non-current asset it is important, however, that the **term of the loan should not exceed** the **economic or useful life** of the asset purchased with the money from the loan. A business will often expect to use the revenues earned by the asset to repay the loan, and obviously, an asset can only do this as long as it is in operational use.

4 Trade payables (creditors) as a source of finance

FAST FORWARD

Trade credit from suppliers is another possible short-term source of finance.

4.1 Trade payables as a source of short-term finance

Taking credit from suppliers is a normal feature of business and nearly every company has at any time a number of suppliers waiting for payment.

It may be thought that this is a form of interest free borrowing, but:

(a) Any available settlement discounts will be lost
(b) It will lead to a loss of supplier goodwill
(c) If the supplier resorts to legal action, this may affect the organisation's future credit rating.

The organisation must weigh up the cost of lost discounts against the value of the number of days borrowing obtained. It may be found that it is more financially worthwhile to pay the supplier early and obtain the discount than to hang onto the funds and invest them for the additional days.

The formula for estimating the cost of lost cash discounts was given in the previous chapter and you may want to refer back to it. This formula is not given to you in the exam, so you should learn it.

5 Export finance

5.1 Finance for foreign trade

FAST FORWARD

It is worth remembering that the exporter can obtain finance from the foreign buyer by insisting on **cash with order** and the importer can obtain finance from the foreign supplier by means of normal trade credit, perhaps evidenced by a term bill of exchange.

Foreign trade raises special **financing problems**, including the following.

(a) When goods are sold abroad, the customer might ask for credit. The period of credit might be 30 days or 60 days, say, after receipt of the goods; or perhaps 90 days after shipment. Exports take time to arrange, and there might be **complex paperwork**. Transporting the goods can be slow, if they are sent by sea. These delays in foreign trade mean that exporters often build up large investments in inventory and receivables.

(b) The risk of bad debts can be greater with foreign trade than with domestic trade. If a foreign customer refuses to pay a debt, the exporter must pursue the debt in the customer's own country, where procedures will be subject to the laws of that country.

There are various measures available to exporters to overcome these problems. (Apart from credit risks, there are other risks, including the risk of currency (exchange rate) fluctuations and political risks.)

5.2 Reducing the investment in foreign receivables

A company can reduce its **investment in foreign receivables** by insisting on earlier payment for goods. Another approach is for an exporter to **arrange for a bank to give cash for a foreign debt**, sooner than the exporter would receive payment in the normal course of events. There are several ways in which this might be done.

METHODS OF OBTAINING CASH FOR FOREIGN DEBTS	
Advances against collections	Exporter asks bank to handle, and bank makes 80-90% advance against value of collection. Banks expect repayment from proceeds. Used when the bill/cheque is payable in exporter's own country
Documentary credits	Described later in the chapter
Negotiation of bills or cheques	Similar to an advance against collection, used when the bill/cheque is payable outside exporter's country (eg in foreign buyer's country)

5.3 Advantages of using bills of exchange in international trade

(a) They provide a **convenient method** of **collecting payments** from foreign buyers.

(b) The exporter can seek **immediate finance**, using term bills of exchange, instead of having to wait until the period of credit expires (ie until the maturity of the bill). At the same time, the foreign buyer is allowed the full period of credit before payment is made.

(c) On payment, the foreign buyer keeps the bill as **evidence of payment**, so that a bill of exchange also serves as a receipt.

(d) If a bill of exchange is dishonoured, it may be used by the drawer to **pursue payment** by means of legal action in the drawee's country.

(e) The buyer's bank might add its name to a term bill, to indicate that it **guarantees payment** at maturity. On the continent of Europe, this procedure is known as **'avalising'** bills of exchange.

5.4 Reducing the bad debt risk

Methods of minimising bad debt risks are broadly similar to those for domestic trade. An exporting company should vet the creditworthiness of each customer, and grant credit terms accordingly. Methods of reducing the risks of bad debts in foreign trade are described below.

5.5 Export factoring

FAST FORWARD

Export factoring provides all the advantages of factoring generally and is especially useful in assessing credit risk.

Export factoring relates to export trade and is similar to the factoring of domestic trade debts.

Key term

Factoring is the sale of debts to a third party (the factor) at a discount, in return for prompt cash. A factoring service may be with recourse, in which case the supplier takes the risk of the debt not being paid, or without recourse when the factor takes the risk. *(OT 2000)*

5.6 Main aspects of factoring

(a) **Administration** of the **client's invoicing**, **sales accounting** and debt collection services are generally involved.

(b) The arrangement is likely to provide **credit protection** for the client's debts, whereby the factor takes over the risk of loss from bad debts and so 'insures' the client against such losses.

(c) The factor will **make payments** to the client **in advance** of collecting the debts. This is sometimes referred to as 'factor finance' because the factor is providing cash to the client against outstanding debts.

A factoring service typically offers prepayment of up to 80% against approved invoices. Service charges vary between around 0.75% and 3% of total invoice value, plus finance charges at levels comparable to bank overdraft rates for those taking advantage of prepayment arrangements.

Factoring, as compared with forfaiting (which we discuss below), is widely regarded as an appropriate mechanism for trade finance and collection of receivables for small to medium-sized exporters, especially where there is a flow of small-scale contracts.

5.7 Forfaiting

FAST FORWARD

Forfaiting provides medium term finance for importers of capital goods.

Key term

Forfaiting is a method of export finance whereby a bank purchases from a company a number of sales invoices or promissory notes, usually obtaining a guarantee of payment of the invoices or notes.

Forfaiting is the most common method of providing medium-term (say, three to five years) export finance. It has normally been used for export sales involving capital goods (machinery etc), where payments will be made over a number of years.

Forfaiting works as follows.

(a) An exporter of capital goods finds an overseas buyer who wants medium-term credit to finance the purchase. The buyer must be willing:

- To pay **some of the cost** (perhaps 15%) at once
- To pay the balance in **regular instalments** normally for the next five years

(b) The buyer will either:

- Issue a **series** of **promissory notes**, or
- Accept a **series of drafts**

with a final maturity date, say, **five years ahead** but providing for regular payments over this time: in other words, a series of promissory notes maturing every six months, usually each for the same amount.

(c) In most cases, however, the buyer will be required to find a bank which is willing to guarantee **(avalise)** the notes or drafts.

(d) At the same time, the exporter must find a bank that is willing to be a **'forfaiter'**.

(e) The exporter will deliver the goods and receive the avalised promissory notes or accepted bills. He will then sell them to the forfaiter, who will purchase them **without recourse to the exporter.** The forfaiter must now bear the risk, ie:

- Risks of non-payment
- Political risks in the buyer's country
- Transfer risk, the buyer's country not meeting its foreign exchange obligations
- Foreign exchange risk
- The collection of payment from the avalising bank

The diagram below should help to clarify the procedures.

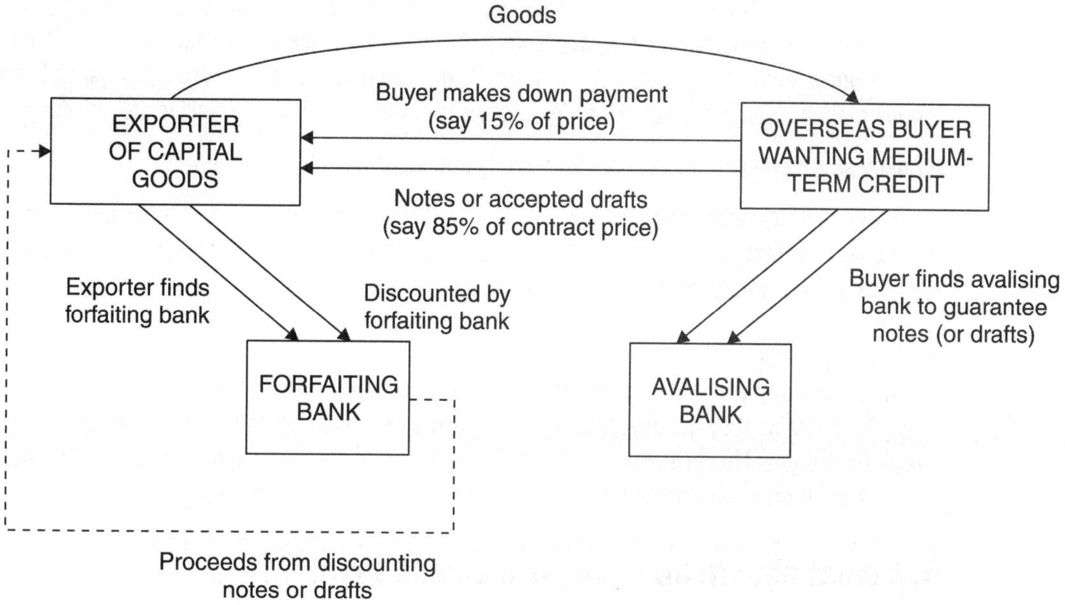

Forfaiting can be an expensive choice, and arranging it takes time. However, it can be a useful way of enabling trade to occur in cases where other methods of ensuring payment and smooth cash flow are not certain, and in cases where trade may not be possible by other means.

5.8 Documentary credits

Documentary credits ('letters of credit') provide a method of payment in international trade which gives the exporter a risk-free method of obtaining payment.

(a) The exporter receives **immediate payment** of the amount due to him, less the discount, instead of having to wait for payment until the end of the credit period allowed to the buyer.

(b) The buyer is able to get a **period of credit** before having to pay for the imports.

The process works as follows:

(a) The buyer (a foreign buyer, or a UK importer) and the seller (a UK exporter or a foreign supplier) first of all agree a contract for the sale of the goods, which provides for payment through a documentary credit.

(b) The **buyer** then requests a bank in his country to issue a **letter of credit** in favour of the exporter. This bank which issues the letter of credit is known as the **issuing bank.**

(c) The issuing bank, by issuing its letter of credit, guarantees payment to the beneficiary.

Documentary credits are slow to arrange, and administratively cumbersome; however, they might be considered essential where the risk of non-payment is high, or when dealing for the first time with an unknown buyer.

6 Cash surpluses

FAST FORWARD

A company has a variety of opportunities for using its **cash surpluses**, but the choice of obtaining a return is determined by considerations, of **profitability**, **liquidity** and **safety**.

6.1 Managing cash

Many companies have temporary cash surpluses which they need to manage so as to earn a return. **Banks** provide one avenue for investment, but larger firms can invest in other forms of financial instrument in the money markets. Generally speaking, the greater the return offered, the riskier the investment.

A business's management of cash should be conducted with:

- Liquidity
- Safety
- Profitability

in mind.

Clearly a company which runs persistent cash surpluses has little problem with liquidity: it should be able to pay its debts as they fall due. Moreover the firm's expenses are lower as it does not have to pay overdraft charges. However, the other factors identified still apply. Cash is an asset of a business; if it is to be invested, it must be invested profitably, and the investment must be secure.

6.2 What should be done with a cash surplus?

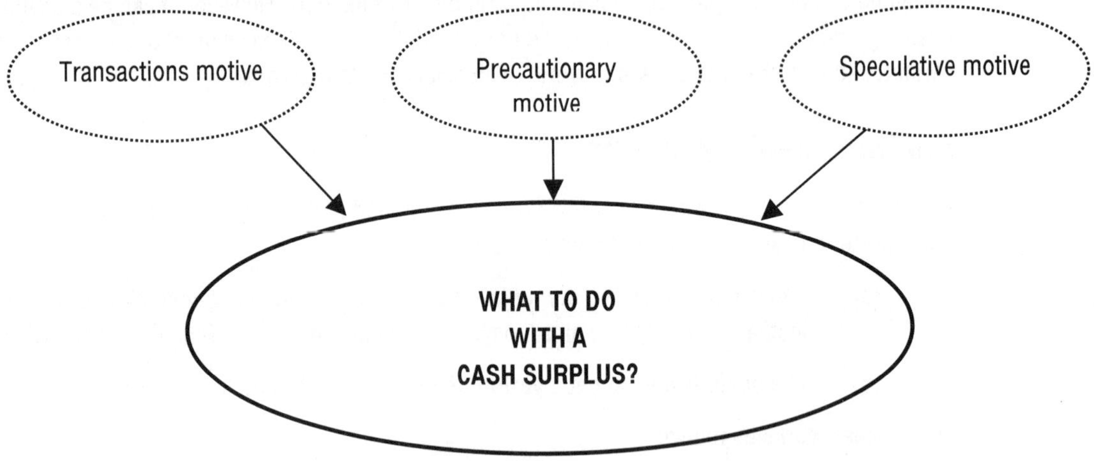

Firstly, a business needs cash to meet its **regular commitments** of paying its suppliers, its employees' wages, its taxes, its annual dividends to shareholders and so on. This reason for holding cash is what the economist J M Keynes called the **transactions motive**.

Keynes identified the **precautionary motive** as a second motive for holding cash. This means that there is a need to maintain a 'buffer' of cash for **unforeseen contingencies**. In the context of a business, this buffer may be provided by an **overdraft facility**, which has the advantage that it will cost very little until it is actually used.

Keynes identified a third motive for holding cash – the **speculative motive**. However, most businesses do not hold surplus cash as a speculative asset (eg in the hope that interest rates will rise).

The cash management policy of a business will reflect its **strategic position**.

(a) Thus, if a company is planning future major **non-current asset purchases**, or if it is planning to **acquire another business**, it will consider whether any cash surplus should be retained and invested in marketable securities until it is needed. Using surplus cash to make such future investments will reduce the extent to which it may need to borrow.

(b) If a company has no plans to grow or to invest, then surplus cash not required for transactions or precautionary purposes should be returned to shareholders.

Surplus cash may be returned to shareholders by the following methods.

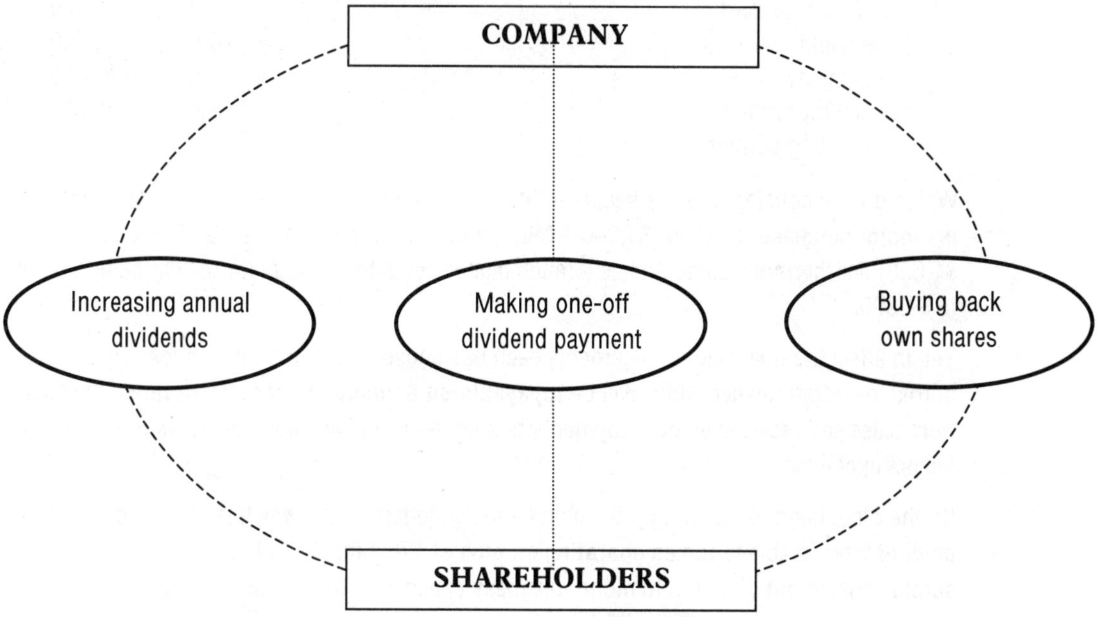

6.3 How much cash will a business require for transactions and precautionary purposes?

A number of mathematical **cash management models** have been developed to try to establish a theoretical basis to the idea of an **optimal cash balance.**

Although many larger companies use such models in practice, for the medium-sized or smaller business, deciding how to manage cash balances is more often a matter left to the judgement and skill of the financial manager, in the light of the cashflow forecast. Once an 'optimal' cash balance is established, the remainder of a surplus should be invested in marketable securities.

6.4 Liquidity

We need to consider what we mean by surplus. Take the following example.

6.5 Example: liquidity

(a) Drif Co receives money every month from cash sales and from debtors for credit sales of $1,000. It makes payments, in the normal course of events of $800 a month. In January, the company uses an overdraft facility to buy a car for $4,000.

	Jan	*Feb*	*March*
	$	$	$
Brought forward	–	(3,800)	(3,600)
Receipts	1,000	1,000	1,000
Payments	(800)	(800)	(800)
Car	(4,000)	0	0
Overdrawn balance	(3,800)	(3,600)	(3,400)

The company has been left with a persistent overdraft, even though, in operating terms it makes a monthly surplus of $200.

(b) Guide Co on the other hand has monthly cash receipts of $1,200 and monthly cash payments of $1,050. The company sets up a special loan account: it borrows $5,000 to buy a car. This it pays off at the rate of $80 a month.

	Jan	Feb	March
	$	$	$
Brought forward	–	70	140
Receipts	1,200	1,200	1,200
Payments	(1,050)	(1,050)	(1,050)
Loan repayment	(80)	(80)	(80)
Operating surplus	70	140	210

Which do you consider has the healthier finances? Clearly Drif Co produces an operating surplus (before the motor purchase) of $200 ($1,000 – $800) a month, which is more than Guide ($150, ie $1,200 – $1,050). Furthermore Guide Co has a much higher net debt, the loan for the car being $5,000 as opposed to $4,000.

Yet, in effect the financing arrangements each has chosen has turned the tables. Drif Co is relying on normal overdraft finance which will be **repayable on demand**. Its normal **operating surplus** of receipts from sales and receivables over payments to suppliers has been completely swamped by the long-term financing of a car.

On the other hand, Guide Co, by arranging a separate term loan, which is more secure from Guide Co's point of view, is able to run an **operating surplus** of $70 a month. It has effectively separated an operating surplus arising out of month to month business expenses from its cash requirements for capital investment (in the car), a **financial inflow**.

This shows the following.

(a) A 'surplus' can sometimes be created by the way in which **financial information** is **presented**.

(b) It is often necessary to distinguish **different kinds** of cash transaction (eg capital payments).

(c) Different types of debt have **different risks** for the company attached to them.

Cash surpluses may arise from **seasonal factors**, so that surpluses generated in good months are used to cover shortfalls later. In this case, the management of the business needs to ensure that the surpluses are big enough to cover the later deficits. The mere existence of a surplus in one or two months in a row is no guarantee of liquidity in the long term.

6.6 Safety

Considerations of **safety** are also important. Cash surpluses are rarely hoarded on the company's premises, where they can be stolen: but what should be done with them, in the short term?

(a) They are assets of the company, and do need to be **looked after** as well as any other asset.

(b) In time of inflation, money effectively **falls in value**.

(c) Any surplus must be kept **secure**: as depositors in the collapsed Bank of Credit and Commerce International must be painfully aware, some banks are not as secure as others. Some investments are riskier than others.

6.7 Profitability

FAST FORWARD

Surplus funds can be deposited in **interest bearing accounts** offered by banks, finance houses or building societies. Generally speaking:

- These are for a fixed period of time
- Early withdrawal may not be permitted, or may result in a penalty
- The principal does not decline in monetary value

Question

Investing cash

Compare the following two situations. Steve and Andy are both in the car repair business. Both own equipment worth $4,000 and both owe $200 to suppliers. Steve, however, has accumulated $1,000 in cash which is deposited in a non interest bearing current account at his bank. Andy has $100 in petty cash.

	Steve	*Andy*
	$	$
Non-current assets	4,000	4,000
Cash at bank	1,000	100
Payables	(200)	(200)
Net assets	4,800	3,900
Profit for the year	1,200	1,200

Which would you say is the more profitable?

Answer

(a) Both obviously have made the same amount of profit in the year in question. In absolute terms they are equal.

(b) However, if we examine more closely, we find that the relative performance of Steve and Andy differs.

	Steve	*Andy*
$\frac{\text{Profit}}{\text{Net assets}}$	$\frac{\$1{,}200}{\$4{,}800} = 25\%$	$\frac{\$1{,}200}{\$3{,}900} = 30.8\%$

In other words, Andy is making the same amount out of more limited resources. Steve could have easily increased his profit if he had invested his spare cash and earned interest on it.

There is the other question about cash surpluses: what do you do with them, to make a profit? They are business assets like any other.

(a) In the long term, a company with an ever increasing cash balance can:

 (i) **Invest it in new business opportunities** for profit
 (ii) **Return it to owners/shareholders** by way of increased drawings/dividends

(b) In the short term, surplus funds need to be invested so that they can earn a return when they are not being used for any other purpose.

 (i) A return can be earned perhaps by an earlier payment of business debts. The return is the **'interest' saved**.

 (ii) Otherwise, there is a variety of deposit accounts and financial instruments which can be used to earn a return on the cash surpluses until they are needed. These are discussed in the next section of this chapter.

6.8 Guidelines for investing

Any business will normally have a number of guidelines as to how the funds are invested. A firm will try and maximise the return for an **acceptable** level of risk. What is acceptable depends on the preferences of the firm in question.

To maintain liquidity, it is often company policy that the surplus funds should be **invested** in financial instruments which are **easily converted** into cash; in effect, enough of the surplus funds should be invested to maintain liquidity.

There have been a number of reported incidents where a firm's corporate treasury department took too many risks with the firm's funds, investing them in risky financial instruments to gain a profit. These went sour, and firms have been left with high losses, arising solely out of treasury operations, with little relevance to the firm's main business.

Guidelines can cover issues such as the following.

(a) Surplus funds can only be invested in **specified types of investment** (eg no equity shares).

(b) All investments must be **convertible into cash** within a set number of days.

(c) Investments should be **ranked**: surplus funds to be invested in higher risk instruments only when a sufficiency has been invested in lower risk items (so that there is always a cushion of safety).

(d) If a firm invests in certain financial instruments, a **credit rating** should be obtained. Credit rating agencies, issue gradings according to risk.

6.9 Legal restrictions on investments

The type of investments an organisation can make is restricted by law in certain special cases:

(a) Where public (ie taxpayers') money is invested by a **public sector** (central or local government) institution

(b) Where the money is invested by a company on behalf of personal investors in cases such as **pension schemes**

(c) In the case of **trusts** (as determined by the relevant Act)

7 Cash investments: bank and building society accounts

7.1 High street bank deposits

Commercial banks in most countries offer a wide range of different types of interest earning account. The main banks and many building societies may also pay interest on some types of **current account** (for day-to-day transactions). Some of these may be of limited relevance to large corporations, but for sole traders and small businesses, high street bank products are important.

For someone who wishes to invest a small sum for a short period, **deposit account** facilities may be available from the banks.

7.2 High interest deposit accounts and high interest cheque accounts

If you have a larger amount of money to invest (typically a minimum of $500), you may be able to place the money in a high interest account. Access is usually still immediate, but the rate of interest offered will be higher.

7.3 Option deposits

These arrangements are offered in many countries for predetermined periods of time ranging from 2 to 7 years with minimum deposits of (say) $2,500. The interest rates, which may be linked to base rates, reflect the longer term nature of the arrangement and the corresponding lack of withdrawal facilities before the expiry of the agreed term. For businesses, these might be of limited relevance.

7.4 Other facilities

Banks may offer special facilities for larger amounts.

(a) With amounts of, say, over $50,000 it may be possible to get fixed rate quotes for **money market deposits** for varying intervals such as seven days up to eighteen months or longer.

(b) For still larger amounts it is possible to arrange for the money to be deposited with the bank's finance company at better rates than that available for normal deposits. Alternatively the business can go direct to a finance company itself.

8 Marketable securities: prices and interest rates

8.1 Marketable securities

In the cash investments discussed in the previous section, the investor's initial capital is secure. He cannot get back less than he put in. Another common feature is that such investments are not marketable.

However, there are also **marketable securities**, such as gilts, bonds and certificates of deposit. Such securities are bought and sold, and they earn interest. What determines their price?

8.2 Prices of fixed interest stocks

The price of marketable securities is affected by the following.

(a) The **interest rate** (known as the **coupon rate**) on a stock is normally fixed at the outset, but it may become more or less attractive when compared with the interest rates in the money markets as a whole. Let us take an example. Suppose that investors in the market expect a return of 6.47%.

(i) $2\frac{1}{2}$% Consolidated Stock pays $2.50 interest for every $100 of the stock's nominal value. However, the increased return means that:

$$\frac{\$2.50}{\text{Price of £100 nominal}} = 6.47\%$$

therefore, the expected price is $\frac{\$2.50}{0.0647} = \$38.64$

Where general interest rates rise, the price of stocks will fall.

(ii) Where general interest rates fall, the price of stocks will rise. For example, if the market required a return of 6%, the price of $100 nominal of a non-redeemable $2\frac{1}{2}$% stock would be:

$\frac{\$2.50}{\text{Price}} = 6\%$ therefore, the expected price is $41.67.

Both these examples ignore two other features affecting prices of stocks.

(b) The **risk** associated with the payment of interest and the **eventual repayment of capital**. British Government securities are considered virtually risk-free but other fixed interest stocks may not be.

(c) The **length of time to redemption** or **maturity**. Suppose the following market values were quoted on 25 March 20X2.

9% Treasury Stock 20X5	$113.8029
9% Treasury Stock 20X9	$142.6311

The first stock is due to be redeemed in 20X5, whereas the second will not be redeemed until the year 20X9. In both cases, as with all government securities except those that are index-linked, the stocks will be redeemed at their nominal value of $100. The closer a stock gets to its redemption date the closer will the price approach $100. This is known as the **pull to maturity**.

8.3 Yields on fixed interest stocks

FAST FORWARD

The **yield** (profitability) of a money market instrument depends on:

- Its face value
- The interest rate offered
- The period of time before it is redeemed (ie converted into cash) by the issuer

The paragraphs below concentrate on gilts (government securities) but the principles involved apply equally to any other fixed interest stocks including, for example company loan stock.

8.4 Interest yield

The yield for a particular gilt is an expression for the return on the stock if it was bought at the price ruling and held for one year.

Key term

The **interest yield** (also known as the flat yield or running yield) is the interest or coupon rate expressed as a percentage of the market price.

Question — Interest yield

On 19 March 20X0 the market price of 9% Treasury Stock 20X9 is $134.1742. What is the interest yield?

Answer

$$\text{Interest yield} = \frac{\text{Gross interest}}{\text{Market price}} \times 100\%$$

$$= \frac{9}{134.1742} \times 100\% = 6.71\%$$

The interest yield in practice is influenced by two other factors.

(a) **Accrued interest**

The interest on 10% Treasury Stock 2003 is paid in two equal instalments on 8 March and 8 September each year. Thus, if an investor were to sell his stock on 1 June 2000, in the absence of any other rules he would be forgoing a considerable amount of interest which will be received on 8 September 2000 by the purchaser. **The price paid by the purchaser must reflect this amount of accrued interest**, and this type of calculation is tested in Question: Cost of purchase in paragraph 4.6

(b) **Cum int** and **Ex int**

For administrative reasons, issuers of securities (eg the government) must close their books some time before the due date for the payment of interest, so that they can prepare and send out the necessary documentation in time for it to reach the registered owners of securities before the due dates. Any person who buys stocks **ex int** will not receive the next interest payment. This will be sent to the former owner.

8.5 Redemption yields

Key term

> **Redemption yield** is the rate of interest at which the total of the discounted values of any future payments of interest and capital is equal to the current price of a security. *(OT 2000)*

The interest yield takes no account of the fact that most Government stocks are redeemable (ie that their face value will be repaid) nor of the proximity of the redemption date although we have seen how the pull to maturity can affect the price. A more realistic measure of the overall return available from a stock is the **gross redemption yield**. This takes account of both the **interest payable until redemption** and the **redemption value**.

8.6 Example: redemption yield (yield to maturity)

A bond with a coupon rate of 8% is redeemable in 9 years time for $100. Its current market price is $91. What is the percentage yield to maturity?

Solution

This is an internal rate of return calculation. We will take two discount rates (see appendix 2) and see where the IRR is likely to fall.

Nine annual receipts of $8 and the final receipt in 9 years' time of $100, discounted at the IRR, will give us the current market price of $91.

We will begin by taking 10% as the discount rate.

t = 9, r = 10

($8 × 5.759) + ($100 × 0.424) = $46.07 + $42.40 = $88.47

This is very close to $91. Now we will try 9%.

t = 9, r = 9

($8 × 5.995) + ($100 × 46.0) = $47.96 + $46 = $93.96

We can see that the IRR must be midway between 10% and 9%.

(88.47 + 93.96)/2 = 91.21

So the percentage yield to maturity is 9.5%.

Exam focus point

> Both the May 2005 and November 2005 exams had questions on calculating the percentage yield to maturity.

Yields are determined by **market prices** which in turn reflect the **demand for particular stocks**. Thus, if a yield is relatively low it can be concluded that the price is relatively high and that the demand for the stock is also relatively high. Conversely, a high yield means that a stock is relatively unpopular.

The major factors affecting choice are these.

(a) Whether the investor is looking for **income or capital appreciation**

(b) The investor's **tax position**

(c) The investor's **attitude to the risk** inherent in gilts resulting from changes in interest rates. (It is important to remember that although the eventual repayment of a gilt is not in doubt, the market price may fluctuate widely between the date of purchase and the eventual redemption)

(d) **Other aspects** of the **investor's business** (The banks and building societies tend traditionally to concentrate on holding short-dated stocks (redeemable soon) while the insurance companies and pension funds which have long-term liabilities often match these with long-dated gilts (redeemable further in the future).)

9 Other types of investment

9.1 Government securities: example – gilts

FAST FORWARD

Gilts are securities issued by the UK government. Other fixed interest marketable securities include **local authority bonds**, and **corporate debt**.

Key term

The term **gilts** is short for 'gilt-edged securities' and refers to marketable British Government securities. These stocks, although small in number (around 100), dominate the fixed interest market in the UK.

The *Financial Times* classifies gilts according to the length of their lives.

(a) Shorts – lives up to five years (Stock Exchange up to seven years)

(b) Mediums – lives from five to fifteen years (Stock Exchange seven to fifteen years)

(c) Longs – lives of more than fifteen years

(d) Undated stocks (Issued many years ago these are sometimes known as irredeemable or one-way option stocks. These include *War Loan* $3^1/_2$*%, Conversion Loan* $3^1/_2$*%, Consolidated Stock* $2^1/_2$*%.* Each has certain other peculiarities)

(e) Index-linked stocks

By 'life' is meant the **number of years** before the issuer repays the principal amount.

9.1.1 Fixed interest gilts

Most gilts are fixed interest, and their prices and yields follow the principles outlined in Section 8 above.

9.1.2 Treasury bills

Key term

A **treasury bill** is government short-term debt, maturing in less than one year, and generally issued at a discount. *(OT 2000)*

Treasury bills are issued weekly by the government to finance short-term cash deficiencies in the government's expenditure programme. The holder is paid the full value of the bill on maturity. Since they are negotiable, they can be re-sold, if required, before their maturity date.

Treasury bills do not pay interest, but the purchase price of a Treasury bill is less than its face value, the amount that the government will eventually pay on maturity. There is thus an **implied rate of interest** in the price at which the bills are traded.

9.1.3 Index-linked stocks

There are various **index-linked Treasury stocks** in issue. The first such stock, 2% Treasury Stock 1996, was issued in March 1981. Both the interest and the eventual redemption value are linked to inflation.

These gilts offer a **guaranteed real return** equal to the **coupon rate**. Many investment fund managers would have considered such a return highly satisfactory over the last fifteen years.

9.1.4 Gilt prices in the Financial Times

Gilt prices are to be found in the *Financial Times*. For all categories other than index-linked gilts, the information is presented as follows.

Monday edition

Notes	*Price ($)*	*Wk% +/–*	*Amount $m*	*Interest due*	*Last xd*
Treas 10pc 20X3	121.0801	0.4	2,506	Mr 8 Se 8	22.2

Tuesday to Saturday editions

	Yield				*52 week*	
Notes	*Int*	*Red*	*Price ($)*	*+ or –*	*High*	*Low*
Treas 10pc 20X3	8.27	4.72	120.9273	+0.0600	123.52	115.44

The first (Monday) example above shows that:

(a) 10% Treasury Stock 20X3 was quoted at $121.0801 at the close of business on the previous Friday, a change of +0.4% in the week.

(b) $2,506 million of the stock was in issue.

(c) Interest is due on 8 March and 8 September.

(d) The stock last went **ex-interest** on 22 February. In other words, if you bought the stock after 22 February, you will not receive the interest due on 8 March. This interest will be paid to whoever held the stock up to 22 February.

The second (Tuesday to Saturday) example shows that:

(a) The current price of the same stock was $120.9273 at the close of business on the previous day, which is $0.06 higher than the price on the day before.

(b) The highest quoted price in the 52 weeks to date is $123.52; the lowest is $115.44.

(c) The gross interest yield and the gross redemption yield are given in the first two columns.

9.1.5 Purchase, sale and issue of gilts

Question — **Cost of purchase**

Suppose that a client wishes to purchase 13¾% Treasury Stock 2002-05 with a nominal value of $5,000. The transaction is executed by a stockbroker, who charges commission of 0.8%, in March 2001 at a price of $111.5064. Accrued interest is 56 days. What will be the total cost?

Answer

	$
Purchase consideration $5,000 @ 111.5064 per $100	5,575.32
Accrued interest: 56 days at 13¾% ($5,000 × 0.1375 × 56/365)	105.48
Broker's commission on consideration 0.8% on $5,575.32	44.60
Total purchase cost	5,725.40

Gilts can be dealt in any amount down to 1c. It is therefore quite possible to buy, say, $13,456.83 nominal value of a particular stock. This facility is often useful to investors who wish to round up an existing holding to some convenient figure. Similarly, it is quite possible to spend an exact amount on a particular stock. For example, an investor might ring up his stockbroker and ask him to buy $5,000 worth of the

13¾% Treasury Stock on the day referred to in the Question above. The broker would then buy stock with a nominal value of:

$$\$5{,}000 \times \frac{\$100}{\$111.5064} = \$4{,}484.05$$

9.2 Local authority stocks

We have already mentioned that it is possible for investors to deposit their money with local authorities. In addition to these investments there are a very large number of marketable local authority securities.

These stocks may, in most respects, be considered as being very similar to British Government Stocks. The main differences are as follows.

(a) The security of a local authority is not considered quite as **good** as that of the central government.

(b) The market in most of the stocks is **much thinner** (ie there are not many transactions) than for gilts, since the amounts involved are smaller and the stocks tend to be held by just a few institutions.

As a result of the points listed above, the yield on local authority stocks tends to be rather higher than on gilts.

9.3 Certificates of deposit

FAST FORWARD

A **certificate of deposit** is a certificate indicating that a sum of money has been deposited with a bank and will be repaid at a later date. As CDs can be bought and sold, they are a liquid type of investment.

Key term

A **certificate of deposit** is a negotiable instrument that provides evidence of a fixed term deposit with a bank. Maturity is normally within 90 days, but can be longer. *(OT 2000)*

9.3.1 Issue of CDs

Certificates of deposit (CDs) are issued by an institution (bank or building society), certifying that a specified sum has been deposited with the issuing institution, to be repaid on a specific date. The term may be as short as seven days, or as long as five years. The minimum nominal amount is usually $50,000, or its foreign currency equivalent.

Since CDs are negotiable, if the holder of a CD cannot wait until the end of the term of the deposit and wants cash immediately, the CD can be sold. The certificates of deposit market is one of the London money markets, and there is no difficulty for a CD holder to sell if the wish to do so arises. The appeal of a CD is that it offers an attractive rate of interest, *and* can be easily sold. CDs are sold on the market at a discount which reflects prevailing interest rates.

The document recognises the obligation of the amount to the **bearer** (with or without interest) at a future date. The holder of a certificate is therefore entitled to the money on deposit, usually with **interest**, on the stated date. Payment is obtained by presenting the CD on the appropriate date to a recognised bank (which will in turn present the CD for payment to the bank or building society that issued it).

CDs have one major advantage over a money-market time deposit with the same bank or building society, namely **liquidity**. Unlike a money market deposit which cannot be terminated until it matures, CDs can be liquidated **at any time** at the prevailing market rate. In return for this liquidity, the investor must, however, accept a lower yield than a money market deposit would command.

9.4 Bills of exchange

FAST FORWARD

A **bill of exchange** is like a cheque, only it is not drawn on a bank. It orders the drawee to pay money.

A **bill of exchange** is similar to a cheque although, strictly speaking, a cheque is a type of bill of exchange.

Key term

A **bill of exchange** is a negotiable instrument, drawn by one party on another, for example by a supplier of goods on a customer, who by accepting (signing) the bill, acknowledges the debt, which may be payable immediately (a sight draft) or at some future date (a time draft). The holder of the bill can, thereafter, use an accepted time draft to pay a debt to a third party, or can discount it to raise cash. *(OT 2000)*

9.4.1 Features

Term bills of exchange have the following features.

(a) Their **duration or maturity** may be from **two weeks** to **six months**.
(b) They can be **denominated** in any **currency**.
(c) They can be for a value of up to **$500,000** per bill.

Bills may be drawn in any currency.

9.4.2 Definitions

(a) The **bill** is **drawn** on the company or person who is being ordered to pay.
(b) The **drawer** orders payment of the money.
(c) The **drawee** is the party who is to pay, and to whom the bill is addressed.
(d) The **payee** receives the funds.

Let us take the example of a cheque. A (**the drawer**), writes out a cheque to B (the payee). The cheque instructs A's bank (**the drawee**), to pay B a sum of money. The drawee of a bill of exchange does not have to be a bank, and the payment date does not have to be immediate.

The **date of the bill** is normally the date when it is signed by the drawer. The place of drawing (which might be shown just as a town or city name) is also included. The amount payable must be shown in words and figures as in a cheque).

There are three ways of specifying the **due date for payment** of a term bill.

(a) On a stated date

(b) A stated period after sight (sighting date is when the drawee signs his acceptance of the bill)

(c) A stated period after the date of the bill

A bill is an unconditional order to pay, and it will always include the word 'pay' and be phrased so as to make it clear that the order is unconditional. The bill must also specify the name of the payee, which might be the drawer ('Pay... to our order') or a third party ('Pay.... to XYZ or order....').

For a term bill with a future payment date, the **drawee** signs his acceptance of the order to pay (**accepts the bill** in other words, agrees to pay) and returns the bill to the drawer or the drawer's bank. When a bill is accepted, it becomes an IOU or promise to pay. Acceptance of a term bill is by signature across the front of the bill. To an accepted bill there will also be added details of where the payment will be made.

For example, an accepted bill might have wording such as 'Accepted payable at Epsilon Bank, for and on behalf of Omega Tango Co' followed by the signature of an authorised person.

An example of an accepted bill is shown below. The name of the drawee is shown in the example on the bottom left-hand side.

9.4.3 Discounting bills

As an IOU, an accepted bill of exchange is a form of debt. It is a **negotiable instrument**.

(a) The holder of the bill can hold on to the bill until maturity, then present it to the specified bank for payment.

(b) Alternatively, the bill holder can **sell the bill** before **maturity**, for an amount below its payment value (ie at a discount). A bill of exchange can be transferred by a simple endorsement. (An authorised signatory of the drawer or bill holder signs the back of the bill, and gives the bill to the buyer. The buyer, as the new bill holder, will claim payment at maturity, unless the bill is sold on again.)

The ability of a bill holder to sell the bill for a reasonable price depends on:

(a) The **credit quality** of the drawee
(b) The **existence** of a liquid secondary market in bills

The **buyer** of a bill expects to make a profit by purchasing the bill at a discount to its face value and then either receiving full payment at maturity on presenting the bill for payment, or reselling the bill before maturity. The profit from buying a bill therefore represents an **interest yield** on a short-term investment (to maturity of the bill).

The seller obtains immediate cash from the buyer of the bill, but in effect is borrowing short-term funds, with the interest rate for borrowing built into the discount price.

Bills of exchange are also used to finance domestic and international trade, because they are tradeable instruments for short-term credit. There are two main types of bills of exchange.

(a) **Trade bills** are bills drawn by one non-bank company on another company, typically demanding payment for a trade debt. The ability of the drawer (bill holder) to discount a trade bill before maturity (ie resell the bill at a discount) depends on the financial status of the two companies concerned. Institutions will only buy the 'finest' trade bills, where both companies have a high credit standing.

(b) **Bank bills** are bills of exchange drawn and payable by a bank. The most common form of bank bill is a **banker's acceptance**, whereby a bank accepts a bill on behalf of a customer, and promises to pay the bill at maturity.

Money market instruments are traded on either an interest rate basis or a discount basis.

(a) When an **interest rate** basis applies, a **principal sum** is lent and the borrower repays the **principal plus interest** at maturity. The interest rate is specified and applied to the principal amount for the term of the loan to calculate the amount of interest payable. Bank loans are made on this basis.

(b) When a **discount basis** applies, a **specified sum** is **payable at maturity** to the holder of a money market instrument. If the instrument is purchased before maturity, the price will be less than the amount payable at maturity. For example, a bill of exchange for $50,000 payable in six months' time might be discounted (sold) for $47,500.

Size of discount

The **size of the discount** will reflect the interest rate that the buyer of the instrument wishes to receive, and the term to the instrument's maturity.

9.5 Other commercial stocks

FAST FORWARD

Commercial paper and **loan stock** are debt instruments issued by companies: commercial paper is unsecured.

9.5.1 Bonds

Key terms

A **bond** is a debt instrument normally offering a fixed rate of interest (coupon) over a fixed period of time, with a fixed redemption value.

Coupon is the annual interest payable on a bond, expressed as a percentage of the nominal value.

(OT 2000)

Bond is a term given to any fixed interest (mostly) security, whether it be issued by the government, a company, a bank or other institution. (Gilts are therefore **UK government bonds**.) Businesses also issue bonds. They are usually for the long term. They may or may not be secured.

9.5.2 Commercial paper

Key term

Commercial paper is unsecured short-term loan notes issued by companies, and generally maturing within three months.

Like a gilt, CP is traded often at a discount reflecting the yield required. It is a type of promissory note, and companies find them useful for short term borrowing (usually 3 months), and is unsecured. It is therefore risky. Although formal **credit ratings** are not required in some countries, they do help investors make rational choices: a firm's CP is therefore given a credit rating by third party agencies to assess its risk.

Loan stocks are issued in return for loans **secured on a particular asset of the business**. The factory, for example, may be offered as **security**. The loan is for the long term. Loan stock holders take priority over other payables when a business is wound-up. They can force a liquidation.

Key term

Permanent interest bearing shares (PIBS) are a type of security specially created to enable building societies to raise funds while improving their capital ratios.

PIBS are quoted on the London Stock Exchange and the market totals about $1 billion.

10 Risk and exposure

FAST FORWARD

Businesses should have guidelines in place covering **what sort of investments** are **allowed** and how much should be **invested** in **lower risk** securities.

10.1 Risk

Risk may be considered in terms of its effect on income, capital or both.

(a) **Income only**

For *most* cash investments there is virtually no risk that the *capital* invested will not be repaid. Also while there may be little doubt that the interest will be paid, those cash investments which carry a variable rate of interest also carry the risk that the rate will fall in line with conditions prevailing in the market.

(b) **Capital only**

With an investment in gilts or other 'undoubted' marketable fixed interest stocks, there is always a risk of a capital loss if prices fall, even though the payment of interest may be considered completely secure.

(c) **Capital and income**

For many investments both income and capital are at risk. Often a loss of income will precede a loss of capital. A company may reduce its ordinary share dividend, precipitating a fall in the share price.

Risk may be caused by general factors, or by factors specific to an individual security or sector.

(a) **General factors**

All investments are affected, to some extent, by changes in the political and economic climate. In October 1987 all major stockmarkets fell dramatically, apparently taking their cue from one another.

(b) **Inflation**

Investments are also at risk from inflation. A fall in the value of money may affect both income and capital. Cash and other non-equity investments are particularly susceptible, although the high yield may provide some compensation.

(c) **Special factors**

The results of an individual company will be affected not only by general economic conditions but also by:

(i) Its type of products or services
(ii) Its competitive position within the industry
(iii) Management factors

10.2 The relationship between risk and return

The return expected by an investor will, as you will now be aware, depend on the level of risk. The higher the risk, the higher the required return. This can be illustrated as in the diagram below.

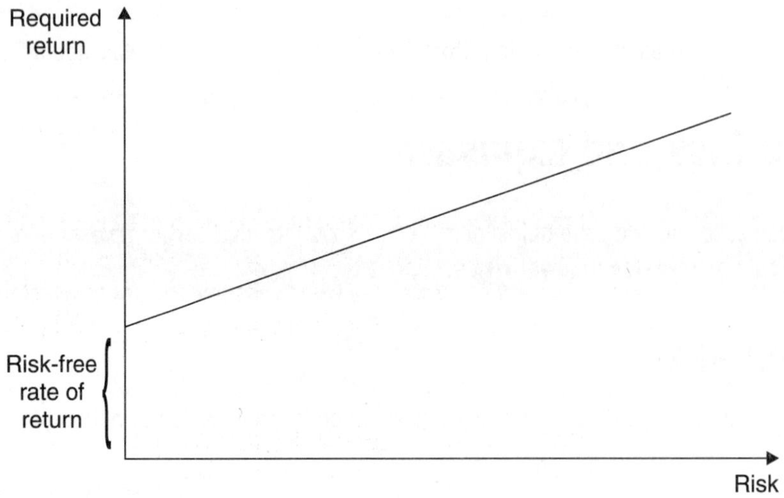

Marketable UK securities can be ranked in order of increasing risk and increasing expected return.

- Government securities — *Low risk*
- Local authority stocks
- Other 'public' corporation stocks
- Company loan stocks
- Other secured loans
- Unsecured loans
- Convertible loan stocks
- Preference shares
- Equities — *High risk*

(a) **Government stock**

The risk of default is negligible and hence this tends to form the base level for returns in the market. The only uncertainty concerns the movement of interest rates over time, and hence longer dated stocks will tend to carry a higher rate of interest.

(b) **Company loan stock**

Although there is some risk of default on company loan stock (also called corporate bonds), the stock is usually secured against corporate assets.

(c) **Preference shares**

These are generally riskier than loan stock since they rank behind debt in the event of a liquidation, although they rank ahead of equity. The return takes the form of a fixed percentage dividend based on the par value of the share. Sometimes it is possible for investors to receive a higher rate of return if distributable profits exceed a given level. However, the dividend may be missed if results are particularly poor.

(d) **Ordinary shares**

Ordinary shares carry a high level of risk. Dividends are paid out of distributable profits after all other liabilities have been paid and can be subject to large fluctuations from year to year. However, there is the potential for significant capital appreciation in times of growth. In general, the level of risk will vary with the operational and financial gearing of the company and the nature of the markets in which it operates.

(e) **CDs and Bills of Exchange**

The riskiness of CDs and bills of exchange varies with the creditworthiness of the issuers. They are riskier than government (and probably local government) securities, but less risky than shares.

What combination of risk and return is appropriate? Given that an investor is faced with a range of investments with differing risk/return combinations, what sort of investment should he choose? This is a very difficult question to answer. Whilst it is safe to assume that most investors are risk-averse (they prefer less risk to more risk, given the same return), the intensity of that aversion varies between individuals.

10.3 Diversification and holding a portfolio

FAST FORWARD

The relative attractiveness of investing in any of these securities derives from their **return** and the **risk**. **Diversification** across a range of separate investments can reduce risk for the investor.

As we saw earlier, holding more than one investment always carries less risk than holding only one. If only one investment is held, the investor could lose a lot if this one investment fails. The extent to which risk can be reduced will depend on the relationship which exists between the different returns. The process of reducing risk by increasing the number of separate investments in a portfolio is known as **diversification**.

Chapter Roundup

- Maintenance of **liquidity** is an important corporate objective. Organisations may have problems due to **timing differences**, **risk** and **contingencies**.
- **Overdrafts** are a form of short-term lending, technically repayable on demand. Businesses may not need to use the overdraft facilities that they have been granted.
- Bank loans can be a **source** of **short medium or long-term finance**, linked with the purchase of specific assets. Interest and repayments will be set in advance.
- **Trade credit** from suppliers is another possible short-term source of finance.
- It is worth remembering that the **exporter** can obtain finance from the foreign buyer by insisting on **cash with order** and the **importer** can obtain finance from the foreign supplier by means of normal trade credit, perhaps evidenced by a term bill of exchange.
- **Export factoring** provides all the advantages of factoring generally and is useful in assessing credit risk.
- **Forfaiting** provides medium-term finance for importers of capital goods.
- A company has a variety of opportunities for using its **cash surpluses**, but the choice of obtaining a return is determined by considerations of **profitability**, **liquidity** and **safety**.
- Surplus funds can be deposited in **interest bearing accounts** offered by banks, finance houses or building societies. Generally speaking:
  - These are for a fixed period of time
  - Withdrawal may not be permitted, or may result in a penalty
  - The principal does not decline in monetary value
- The **yield** (profitability) of a money market instrument depends on:
  - Its face value
  - The interest rate offered
  - The period of time before it is redeemed (ie converted into cash) by the issuer
- **Gilts** are securities issued by the UK government. Other fixed interest marketable securities include **local authority bonds**, and **corporate debt**.
- **Commercial paper** and **loan stock** are debt instruments issued by companies: commercial paper is unsecured.
- A **certificate of deposit** is a certificate indicating that a sum of money has been deposited with a bank and will be repaid at a later date. As CDs can be bought and sold, they are a liquid type of investment.
- A **bill of exchange** is like a cheque, only it is not drawn on a bank. It orders the drawee to pay money.
- The relative attractiveness of investing in any of these securities derives from their **return** and the **risk**. **Diversification** across a range of separate investments can reduce risk for the investor.
- Businesses should have guidelines in place covering **what sort of investments** are **allowed** and how much should be **invested** in **lower risk** securities.

Quick Quiz

1 Which of the following is **not** a type of bank borrowing?

A Term loan
B Certificate of deposit
C Revolving facility
D Uncommitted facility

2 Match the name of the bank borrowing facilities detailed below with the relevant description.

Facility		*Description*	
A	Overdraft	1	Renewable after a set period.
B	Revolving facility	2	Borrowing of a fixed amount for a fixed period.
C	Term loan	3	Borrowing through the customer's current account up to a certain limit. Repayable on demand.

3 What reasons may make a business ask for an overdraft to reduce trade payables?

4 Which of the following is normally an advantage of an overdraft over a term loan?

A No risk of the bank withdrawing the facility
B Interest only paid to the extent that funds are required
C Better for borrowing to finance purchase of non-current assets
D Planning and budgeting are simpler

5 Banks are generally likely to grant an overdraft facility when a business is building up its inventory.

True ☐

False ☐

6 Which of the following methods could *not* be used to reduce the risk of bad debts in foreign trade?

A Export factoring
B Forfaiting
C Advances against collections
D Documentary credits

7 Apart from liquidity, what are the other two key considerations which a business should bear in mind in managing cash?

8 .... is an unsecured short-term loan note issued by companies, and generally maturing within three months.

9 Interest yield = $\frac{\boxed{}}{\boxed{}}$ × 100%. Fill in the boxes.

10 On a particular day, 9% Treasury Stock 2012 is quoted at a price of $141. What is the coupon rate?

11 The market prices of gilts will generally fall if interest rates rise.

True ☐

False ☐

12 Rank the following in order of risk (1 for the lowest risk).

☐	Preferred shares
☐	Government securities
☐	Company loan stock
☐	Ordinary shares
☐	Local authority stocks

13 Ms Archer is intending to purchase 8% Treasury Stock 2003-06 with a nominal value of $10,000. The transaction is executed by a broker, who charges commission of 0.8%, at a price of $105.50. Accrued interest is 30 days. What will be the total cost?

A $10,700
B $10,634
C $10,616
D $10,550

Answers to Quick Quiz

1 B This is a type of investment, not a debt.

2 A3; B1; C2

3 (a) To take advantage of early settlement discounts
(b) To pay suppliers who are pressing for payment

4 B Interest only paid to the extent funds are required

5 False. Some reasons for building up inventories (coping with seasonal demand, taking advantage of favourable purchase terms) will probably be acceptable to the bank, but generally such build-ups will be temporary. Banks are less likely to grant an increase to support a permanent increase in inventory level.

6 C This can reduce the investment in foreign receivables, but it does not reduce the risk of bad debts.

7 Safety; profitability

8 Commercial paper

9 $\text{Interest yield} = \frac{\text{Coupon rate}}{\text{Market price}} \times 100\%$

10 9%

11 True

12 Preferred shares, 4; Government securities, 1; Company loan stock, 3; Ordinary shares, 5; Local authority stocks, 2.

13 A

	$
Purchase consideration: $10,000 @ $105.50 per $100	10,550
Accrued interest: 30 days at 8% ($10,000 × 0.08 × 30/365)	66
Broker's commission: $10,550 × 0.8%	84
	10,700

Now try the question below from the Exam Question Bank

Number	Level	Marks	Time
Q32	Examination	20	36 mins

19

Receivables and payables

Introduction

The previous chapters have discussed some of the issues of managing cash, and you will have noted the **time lag** between the provision of goods and services and the receipt of cash for them. This time lag, as we have seen, can result in a firm making considerable demands on its bank to finance its working capital. Any increase in the time lag can make it significantly more difficult for a business to pay **its** own debts as they fall due.

This chapter introduces receivables management by considering the policy decisions that a business has to take in relation to **all** receivables.

An important decision in this area is whether to offer **settlement discounts** in return for quicker payment.

The credit controller also has to monitor the ongoing creditworthiness of customers and the **aged receivables listing** is a principal instrument used.

Section 7 deals with ways of limiting or managing the risk from bad debts.

In sections 8 and 9 we look at the need to monitor payables and describe payment methods and procedures. As with receivables, the effect of discounts is important.

Topic list	Learning outcomes	Syllabus references	Ability required
1 What is credit control?	D (v)	D (7)	Evaluation
2 Total credit	D (v)	D (7)	Evaluation
3 The credit cycle	D (v)	D (7)	Evaluation
4 Payment terms and settlement discounts	D (vi)	D (8)	Analysis
5 Maintaining information on receivables	D (vi)	D (9)	Analysis
6 Collecting debts	D (vi)	D (10)	Evaluation
7 Credit insurance, factoring and invoice discounting	D (vi)	D (10)	Analysis
8 Managing payables	D (vi)	D(9)	Evaluation
9 Methods of paying suppliers	D (vi)	D(11)	Evaluation

1 What is credit control?

FAST FORWARD

Credit control deals with a firm's management of its working capital. **Trade credit** is offered to business customers. **Consumer credit** is offered to household customers.

1.1 Credit

There are two aspects to **credit** we shall consider here.

(a) **Trade credit**

This is credit issued by a business to another business. For example, many invoices state that payment is expected within thirty days of the date of the invoice. In effect this is giving the customer thirty days credit. The customer is effectively borrowing at the supplier's expense.

(b) **Consumer credit**

This is credit offered by businesses to the end-consumer.

(i) Many businesses offer **hire purchase terms**, whereby the consumer takes out a loan to repay the goods purchased. Failure to repay will result in the goods being repossessed.

(ii) In practice, much of the growth in consumer credit has been driven not so much by retailers as by banks. **Credit cards** are largely responsible for the explosive growth in consumer credit.

Credit control issues are closely bound up with a firm's management of liquidity, discussed in earlier chapters. Credit is offered to enhance sales and profitability, but this should not be to the extent that a company becomes illiquid and insolvent.

Credit is also vital in securing orders in certain specified situations.

(a) **Economic conditions** can influence the type and amount of credit offered. In 'boom times, when customers are queuing with orders' (Bass, in *Credit Management Handbook*), new customers can be asked for security, and risk can be minimised. In other times, credit must be used to entice customers in, and so the credit manager's job is to control risk.

(b) **High-risk or marginal customers** require flexible payment arrangements. High risk customers are often profitable, but the risk has to be managed. The customer may require a credit limit of $50,000, on standard terms, but may only deserve $35,000. The supplier might choose instead to offer a $30,000 credit limit, together with a discount policy to encourage early payment.

Just as there is a relationship between offering credit and securing sales, so too there has to be a suitable working relationship between credit control personnel and sales and marketing staff. This is because, in the words of Bass, 'a sale is not complete until the money is in the bank' and the cost of chasing after slow payers and doubtful debts is considerable.

1.2 A firm's credit policy

A firm should have policies for credit and credit control.

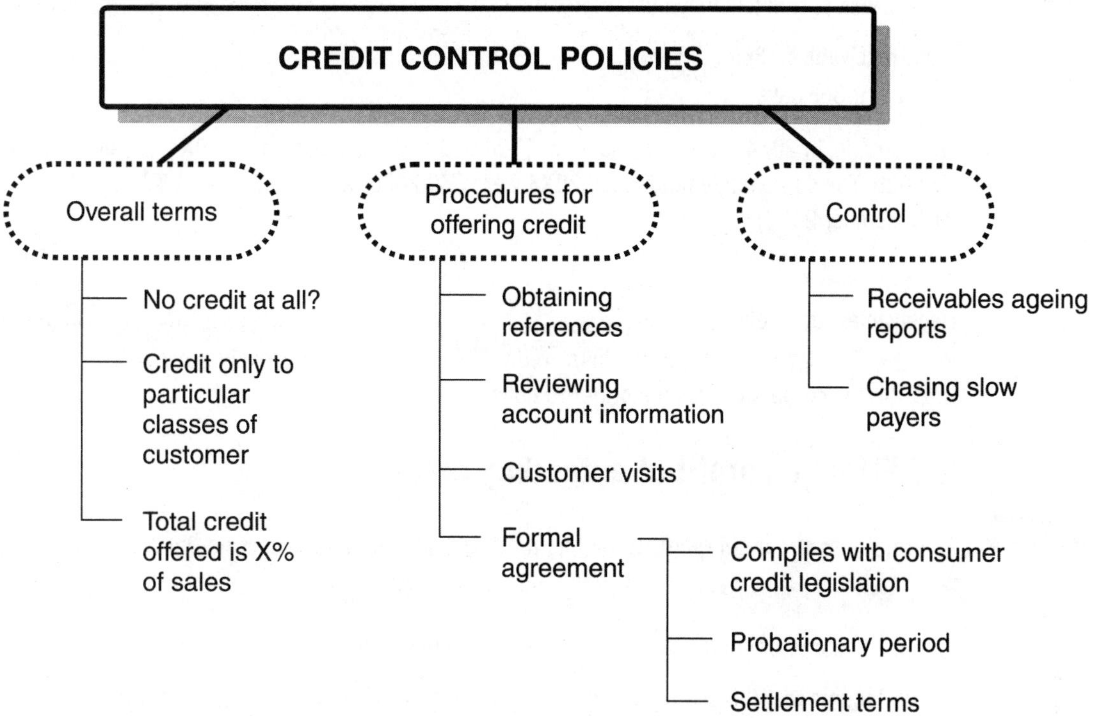

When a new customer applies for credit, their credit status will be assessed in a number of ways:

(a) References. Standard practice is to require a banker's reference and two trade references.
(b) The company's published accounts.
(c) The use of credit reference agencies such as Dun and Bradstreet.

2 Total credit

FAST FORWARD

Total credit can be measured in a variety of ways. Financial analysts use days sales in receivables, but as this is an annualised figure it gives no idea as to the make-up of total receivables.

2.1 The cost of credit

A bank's decision to lend money to a customer is determined by many factors over which the customer has little control. The bank, for example, might only wish to extend so much credit to firms in a particular industry.

Similarly, the firm itself has to maintain a 'global' approach to credit control in the light of the firm's objectives for **profit**, **cash flow**, **asset use** and **reducing interest costs**.

Finding a **total level of credit** which can be offered is a matter of finding the least costly balance between enticing customers, whose use of credit entails considerable costs, and refusing opportunities for profitable sales.

Firstly it helps to see what receivables, which often account for 30% of the total assets of a business, actually represent.

2.2 Measuring total receivables

The **days sales in receivables ratio**, sometimes called **receivables payment period** represents the length of the credit period taken by customers.

$$\frac{\text{Total receivables} \times 365}{\text{Sales in 365 days}} \text{ Days sales}$$

For example, in 20X4 X Co made sales of $700,000 and at 31 December 20X4, receivables stood at $90,000. The comparable figures for 20X3 were $600,000 (annual sales) and $70,000 (receivables at 31 December 20X3).

	20X4	*20X3*
Receivables represent	$\frac{\$90,000 \times 365}{\$700,000}$ = 47 days	$\frac{\$70,000 \times 365}{\$600,000}$ = 43 days

In 20X4, the company is taking longer to collect its debts.

2.3 Effect on profit of extending credit

FAST FORWARD

The **total investment in receivables** has to be considered in its impact on the general investment in working capital.

The main cost of offering credit is the interest expense. How can we assess the effect on profit?

Let us assume that the Zygo Company sells widgets for $1,000, which enables it to earn a profit, after all other expenses except interest, of $100 (ie a 10% margin).

(a) Aibee buys a widget for $1,000 on 1 January 20X1, but does not pay until 31 December 20X1. Zygo relies on overdraft finance, which costs it 10% pa. The effect is:

	$
Net profit on sale of widget	100
Overdraft cost $1,000 × 10% pa	(100)
Actual profit after 12 months credit	Nil

In other words, the entire profit margin has been wiped out in 12 months.

(b) If Aibee had paid after six months, the effect would be:

	$
Net profit	100
Overdraft cost $1,000 × 10% pa × $^6/_{12}$ months	(50)
	50

Half the profit has been wiped out. (*Tutorial note.* The interest cost might be worked out in a more complex way to give a more accurate figure.)

(c) If the cost of borrowing had been 18%, then the profit would have been absorbed before seven months had elapsed. If the net profit were 5% and borrowing costs were 15%, the interest expense would exceed the net profit after four months.

A second general point is the relation of **total credit to bad debts**. Burt Edwards argues that there is a law of 10-to-1: 'Experience in different industries shows that the annual interest expense of borrowings to support overdue debts, ie those in excess of agreed payment terms, is at least ten times the total lost in bad debts'. This is not a 'law', but has been observed to be the case over a variety of UK businesses.

Question

Cost of credit

Winterson Tools has an average level of receivables of $2m at any time representing 60 days outstanding. (Their terms are thirty days.) The firm borrows money at 10% a year. The managing director is proud of the credit control: 'I only had to write off $10,000 in bad debts last year,' she says proudly. Is she right to be proud?

Answer

At the moment, Winterson Tools is paying 10% × $1m (ie $^{30}/_{60}$ days × $2m) = $100,000 in interest caused by customers taking the extra month to pay.

The level of total credit can then have a significant effect on **profitability**. That said, if credit considerations are included in pricing calculations, it may be the case that extending credit can, in fact, increase profitability. If offering credit generates extra sales, then those extra sales will have additional repercussions on:

(a) The **amount of inventory** maintained in the warehouse, to ensure that the extra demand must be satisfied

(b) The **amount of money** the company **owes** to its **suppliers** (as it will be increasing its supply of raw materials)

This means an increase in **working capital**. Working capital is an **investment**, just as a non-current asset (eg new machinery) is, albeit of a different kind.

To determine whether it would be profitable to extend the level of total credit, it is necessary to assess the following.

- The additional sales volume which might result
- The profitability of the extra sales
- The extra length of the average debt collection period
- The required rate of return on the investment in additional receivables

Question

Increase in credit period

A company is proposing to increase the credit period that it gives to customers from one calendar month to one and a half calendar months in order to raise sales from the present annual figure of $24 million representing 4m units per annum. The price of the product is $6 and it costs $5.40 to make. The increase in the credit period is likely to generate an extra 150,000 unit sales. Is this enough to justify the extra costs given that the company's required rate of return is 20%? Assume no changes to inventory levels, as the company is increasing its operating efficiency. Assume that existing customers will take advantage of the new terms.

Answer

The existing value of receivables is:

$$\frac{£24\text{ m}}{12\text{ months}} = \$2\text{m}$$

If sales increased by 150,000 units, the value of receivables would be:

$$1\tfrac{1}{2} \times \frac{\$24m + (150{,}000 \times \$6)}{12 \text{ months}} = \$3{,}112{,}500.$$

The receivables have to be financed somehow, and the additional $1,112,500 will cost $1,112,500 × 20% = $222,500 in financing costs.

The profit on the extra sales is: 150,000 units × ($6 – $5.40) = $90,000

The new credit policy is not worthwhile, mainly because existing customers would also take advantage of it.

2.4 Example: total investment in receivables

RB Co is considering a change of credit policy which will result in a slowing down in the average collection period from one to two months. The relaxation in credit standards is expected to produce an increase in sales in each year amounting to 25% of the current sales volume.

Sales price per unit	$10.00
Profit per unit (before interest)	$1.50
Current sales revenue per annum	$2.4 million

The required rate of return on investment is 20%.

Assume that the 25% increase in sales would result in additional inventories of $100,000 and additional payables of $20,000. Advise the company on whether or not it should extend the credit period offered to customers, in the following circumstances.

(a) If all customers take the longer credit of two months

(b) If existing customers do not change their payment habits, and only the new customers take a full two months' credit

Solution

The change in credit policy would be justifiable, in the context of this question, if the rate of return on the additional investment in working capital exceeds 20%.

Extra profit	
Profit margin $^{\$1.50}/_{\$10}$ =	15%
Increase in sales revenue $2.4m × 25%	$0.6 million
Increase in profit (15% × $0.6m)	$90,000

The total sales revenue is now $3m ($2.4m + $0.6m)

(a) *Extra investment, if all customers take two months credit*

	$
Average receivables after the sales increase (2/12 × $3 million)	500,000
Current average receivables (1/12 × $2.4 million)	200,000
Increase in receivables	300,000
Increase in inventories	100,000
	400,000
Increase in payables	(20,000)
Net increase in 'working capital'	380,000

$$\text{Return on extra investment } \frac{\$90{,}000}{\$380{,}000} = 23.7\%$$

(b) *Extra investment, if only the new customers take two months credit*

	$
Increase in receivables (2/12 × $0.6 million)	100,000
Increase in inventories	100,000
	200,000
Increase in payables	(20,000)
Net increase in working capital investment	180,000

Return on extra investment $\frac{\$90,000}{\$180,000} = 50\%$

In both case (a) and case (b) the new credit policy appears to be worthwhile.

Furthermore, the cost profile of the product can also support extra sales. If the firm has high fixed costs but low variable costs, the extra production and sales could provide a substantial contribution at little extra cost.

Exam focus point

You may be required to evaluate whether a proposed change in credit policy is financially justified. This is the procedure you should follow.

2.5 Receivables quality and liquidity

Another objective of any credit control system is to minimise any risks to **cash flow** arising from insolvent customers. The **quality** of receivables has an important impact on a firm's overall liquidity. Receivable quality is determined by their **age** and **risk**.

Some **industries** have a higher level of risk than others, in other words, there is a higher probability that customers will fail to pay. Some markets are riskier than others. Selling goods to a country with possible payment difficulties is riskier than selling them in the home market.

For many customers, delaying payment is the cheapest form of finance available and there has been much publicity recently about the difficulties that delayed payments cause to small businesses. There is no easy answer to this problem.

2.6 Policing total credit

The total amount of credit offered, as well as individual accounts, should be policed to ensure that the senior management policy with regard to the total credit limits is maintained. A **credit utilisation report** can indicate the extent to which total limits are being utilised. An example is given below.

Customer	*Limit*	*Utilisation*	
	$'000	$'000	%
Alpha	100	90	90
Beta	50	35	70
Gamma	35	21	60
Delta	250	125	50
	435	271	
		62.3%	

This might also contain other information, such as days sales outstanding and so on.

Reviewed in aggregate, this can reveal the following.

- The number of customers who might want more credit
- The extent to which the company is exposed to receivables
- The 'tightness' of the policy
- Credit utilisation in relation to total sales

It is possible to design credit utilisation reports to highlight other trends.

- The degree of exposure to different countries
- The degree of exposure to different industries

Trade receivables analysis as at 31 December

Industry	*Current credit utilisation*	*% of total receivables*	*Annual sales*	*As a % of total sales*
	$'000	%	$ million	%
Property	9,480	25.0	146.0	19.2
Construction	7,640	20.2	140.1	18.4
Engineering	4,350	11.5	112.6	14.8
Electricals	4,000	10.6	83.7	11.0
Electricity	2,170	5.7	49.2	6.5
Transport	3,230	8.5	79.9	10.5
Chemicals, plastics	1,860	4.9	43.3	5.7
Motors, aircraft trades	5,170	13.6	105.8	13.9
	37,900	100.0	760.6	100.0

Analysis

(a) An industry analysis of credit exposure shows in this case that over 45% of the company's trade receivables (about $17 million) are in the property and construction industries. Management should have a view about this exposure to industry risk.

(b) The size of the exposure to property and construction could seem excessive, in view of the cyclical nature of these industries, the current economic outlook, and the comparatively slow payment rate from these customers. (These industries account for only 37.6% of annual sales, but 45.2% of trade receivables.) Management might wish to consider whether the company should try to reduce this exposure.

(c) A decision might also be required about whether the company should be willing to accumulate trade receivables in these sectors, in order to sustain sales, or whether the credit risk would be too high.

2.7 Conclusion

The amount of **total credit** that a business offers is worthy of consideration at the highest management levels. Two issues are:

- The firm's working capital needs and the investment in receivables
- The management responsibility for carrying out the credit control policy

Question **Inflation**

Your company is concerned about the effect of inflation, which (you should suppose) currently stands at 6%, on its credit control policy. Outline the main points to consider, for discussion with your manager.

Answer

Inflation accentuates the importance of credit control, because the cost of the investment in receivables, in real terms, is higher. If a company grants credit of $100,000 for 3 months, and the rate of inflation is 6% per annum, the value in 'today's money' of the eventual receipts in 3 months' time would be about 1½% less – ie about $1,500 less. If the rate of inflation went up to, say, 12%, the value of the same receipts in 3 months' time would be about $3,000 less. In other words, the cost of granting credit increases as the rate of inflation gets higher. Also, with higher inflation, customers have an increased incentive to pay late.

3 The credit cycle

FAST FORWARD

The **credit control department** is responsible for those stages in the collection cycle dealing with the offer of credit, and the collection of debts.

3.1 The credit cycle

The credit control function's jobs occupy a number of stages of the **order cycle** (from customer order to invoice despatch) and the **collection cycle** (from invoice despatch to the receipt of cash), which together make up the **credit cycle.** The job of the credit control department can comprise all those activities within the dotted line **in the diagram on the next page**.

(a) **Establish credit status for new customers or customers who request a credit extension.**

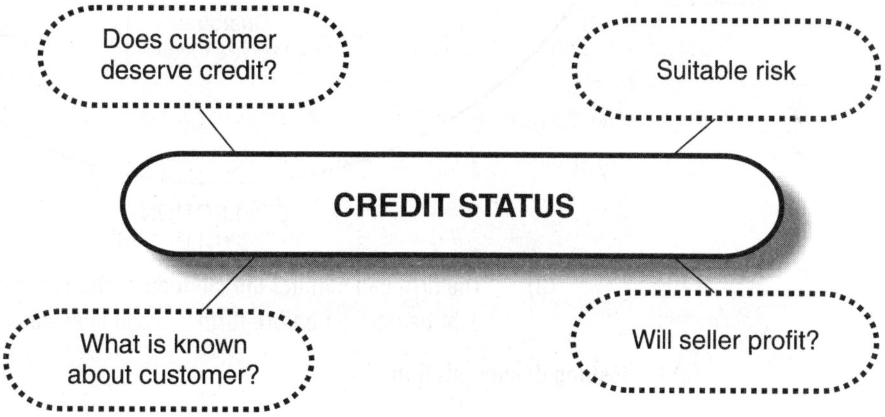

(b) **Check credit limit**

If the order is fairly routine, and there is no problem with credit status, then credit control staff examine their records or at least the sales ledger records to see if the new order will cause the customer to exceed the credit limit. There are a number of possible responses, as follows.

(i) **Authorisation**

If the credit demanded is within the credit limit, and there are no reasons to suspect any problems, then the request will be authorised.

(ii) **Referral**

It is possible that the credit demanded will exceed the limit offered in the agreement.

(1) The firm can simply **refuse the request for credit**, at the risk of damaging the business relationship. However, credit limits are there for a reason – to protect the business's profitability and liquidity.

(2) The firm can offer a **revised credit limit**. For example, the customer may be solvent and a regular payee, therefore a low risk. The company might be able to offer a higher credit limit to this customer.

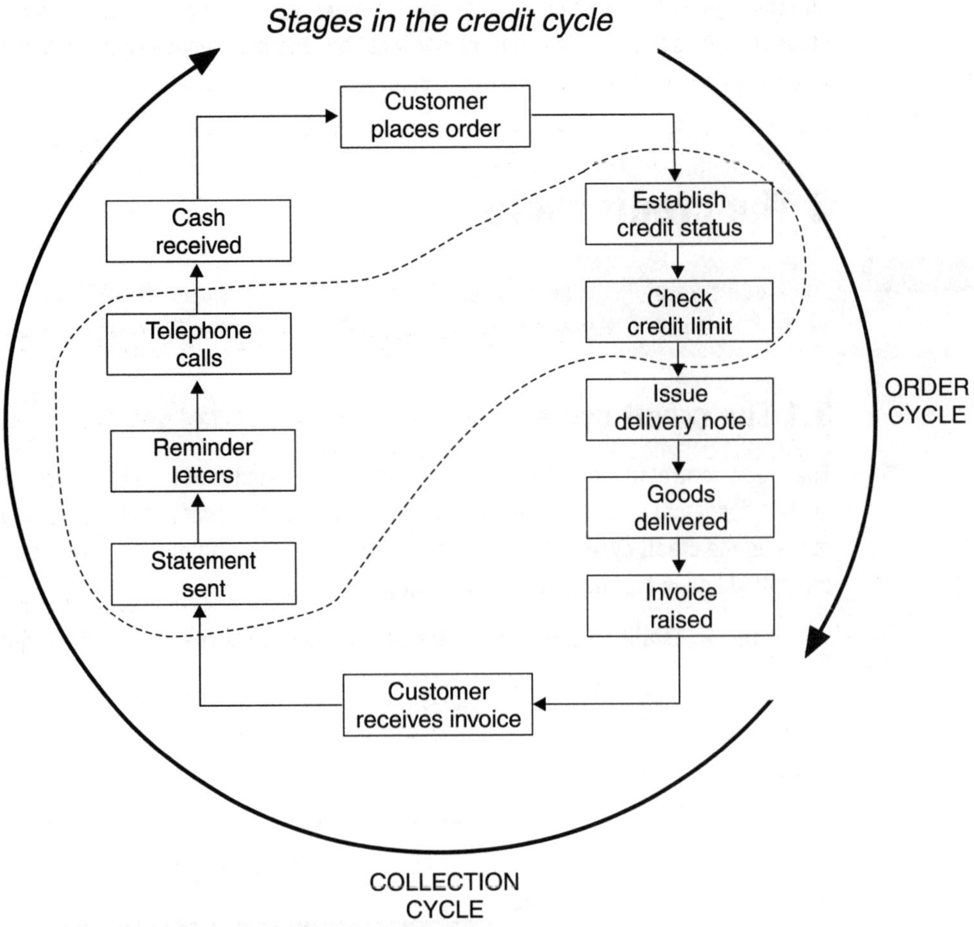

(3) The firm can **contact the customer**, and request that some of the outstanding debt be paid off before further credit is advanced.

(c) **Issuing documentation**

Issuing the delivery note, invoicing and so on is not the job of the credit control department, but the credit control department will need to have **access to information** such as invoice details to do its job.

(d) **Settlement**

The credit control department takes over the collection cycle, although the final payment is ultimately received by the accounts department. Collection involves reviewing overdue debts, and chasing them.

Question — Credit control and working capital

See if you can explain the likely effects of a company's credit control policy on the control of working capital in general.

Answer

Working capital includes inventory, receivables, payables and cash. The effect of credit policy on working capital is that if **more credit** is granted, there will be a **slowdown** in the **inflow of cash** (unless the extension of credit also results in an increase in sales). **Discounts** for **early payment** would also affect cash flows. Similarly, **tightening up on credit** and so granting less credit will result in a **speeding up** of **cash inflows**, provided that there is no reduction in sales as a consequence of the restriction of credit.

The total amount of working capital should be kept under control because the investment in working capital must be financed, and so excessive receivables are unnecessarily costly and would reduce the organisation's return on capital employed.

Credit policy is therefore significant both from the point of view of **liquidity** (cash flow) and the **management of finance** (investment).

4 Payment terms and settlement discounts

FAST FORWARD

A firm must consider suitable **payment terms** and **payment methods**. **Settlement discounts** can be offered, if cost effective and if they improve liquidity.

4.1 Payment terms

An important aspect of the credit control policy is to devise suitable **payment terms**, covering when should payment be made and how this should be achieved.

(a) Credit terms have to take into account the **expected profit** on the sale and the seller's cash needs.

(b) Credit terms also establish when **payment is to be received**, an important matter from the seller's point of view.

TERMS AND CONDITIONS OF SALE

- **Nature of goods to be supplied**
- **Price**
- **Delivery**
- **Date of payment**
- **Frequency of payment**
- **Discounts**

The credit terms the seller offers depend on many factors.

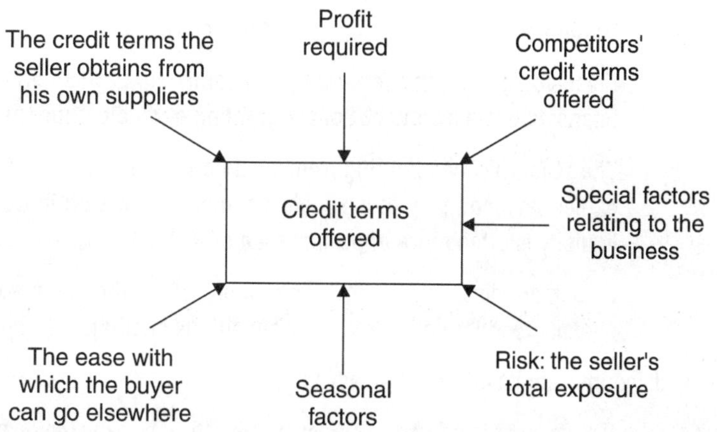

The terms must be simple to understand and easily enforceable. If the seller does not enforce his terms he is creating a precedent.

All sale agreements are **contracts**, as described earlier: credit terms are part of the contract. Although contracts do not have to be in writing, it helps if they are, and these are confirmed by the invoice.

PAYMENT TERMS	
Payment a specified number of days after delivery	Eg Net 10 (10 days)
Weekly credit	All supplies in a week must be paid for by a specified date in the next week
Half monthly credit	All supplies in one half of month must be paid for by a specified date in the next
10th and 25th	Supplies in first half of the month must be paid for by 25th, supplies in second half must be paid for by 10th of next month
Monthly credit	Payment for month's supplies must be paid by specified date in next month; if date 7th might be written Net 7 prox. Some monthly credit called Number MO; 2MO means payment must be in next month but one
Delivery	Certain payment terms geared to delivery • CWO Cash with order • CIA Cash in advance • COD Cash on delivery • CND Cash on next delivery

4.2 Methods of payment

Payment can be accepted in a variety of forms.

- Cash
- BACS
- Cheques
- Banker's draft
- Travellers' cheques or Eurocheques
- Postal orders
- Standing order
- Direct debit
- Credit card
- Debit card
- Bills of exchange, promissory notes
- Internet transfers

4.3 Payment times: settlement discounts

Some firms offer settlement discounts if payment is received early.

(a) If sensibly priced, they encourage customers to pay earlier, thereby avoiding some of the financing costs arising out of the granting of credit. Thus they can affect **profitability**.

(b) The seller may be suffering from cash flow problems. If settlement discounts encourage earlier payment, they thus enable a company to **maintain liquidity**. In the short term, liquidity is often more important than profitability.

(c) Settlement discounts might, conceivably, **affect the volume of demand** if, as part of the overall credit terms offered, they encourage customers to buy.

However discounts can have certain disadvantages.

(a) If a discount is offered to **one customer**, the company may have to offer it to other customers.
(b) **Discounts** may be **difficult to withdraw**.
(c) They establish a **set settlement period**, which might otherwise be lowered in the future.

To consider whether the offer of a discount for early payment is financially worthwhile it is necessary to compare the **cost** of the discount with the **benefit** of a reduced investment in receivables.

4.4 Example: settlement discounts

Wingspan currently has sales of $3m, with an average collection period of two months. No discounts are given. The management of the company are undecided as to whether to allow a discount on sales of 2% to settle within one month. The company assumes that all customers would take advantage of the discount. The company can obtain a return of 30% on its investments.

Advise the management whether or not to introduce the discount.

Solution

In this example the offer of a discount is not expected to increase sales demand. The advantage would be in the **reduction of the collection period**, and the resulting saving in the working capital investment required.

Our solution will value receivables at sales value.

(a) *Change in receivables*

	Receivables valued at sales price
	$
Current value of receivables (2/12 × $3m)	500,000
New value of receivables (1/12 × $3m)	250,000
Reduction in investment in receivables	250,000

(b) The cost of reducing receivables is the cost of the discounts, ie

2% × $3 million = $60,000

(c) The reduction in receivables of $250,000 would cost the company $60,000 per annum. If the company can earn 30% on its investments, the benefit is:

30% × $250,000 = $75,000

The discount policy would be worthwhile, since the benefit of $75,000 exceeds the cost of $60,000.

The percentage cost of an early settlement discount to the company giving it can be estimated by the formula:

Formula to learn

$$\left(\frac{100}{100-d}\right)^{\frac{365}{t}} - 1$$

Where: d is the discount offered (5% = 5, etc)
t is the reduction in payment period in days

In the example above, the formula can be applied as follows.

$$\text{Cost of discount} = \left(\frac{100}{100-2}\right)^{\frac{365}{30}} - 1$$

$$= 27.9\%$$

Since 27.9% is less than the 30% by which the company judges investments, offering the discount is worthwhile.

Question — Discount

Gamma grants credit terms of 60 days net to customers, but offers an early settlement discount of 2% for payment within seven days. What is the cost of the discount to Gamma?

Answer

Gamma is offering customers the option of paying $98 after seven days per $100 invoiced, or payment in full after 60 days.

Using the formula

$$\text{Cost of discount} = \left(\frac{100}{100-d}\right)^{\frac{365}{t}} - 1$$

$$= \left(\frac{100}{100-2}\right)^{\frac{365}{53}} - 1$$

$$= 14.9\%$$

Exam focus point

> The examiner has made it clear that he expects you to know this formula. There are other, simpler ways of calculating the cost of discount but you should not use them in the exam. The November 2005 exam had a 4-mark question similar to the one above. Discounts also appeared in the pilot paper and the May 2005 exam.

As far as an **individual customer** is concerned, the principles are similar. For example, assume Boris has an average $10,000 outstanding, representing two months sales. You offer Boris a 1% settlement discount which would reduce the average amount outstanding to $5,000 (before discounts). You borrow money at 5%. A 1% discount on annual sales of $60,000 would cost you $600. Overdraft interest saved is $250 ($5,000 × 5%) so it is not worth offering the discount.

4.5 Late payment

It has been suggested that businesses should charge interest on overdue debts, however:

(a) **Charging for late payment** might be misconstrued (The supplier might assume that charges for late payment give the customer the authority to pay late.)

(b) A statutory **rate for interest** on overdue debts may not have been established in the country.

(c) Charging for payments relates only to the effect of the late payment on **profitability**, not on liquidity

Question — Good cash management

Thinking back to topics covered in earlier chapters, explain how good cash management may realise each of the following benefits.

(a) Better control of financial risk
(b) Opportunity for profit
(c) Strengthened balance sheet
(d) Increased confidence with customers, suppliers, banks and shareholders

Answer

(a) **Better control of financial risk.** By determining and maintaining the proper level of cash within a company in accordance with the organisation's financial procedures and within defined authorisation limits.

(b) **Opportunity for profit**. By reducing to a minimum the opportunity cost associated with maintaining cash balances in excess of company's operating needs. Earnings (or surpluses) are improved by freeing up surplus cash for investment purposes while reducing interest charged through minimising borrowing.

(c) **Strengthened balance sheet**. By reducing or eliminating cash balances in excess of target balances and putting surplus cash to work by investing it (eg in the overnight money market); by reducing or eliminating cash borrowing and keeping interest costs as low as possible.

(d) **Increased confidence with customers, suppliers, banks and shareholders**. By having access to funds to disburse to suppliers (creditors), banks (interest, fees and principal payments) and shareholders (dividends) when due. By providing good instructions to customers (receivables) to enable the organisation to convert receipts into usable bank deposits.

Question — Credit control policy

Your company has been growing rapidly over the last two years and now wishes to introduce a more formal credit control policy. You are asked to give a brief presentation on the factors involved in setting up such a policy.

Answer

The factors involved in establishing a credit control policy are as follows.

(a) **A total credit policy** must be **decided**, whereby the organisation decides how much credit it can and should allow to customers in total. Receivables should not be excessive in relation to total sales revenues, and the cost of financing receivables should also be considered. The receivables policy that is established will include maximum periods for payment.

(b) A **credit policy** must be **set** for deciding credit terms for individual customers. This will include establishing a system of credit rating, and procedures for deciding the maximum credit limit and terms for the payment period.

(c) The **purpose of allowing credit** is to **boost sales demand**. Management must consider how 'generous' credit terms should be to encourage sales, whilst at the same time avoiding excessive increases in bad debts, and problems with chasing payment from slow payers.

(d) Granting credit will inevitably mean that **problems will arise with slow payers** and bad debts. Procedures must be established for collecting debts from slow payers and writing off bad debts.

(e) **Discounts** might be **offered** for **early payment of debts**, and a decision should be taken as to how much discount, if any, should be offered to encourage early payment, thereby reducing the volume of receivables.

5 Maintaining information on receivables

FAST FORWARD

For control purposes, **receivables** are generally analysed by age of debt.

5.1 Receivables age analysis

An **aged receivables listing** will probably look very much like the schedule illustrated below. The analysis splits up the total balance on the account of each customer across different columns according to the dates of the transactions which make up the total balance. Thus, the amount of an invoice which was raised 14 days ago will form part of the figure in the column headed 'up to 30 days', while an invoice which was raised 36 days ago will form part of the figure in the column headed 'up to 60 days'. (In the schedule below, 'up to 60 days' is used as shorthand for 'more than 30 days but less than 60 days'.)

HEATH CO
AGE ANALYSIS OF RECEIVABLES AS AT 31.1.X2

Account number	*Customer name*	*Balance*	*Up to 30 days*	*Up to 60 days*	*Up to 90 days*	*Over 90 days*
B004	Brilliant	804.95	649.90	121.00	0.00	34.05
E008	Easimat	272.10	192.90	72.40	6.80	0.00
H002	Hampstead	1,818.42	0.00	0.00	724.24	1,094.18
M024	Martlesham	284.45	192.21	92.24	0.00	0.00
N030	Nyfen	1,217.54	1,008.24	124.50	0.00	84.80
T002	Todmorden College	914.50	842.00	0.00	72.50	0.00
T004	Tricorn	94.80	0.00	0.00	0.00	94.80
V010	Volux	997.06	413.66	342.15	241.25	0.00
Y020	Yardsley Smith & Co	341.77	321.17	20.60	0.00	0.00
Totals		6,745.59	3,620.08	772.89	1,044.79	1,307.83
Percentage		100%	53.6%	11.5%	15.5%	19.4%

An age analysis of receivables can be prepared manually or, more easily, by computer. In theory this should represent actual invoices outstanding, but there are problems, which we shall discuss later in this chapter, of unmatched or 'unallocated' cash and payments on account.

The age analysis of receivables may be used to help decide what action to take about older debts. Going down each column in turn starting from the column furthest to the right and working across, we can see that there are some rather old debts which ought to be investigated.

A number of **refinements** can be suggested to the aged receivables listing to make it easier to use.

(a) A report can be printed in which **overdue accounts** are seen first: this highlights attention on these items.

(b) It can help to aggregate data by **class of customer**.

(c) There is no reason why this should not apply to individual receivable accounts as below. You could also include the date of the last transaction on the account (eg last invoice, last payment).

Account number	*Customer name*	*Balance*	*Up to 30 days*	*Up to 60 days*	*Up to 90 days*	*Over 90 days*	*Sales revenue in last 12 months*	*Days sales outstanding*
B004	Brilliant	804.95	649.90	121.00	0.00	34.05	6,789.00	43

We can see from the age analysis of Heath's receivables given earlier that the relatively high proportion of debts over 90 days (19.4%) is largely due to the debts of Hampstead. Other customers with debts of this age are Brilliant, Nyfen and Tricorn.

Additional ratios which might be useful in management of receivables, in addition to days sales outstanding, are as follows.

(a) **Overdues as a percentage of total debt.** For example, assume that Heath (Paragraph 1.1) offers credit on 30 day terms. Brilliant's debt could be analysed as:

$$\frac{\$121.00 + \$34.05}{\$804.95} = 19.3\% \text{ overdue.}$$

(b) **If debts are disputed**, it is helpful to see what proportion these are of the total receivables and the total overdue. If, of Heath's total receivables of $6,745.59, an amount of $973.06 related to disputed items, the ratio of disputed debts to total outstanding would be:

$$\frac{\$973.06}{\$6,745.59} = 14.4\%$$

As a percentage of total items *over* 30 days old:

$$\frac{\$973.06}{\$6,745.59 - \$3,620.08} = 31\%$$

An increasing disputes ratio can indicate:

(i) Invoicing problems
(ii) Operational problems

Exam focus point

Make sure you show workings clearly if you are asked to give a receivables' age analysis.

5.2 Receivables' ageing and liquidity

Also of interest to the credit controller is the *total* percentage figure calculated at the bottom of each column. In practice the credit controller will be concerned to look at this figure first of all, in order to keep the ageing figures consistent. Why might a credit controller be worried by an increase in the **ageing**? If the credit controller knows the customers are going to pay, should it matter?

Think back to your work on cash forecasting. This is based on the expectation that a company's debts will be paid within, say, 30 days after receipt of goods. In other words revenue booked in Month 1 would be followed up by cash in Month 2. The cash forecast also has an outflow side. Any reduction in the inflow caused by an overall increase in the receivables period affects the company's ability to pay its debts and increases its use of overdraft finance: unauthorised overdrafts carry a hefty fee as well as interest.

5.3 Delays in payments by specific customers

FAST FORWARD

Some customers are **reluctant** to pay. The debt collector should keep a record of every communication. A **staged process** of reminders and demands, culminating in debt collection or legal action, is necessary.

It may be the case that an increase in the overall receivables ageing is caused by the activities of one customer, and there is always the possibility that cut-off dates for producing the report can generate anomalies. (For example, a customer might pay invoices at the end of every calendar month, whereas the receivables ageing analysis might be run every 30 days.)

However, the credit controller should try and avoid situations where a customer starts to delay payment. He or she should review information from:

- Sales staff regarding how the company is doing
- The press for any stories relevant to the company
- Competitors
- The trade 'grapevine'

These can supply early warning signals.

If, however, there is a persistent problem, the credit controller might have to insist on a **refusal of credit**.

(a) This is likely to be resented by sales staff who will possibly receive less commission as a result of lower sales.

(b) However, if there is a possibility of default, the loss of a *potential* sale is surely less severe than the failure of *actual* money to arrive.

6 Collecting debts

FAST FORWARD

There should be efficiently organised procedures for ensuring that **overdue debts** and **slow payers** are dealt with effectively.

Exam focus point

A question might require you to evaluate different methods of debt collection and to recommend the most appropriate method.

6.1 Collecting debts

Collecting debts is a two-stage process.

(a) Having agreed credit terms with a customer, a business should issue an invoice and expect to receive payment when it is due. **Issuing invoices** and **receiving payments** is the task of sales ledger staff. They should ensure that:

- The **customer is fully aware** of the terms.
- The **invoice is correctly drawn up** and issued promptly.
- They are aware of any **potential quirks** in the customer's system.
- **Queries** are **resolved quickly.**
- **Monthly statements** are **issued promptly.**

(b) If payments become overdue, they should be 'chased'. Procedures for pursuing overdue debts must be established, for example:

(i) **Instituting reminders or final demands**

These should be sent to a named individual, asking for repayment by return of post. A second or third letter may be required, followed by a final demand stating clearly the action that will be taken. The aim is to goad customers into action, perhaps by threatening not to sell any more goods on credit until the debt is cleared.

(ii) **Chasing payment by telephone**

The telephone is of greater nuisance value than a letter, and the greater immediacy can encourage a response. It can however be time-consuming, in particular because of problems in getting through to the right person.

(iii) **Making a personal approach**

Personal visits can be very time-consuming and tend only to be made to important customers who are worth the effort.

(iv) **Notifying debt collection section**

This means not giving further credit to the customer until he has paid the due amounts.

(v) **Handing over debt collection to specialist debt collection section**

Certain, generally larger, organisations may have a section to collect debts under the supervision of the credit manager.

(vi) **Instituting legal action to recover the debt**

Premature legal action may unnecessarily antagonise important customers.

(vii) **Hiring an external debt collection agency to recover the debt**

This is an expense which must be justified.

6.2 Special cases

6.2.1 'Key account' customers

In most businesses, major **'key account' customers** will receive special treatment in the sales effort, and it is appropriate that special treatment is also given in managing the debts in these cases. In such circumstances, a more personal approach to debt collection is advisable, with the salesman or a debt collection officer (perhaps the credit manager himself) making an approach to the customer to request payment.

6.2.2 Reconciliation and 'on account' payments

A problem you might encounter is a customer who pays a round sum to cover a variety of invoices. The round sum may be a **payment 'on account'**: in other words, the customer might not state which invoices the payment refers to. This might occur because the customer is having liquidity problems. Unallocated payments on account, which have not been agreed, should be investigated.

7 Credit insurance, factoring and invoice discounting

FAST FORWARD

The earlier **customers** pay the better. **Early payment** can be encouraged by good administration and by **discount policies**. The risk that some **customers** will never pay can be partly guarded against by **insurance**.

7.1 Credit insurance

Companies might be able to obtain **credit insurance** (**default insurance**) against certain approved debts going bad through a specialist credit insurance firm.

When a company arranges credit insurance, it must submit specific proposals for credit to the insurance company, stating the name of each customer to which it wants to give credit and the amount of credit it wants to give. The insurance company will accept, amend or refuse these proposals, depending on its assessment of each of these customers.

Credit insurance is normally available for only up to about 75% of a company's potential bad debt loss. The remaining 25% of any bad debt costs are borne by the company itself. This is to ensure that the company does not become slack with its credit control.

7.2 Domestic credit insurance

FAST FORWARD

Credit insurance can be obtained against some bad debts. However, the insurers will rarely insure an entire bad debt portfolio - as they are unwilling to bear the entire risk. Also the client's credit control procedures should be of a suitable standard to avoid any unnecessary exposure.

Credit insurance for **domestic** (ie not export) businesses is available from a number of sources.

Insurance companies are prepared to assume for themselves the risk of the debt going bad, and they hope to profit from this. Furthermore, they are less vulnerable, as institutions, to the possibility that debt will ruin their business.

There are several types of credit insurance on offer. These are briefly described below.

7.2.1 'Whole turnover' policies

Whole turnover policies can be used in two ways.

(a) It can **cover** the **firm's entire receivables ledger**, although, normally speaking, the actual amount paid out will rarely be more than 80% of the total loss for any specific claim.

(b) Alternatively, the client **can select** a **proportion of its receivables** and insure these for their entire amount.

In other words, perhaps 80% of each debt is insured; or the entire amount of the debts incurred, say, by perhaps 80% of the customers.

Premiums on a whole turnover policy are usually **1% of the insured sales**.

Question — **Compensation**

Gibbony Whey has a whole turnover policy for its debts. The policy is underwritten by Broaken Amis Assurance and is on a whole turnover basis, whereby 80% of the receivables ledger is covered, provided that the total credit offered to customers does not exceed $1m. In the first quarter of 20X4, the company made total sales of $4m: at the end of the quarter receivables for credit sales stood at $1.4m. Gibbony Whey has traded with Sloe Pears: the underwriters approved a credit limit for Sloe Pears of $1,700. At the end of the quarter, Sloe Pears had outstanding debts of $2,100. Sloe Pears turns into a 'bad receivable' when the company's buildings are completely destroyed by a falling asteroid.

Gibbony Whey writes to Broaken Amis claiming for the bad debt. How much will Gibbony Whey be entitled to as compensation?

Answer

$1,700 × 80% = $1,360.

Gibbony Whey gave more credit than was underwritten by the insurance company.

7.2.2 Annual aggregate excess of loss

Under an **annual aggregate excess of loss policy**, the insurer pays 100% of debts above an agreed limit. This is similar to motor insurers requiring that the first amount (eg $50) of a loss is borne by the insured.

7.2.3 Specific account policies

Insurance can be purchased to cover a **specific customer account** in the event of some contingency. For example, a policy might depend on the customer being formally declared insolvent.

7.3 Factoring

FAST FORWARD

Some companies use **factoring** and **invoice discounting** to help short-term liquidity or to reduce administration costs.

Key term

Factoring is an arrangement to have debts collected by a factor company, which advances a proportion of the money it is due to collect.

Some businesses might have difficulties in financing the amounts owed by customers. There are two main reasons for this.

(a) If a business's **sales** are rising **rapidly**, its **total receivables** will **rise quickly too**. Selling more on credit will put a strain on the company's cash flow. The business, although making profits, might find itself in difficulties because it has too many receivables and not enough cash.

(b) If a business grants **long credit** to its customers, it might run into **cash flow difficulties** for much the same reason. Exporting businesses must often allow long periods of credit to foreign buyers, before eventually receiving payment, and their problem of financing receivables adequately can be a critical one.

Factors are organisations that offer their clients a financing service to overcome these problems. They are prepared to advance cash to the client against the security of the client's receivables. The business will assign its receivables to the factor and will typically ask for an advance of funds against the debts which the factor has purchased, usually up to 80% of the value of the debts.

For example, if a business makes credit sales of $100,000 per month, the factor might be willing to advance up to 80% of the invoice value (here $80,000) in return for a commission charge, and interest will be charged on the amount of funds advanced. The balance of the money will be paid to the business when the customers have paid the factor, or after an agreed period.

This service gives the business immediate cash in place of a debt (which is a promise of cash in the future). If the business needs money to finance operations, borrowing against trade debts is therefore an alternative to asking a bank for an overdraft.

The main aspects of factoring

These are as follows.

(a) Administration of the client's invoicing, sales accounting and debt collection service.

(b) Credit protection for the client's debts, whereby the factor takes over the risk of loss from bad debts and so 'insures' the client against such losses. Factoring is often **with recourse**, which means that the client carries the risk of bad debts. However the arrangement can be made **without recourse**, which means that the risk of bad debts has been transferred to the factor.

(c) Making payments to the client in advance of collecting the debts. This is sometimes referred to as '**factor finance**' because the factor is providing cash to the client against outstanding debts.

The appeal of factor financing to **growing firms** is that factors might advance money when a bank is reluctant to consider granting a larger overdraft. Advances from a factor are therefore particularly useful for companies needing more and more cash to expand their business quickly.

7.4 The advantages of factoring

Benefits of factoring for a business customer

(a) The business can **pay** its **suppliers promptly**, and so be able to take advantage of any early payment discounts that are available.

(b) **Optimum inventory levels** can be **maintained**, because the business will have enough cash to pay for the inventories it needs.

(c) **Growth** can be **financed** through **sales** rather than by injecting fresh external capital.

(d) The business gets **finance linked** to its **volume of sales**. In contrast, overdraft limits tend to be determined by historical balance sheets.

(e) The managers of the business do **not** have to **spend their time** on the **problems of slow paying receivables.**

(f) The business does **not incur** the **costs** of running **its own receivables ledger** department.

An important **disadvantage of factoring** is that customers will be making payments direct to the factor, which is likely to present a **negative picture of the firm**.

7.5 Invoice discounting

FAST FORWARD

Factoring involves **debt collection** by the **factoring company** which advances a proportion of the monies due. **Invoice discounting** is the sale of debts at a discount in return for cash.

Key term

Invoice discounting is the sale of debts to a third party at a discount, in return for prompt cash. The administration is managed in such a way that the debtor is unaware of the discounter's involvement and continues to pay the supplier. *(OT 2000)*

Invoice discounting is related to factoring and many factors will provide an invoice discounting service. For example, if your business had just redecorated the Town Hall it might have sent the Council an invoice for $5,000. This would be an easy invoice to sell on for cash because the Council are very likely to pay. An invoice for $5,000 sent to 'A Cowboy & Co' would not be so easy to sell for immediate cash!

The invoice discounter does **not** take over the administration of the client's sales ledger, and the arrangement is purely for the **advance of cash**. A business should only want to have some invoices discounted when it has a temporary cash shortage.

Confidential invoice discounting is an arrangement whereby a debt is confidentially assigned to the factor, and the client's customer will only become aware of the arrangement if he does not pay his debt to the client.

Question — Factoring

The Managing Director, the Chief Accountant and the Chief Internal Auditor were meeting to discuss problems over debt collection recently identified in the Forward Company. One point made strongly by the Chief Internal Auditor was that his staff should be involved in much more than the routine verification tasks normally undertaken. It is, therefore, agreed that the internal audit section should look at the problem and consider the possibility of using the services of a factor to take over some, or all, of the work of the receivables credit section.

Required

Outline the advantages and disadvantages of using the services of a factor.

Answer

The decision to factor the debts should only be taken once a wide ranging assessment of the costs and benefits of so doing has been carried out. This will involve the following steps.

(a) Find out **which organisations** provide debt factoring services. These may include the firm's own bankers, but there might be specialist agencies available who could also do the job.

(b) **Some assessment** of the **services provided** should also be made. Factors take on the responsibility of collecting the client firm's debts. There is a variety of factoring services.

   (i) **With recourse factoring**. This is the most basic service, whereby the bank undertakes to collect the debts and offer an advance, perhaps 80% thereon. The remainder is paid over once the cash has been received from customers. If the debt cannot be collected, the bank can claim back the advance from the client firm.

   (ii) **No recourse factoring**. The bank undertakes to pay the debts, but cannot claim the advance back from the client if the debt does not prove collectable.

   (iii) Some factors are willing to **purchase a number of invoices**, at a **substantial** discount. The factor would not be taking responsibility for the client's overall credit administration. In a way, this is like receiving an advance from a debt collector.

(c) The **costs of the factoring** service can then be assessed. The cost is often calculated as a percentage of the book value of the debts factored, so that if the factor took over $1,000,000 of debt at a factoring cost of 1.5%, then the client would pay a fee of $15,000. Moreover interest might also be charged on the advance, in some cases before the debt was recovered.

(d) This can then be compared with the **costs of doing nothing**. If the choice is between either employing a factor or leaving things as they are, then the costs included in the decision include administration, salaries, interest costs on the overdraft, and other cash flow problems (eg delayed expenditure on purchases owing to bad debts, might mean that the company cannot take advantage of settlement discounts offered).

(e) However, before any final decision is taken, the organisation can try to ensure that factoring is still better value than other choices. These can include:

   (i) The **introduction** of **settlement discounts** as an inducement to pay early might improve the collection period, and hence reduce the outstanding debt

   (ii) The **use** of **credit insurance** in some cases

   (iii) A **stronger credit control policy**

   (iv) Perhaps **appointing more credit control staff** might in the long run be cheaper than factoring if the collection rate increases

There may well be operational or management solutions to this problem. These should be investigated first as customers might not like dealing with a third party.

Exam focus point

The management of receivables and other elements of working capital gets right down to the day-to-day practicalities of running a business. In questions involving working capital management, you should always consider whether any proposed course of action really makes business sense.

8 Managing payables

FAST FORWARD

Effective management of **trade payables** involves seeking satisfactory credit terms from suppliers, getting credit extended during periods of cash shortage, and maintaining good relations with suppliers.

8.1 Trade credit

Trade payables are those suppliers who are owed money for goods and services which they have supplied for the trading activities of the enterprise. For a manufacturing company, trade payables will be raw materials suppliers.

The **management of trade payables** involves:

- Attempting to obtain satisfactory credit from suppliers
- Attempting to extend credit during periods of cash shortage
- Maintaining good relations with regular and important suppliers

Question — **Obtaining credit**

What might your firm have to do to obtain credit from a supplier?

Answer

A firm would have to provide good references, maintain a good payment record, allow the supplier to pay a visit, and generally be *known* to be a successful business and a good credit risk.

Taking credit from suppliers is a normal feature of business. Nearly every company has some trade payables waiting for payment. Trade credit is a source of short-term finance because it helps to keep working capital down. It is usually a cheap source of finance, since suppliers rarely charge interest. However, trade credit *will* have a cost, whenever a company is offered a discount for early payment, but opts instead to take longer credit.

8.1.1 Trade credit and the cost of lost early payment discounts

Trade credit from suppliers is particularly important to small and fast growing firms. The costs of making maximum use of trade credit include:

(a) The loss of suppliers' goodwill
(b) The loss of any available cash discounts for the early payment of debts

The cost of lost cash discounts can be estimated by the formula:

Formula to learn

$$\left(\frac{100}{100-d}\right)^{\frac{365}{t}} - 1$$

where d is the size of the discount. For a 5% discount, d = 5.

t is the reduction in the payment period in days which would be necessary to obtain the early payment discount

8.2 Example: trade credit

X has been offered credit terms from its major supplier of 2/10, net 45. That is, a cash discount of 2% will be given if payment is made within ten days of the invoice, and payments must be made within 45 days of the invoice. The company has the choice of paying 98c per $1 on day 10 (to pay before day 10 would be unnecessary), or to invest the 98c for an additional 35 days and eventually pay the supplier $1 per $1. The decision as to whether the discount should be accepted depends on the opportunity cost of investing 98c for 35 days. What should the company do?

Solution

If the company refuses the cash discount, and pays in full after 45 days, the implied cost in interest per annum would be approximately:

$$\left(\frac{100}{100-2}\right)^{\frac{365}{35}} - 1 = 23.5\%$$

Suppose that X can invest cash to obtain an annual return of 25%, and that there is an invoice from the supplier for $1,000. The two alternatives are as follows.

	Refuse discount	*Accept discount*
	$	$
Payment to supplier	1,000.0	980
Return from investing $980 between day 10 and day 45:		
$\$980 \times \frac{35}{365} \times 25\%$	(23.5)	
Net cost	976.5	980

It is cheaper to refuse the discount because the investment rate of return on cash retained, in this example, exceeds the saving from the discount.

Although a company may delay payment beyond the final due date, thereby obtaining even longer credit from its suppliers, such a policy would be inadvisable (except where an unexpected short-term cash shortage has arisen). Unacceptable delays in payment will worsen the company's credit rating, and additional credit may become difficult to obtain.

8.3 Other payables

There is usually less scope for flexibility with other types of short-term payables. Things like rent and tax and dividends have to be paid out in full on certain specific dates.

'Management' in such cases is a matter of ensuring that what is due gets paid on time and that the finance is available when needed.

Age analysis of payables

You will be able to appreciate what an age analysis of payables is, having looked at the age analysis of receivables earlier in the last chapter.

8.4 Example: age analysis of payables

Here is an age analysis of payables for Heath Co.

HEATH CO
AGE ANALYSIS OF TRADE PAYABLES AS AT 31.1.X2

Account code	*Supplier name*	*Balance*	*Up to 30 days*	*Up to 60 days*	*Up to 90 days*	*Over 90 days*
V001	Vitatechnology	3,284.00	2,140.00	1,144.00	–	–
P002	Prendergast Tubes	1,709.50	1,010.50	699.00	–	–
G072	Gerald Printers	622.64	622.64	–	–	–
P141	Plates of Derby	941.88	510.92	290.75	–	140.21
P142	Plates of Derby	604.22	514.42	–	–	89.80
G048	Greenlands Centre	34.91	–	–	–	34.91
Totals		7,197.15	4,798.48	2,133.75	–	264.92
Percentage		100%	66.7%	29.6%	0.0%	3.7%

Various points of analysis and interpretation could arise from an age analysis of payables.

(a) Is the company **paying its suppliers earlier** than it needs to?

(b) Is the company taking **advantage of suppliers' discounts** where this is advantageous?

(c) Do older amounts represent **disputes**, disagreements or accounting errors that ought to be looked into?

(d) In the case of Heath Co, is it possible that the fact that there are two accounts for Plates of Derby has led to confusion, perhaps resulting in the older unsettled items?

8.5 The purchasing cycle

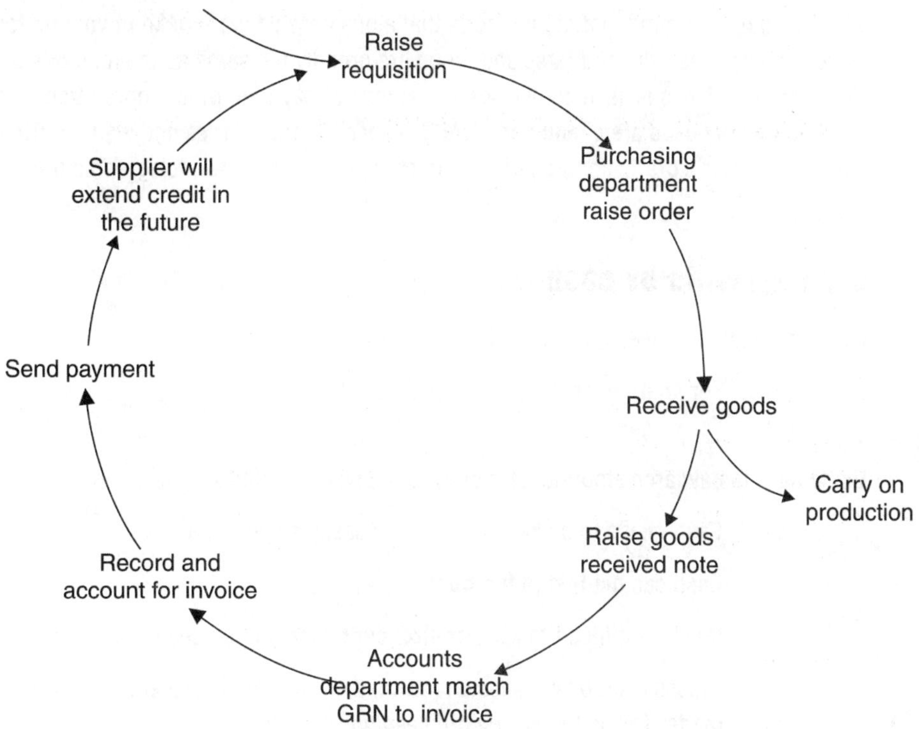

The purchasing business is now the customer, which has its credit status checked, takes delivery of goods and invoice, and pays for the goods or services.

8.6 Payment terms as part of the order

The **payment terms** offered by or agreed with the supplier form part of the contract with the supplier.

8.7 Controls over purchasing

In the same way as controls are maintained over receivables, controls should also be in place over purchase commitments. The **documentation** in the diagram above is an important control. In addition, there should be restrictions on who is allowed to place an order; perhaps only a **centralised purchasing function** should be permitted to order goods. When goods arrive the goods received department should check they **agree to the order** and are of **acceptable quality**. The details of invoices should be **carefully checked**, and the purchasing department should confirm that the goods have been received.

Businesses with several sites should decide whether purchasing should be **centralised** in one location or devolved to each site. A central location may be able to **co-ordinate inventory holdings better, obtain better prices or bulk discounts**, and have access to a **wider range of suppliers**. Local ordering may be more **flexible** to **individual locations'** needs, and local purchasing managers may form **stronger relationships** with **local suppliers**.

9 Methods of paying suppliers

FAST FORWARD

Trade payables are a useful and cheap **source of finance,** but a successful business needs to ensure that it is seen as a good credit risk by its suppliers. Some suppliers must be paid on specific dates. This must be remembered and cash must be available.

9.1 Introduction

We should bear in mind that the methods that a business uses to **make payments** for goods and services, wages and salaries, rent and rates and so on are broadly the same as the methods of **receiving payments**. However, a business is likely to use some methods of payment much more often than others, and the most commonly used are **cheque** and **BACS** (especially for salaries and wages). **Other payment methods** are cash, banker's draft, standing order, direct debit, mail transfer, telegraphic transfer and online payment.

9.2 Payments by cash

Cash payments are used quite often by a business:

(a) For **small payments** out of petty cash
(b) For **wages**

Using cash to pay large amounts of money to suppliers ought to be very rare indeed.

(a) Cash needs to be kept **secure**: it is easily stolen.

(b) Cash can get **lost in the post**.

(c) It will be difficult to keep **control over cash** if it is used often for making payments.

(d) Unless a supplier issues a **receipt**, there will be no evidence that a cash payment has been made. This is bad for record keeping.

9.3 Advantages and disadvantages of paying by cheque

Cheques are widely used in business to pay for supplies and other expenses. It is worth thinking briefly about the advantages and disadvantages of using cheques as a method of payment.

Advantages of cheque payments	Disadvantages of cheque payments
Cheques are **convenient to use** for payments of any amount (provided sufficient money is in the bank, or the organisation has a large enough overdraft facility).	There are **security problems** with keeping cheques safe from theft and misuse (forged signatures), although cheques are certainly more secure than cash as a method of payment.
The cheque **counterfoil** and cheque number can be used to provide a useful method for tracing past payments whenever any queries arise.	Cheques can be a **slow method of payment**, and a supplier might insist on a different method that is more prompt and reliable, such as standing order.
They are commonly used and **widely accepted**.	

9.4 Bank giro credits

Bank giro credits (**credit transfers**) are a means by which payments might be **received** from customers. Bank giro credits can also be used by businesses to **make payments**.

In practice, bank giro credits are rarely used by businesses to pay suppliers, except in cases where the supplier sends an invoice with a detachable preprinted bank giro credit transfer paying-in slip. Suppliers who use their own preprinted bank giro credit transfer forms include the various utility companies.

Bank giro credit transfers are sometimes used by small companies to pay monthly salaries.

9.5 Payments by banker's draft

A supplier might sometimes ask a customer to pay by **banker's draft**. Banker's drafts are not used for small value items, but might be used when a large payment is involved, such as for the purchase of a company car.

9.6 Standing orders

Standing order payments might be used by a business to make regular payments of a fixed amount.

(a) **Hire purchase (HP) payments** to a hire purchase company (finance house), where an asset has been bought under an HP agreement

(b) **Rental payments** to the landlord of a building occupied by the business

(c) Paying **insurance premiums** to an insurance company

9.7 Direct debits

Payments by direct debit **might** be made by some companies for regular bills such as telephone, gas, electricity and water bills. The company being paid by direct debit will inform the payer of the amount and date of each payment in a printed statement.

Question

Payment methods

Libra has to make the following payments.

(a) $6.29 for office cleaning materials bought from a nearby supermarket.

(b) $231.40 monthly, which represents hire purchase instalments on a new van. The payments are due to Marsh Finance over a period of 36 months.

(c) $534.21 to Southern Electric for the most recent quarter's electricity and standing charge. A bank giro credit form/payment counterfoil is attached to the bill. There is no direct debiting mandate currently in force.

(d) $161.50 monthly for ten months, representing the business rates payable to Clapperton District Council, which operates a direct debiting system.

(e) $186.60 to Renton Hire for a week's hire of a car on company business by the Sales Director. The Sales Director must pay on the spot, and does not wish to use a personal cheque or cash.

(f) $23,425.00 to Selham Motors for a new car to be used by the Finance Director. Selham Motors will not accept one of the company's cheques in payment, since the Finance Director wishes to collect the vehicle immediately upon delivering the payment in person and Selham Motors is concerned that such a cheque might be dishonoured.

Recommend the method of payment which you think would be most appropriate in each case, stating your reasons.

Answer

(a) This is a small business payment which should be paid out of petty **cash** for the sake of convenience.

(b) A **standing order** is convenient for regular fixed payments. Once the standing order instruction is made, the bank will ensure that all payments are made on the due dates and will stop making payments at the date specified in the instruction. Some finance companies may insist on a standing order being set up, as it is convenient for them to receive instalments regularly without having to issue payment requests or reminders.

(c) **Pay by cheque at the bank**, accompanied by the bill and completed bank giro credit form. The bank clerk will stamp the bill as evidence that the payment was made. Paying by cheque is safer than paying by cash and is more usual for such a large payment. Handing the cheque over at the bank will be convenient and evidence of payment will be obtained. If the payment is made at a bank other than that at which Libra holds an account, the bank receiving the payment will probably make a small charge for processing it. An alternative method is to send a **crossed cheque by post**, enclosing the payment counterfoil.

(d) The **direct debit mandate** will allow the Council to debit the amounts due direct from Libra's bank account on the due dates. The mandate will be effective until it is cancelled. The Council must inform Libra in advance of the amounts it will be debiting.

(e) Payment by **credit card** or **charge card** avoids the need to pay immediately by cash or cheque. The amount paid will appear on the monthly statement for the card used. If the Sales Director's personal card is used, he will claim payment later from the company, which may pay him by cheque or with his monthly salary payment. If a company credit or charge card is used, the company will be responsible for paying the amounts shown on the monthly statement.

(f) A **banker's draft** cannot be stopped or cancelled once it is issued. Being effectively like a cheque drawn on the bank itself, it is generally accepted as being as good as cash. It is therefore most likely to be accepted by Selham Motors.

9.8 BACS

FAST FORWARD

The most common and convenient methods of payment are by cheque, BACS and **Internet transfer**. Other payment methods are often arranged at the insistence of the supplier, and this explains much of the use of banker's drafts, standing orders and telegraphic transfers.

When a business uses **Bankers' Automated Clearing Services (BACS)**, it sends information (which will be input into the books of the business) to BACS for processing. Many different businesses use BACS; even small businesses can do so because their bank will help to organise the information for BACS. To give examples, BACS is widely used for monthly salaries by an employer into employees' bank accounts, as already mentioned, and for standing order payments, as well as for payments to suppliers.

9.9 Internet payments

Many organisations now have access to online banking and use this to pay employees and suppliers. Funds can be transferred between accounts with a few clicks. It is very important to prevent unauthorised access to the system and to keep records, such as printouts, of all transactions.

Exam focus point

Don't neglect payables management, as a business can gain cash flow advantages from careful management of payables.

Chapter Roundup

- **Credit control** deals with a firm's management of its working capital. **Trade credit** is offered to business customers. **Consumer credit** is offered to household customers.
- **Total credit** can be measured in a variety of ways. Financial analysts use days sales in receivables, but as this is an annualised figure it gives no idea as to the make-up of total receivables. Many firms need to consider the **cost of excess credit**.
- The **total investment in receivables** has to be considered in its impact on the general investment in working capital.
- The **credit control department** is responsible for those stages in the collection cycle dealing with the offer of credit, and the collection of debts.
- A firm must consider suitable **payment terms** and **payment methods**. **Settlement discounts** can be offered, if cost effective and if they improve liquidity.
- For control purposes, **receivables** are generally analysed by age of debt.
- There should be efficiently organised procedures for ensuring that **overdue debts** and **slow payers** are dealt with effectively.
- Some customers are **reluctant** to pay. The debt collector should keep a record of every communication. A staged process of reminders and demands, culminating in debt collection or legal action, is necessary.
- The earlier customers pay the better. **Early payment** can be encouraged by good administration and by **discount policies**. The risk that some receivables will never pay can be partly guarded against by **insurance**.
- **Credit insurance** can be obtained against some bad debts. However, the insurers will rarely insure an entire bad debt portfolio - as they are unwilling to bear the entire risk. Also the client's credit control procedures should be of a suitable standard to avoid any unnecessary exposure.
- Some companies use **factoring** and **invoice discounting** to help short-term liquidity or to reduce administration costs.
- Factoring involves **debt collection** by the **factoring company** which advances a proportion of the monies due. **Invoice discounting** is the sale of debts at a discount in return for cash.
- Effective management of **trade payables** involves seeking satisfactory credit terms from suppliers, getting credit extended during periods of cash shortage, and maintaining good relations with suppliers.
- Trade payables are a useful and cheap **source of finance**, but a successful business needs to ensure that it is seen as a good credit risk by its suppliers. Some suppliers must be paid on specific dates. This must be remembered and cash must be available.
- The most common and convenient methods of payment are by **cheque**, **BACS** and **internet transfer**. **Other payment methods** are often arranged at the insistence of the supplier, and this explains much of the use of banker's drafts, standing orders and telegraphic transfers.

Quick Quiz

1 Goods and Chattels are considering increasing the period of credit allowed to customers from one calendar month to two months. Annual sales are currently $2.4m, and annual profits are $120,000. It is anticipated that allowing extended credit would increase sales by 20%, while margins would be unchanged. The company's required rate of return is 15%. What is the financial effect of the proposal?

A Reduction in profit of $102,000
B Reduction in profit of $18,000
C Increase in profit of $102,000
D Increase in profit of $18,000

2 The .... cycle and the .... cycle together make up the .... cycle. *Fill in the blanks*, using the following words: credit; collection; order.

3 How can we calculate the number of days sales represented by receivables?

4 What matters should the terms and conditions of sale cover?

5 What is meant by COD?

6 Which of the following would be the last document issued to a customer in the order processing and debt collection cycle?

A Statement
B Reminder
C Advice note
D Invoice

7 List typical column headings that you would expect to see in an aged analysis of receivables.

8 List three types of credit insurance policy.

9 What service involves collecting debts of a business, advancing a proportion of the money it is due to collect?

10 What service involves advancing a proportion of a selection of invoices, without administration of the receivables ledger of the business?

11 Which of the following is likely to be the most effective way of obtaining payment from a difficult customer?

A Personal visit
B Telephone request
C Sending a fax reminder
D Sending an e-mail reminder

12 In what order would a company normally undertake the following actions to collect a debt?

A Hiring an external debt collection agency to recover the debt
B Notifying the debt collection service
C Sending a reminder
D Instituting legal action to recover the debt

13 The premium for whole turnover policies is usually ......% of insured sales, and whole turnover policies rarely cover more than ......% of the total loss.

14 Cost of lost cash discount = $\left(\frac{100}{100-d}\right)^{\frac{365}{t}} - 1$. What do d and t represent?

15 Avery has been offered a cash discount of 2% by one of its suppliers if it settles its accounts within 10 days. Avery currently takes 60 days credit from the supplier. What is the implied cost in interest per annum to the nearest whole % if Avery decides not to take the discount?

A 2%
B 12%
C 16%
D 24%

Answers to Quick Quiz

1 B

Existing receivables	\$2.4m ÷ 12	\$200,000
New level of receivables	\$2.4m × 1.2 ÷ 6	\$480,000
Increase in receivables		\$280,000
Additional financing cost	\$280,000 × 15%	\$42,000
Additional profit	\$2.4m × 20% × 5%	\$24,000
Net decrease in profit	\$42,000 – \$24,000	\$18,000

2 The order cycle and the collection cycle together make up the credit cycle.

3 $\dfrac{\text{Total receivables}}{\text{Annual credit sales}} \times 365 = \text{Days sales}$

4 Price, delivery, date of payment, frequency of payment (if instalments), discount

5 Cash On Delivery

6 B The normal sequence is advice note, invoice, statement, reminder.

7
- Account number
- Customer name
- Total balance
- Up to 30 days
- Up to 60 days
- Up to 90 days
- Over 90 days

8 Whole turnover; excess of loss; specific account

9 Factoring

10 Invoice discounting

11 A Personal visit is the most expensive option, but is the most likely to obtain results. It is therefore recommended in the case of high value receivables.

12 C Sending a reminder
B Notifying the debt collection service
D Instituting legal action to recover the debt
A Hiring an external debt collection agency to recover the debt

13 The premium for whole turnover policies is usually **1%** of insured sales, and whole turnover policies rarely cover more than **80%** of the total loss.

14 d is the percentage discount given.
t is the reduction in payment period to obtain this discount (in days)

15 C In this case:

$$\left(\frac{100}{100-2}\right)^{\frac{365}{50}} - 1 = 15.9\%, \text{ say } 16\%$$

Now try the questions below from the Exam Question Bank

Number	Level	Marks	Time
Q30	Examination	20	36 mins
Q31	Examination	20	36 mins

20

Managing inventory

Introduction

You should be able to apply the **EOQ** model for inventory ordering; it is likely to feature somewhere in every paper. As well as doing the calculations, you need to explain its assumptions and the components of inventory costs.

We also discuss in overview the impact of **lean manufacturing** and **just-in-time** on inventory control and other important aspects of purchasing.

Topic list	Learning outcomes	Syllabus references	Ability required
1 Managing inventories	D (vii)	D (12)	Evaluation
2 Purchasing	D (vii)	D (14)	Evaluation

1 Managing inventories

FAST FORWARD

Business should consider at what level of inventory orders should be made, taking account of demand levels, delivery times and any uncertainties. **Safety inventory** may be held if uncertainties are particularly large.

1.1 Controlling inventory

Almost every company carries inventories of some sort, even if they are only inventories of consumables such as stationery. For a manufacturing business, inventories, in the form of **raw materials**, **work in progress** (goods or projects on which work has been carried out but which are not yet ready for sale) and **finished goods**, may amount to a substantial proportion of the total assets of the business.

Some businesses attempt to control inventories on a scientific basis by balancing the costs of inventory shortages against those of inventory holding.

(a) The **economic order quantity (EOQ) model** can be used to decide the optimum **order size** for inventories which will minimise the costs of ordering inventories plus inventory holding costs.

(b) If **discounts** for **bulk purchases** are **available**, it may be cheaper to buy inventories in **large order sizes** so as to obtain the discounts.

(c) Uncertainty in the demand for inventories and/or the supply lead time may lead a company to **decide to hold buffer inventories** or **safety inventories** (thereby increasing its investment in working capital) in order to reduce or eliminate the risk of running out of inventory

Key term

Safety inventory is the quantity of inventories of raw materials, work in progress and finished goods which are carried in excess of the expected usage during the lead time of an activity. The safety inventory reduces the probability of operations having to be suspended due to running out of inventories. *(OT 2000)*

1.2 Inventory costs

Inventory costs can be conveniently classified into four groups.

(a) **Holding costs** comprise the cost of capital tied up, warehousing and handling costs, deterioration, obsolescence, insurance and pilferage.

(b) **Procuring costs** depend on how the inventory is obtained but will consist of **ordering costs** for goods purchased externally, such as clerical costs, telephone charges and delivery costs.

(c) **Shortage costs** may be:

   (i) The loss of a sale and the contribution which could have been earned from the sale

   (ii) The extra cost of having to buy an emergency supply of inventories at a high price

   (iii) The cost of lost production and sales, where the stock-out (running out of inventory) brings an entire process to a halt

(d) The **cost of the inventory** itself, the supplier's price or the direct cost per unit of production, will also need to be considered when the supplier offers a discount on orders for purchases in bulk.

Businesses need to be aware of rates of **consumption/usage, and lead times**, the time between placing an order with a supplier and the inventory becoming available for use.

1.3 Re-order quantities: the basic EOQ model

Key term

Economic order quantity (EOQ) is the most economic inventory replenishment order size, which minimises the sum of inventory ordering costs and inventory holding costs. EOQ is used in an 'optimising' inventory control system. *(OT 2000)*

FAST FORWARD

Inventory holding and ordering costs can be minimised using the **economic order quantity** model. If **discounts** are offered for bulk purchases, the higher holding costs should be weighed against the lower ordering and purchasing costs.

Let D = the usage in units for one year (the demand)
C_o = the cost of making one order
C_h = the holding cost per unit of inventory for one year
(relevant costs only)
Q = the reorder quantity

Assume that:

(a) Demand is constant
(b) The lead time is constant or zero
(c) Purchase costs per unit are constant (ie no bulk discounts)

The total annual cost of having inventory (T) is:

Holding costs + ordering costs

$$\frac{QC_h}{2} + \frac{C_oD}{Q}$$

The order quantity, Q, which will minimise these total costs (T) is given by the following formula. (You do not need to know how this formula is derived.) Note that it is similar in form to the formula for the optimum sale quantity in Baumol's cash management model.

Formula to learn

Economic Order Quantity EOQ = $\sqrt{\dfrac{2C_oD}{C_h}}$

Where C_o = cost of placing an order
C_h = cost of holding one unit in inventory for one year
D = annual demand

1.4 Example: economic order quantity

The demand for a commodity is 40,000 units a year, at a steady rate. It costs \$20 to place an order, and 40c to hold a unit for a year. Find the order size to minimise inventory costs, the number of orders placed each year, and the length of the inventory cycle.

Solution

$Q = \sqrt{\dfrac{2C_oD}{C_h}} = \sqrt{\dfrac{2 \times 20 \times 40{,}000}{0.4}}$ = 2,000 units. This means that there will be

$\dfrac{40{,}000}{2{,}000}$ = 20 orders placed each year, so that the inventory cycle is once every 52 ÷ 20 = 2.6 weeks. Total

costs will be (20 × \$20) + $\left(\dfrac{2{,}000}{2} \times 40c\right)$ = \$800 a year.

Exam focus point

In the exam, you will be given the EOQ formula.

1.5 The effect of discounts

The solution obtained from using the simple EOQ formula may need to be modified if bulk discounts (also called quantity discounts) are available.

To decide mathematically whether it would be worthwhile taking a discount and ordering larger quantities, it is necessary to minimise the total of:

- Total material costs
- Ordering costs
- Inventory holding costs

The total cost will be minimised:

- At the pre-discount EOQ level, so that a discount is not worthwhile, or
- At the minimum order size necessary to earn the discount

1.6 Example: bulk discounts

The annual demand for an item of inventory is 45 units. The item costs $200 a unit to purchase, the holding cost for one unit for one year is 15% of the unit cost and ordering costs are $300 an order. The supplier offers a 3% discount for orders of 60 units or more, and a discount of 5% for orders of 90 units or more. What is the cost-minimising order size?

Solution

(a) The EOQ ignoring discounts is:

$$\sqrt{\frac{2 \times 300 \times 45}{15\% \text{ of } 200}} = 30 \text{ units}$$

	$
Purchases (no discount) 45 × $200	9,000
Holding costs 15 units × $30 (Ch)	450
Ordering costs 1.5 orders × $300	450
Total annual costs	9,900

(b) With a discount of 3% and an order quantity of 60 units costs are as follows.

	$
Purchases $9,000 × 97%	8,730
Holding costs 30 units × 15% of 97% of $200	873
Ordering costs 0.75 orders × $300	225
Total annual costs	9,828

(c) With a discount of 5% and an order quantity of 90 units costs are as follows.

	$
Purchases $9,000 × 95%	8,550.0
Holding costs 45 units × 15% of 95% of $200	1,282.5
Ordering costs 0.5 orders × $300	150.0
Total annual costs	9,982.5

The cheapest option is to order 60 units at a time.

Note that the value of Ch varied according to the size of the discount, because Ch (see para 3.4) was a percentage of the purchase cost. This means that total holding costs are reduced because of a discount.

This could easily happen if, for example, most of Ch was the cost of insurance, based on the cost of inventory held.

Question — Order quantity

A company uses an item of inventory as follows.

Purchase price:	$96 per unit
Annual demand:	4,000 units
Ordering cost:	$300
Annual holding cost:	10% of purchase price
Economic order quantity:	500 units

Should the company order 1,000 units at a time in order to secure an 8% discount?

Answer

The total annual cost at the economic order quantity of 500 units is as follows.

	$
Purchases 4,000 × $96	384,000
Ordering costs $300 × (4,000/500)	2,400
Holding costs $96 × 10% × (500/2)	2,400
	388,800

The total annual cost at an order quantity of 1,000 units would be as follows.

	$
Purchases $384,000 × 92%	353,280
Ordering costs $300 × (4,000/1,000)	1,200
Holding costs $96 × 92% × 10% × (1,000/2)	4,416
	358,896

The company should order the item 1,000 units at a time, saving $(388,800 – 358,896) = $29,904 a year.

Exam focus point

The November 2005 exam had a 5-mark question on calculating the EOQ with discount.

1.7 Economic batch quantity

The economic batch quantity is related to the economic order quantity, and is used when replenishment of inventory is gradual rather than instantaneous. It can be used when a company is making the items itself rather than ordering them. Production runs will be set up when necessary and production will take place until the order is completed. No further order is made, or inventory delivered, until the company is next on the point of running out of inventory.

The extra information required for the economic batch quantity model is the annual rate at which inventories arrive in stores, R, and the formula is:

Formula to learn

$$\text{Economic Batch Quantity EBQ} = \sqrt{\frac{2C_0D}{C_h(1-D/R)}}$$

Exam focus point

You are not given the formula for the economic batch quantity and it is unlikely that you will be required to calculate it, but make sure that you understand when it is applicable and that you can follow the workings

Question

EOQ and EBQ

Maurice sells one product for which the annual demand is 50,000 units. Ordering costs are $40 per order, holding costs $0.50 per item per year.

Required

Calculate

(a) The economic order quantity

(b) The economic batch quantity if Maurice is able to replenish its inventories at a rate of 200,000 units per year.

Answer

(a) EOQ $= \sqrt{\dfrac{2C_0D}{C_h}}$

$= \sqrt{\dfrac{2 \times 40 \times 50{,}000}{0.50}}$

= 2,828 units

EBQ $= \sqrt{\dfrac{2C_0D}{C_h(1 - D/R)}}$

$= \sqrt{\dfrac{2 \times 40 \times 50{,}000}{0.50(1 - 50{,}000/200{,}000)}}$

= 3,266 units

1.8 Uncertainties in demand and lead times: the re-order level system

Key term

Re-order level = maximum usage × maximum lead time.

It is the measure of inventory at which a replenishment order should be placed. Use of the above formula builds in a measure of safety inventory and minimises the possibility of the organisation running out of inventory.

The EOQ model assumes a level of stability which does not always apply in business.

When the volume of demand is uncertain, or the supply lead time (time taken for the supplier to deliver) is variable, there are problems in deciding what the re-order level should be. By holding a **safety inventory**, a company can reduce the likelihood that inventories run out during the re-order period (due to high demand or a long lead time before the new supply is delivered). The **average annual** cost of such a safety inventory would be:

Quantity of safety inventory (in units) × Inventory holding cost per unit per annum

The diagram below shows how the inventory levels might fluctuate with this system. Points marked 'X' show the re-order level at which a new order is placed. The number of units ordered each time is the EOQ. Actual inventory levels sometimes fall below the safety inventory level, and sometimes the re-supply arrives before inventories have fallen to the safety level, but on average, extra inventory holding amounts to the volume of safety inventory. The size of the safety inventory will depend on whether running out of inventory is allowed.

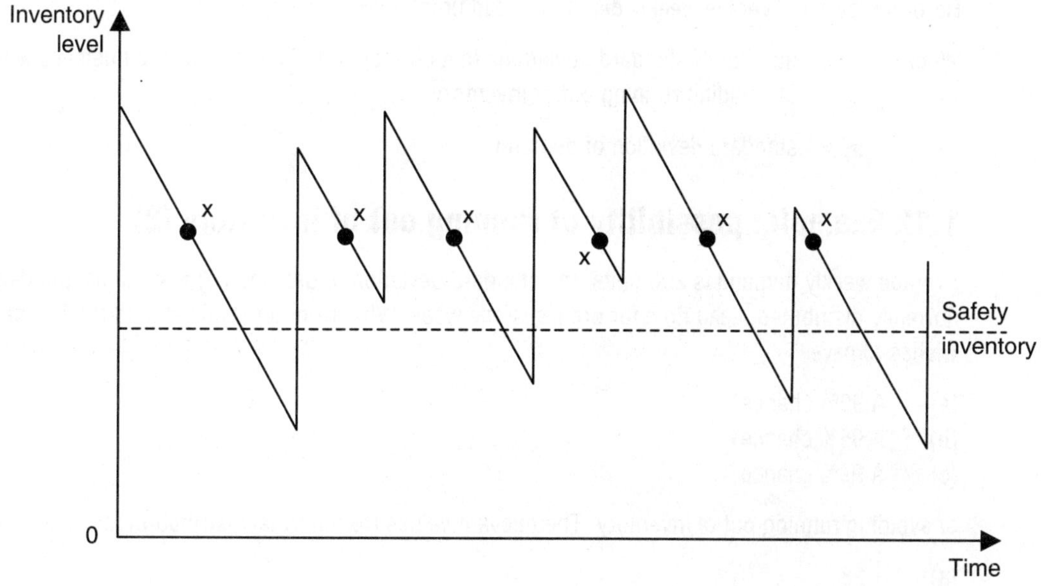

In the modern manufacturing environment running out of inventory can have a disastrous effect on the production process. Nevertheless you may encounter situations where the risk of running out is assumed to be worth taking. In this case the re-order level may not be calculated in the way described above.

1.9 Periodic review

An alternative to the re-order level system is a periodic review system. Using this system, inventory levels are reviewed at fixed intervals, for instance the same day each month. Orders are then put through to top inventory up to pre-set levels.

1.10 Finite number of re-order levels

You may see a question where you are given a list of the re-order levels from which the business will select one. For each **possible re-order level**, and therefore each level of buffer inventory, **calculate**:

- The **costs of holding buffer inventory** per annum
- The **costs of running out of inventory** (Cost of running out of inventory × expected number of times running out per order × number of orders per year)

The expected number of times running out per order reflects the various levels by which demand during the lead time could exceed the re-order level.

1.11 Example: possibility of running out of inventory (1)

If re-order level is 4 units, but there was a probability of 0.2 that demand during the lead time would be 5 units, and 0.05 that demand during the lead time would be 6 units, then expected number of times running out = ((5 – 4) × 0.2) + ((6 – 4) × 0.05) = 0.3.

Demand normally distributed

Alternatively you may be told that demand is normally distributed. If this is the case you need to know:

- Average weekly demand
- Standard deviation of demand
- Lead time
- Acceptable risk levels

Re-order level = (Average weekly demand × lead time) + xσ

Where x = number of standard deviations that correspond to the chance the business wishes to have of avoiding running out of inventory

σ = standard deviation of demand

1.12 Example: possibility of running out of inventory (2)

Average weekly demand is 200 units, the standard deviation of demand (σ) is 40 units and demand is normally distributed. Lead time for orders is one week. What re-order levels should the business set if it wishes to have

(a) A 90% chance
(b) A 95% chance
(c) A 99% chance

of avoiding running out of inventory. The relevant values from normal distribution tables are respectively:

(a) 1.28
(b) 1.65
(c) 2.33

Solution

Re-order level = (Average weekly demand × lead time) + xσ

(a) Re-order level = (200 × 1) + (1.28 × 40)
= 251.2 units

(b) Re-order level = 200 + (1.65 × 40)
= 266 units

(c) Re-order level = 200 + (2.33 × 40)
= 293.2 units

1.13 Maximum and minimum inventory levels

Key term

Maximum inventory level = re-order level + re-order quantity – (minimum usage × minimum lead time)

It is the inventory level set for control purposes which actual inventory holding should never exceed.

The maximum level acts as a warning signal to management that inventories are reaching a potentially wasteful level.

Key term

Minimum inventory level or **safety inventory** = re-order level – (average usage × average lead time)

It is the inventory level set for control purposes below which inventory holding should not fall without being highlighted.

The minimum level acts as a warning to management that inventories are approaching a dangerously low level and that inventory may run out.

Key term

Average inventory = Minimum level + $\frac{\text{re-order quantity}}{2}$

This formula assumes that inventory levels fluctuate evenly between the minimum (or safety) inventory level and the highest possible inventory level (the amount of inventory immediately after an order is received, safety inventory and reorder quantity).

1.14 Just-in-time (JIT) procurement

FAST FORWARD

The aim of **Just-in-time** is to hold as little inventory as possible and production systems need to be very efficient to achieve this.

Just-in-time procurement means obtaining goods from suppliers at the **latest possible time** (ie when they are needed on the production line), thus **avoiding the need to carry** any materials or component inventory. **Deliveries** will be **small and frequent** rather than in bulk.

Just-in-time procurement thus implies a mutually beneficial working relationship with suppliers. The aim is that suppliers **guarantee to deliver** raw materials components of **appropriate quality** always **on time**. In return the suppliers receive a long – term commitment to purchase their goods. **Unit purchasing prices** may need to be **higher** than in a conventional system to meet more rigorous quality and delivery requirements. However savings in production costs and reductions in working capital should offset these costs.

Lean manufacturing implies a smooth and predictable production flow, with setup costs and time minimised. The aim is to **match production** with ultimate **demand**, and so work is only carried out in response to customer wishes.

Production should be organised so that **transfer times** of raw materials and work-in-progress are **kept** to an **absolute minimum**. The maintenance programme should be sufficiently rigorous to stop machinery breaking down.

The **workforce** is a key element in lean manufacturing. **Flexibility** and **multi-skilling** will minimise production delay caused by shortage or absence of staff. There also needs to be an emphasis on **eliminating poor quality production**, as scrapping work in progress and producing additional units can lead to delays.

Introducing JIT/lean manufacturing might bring the following potential benefits.

- Reduction in inventory holding costs
- Reduced manufacturing lead times
- Improved labour productivity
- Reduced scrap/rework/warranty costs

JIT will not be appropriate in all cases. For example, a restaurant might find it preferable to use the traditional economic order quantity approach for staple non-perishable food inventories but adopt JIT for perishable and 'exotic' items. In a hospital, running out of inventory could quite literally be fatal and JIT would be quite unsuitable.

2 Purchasing

FAST FORWARD

Purchasing may be **centralised** or **decentralised**. The optimal mix of **quantity, quality, price** and **delivery arrangements** should be sought.

2.1 The purchasing function

Purchases can account for a major part of a company's expenditure, but rarely get subjected to the planning and control constraints that are experienced by other business functions. This comment is not true of all branches of industry and commerce. In high street stores, 'buying' is recognised as one of the most important functions of the business.

The effectiveness of the purchasing function affects profit in three ways.

(a) Effective purchasing ensures the best **value for money** is obtained by the firm.

(b) Effective purchasing assists in **meeting quality targets**. Again this has an impact on a firm's long-term marketing strategy, if quality is an issue.

(c) An effective purchasing strategy minimises the amount of purchased **material held in inventory**.

2.2 The purchasing mix

The purchasing manager has to obtain the best purchasing **quantity**, **quality**, **price**, and **delivery arrangements**. Purchasing may be **centralised** or **decentralised**. The **purchasing mix** has implications for JIT and quality management.

PURCHASING MIX	
Quantity	Size and timing of orders dictated by balance between delays in production caused by insufficient inventory and costs of inventory-holding
Quality	Quality of goods required for the manufacturing process, and the quality of goods acceptable to customers
Price	Short-term trends may influence, but best value over period of time is most important
Delivery	Lead time between placing and delivery of an order and reliability of suppliers' delivery arrangements

Question

JIT

If a company operates a JIT production system, what does this imply for purchasing?

Answer

(a) JIT systems and no-inventory production require the receipt of goods from suppliers at the latest possible time (ie when they are needed), to avoid the need to carry any materials or components in inventory.

(b) JIT seeks to avoid defects. Supplies must be of high quality to eliminate waste, as the quality of components can affect the quality of the end product.

Thus reliability of delivery and certainty of quality are as important (if not more so) as price.

SUPPLY STRATEGY	
Sources of supply	Available sources, their location, reliability, importance of yourself to them
Spread of supply	Single source to get bulk discounts and minimise costs, or dual sourcing to avoid lost production and complacency
Cost of supplies	Speed of achievement of cost discounts through volume purchases
Make or buy decision	More efficient to make goods in-house?
Suitability of existing supplier	Producing goods to required standard, ability to improve quality

SUPPLY STRATEGY	
Image or reputation of supplier	Selling point to buyer's customers eg makes of car supplied by car rental firms

2.3 Building supplier relationships

Many companies are seeking to build up **long-term relationships with suppliers**, often offering them advice and help with product development, manufacturing processes and quality. This often leads to a reduction in the number of suppliers a firm deals with. This policy is a means of **ensuring consistency** of bought-in component quality, and facilitates JIT production.

(a) **Advantages** of closer relationships with suppliers include:

- Sharing of information
- Better co-ordination
- The security of the relationship enables long-term planning
- Equipment and components are consistent and compatible
- Convenience for ordering supplies
- Discounts for bulk purchases
- Preferred customer status and better service agreements
- Products, upgrades and advice tailored to specific needs

(b) **Disadvantages**

- Dependence on a supplier inhibits a firm's freedom
- It may turn out more expensive
- The balance of power might be unequal

2.4 Centralised versus decentralised purchasing

There are advantages to both centralised and decentralised purchasing. Each organisation will make this decision on the basis of their own business and their own business environment.

2.4.1 Advantages of centralised purchasing

- The firm will be buying in larger quantities and so will be able to negotiate more substantial discounts.
- The organisation as a whole should be able to arrange more favourable credit terms than an individual branch.
- Inventory handling functions will be mainly centralised, which should save costs – but some handling will still have to be done at branch level.
- It should be possible to hold lower overall levels of inventory than if inventory was being held at each branch.
- Only one buying department will be needed, which will save costs.

2.4.2 Advantages of decentralised purchasing

- Local branches will be more in control of their production and sales if they have local control of purchasing.
- The purchasing requirements of individual branches may vary. For instance, some lines of inventory may sell better in some areas than others.

- Local branches will be able to form their own relationships with suppliers. There may be more mutual co-operation between a smaller organisation and its supplier than between a large purchasing department and a supplier.
- A local branch can be made more accountable for its own profitability and cash management if it has control of its own purchasing function.

Chapter Roundup

- Inventory holding and ordering costs can be minimised using the **economic order quantity** model. If **discounts** are offered for bulk purchases, the higher holding costs should be weighed against the lower ordering and purchasing costs.
- Businesses should consider at what **level** of inventory orders should be made, taking account of demand levels, delivery times and any uncertainties. **Safety inventory** may be held if uncertainties are particularly large.
- The aim of **Just-in-Time** is to hold as little inventory as possible and production systems need to be very efficient to achieve this.
- Purchasing may be **centralised** or **decentralised**. The optimal mix of **quantity**, **quality**, **price** and **delivery arrangements** should be sought.

Quick Quiz

1 The basic EOQ formula for inventories indicates whether bulk discounts should be taken advantage of.

True ☐

False ☐

2 What do BACS and CHAPS stand for?

3 Identify the potential benefits of JIT manufacturing.

4 The Economic Order Quantity can be expressed as follows:

$$\sqrt{\frac{2C_oD}{C_h}}$$

What does C_h describe in this formula?

A The cost of holding one unit of inventory for one year
B The cost of placing one order
C The cost of a unit of inventory
D The customer demand for the item

5 Using the following information:

Max lead time = 5 days
Min lead time = 2 days
Average lead time = 3 days
Reorder level = 100 units
Reorder quantity = 150 units
Maximum usage = 60 units per day
Average usage = 30 units per day
Minimum usage = 20 units per day

Calculate the maximum level of inventory.

6 Calculate the minimum level of inventory, using the information in question 7.

Answers to Quick Quiz

1 False. It may be necessary to modify the formula to take account of bulk discounts.

2 Bankers' Automated Clearing Services; Clearing House Automated Payments System.

3 (a) Reduction in inventory holding costs
(b) Reduced manufacturing lead times
(c) Improved labour productivity
(d) Reduced scrap/rework/warranty costs

4 A The cost of holding one unit of inventory for one year

5 Maximum level of inventory = re-order level + re-order quantity – (minimum usage × minimum lead time)
= 100 + 150 – (20 × 2)
= 210 units

6 Minimum level of inventory = re-order level – (average usage × average lead time)
= 100 – (30 × 3)
= 10 units

Appendix 1

International Accounting Terminology and Formats

International Accounting Terminology and Formats

Terminology

Below is a short list of the most important terms you are likely to use or come across, together with their international equivalents.

UK term	International term
Profit and loss account	Income statement
Profit and loss reserve (in balance sheet)	Retained earnings, or accumulated profits
Turnover	Revenue
Debtor account	Account receivable
Debtors (eg 'debtors have increased')	Receivables
Debtor	Customer
Creditor account	Account payable
Creditors (eg 'creditors have increased')	Payables
Creditor	Supplier
Debtors control account	Receivables control account
Creditors control account	Payables control account
Stock	Inventory
Fixed asset	Non-current asset (generally). Tangible fixed assets are also referred to as 'property, plant and equipment'.
Long-term liability	Non-current liability
Provision (eg for depreciation)	Allowance (You will sometimes see 'provision' used too.)
General ledger	Nominal ledger
VAT	Sales tax
Debentures	Loan notes
Preference shares/dividends	Preferred shares/dividends

Formats

Note that the financial statements are generally expressed in dollars rather than pounds.

In general the format for the income statement (international) is the same as the profit and loss account (UK) except for a couple of differences in terminology. Here is a simple example, with the differences highlighted.

CHEAPSTAKE
INCOME STATEMENT
FOR THE YEAR ENDED 31 DECEMBER 20X6

		$'000
= Turnover in UK	Revenue	9,000
	Cost of sales	4,529
	Gross profit	4,471
	Distribution expenses	918
	Administration expenses	1,598
	Finance cost	50
	Profit before tax	1,905
= Tax/corporation tax in UK	Income tax expense	105
	Profit for the year	1,800

[redacted]

The format of the balance sheet is different from the UK. **Instead of having net assets (assets less liabilities) equal to capital and reserves, it has total assets in the top half equal to equity and liabilities in the bottom half.**

CHEAPSTAKE
BALANCE SHEET AS AT 31 DECEMBER 20X6

ASSETS	$'000	$'000
Non-current assets		
Intangible asset: goodwill		270
Tangible assets: property and plant and equipment		2,720
		2,990
Current assets		
Inventory	1,950	
Receivables	1,544	
Bank	200	
		3,694
		6,684
EQUITY AND LIABILITIES		
Equity		
$1 Ordinary shares		400
10% preferred shares (non-redeemable)		600
Revaluation reserve		350
Retained earnings		2,274
		3,624
Non-current liabilities		
5% Loan notes	1,000	
Deferred tax	120	1,120
Current liabilities		1,940
		6,684

(As you can see, assets = capital plus liabilities, rather than assets less liabilities = capital.)

Appendix 2
Mathematical tables and exam formulae

Present value table

Present value of $1 ie $(1+r)^{-n}$ where r = interest rate, n = number of periods until payment or receipt.

Periods					Interest rates (r)					
(n)	1%	2%	3%	4%	5%	6%	7%	8%	9%	10%
1	0.990	0.980	0.971	0.962	0.952	0.943	0.935	0.926	0.917	0.909
2	0.980	0.961	0.943	0.925	0.907	0.890	0.873	0.857	0.842	0.826
3	0.971	0.942	0.915	0.889	0.864	0.840	0.816	0.794	0.772	0.751
4	0.961	0.924	0.888	0.855	0.823	0.792	0.763	0.735	0.708	0.683
5	0.951	0.906	0.863	0.822	0.784	0.747	0.713	0.681	0.650	0.621
6	0.942	0.888	0.837	0.790	0.746	0.705	0.666	0.630	0.596	0.564
7	0.933	0.871	0.813	0.760	0.711	0.665	0.623	0.583	0.547	0.513
8	0.923	0.853	0.789	0.731	0.677	0.627	0.582	0.540	0.502	0.467
9	0.914	0.837	0.766	0.703	0.645	0.592	0.544	0.500	0.460	0.424
10	0.905	0.820	0.744	0.676	0.614	0.558	0.508	0.463	0.422	0.386
11	0.896	0.804	0.722	0.650	0.585	0.527	0.475	0.429	0.388	0.350
12	0.887	0.788	0.701	0.625	0.557	0.497	0.444	0.397	0.356	0.319
13	0.879	0.773	0.681	0.601	0.530	0.469	0.415	0.368	0.326	0.290
14	0.870	0.758	0.661	0.577	0.505	0.442	0.388	0.340	0.299	0.263
15	0.861	0.743	0.642	0.555	0.481	0.417	0.362	0.315	0.275	0.239
16	0.853	0.728	0.623	0.534	0.458	0.394	0.339	0.292	0.252	0.218
17	0.844	0.714	0.605	0.513	0.436	0.371	0.317	0.270	0.231	0.198
18	0.836	0.700	0.587	0.494	0.416	0.350	0.296	0.250	0.212	0.180
19	0.828	0.686	0.570	0.475	0.396	0.331	0.277	0.232	0.194	0.164
20	0.820	0.673	0.554	0.456	0.377	0.312	0.258	0.215	0.178	0.149

Periods					Interest rates (r)					
(n)	11%	12%	13%	14%	15%	16%	17%	18%	19%	20%
1	0.901	0.893	0.885	0.877	0.870	0.862	0.855	0.847	0.840	0.833
2	0.812	0.797	0.783	0.769	0.756	0.743	0.731	0.718	0.706	0.694
3	0.731	0.712	0.693	0.675	0.658	0.641	0.624	0.609	0.593	0.579
4	0.659	0.636	0.613	0.592	0.572	0.552	0.534	0.516	0.499	0.482
5	0.593	0.567	0.543	0.519	0.497	0.476	0.456	0.437	0.419	0.402
6	0.535	0.507	0.480	0.456	0.432	0.410	0.390	0.370	0.352	0.335
7	0.482	0.452	0.425	0.400	0.376	0.354	0.333	0.314	0.296	0.279
8	0.434	0.404	0.376	0.351	0.327	0.305	0.285	0.266	0.249	0.233
9	0.391	0.361	0.333	0.308	0.284	0.263	0.243	0.225	0.209	0.194
10	0.352	0.322	0.295	0.270	0.247	0.227	0.208	0.191	0.176	0.162
11	0.317	0.287	0.261	0.237	0.215	0.195	0.178	0.162	0.148	0.135
12	0.286	0.257	0.231	0.208	0.187	0.168	0.152	0.137	0.124	0.112
13	0.258	0.229	0.204	0.182	0.163	0.145	0.130	0.116	0.104	0.093
14	0.232	0.205	0.181	0.160	0.141	0.125	0.111	0.099	0.088	0.078
15	0.209	0.183	0.160	0.140	0.123	0.108	0.095	0.084	0.074	0.065
16	0.188	0.163	0.141	0.123	0.107	0.093	0.081	0.071	0.062	0.054
17	0.170	0.146	0.125	0.108	0.093	0.080	0.069	0.060	0.052	0.045
18	0.153	0.130	0.111	0.095	0.081	0.069	0.059	0.051	0.044	0.038
19	0.138	0.116	0.098	0.083	0.070	0.060	0.051	0.043	0.037	0.031
20	0.124	0.104	0.087	0.073	0.061	0.051	0.043	0.037	0.031	0.026

Cumulative present value table

This table shows the present value of $1 per annum, receivable or payable at the end of each year for *n* years $\frac{1-(1+r)^{-n}}{r}$.

Periods (n)	Interest rates (r) 1%	2%	3%	4%	5%	6%	7%	8%	9%	10%
1	0.990	0.980	0.971	0.962	0.952	0.943	0.935	0.926	0.917	0.909
2	1.970	1.942	1.913	1.886	1.859	1.833	1.808	1.783	1.759	1.736
3	2.941	2.884	2.829	2.775	2.723	2.673	2.624	2.577	2.531	2.487
4	3.902	3.808	3.717	3.630	3.546	3.465	3.387	3.312	3.240	3.170
5	4.853	4.713	4.580	4.452	4.329	4.212	4.100	3.993	3.890	3.791
6	5.795	5.601	5.417	5.242	5.076	4.917	4.767	4.623	4.486	4.355
7	6.728	6.472	6.230	6.002	5.786	5.582	5.389	5.206	5.033	4.868
8	7.652	7.325	7.020	6.733	6.463	6.210	5.971	5.747	5.535	5.335
9	8.566	8.162	7.786	7.435	7.108	6.802	6.515	6.247	5.995	5.759
10	9.471	8.983	8.530	8.111	7.722	7.360	7.024	6.710	6.418	6.145
11	10.368	9.787	9.253	8.760	8.306	7.887	7.499	7.139	6.805	6.495
12	11.255	10.575	9.954	9.385	8.863	8.384	7.943	7.536	7.161	6.814
13	12.134	11.348	10.635	9.986	9.394	8.853	8.358	7.904	7.487	7.103
14	13.004	12.106	11.296	10.563	9.899	9.295	8.745	8.244	7.786	7.367
15	13.865	12.849	11.938	11.118	10.380	9.712	9.108	8.559	8.061	7.606
16	14.718	13.578	12.561	11.652	10.838	10.106	9.447	8.851	8.313	7.824
17	15.562	14.292	13.166	12.166	11.274	10.477	9.763	9.122	8.544	8.022
18	16.398	14.992	13.754	12.659	11.690	10.828	10.059	9.372	8.756	8.201
19	17.226	15.679	14.324	13.134	12.085	11.158	10.336	9.604	8.950	8.365
20	18.046	16.351	14.878	13.590	12.462	11.470	10.594	9.818	9.129	8.514

Periods (n)	Interest rates (r) 11%	12%	13%	14%	15%	16%	17%	18%	19%	20%
1	0.901	0.893	0.885	0.877	0.870	0.862	0.855	0.847	0.840	0.833
2	1.713	1.690	1.668	1.647	1.626	1.605	1.585	1.566	1.547	1.528
3	2.444	2.402	2.361	2.322	2.283	2.246	2.210	2.174	2.140	2.106
4	3.102	3.037	2.974	2.914	2.855	2.798	2.743	2.690	2.639	2.589
5	3.696	3.605	3.517	3.433	3.352	3.274	3.199	3.127	3.058	2.991
6	4.231	4.111	3.998	3.889	3.784	3.685	3.589	3.498	3.410	3.326
7	4.712	4.564	4.423	4.288	4.160	4.039	3.922	3.812	3.706	3.605
8	5.146	4.968	4.799	4.639	4.487	4.344	4.207	4.078	3.954	3.837
9	5.537	5.328	5.132	4.946	4.772	4.607	4.451	4.303	4.163	4.031
10	5.889	5.650	5.426	5.216	5.019	4.833	4.659	4.494	4.339	4.192
11	6.207	5.938	5.687	5.453	5.234	5.029	4.836	4.656	4.486	4.327
12	6.492	6.194	5.918	5.660	5.421	5.197	4.988	4.793	4.611	4.439
13	6.750	6.424	6.122	5.842	5.583	5.342	5.118	4.910	4.715	4.533
14	6.982	6.628	6.302	6.002	5.724	5.468	5.229	5.008	4.802	4.611
15	7.191	6.811	6.462	6.142	5.847	5.575	5.324	5.092	4.876	4.675
16	7.379	6.974	6.604	6.265	5.954	5.668	5.405	5.162	4.938	4.730
17	7.549	7.120	6.729	6.373	6.047	5.749	5.475	5.222	4.990	4.775
18	7.702	7.250	6.840	6.467	6.128	5.818	5.534	5.273	5.033	4.812
19	7.839	7.366	6.938	6.550	6.198	5.877	5.584	5.316	5.070	4.843
20	7.963	7.469	7.025	6.623	6.259	5.929	5.628	5.353	5.101	4.870

Exam formulae

Valuation models

(i) Future value S, of a sum X, invested for n periods, compounded at r% interest per annum:

$$S = X[1 + r]^n$$

(ii) Present value of \$1 payable or receivable in n years, discounted at r% per annum:

$$PV = \frac{1}{[1+r]^n}$$

(iii) Present value of an annuity of \$1 per annum, receivable or payable for n years, commencing in one year, discounted at r% per annum:

$$PV = \frac{1}{r}\left[1 - \frac{1}{[1+r]^n}\right]$$

(iv) Present value of \$1 per annum, payable or receivable in perpetuity, commencing in one year, discounted at r% per annum:

$$PV = \frac{1}{r}$$

(v) Present value of \$1 per annum, receivable or payable, commencing in one year, growing in perpetuity at a constant rate of g% per annum, discounted at r% per annum:

$$PV = \frac{1}{r-g}$$

Inventory management

(i) Economic Order Quantity $EOQ = \sqrt{\frac{2C_oD}{C_h}}$

Where C_o = cost of placing an order D = annual demand

C_h = cost of holding one unit in inventory for one year

Cash management

(i) Optimal sale of securities, Baumol model:

$$\text{Optimal sale} = \sqrt{\frac{2 \times \text{Annual cash disbursements} \times \text{Cost per sale of securities}}{\text{Interest rate}}}$$

(ii) Spread between upper and lower cash balance limits, Miller-Orr model:

$$\text{Spread} = 3\left[\frac{\frac{3}{4} \times \text{transaction cost} \times \text{variance of cash flows}}{\text{Interest rate}}\right]^{\frac{1}{3}}$$

Objective test question and answer bank

1 A company makes an accounting profit of $300,000 during the year. This includes non-taxable income of $50,000 and book depreciation of $30,000. In addition, expenses of $25,000 are disallowable for tax purposes. If the tax allowable depreciation totals £24,000, what is the taxable profit?

A $279,000
B $281,000
C $319,000
D $321,000

2 A company has sales of $200,000, excluding sales tax, in a period. Its purchases, excluding sales tax, total $150,000. It has no zero-rated sales but 20% of its purchases are zero-rated. Sales tax is 17.5%. What is the sales tax payable for the period?

A $7,447
B $8,750
C $14,000
D $29,750

3 Fill in the four missing words.

The accruals basis of accounting requires that the impact of transactions should be reflected in the financial statements for the period in which they ...., and not, in the period any .... involved is .... or ....

4 When carrying out an audit an external auditor must satisfy himself of a number of matters. Which of the following are not one of those matters?

A The accounts have been prepared by a qualified accountant
B Proper accounting records have been kept
C The accounts have been prepared in accordance with the legislation
D The accounts are in agreement with accounting records

5 According to the IASB *Framework* the qualitative characteristics of financial statements are

A Understandability, consistency, reliability and going concern
B Understandability, prudence, reliability and relevance
C Understandability, relevance, reliability and comparability
D Prudence, consistency, relevance and accruals

6 T purchases production machinery costing $200,000 and having an estimated useful life of 20 years with a residual value of $4,000. After being in use for 6 years the remaining useful life of the machinery is revised and estimated to be 25 years, with an unchanged residual value. The annual depreciation charge after these events is $...................

7 Fill in the two series of missing words.

An asset is a resource controlled by an entity as a result of .... and from which .... are expected to flow to the entity.

8 IAS 37 *Provisions, contingent liabilities and contingent assets* requires that material contingencies, other than those where the probability of the outcome is remote, existing at the balance sheet date should be treated as follows.

A Contingent assets and contingent liabilities must always be either accrued or disclosed in the financial statements

B Contingent liabilities must always be accrued and contingent assets must always be disclosed in the financial statements

C Contingent liabilities must always be either accrued or disclosed and contingent assets must always be disclosed in the financial statements

D Neither contingent assets nor contingent liabilities can be accrued in the financial statements

9 A company purchases a new machine and the costs involved in this are given below.

	$
Purchase price	680,000
Delivery costs	30,000
Installation costs	80,000
Cleaning costs after first production run	4,000

At what figure would the machine initially be included in the balance sheet? $......................

10 Which of the following is a source of tax rules?

A International accounting standards
B Local company legislation
C Local tax legislation
D Domestic accounting practice

11 H has prepared its financial statements for the year ending 30 June 20X8. On 15 July a major fraud was uncovered by the auditors which had taken place during the year to 30 June. On 31 July the company made a large loan stock issue which has significantly increased the company's gearing level.

In accordance with IAS 10 *Events after the balance sheet date*, how should the two events be treated in the financial statements?

	Fraud	*Loan stock issue*
A	Accrued in accounts	Disclosed in notes
B	Accrued in accounts	Accrued in accounts
C	Disclosed in notes	Disclosed in notes
D	Disclosed in notes	Accrued in accounts

12 A company pays a dividend of $400,000. The rate of advanced tax is 20%. What is the advanced tax payable?

A $80,000
B $90,000
C $100,000
D $110,000

13 According to IAS 36 *Impairment of assets* what is the recoverable amount of a non-current asset?

A Net selling price
B Value in use
C The higher of net selling price and value in use
D The lower of net selling price and value in use

14 Which of the following types of research and development expenditure must be written off in the year it is incurred?

A Market research costs confirming the ultimate commercial viability of a product
B Legal costs in connection with registration of a patent
C Costs of searching for possible alternative products
D Costs of research work which are to be reimbursed by a customer

15 If an auditor disagrees with the director's treatment of an item and he considers that the effect on the financial statements is *material,* but not *pervasive*, what type of audit report would be issued?

A Unqualified report
B Qualified report with 'except for' paragraph
C Disclaimer of opinion
D Adverse opinion

16 At 31 December 20X8 Jiang Co has trade receivables of $14,000, trade payables of 75% of this figure, inventory of finished goods of $7,000 and inventory of raw materials of $5,000. The business also has a bank overdraft of $2,500 and $25,000 6% loan stock. There were also accruals of $1,000, prepayments of $500 and petty cash of $100.

What is the current ratio at 31 December 20X8?

A 0.68
B 0.69
C 1.90
D 2.00

17 A provision for the cost of removing pollution arising from a company's operations should be recognised if?

A The accounts would reveal an understated net profit figure without the provision

B The directors recognise that there is a legal or constructive obligation to remove the pollution by spending money in the future

C Other companies in the same industry have recognised similar provisions

D The company auditors instruct the directors to set up a provision.

18 According to IAS 36 *Impairment of assets*, how often should assets be tested for impairment?

A Every year
B Every 3 years
C Every time non-current assets are revalued
D When there is an indication that impairment may have occurred

19 G has revalued one of its buildings to $1,200,000 at 31 December 20X8. The building was purchased 8 years ago at a cost of $840,000 and is being depreciated over a period of 40 years.

The depreciation charge for the year ending 31 December 20X9 will be $........................

20 Given below are details of one of S's construction contracts.

	$
Costs incurred to date	240,000
Estimated costs to completion	280,000
Progress payments invoiced	280,000
Total contract price	680,000

The contract is estimated to be 45% complete.

What figure would appear on the balance sheet for the gross amount due from customers?

$ ....

21 According to IAS 24 *Related party disclosures,* which of the following would not be a related party of Chen Co?

A An associated undertaking of Chen Co
B The managing director of Chen Co's parent company
C A company in which Chen Co holds a 10% investment
D Chen Co's pension fund for its employees

22 State the definition of a non-adjusting event in no more than twenty-five words.

23 Define a provision in no more than ten words.

24 Which of the following does **not** accurately describe *'true and fair view'*?

A It is a dynamic concept that evolves in response to changes in accounting and business practice

B Even reasonable business people and accountants may not share a consensus as to the degree of accuracy and completeness required

C Courts are likely to examine the meanings of the word 'true' and the word 'fair' in interpreting the meaning of 'true and fair'

D Courts are likely to look to the ordinary practices of professional accountants

25 A company is resident in Country Z. It has a branch in Country Y. The branch has taxable profits of $100,000, on which tax of $5,000 is paid. The tax rate in Country Z is 20% and there is a double taxation treaty between Countries Y and Z that allows tax relief on the full deduction basis. If the company has total taxable profits including those of the branch of $200,000, how much tax will it pay in Country Z?

A $20,000
B $25,000
C $35,000
D $40,000

26 Where is employee tax recorded in a set of financial statements?

A Charged to employee costs in the income statement
B Not included in the financial statements at all
C Included as a creditor in the balance sheet
D Included as a debtor in the balance sheet

27 A company has sales of $800,000, excluding sales tax, in a period. Its purchases, including sales tax, total $550,000. The rate of sales tax is 10%. If 25% of all sales are zero rated, what is the sales tax payable for the period?

A $10,000
B $20,000
C $22,500
D $30,000

28 Which of the following statements provides the best definition of the term 'interest yield'?

A The amount of interest paid on $100 of stock in one year
B The quoted percentage rate of interest on a stock
C The interest rate on a stock quoted as a percentage of the market price
D The coupon rate

29 A company has an accounting profit of $200,000 for the year. This includes depreciation of $25,000 and disallowable expenses of $10,000. If the tax allowable depreciation totals £30,000 and the tax rate is 30%, what is the tax payable?

A $55,500
B $58,500
C $60,000
D $61,500

30 Which of the following could normally be covered under a company's export credit insurance policy?

A All its export business on a regular basis
B Selected parts of its export business
C Occasional, high value export sales
D All of the above

The figures below have been extracted from the accounts of PR Co and apply to questions 31 to 34

	$
Sales revenue	750,000
Cost of sales	500,000
Gross profit	250,000
Current assets	
Inventory	75,000
Trade receivables	100,000
Other receivables	10,000
Cash at bank and in hand	5,000
	190,000
Current liabilities	
Overdraft	30,000
Dividend	40,000
Trade payables	80,000
Other payables	10,000
	160,000
Net current assets	30,000

31 What is the current ratio?

A 0.72
B 0.82
C 1.19
D 1.58

32 What is the customers' payment period?

A 48.67 days
B 53.53 days
C 73.00 days
D 80.30 days

33 What is the suppliers' payment period?

A 38.9 days
B 43.8 days
C 58.4 days
D 65.7 days

34 What is the inventory turnover period?

A 36.50 days
B 54.75 days
C 109.50 days
D 171.09 days

35 ICE had sales in the last year of $150,000, and purchases of $115,000. At the start of the year inventory was $15,000, receivables were $5,000 and payables were $10,000. At the end of the year inventory was $10,000, receivables were $8,000 and payables were $12,000.

What was the gross profit for the period?

A $30,000
B $32,000
C $34,000
D $40,000

36 CHEM produces quarterly cash forecasts. It uses 1,500 units of Chemical A per quarter, for which it currently pays $20 per unit. The price of Chemical A is expected to rise by 3% per quarter for the foreseeable future, and CHEM plans to increase production by 2% per quarter for the next year.

It is now nearing the end of quarter 1. What figure for Chemical A should be included in the cash flow forecast for Quarter 3 (to the nearest $)?

A $34,792
B $33,113
C $32,467
D $31,518

37 DEL is a specialist delicatessen chain with average daily takings of $10,000. The shops are open for six days each week and takings are banked every other day. The overdraft rate is 10% simple interest. What is the annual cost to DEL of not banking daily?

(You can assume that the shops are open for six days a week throughout the year, and that the banks are open every day that the shops are open. Work to the nearest $.)

A $156
B $427
C $855
D $1,560

38 The percentage cost of an early settlement discount to the company giving it can be estimated by the formula:

$$\left(\frac{100}{100-d}\right)^{\frac{365}{t}} - 1$$

What does 'd' represent in this formula?

A The number of days credit allowed with the discount
B The number of days credit allowed without the discount
C The reduction in days credit allowed with the discount
D The discount percentage offered

39 CENT is offering customers the option of paying $98.50 after seven days per $100 invoiced, or payment in full after 45 days. What is the annual cost of this policy in percentage terms?

A 1.5%
B 12.4%
C 14.4%
D 15.6%

40 You are the Credit Controller of WTP. The sales manager has asked you to open accounts for four new customers (A, B, C and D), and he is suggesting payment terms of 30 days with a credit limit of $10,000 for each customer. You have extracted the following information from their accounts. Which of the customers would you feel the most confident in supplying as requested?

	Cost of goods sold	*Trade payables*
A	$1,800,000	$450,000
B	$180,000	$45,000
C	$120,000	$10,000
D	$1,200,000	$100,000

41 What is the maximum percentage of bad debt loss that will normally be covered by a credit insurance policy?

A 65%
B 75%
C 85%
D 95%

42 Which of the following would **not** be a preferential creditor in the event of a bankruptcy?

A Subcontractors in the building industry
B Pension scheme contributions
C Preferred shareholders
D Staff salaries

43 The annual demand for an item of inventory is 90 units. The item costs $225 a unit to purchase, the holding cost for one unit for one year is 10% of the unit cost, and ordering costs are $200 per order. What is the economic order quantity?

A 20 units
B 30 units
C 40 units
D 50 units

44 Further to the information in the previous question, the company has decided to accept the offer of a 2% discount for orders over 45 units. What will be the total annual purchasing costs?

A $21,257
B $21,156
C $21,150
D $20,741

45 Which of the following effects is the **least likely** to be associated with the introduction of a just-in-time procurement system?

A Improved labour productivity
B Reduction in the number of goods inwards transactions
C Reduction in inventory holding costs
D Reduced manufacturing lead times

1 B

		$	$
Accounting profit			300,000
Add:	depreciation	30,000	
	disallowed expenses	25,000	
			55,000
			355,000
Less:	non-taxable income	50,000	
	tax allowable depreciation	24,000	
			74,000
Taxable profit			281,000

2 C

	$
Output tax (200,000 x 17.5%)	35,000
Input tax ((150,000 x 80%) x 17.5%)	21,000
Payable	14,000

3 The accruals basis of accounting requires that the **impact of transactions** should be reflected in the financial statements for the period in which they **occur**, and not, in the period any **cash** involved is **received** or **paid**.

4 A In order to state that the financial statements show a true and fair view the auditor must satisfy himself that the other three matters are valid.

5 C

6 D

		$
Cost		200,000
Depreciation	$6 \times \left(\frac{200{,}000 - 4{,}000}{20}\right)$	58,800
NBV end year 6		141,200
Depreciation year 7	$\frac{141{,}200 - 4{,}000}{25}$ =	$5,488

7 An asset is a resource controlled by an entity as a result of **past transactions or events** and from which **future economic benefits** are expected to flow to the entity.

8 D Probable liabilities should be accrued
Possible liabilities should be disclosed
Contingent assets are only disclosed if they are probable

9 $790,000. The cost to appear initially in the balance sheet is the cost of getting the machine ready for production. This will include the delivery and installation costs but not the cleaning costs after the first production run.

10 C Local tax legislation forms the basis of local taxation and so is a source of tax rules. The other options are all sources of accounting rules.

11 A The fraud is an adjusting event as it took place during the year to 30 June although it was not discovered until after the year end. The loan stock issue is a non-adjusting event but due to its materiality should be disclosed in the notes.

12 C The dividend is 80% of the total payment and so the advanced tax is 20/80 or ¼ of the dividend.

$400,000 x ¼ = $100,000

Tutor's note: Another way of looking at this is to say that the dividend is 80% of the total payment, therefore the total payment must be:

$400,000/80 x 100 = $500,000

So the advanced tax due must be:

$500,000 x 20% = $100,000

13 C The higher of net selling price and value in use.

14 C Items A and B are costs incurred in the *development* of a product. Note that while market research costs are not normally development costs, they *may be* treated as such when confirming ultimate commercial viability.

C is research and therefore must be written off.

D is work in progress (inventory) which you are being paid to do.

15 B Qualified report with 'except for' paragraph.

16 C Current ratio = $\frac{\text{Current assets}}{\text{Current liabilities}}$

Current assets	
Receivables	14,000
Finished goods inventory	7,000
Raw materials inventory	5,000
Prepayments	500
Petty cash	100
	26,600
Current liabilities	
Payables ($14,000 × 75%)	10,500
Bank overdraft	2,500
Accruals	1,000
	14,000

Current ratio = $\frac{\$26,600}{\$14,000}$ = 1.9

17 B It is the existence of an obligation which creates the need for a provision.

18 D

19 Depreciation charge = $\frac{\$1,200,000}{32 \text{ years}}$

= $37,500

20 $32,000

	$
Costs to date	240,000
Attributable profit (45% × (680 – 240 – 280))	72,000
Progress billings	(280,000)
Gross amount due from customers	32,000

21 C IAS 24 states that two or more parties are related if:

- One party has control of the other
- The parties are subject to common control
- One party has significant influence over the financial and operating policies of the other party
- One party has joint control over the other

A 10% investment in another company does not fall into any of these categories.

22 Non-adjusting events **arise after the balance sheet date** and concern **conditions** which did **not exist** at that time.

23 A provision is a liability of uncertain timing or amount.

Note. Although the amount is uncertain, it should be susceptible to **measurement** with **sufficient reliability**. Where no reliable estimate can be made, a liability exists which cannot be recognised. Such a liability should be disclosed as a contingent liability.

24 C Courts are **not likely** to examine the individual meanings of the word 'true' and the word 'fair' in interpreting the meaning of 'true and fair'. The courts are likely to use an approach that applies the **concepts implied** by the **expression** *'true and fair'*.

25 C Total tax due is $40,000 ($200,000 x 20%) less double taxation relief for $5,000, leaves $35,000 to pay.

26 C The company acts as a tax collector on behalf of the tax authority. Therefore any tax deducted is put in a creditor account until the money is actually paid to the tax authority. The balance on the creditor account represents the amount collected but not yet paid over.

27 A

	$
Output tax (800,000 x 75% x 10%)	60,000
Input tax (550,000/110 x 10)	50,000
Payable	10,000

The important point to remember is that zero rated sales are still taxable supplies; they just pay tax at 0%. Therefore input tax does not need to be restricted.

28 C The interest rate on a stock quoted as a percentage of the market price.

29 D

	$	$
Accounting profit		200,000
Add: depreciation	25,000	
disallowed expenses	10,000	
		35,000
		235,000
Less: tax allowable depreciation		30,000
Taxable profit		205,000

Tax payable = $205,000 x 30% = $61,500.

30 D All of the above.

31 C The current ratio is the ratio of current assets to current liabilities.

In this case: $190,000 ÷ $160,000 = 1.19

32 A The customers payment period is calculated as:

$$\frac{\text{Trade receivables}}{\text{Credit sales}} \times 365$$

In this case it is assumed that there are no cash sales:

$$\frac{100{,}000}{750{,}000} \times 365 = 48.67 \text{ days}$$

33 C The suppliers payment period is calculated as:

$$\frac{\text{Trade payables}}{\text{Purchases}} \times 365$$

In this case the purchases figure is not known, and therefore the cost of sales will be used as an approximation:

$$\frac{80{,}000}{500{,}000} \times 365 = 58.4 \text{ days}$$

34 B The inventory turnover period is calculated as:

$$\frac{\text{Average inventory}}{\text{Cost of sales}} \times 365$$

In this case it is assumed that the closing inventory approximates to the average inventory figure:

$$\frac{75{,}000}{500{,}000} \times 365 = 54.75 \text{ days}$$

35 A

	$	$
Sales		150,000
Less cost of sales		
Purchases	115,000	
Add opening inventory	15,000	
Less closing inventory	(10,000)	
		(120,000)
Gross profit		30,000

36 B Usage of Chemical A:

Current	1,500.0 units
Quarter 2	1,530.0 units
Quarter 3	1,560.6 units

Price of Chemical A per unit:

Current	$20.00
Quarter 2	$20.60
Quarter 3	$21.218

Cost of Chemical A for Quarter 3: 1560.6 units × $21.218 = $33,113

37 B There are three days each week when there is $10,000 unbanked, ie 156 days per year.

The daily rate of overdraft interest is 10%/365 = 0.0274%

The annual cost is therefore $10,000 x 156 x 0.0274% = $427

38 D The discount percentage offered.

39 D The following formula can be used:

$$r = \left(\frac{100}{100-d}\right)^{\frac{365}{t}} - 1$$

Where: r = percentage cost of policy
d = discount offered
t = reduction in payment period in days

In this case:

$$r = \left(\frac{100}{98.5}\right)^{\frac{365}{38}} - 1$$

$$= 15.6\%$$

40 D Companies A and B both have supplier payment periods of three months ($45,000 × 12/$180,000), which is well in excess of the terms that would be offered, and suggests that there may be problems with collection.

Companies C and D both pay their suppliers within one month ($10,000 × 12/$120,000) and would therefore cause less concern over collection. However, Company C only purchases $120,000 in total, and therefore a monthly credit limit of $10,000 is too high. Company D will therefore give the least cause for concern.

41 B 75%

42 C Preferred shareholders

43 C Use the EOQ model:

$$EOQ = \sqrt{\frac{2C_0D}{C_h}}$$

Where C_0 = cost of placing an order
D = annual demand
C_h = cost of holding one unit of inventory for one year

In this case:

$$EOQ = \sqrt{\frac{2 \times 200 \times 90}{22.50}}$$

$$EOQ = \sqrt{1{,}600}$$

EOQ = 40 units

44 D It is assumed that the company will order 45 units at a time.

		$
Purchases	90 × $225 × 98%	19,845
Holding costs	45 × 0.5 × $22.50 × 98%	496
Ordering costs	2 × $200	400
		20,741

45 B There are likely to be **more** deliveries by suppliers since goods are only obtained just before they are needed, and inventory levels are reduced.

Exam question and answer bank

1 Convex 9 mins

Learning outcome A(vii)

Convex is a limited liability company incorporated in Switzerland. However its board are all English and board meetings are held regularly in London. Head office is in Switzerland but the main accountancy offices are in London and the chairman and the chief executive are based in London.

Required:

(a) Where is the place of management of Convex? **2 marks**

(b) Would your answer to part (a) change if the following were the case?

(i) The Board are all Swiss nationals?

(ii) Board meetings are held in Switzerland with the main accounts offices in London and the chairman and chief Executive based in Switzerland? **3 marks**

Total Marks = 5

2 AB 18 mins

Learning outcome A(viii)

AB has an allotted capital of $350,000 in fully paid 50c ordinary shares. At 31 December 20X6 the following balances were included in the company's balance sheet.

	$
Agreed income tax liability on 20X5 profits	16,300
Estimated income tax liability on 20X6 profits	5,000
Deferred taxation account	29,400
Retained earnings b/f (credit)	43,000

The following information relates to the year ended 31 December 20X7.

(a) Income tax liability for 20X5 profits was settled (January).

(b) Income tax liability for 20X6 was agreed at $3,800 (December), paid January 20X8.

(c) Net profit for 20X7 (before tax) was calculated at $100,000.

(d) Income tax based on the 20X7 profits was estimated at $36,000.

(e) A transfer to the deferred taxation account of $7,000 for 20X7 is to be made in respect of capital allowances in excess of depreciation charges (the entire balance on the deferred tax account being of a similar nature).

Required

(a) Make all relevant entries in the ledger accounts (except bank and share capital).

(b) Complete the income statement for 20X7 and show how the final balances would be included in the balance sheet at 31 December 20X7. Show the details given in the notes to the accounts.

Assume income tax at 25%. **10 marks**

3 Tax and dividends 9 mins

Learning outcome A(i)

(a) Company A has an accounting profit of $750,000. This total is after charging book depreciation of $300,000, formation expenses of $15,000 and entertaining expenses of $75,000. The figure also includes government grants received of $25,000.

The tax rate is 25%. Under A's tax regime, government grants are tax-free and formation and entertaining expenses are disallowable. If the tax allowable depreciation is $350,000, calculate the tax due for the current period. **2 marks**

(b) A has paid a dividend during the accounting period of $1,500,000. It operates in a country where a full imputation system applies. Personal income tax is 30%.

How much tax will be paid by its shareholders? **3 marks**

Total Marks = 5

4 VAT 9 mins

Learning outcome A(ii)

A company has sales of $570,000 including VAT. Its purchases for the same period were $300,000 excluding VAT. The sales tax rate is 17.5%. Calculate the tax payable to the tax authorities if 20% of sales are zero-rated but only 15% of its purchases are zero-rated. **5 marks**

5 Company tax 9 mins

Learning outcome A(ii)

J is a retail enterprise. Its tax rate is 25%. It has a current tax creditor brought forward from the year ended 30 June 20X4 of $765,000 and a deferred tax creditor of $200,000.

On 30 June 20X5, the estimated tax charge for the year ended 30 June 20X5 was $976,000. The actual tax charge for the year ended 30 June 20X4 was agreed with the tax authority and settled with a payment of $794,000. The deferred tax creditor needs to be increased to $300,000 as at 30 June 20X5.

Required

Prepare the notes in respect of current and deferred tax as they would appear in the income statement and balance sheet of J for the year ended 30 April 20X5. **5 marks**

6 Regulatory influences 9 mins

Learning outcome B(i)

State three different regulatory influences on the preparation of the published accounts of quoted companies and briefly explain the role of each one. Comment briefly on the effectiveness of this regulatory system. **5 marks**

7 Accounting standards 9 mins

Learning outcome B(iii)

There are those who suggest that any standard setting body is redundant because accounting standards are unnecessary. Other people feel that such standards should be produced, but by the government, so they are legislated.

Required

Discuss the statement that accounting standards are unnecessary for the purpose of regulating financial statements. **5 marks**

8 IASB — 9 mins

Learning outcome B(iii)

Consider to what extent the IASB has succeeded in its aims and what problems it still faces. **5 marks**

9 Accounting concepts — 9 mins

Learning outcome B(ii)

Define the following accounting concepts.

(a) The business entity concept
(b) The money measurement concept
(c) The historical cost convention
(d) The stable monetary unit
(e) Objectivity
(f) The realisation concept
(g) The duality concept

5 marks

10 External auditors — 9 mins

Learning outcome B(vii)

Describe the external auditors' responsibilities with respect to the financial statements. **5 marks**

11 Audit report — 9 mins

Learning outcome B(vii)

Explain what is meant by a 'qualified' audit report and describe the differences between a 'qualified' and an 'unqualified' report. **5 marks**

12 C — 36 mins

Learning outcome C(v)

C is a civil engineering company. It started work on two long-term projects during the year ended 31 December 20X0. The following figures relate to those projects at the balance sheet date.

	Maryhill bypass	*Rottenrow Centre*
	$'000	$'000
Contract price	9,000	8,000
Costs incurred to date	1,400	2,900
Estimated costs to completion	5,600	5,200
Value of work certified to date	2,800	3,000
Cash received from contractee	2,600	3,400

An old mineshaft has been discovered under the site for the Rottenrow Centre and the costs of dealing with this have been taken into account in the calculation of estimated costs to completion. C Co's lawyers are reasonably confident that the customer will have to bear the additional costs which will be incurred in stabilising the land. If negotiations are successful then the contract price will increase to $10m.

C recognises revenues and profits on long-term (construction) contracts on the basis of work certified to date.

Required

(a) Calculate the figures which would appear in C's financial statements in respect of these two projects. **14 marks**

(b) It has been suggested that profit on construction contracts should not be recognised until the contract is completed. Briefly explain whether you believe that this suggestion would improve the quality of financial reporting for long-term contracts. **6 marks**

Total Marks = 20

13 IFRS 5 — 9 mins

Learning outcome C(iii)

At 30 November a manufacturing company decided to sell one of its processing plants and steps were taken to locate a buyer. After consultation with a property agent, who advised that prices in the area were expected to rise sharply over the next twelve months, senior management decided to raise the price of the building in anticipation of this. The buyers who were interested have now withdrawn due to the price rise but the directors are confident that in the new year, when property prices rise, they will obtain the price required. In the meantime, the processing plant is continuing to operate and handle customers orders.

At 31 December, will this plant be classified as 'held for sale' under IFRS 5? Explain your answer. **5 marks**

14 Leases — 9 mins

Learning outcome C(v)

The following definitions have been taken from the International Accounting Standards Board's *Framework for the Preparation and Presentation of Financial Statements.*

- 'An asset is a resource controlled by the entity as a result of past events and from which future economic benefits are expected to flow to the entity.'
- 'A liability is a present obligation of the entity arising from past events, the settlement of which is expected to result in an outflow from the entity of resources embodying economic benefits.'

IAS 17 *Leases* requires lessees to capitalise finance leases in their financial statements.

Required

Explain how IAS 17's treatment of finance leases applies the definitions of assets and liabilities. **5 marks**

15 T

36 mins

Learning outcome C(i)

T is a quoted company which owns a large number of hotels throughout the UK. The company's latest trial balance at 31 December 20X0 is as follows.

			$'000	$'000
Administrative expenses			3,000	
Bank			300	
Payables				1,700
Distribution costs			4,000	
Food purchases			2,100	
Heating and lighting			3,000	
Hotel buildings:	cost		490,000	
	depreciation to date			46,200
Hotel fixtures and fittings:		cost	18,000	
		depreciation to date		9,400
Interest			4,950	
Interim dividend paid			1,000	
Loans, repayable 20X8				110,000
Retained earnings				86,000
Sales of accommodation and food				68,500
Share capital: $1 shares, fully paid				220,000
Inventory as at 31 December 20W9			400	
Taxation			50	
Wages:	administrative staff		6,000	
	housekeeping and restaurant staff		9,000	
			541,800	541,800

Additional information

(a) During the year the company spent a total of $12m on a new hotel and purchased new fixtures for $7m. These acquisitions have been included in the relevant trial balance totals.

(b) Hotels are to be depreciated by 2 per cent of cost, and fixtures and fittings by 25 per cent of the reducing balance, with a full year's depreciation to be charged in the year of acquisition.

(c) Closing inventories of foodstuffs and other consumables were valued at $470,000 on 31 December 20X0.

(d) The balance on the taxation account is the amount remaining after the settlement of the corporation tax liability for the year ended 31 December 20W9. The directors have estimated the corporation tax liability for the year ended 31 December 20X0 at $10.2m.

Required

Prepare T's income statement for the year ended 31 December 20X0 and its balance sheet at that date.

Notes to the accounts are not required. **20 marks**

16 CEC

36 mins

Learning outcome C(iii)

After its end of year physical inventory count and valuation, the accounts staff of CEC have reached a valuation of $153,699 at cost for total inventories held as at the year end.

However, on checking the figures, the chief bookkeeper has come across the following additional facts.

(a) On one of the inventory sheets, a sub-total value of $6,275 had been carried forward on to the next sheet as $6,725.

(b) 260 units of inventory number 73113X which cost $0.60 each have been extended into the total value column at $6 each.

(c) The purchasing department has informed the accounts department that it is in possession of a number of free samples given to them by potential suppliers. Their estimated value, at purchase cost, would be $1,750. They were not included in the inventory referred to above.

(d) The count includes $4,658 of goods bought on credit and still not paid for as at the year end.

(e) The count includes damaged goods which originally cost $2,885. These could be repaired at a cost of $921 and sold for $3,600.

(f) The count excludes 300 units of item 730052 which were sold to a customer SC on a sale or return basis, at a price of $8 each. The original cost of the units was $5 each. SC has not yet indicated to CEC whether these goods have been accepted, or whether they will eventually be returned.

(g) The count includes 648 units of item 702422. These cost $7.30 each originally but because of dumping on the market by overseas suppliers, a price war has flared up and the unit cost price of the item has fallen to $6.50. The price reduction is expected to be temporary, lasting less than a year or so, although some observers of the market predict that the change might be permanent. CEC has already decided that if the price reduction lasts longer than six months, it will reduce its resale price of the item from $10.90 to about $10.

Required

Calculate the closing inventory figure for inclusion in the annual accounts of CEC, making whatever adjustments you consider necessary in view of items (a) to (g). Explain your treatment of each item.

20 marks

17 Plant and equipment — 9 mins

Learning outcome C(iii)

A business's plant and equipment account and depreciation account at 31 December 20X8 show the following:

Year of purchase	*Cost*	*Accumulated depreciation*
	$	$
20X5	100,000	80,000
20X6	70,000	42,000
20X7	50,000	20,000
20X8	30,000	6,000
	250,000	148,000

Depreciation is calculated at 20% on a straight line basis with a full year's charge in the year of acquisition and none in the year of disposal.

During 20X9 the following transactions took place:

(a) Purchases of plant and equipment amounted to $150,000
(b) Plant that had been bought in 20X5 for $40,000 was sold for $5,000
(c) Plant that had been bought in 20X7 for $10,000 was damaged and had to be scrapped.

Required

Prepare the following ledger accounts as at 31 December 20X9:

Plant and equipment – cost
– accumulated depreciation
– disposals

5 marks

18 IT — 9 mins

Learning outcome C(v)

The accounts of IT at 1 January 20X6 include capitalised development costs of $26,500. During the year ended 31 December 20X6 IT purchased a new business. The consideration paid to the proprietor included $4,800 in respect of goodwill. The company also spent $7,900 in research and $3,500 on development activities.

The directors of IT intend to write off $1,200 in respect of impairment of goodwill. They believe that $22,600 of development costs should be carried forward at 31 December 20X6, in accordance with IAS 38.

Show the ledger accounts for goodwill and research and development in the books of IT. **5 marks**

19 F — 36 mins

Learning outcome C(v)

F, an engineering company, makes up its financial statements to 31 March in each year. The financial statements for the year ended 31 March 20X1 showed revenue of $3m and trading profit of $400,000.

Before approval of the financial statements by the board of directors on 30 June 20X1 the following events took place.

(a) The financial statements of P for the year ended 28 February 20X1 were received which indicated a permanent decline in that company's financial position. F had bought shares in P some years ago and this purchase was included in unquoted investments at its cost of $100,000. The financial statements received indicated that this investment was now worth only $50,000.

(b) There was a fire at the company's warehouse on 30 April 20X1 when inventory to the value of $500,000 was destroyed. It transpired that the inventory in the warehouse was under-insured by some 50%.

(c) It was announced on 1 June 20X1 that the company's design for tank cleaning equipment had been approved by the major oil companies and this could result in an increase in the annual revenue of some $1m with a relative effect on profits.

The following points have also to be taken into consideration.

(d) Bills receivable of $150,000 were discounted with the banks on 15 March 20X1 and are due for maturity on 15 September 20X1. If the customer does not pay the bill, F will be liable to make up the shortfall to the bank.

(e) The company is expecting to receive orders worth up to $2 million for a new item of equipment which is at present on field trials. The equipment is being imported by the company at selling price less a trade discount of 25%. A quantity of this new equipment was held in inventory on 31 March 20X1.

Required

You are required to explain how, if at all, items (a) to (e) above should be reflected in the accounts of F for the year ended 31 March 20X1. **20 marks**

20 B

36 mins

Learning outcome C(ii)

The draft financial statements for B, a limited liability company, are set out below.

INCOME STATEMENT FOR THE YEAR ENDED 30 SEPTEMBER 20X1

	$000
Sales revenue	600
Cost of sales	(410)
Gross profit	190
Profit on sale of non-current asset	10
	200
Depreciation	(30)
Other expenses	(70)
Interest expense	(15)
Profit for the period	(85)

BALANCE SHEET AS AT 30 SEPTEMBER

	20X1		*20X0*	
	$'000	$'000	$'000	$'000
Non-current assets (see note)		450		520
Current assets				
Inventory	65		50	
Receivables	80		30	
Bank and cash	30		15	
		175		95
Total assets		625		615
Equity and liabilities				
Share capital		400		400
Retained earnings		145		95
Non-current liability				
Loan		20		100
Current liabilities				
Payables		60		20
		625		615

Notes

The company purchased non-current assets for $40,000 during the year ended 30 September 20X1.

Dividends of $35,000 were paid during the year.

Ignore taxation.

Required

(a) Prepare a cashflow statement for B for the year ended 30 September 20X1. The format need not comply with the accounting standard.

(b) Discuss whether a cashflow statement is more important than an income statement to users of accounts.

20 marks

21 Cat

36 mins

Learning outcome C(ii)

Set out below are the balance sheets of Cat Co as at 30 June 20X1 and 20X2.

CAT CO

BALANCE SHEET AS AT 30 JUNE

	20X1		*20X2*	
Assets	$	$	$	$
Non-current assets				
Cost	85,000		119,000	
Depreciation	26,000		37,000	
		59,000		82,000
Current assets				
Inventories	34,000		40,000	
Receivables (trade)	26,000		24,000	
Cash at bank	10,000		13,500	
		70,000		77,500
Total assets		129,000		159,500
Equity and liabilities				
Equity				
Ordinary $1 shares	26,000		28,000	
Share premium	12,000		13,000	
Retained earnings	44,000		70,500	
		82,000		111,500
Non-current liabilities				
10% loan stock		20,000		10,000
Current liabilities				
Payables (trade)	15,000		23,000	
Taxation	12,000		15,000	
		27,000		38,000
Total equity and liabilities		129,000		159,500

Notes

(a) No non-current assets were disposed of during the year.

(b) Of the 10% loan stock, $10,000 was redeemed at par on 31 December 20X1.

(c) Dividends of $13,000 were paid during the year.

Required

Prepare a cash flow statement and related notes for the year to 30 June 20X2, using the format specified in IAS 7.

20 marks

22 ABA

9 mins

Learning outcome C(v)

The directors of ABA, a limited liability company, are reviewing the draft accounts for the year ended 30 June 20X9. The net profit before tax currently stands at $923,000. The auditors have drawn their attention to the following matters:

(a) An announcement was made on 4 July that one of their customers, IMX, had gone into liquidation. The liquidator is estimating that suppliers will receive 30c in the $. The receivable in ABA's accounts regarding IMX stands at $325,000 at 30 June.

(b) A line of inventory valued at cost of $150,000 has become obsolete. It can only be disposed of for $200,000 via an agent who will require 20% of selling price. Other disposal costs will amount to $25,000.

(c) An outstanding claim for damages by an ex-employee who was injured in the warehouse is likely to amount to $50,000. No provision has been made for this as it was expected to be covered by insurance. However the insurance company are now claiming that certain safety procedures were not in place, rendering the cover invalid.

Required

Explain how each of these issues should be dealt with and show the effect on the net profit before tax.

5 marks

23 L

Learning outcome C(iv)

L, a limited liability company, has the following capital structure:

	$'000
Share capital	
50c ordinary shares (fully paid)	15,000
Share premium	3,000
Retained earnings	27,000
	45,000

The following share issues are made:

(a) A '3 for 2' bonus issue, and then

(b) A '1 for 2' rights issue at 80c.

Show the capital structure following these issues, assuming all rights are taken up. **5 marks**

24 International tax

Learning outcome A(viii)

J has an overseas branch L, which made a profit adjusted for tax purposes of $8 million for the year ended 30 June 20X6. This figure is included in the financial statements to 30 June 20X6. Taxable profits of the overseas branch have suffered local tax at a rate of 15%. J calculates that its tax liability for the year to 30 June 20X6 will be $1.5m. Overseas tax has not been taken into account in computing this tax liability. The liability for the year ended 30 June 20X5 has been agreed at $970,000. The deferred tax creditor needs to be reduced to $290,000 as at 30 June 20X6. J has the following balances brought forward: Current tax: $976,000; Deferred tax: $300,000.

Required

Prepare the notes in respect of current and deferred tax as they would appear in the financial statements of J for the year ended 30 April 20X6.

5 marks

25 Debt **36 mins**

Learning outcome D(ix)

AB is a medium-sized private company to which you have recently been appointed as the assistant financial controller. The company is currently engaged in a business expansion programme for which additional finance will be required. It is not currently feasible to raise additional equity finance, consequently debt finance is being considered. The decision has not yet been finalised whether this debt finance will be short or long term and if it is to be at fixed or variable rates. The financial controller has asked you, as part of your first assignment, to assist her in the preparation of information for a forthcoming meeting of the Board of Directors.

Required

Prepare a draft report to the Board of Directors which identifies and briefly discusses:

(a) Four main factors to be considered when deciding on the appropriate mix of long-term or short-term sources of debt finance for the company.

(b) Two main advantages of fixing interest rates on debt.

20 marks

26 ARD — 36 mins

Learning outcome D(x)

ARD has been having some difficulty with the collection of debts from export customers. At present the company makes no special arrangements for export sales.

As a result the company is considering either employing the services of a non-recourse export factoring company, or insuring its exports against non-payment through an insurer. The two alternatives also provide possible ways of financing sales.

An export factor will, if required, provide immediate finance of 80% of export credit sales at an interest rate of 2% above bank base rate (the base rate is 8%). The service fee for debt collection is 3% of credit sales. If the factor is used, administrative savings of $35,000 a year should be possible.

A comprehensive insurance policy costs 35 cents per $100 insured and covers 90% of the risk of non-payment for exports. The insurer will probably allow ARD to assign its rights to a bank, in return for which the bank will provide an advance of 70% of the sales value of insured debts, at a cost of 1.5% above base rate.

ARD's annual exports total $1,000,000. Export sales are on open account terms of 60 days credit, but on average payments have been 30 days late. Approximately 0.5%, by value, of credit sales result in bad debts which have to be written off. The company is able to borrow on overdraft from its bank, unsecured, at 2.5% above base rate. Assume a 360 day year.

Required

Recommend which combination of export administration and financing ARD should use. **20 marks**

27 GUS — 36 mins

Learning outcome D(i)

GUS is a toy manufacturing company. It manufactures Polly Playtime, the latest doll craze amongst young girls. The company is now at full production of the doll. The final accounts for 20X9 have just been published and are as follows. 20X8's accounts are also shown for comparison purposes.

INCOME STATEMENT YEAR ENDED 31 DECEMBER

	20X9	20X8
	$'000	$'000
Sales	30,000	20,000
Cost of sales	20,000	11,000
Gross profit	10,000	9,000
Interest	450	400
Profit before tax	9,550	8,600
Tax	2,000	1,200
Profit for the period	7,550	7,400

Note: Dividends of $2,500,000 were declared in 20X8 and 20X9.

BALANCE SHEET AS AT 31 DECEMBER

	20X9		20X8	
	$'000	$'000	$'000	$'000
Non-current assets		1,500		1,400
Current assets				
Inventory	7,350		3,000	
Receivables	10,000		6,000	
Cash	2,500	19,850	4,500	13,500
Total assets		21,350		14,900
Equity and liabilities				
Ordinary shares (25c)		5,000		5,000
Retained earnings		8,950		3,900
		13,950		8,900
Non-current liabilities				
8% loan stock		1,200		3,500
Current liabilities				
Overdraft	2,000		–	
Trade payables	4,200		2,500	
		6,200		2,500
Total equity and liabilities		21,350		14,900

(a) By studying the above accounts and using ratio analysis, identify the main problems facing GUS. **15 marks**

(b) Provide possible solutions to the problems identified in (a). **5 marks**

Total Marks = 20

28 VX **36 mins**

Learning outcome D(ii)

The VX Company has produced the following information from which a cash budget for the first six months of next year is required.

The company makes a single product which sells for $50 and the variable cost of each unit is as follows.

Material	$26
Labour (wages)	$8
Variable overhead	$2

Fixed overheads (excluding depreciation) are budgeted at $5,500 per month payable on the 23rd of each month.

Notes

(a) Sales units for the last two months of this year.

November	*December*
1,000	1,200

(b) Budgeted sales for next year.

January	*February*	*March*	*April*	*May*	*June*
1,400	1,600	1,800	2,000	2,200	2,600

(c) Production quantities for the last two months of this year.

November	*December*
1,200	1,400

(d) Budgeted production units for next year.

January	*February*	*March*	*April*	*May*	*June*
1,600	2,000	2,400	2,600	2,400	2,200

(e) Wages are paid in the month when output is produced.
(f) Variable overhead is paid 50% in the month when the cost is incurred and 50% the following month.
(g) Suppliers of material are paid two months after the material is used in production.
(h) Customers are expected to pay at the end of the second month following sale.
(i) A new machine is scheduled for January costing $34,000, this is to be paid for in February.
(j) An old machine is to be sold for cash in January for $1,200.
(k) The company expects to have a cash balance of $35,500 on 1 January.

Tasks

(a) Prepare a month by month cash budget for the first six months of next year.

(b) Discuss the actions management might take in the light of the cash budget you have prepared.

(c) Explain how depreciation would affect the following.

(i) A cash budget
(ii) The calculation of profit in a business

20 marks

29 Cash management — 36 mins

Learning outcome D(iv)

The treasurer of a local government department is reviewing her cash management procedures. She plans to introduce the use of cash management models and has asked you to investigate their applicability to the department. The following information is available.

(i) The department has agreed with its bank that it will maintain a minimum daily cash balance of $15,000. Severe financial penalties will apply if this balance is not maintained.

(ii) A forecast of daily cash movements for the next twelve months shows a standard deviation of daily cash flows of $3,000.

(iii) The daily interest rate is at present 0.0236% and this is not expected to change for the foreseeable future.

(iv) The transaction cost for each sale or purchase is $25.

Assume you are a newly recruited accountant in the department.

Required

Write a report to the treasurer which discusses:

(a) The advantages of cash management models over more traditional methods of cash forecasting, making specific reference to their applicability to a public sector organisation such as a local authority; **6 marks**

(b) How the Miller-Orr model would operate in practice, using the information given above. Your report should include calculations of the upper and lower limits for cash balances and the return point. Assume a spread of $26,820. **8 marks**

(c) How the Baumol model would operate and what its disadvantages are. **6 marks**

Note. You do not need to calculate the spread as this is given above, but you should explain the terms used in the Miller-Orr model.

Total Marks = 20

30 Factoring 36 mins

Learning outcome D(iii)

ABC is a small manufacturing company which is suffering cash flow difficulties. The company already utilises its maximum overdraft facility. ABC sells an average of $400,000 of goods per month at invoice value, and customers are allowed 40 days to pay from the date of invoice. Two possible solutions to the company's cash flow problems have been suggested.

- Option 1 The company could factor its trade debts. A factor has been found who would advance ABC 75% of the value of its invoices immediately on receipt of the invoices, at an interest rate of 10% per annum. The factor would also charge a service fee amounting to 2% of the total invoices. As a result of using the factor, ABC would save administration costs estimated at $5,000 per month.
- Option 2 The company could offer a cash discount to customers for prompt payment. It has been suggested that customers could be offered a 2% discount for payments made within ten days of invoicing.

Required

(a) Identify the services that may be provided by factoring organisations. **4 marks**

(b) Calculate the annual net cost (in $) of the proposed factoring agreement. **6 marks**

(c) Calculate the annualised cost (in percentage terms) of offering a cash discount to customers. **4 marks**

(d) Discuss the merits and drawbacks of the two proposals. **6 marks**

Total Marks = 20

31 Debt collection targets 36 mins

Learning outcome D(vi)

(a) Using an example, describe how you would devise a system of targets for credit control staff to ensure a consistent receivables ageing ratio.

(b) Describe the features of debt factoring, and explain why small, rapidly growing firms might employ a debt factor.

20 marks

32 SF **36 mins**

Learning outcome D(ix)

SF is a family-owned private company with five main shareholders.

SF has just prepared its cash budget for the year ahead, details of which are shown below. The current overdraft facility is $50,000 and the bank has stated that it would not be willing to increase the facility at present, without a substantial increase in the interest rate charged, due to the lack of assets to offer as security.

The shareholders are concerned by the cash projections, and have sought advice from external consultants.

All figures, $'000						*Month*						
	J	*F*	*M*	*A*	*M*	*J*	*J*	*A*	*S*	*O*	*N*	*D*
Collections from customers	55	60	30	10	15	20	20	25	30	40	55	80
Dividend on investment						10						
Total inflows	55	60	30	10	15	30	20	25	30	40	55	80
Payments to suppliers		20		20		25		28		27		25
Wages and salaries	15	15	15	15	15	20	20	15	15	15	15	15
Payments for non-current assets			2		5	10		15				
Dividend payable				25								
Corporation tax									30			
Other operating expenses	5	5	5	5	7	7	7	7	7	7	8	8
Total outflows	20	40	22	65	27	62	27	65	52	49	23	48
Net in or (out)	35	20	8	(55)	(12)	(32)	(7)	(40)	(22)	(9)	32	32
Bank balance (overdraft)												
Opening	20	55	75	83	28	16	(16)	(23)	(63)	(85)	(94)	(62)
Closing	55	75	83	28	16	(16)	(23)	(63)	(85)	(94)	(62)	(30)

The following additional information relating to the cash budget has been provided by SF.

(i) All sales are on credit. Two months' credit on average is granted to customers.

(ii) Production is scheduled evenly throughout the year. Year-end inventories of finished goods are forecast to be $30,000 higher than at the beginning of the year.

(iii) Purchases of raw materials are made at two-monthly intervals. SF typically takes up to 90 days to pay for goods supplied. Other expenses are paid in the month in which they arise.

(iv) The capital expenditure budget comprises:

Office furniture	March	$2,000
Progress payments on building extensions	May	$5,000
Car	June	$10,000
New equipment	August	$15,000

Required

Assume you are an external consultant employed by SF. Prepare a report for the board:

(a) Advising on the possible actions it might take to improve its budgeted cash flow for the year, and the possible impact of these actions on the company's business **12 marks**

(b) Explaining the advantages of borrowing by means of a term loan rather than an overdraft **5 marks**

(c) Identifying possible short-term investment opportunities for the cash surpluses identified in the first part of the budget year **3 marks**

Total Marks = 20

1 Convex

(a) Although the head office is in Switzerland, board meetings are held in London and the chairman and chief executive are based in London. **Therefore the place of management is London.**

(b) (i) The nationality of the Board Members is irrelevant to the place of management. Therefore the place of management is London.

(ii) As board meetings are held in Switzerland and the chairman and chief executive are based in Switzerland, **the place of management is Switzerland**. Although the accounting offices are in London, this does not affect the place where management decisions are made.

2 AB

Top tips

This is a longer tax question than you will meet in the exam, but it covers a lot of issues. Go through it methodically.

(a)

INCOME TAX (20X5) ACCOUNT

	$		$
Bank	16,300	Balance b/f	16,300

INCOME TAX (20X6) ACCOUNT

	$		$
Income statement over-provision	1,200	Balance b/f	5,000
Balance c/f	3,800		
	5,000		5,000

INCOME TAX (20X7) ACCOUNT

	$		$
		Income statement	36,000
Balance c/f	39,800	B/f re 20X6	3,800
	39,800		39,800

DEFERRED TAXATION ACCOUNT

	$		$
		Balance b/f	29,400
Balance c/f	36,400	Income statement (increase in provision)	7,000
	36,400		36,400

INCOME TAX EXPENSE (20X7)

	$		$
Charge for 20X7	36,000	Over provision re 20X6	1,200
Transfer to deferred tax	7,000	Balance c/f	41,800
	43,000		43,000

(b) INCOME STATEMENT
FOR THE YEAR ENDED 31 DECEMBER 20X7 (EXTRACT)

	Note	$
Profit before tax		100,000
Income tax expense	3	(41,800)
Profit for the period		58,200

BALANCE SHEET AS AT 31 DECEMBER 20X7 (EXTRACT)

	$	Note
Equity and liabilities		
Issued capital of 700,000 50c ordinary shares fully paid	350,000	
Retained earnings	101,200	4
Non current liabilities		
Deferred tax	36,400	2
Current liabilities		
Current tax	39,800	1

Notes to the balance sheet and income statement

1 *Current tax comprises*

	$
Income tax (3,800 + 36,000)	39,800

2 *Deferred tax*

	$
Balance at 1.1.20X7	29,400
Deferred tax expense related to temporary differences	7,000
Balance at 31.12.20X7	36,400

3 *Tax on profit for the year*

	$
Income tax (at 25% on taxable profits of 20X7)	36,000
less overprovision on profits of 20X6	(1,200)
Transfer to deferred tax for temporary differences	7,000
	41,800

4 *Retained earnings*

	$
Profit for the period	58,200
Retained brought forward	43,000
Retained carried forward	101,200

3 Tax and dividends

Top tips

Remember that the dividend is a **net** amount.

(a)

		$'000	$'000
Accounting profit			750
Add: disallowable expenditure:	entertaining	75	
	formation expenses	15	
	book depreciation	300	
			390
			1,140
Less: non-taxable income		25	
tax allowable depreciation		350	
			(375)
Taxable profit			765

The tax rate is 25%, so the tax due is $191,250 (25% × $765,000).

(b)

	$'000
Net dividend paid	1,500
Tax credit ($^{25}/_{75}$)	500
Gross dividend	2,000
Tax due at 30%	600
Less tax credit	(500)
Payable by shareholders	100

Note that this represents 5% of the gross dividend ie. the difference between the corporate and individual tax rates. If the individual tax rate is the same as the corporate rate, the shareholders have no additional tax to pay.

4 VAT

	$
Output tax (see note)	70,000
Input tax (300,000 x 85%) x 17.5%	44,625
Tax payable	25,375

Note

Assume sales excluding VAT are Y.

Then zero-rated sales are 20% x Y and standard rated gross sales are Y x 80% x 1.175%.

So:

(20% x Y) + (Y x 80% x 1.175%) = 570,000

0.2Y + 0.94Y = 570,000

1.14Y = 570,000

Y = 500,000

Check: Net sales are $500,000, so VAT due is $500,000 x 80% x 17.5% ($70,000). This gives sales including VAT of $570,000.

5 Company tax

Top tips

Writing out T accounts will probably help here.

Tax on profit on ordinary activities – note to income statement

	$'000
Current tax	
Tax on profit for the period	976
Underprovision for previous period ($794,000 – $765,000)	29
Deferred tax	
Increase in provision ($300,000 - $200,000)	100
Total tax charge	1,105

Balance sheet

	$'000
Payables	
Current tax	976
Deferred tax	300

6 Regulatory influences

Top tips

Do not omit the requirement to **explain**.

The EC decision that listed companies in the EU had to comply with International Accounting Standards from 2005 gave the IASB a more dominant role.

Stock Exchange

A quoted company is a company whose shares are bought and sold on a stock exchange. This involves the signing of an agreement which requires compliance with the rules of that stock exchange. This would normally contain amongst other things the stock exchange's detailed rules on the information to be disclosed in listed companies' accounts. This, then, is one regulatory influence on a listed company's accounts. The stock exchange may enforce compliance by monitoring accounts and reserving the right to withdraw a company's shares from the stock exchange: ie the company's shares would no longer be traded through the stock exchange. In many countries there is, however, no statutory requirement to obey these rules.

Local legislation

In most countries, companies have to comply with the local companies legislation, which lays down detailed requirements on the preparation of accounts. Company law is often quite detailed, partly because of external influences such as EU Directives. Another reason to increase statutory regulation is that listed companies are under great pressure to show profit growth and an obvious way to achieve this is to manipulate accounting policies. If this involves breaking the law, as opposed to ignoring professional guidance, company directors may think twice before bending the rules - or, at least, this is often a government's hope.

Standard-setters

Professional guidance is given by the national and international standard-setters. Prescriptive guidance is given in accounting standards which must be applied in all accounts intended to show a 'true and fair view' or 'present fairly in all material respects'. IASs, IFRSs and national standards are issued after extensive consultation and are revised as required to reflect economic or legal changes. In some countries, legislation requires details of non-compliance to be disclosed in the accounts. 'Defective' accounts can be revised under court order if necessary and directors signing such accounts can be prosecuted and fined (or even imprisoned).

The potential for the IASB's influence in this area is substantial.

7 Accounting standards

The users of financial information – shareholders, suppliers, management, employees, business contacts, financial specialists, government and the general public - are entitled to this information about a business entity to a greater or lesser degree. However, the needs and expectations of these groups will vary.

The preparers of the financial information often find themselves in the position of having to reconcile the interests of different groups in the best way for the business entity. For example whilst shareholders are looking for increased profits to support higher dividends, employees will expect higher wage increases; and yet higher profits without corresponding higher tax allowances (increased capital allowances for example) will result in a larger corporation tax bill.

Without accounting standards to prescribe how certain transactions should be treated, preparers would be tempted to produce financial information which meets the expectations of the favoured user group. For example creative accounting methods, such as off balance sheet finance, could be used to enhance a company's balance sheet to make it more attractive to investors/lenders.

The aim of accounting standards is that they should regulate financial information in order that it shows the following characteristics, amongst others.

(i) Objectivity
(ii) Comparability
(iii) Completeness
(iv) Consistency

8 IASB

The main aims of the IASB are:

(i) To develop, in the public interest, a single set of understandable and enforceable accounting standards

(ii) To promote the use and rigorous application of those standards

(iii) To bring about the convergence of national accounting standards and International Accounting Standards.

The tendency of the IASB has been to concentrate on the first very specific aim, and to leave the second and third slightly more vague aims to follow behind.

The IASB's recent target has been to produce a set of 'core standards' which the worldwide body representing stock exchanges, IOSCO, can accept for all cross-border listings. In theory, this would mean that, say, a German company that prepares its accounts using IASs would be accepted for a listing on the Tokyo Stock Exchange.

IOSCO has given the core standards qualified endorsement and with the new standards and improvements to existing standards issued in 2003 and 2004, the IASB claims to have now established a 'stable platform' of standards.

However, individual stock exchanges may still make life difficult for foreign companies by insisting on substantial additional disclosures. The IASB is facing an uphill struggle, but there have been substantial successes, notably the EC decision that the consolidated accounts of listed companies must comply with IFRS from 2005.

9 Accounting concepts

Top tips

These are longer definitions than you would be required to produce for 5 marks. One sentence defining each concept would be sufficient.

(a) **The business entity concept**

The concept is that accountants regard a business as a separate entity, distinct from its owners or managers. The concept applies whether the business is a limited liability company (and so recognised in law as a separate entity) or a sole proprietorship or partnership (in which case the business is not separately recognised by the law).

(b) **The money measurement concept**

This concept states that accounts will only deal with those items to which a monetary value can be attributed. For example, in the balance sheet of a business monetary values can be attributed to such assets as machinery (eg the original cost of the machinery; or the amount it would cost to replace the machinery) and inventories (eg the original cost of the goods, or, theoretically, the price at which the goods are likely to be sold).

(c) **The historical cost convention**

A basic principle of accounting (some writers include it in the list of fundamental accounting assumptions) is that resources are normally stated in accounts at historical cost, ie at the amount which the business paid to acquire them. An important advantage of this procedure is that the objectivity of accounts is maximised: there is usually objective, documentary evidence to prove the amount paid to purchase an asset or pay an expense.

(d) **Stable monetary unit**

The financial statements which an accountant prepares must be expressed in terms of a monetary unit (eg in the UK the £, in the USA the $). It is assumed that the value of this unit remains constant.

In practice, of course, the value of the unit is not usually constant and comparisons between the accounts of the current year and those of previous years may be misleading.

(e) **Objectivity**

An accountant must show objectivity in his work. This means he should try to strip his conclusions of any personal opinion or prejudice and should be as precise and as detailed as the situation warrants. The result of this should be that any number of accountants will give the same answer independently of each other.

In practice, objectivity is difficult. Two accountants faced with the same accounting data may come to different conclusions as to the correct treatment. It was to combat subjectivity that accounting standards were developed.

(f) **The realisation concept**

The realisation concept states that revenue and profits are not anticipated but are recognised by inclusion in the income statement only when *realised* in the form either of cash or of other assets the ultimate cash realisation of which can be assessed with reasonable certainty. Provision is made for all known liabilities (expenses and losses) whether the amount of these is known with certainty or is a best estimate in the light of the information available.

(g) **The duality concept**

This convention underpins double entry bookkeeping. Every transaction has two effects. For example, if goods are purchased for cash, the accounts must reflect both the purchase and the payment of cash.

10 External auditors

The external auditors' responsibilities with respect to the financial statements are concerned with deciding whether the accounts show a true and fair view of the affairs of the company for the year. The auditors must express an opinion on the financial statements to this effect.

The auditors conduct an audit which examines the figures in the financial statements and agrees them back to the underlying accounting information. They are required to satisfy themselves that the directors have prepared the accounts correctly and that there is no materially misleading information within them. To this end the auditors have a statutory right to all information and explanations deemed necessary to perform the audit.

The external auditors report to the members of the company and their responsibility is limited to the expression of this opinion.

They are not responsible for the accounting systems, or for the detection of all fraud and error. While auditors will report on whether or not the accounting system is satisfactory, and will design their tests in order to have a good chance of detecting any material fraud or error, these issues are the responsibility of the **directors**.

11 Audit report

If the auditors' work leads them to conclude that the financial statements are free from material error or misstatement and that they give a true and fair view of the financial affairs of the company then they will issue an unqualified opinion. This opinion covers the income statement, the balance sheet and the notes to the accounts. By convention the opinion usually covers the cash flow statement as well. They also review the directors report to ensure that this does not contain information which is materially misleading or which conflicts with elements of the financial statements. The auditors' report is the statement of their opinion on these elements of the financial statements. They state explicitly that the balance sheet reflects the state of the company's affairs at the year end and that the income statement gives the company's profit or loss for the year. The report also covers a number of other elements, such as the fact that proper accounting records were kept, by exception.

A qualified report contains a qualified opinion because the auditors are concerned that the financial statements do not or may not give a true and fair view. This may occur due to disagreement or uncertainty. Disagreement occurs when the auditors form an opinion which conflicts with the view given by the financial statements. Uncertainty arises when there is a limitation in scope and the auditors are unable to form an opinion.

The extent of the qualification is determined by whether the disagreement or uncertainty is merely material or is pervasive.

When the auditors issue a qualified report it must contain a full explanation of the reasons for the qualification and, where possible, a quantification of the effects on the financial statements. This means that a qualified report will contain at least one more paragraph than an unqualified report.

The qualified report should leave the reader in no doubt as to its meaning and the implications it has on an understanding of the financial statements.

12 C

Top tips

Begin by working out the profit/loss on each contract. Will the expected increase in the contract value at Rottenrow be taken into account?

(a)

	Maryhill bypass	*Rottenrow centre*
	$'000	$'000
Income statement		
Revenue	2,800	2,900
Cost of sales	(2,178)	(3,000)
Profit/(loss)	622	(100)
Balance sheet		
Costs to date plus recognised profits (1,400 + 622/2,900)	2,022	2,900
Progress billings plus recognised losses (2,600/3,400 + 100)	(2,600)	(3,500)
Gross amount due to customers for contract work (liability)	(578)	(600)

Working

Maryhill: $[9{,}000 - (1{,}400 + 5{,}600)] \times \frac{2{,}800}{9{,}000} = 622$

Rottenrow: 8,000 – (2,900 + 5,200) = (100)

(b) Construction contracts are recognised as such when they cover at least two accounting periods. If they were not to be treated as they are under IAS 11 then the costs incurred during the early years of the contract would be recognised but with no corresponding revenue. This would lead to several years of no profits then one year of high profits regardless of how profitable the contract really was. The advantage of this approach however would be that there would be no need to use estimates and forecasts.

The current treatment matches an element of the revenue to the costs incurred. There is an attempt to maintain prudence by ensuring that any foreseeable losses are accounted for immediately. This gives a fairer representation of the underlying financial substance of the transaction and makes it easier for the user of the accounts to assess the financial position of the company.

13 IFRS 5

Top tips

Read this question carefully. The definition of 'held for sale' is quite specific.

The plant will not be classified as 'held for sale'.

For this to be the case, the asset must be available for immediate sale and its sale must be **highly probable**. For the sale to be highly probable, the asset must be actively marketed for sale at a price that is reasonable in relation to its current fair value.

This property is being marketed at a price which is **above** its current fair value. It is improbable that it will be sold at that price until property prices rise. This delay has been imposed by the seller, so it cannot be said that his intention is to sell the plant immediately. Therefore it cannot be classified as 'held for sale'.

14 Leases

> **Top tips**
>
> The principle of 'substance over form' is important here. Consider what the position would be if lessees were not required to capitalise finance leases.

IAS 17 is an example of substance triumphing over form. In legal terms the lessor may be the owner of the asset, but the lessee enjoys all the risks and rewards which ownership of the asset would convey. This is the key element to IAS 17. The lessee is deemed to have an asset as they must maintain and run the asset through its useful life.

The lessee enjoys the future economic benefits of the asset as a result of entering into the lease. There is a corresponding liability which is the obligation to pay the instalments on the lease until it expires. Assets and liabilities cannot be netted off. If finance leases were treated in a similar manner to the existing treatment of operating leases then no asset would be recognised and lease payments would be expensed through the income statement as they were incurred. This is off balance sheet finance. The company has assets in use and liabilities to lessors which are not recorded in the financial statements. This would be misleading to the users of the accounts and make it appear as though the assets which were recorded were more efficient in producing returns than was actually the case.

15 T

> **Top tips**
>
> This is similar to Section C questions in the exam. Make all your workings very clear, so you can see what you are doing.

INCOME STATEMENT
FOR THE YEAR ENDED 31 DECEMBER 20X0

	$'000
Revenue	68,500
Cost of sales (W2)	(25,980)
Gross profit	42,520
Distribution costs	(4,000)
Administrative expenses (W3)	(9,000)
	29,520
Interest	(4,950)
Profit before tax	24,570
Taxation (10,200 + 50) (W5)	(10,250)
Profit for the period	14,320

BALANCE SHEET AS AT 31 DECEMBER 20X0

	$'000	$'000
Non-current assets		
Property, plant and equipment		440,450
Current assets		
Inventory	470	
Cash at bank	300	
		770
Total assets		441,220

	$'000	$'000
Equity and liabilities		
Equity		
Share capital		220,000
Retained earnings (W6)		99,320
Non-current liabilities		
Loans		110,000
Current liabilities		
Trade payables	1,700	
Taxation	10,200	
		11,900
Total equity and liabilities		441,220

Workings

1 *Depreciation*

	$'000
Hotels 490,000 @ 2%	9,800
Fixtures and fittings (18,000 – 9,400) @ 25%	2,150
	11,950

2 *Cost of sales*

	$'000
Food purchases	2,100
Heating and lighting	3,000
Housekeeping and restaurant staff	9,000
Opening inventory	400
Closing inventory	(470)
Depreciation	11,950
	25,980

3 *Administrative expenses*

	$'000
Administration	3,000
Staff wages	6,000
	9,000

4 *Property, plant and equipment*

	Hotels $'000	*Fixtures and fittings* $'000	*Total* $'000
Cost or valuation			
As at 1 January 20X0	478,000	11,000	489,000
Additions	12,000	7,000	19,000
As at 31 December 20X0	490,000	18,000	508,000
Depreciation			
As at 1 January 20X0	46,200	9,400	55,600
Charge for the year	9,800	2,150	11,950
As at 31 December 20X0	56,000	11,550	67,550
Net book value as at 31 December 20X0	434,000	6,450	440,450
Net book value as at 1 January 20X0	431,800	1,600	433,400

5 *Taxation*

	$'000
Taxation charge for the year	10,200
Underprovision from the previous year	50
	10,250

6 *Retained earnings*

	$'000
Profit for the period	14,320
Dividend	(1,000)
Retained for the period	13,320
Retained earnings b/f	86,000
Retained earnings c/f	99,320

16 CEC

Top tips

This is a fairly easy question. Remember to **explain** each item.

		Adjustment	
Item	*Explanation*	*Add to inventory value* $	*Subtract from inventory value* $
(a)	The sub-total error has over-valued inventories by $(6,725 – 6,275)		450
(b)	This arithmetical error has over-valued the item by $(6 – 0.6) per unit for 260 units		1,404
(c)	Free samples are not trading items and should be excluded from the valuation		
(d)	Goods held should be included in the valuation regardless of whether or not they have been paid for yet.		
(e)	Cost $2,885. Net realisable value $(3,600 – 921) = $2,679. The inventory should be valued at the lower of cost and NRV. Since NRV is lower, the original valuation of inventories (at cost) will be reduced by $(2,885 – 2,679)		206
(f)	Inventory issued on sale or return and not yet accepted by the customer should be included in the valuation and valued at the lower of cost and NRV, here at $5 each (cost)	1,500	
(g)	The cost ($7.30) is below the current and foreseeable selling price ($10 or more) which is assumed to be the NRV of the item. Since the current valuation is at the lower of cost and NRV, no change in valuation is necessary		
		1,500	2,060

s	$	$
Original valuation of inventories, at cost		153,699
Adjustments and corrections:		
to increase valuation	1,500	
to decrease valuation	(2,060)	
		(560)
Valuation of inventories for the annual accounts		153,139

17 Plant and equipment

Top tips

Do not forget the annual depreciation charge.

PLANT AND EQUIPMENT – COST

	DR		*CR*
	$		$
Balance b/f	250,000	Plant 20X5 disposal	40,000
Purchases	150,000	Plant 20X7 disposal	10,000
		Balance c/d	350,000
	400,000		400,000
Balance b/d	350,000		

PLANT AND EQUIPMENT – ACCUMULATED DEPRECIATION

	DR		*CR*
	$		$
Plant 20X5 disp	32,000	B/f	148,000
Plant 20X7 disp	4,000	Current year chg – 350,000 x 20%	70,000
Balance c/d	182,000		
	218,000		218,000
		Balance b/d	182,000

PLANT AND EQUIPMENT – DISPOSALS

	DR		*CR*
	$		$
Plant 20X5	40,000	Plant 20X5 depn	32,000
Plant 20X7	10,000	Plant 20X7 depn	4,000
		Plant 20X5 proceeds	5,000
		Losses on disposals	9,000
	50,000		50,000

18 IT

Top tips

The important point is to distinguish between the amounts actually spent during the year and the amounts charged to the income statement.

PURCHASED GOODWILL

	$		$
Cash	4,800	Income statement: impairment loss	1,200
		Balance c/d	3,600
	4,800		4,800
Balance b/d	3,600		

RESEARCH AND DEVELOPMENT EXPENDITURE

	$		$
Balance b/f	26,500	∴ Income statement (7,900 +	
Cash: research	7,900	(26,500 + 3,500 – 22,600))	15,300
development	3,500	Development costs c/d	22,600
	37,900		37,900
Balance b/d	22,600		

19 F

Top tips

Make sure you know what constitutes an 'adjusting event'.

The treatment of the events arising in the case of F would be as follows.

(a) The fall in value of the investment in P has arisen over the previous year and that company's financial accounts for the year to 28 February 20X1 provide additional evidence of conditions that existed at the balance sheet date. The loss of $50,000 is material in terms of the trading profit figure and it should therefore be reflected in the financial statements of F. Due to the size and nature of the loss, it should be disclosed separately either on the face of the income statement or in the notes, according to IAS 1.

(b) The destruction of inventory by fire on 30 April (one month after the balance sheet date) must be considered as a new condition which did not exist at the balance sheet date. Since the loss is material, being $250,000, it should be disclosed separately, by way of a note describing the nature of the event and giving an estimate of its financial effect. Non-reporting of this event would prevent users of the financial statements from reaching a proper understanding of the financial position.

(c) The approval on 1 June of the company's design for tank cleaning equipment creates a new condition which did not exist at the balance sheet date. This is, therefore, an event which does not require adjustment under IAS 10. It is not clear, however, that it is of such material significance that non-reporting would prevent a proper understanding of the financial position. Disclosure may therefore be unnecessary.

(d) The bills have been discounted with recourse (ie if they are dishonoured the bank can claim the money off F) and hence there is a possibility of a liability arising if the bills are not honoured. Under IAS 37, the contingent liability of $150,000 in respect of bills discounted should be disclosed in the financial statements as a note to the accounts, but not recognised as an expense and liability because the loss is not probable.

(e) If the field trials are not successful, then there is a possibility that it will be difficult to sell the equipment. Therefore, consideration should be given as to whether the equipment should be written down in the accounts to net realisable value. If the loss is not probable, a write down would not be required but consideration should be given as to whether the contingent liability should be disclosed by way of note. In the circumstances given, it would appear that the possibility of loss is remote and therefore, under IAS 37, no disclosure would be required. The expected future sales which might arise should not be included in the financial statements.

20 B

Top tips

This is very likely to be examined. Make sure you know the format. Do not neglect part (b).

(a) **Cash-flow statement for the year ended 30 September 20X1**

	$'000	$'000
Cash flow from operating activities – see workings		95
Sale of non-current assets – see workings		90
Interest		(15)
Purchase of non-current asset		(40)
Dividends		(35)
Repayment of loan		(80)
		15
Opening bank and cash	15	
Closing bank and cash	30	
Increase in cash		15

Workings

	$'000
Cash flow from operating activities	
Profit before tax (85 + 15)	100
Adjustment for non-cash-flow items	
Profit on sale of non-current asset	(10)
Depreciation	30
Adjustment for working capital	120
Inventory	(15)
Receivables	(50)
Payables	40
Cash flow from operating activities	95
Sale of non-current assets	
Net book value (520 + 40 – 30 – 450)	80
Profit from sale	10
Proceeds on sale	90

(b) A cashflow statement (CFS) helps users to assess the liquidity, solvency and financial adaptability of an entity. The liquidity of an entity is revealed by the change in the bank/cash balances between the beginning and end of the period. The solvency of an entity, and whether it is a going concern, may be assessed by using the historical cash flow to forecast future cash flows. The financial adaptability of an entity is its ability to use its cash to meet changes in its business environment.

A CFS is easier to understand than the accruals-based concept of an income statement, since it simply records the receipt and payment of cash, and is therefore likely to be more important to the user of accounts than the more complex income statement.

A CFS is more objective than accruals-based financial statements and it is less capable of manipulation. Users are therefore likely to place greater importance on this statement than the more subjective income statement.

Cash is the life-blood of a business and it is, therefore, vital that users of accounts assess cash flow when appraising a business. The CFS shows how finance is raised and where this is invested in the business. It thus provides a link between the income statement and the balance sheet.

Cash flow provides a basis for determining the amount of dividends to pay, and this is of interest to the users of accounts; similarly, cash flow is useful in valuing a business, which is also of interest to users.

Cash flow from operations is a measure of the 'quality' of the profit: the more closely cash approximates to profit, then the higher the quality.

However, although CFS is conceptually easier to understand than an income statement, the information it gives may be less easy to interpret. An increase in profit gives a positive message; a decrease in profit gives a negative message. Such a direct correlation does not apply to the CFS. Cash may increase, but this may be as a result of selling all the non-current assets; it may decrease, although this may be the result of buying non-current assets which will yield long-term advantages.

The CFS focuses on cash, not working capital, and thus there may be a temporary decrease/increase in cash depending on whether a large receivable has paid or inventory has been built up.

The pattern of cash flows may be erratic and these are not smoothed out by the accruals policy as used in the income statement. The CFS is not, therefore, a measure of economic performance.

Thus the income statement and the CFS are both relevant to the users of accounts and neither should be used in isolation.

21 Cat

Top tips

Note that this question does require the IAS 7 format.

CAT CO

CASH FLOW STATEMENT FOR THE YEAR ENDED 30 JUNE 20X2

	$'000	$'000
Cash flows from operating activities		
Profit before tax (W1)	54,500	
Interest expense	1,500	
Depreciation	11,000	
Increase in inventories	(6,000)	
Decrease in receivables	2,000	
Increase in payables	8,000	
Interest paid	(1,500)	
Dividends paid	(13,000)	
Income tax paid (W2)	(12,000)	
Net cash from operating activities		44,500
Cash flows from investing activities		
Payments to acquire non-current assets (W3)		(34,000)
Net cash used in investing activities		10,500
Cash flows from financing activities		
Issue of ordinary share capital	3,000	
Redemption of loan stock	(10,000)	
Net cash used in financing activities		(7,000)
Net increase in cash and cash equivalents (Note)		3,500

NOTES TO THE CASH FLOW STATEMENT

Note: analysis of the balances of cash and cash equivalents as shown in the balance sheet

	20X1	*20X2*	*Change in year*
	$'000	$'000	$'000
Cash at bank	10,000	13,500	3,500

Workings

1 *Profit before tax*

RETAINED EARNINGS

	$'000		$'000
Taxation	15,000	Balance b/f 1.7.X1	31,000
Dividends	17,000	Profit before tax (bal fig)	54,500
Balance c/f 30.6.X2	53,500		
	85,500		85,500

Profit for the year is after charging loan interest of 10% × 10,000 for 12 months and 10% × 10,000 for 6 months.

2 *Tax paid*

TAXATION

	$'000		$'000
Tax paid*	12,000	Balance b/f 1.7.X1	12,000
Balance c/f 30.6.X2	15,000	Tax charge	15,000
	27,000		27,000

*Note. The tax paid will be last year's year-end provision

3 *Non-current assets*

NON-CURRENT ASSETS

	$'000		$'000
Balance b/f 1.7.X1	85,000		
Purchases (bal fig)	34,000	Balance c/f 30.6.X2	119,000
	119,000		119,000

22 ABA

Top tips

Do not forget to show effect of these adjustments on the net profit before tax.

(a) The value of the IMX receivable will have to be written down. If, as appears likely, something can be recovered, then the debt will not need to be written off entirely. It can be written down to 30c in the $. The write-down needed will be $227,500.

(b) NRV of this inventory is now:

	$
Sales proceeds	200,000
Less agents commission 20%	(40,000)
Less disposal costs	(25,000)
	135,000

As this is less than cost, the inventory should be written down by $15,000.

(c) It currently looks probable that this liability will not be met by the insurance company, so it should be provided for in full in accordance with IAS 37.

Effect on net profit before tax

	$
Draft net profit	923,000
IMX write-down	(227,500)
Inventory write-down	(15,000)
Provision for damages	(50,000)
Adjusted net profit	630,500

23 L

(a) '3 for 2' bonus issue

This involves the issue of 45m new 50c shares, financed from the share premium account and the retained earnings. The capital structure following this issue will be:

	$'000
Share capital (15,000 + 22,500)	37,500
Share premium	–
Retained earnings (27,000 – 19,500)	7,500
	45,000

(b) '1 for 2' rights issue at 80c

37.5m shares are now issued at 80c.

	$'000
Share capital (37,500 + 18,750)	56,250
Share premium (37.5m × 30c)	11,250
Retained earnings	7,500
	75,000

24 International tax

> **Top tips**
>
> This question covers a number of issues. Deal with each one separately.

Tax on profit on ordinary activities – note to income statement

	$'000
Current tax	
Tax on profit for the period	1,500
Overseas tax paid (note)	(1,200)
Overprovision for previous period ($976,000 - $970,000)	(6)
Deferred tax	
Decrease in provision ($300,000 - $290,000)	(10)
Total tax charge	284

Note: Tax paid by overseas branch = $8m x 15% = $1.2m.

Balance sheet

	$m
Payables	
Current tax	300
Deferred tax	290

25 Debt

> **Top tips**
>
> This is unlikely to appear as a 20-mark question, but could be a 5-mark question. You should know all the main points.

To:	Board of Directors of AB
From:	Assistant Financial Controller
Date:	29 January 20X1
Subject:	Factors to be considered in deciding the financing mix

Introduction

The purpose of this report is to identify the main factors to be considered when deciding on the appropriate mix of long-term or short-term sources of debt finance, and to consider the advantages of fixing interest rates on debt.

Main factors to be considered

1 **The purpose of the borrowing**

The type of funds must be matched to the **purpose** for which they are required. The **business expansion programme** is likely to **require finance** both for the purchase of additional non-current assets, and for an increase in the level of working capital. In general cheaper **short-term funds** should only be used to **finance short-term requirements**, such as a larger level of fluctuations in the level of working capital. Short-term debt, usually in the form of an overdraft, is repayable on demand, and it would therefore be risky to finance long-term capital investments in this way.

2 **Flexibility**

Short-term finance is a **more flexible** source of finance; there may be penalties for repaying long-term debt early. However, we do have to be sure that further short-term debt will be available if we need to renew our facility.

3 **Our ability to borrow and repay**

We must be able to convince a lender of our ability to service the debt and to repay it at the end of the term. We must therefore put together a **business plan** for the expansion that shows how earnings from the additional sales will be sufficient to cover interest costs, and also shows how we intend to fund repayment at the end of the loan period. We must also confirm that we have the **legal capacity** to borrow in the manner required by checking the articles of association, and that we will not breach any restrictive covenants on our existing borrowings.

4 **The cost of the debt and the repayment terms**

The **relative costs** of the alternative sources of finance must be considered. For example, short-term debt is usually cheaper than long-term debt, but will carry a higher level of risk, as discussed above. The interest rate charged will also depend on the **perceived risk** of the investment to the lender, and this is another reason for putting together a comprehensive business plan. The **repayment terms** must also be **matched** to the pattern of cash flows coming from the new enterprise.

5 **The effect on gearing**

The gearing of the business is a measure of the amount of debt relative to equity. If a company is seen as being too highly geared, finance providers will judge that the **risk of default** is high, and are likely to seek higher compensation for this risk. This could take the form of a higher interest rate, restrictive covenants, or shorter repayment terms. If they perceive the risk to be high, some finance providers may be unwilling to lend at all. If gearing is likely to be a problem, we could consider acquiring some of the new assets using leases, since operating leases are not included in the company's balance sheet.

The advantages of fixing interest rates on debt

The two main advantages of fixed interest rates are as follows:

1 **Cash flow planning**

With a fixed rate loan, we will know exactly how much we need to pay, and when. This will make it easier to **plan** the **cash flow** and to ensure that we have **funds available** when required.

2 **Cost**

If we believe that interest rates are likely to rise over the period of the loan, then taking out a **fixed rate loan** will **limit our interest rate liability.**

Conclusions

The key factor in the choice of financing method is the purpose for which the funds are required. A detailed business plan for the new investment should be prepared in order to identify the most appropriate financing mix, and to support our case to potential lenders.

26 ARD

Top tips

This is a difficult question. If you had trouble, go through the answer carefully and make sure you understand it.

ARD has the following options.

(a) It can **continue its existing policy**.

(b) It can **use the export factor**, either in combination with its existing overdraft, or using the 80% finance offered by the factor.

(c) It can **use the insurer** with the assignment of policy rights (since cheaper finance is available at no extra cost).

It is assumed that all export debts will be financed by an overdraft or by special lending arrangements.

(a) **Use of the export factor for debt collection only**

	$
Service fee (3% × $1,000,000)	(30,000)
Bad debts saved (by insurance) (0.5% × $1,000,000)	5,000
Administration costs saved	35,000
Net saving	10,000

(b) **Use of the export factor for debt collection and finance**

There will be a saving in finance charges of 0.5% a year on 80% of the average receivables required.

	$
Service fee for debt collection	(30,000)
Interest costs saved (0.5% × 80% × $1,000,000 × 90/360)	1,000
Bad debts saved	5,000
Administrative costs saved	35,000
Net saving	11,000

(c) **Use of the insurer**

If the insurer was used, there is a saving of 1% on 70% of the finance required, since 70% of finance will be obtained at just 1.5% above base rate, instead of 2.5% above base rate.

	$
Insurance costs (0.35% × $1,000,000)	(3,500)
Savings in bank interest (1% × 70% × $1,000,000 ×90/360)	1,750
Savings in bad debts (90% × 0.5% × $1,000,000)	4,500
Net saving	2,750

Conclusion

ARD should use the services of the export factor, and obtain finance for 80% of export credit sales from the factor.

27 GUS

Top tips

This is a good example of *using* ratios to explain what is happening. The ratios alone do not explain anything.

(a) The company has become significantly more reliant on short term liabilities to finance its operations as shown by the following analysis:

	20X9		*20X8*	
	$'000		$'000	
Total assets	21,350		14,900	
Short-term liabilities	8,700	40.7%	5,000	33.6%
Long term funds (equity and debt)	12,650	59.3%	9,900	66.4%
	21,350		14,900	

Overtrading

A major reason for this is classic overtrading: sales increased by 50% in one year, but the operating profit margin fell from 9,000/20,000 = 45% in 20X8 to 10,000/30,000 = 33% in 20X9.

Refinancing

However, the effect is **compounded** by the **repayment** of $2.3 million (66%) of the 8% loan stock and replacement with a $2 million bank overdraft and increased trade payable finance. Although this may be because the interest rate on the overdraft is cheaper than on the loan stock, it is generally not advisable in the context of the risk of short term debt.

However, if it is felt that the current sales volume is abnormal and that, when the Polly Playtime doll reaches the end of its product life cycle, sales will stabilise at a lower level, the use of shorter term debt is justified.

Liquidity ratios

As a result of overtrading, the company's **current ratio** has deteriorated from 13,500/5,000 = 2.7 in 20X8 to 19,850/8,700 = 2.28 in 20X9. The **quick assets ratio** (or 'acid test') has deteriorated from 10,500/5,000 = 2.1 to 12,500/8,700 = 1.44. However these figures are acceptable and only if they continue to deteriorate is there likely to be a liquidity problem. In the 20X9 accounts the company continues to have a healthy bank balance, although this has been achieved partly by halting dividend growth.

Investment in non-current assets

The company has **not maintained an investment in non-current assets** to match its sales growth. Sales/non-current assets has increased from 20,000/1,400 = 14.3 times to 30,000/1,500 = 20 times. This may be putting the quality of production at risk, but may be justified, however, if sales are expected to decline when the doll loses popularity.

Working capital ratios

An investigation of working capital ratios shows that:

(1) **Inventory turnover** has **decreased** from 11,000/3,000 = 3.67 times to 20,000/7,350 = 2.72 times. This indicates that there has been a large investment in inventory. The question of whether this is justified again depends on expected future sales, but the strategy appears to be the opposite of that adopted for non-current assets.

(2) The **average receivables payment period has increased** from 6,000/20,000 $\times$ 365 = 110 days to 10,000/30,000 $\times$ 365 = 122 days, indicating a lack of credit control. This has contributed to a weakening of the cash position. There appears to be no evidence of prompt payment discounts to customers.

(3) The **payment period to suppliers** (roughly estimated) has **decreased** from 2,500/11,000 $\times$ 365 = 83 days to 4,200/20,000 $\times$ 365 = 77 days. This result is unexpected, indicating that there has been no increase in delaying payment to suppliers over the year. Suppliers are being paid in a significantly shorter period than the period of credit taken by customers.

Conclusion

In summary, the main problem facing GUS is its increasing overdependence on short term finance, caused in the main by:

(1) A major investment in inventory to satisfy a rapid increase in sales volumes
(2) Deteriorating profit margins
(3) Poor credit control of receivables
(4) Repayment of loan stock

(b) **Future sales**

Possible solutions to the above problems depend on **future sales** and **product projections**. If the rapid increase in sales has been a one-product phenomenon, there is little point in over-capitalising by borrowing long term and investing in a major expansion of non-current assets. If, however, sales of this and future products are expected to continue increasing, and further investment is needed, the company's growth should be underpinned by an injection of equity capital and an issue of longer term debt.

Better working capital management

Regardless of the above, various working capital strategies could be improved. **Customers** should be encouraged to **pay more promptly**. This is best done by instituting **proper credit control procedures. Longer credit periods** could probably be negotiated with suppliers and quantity discounts should be investigated.

28 VX

Top tips

This has been examined and is not difficult. Set it all out neatly, so that you do not miss anything.

(a) *Initial workings*

(i) Sales value

	Nov	*Dec*	*Jan*	*Feb*	*Mar*	*Apr*
Sales units	1,000	1,200	1,400	1,600	1,800	2,000
Sales value at $50 ($)	50,000	60,000	70,000	80,000	90,000	100,000

Sales revenue will be received two months after the sale is made.

(ii) Production costs

	Nov	*Dec*	*Jan*	*Feb*	*Mar*	*Apr*	*May*	*June*
Production units	1,200	1,400	1,600	2,000	2,400	2,600	2,400	2,200
	$'000	$'000	$'000	$'000	$'000	$'000	$'000	$'000
Wages at $8			12.8	16.0	19.2	20.8	19.2	17.6
Variable o/h at $2	2.4	2.8	3.2	4.0	4.8	5.2	4.8	4.4
50% paid in month	1.2	1.4	1.6	2.0	2.4	2.6	2.4	2.2
50% in following month		1.2	1.4	1.6	2.0	2.4	2.6	2.4
Total payment			3.0	3.6	4.4	5.0	5.0	4.6
Material at $26	31.2	36.4	41.6	52.0	62.4	67.6	62.4	57.2
Payment after two months			31.2	36.4	41.6	52.0	62.4	67.6

CASH BUDGET FOR FIRST SIX MONTHS OF NEXT YEAR

	Jan	*Feb*	*Mar*	*Apr*	*May*	*June*
	$'000	$'000	$'000	$'000	$'000	$'000
Receipts						
Sales revenue	50.0	60.0	70.0	80.0	90.0	100.0
Sale of old machine	1.2	–	–	–	–	
	51.2	60.0	70.0	80.0	90.0	100.0
Payments						
Wages	12.8	16.0	19.2	20.8	19.2	17.6
Variable overhead	3.0	3.6	4.4	5.0	5.0	4.6
Material	31.2	36.4	41.6	52.0	62.4	67.6
Fixed overhead	5.5	5.5	5.5	5.5	5.5	5.5
New machine		34.0				
	52.5	95.5	70.7	83.3	92.1	95.3
Net cash flow	(1.3)	(35.5)	(0.7)	(3.3)	(2.1)	4.7
Opening cash balance	35.5	34.2	(1.3)	(2.0)	(5.3)	(7.4)
Closing cash balance	34.2	(1.3)	(2.0)	(5.3)	(7.4)	(2.7)

(b) The cash budget shows that the company will require more cash than is available from February onwards. Management might decide to arrange an overdraft to cover the deficit. Alternatively they could reduce or avoid the deficit by taking actions such as the following.

(i) **Negotiate credit facilities** or stage payments for the purchase of the machine.

(ii) **Defer** the **purchase** of the **machine** or lease it instead of buying.

(iii) **Defer payments** to **material suppliers**, although the company already takes two months credit for these purchases.

(iv) **Attempt to collect payments** from customers more quickly.

(c) (i) **Depreciation** is not a cash flow and so would have no effect on a cash budget.

(ii) **Depreciation is charged** in the **income statement** for the year and therefore reduces the profit of a business.

29 Cash management

Top tips

Part (a) could be answered just using common sense. In the exam you are given the formulae for the Baumol and Miller-Orr models.

To: The Treasurer
From: A N Recruit, Accounts
Date: 15 May 20X2
Subject: Cash management models

(a) **Advantages of such models**

Cash management models take into account the trade-off between **the rate of return** which can be earned on surplus funds and the **need to maintain liquidity**. For example, a company will need to keep a certain amount of cash in a non-interest or low-interest current account in order to meet known and expected liabilities. If, however, the balance in this account becomes unnecessarily high, the company is losing the interest which could be earned by transferring the funds to a higher interest deposit account or other form of investment.

Cash management in the public sector

For our department, this is particularly important as the more we can earn in additional interest the more we have to spend on the local community. Local authorities are increasingly being asked to demonstrate **efficiency and effective** use of resources and one of our largest resources is cash.

Similarity to inventory models

Cash management models effectively regard **surplus cash** as a form of inventory. Inventory management models attempt to minimise the sum of inventory-holding costs, inventory ordering costs and stock-out costs. Equivalent costs can be identified for cash balances. The cash model which is closest to the 'Economic Order Quantity' inventory model is the **Baumol model**, but this is unrealistic in that it assumes that cash is used up at an even rate.

(b) **Miller-Orr model**

The **Miller-Orr model**, illustrated below, is more useful because it deals with receipts and payments of cash and provides trigger points for transferring cash to and from investment accounts when the current account balance becomes too high or low respectively. It does, however, make an unrealistic assumption that **cash flows** are entirely **unpredictable**.

Lower and upper limits

We have already agreed with our bank that the minimum balance on our current account will be \$15,000. This is referred to as the 'lower limit'. Thus when the balance falls to that level we will need to transfer money out of the investment account into the current account. To compute the 'upper limit' the Miller-Orr model uses three data items:

- The transaction cost for each cash transfer in or out of the account: \$25
- The variance of daily cash flows: $(\$3,000)^2 = \$9,000,000$
- The daily interest rate on invested cash: 0.0236%

Using these items of data it can be shown that the 'spread' between the upper and lower limits is \$26,820. This means that the upper limit is \$15,000 + \$26,820 = \$41,820. When the current account reaches this high level, money will be transferred out into the investment account.

Transfers

The final question is how much needs to be transferred in and out when the lower and upper limits are reached. The Miller-Orr model sets the 'return point' at a figure one third of the way between the upper and lower limits.

The return point is $\$15,000 + \frac{1}{3} \times \$26,820 = \$15,000 + \$8,940 = \$23,940$.

In summary, then, when the balance falls to \$15,000, \$8,940 is transferred into the account to bring it up to \$23,940. When the balance rises to \$41,820, \$17,880 is transferred out of the account to return the balance to \$23,940.

Note. You do not need to compute the spread in this question because it is given to you. Using the formula for the Miller-Orr model, the spread is

$$3\left[\frac{3}{4} \times \frac{\text{transaction cost} \times \text{variance of cash flows}}{\text{interest rate}}\right]^{\frac{1}{3}}$$

$$\text{Hence the spread is } 3\left(\frac{\frac{3}{4} \times 25 \times 9,000,000}{0.0236\%}\right)^{\frac{1}{3}} = \$26,827$$

(c) **Baumol's model**

The model is based on determining the optimal amount of cash that will be raised in each transaction, and hence the number of transactions and the level of transaction costs.

$$Q = \sqrt{\frac{2FS}{i}}$$

where: i = interest rate
F = annual cash payments
S = cost per sales of securities

Limitations of the model

(1) **Return from securities**

It assumes a **steady rate of return** from the securities although this may be very uncertain. The treasurer should consider the effect of fluctuations in this rate on the model.

(2) **Lack of buffer inventory**

It **does not allow** for a **buffer inventory** of cash but assumes that further securities will only be sold when the cash balance reduces to zero. This is unlikely to be realistic in practice.

(3) **Independence of transaction costs**

It assumes that the level of **transaction costs** is independent of the size of the transaction - again this is unlikely to be true in practice.

(4) **Payment intervals**

In reality, **payments** will **not be made continuously** but at regular intervals. The effect of this 'stepped' effect on the operation of the model should be considered.

Signed: AN Recruit

30 Factoring

Top tips

Note that you are asked for the factoring cost in $ and the discount cost in %. You must learn the formula for the cost of a discount.

(a) A factor normally manages the debts owed to a client on the client's behalf.

Services provided by factoring organisations

(i) **Administration** of the client's invoicing, sales accounting and debt collection service.

(ii) **Credit protection** for the client's debts, whereby the factor takes over the risk of loss from bad debts and so 'insures' the client against such losses. The factor may purchase these debts 'without recourse' to the client, which means that if the client's customers do not pay what they owe, the factor will not ask for the money back from the client.

(iii) **'Factor finance'** may be provided, the factor advancing cash to the client against outstanding debts. The factor may advance up to 85% of approved debts from the date of invoice.

(iv) A **confidentiality agreement** may be offered to conceal the existence of the arrangement from customers.

(b) It will be assumed that the factor finance will **not** be **replacing** any **existing credit lines**, and therefore the full interest cost of the agreement will be relevant when determining the cost of factoring.

Annual sales are $400,000 × 12 = $4.8m

Daily sales are $4.8m/365 = $13,151

The annual cost of factoring can now be found:

	$
Interest ($13,151 × 40 days × 75% × 10%)	39,453
Service fee ($4.8m × 2%)	96,000
Total annual charge	135,453
Less internal cost savings ($5,000 × 12)	60,000
Net annual cost	75,453

(c) $$\text{Cost} = \left(\frac{100}{100-d}\right)^{\frac{365}{t}} - 1$$

t = 40 – 10 = 30 days

d = 2%

$$\text{Cost} = \left(\frac{100}{100-2}\right)^{\frac{365}{30}} - 1$$

$$= 27.9\%$$

(d) **Key issues in the discount option**

(i) The **proposal is expensive**. The company should be able to get cheaper overdraft finance than this, and longer-term debt may cost even less.

(ii) The company may need to **offer a discount** in order to make its terms competitive with other firms in the industry.

(iii) The **level of take-up** among customers is **uncertain**, and will affect the cash flow position.

(iv) Problems may arise when customers take both the discount and the full forty day credit period. This will **increase administrative costs** in seeking repayment.

Key issues in the factoring option

(i) The factor may be able to **exercise better credit control** than is possible in a small company.

(ii) The **amount of finance** that will be received is **much more certain** than for the discounting option as 75% of the value of the invoices will be provided immediately.

(iii) The **relationship with the customers** may **deteriorate** due partly to the reduction in the level of contact with the company, and partly to the historical view of the factor as the lender of last resort.

Conclusion

The final decision must take into account all the above issues. However, the **most important points** to consider are the ability of each proposal to meet the financing requirements, and the relative costs of the different sources of finance.

31 Debt collection targets

Top tips

Part (a) does require you to come up with some **numbers**. This makes it much easier to construct an example.

(a) Receivables are assets which it is hoped can be converted into cash, and many companies promote the use of **cash targets** as aids to motivate credit controllers. A cash target is the amount that should be collected in order to arrive at an 'ideal' figure for receivables ageing. For example, assume at the end of November that receivables outstanding of $2m amount to approximately 61 days. This figure is made up as follows.

		$
November	30 days	900,000
October	31 days	1,100,000
		2,000,000

There are no debts older than this.

Sales in December are $700,000, and the target receivables ageing at the end of December is 55 days. The December sales add $700,000 which would mean that if no money were collected total receivables at the end of December would be $2,700,000 or 92 days. Therefore, to reach a target of 55 days receivables outstanding requires that the oldest 37 days receivables (92 – 55) should be collected. These are:

		$
October	31 days	1,100,000
November	6 days $^{6}/_{30}$ × $900,000	180,000
Cash to be collected		1,280,000

The firm should thus aim to collect $1,280,000. Note the emphasis on collecting the oldest debts. If we simply aggregated the figures for December we would have a target receivables of 55/92 × $2,700,000 = $1,614,130 suggesting a cash recovery of only $1,085,870.

The advantages of highlighting efforts on the oldest debts are that:

(i) Older debts imply that customers are taking more credit.

(ii) Staff are not encouraged to ask for *early* payment as a special favour from recent customers.

(iii) Effort is expended on debts which are proving hard to collect anyway.

(b) **Factoring** is a service that does not have a concise definition. A factor is defined as 'a doer or transactor of business for another', but a factoring organisation specialises in trade debts, and so manages the receivables of a client (business customer) on the client's behalf. There are the following aspects of factoring.

(i) Administration of the client's invoicing, sales accounting and debt collection service.

(ii) Credit protection for the client's debts, whereby the factor takes over the risk of loss from bad debts and so 'insures' the client against such losses. This service is also referred to as 'debt underwriting' or the 'purchase of a client's debts'.

(1) The **factor might purchase** these **debts 'without recourse'** to the client, which means that, in the event that the client's customers are unable to pay what they owe, the factor will not ask for his money back from the client.

(2) Not every factoring organisation will purchase approved debts without recourse and **'with recourse' factoring might be provided**, especially in cases where the size of the debt is particularly high, or the factor would not approve the debts for a 'without recourse' agreement.

(3) **Credit protection is credit insurance** and so the factoring organisation will want to give its approval to a credit sale before it goes ahead; in other words, the factoring organisation will want to act as a credit controller.

(iii) **Making payment** to the **client** in advance of collecting the debts. This might be referred to as 'factor finance' because the factor is providing cash to the client as a prepayment of outstanding debts.

A factoring organisation might be asked by a client to **advance funds** to the client against the **debts** which the factor has purchased, up to 80% of the value of the debts. This service gives the client **immediate cash** in place of a debt (which is a promise of cash in the future). The remainder, less the fees, is received later. If the client needs money to finance operations, borrowing against trade debts is therefore an alternative to asking a bank for an overdraft, although the factor will probably charge higher interest. Whereas a bank overdraft would have shown in the client's balance sheet as a current liability, factor financing does **not show up** in the client's balance sheet at all.

In the client's balance sheet, the amount of **receivables** would be **reduced** and **cash** would initially **increase** by the same amount (although the cash would be used immediately by the client to buy more inventory, make more sales, and create even more receivables – ie the cash advance from the factor would be to put to operational use). For this reason, advances from a factor are particularly useful for **rapidly-growing companies**, that need more and more cash to expand their business quickly, by purchasing more inventory and allowing more credit sales than they would otherwise be able to do. The appeal of factor financing to growing firms is that factors might advance money when a bank is reluctant to consider granting a larger overdraft.

32 SF

Top tips

This question requires you to apply what you have learned in the finance section of the syllabus. Read the information through twice – the situation will become clearer.

To: Board of Directors, SF
From: External consultant
Date: 12 November 20X1
Subject: Cash flow budget

Introduction

The budget shows that the company will experience a **positive cash position** for the first quarter of the year, there being a net inflow of cash during this time as well as no use of the overdraft facility. However, thereafter the position deteriorates, with the company being forecast to exceed its overdraft limit from August to November. By the end of the year, the company's cash reserves will be $50,000 lower than at the start of the period.

Possible remedial actions

1 **Production scheduling**

Sales show a cyclical movement, with receipts from customers being highest during the winter months. However, production is scheduled evenly throughout the year. If production could be **scheduled** to **match the pattern of demand**, the cash balance would remain more even throughout the year. Any resulting increase in the overall level of production costs could be quantified and compared with the savings in interest costs to assess the viability of such a proposal.

2 **Defer the corporation tax payment**

This might be possible by **agreement with the tax authorities**. The company should consider the relative **costs of the interest** that would be charged if this were done, and the **cost of financing** the payment through some form of debt.

3 **Dividend**

SF is a private company, and therefore the shareholders could agree to **forgo** or **defer the dividend**. The practicality of this will depend on the personal situation of the five shareholders.

4 **Defer payment for non-current assets**

(a) Presumably the **purchase** of the **office furniture** could be deferred, although the sums involved are relatively insignificant.

(b) The **progress payment** on the **building extension** is likely to be a contractual commitment that cannot be deferred.

(c) The **purchase of the car** could reasonably be **deferred** until the cash position improves. If it is essential to the needs of the business, the company could consider spreading the cost through some form of leasing or hire purchase agreement.

(d) It is not clear why the new **equipment** is being **purchased**. Presumably some form of investment appraisal has been undertaken to establish the financial benefits of the acquisition. However, if it is being purchased in advance of an increase in production then it may be possible to defer it slightly. The company could also look at alternative methods of financing it, as have been suggested in the case of the car.

5 **Realise the investment**

The dividend from this is $10,000, and therefore assuming an interest rate of, say, 5%, it could be worth in the region of $200,000. It is not clear **what form** this takes or for **what purpose** it is being held, but it may be possible to dispose of a part of it without jeopardising the long-term strategic future of the business.

6 **Reduce the inventory holding period**

At present it is forecast that inventories will be $30,000 higher by the end of the year. This represents three months' worth of purchases from suppliers. It is not clear to what extent this increase is predicated upon **increasing sales**, although since the building is being extended it is assumed that there will be some increase in the level of production and sales in the near future. However, the size of the increase seems excessive.

7 **Tighten credit control procedures**

It is not known what level of bad debts is incurred by SF, but even if it is low, **tightening up** the **credit control** and **debt collection procedures** could improve the speed with which money is collected.

8 **Factor the receivables ledger**

The use of a factor to administer the receivables ledger might **reduce the collection period** and **save administration costs**. An **evaluation** of the **relevant costs and benefits** could be undertaken to see whether it is worth pursuing this option.

9 **Reduce the debt collection period**

SF currently allows its customers two months' credit. It is not known how this compares with the industry norms, but it is unlikely to be excessive. However, there may be some scope for **reducing the credit period** for at least some of the customers, and thereby reducing the average for the business as a whole.

10 **Increase the credit period taken**

Since SF already takes 90 days credit, it is unlikely that it will be able to increase this further without **jeopardising** the **relationship** with its suppliers.

11 **Inject additional long-term capital**

The budget assumes that both non-current and working capital will increase by $30,000 during the year, and the directors should therefore consider seeking **additional long term capital** to finance at least the non-current asset acquisitions. Possible sources of capital include:

- Injection of funds from the existing shareholders
- The use of venture capital
- Long-term bank loan, loan stock issue or mortgage

Loans and overdrafts

Companies often have a greater proportion of their debt in the form of overdraft due to the problems of providing sufficient security to lenders. However, a term loan will often be more attractive than an overdraft for the following reasons.

1 Overdraft finance is generally **repayable on demand**. It therefore carries a higher level of financial risk than does a term loan.

2 The bank may become uncomfortable with a growing overdraft and seek to secure scheduled repayment or other **conditions** from the company. This can present a growing firm with cash flow problems.

3 Overdraft finance is generally floating rate, thus exposing the company to **interest rate risk**. Term loans can often be negotiated at a fixed rate thus reducing this element of risk and assisting with cash flow forecasting.

4 Term loans can be negotiated over a timescale that can be related to the company's forecast need for financing, and with a **repayment schedule** that can be tailored to the company's requirements. For example, capital may be repaid in stages or at the end of the period.

5 If the company has a good trading record and/or a good asset base and can therefore offer reasonable security, it may be able to negotiate a **lower interest rate** than would be payable on an overdraft.

Cash surpluses

The company should also consider investing its cash surpluses during the first quarter of the year to earn at least some interest, although this will be restricted by the short periods for which funds are likely to be available. Possible investments include:

- Bank deposits
- Short-term gilts
- Bills of exchange

Conclusions

It can be seen that there are a number of avenues that SF could explore. It appears that the company is fundamentally profitable, given the size of the corporation tax bill, and the fact that were it not for the non-current asset additions and the investment in inventory the cash balance would increase by $10,000 during the year. However, the liquidity issues must be addressed now to avoid exceeding the overdraft limit.

Index

Note: Key Terms and their references are given in **bold.**

Review Form & Free Prize Draw – Paper P7 Financial Accounting and Tax Principles (5/06)

All original review forms from the entire BPP range, completed with genuine comments, will be entered into one of two draws on 31 January 2007 and 31 July 2007. The names on the first four forms picked out on each occasion will be sent a cheque for £50.

Name: ______________________ **Address:** ______________________

How have you used this Text?
(Tick one box only)

☐ Home study (book only)
☐ On a course: college ____________
☐ With 'correspondence' package
☐ Other ____________

Why did you decide to purchase this Text? *(Tick one box only)*

☐ Have used BPP Texts in the past
☐ Recommendation by friend/colleague
☐ Recommendation by a lecturer at college
☐ Saw information on BPP website
☐ Saw advertising
☐ Other ____________

During the past six months do you recall seeing/receiving any of the following?
(Tick as many boxes as are relevant)

☐ Our advertisement in *Financial Management*
☐ Our advertisement in *Pass*
☐ Our advertisement in *PQ*
☐ Our brochure with a letter through the post
☐ Our website www.bpp.com

Which (if any) aspects of our advertising do you find useful?
(Tick as many boxes as are relevant)

☐ Prices and publication dates of new editions
☐ Information on Text content
☐ Facility to order books off-the-page
☐ None of the above

Which BPP products have you used?

Text	☑	*Success CD*	☐	*Learn Online*	☐
Kit	☐	*i-Learn*	☐	*Home Study Package*	☐
Passcard	☐	*i-Pass*	☐	*Home Study PLUS*	☐

Your ratings, comments and suggestions would be appreciated on the following areas.

	Very useful	*Useful*	*Not useful*
Introductory section (Key study steps, personal study)	☐	☐	☐
Chapter introductions	☐	☐	☐
Key terms	☐	☐	☐
Quality of explanations	☐	☐	☐
Case studies and other examples	☐	☐	☐
Exam focus points	☐	☐	☐
Questions and answers in each chapter	☐	☐	☐
Fast forwards and chapter roundups	☐	☐	☐
Quick quizzes	☐	☐	☐
Question Bank	☐	☐	☐
Answer Bank	☐	☐	☐
OT Bank	☐	☐	☐
Index	☐	☐	☐

Overall opinion of this Study Text *Excellent* ☐ *Good* ☐ *Adeqate* ☐ *Poor* ☐

Do you intend to continue using BPP products? *Yes* ☐ *No* ☐

On the reverse of this page are noted particular areas of the text about which we would welcome your feedback.
The BPP author of this edition can be e-mailed at: marymaclean@bpp.com

Please return this form to: Nick Weller, CIMA Publishing Manager, BPP Professional Education, FREEPOST, London, W12 8BR

Review Form & Free Prize Draw (continued)

TELL US WHAT YOU THINK

Because the following specific areas of the Text contain new material and cover highly examinable topics etc, your comments on their usefulness are particularly welcome.

Please note any further comments and suggestions/errors below

Free Prize Draw Rules

1. Closing date for 31 January 2007 draw is 31 December 2006. Closing date for 31 July 2007 draw is 30 June 2007.
2. Restricted to entries with UK and Eire addresses only. BPP employees, their families and business associates are excluded.
3. No purchase necessary. Entry forms are available upon request from BPP Professional Education. No more than one entry per title, per person. Draw restricted to persons aged 16 and over.
4. Winners will be notified by post and receive their cheques not later than 6 weeks after the relevant draw date.
5. The decision of the promoter in all matters is final and binding. No correspondence will be entered into.